THE CHANGING
SOUTH PACIFIC

THE CHANGING SOUTH PACIFIC

Identities and Transformations

Edited by
Serge Tcherkézoff and
Françoise Douaire-Marsaudon

Translated by Nora Scott

ANU
THE AUSTRALIAN NATIONAL UNIVERSITY

E PRESS

ANU

E PRESS

Published by ANU E Press
The Australian National University
Canberra ACT 0200, Australia
Email: anuepress@anu.edu.au

Cover: Photography by Bob Cooper

Previously published by Pandanus Books

National Library in Australia Cataloguing-in-Publication entry

Title: The changing South Pacific : identities and transformations / edited by Serge Tcherkézoff.

ISBN: 9781921536144 (pbk.)
9781921536151 (pdf)

Notes: Bibliography.

Subjects: Ethnology--Oceania.

            Oceania--Politics and government.

Other Authors/Contributors:

            Tcherkézoff, Serge.

Dewey Number: 305.800995

Acknowledgments

In 1990, a member of our temporary research group — *Identités et transformations des sociétés océaniennes* — in the *Centre National de la Recherche Scientifique* suggested that each member of the group contribute an article on the theme of identity and transformation. We were all researchers from various cross-cultural 'laboratories', that is, more permanent centres of research jointly organised by the CNRS and universities (*Laboratoire d'anthropologie sociale, Laboratoire de langues et civilisations orientales, Techniques et Cultures*, and so on), who had met through seminars and common research programs. At that time, a permanent multidisciplinary research centre focused on Pacific Studies did not exist (CREDO was not established until 1995). Everyone agreed on the idea, even if some added that they were unlikely to have the time to write an article, while others who had originally committed were later obliged to respond to other priorities. Their contributions were written from 1990 to 1995 and the resulting book was published in French in 1997 as *Le Pacifique-sud aujourd'hui: Identités et transformations culturelles*, by CNRS Press. No significant changes have been introduced in the current translation, although some additional bibliographical references have been given.

Our thanks go to the French Ministry of Foreign Affairs (Comité du Fonds Pacifique), who agreed to fund the translation, to Nora Scott who undertook this immense task, and to our friends and colleagues at the Research School of Asian and Pacific Studies, The Australian National University, who accepted to publish it: David Hegarty, Director of the Centre for Contemporary Pacific and the State, Society and Governance in Melanesia Project, and Darrell Tryon, Deputy Director of the Research School of Pacific and Asian Studies.

S. Tcherkézoff,
Canberra, October 2004

Preface

Scientific collaboration between France and Australia in the social sciences and humanities has come a long way since the joint signing of the Cultural, Scientific and Technical Agreement in 1977. Today there exist collaborative agreements between French and Australian higher education and research institutions that cover a wide variety of disciplines.

Not the least of these was the International Program of Scientific Collaboration (PICS) 2001–2004, between the Centre National de la Recherche Scientifique (CNRS), France's national scientific research body, and The Australian National University (ANU). This program, entitled 'Early Encounters in the Pacific', was conducted by the Centre de Recherche et de Documentation sur l'Océanie (CREDO), a research centre of the Maison de l'Asie-Pacifique, housed at the University of Provence, Marseilles and the Research School of Pacific and Asian Studies (RSPAS), at The Australian National University. This multi-disciplinary research program has now entered a second phase, looking at modern political, economic and cultural encounters in Pacific societies, as seen through the prism of earlier traditional Oceanic values and social institutions. The results of the first phase of the CNRS-ANU collaboration are currently in press.

The publication of *The Changing South Pacific: Identities and Transformations* by Pandanus Books and the Centre for the Contemporary Pacific at the Research School of Pacific and Asian Studies is a further step in the collaboration between our sister institutions. First published under the leadership of Serge Tcherkézoff and Françoise Douaire-Marsaudon, this translation of Le Pacifique-Sud aujourd'hui makes accessible to an English-speaking readership the fruits of the research of a leading group of French social scientists on a subject which has been at the heart of much of the social science research carried out in the Pacific region over the past decade, namely the cultural and political transformations taking place in Oceanic societies and the concomitant emergence of new regional and national identities.

Collaboration between the French Centre National de la Recherche Scientifique and the Research School of Pacific and Asian Studies at The Australian National University is now well established in a number of disciplines. However, in many areas, this collaboration and sharing of research results is in need of further enhancement. Indeed, one of the principal findings from the French Assises de la Recherche Française dans le Pacifique — a French government review of French research in the Pacific over the last twenty years, held in Noumea in August 2004 — was that a major effort should be mounted to make francophone research more accessible to the English-speaking world. The publication of *The Changing South Pacific: Identities and Transformations* is an important step in this direction.

Darrell Tryon
Research School of Pacific and Asian Studies
The Australian National University
August 2005

Foreword to the original edition

Bernard Juillerat

Mention Oceania, and what springs to mind is hardly a 'continent' on the lines of Africa or America, but rather an ocean — more nearly a void — surrounded by continents, among which the subcontinent of Australia. And yet the unity of this space that is home to so many island peoples and cultures no longer needs proving: it is based on a common origin in Asia, and on the large linguistic groups that grew from this single root, of which the Austronesian group populates nearly the whole of the Pacific.

Today, however, the peoples of the Pacific are in search of a unified identity built on cultural and political foundations that reach beyond the borders of the independent nations, of the protectorates or of the French overseas territories. The many aboriginal groups of Australia described by classical Anthropology increasingly recognise themselves in a 'pan-aboriginal identity' opposed to white power; likewise, Melanesians are seeking stronger ties among themselves, independently of their cultural diversity and the borders left them by the colonial powers, but they would also like to join the people of Oceania as a whole, whether by the intermediary of pluri-governmental institutions or a common identity — the Pacific Way — which has room for all particularisms.

On the large islands — in particular New Guinea, the Solomon and Vanuatu — a number of human groups are still feeling the aftershocks of their first contact with the colonisers and missionaries: they remain deeply rooted in the old culture, although these roots are already growing weaker, but the members of these groups are also attempting to interpret what history is in the process of offering them or imposing on them; it is a time of doubt, of rejection, of enthusiasms and sometimes of millenarian illusions. A second stage in the transition towards Westernization can be seen in a form of biculturalism: the societies in this situation have assimilated Christianity and Western education, have invested in political life and local development programs and thus feel endowed with a new identity, although they remain relatively isolated. Lastly, in the archipelagos that have been administered and Christianised since the nineteenth century, like Polynesia or New Caledonia, today's populations are experiencing what could be called a third phase of transition: Christianity has been assimilated and the ancestral culture partially forgotten; the inhabitants have understood the issues of political life and are part of the market economy. If they are an independent State, they have assumed responsibility for their own destiny and are debating the changes to be made in their constitutional system, their relations with the other countries in the South Pacific as well as national development and their membership in the world community. At the same time, however, they are anxious to continue the traditions that make their cultural difference, in the growing globalization, to preserve something of their past.

The present work is divided into three parts corresponding roughly to these three 'phases' of transformation. Needless to say, these stages are connected by a historical continuum and should be seen as merely a reading aid, to help follow this book, but also the never-ending story of change in the cultures of the South Pacific.

This book is the outcome of a collective effort. Since the 1960s a group of French anthropologists has been studying some societies in Oceania. Over the years, the group has changed names, lost members and gained new ones, grown younger and contained in the 1990s some twenty researchers, belonging to diverse laboratories and research groups. A dozen texts are gathered in this volume, each presenting a society, captured in its generality or seen from a specific point of view, but always with reference to the issue of collective identity and its confrontation with history and change. All of the present studies stem from work conducted 'in the field' over many long months and many trips, sometimes extending over a period of twenty years or more. For history happens in the field, and that is where the anthropologist must tirelessly follow these societies into their future.

CONTENTS

INTRODUCTION

The cargo will not come …

Serge Tcherkézoff and Françoise Douaire-Marsaudon

The French reader was the initial target of this introduction. He usually knows little about the South Pacific cultures. For instance, while he has had more than one occasion to see pictures of 'Tahiti' or 'Easter Island' in eastern Polynesia, he knows almost nothing about the political, social and cultural realities of the western half of the region. With the exception of the two islands of Wallis and Futuna, this part of the Pacific has no French territories; instead, there are a variety of small independent States which have kept their own Polynesian tongue as the official language. The present work will take the reader to Wallis, as well as to the States of Tonga and (Western) Samoa.

Another example: the word 'Aboriginal' is well known as a term for the first inhabitants of Australia. But the extent to which this identity was imposed from outside on a set of extremely diversified groups is generally less known. The reader will be able to make a closer examination of the political and cultural stakes involved in this identity and to measure the role they play in building today's Australia.

And if he has heard about the Melanesian 'cargo cults' — perhaps the only social phenomenon in this region to have gained worldwide fame — the reader probably has little idea of their variety. These messianic cults can be quite different from the media image of an illusory expectation kept alive by magical practices concerning a miraculous cargo supposed to be brought by great ships. Their variety is enriched by equally ill-known contemporary changes. Today's cargo cults present a new face of which this work gives a few examples.

In 1957, Peter Worsley published a study of these cults entitled 'The Trumpet Shall Sound', alluding to the Biblical announcement of the final coming, the advent of heaven on earth … and the arrival of the mythic ships bearing the long-awaited cargo.[1] But the metaphor could no longer be used today.

Beginning in the early 1900s, a time when Europeans were already present, Melanesians could contemplate from afar the wealth brought by the Whites but which they rarely distributed. The Melanesians also saw them waiting for the ships, impatiently scanning the horizon: the isolated missionary stations and military posts were dependent on supplies from outside. The cargo cults which sprang up at this time were founded on the belief that, by going through certain motions, the White people's merchandise would come to the indigenous inhabitants as well; some even said that the cargo was sent by the ancestors, but that the Whites had intercepted it and taken it for themselves. At the same time, local groups sought, through this imaginary appropriation, to couch a certain form of power in thinkable terms — which would play a role in their resistance to colonisation. They also sought to understand the Christian message and, in so doing, transformed it. Other, more recent cults awaited not only shipments of cargo but also the arrival of white leaders, like the movement waiting for the American president L. B. Johnson to come and govern them.[2] But today the time has come for realism: the trumpet will not sound, the cargo will not come.

And yet, while they no longer wait for the mythic ships, the contemporary attitude of the Pacific peoples is not one of societies having decided to turn inwards, cloistered in their gardens wrested from the forest. One can, for instance, decide to create one's own cargo and its containers, as in the case of the Sulka, which will be described. The 1990s were also a time of new hope — and new illusions — prompted by the increasingly rapid integration of these societies into a world system encompassing the Pacific basin or the entire globe. Our book will propose several illustrations of this. A good number of these societies are now caught up in such accelerating change. Nevertheless, they have preserved an intense awareness of their own identity. This is anything but immutable, but after all, isn't what counts the representation of a specific 'us' shared by the members of a group?

As this work puts in at several islands in the immensity of the Pacific Ocean,[3] it invites the reader to understand how the inhabitants of these islands, large and small, seek to affirm both an individual identity and their belonging to the contemporary world.

Social and cultural anthropology has always considered that it makes sense to speak of *a* society or culture, at least for a given period of time. In so doing, it observes phenomena connected with identity: expressed values and ways of conducting social relations. Even if such relations sometimes imply profound differences of status, class and obligations between individuals, they have a sufficient number of references in common for those concerned to share, on certain points, a similar representation of this place — that we call 'society' — which, they say, founds these obligations and these prohibitions, these duties and these rights. Each of the examples set out in this book underscores the weight and import of this identity: it speaks to everyone, even if, at times, it works to the benefit of only a few.

The same anthropology is immediately faced with the diachronic dimension: history — is any society exempt? — and its major phases, its *longues durées* which stack up one upon the next and imprint themselves on memory; but also the subtle, imperceptible day-to-day changes of which the observer becomes aware only when he returns several years later (two examples in the present volume benefit from a series of studies carried out over a span of more than 20 years); and finally the fundamental transformations sparked by cultural interpretations desperately seeking to make sense of the impact of a radically new element, such as the arrival of Westerners in societies which did not even imagine such beings existed. Such are the changes whose consequences the anthropologist feels compelled to incorporate into his or her narrative.

Inclusion of the diachronic dimension also leads to regional comparisons, especially if the variations observed between neighbouring groups offer regular similarities or term-for-term inversions recurring too often to be a matter of chance, thus imposing the question of a possible common origin. Is it legitimate to speak of a unitary culture when it comes to the groups under study? The query is particularly apposite in the absence of historical documents, and the articles on Papua-New Guinea provide an enlightening example of this type of research. The notion of change is thus understood here in both a historical and a structural perspective.[4]

Each of these two dimensions — identity and change — raises a series of methodological problems, and their interrelation raises even more. However, rather than going into a long theoretical discussion of the models available today,[5] the authors of this work all agree that anthropology is comparative or it is not anthropology, that there have never been 'societies without a history' and that the anthropology of change is simply anthropology. They have therefore chosen to contribute to the debate by means of numerous and specific examples. What has brought them together is first of all the fact that they all work in the South Pacific, that their fieldwork consists of long and repeated studies and that, during the seminars held by the research group of which they were all members,[6] they have noted the convergence of the questions raised by these studies.

In all these examples, we will see how local identity is confronted with another dimension, an interaction whose effects are observed by each author. Because the Pacific peoples have long lived in their islands and, until the arrival of the Europeans, had never encountered large-scale wars of conquest imposing a social and linguistic unification, all of these groups, whether they inhabit the space of an island or a valley, developed notions of identity rich in a diversity of symbols. Then, in the space of two centuries — and sometimes thirty years — they saw it all. They experienced the arrival of the mission. Immense quantities of wealth passed before their eyes, in the possession of the army, the government functionaries, the colonists and the businessmen — objects which seemed to contain a power until then held only by the gods or the dead, 'things with *mana*', we should say, borrowing an expression from Marcel Mauss.[7] They heard talk of universalist values, and later some, who had stayed in their valley, discovered they were citizens of a nation-State or inhabitants of a 'territory' belonging to some remote power. Others were driven from their valley; they made war (Whites spoke of 'uprisings') and they lost. Others still were never colonised; but even though no foreign administration ever established itself, the new laws of the world monetary system nevertheless commanded recognition. At the same time, new terms appeared, general ones, like 'Aboriginals' or 'Pacific Way', or regional ones — as the example of the 'Anga culture' will show — attesting that the articulation between identity and change has undergone a change of scale.

The texts collected here are all based on fieldwork. This is characteristic of the anthropological study, even when its object includes some history — for here we are talking about the history of local representations, experienced on a day-to-day basis, about representations of identity, at times those which singularise an individual, at other times those in which the 'us' of local speech refers to the whole group. The exposition of the facts favours such fieldwork.

There is an urgent need to bear witness, owing to the rapidity, the magnitude and the diversity of the changes under way in the Pacific, a continent-sized region which is gaining international importance as a point of contact and encounter between the economic powers of Southeast Asia and those of the Near East and the Anglo-American world.[8] It is also increasingly perceived as holding values which could be useful to other continents, as certain religious or cultural movements proclaim. Compared with a Western world in the grip of massive 'deconstructions' (whether the collapse of ideological 'systems' or the break-up of States into numerous communities each claiming its own 'ethnic' identity) and ill-compensated by 'reconstructions', some of which seem troubling to say the least, the Pacific world — without being absolutely peaceful, far from it — seems, to a certain extent, to be going through a period of restructuring. Broader identities are being held up to the West, forms of thought seek to adapt to the dimensions of the Pacific basin, if not to those of the whole globe. One astonishing but typical example of these new visions is the 'Alliance of Pacific Cultures', recently put forward by a delegation of several hundreds of traditional Samoan chiefs: in 1994 these chiefs travelled thousands of kilometres to confer with their Hawaiian counterparts and, pushing on to the shores of America, with representatives of the Amerindian nations, with a view to proclaiming the utility and the universal value of certain aspects of the 'Pacific cultural tradition'. Their idea was that the adoption and implementation, by Western societies themselves, of certain features common to the Pacific cultures could lead to the construction of viable societies in a West which appears, to these Pacific peoples, to be in many ways socially and morally bankrupt.[9]

This recent initiative shows that the consensual ideal of the 1970s — the 'Pacific Way' — is still alive, here and there. The term was launched in a speech pronounced before the United Nations by the Fijian Prime Minister, Ratu Sir Kamisese Mara, in 1970 as it happens, and immediately caught on. A few years later, Ron Crocombe, professor at the University of the South Pacific (USP, Fiji), wrote an entire article bearing this title[10] — and subtitled: 'An Emerging Identity' — which enumerated the contexts in which the expression was meaningful. It was a 'brotherhood' of 'all islands people' in the image of the brotherhood underlying the naming and kinship systems of the cultures of this region (where the classificatory extension of consanguineous kin terms is very broad: for instance, all older female cousins, and even all older women, are called 'mother'). It is a 'unity' between the countries, which is felt by the politicians, church administrators and sometimes by businessmen, and affirmed 'vis-à-vis Europeans and Asians'. This ideal was expressed first and most strongly in Fiji, Samoa and Tonga, then it reached Papua New Guinea, the Cook Islands, Kiribas, Tuvalu, the Solomon Islands, Vanuatu, Nauru, etc., keeping pace with the advent of autonomy or independence. In effect, the term also implies rejection of the colonial situation, thus suiting the newly independent States and the ideology of those working in this direction. The case of the two major regional powers is clearly more ambiguous: at the time of Crocombe's article, Australia and New Zealand were beginning periodically to show that they felt a part of the 'Pacific unity'. Last, and most importantly, this unity is affirmed at the cultural level. The differences of culture and social organisation so often underscored by the foreign experts (for instance the system of 'aristocratic' chiefly families in Polynesia as opposed to the more 'egalitarian' system in Melanesia) were pushed into the background,[11] and into the foreground moved whatever seemed to constitute shared strong points, namely the ethic of 'peace' and 'consensus', involving a purportedly specific tradition of negotiation and decision-making.[12]

But this restructuring had its flaws, if we include in the picture the internal frictions and the contrast between the small States and the great regional powers. As M. Panoff wrote in 1991, this consensual ideal of the Pacific Way, born during that honeymoon which characterised the early stages of decolonisation, 'shattered in Vanuatu, in Papua New Guinea, in Fiji, and developed cracks in Samoa and the Cook Islands'.[13] By an appalling irony of history, Papua New Guinea now finds itself, with the secession of Bougainville fifteen years after its own independence, in the situation of a dominant, repressive power in its own right. Fiji is being torn apart by strife between two numerically comparable populations, one of Indian origin and the other indigenous. And Samoa (formerly Western Samoa), whose social system has always vaunted the merits of political consensus (at least within the sacred order instituted by genealogical ties), underwent in 1994 a political crisis fuelled by a divide, as new as it was deep, between town and country, salaried workers and farmers, new political cadres and traditional chiefs.

In the Pacific as in other parts of the world conflicts are a legacy of the preceding period. But today, the situations inherited from the colonial era are complicated by wider problems, in particular with the burden of economic constraints. There are few societies, few States in the Pacific which today could be said to be in a position to control their own economic choices, and these external constraints have serious internal consequences, as shown by the two examples just mentioned, that of Papua-New Guinea (hereafter PNG) and that of Samoa. There more than elsewhere one can measure the inequality among the societies of this region: those the size of no more than a small community, highly dependent on international aid packages — which come with requirements intended to modify custom so as to promote 'development', itself the cause of more inequalities and conflicts[14] — and the others, the major regional powers, those which, like Australia and New Zealand, can compete in what has come to be called the 'concert of nations'.

Another feature of this collection of texts: despite the specific nature of the situations described, and underscored by the space given to directly observed facts, the present analyses illustrate an Anglo-American debate which has gone through a number of phases since it first arose more than fifteen years ago. Initially centred on the issue of the 'invention of tradition',[15] where values reputed to be, but which are not necessarily, 'traditional' are invoked as authoritative arguments in the new conflicts spawned by the contemporary situation, it has ultimately brought anthropologists face to face with themselves: is it legitimate to inquire into the 'authenticity' of the ideas and practices used by the societies one is studying?[16] The debate continues, but it has taken more open forms.[17] In reality the question raised is an ambiguous one, for it touches on two different debates. It is clear that it is not for the observer to say whether a given fact 'belongs to this or that culture', nor whether it is 'traditional' or not (or 'authentic', 'genuine', 'modern' or the outcome of 'acculturation'). He merely observes the way the parties include, exclude or hold this practice at a distance. Alternatively, he may speak of 'a society', in the simple sense in which, by observing the practices through which the people themselves agree that a given individual holds or loses his or her place in the social space designated by the personal pronoun 'we', he identifies the boundaries beyond which these practices are no longer valid or no longer have consequences; in this case he will say that one has reached the bounds of the society concerned.

If the question of identity, that of the individual or that of the group (the latter sometimes being considered from the problematic standpoint of 'ethnicity'[18]), has run through this debate from its inception down to the most recent developments, one can nevertheless note that this inquiry into the identity of South Pacific societies — or those elsewhere for that matter — long a preserve of 'ethnologists', has now been taken up by the societies themselves. The question one needs to hear is no longer 'Who are they?', but the one 'they' are asking loud and clear: 'What are we becoming?' A double transformation of the investigation: the object has become the subject, and the historical dimension is taken into account.

Indeed, a good number of societies in this region went through the missionary and colonial era while preserving — or creating in reaction to the foreign presence — the sentiment of a collective identity. Today the social groups of the South Pacific, whether they locate the identity of their 'we' in a few valleys, like the Baruya or the Ankave of PNG, or in a province with respect to the whole nation of PNG, like the new Kivung cult of the Sulka, in a recently forged national identity (the 'Aboriginals') or in a continuity with the past (like the State of Samoa: 'our *FaaSamoa*'), all these groups have representations of this identity sufficiently alive and strong to be able to ask themselves and others the essential questions about their future. One of these crops up time and again, and, although it springs from the pressure of the economic constraints mentioned above, it is still the expression of the minimum degree of liberty, that conferred by political independence: what will the model for 'becoming' be and up to what point should one try to fit the model provided by the West? Though not really new, the question has grown singularly acute of late, and the Western model, including its heretofore least-contested aspects, is now being challenged: development, yes; democracy, yes; but not necessarily in their imported forms.[19]

Both Melanesia and Polynesia are present in these articles. One major figure, however, is missing: Micronesia, where French researchers have just begun to work.[20] Australia too is present, but not New Zealand, where here too the question of identity, under intense debate, would call for a thorough study. Relations between Maori and Pakeha (New Zealanders of European stock) raise problems identical to those governing relations between Aboriginals and non-Aboriginals in Australia; this is especially true for ancestral land rights. In addition, both cases show a constant growth of the Asian immigrant communities, which fill the business sector; and the resulting changes are also comparable.[21] Yet in spite of obvious shortcomings, what is proposed here already permits a response to one pressing demand: until now there was no recent retrospective on Papua-New Guinea research, and there was a deplorable lack of any general work on identity and change concerning both Australia[22] and western Polynesia.[23]

We have organised the texts around three categories of situations and analyses. First we will look at the confrontation following on the relatively recent arrival of Europeans in the Pacific, the effects of which are still clearly perceptible in Papua-New Guinea, for instance. The changes in particular will be observed. They run deep and have happened quickly, so that local identities are obliged to invent a new vision of the future.

Next we will study the relationship with a new regional or national identity, rooted, to be sure, in past history, but formulated explicitly under pressure from recent circumstances

— or through the intermediary of the anthropologist's comparative outlook — as well as the multiple consequences resulting from the confrontation between local and global points of view (Australia, PNG, Polynesia). The study, centred on identities, shows how communities preserve, rediscover, restructure or re-create their references. It even happens that the anthropologist has a hand in bringing about this new awareness.

Finally, even in societies in contact with Europeans since the eighteenth or nineteenth centuries, as in Polynesia, we will look into their relatively recent entry into the international dimension, the market economy, but also law and human rights, a political dimension therefore which cannot avoid dialogue with 'Western' notions, whether these be exchange rates, private ownership or democracy.

These three situations create new areas of inquiry, those already mentioned in the case of 'cargo' or still others concerning money, the notion of personhood, and so on. Some of the new cases of integration have surprising side-effects For example, money is given in ceremonial exchanges as were formerly pigs or shells … but money can also be obtained outside the social group, which gives rise to totally different cargo cults or to the overwhelming place now occupied by ceremonial exchanges in the individual's inscription in society. Or a group aspires to 'democracy', but paradoxically this is pursued in the name of tradition and even, in western Polynesia, in the name of the sacred chiefdom.

The examples presented in these articles are grouped around these three poles, although they sometimes partake of all three.

———————

The first group takes us to Papua New Guinea, a young nation (created in 1975), but a land that has been inhabited for at least the past forty thousand years. Studies conducted on three of the islands, New Guinea, New Britain, New Ireland (all three part of PNG) find slow or radical changes subsequent to the arrival of Europeans. These articles examine recent or already old situations, sometimes using fieldwork conducted over a span of more than twenty years, as Maurice Godelier and Bernard Juillerat have done. The examples show simultaneously three orders of facts: (1) the changes subsequent to the arrival of the mission (some of these islands have only recently heard of Christianity), hence the possibility of directly observing this type of encounter so instrumental in shaping world history but which is now a thing of the past, with the exception, precisely, of PNG (and perhaps Amazonia); (2) the changes prompted by the introduction of European objects, of which the cargo cults represent a particular manifestation; (3) finally, the changes induced by the political evolution of these cultures and their integration into a much broader structure based on a new principle — the nation — which imposes on former 'tribes' an unfamiliar and completely unexpected conceptual and administrative framework.

Maurice Godelier's text speaks of a half century of contact between the Baruya of New Guinea and the White world, a very short span of time considering the number of changes that have come about. The appearance of metal objects, first of all, which replaced their stone tools even before the Baruya had actually seen their first White man; then the 'first contact' in 1951: the demonstration of White power using firearms, the punitive expeditions starting in 1960, the arrival of the missionaries a short time later. Then came the market, the transformation of gift-exchange into buying and selling, wage labour for some, the appearance of coffee plantations. In 1975, the Baruya became citizens of a new nation, whereas their world still ended with their valleys or with a few neighbouring valleys with whom they fought. Quickly the Baruya realized that the new administration had nothing to offer, and neo-traditional values asserted themselves. The initiations were resumed on a wider scale, but without the rites associated with war, which was banned by the Australian administration in the 1960s (even though one short but lethal conflict did break out). Since the late 1980s, the desire for a place in a wider world has once more manifested itself, and the idea of 'doing business' (*makim bisnis*) appears to have carried the day. Is this process irreversible? The text leaves the question open.

Bernard Juillerat invites us to a parallel analysis, in the form of concise, direct fieldnotes which report work also done in New Guinea, but this time among the Yafar of West Sepik. The first section is entitled '1970': this is the era of the first Australian patrol officers, who had arrived some ten years before, like the missionaries; it is the time of new horizons, discovered by those who hired out to the plantations in New Britain or New Ireland. Next comes '1973', with the beginning of self-government, which becomes the local figure of 'Selfgavman', a sort of boogeyman waiting to grab all the food, a sort of 'cargo' ship in reverse. '1976' is the era of the new government school, but also that of the secret Yangis rite, which had not been performed for over ten years. It is also the first time the Yafar, feeling the inevitable changes in the wind, have asked a foreigner — the anthropologist — to take custody of some of their secrets. '1978', disappointment: the new administration (of the PNG government) doesn't give anything, but it collects taxes. '1981', too many people have died of sickness: an epidemic — usually one of the first gifts of contact — creates too much friction (accusations of witchcraft). It is also the birth of a singular new cargo cult. '1986' … '1991' '1995'. Much else happens. Fieldnotes are not amenable to summary. Nor is it necessary to present the reader with a problematic, for the narrative does not contain any difficulties, even for someone who knows next to nothing about the Pacific cultures. But each paragraph taken alone paints an evocative picture which places the reader, not without emotion, at the very heart of these Yafar villages. Like the other peoples of PNG, the Yafar are caught between the hope for cargo and the constraints of a slow, uneven 'development' in the midst of a seriously deteriorated health situation. Here too the article ends on a question.

We remain in the Sepik with the analysis of Philippe Peltier, who also has some questions about the changes that have come to this part of PNG. But this time the attention focuses on the creativity that once went into the architecture and decoration of their famous 'men's houses'. Indisputably an art form, but in this region the artistic creation also expressed a 'position with respect to society'; furthermore the men's house was also a central site for ritual activities. Today a good number of these houses have disappeared while others are only empty shells; but their forms have taken over new sites, such as schools and churches.

A considerable quantity of objects used to be amassed in these houses, arranged according to a spatial division based on degree of symbolic power: objects for more-or-less everyday use, head trophies, then further back, ancestral skulls overmodelled with red earth, and in the most secret recess, objects which probably served as clan emblems. These accumulated items were the memory of these groups and constituted the individuality of each men's house, even as they were the guarantee of an identity constantly under reconstruction. The analysis of two myths shows that the men's houses 'are also … a story of the exchange of women', in other words of alliances which placed each group within a wider network.

The intrusion of modernity into this region had two high points: first of all general pacification and the ban on headhunting; and then in the 1960s, the end of the initiations and the public exposure of the objects kept in the men's houses out of sight from the women, objects which were subsequently confiscated or sold by the missionaries and merchants. At the end of this period these houses stood empty. Then came the 1970s, the arrival of a missionary converted to the idea of using 'indigenous styles', and the construction of the church in the image of a men's house. In reality the decoration takes a double reading, for the encounter between local and Christian traditions gave rise to a new version of Genesis. But the church is not really a men's house, it is more like a pantheon charged with creating ties between old and new. As for the school, also built on traditional lines, it may denote a process of folklorisation which, via the school, permeates every sector of the society. The changes made to the men's houses were also a 'political tool that enabled [Sepik] societies to find a place in the modern world by playing on Western expectations: after all, isn't the Sepik synonymous with art and Men's Houses?'

The region of Porapora, where Peltier carried out intensive investigations, has seldom been studied because of the difficulty of access. No foreign authority arrived until 1930, so the situation was very different from that of the neighbouring regions like, for example, that of the Banaro, where Thurnwald lived at the beginning of the twentieth century and where B. Juillerat worked more recently.[24] Peltier is therefore in a position to describe many little-known features of these houses and the changes they have undergone.

From the 'men's houses in the Sepik', we move on to the Sulka 'ancestors' house' in the neighbouring island of New Britain. Monique Jeudy-Ballini shows us how, as in the preceding case, this house is the vehicle for creating traditions: here it becomes the temple of a new cult — the missionaries called it a 'cargo cult', but it is a special kind. Adamantly rejecting the term 'cargo', it asks its members to work for the 'redemption of the sins' of all men, Sulka and others. As in the Sepik, where the men's house became a church, the Sulka ancestors' house features both the local ancestors and Biblical characters, a list of the Sulka dead and a written tablet of the Ten Commandments. Juillerat, in his article on the Yafar, mentions a new-fashioned cargo cult whose representations have to do with guerilla warfare.[25] The cult described by Jeudy-Ballini is another of these new forms where the members are no longer waiting for 'cargo'. It is still tempting to speak of a cargo cult, but in these two examples, while the hope of wealth is indeed present, these representations reverse those of the previous cults described by Worsley: here cult members themselves help create their own cargo.

In effect, the Sulka Kivung movement demands important financial sacrifices thanks to which its members have begun building a veritable new city which outstrips the wildest hopes of the classic cargo cults. Their success has to do with local politics and 'keeping up with the Joneses'. They play on the opposition between the central government of Papua

New Guinea and the provincial government, a clear sign of the change of scale to which the Melanesian populations have recently been subjected. At the same time, the notion of sin and that of the buying-power conferred by money have been combined in a strange way. To constitute one's own cargo — which is materialised in the unexpected shape of a new city — is to redeem the sins of the entire world. Jeudy-Ballini gives a detailed account of the sequences of representations which show the members of the Kivung movement to be true acrobats in the art of negotiating the tangled logic typical of the simplistically termed 'syncretic' movements. To 'follow the custom of the ancestors', to do what they demand today, is to redeem the fact that the ancestors themselves followed the 'custom of the ancestors'. The latter sinned unwittingly. Today new knowledge enables one to sin and then to pay for redemption. Furthermore, since the sins that need redeeming are those of the whole world, the supply becomes inexhaustible. This redemption is actually the conversion of a sacrifice, the effect of which is to funnel millions of dollars into bank accounts. As a supreme paradox, the money is used both to make gifts to the central government (whereas the movement refuses to pay provincial taxes) and to construct modern buildings, nullifying, as it were, a question left unanswered for the Sulka: why was this Western wealth never given to them? It is not a question of simply imitating the Europeans and, when the cargo did not come, of making it on the spot. It is a question of speaking with the outside world (from the PNG government to the Europeans) the only language they are, so the Sulka believe, capable of understanding, and of applying the principle of 'the rich get richer'; in short, of making the Whites envious. The ultimate paradox is that part of the money collected is given to the Catholic mission. 'No doubt,' Jeudy-Ballini writes, 'the God the Kivung strives to better will recognise His own', as should the Europeans when they see the bright shiny new city.

This first set of texts ends with a reconstruction proposed by Brigitte Derlon: the analysis of a cargo cult in New Ireland, in the Mandak linguistic zone, which was totally or almost totally unknown. Here too the cultural process obeys a sacrificial logic, but this time it no longer hinges on money, as among the Sulka. It seems that this cult demanded the killing of a human being. Here, too, one of the author's conclusions was that the aim was not to accumulate wealth, but to establish a dialogue and a balanced exchange with the Whites.

The study invites the reader along on a meticulous investigation. First of all this cult was popular in the early twentieth century and lasted only a few years. The author therefore had to work from the texts she was able to collect on the spot; there are no other studies on this cargo cult in Mesi, an area where no one else has worked. Secondly, Christianity has cast a shadow of shame over these memories and accounts. The ethnological study thus turns into an exercise in ethno-history. Derlon uncovers the particular circumstances of the time (a famine, the arrival of White wealth) as well the long-term social logic which guided the whole kinship system, land-holding, the theories of conception and the reproduction rights on certain sacred objects — *malanggan* are famous in Melanesian museography. As in Peltier's study on the men's houses, these art objects renowned in Europe are replaced in their context, thus taking the museum visitor to the very heart of this society.

In such a social organisation where identity and rights are transmitted in the group through the maternal line, the wife and her children enjoy only a use right on the lands of the matrilineal group of their husband and father, and this right ceases when he dies. But if, in the framework of his funeral rites, the wife's group makes an offering of her corpse or that of one of her children, the group acquires a permanent right on a share of the land. This is not a commercial transaction. The particular method of killing causes the victim to be identified with the deceased man and, as a consequence, to be affiliated to his group. Through a logic which combines the efficacy of a sacrificial rite with local conceptions of the transmission of the substances constituting the identity of persons or groups, the victim's descendants cease to be outsiders. It so happens that the logic governing land rights also operates in the transmission of rights on the *malanggan* ritual objects, these being themselves representations of the clan's identity. Human sacrifice played the same role.

With these elements in hand, the investigation returns to the village which was the site of this cargo cult and shows that the sacrifices were meant to give a victim 'to the White people's *malanggan*' so as to create a spiritual kinship leading to a sharing of the wealth. Once again the cluster of available details has a number of aspects. We find a mythology peculiar to this village as well as the familiar theme of the cargo sent to the Black men by the Whites, but also an unexpected sequel to the classic story: once the Whites had learned to manufacture the wealth they had captured, this wealth became a symbol of their identity, and the cult conceived a sacrifice aimed at the Whites, at the White people's *malanggan*, which would gain them affiliation to this source. Another surprise: the wealth was comprised essentially of … books. The word 'to write' is formed from '*malanggan*': the capture through affiliation in accordance with a traditional ritual of a specifically White knowledge, which nevertheless was part of the wealth stolen from the New Irelanders' ancestors. Is this to say that communication — at least in writing — has become possible between Melanesians and Europeans?

———————

The second set of texts presents the process of establishing a communal identity in which we see simultaneously the affirmation of the singularity of many fragmented small groups and an investment in a collective identity which is taking and changing shape at a rapid pace.

The Aboriginal peoples of Australia descend from over four hundred different language groups. In the 1960s, the term Aboriginal (written until then in French with a small *a*), a term remaining from a colonial segregationist discourse, acquired a capital A and became the emblem of a new identity, which stressed the ancestral customs, but also an instrument of resistance and the advancement, in particular, of demands for the recognition of ancestral land rights. As it grew, the notion of collectivity paradoxically also reinforced a new assertion of the singularity of the different local groups, which redefined themselves only partially in terms of traditional elements.

Inclusion in a larger identity can be explicit, engaged or political, like the notion of 'Aboriginal'. It can also be implicit, giving rise locally to a few comments, as when a member of one of the twelve linguistic groups comprising the Anga culture zone in Papua New Guinea discovered and remarked on the initiation or marriage practices of another group a few valleys away. But here too awareness of a certain similarity with more-or-less distant neighbours is expressed, and the regional government is there as a reminder. The chief discourse, however, is that of the observer. He knows from the linguistic and genetic studies and from comparing the features central to their social organisation, that the Anga constitute a single culture, as far back as their history can be traced. The term 'Anga', however, is a recent invention, referring to an entity whose exact boundaries are known only to anthropologists, a few politicians and a handful of patrol officers. Furthermore, no sooner is this unity affirmed by the analysis than the field of investigation finds itself awash in diversity. Yet the differences present a systematic character revealed by a process of observation which alternates between the most comparative point of view and the most local, so as to pin down the different levels of Anga identity.

In the present example, the anthropologist's knowledge contributes to the construction of at least part of this vision of identity. This is also the case in Australia: earlier anthropological work, like the opinions of experts called upon to testify in land-rights cases, is used to define, with the plaintiffs, the references of the 'group' pressing its claim. In Polynesia, the role of the anthropologist can be even more marked when he is an ethno-archaeologist trying to unearth forgotten food-growing practices — cultivation pits in this case — which the population reinvests with a both new and rediscovered identity. The example comes from the Tuamotu archipelago.

Some twenty years ago in Australia, the word 'Aboriginal' acquired a capital A. Barbara Glowczewski-Barker explains why and gives us an ethno-history of relations between Europeans and Aboriginal peoples. The notion of 'Aboriginal', left over from the colonial discourse, today is based on a double claim to identity: a persistent identity (identification by language, beliefs and ancestral songlines) and a resistant identity (revision of the official history of contact, land-right claims, critique of exclusion and exploitation). In addition to this pan-Aboriginal policy and ethic, new values stress the singularity of local identities, in which one can see a redefinition if not a reinvention of tradition.

Land claims are a priority for Aboriginal peoples. Recognition of a native title which would confirm once and for all that the Aboriginals are the original owners of the land has become a question of principle. But could any one authority legitimately represent all groups concerned? In addition, non-Aboriginals obviously reject the idea of a national treaty which would ratify any division of the nation. This has become a burning question since, for the first time in their history, a court case (the 'Mabo case' from the name of the representative of a group of Torres Strait Islanders) recognised an Aboriginal group's native title on lands.

When studying Aboriginal identity, one usually forgets the specificity of 'essentialist' indigenous theories, no doubt because these are so complicated. Glowczewski-Barker presents an enlightening exposé. In Australia, the spirit-child traditionally transmits 'essences' which identify the child in spirit and flesh with its kinsmen, but also with natural species and with places. It is this 'elsewhere' which links a person 'from the inside' to his or her ancestors and to certain animals and plants. The body not only gives each person their humanness and singularity, their individual and collective identities, it also comprises 'essences' which surpass the human dimension. The famous but often badly understood question of the 'Dreaming' concerns these ties, which identify an individual with an itinerary, with places and with natural species as well as with other individuals.

As for the boundaries between tribal identities, these used to be under constant negotiation, subject to encounters and alliances between various groups, owing to the kinship system, to the exchanges of goods, but also to the exchanges of rituals and narratives which thus connected the itineraries with the places associated with them. This confirmed the singularities of a filiation common to humans, ancestors and places: the alliances preserved or negotiated these singularities. Despite being relegated to reserves, some Aboriginal people have managed to establish a wide circulation of an increasingly large number of rituals elaborated so as to include various changes induced by colonisation. This accelerated circulation has not resulted in a uniformisation of beliefs but, on the contrary, in the constitution of the varied local versions into a new body of mythical-historical lore.

Aboriginal laws have a long and often tragic history, running from apartheid to 'self-management', by way of assimilation; the latter has taken several forms, for example, 'whitening' (the separation of half-caste girls from their families and marrying them to 'quadroon' boys), etc. Today the notion of Aboriginal has positive connotations and, for Aboriginal people themselves, the dichotomy between 'half-caste and full blood' no longer describes skin colour or the amount of Aboriginal blood in their veins, but life-styles and ways of thinking, (those who opt for an Aboriginal life-style being known as 'full-bloods' and those who live in town, in the White world, being called half-caste[26]). Activists using Aboriginal roots as a reference, call all people of mixed blood 'Aboriginal'.

The debate between religion and ethnic identity is also a major thread running through the issue of Aboriginality. Aboriginal spirituality is based on a network of links between individuals, their lands and their myths; but this network does not relate to the Aboriginal groups or to the land of Australia as a whole. The Aboriginal notion of 'place' stands in opposition to the Christian idea of universal space. Furthermore Christianisation was violently imposed (children were removed from their parents) and went hand in hand with a ban on a number of traditional practices, thus destroying one whole dimension of what it meant to attain adulthood as well as the representations of the gender roles. In addition the ban on mixed marriage resulted at times in the destitution of paternal authority and, for the youngest, in a lack of identification, phenomena which contributed largely to the development of alcoholism and delinquency.

After the 'Mabo case', the passage of a federal 'Mabo law' and the institution of a set of special courts, one might have thought that the land-rights question was headed in the right direction. But the States brought in their own laws as a check on the federal decisions. Even so, today 'reconciliation' is encouraged and the recognition of a history free of a simplistic and unilateral vision. The reconciliation commission is looking for inspiration in the territorial rights treaties recently passed with the Maori in New Zealand or with the Indians in Canada, and activists are starting to promote a many-facetted aboriginality and to develop ties with other indigenous peoples in the Pacific, whether within the framework of the UN or in the Festival of the Pacific, etc.

In Melanesia it is the Anga culture group which provides a glimpse into two dimensions of identity: a regional dimension, with the article by Pierre Lemonnier, who asks in what way the twelve Anga language groups constitute a specific culture representative of an original mode of social organisation, and a local dimension, with the contribution by Pascale Bonnemère, who, in counterpoint to Lemonnier's article, examines a specific attribute of personhood in one of these groups.

By looking into the various definitions of the Anga culture group, which inhabits the Highlands of PNG, Lemonnier also raises a methodological problem that cannot be avoided for a region like New Guinea, which counts no fewer than 850 languages and over 1000 tribes or local groups. Seeking to discover what — technical systems, language, way of exploiting nature, social organisation — in various areas distinguishes the Anga from the other human groups in the great island, the author demonstrates that the specificity of this set of groups, that is its identity in the eyes of anthropologists, results from an original combination of practices and representations consistently found in all the tribes of this group.

Lemonnier's article also presents itself as a defence and illustration of the use of comparative models in Melanesian anthropology. He shows how a constant give-and-take between the detailed ethnography of individual societies and the descriptive models of various 'types' of economic and social organisations encountered in New Guinea enables us at once to refine our knowledge of Anga societies (and of 'Great-Men' societies, of which one Anga group, the Baruya, furnishes the prototype) and to specify how they contrast with other New Guinea systems (Big-Men societies, the system found on the island's southern coast). By the way war, male initiations and gender relations dominate social life and, above all, constantly refer back and forth to each other, the set of Anga societies provides a rigorous illustration of the social logics which Godelier has shown to lie at the heart of the world of 'Great Men'. This social landscape stands in sharp contrast to those societies a few hundred kilometres away which focus on Big Men, organisers of large-scale exchanges of pigs and shells. Among the Anga, who do not practice intergroup ceremonial exchanges, the great warriors, the masters of the initiations and, to a lesser extent, the shaman healers, are the 'Great Men' who occupy the principal political positions. Nevertheless, as Lemonnier stresses, in several of these groups, the use of wealth differs measurably from that observed among the Baruya, so that, in view of the ethnographic material now available on other Anga groups, one point of the model based on the Baruya case needs modifying: rather than limited use of wealth in marriages, it is the compartmentalisation of the exchanges in which these items are used which opposes 'Great-Men' societies to the Big-Men systems. Which in turn means that the question of the absence of large-scale economic exchanges and of political status linked to the manipulation of wealth in the Anga groups must be recast. And the debate is relaunched.

The third part of the study deals with the ways in which the Anga go about defining themselves and constructing an ethnic or tribal identity. We see how the same institutions, practices and behaviours which struck anthropologists by their consistency among the Anga, but also because they were the opposite of logics observed in other parts of New Guinea, are precisely those elements which enable each tribe to perceive itself as different from its neighbours and which reproduce its identity.

Pascale Bonnemère analyses the name-forms used by the Ankave. Personal names provide a way to investigate the definition of personal identity. Detailed examination of the names of all inhabitants of one valley revealed the rules underlying their construction. It appears that these rules are fundamentally different depending on whether the person is a man or a woman. Not only do the elements which go into most of the names given to either sex refer to different realities (clan versus toponym or bird names, for example), their structures, too, obey opposite logics. Men's names situate the individual with respect to his genealogy — they mention certain ancestral clans — and to time, while women's names refer rather to the space and territory of a single clan, her father's. Bonnemère compares these differences with the specific features of the Ankave kinship system: the differences in personal names according to the gender of the person named, like the practice of using another name form, the 'name of endearment', which depends chiefly on the mother's clan.

But Ankave personal names display other features than gender difference, and their analysis enables us to advance the question of personhood in this society. Chief among these characteristics is homonymy: several people can have the same name. This implies that the name is not where the Ankave have chosen to express the individual's most personal attributes. Another specificity lies in the system used for naming siblings, which gives younger children the same name as the eldest and simply tacking on a qualifier of birth order. Analysis of the names of several sets of siblings reveals that same-sex classificatory siblings (close or distant cousins) are considered to possess a greater degree of sameness than opposite-sex real siblings (brothers and sisters).

In the context of the changes Ankave society has been experiencing of late, it seems that these two characteristics will have opposite effects on the evolution of the naming system. The Ankave's penchant for homonymy leaves them perfectly free to adopt Biblical names, the limited number of which inevitably leads to repetition. But these names do not readily lend themselves to the addition of a qualifier of birth order. It is therefore most likely that the Ankave will continue for a long time to use personal names and other forms of address as their ancestors did.

This second set of texts ends with an example from Polynesia containing one very special feature. The role played by the researcher-observer was decisive here. Jean-Michel Chazine gives us 'an attempt at participant ethno-archaeology' in Tuamotu. The Tuamotu archipelago is comprised of atolls, which form a very special environment owing to a number of problematic natural conditions. For the ethno-archaeologist, their interest lies in permitting a time-study of the relationship between these natural conditions and the past and present adaptability of the inhabitants of these atolls. The author tells us how conducting this general study ultimately led to an altogether original experiment: following an attempt on the part of the researchers at rehabilitating some old cultivation pits, at a time when local food sources had almost entirely disappeared from the atolls, a few inhabitants took the initiative of using the old and new techniques placed at their disposal by these researchers to create their own subsistence gardens.

At the outset, a double approach had been decided on which combined environmental analysis (sea-level fluctuations, climatic conditions, growth rate of the outer reef, etc.) with properly anthropological analyses (interviews, collecting oral traditions, etc.). Subsequent field observation made it possible to take into consideration the widespread remains of old cultivation practices, embodied in the cultivation pits. In former times, these pits enabled the inhabitants to grow what were probably large quantities of taros just above the water table, thus providing the islanders with a ready supply of food. This is all the more interesting since, on the one hand, the Tuamotu atolls have long been reputed to be almost totally non-productive — if one excepts the growing of coconuts, introduced by the Europeans — and, on the other hand, today's inhabitants, having become entirely dependent on outside resources, now exhibit serious nutritional deficiencies. The idea of refurbishing these cultivation pits gradually gained ground: the goal was to use these pits to demonstrate 'the important autochthonous food-producing potential', and a program was developed by the research team. In addition to mapping the pits, this consisted in interviewing elderly inhabitants who were 'eye-witnesses or themselves possessors of ancestral knowledge' in the hope of recovering the cultivation techniques formerly used in these pits. The experimental rehabilitation, planned to last at least two years, was accompanied by a program of demonstrations and audio-visual displays geared to the inhabitants and explaining the complete arsenal of old and modern techniques available to them.

Despite the many problems (presence of plant-eating crabs on the floor of the pits and difficulty obtaining taro shoots, notably), the experiment went ahead. But most surprising was that, as the experiment unfolded, a dozen householders took the initiative of establishing their own subsistence gardens using the techniques explained during the experiment. These gardens, made unbeknown to the research team, show how old skills can be reappropriated; but they also indicate that this kind of 'transplant from the past' can take an unexpected turn and totally unforeseen forms.

The third set of texts deals with western Polynesia. Here the representations of the various identities were elaborated in a particular context: these were societies that had never been colonised (Tonga) or that had known colonial rule for only a short time (Samoa), whose land had never been confiscated, and which had never been chosen for settlement colonies, including a French territory such as Wallis. The analyses also underscore the series of changes that have occurred. These are not, however, the consequences of the 'first contact' — which took place a century and a half or two centuries ago, and sometimes more — they are phenomena resulting from the insertion of these countries into the modern world: the impact of the market economy and money or the encounter between traditional models for managing society and Occidental systems, such as democracy, for instance.

Of the three Polynesian societies considered here, two are now independent States: Tonga and (Western) Samoa. They are nation-States in their own right, members of the United Nations, even if their size has won them the label of 'micro-States'. Both present one very particular feature: the traditional socio-cultural unit — 'ethnic' group as it used to be called (at least from the linguistic standpoint and from the point of view of their origin myths, obligations and prohibitions, which all have a number of points in common) — coincides with the new political entity — the State. It is a bit as though each of the hundreds of 'tribes' in New Guinea had become a separate State rather than all being gathered into what is today Papua-New Guinea. These States thus have the means — in terms of ability to represent what their identity is or 'should be' — to cope with the changes that they can avoid no more than anyone else. It should therefore be no surprise, for instance, that cargo cults were virtually non-existent and that today the chief problem, among others, is how to realise the coexistence of democratic values with traditional chiefdoms. As for Wallis, which together with the island of Futuna, makes up the French overseas territory of Wallis-and-Futuna, its ties with France clearly pose their own problems of identity, unknown in Tonga or Samoa, and which call for a separate study. Nevertheless, as we will see, even in Wallis there are strong identity signposts, based on tradition but also open to integrating certain aspects of modern culture. This is the case, in particular, of the objects circulated ceremonially; and in this matter, Wallis and Tonga can be considered together.

Françoise Douaire-Marsaudon shows us, for instance, that in both Tonga and Wallis, the ceremonial objects which, from time immemorial, have borne the signs of this identity are still the focus of village life: the food items and 'riches' (tapa and mats) which drive the exchanges at an undiminished rate — which may have even increased with the entry of paper money into the circuit and thus the possibility of buying pigs and mats to circulate. Ever since Mauss', *Essai sur le don* (1925), theories on ceremonial gift-exchange in Polynesia have enjoyed a certain popularity. Yet most of the studies use the example of New Zealand's Maori people. The objects and practices involved in ceremonial gift-exchange in Tonga and Wallis reveal features which are at the same time different and the same. Starting from the study of specific cases drawn from field material and history, Douaire-Marsaudon shows first of all that some of these objects, like food and wealth, function, in the representational system of the societies in question, as individual and collective tokens of identity. But these tokens of identity are not merely static emblems for the individuals and the groups. The author demonstrates that they are no doubt called to represent the individuals and the groups as they are engaged in 'becoming', and she points out some of the implications of this dynamic aspect of these representations of identity; at the same time, she discusses new ways of giving which seem to make a complete break with the traditional conception of gift-exchange.

Food and wealth are not only the primary objects exchanged ceremonially, they are also strongly 'gendered' objects: in both Tonga and Wallis, food is produced, cooked and presented by the men, while 'riches' — essentially mats, barkcloth and coconut oil — are prepared, manufactured and offered by the women. Polynesia is renowned for the considerable quantities of food, especially pig meat and tubers,[27] which can be accumulated for a gift-giving ceremony. The stacking, distribution and collective consumption of these food items have a variety of functions: affirming oneself as a group, establishing or reestablishing relations disrupted by some event (death, birth, transmission of a title, a chief's visit, or today the swearing-in of a member of Parliament).

The 'riches' are mainly objects manufactured by women: lengths of barkcloth, mats and coconut oil. These used to be made by commoners, together with and under the direction of women from the aristocracy who controlled them. Among the aristocracy, certain fine mats and tapas, duly embossed with individual insignia, were passed down from generation to generation and made up the 'treasure' of the *kainga* group, while others circulated between groups, all of which corresponds to Annette Weiner's definition of the paradox of 'keeping-while-giving' or even Godelier's 'keeping-for-giving'.[28] Today the manufacture of these 'riches' has become more democratic, but the noble families still preserve and transmit their highly valuable objects. Thus these female gift-objects are both wealth, 'signs' of wealth and 'talismans' — to borrow Mauss's expression (1925) — believed to attract more 'riches'.

In Tonga as in Wallis, food and wealth are always displayed and given together. Formerly, and to a large extent even today, these gifts were the sign of the debt underpinning the reciprocal obligations between a chief and his people. Today as yesterday, they measure the status and the wealth of the exchange groups, and in other parts of the world, such exchanges often assume a strongly agonistic character.[29] But above all the author stresses the meaning of these male and female gift-objects, located in the traditional system of representations of the life cycle: she interprets them as being held to represent not only the productive or creative capacities of the men and women of the groups present, but also the promise of life carried by these women and men and hence the token of the continuity of generations.

Alongside the traditional food and 'riches', other objects, from the West, have appeared in more recent times, in particular hard currency. And yet, all these items, including the money, which have come to be included in ritual gift-giving, are vested with the same function as the traditional objects. Certain new practices however are altering the logic of gift-giving by making it a means of personal enrichment. The author wonders about the coexistence of apparently entirely contradictory values within the same set of social practices.

We are still in Tonga with the text of Marie-Claire Bataille-Benguigui and Georges Benguigui. The authors show us how, in a Polynesian society where traditional hierarchy still plays a crucial role, aspirations to a new way of managing society and its conflicts — known as democracy — are beginning to emerge. Behind the demands for democracy, we also catch a glimpse of the issue of identity.

Although the present political regime is far from being a model of democracy, it represents the efforts of a nineteenth-century ruler, regarded as the founding father of Tonga, to protect this country from the voracity of the great powers by endowing it with a European-style Constitution containing the first affirmations of democracy and individual rights. By preaching that all people are equal before God, the Christian Churches also helped sow the seeds of equality and individualism. These continued to grow with Tonga's entry into the capitalist market economy and its mutation into a consumer society. Other facts too played a role in the emergence of the democracy debate: the growing demand for education, large-scale Tongan emigration, the birth of a so-called 'middle' class and the appearance of an intelligentsia. The pro-democracy movement crystallised around a newsletter and a group of leaders — often teachers — from middle-class backgrounds.

At the outset, the opposition denounced excesses and corruption in general. A second phase opened with the demand to oversee the activities of the government ministers — almost all nobles — a much more 'sacrilegious' exigency in the eyes of the traditionalists. A third phase began with the calling of a massive Convention, inviting all of Tonga's intellectuals and religious leaders living at home or abroad. This Convention ended with a call for a new Constitution which would limit the king's function to an apolitical role, thus provoking a split in the opposition between those who, desirous of reform, still supported the monarchy, and the others who challenged the idea.

The identity debate broke out over the 'passports' affair, in which the government had sold, at fabulous prices, the Tongan passport to citizens of Asian countries in a 'delicate' or precarious situation. Following a series of petitions and mass demonstrations, the government was forced to call an emergency meeting of the Parliament to 'regularise' the affair by constitutional amendment.

One measures in this instance the distinctive nature of these States. Their smallness (Tonga numbers 100,000 inhabitants) means that news spreads fast and that a government cannot conceal its actions for long. Furthermore, their already long history of contact but also a tradition of reciprocal obligations between chiefs and subjects result in the formulation of a certain number of demands for democracy in political life. At the same time, owing to the sentiment that the existence of sacred chiefs rests on a millennia-old tradition, any clever appeal, in case of conflict, to a transcendent reference is still effective. Thus today many members of the democratic opposition do not want to hear about any revolution which might topple the royal family by force.

That is why, running through all these debates, we see various ideas which may even seem contradictory. Intermixed with the question of Tonga's identity, we find elements of xenophobia. Some of the most fervent supporters of democratisation have at times taken the defence of tradition. Alternatively, a good many churchmen are highly critical. Royalists oppose Western-style democracy to traditional Tongan consensus. Here, too, the debate is complex because, in Tonga, consensus depends on a distinction between nobles and commoners which gives the former an absolute majority in parliamentary decisions.[30] Lastly, the question of economic development has produced some unexpected alliances: the king and certain nobles involved in business have turned out to be fervid supporters of rapid development, while the opposition leader leans towards a slow-paced economic program which would take into consideration Tonga's specificities.[31]

The two authors have collected a large number of quotations from recent stands taken by the various protagonists. They thus provide a very direct picture of the ideological complexity of the ongoing debates. We see how the usual analytical notions of 'syncretism' and 'acculturation' must be set aside. Tongans are well aware of what, on the one hand, the tradition of 'being Tongan' and, on the other, Western values mean for them, and they express their opinion: 'I want to be a modern man and a Tongan, not a modern man who happens to live in Tonga'. Another makes substantially the following analysis: freedom is what people are looking for, therefore democracy is good because of the freedom it contains; but freedom is more important than democracy; now this democracy, when it is 'Lincoln's democracy', leads to political parties and from there opens the way for a new logic of people dominating each other.

The States of this region thus challenge the analysis and ask it to refine its concepts: for one thing, the traditional hierarchical organisation can contain a discrepancy with regard to the idea of political inequality. The first makes the superior the source of the inferior's authority, whereas in inequality the superior and the inferior have simply different access, more or less, to the source of power, which is established or imported from outside. In Tonga, and to an even greater degree in Samoa, a divine-right or ancestral authority, to be brief, based on genealogical ties (a link between the ancestors of the two ranked individuals) does not seem to be experienced in the same way as an authority established by democratic vote. The first is visible because it was already there (even if certain circumstances are needed to reveal or to underscore it — this is the logic of *mana*); the second is unpredictable, subject to the whims of opinion and alliances of the moment. In a word, the first is divine, the second merely human. This is why the debates unfolding in these countries over a switch to a Western-style system of government are much more complex than they might seem: it is not simply a matter of replacing an inequality with an equality.

Serge Tcherkézoff describes the situation in (Western) Samoa. As we mentioned in passing, it presents a number of parallels with the Tongan case when it comes to the ongoing political and economic debate. Although Samoa does not have a royal family but a State, with a head of State, an elected Parliament and a government chosen from the Parliament, the situation is comparable in a somewhat multiplied form. Here the sacred chiefs are all heads of extended families, enthroned in the name of the family founding ancestor: there are over 10,000 of these chiefs (for a population of 160,000). No distinction is made between 'noble' and 'commoner' families, but one is made between those individuals selected by their extended family to carry the ancestor's name (who, from that moment on 'are' the founding ancestor) and the rest. To be elected and thus become the (family) 'chief' or *matai* is not a matter of birthright; the family chooses from among all the descendants according to their assessment of the candidate's capacity to represent the family with dignity in the ceremonial exchanges (oratory, ability to organise work in the gardens but also to amass sums of money, with the abuses such criteria can entail).

The Constitution, voted at Independence, follows the British model in terms of individual rights, but not for elections: only the *matai* can vote and run for Parliament. This is the reason for the debate between tradition and 'democracy'. It is thus a very specific debate, but the ideological positions are similar to those mentioned for Tonga. Does access to political democracy imply the total abolition of the *matai* system? If this were the case, few would support the project because it would mean calling into question the form of society represented by the extended family. This notion of family is the basis of village organisation — the country is essentially one big set of villages — and above all, the keystone of the land-holding system: there is scarcely any private ownership of the land, and 80 per cent of the country is comprised of so-called 'family' lands, managed collectively by the extended family, the sole 'owners' being the ancestors who entrust their management to the *matai*. Nevertheless, the present government is moving towards private ownership, something also demanded by the 'development' advisors. This is why the opposition numbers a good share of the country's 'great' *matai* and their families, that is extended families whose genealogy goes way back (and who therefore contain a greater number of members who recognise each other as descending from common ancestors). One of the first steps taken by the government was to redefine eligibility to vote, which recently has been extended to anyone aged twenty-one and over; only *matai*, however, can stand for election.

Because the *matai* system is the backbone of the family organisation and the land-holding system, as Tcherkézoff's text stresses, the debate is as heated here as it is in Tonga. To do away with this organisation so as to establish a full electoral democracy would be to bring about as fundamental a transformation as a switch from a monarchy to a republic would in Tonga. There would be more equality, but more inequality as well, some say. There would be a rich/poor divide for access to the land, whereas today no one is without. A division would grow up between the political class, accustomed to parliamentary give-and-take and to election campaigns, and those whose upbringing rests primarily on traditional principles and family customs. Here people also mention the fact that the *matai* in Parliament is constantly under the eye of his family and village constituency, which can revoke his *matai* title at any time (and therefore his seat in Parliament): that, some say, is true democracy.

The study also analyses the different periods of change. For the democracy debate is only the latest in a long series. It contains elements which shed light on the first contact, at the time of the missionaries' arrival. When it comes to identity, the analysis distinguishes the way the inhabitants express their belonging (1) to a 'Samoan' culture, *FaaSamoa*, which extends beyond the borders of western Samoa, (2) to a social system, *faamatai* (the *matai* system with all its ramifications, organising a sort of universal hierarchy) and (3) to an independent State, Samoa. These three areas of belonging operate simultaneously, but in spaces which only partially overlap.

Tcherkézoff also raises a general question of methodology for the study of social change. What is needed is a two-level model. At present the Samoan government is facing crucial choices for the country's future. The method proposed makes it possible to foresee some of the consequences. First of all there needs to be an analysis of the different facets of identity (cultural, social, national) over a period of time during which the 'encompassing' values of identity are unchanged (the references which made it unthinkable for some of those concerned that certain relations could ever be reversed). These areas, because they are the most global system of belonging for everyone, represent the first level of the model. In these domains, various concomitant facts can be juxtaposed whose simultaneous presence is contradictory only on a second level, where it creates a sort of space in which the superiorities are indeed inverted, but which remains encompassed by the broader space of the initial references. A host of imported technical objects and monetary practices have thus entered into Samoan society without calling the *matai* system into question. Another change which can occur without producing a fundamental transformation: the new element is directly identified with the encompassing references and placed, without creating a contradiction, on the first level. This is obviously more unusual, but it occurred in the case of the integration of the missionaries: they were ascribed a role of sacred authority with regard to the village, a role which was perfectly identified as that of the sister with respect to her brother when he is a *matai*. Other seemingly innocent modifications introduce elements at the second level which subsequently enter into direct contradiction with the encompassing relations, since the values they create resist inclusion (encompassment) in the pre-existing space, but this contradiction becomes apparent only gradually. This is the case, for example, of any change involving land rights or anything which might destroy the ranked unity of the two basic Samoan principles, in which the principle of family-village organisation (the *matai* system of *faamatai*) encompasses the political organisation (voting laws and the principle of government power, *malo*). In some cases, what is intended as a 'technical' change can lead, through a series of unforeseen consequences, to a fundamental ideological transformation — a modification of the representations of identity, an obliteration of certain encompassing relationships which ensured the individual's belonging. This kind of reflection is necessary for countries which are today massively asking themselves the question of identity in the form of 'what kind of society for tomorrow?'

————————

The situations illustrated by the three sets of articles tells us, in sum, that the cargo won't be coming after all. Those who believed in its imminent arrival, because they had discovered that the world was bigger than their island or their valley, lost all hope when the Europeans departed; today they have altered their expectations and are themselves building different cargo. Those trying to cope with newly enlarged or remodelled identities are experiencing other difficulties and creating other, new forms of hope for the future, such as seizing control of their own land or controlling the economic circuits rather than being controlled by them. And those who saw the wealth arrive two hundred years ago, those who explained to the Whites that, in their language, those things which are 'true', 'effective' and 'divine' are all part of the same notion, *mana*,[32] have long since understood that the holds of the European sailing ships were empty of 'true' wealth and full of bogus wealth. Thus, when Polynesians claim Christianity or democracy for their own, they make them part of their tradition: they feel they know the 'true' meaning of these values, an originally imported one — they admit — but which has long since been transformed by the *mana* of these societies which lived and continue to live on these islands in the Pacific Ocean.

The texts collected in this volume take an *anthropological* approach to the variety of societal problems which confront the peoples of the South Pacific today: religious revival, the sociology of relations between local groups, regions and nation-States, the problem of culture areas, the place of democracy in the transition of States founded on sacred chiefdoms, the role of ceremonial exchanges in a market economy, and so forth. All of these questions call for an anthropological outlook in the sense of a truly *interdisciplinary* approach by what are called the 'social sciences', and above all in the sense of a priority given, through long and repeated fieldwork, to the interpretation of lived experience, what the French term the *vécu*: acts, thoughts and attitudes exhibited and voiced by those confronted with these questions.

The ambition of the present book is to inform the reader about the *contemporary realities experienced* by the inhabitants of this region, with a view to contributing to an *intercultural dialogue* between the reader and these inhabitants, and not with the sole aim of encyclopedic knowledge. It would be of no use to learn that, in such and such a South Pacific country there are cargo cults, astonishing naming systems or an animated debate over democracy, if at the same time one did not become aware of the place occupied by these social facts in daily thinking, in these inhabitants' vision of themselves, when they wonder, not without some anxiety, about their future and their identity.[33]

Footnotes

1   See Worsley (1977).

2   Details on this example can be found in Lindstrom's book (1993), which traces the notion of 'cargo' through the discourses of missionaries, colonisers, anthropologists and local movements.

3   The French traditionally speak of *Océanie*: a geographical and culture area. Today there is a tendency to follow the more frequent local use of the English term, 'Pacific': when countries in the area meet, the speeches evoke the Pacific peoples (see below, the Pacific Way, a well-known expression of identity). Our stopovers are located in the southern part of this region: the South Pacific. Researchers working on this area continue to be known as 'Oceanists' though, in both English and French.

4   Which was already the case in an earlier book devoted to the comparative approach to Polynesia, part of the contents of which coincides with the themes developed in the present volume (Hooper and Huntsman, eds., 1985; for the notion of change, see Anthony Hooper's Introduction, pp. 8 and 10).

5   See Babadzan (1982), Baré (1987), Biersack (ed. 1991), Bonnemaison (1986), Borofsky (1987, ed. 1994), Carrier (ed. 1992), Davidson (1966), Dening (1966, 1980), Friedman (1981, 1985), Godelier (1984, 1991, ed. 1991), Hau'ofa *et al.* (eds. 1993), Hooper and Huntsman (eds. 1985), Howard (1990), Howard and Borofsky (eds. 1989), Keesing and Jolly (1992), Linnekin (1991a), Linnekin and Poyer (eds. 1990), Robillard (ed. 1992), Sahlins (1981, 1987, 1995), Thomas (1989), Tonkin *et al.* (eds. 1989), Valeri (1982), White (1991); as well as *op. cit.* below in notes 14-19.

6   See 'Acknowledgments' and, at the end of this volume, 'Biographies'.

7   It should be borne in mind that South Pacific ethnography was determining for the pioneers of French anthropology: this was true for M. Mauss, for his teacher E. Durkheim (in his last period), for his companions, like H. Hubert, with whom Mauss wrote so many pages on magic in Melanesia, for his young colleagues like R. Hertz, who carried out a detailed analysis of Maori practices (see below). The recasting of the notions of forbidden and sacred, the revision of Australian totemism, of the ceremonial circulation of gifts in Melanesia and Polynesia, as well as the concept of *mana*, borrowed from these same culture areas, are all well known. *Mana*, a term that is both Polynesian and Melanesian, is an active, mobile force capable of assuming any shape. It is rooted in the representation shared by all individuals of belonging to a group which defines their identity; this sharing leads to the idea of a sacred element constitutive of the group (whether or not this idea takes the form of a spirit, a god or an ancestor); this 'sacred' component is then ascribed the power to occupy objects (or people) which, at some point or other, represent the group as a whole in the eyes of each of its members (see Durkheim 1968 [1912]; Hertz 1970 [1928], etc.; Mauss 1904, 1906, 1925; for more on *mana* one can also consult Fournier 1994 and Tcherkézoff 1991, 1995a).

8   See the historical, geographical and social atlas published by Antheaume and Bonnemaison (1988).

9   The first aim was to let other parts of the world know that Pacific basin cultures have a tradition of reaching political decisions by 'consensus' (in contrast to majority rule), which is a way of making peace between diverging views, whereas voting ratifies the victory of one group over another (on the logic of consensus, see Chapter 12, this volume and the reference in note 12, below). A few photos of the Hawaiian trip appeared in the magazine *Poliata* (1995, n°1, Apia, W. Samoa).

10 See Crocombe (1976).

11 Furthermore, today we know (Hooper, 'Introduction', in Hooper and Huntsman 1985) just how artificial these great cultural divisions are and how they were exaggerated by a typological division which took an external view (Burrows 1939; Goldman 1955; Sahlins 1958), and how the same authors sometimes later replaced these views with a 'structural' comparison of the socio-cultural forms which, on the contrary, show the unity of the Pacific cultures — the case of Fiji, geographically situated on the borderline of the former dichotomy, is a prime example (Sahlins 1962, 1987).

12 The Prime Minister of the Cooks explained, in 1975, how even when all the regional heads of State but one were in agreement on a decision, they felt they had to continue talking until they achieved unanimity, at least nominally, rather than force the result by the logic of numerical advantage (see Crocombe 1976: 15–17 for this and other examples of the value of 'unanimous compromise' in defining the Pacific Way).

13 See Panoff (1991: 3).

14 On the consequences of Western-style development, see Lockwood *et al.* (eds. 1993) and Tcherkézoff (1992b).

15 See Keesing and Tonkinson (1982), Linnekin (1983), Hanson (1989), Keesing (1989), Linnekin and Poyer (1990), Trask (1991), Keesing (1991), van der Grijp and van Meijl (1993), Friedman (1993), Otto and Thomas (1997), Babadzan (1999).

16 See Trask (1991).

17 See Jolly and Thomas (1992), van der Grijp and van Meijl (1993), van Meijl and van der Grijp (1994).

18 See Keesing (1989), Linnekin and Poyer (1990), Tonkin *et al.* (eds. 1989; the Introduction presents a detailed study of the notion).

19 See Aiono (1992) and all of the articles in *Culture and Democracy in the South Pacific*, Crocombe *et al.* (eds. 1992); see Hau'ofa (1994), Hau'ofa *et al.* (eds. 1993), Jourdan and Philibert (1994), Lockwood *et al.* (eds. 1993), as well as the many articles by public figures in the Pacific published regularly in *The Contemporary Pacific*, a successful journal launched in 1989 by the Center for Pacific Island Studies at the University of Hawaii at Manoa.

20 With the exception of J.-P. Latouche (CNRS), who worked on genealogies as 'mythistory' (Latouche 1984).

21 On this point, see a recent article in the *Pacific Islands Monthly* (Barber 1994).

22 At least before B. Glowczewski, who presents the case of Australia here (see Chapter 6, this volume, and some of her recent publications 1999, 2002, 2004), to which must be added the work of Marika Moisseeff on the cultural objects which play a central role in reproducing the identity of Aboriginal groups (see Moisseeff 1989, 1994, 1995).

23 As in the case of Australia, the work on western Polynesia is of recent date and is published by the authors present in this volume (see Chapters 10–12). We add that the comparative work on identity and changes in the region began with the special issue of *Etudes rurales* devoted to the status of land in the Pacific, which constitutes a veritable collective work (in which most of the present contributors appear; see Baré, ed. 1992); it is well known how important, for these societies, land is as a fundamental source of identity: 'It is the land that owns the people' (and not the other way around), they say in the Pacific (on this theme, see Chapter 1).

24 See Juillerat (1993).

25 Along the border with Irian Jaya (the western half of New Guinea, under Indonesian rule).

26 The very same history could be traced in western Polynesia for the word *afakasi* ('half-caste').

27 Yams, taros, sweet potatoes in Tonga and Wallis; taros in Tikopia, Anuta, Futuna, Samoa; breadfruit in Tahiti.

28 See Weiner (1992), Godelier (1994, 1996: 50ff).

29 The author disagrees on this point with the interpretation of Mauss (1925) for whom the Polynesian gift system is not competitive in the potlatch sense.

30 In Samoa one hears the same debate about consensus, but this time it is a criticism coming from the opposition, led by the traditional chiefs, against the present government's adhesion to the principle of the majority rule and its consequences.

31 The same split today in Samoa pits the government, closely connected with business, against the opposition.

32 See Sahlins (1987: 38) and above, note 7.

33 We thank Bernard Juillerat and Pascale Bonnemère who kindly read [in 1995] the [French] draft of this introduction [The reader of this English edition must be aware that this text has been written ten years ago. That is why the Bougainville war is mentioned as current, the Solomon crisis is not mentioned, etc.]

PART ONE

Chapter One

ASPECTS AND STAGES OF THE WESTERNISATION OF A TRIBAL SOCIETY:

*The Baruya of New Guinea**

Maurice Godelier

I will attempt to describe the various aspects and stages of the 'Westernising' of a so-called 'primitive' society in New Guinea, the Baruya, who were discovered by white Europeans in 1951 and brought under Australian colonial rule in 1960. Fifteen years later, in 1975, when Australia gave Papua New Guinea its independence, the members of this small society found themselves citizens of a new State, member of the United Nations, whose political system was modelled on that of a Western parliamentary democracy — with a few accommodations to allow for the tribal and regional variations found on this the world's largest island.

The Western model

In the years between 1967 and 1988, I had the good fortune of witnessing the changes in the life-style and thinking of the members of this society, changes that were induced by their forced entry into a new world shaped first of all by colonisation and then by decolonisation, but in all events at the instigation of the West and with the Western model in mind. The Westernisation of the world began centuries ago, intensified in the sixteenth century, and today continues, in new forms. Furthermore, there seems to be no end in sight.

Since 9 November 1989 and the fall of the Berlin Wall, we might even say that the process of Westernisation has resumed within Europe itself. The two European blocs that had opposed each other for a number of decades are today making their way along the difficult road to unification and striving to create or to foster in the former communist countries a system that combines the capitalist market with parliamentary democracy, all of which presupposes freedom of opinion and expression for the citizens of these countries and a multi-party political system. But as can be seen from the tragic example of the disintegration of the former Yugoslavia, this process may run afoul of realities that cannot be imputed to communism, but which are survivals of much older historical divisions. However modern-day 'Westernisation' no longer proceeds from the West alone. It is now a product of the East as well: of Japan and of the four or five 'little dragons'. In these cases, Westernisation no longer results from the simple expansion of the West; it also stems from societies that have retained their political sovereignty and their cultural identity, of which one major component is certainly Buddhism. Today, then, Westernisation continues, but not every aspect of the West can be exported with the same degree of success as was once the case.

What is the West? What are its essential components? Elements that occur in association in the West may be dissociated and appear in combination with different social and cultural components in other parts of the world. In my view, the West is a blend of the real and the imaginary, of achievements and standards, of modes of action and ways of thinking, which today are rolled up into a ball of energy that either attracts or repels and which revolves around three axes, three sets of institutions each with its own logic, representations and values: capitalism, parliamentary democracy and Christianity.

Capitalism is the most developed form of market economy that has ever existed. Parliamentary democracy is a system of government that, whether it takes the form of a republic or a constitutional monarchy, entrusts power to representatives elected by universal suffrage and recognises that all citizens have, in principle, equal rights and equal duties in the eyes of the law. And Christianity is a religion that emphasizes the sins and salvation of the individual and also preaches that one should love one's neighbour as oneself and render unto Caesar that which is Caesar's and unto God that which is God's.

The West today derives its strength from the combination of these three components; they emerged at different points in its history and have only lately met and melded. Christianity has exerted its influence for 2000 years and predates the appearance of capitalism by many centuries. Capitalism began to develop before the sixteenth century within seigniorial and monarchical societies. In the beginning, therefore, it had nothing to do with democracy; indeed, as late as 1906, Max Weber even wondered whether there was any necessary link between capitalism and democracy. Taiwan and South Africa, only one of which is Christian, currently prompt the same question.

These examples remind us that the West has its dark side as well: the conquering, colonial, despotic West drawing its wealth from the resources of the rest of the world, closing its eyes whenever convenient to the lack of freedom and rights under some of the regimes that serve it or are associated with it, encouraging not only individualism but also self-centredness. Such denunciations do not apply to the third world alone: in the West equal rights coexist, sometimes successfully and sometimes not, with what are at times enormous disparities in standards of living, and there are still those who believe that the accumulation of capital depends in part on the legal exploitation of labour.

In short, the West is not a flawless model, but it is still today a source more of attraction than repulsion. At the same time, like any historical phenomenon, it runs the risk of one day being dismantled by history as a result of its contradictions and ambiguities. Immediately after the events in Berlin and Bucharest, that day seemed to have been postponed for several decades or even several centuries. But today, the economic and social disparities mounting up in Eastern Europe and in the South, the struggle for the recognition of long-flouted national and ethnic identities, the appearance of political and religious movements combining fundamentalism and terrorism all raise doubts about a peaceful future for the new world order, though not about the reality of one.

Tribal societies and the example of the Baruya

I would now like to turn the Westernisation of pre-industrial societies, confining my remarks to tribal societies, which are still major components of many nations in Africa, Asia, America and Oceania. What is a tribe? A tribe is a local society composed of a set of kinship groups, united by the same principles of social organisation and ways of thinking, interconnected by repeated marriages and cooperating in the defence of a common territory and the exploitation of its resources. Several tribes may share the same language and the same principles of social organisation. What distinguishes them and sets them apart is the control of a part of nature, a territory.

Thus tribal identity is a composite reality consisting of a cultural and social framework and identification with a territory that has been conquered or inherited from the tribal ancestors and which must be passed on to future generations. Tribal societies have always been highly diverse. In general, however, they may be classified on the basis of two criteria: whether they are still sovereign in their own territory (which is extremely rare) or already part of a State (often a pre-colonial one) governed by the members of a dominant tribe or ethnic group; and whether power within the tribe is shared more or less equally between all groups or is concentrated in the hands of a few at the top of a more or less fixed, hereditary hierarchy. In 1951 the Baruya of New Guinea were one such tribal society with their own sovereign territory in which ritual and political power was held for the most part by a number of lineages descended from conquering groups.

I will analyse the forms taken by the processes of Westernisation in that tribal society and the stages through which those processes passed. Then, rather than making comparisons with other societies, I will show that the processes operating among the Baruya have also occurred and recurred elsewhere.

The Baruya live in two high valleys (at an altitude of 2000 metres) in a chain of mountains in the interior of New Guinea. They were discovered in 1951 by an Australian officer who had heard of the 'Batiya', renowned as salt producers, and organised a military expedition to locate them. At the time, New Guinea was divided into three colonial regions: Irian Jaya, controlled by the Netherlands; New Guinea, a German ex-colony placed under Australian trusteeship after the First World War by the League of Nations; and Papua, a former British colony 'given' by Great Britain to Australia in 1904.

The Baruya population of the time amounted to some 1800 people living in ten or so small villages. The society was made up of fifteen clans, eight of which had been formed by invaders who had conquered local groups. The economy was based primarily on a form of extensive slash-and-burn agriculture, but the Baruya also practised more intensive techniques, growing irrigated crops on terraces. Pig-raising was mainly women's work; and hunting, which was an exclusive preserve of the men, had a chiefly ritual significance and contributed to the assertion of male superiority. At the beginning of the twentieth century, their tools were still made of stone, bone or wood, but the Baruya had no good stones on their territory to manufacture their tools, so they obtained them by trading in salt, which they produced from the ashes of a plant.

The organisation of society was and still is based on the interplay of kinship relations and the general subordination of women to men. Descent is reckoned patrilineally and women are forbidden to own land, use weapons and possess the magic and ritual objects which, according to the Baruya, ensure children's growth. Marriage consists of the direct exchange of women among the men. Formerly large-scale male initiation ceremonies were held every three years, and the entire tribe, with all the villages and lineages taking part, would build a large ceremonial house, the *tsimia*, which the Baruya described as a gigantic 'body', each vertical post standing for one of the tribe's young men who was to be initiated.

In sum, then, what we have here is an example of a small local society, politically independent, with a partly autarkic economy — able to provide for its own subsistence but dependent on the salt trade for the acquisition of tools, weapons, ritual objects and other items, in short, its means of production, destruction and other objects essential for its social and cultural reproduction. It was a classless society, but not an egalitarian one. There were various kinds of inequality; generalised inequality between men and women, and another that set 'Big Men' apart from others. These 'Big Men' were 'big' by virtue of either their function or their merit.[1] They were either ritual masters who had inherited from their ancestors the sacred objects necessary to raise children or to ward off evil spirits, or they were great warriors who had killed many enemies, or they were great cassowary hunters.[2] The Baruya had no concept of the creation of the world. They believed that after a period when sky and earth were one and when animals and human beings lived together and spoke the same language, the present order of the world came about, when the sun and moon broke away from the earth and rose above it, pushing the sky before them. For the Baruya the sun and the moon are powers, remote deities whose actions are beneficial. For example, the sun acts in women's wombs together with male semen to make children. What concerns and frightens the Baruya are the evil spirits living in the forest and the caves, especially the spirits of the dead.

In Baruya society there was no direct link between economics and kinship, between the production of wealth and the reproduction of life: a woman could be exchanged only for another woman. In many other societies in New Guinea and in Africa, a woman was exchanged for wealth (bridewealth), and contact with the West has rapidly led to an enormous inflation in dowries. This reminds us of the great variety characterising the societies on which the West has acted.

The first changes (1951 and before)

The Westernisation of the Baruya took place in four stages under the influence of various forces that acted either separately, successively, or jointly.

The first meeting of the two worlds took place in 1951, but by that time the West had already transformed the lives of the Baruya, although there were no Europeans in the area. During the twenty years preceding this contact, the Baruya, through their salt trade, had obtained steel axes and machetes made in Sheffield and Solingen, in an industrial Europe of whose very existence they were unaware. Seeing the effectiveness of these new tools, they discarded their traditional stone tools in the forest. With their more effective steel tools they saved time clearing land, time which they spent either in fighting or in doing nothing. But to acquire the new tools, they were obliged to produce more salt. The women, who were excluded by tradition from the work of tree-felling, continued to use their wooden tools, and, inasmuch as the Baruya began clearing larger gardens and raising more pigs, introduction of the white people's tools meant more work for the women.

Thus, by abandoning their old stone tools, the Baruya had unwittingly placed themselves in a position of material and economic dependence on the West. But other surprising events occurred during the years that led up to the arrival of the Whites. One day, the Baruya saw in the sky two large birds chasing each other and spitting fire. They were terrified. This was an episode of the Second World War, an air battle between Japanese and Australians that probably took place in 1943. Sometime later a Baruya named Dawatnie, who had gone to trade in salt among the Watchakes, a tribe living far to the north of the Baruya, was led by his hosts to the top of a mountain, from where he was shown in the valley below several of these large birds: beings of human form were entering the bellies of these birds. On returning home he related what he had seen and thus, before they had ever seen any Europeans, the Baruya discovered the existence of supernatural beings of human form and with light skin who lived in large firebirds.

In 1951 the first white man, Jim Sinclair, arrived at the head of a column of soldiers and bearers. The Baruya were then at war with their neighbours, whose fortified villages were positioned on top of the mountains on the other side of the same valley. The white man set up a camp, and in the centre he erected a pole on which he hoisted the Australian flag. He drew up his men and ordered them to present arms to the flag. The Baruya were dazzled by the flashing bayonets, and when the flag was raised the following morning, a warrior named Bwarinmac fell into a trance. He believed he had been possessed by the white man's power, which had revealed itself in the glinting bayonets. At that point the Baruya decided to kill the white man and massacre his troops. But Jim Sinclair, who was completely unaware of their intentions, asked for a dozen very thick shields to be brought and invited some powerful warriors to shoot arrows at them. Then he drew up a platoon of soldiers and told them to open fire: the shields shattered. This demonstration of force impressed the Baruya, who abandoned their plans for a massacre. Thus in 1951 another dimension was added to the Baruya's material dependence on Western tools: their military subordination.

Thirty years later, after independence, things would no longer be the same when the Baruya and neighbouring tribes resumed their warfare. The government sent an officer and a few soldiers to arrest the 'ringleaders', and to impress the crowd the officer made as if to order his men to fire on them. The Baruya explained to him that they were not afraid: he would not be able to kill all of them, as they were too numerous, and in any case he and his soldiers would rapidly be overwhelmed.

But let us return to 1951. The first sight of a white man in the flesh produced a great change in the Baruya. They soon discovered that he was a man like themselves and not a supernatural being, a man who was superior but certainly not a spirit or a god.

Colonisation: Introduction of Western power and knowledge (1960–1967)

Soldiers

Several years went by during which no other Whites appeared. Then suddenly in 1960 an impressive column of soldiers and bearers emerged into the Wonenara Valley on the border between the Baruya and their enemies. This was a flat area where the tribes traditionally gave battle, and because it was flat the white men decided to build a landing strip there. A patrol post was constructed at the end of the strip, and then a party of soldiers set off to identify the tribes and inform them that they no longer had the right to fight each other. The officer in charge of establishing the post and the colonial administration next summoned representatives of the various tribes to explain the new order of things. After appointing them 'chiefs' of their villages on behalf of Her Majesty, the Queen of England, he sent them home. Unfortunately, one of these men was captured on the way back by some warriors of the Yunduye tribe with which his own tribe had been at war when the Whites arrived. He was killed, and his body was fed to the dogs.

On hearing this news, the officer organised a punitive expedition. Three people were subsequently killed, including a woman; a column of prisoners was brought back to the post. One of the prisoners, a great shaman, believed that he could escape from the white men by flying away, since the spirit of the shaman is a bird, and he therefore threw himself — in handcuffs — from the top of a cliff. He crashed to the ground but was not killed, and was terribly disabled for the rest of his life. Another incident, this time among the Baruya, gave the local tribes a fresh opportunity to gauge the white men's strength and determination. Following the suicide of a woman, a battle had broken out between the inhabitants of her village and those of her husband's village. When the officer was informed, he went to the scene of the battle and on the way burned the village of the people he believed to have been responsible for the disorder, the dead woman's village. Unfortunately for the Baruya, two of their sacred objects disappeared in this fire: the dried fingers of a great warrior who had led their ancestors in the conquest of the territory and — much more serious — the flints used to rekindle the sacred flame during initiation ceremonies, which exploded in the heat of the fire. The officer never knew anything of these losses.

Thus, within months of being colonised, the local tribes lost a major attribute of their existence: the right to lead their own lives and the right to apply their laws on their own territory. In short, they lost at one and the same time what we would call political sovereignty and cultural autonomy.

A comprehensive census of the population was begun at that time, as a State can exercise its authority only over a registered population. Peace was imposed, and the villages were forcibly relocated on the valley floor for census purposes and ease of control: the people were obliged to cooperate in the census and to submit to the law; they were prohibited from taking the law into their own hands. The Baruya had just been introduced to an institution that has played a major role in the development of humankind and is regarded as an indication of civilisation: the State. Of course, the State that had discovered them was colonial and authoritarian, but it was seen by Europeans as a necessary stage on the way to the democratic parliamentary State that was to replace it after independence.

Missionaries

In 1966 another component of the West, Christianity, entered the Baruya's territory in force. Lutheran missionaries came to settle near the patrol post and built both a mission and a school. They brought with them evangelists from the coastal tribes, which had been converted to Christianity long before, and they placed one in each village, to preach the word of the Lord. They preached in Pidgin English, the language taught at school, together with the rudiments of arithmetic and writing. The Baruya and the neighbouring tribes welcomed this move, and soon more than one hundred children were attending the school. Two years later the best pupils were sent to one of the mission's secondary schools in a town in the interior. One of the boys in this first class later became a forestry engineer, another a mathematics teacher, and a third, a policeman; one even became a Protestant minister.

Throughout the students' secondary schooling, the missionaries forbade them to return to their tribe to take part in initiation ceremonies. They were told that their ancestors had worshipped false gods and that they and their parents had previously been living in sin without knowing it. A split developed between those boys who were to remain 'bush-Kanaka' like their parents, and the minority, the 'school boys', who had begun to 'evolve'. Some of the latter declared at that time that the customs of their ancestors should be abandoned and that they 'spat on the loin cloths' of their fathers. Fifteen years later, however, nearly all of them returned of their own accord to take part in the big initiation ceremonies. We shall now see why.

Kanaka comes from the French word 'canaque', which is used to refer to the tribes of New Caledonia. This term had been taken over by the Australian administration to refer to the scarcely pacified bush tribes. The Baruya had therefore become 'bush-Kanaka', primitive people living in the forests. Yet it was these same 'bush-Kanaka' who had decided to send some of their children to school, thereby demonstrating their determination to join the new world that had been imposed or proposed, a world which, as they quickly realised, they could no longer avoid. The soldiers, evangelists and bearers, black like themselves and coming from unknown tribes, were proof of that. They therefore sent their boys to school either without initiating them, or limiting their initiation to several hours and a few rites, whereas tradition demanded that boys be separated from their mothers and the world of women by the age of nine and that they should live in the men's house up to the age of twenty, when they would marry. The Baruya's leading shaman also sent his own son to the school. Twenty years later the son, now a Protestant minister, returned to his tribe and was made deputy to the German missionary in charge of the Lutheran mission. At the time two Baruya clans had decided, with government encouragement, to establish a sort of sales and purchasing cooperative, and they entrusted its management to him. He was expelled from the mission, however, for making his wife's mother pregnant. Later, under suspicion of having misappropriated the shop's funds, he was obliged to give up his other position. Today he lives in his village, has taken a second wife and still enjoys undisputed prestige.

Civil servants

In 1965 the administration began to recruit up to thirty per cent of the men in certain villages for work on coastal plantations. Many Baruya who wanted to 'see some country' volunteered for this work and went off for a period of two years. At the time, the administration did not allow indigenous people to renew their contracts, as it was afraid they might begin to form organisations if they remained for too long at the same plantation. The men were housed in barracks, fed and paid a few dollars a week. At the end of their contract, they were given roughly two hundred Australian dollars each, which they could spend as they wished. Most of them spent part of this sum on tools, blankets and umbrellas, which they distributed when they got back to the village. The Baruya thus became wage-earners who freely sold their labour.

In fact the money they earned and the food rations they received did not amount to a real salary. They had experienced the discipline of continuous piecework under the supervision of foremen, an experience that was completely foreign to their traditional forms of labour. They had seen the ocean (of whose existence they had not dreamed) and ships and planes. But on their return in 1967 many declared that they would not leave again even if asked.

In 1967, following the soldiers, the missionaries and the civil servants, an academic anthropologist arrived: myself, bringing the Western presence up to full strength. Following Western forms of authority, here was now a Western form of knowledge. After a few months, I was asked by the patrol officer to tell him who the true fight-leaders, the real 'ringleaders', were, since it was obvious that the Baruya had put forward men without importance as their village chiefs. The missionaries, for their part, would have liked to know what went on during the shamanist ceremonies and who the 'sorcerers' were. Like any doctor, I invoked professional ethics to justify my silence.

'Makim bisnis'

In 1968 the administration, in its preoccupation with development, organised huge campaigns to encourage the tribes to plant coffee and distributed thousands of coffee plants free of charge. Agronomists came to explain what types of soil and what exposure were suitable for the crop. Coffee fetched a good price at the time, since Brazil was going through a production crisis, something of which the Baruya were completely unaware. As producers of salt, they knew what it meant to produce for exchange or for sale. But their salt was at one and the same time a commodity and their currency. In the case of coffee, they were producing a commodity that they did not consume themselves, and which brought in a currency that was produced and controlled by others.

The Baruya set to planting coffee trees in the belief that they would be able to make money without leaving their valleys and without subjecting themselves to the discipline of plantation work. But a problem soon arose: certain families had good coffee-growing ground, and others did not. Initially the old rule of reciprocity between families allied by marriage applied, and the lineages that had a large area of good land allowed their brothers-in-law to plant coffee trees there. But a coffee tree has a life of some twenty years. Allowing someone to use one's land to plant coffee was therefore entirely different from allowing him to plant sweet potatoes or vegetables, which are harvested at the end of a single season. Economic differentiation began to develop between lineages and between individuals, a phenomenon that had not existed with subsistence agriculture, with the exception of salt-producing land. In short, the Baruya began to *makim bisnis*, to do business in the way the administration did, which was widespread in those regions that had been colonised for a long time. But *makim bisnis* meant selling to the Whites, not — yet — to one's brother, to a member of one's own tribe, to a Baruya.

That threshold was crossed the day the Baruya decided to sell the meat of a pig they had killed. Among the Baruya, pigs had always been exchanged as gifts between relatives, allies, initiates, and so forth. The selling of pig meat meant turning a gift into a commodity; it meant accepting the idea that anyone with money, even someone with no personal link with the pig's owner, could apply to purchase that commodity. Impersonal commodities and an abstract *Homo economicus* made their appearance in a society that had traditionally operated on the basis of personal relationships.

Independence: learning about parliamentary government, involution, recombining models

At the end of 1968, Australia decided to organise countrywide elections in order to establish an assembly of representatives drawn from the various regions, the first step towards the parliamentary democracy that was to replace the colonial administration after independence. A number of parties already existed, including the PANGU party, which was nearly the only one demanding independence; its secretary, Michael Somare of the Sepik, was to become Prime Minister of the first government of the independent State of Papua New Guinea. But in 1968 the Baruya were entirely unaware of the existence of these parties and of the significance of the elections. By a stroke of luck, I was present when they took place.

The various tribes of the region were assembled at several easily accessible points in the mountains. A European officer arrived with his interpreters and set up a polling station in a tent. He explained that all the registered adults should vote and that by so doing they would send to the capital people who would speak up for them to the government. Then, as hardly anyone could read and therefore choose between ballot papers, the crowd was shown posters with the pictures of nine candidates, black and white: all were unknown to the tribes. The officer provided some information about the candidates and their programs. Each man and woman was then called by name and asked to point to one of the photos. The men were bashful, and the women were terrified. For example, one of them who placed her finger between two photos was shouted at; she then pointed to one photo at random. She had 'voted'. Such were the Baruya's first lessons in parliamentary government. Since then the Baruya have come to be perfectly aware of the importance of having their own representative in the National Assembly. But they have encountered two problems, which they have not yet solved. It is essential to win a seat for lineages to agree on a single candidate and that other tribes be prepared to back that candidate. But each tribe wants to be represented by one of its own members, and each lineage would prefer to choose the representative from within its own ranks.

In 1975, without asking, the Baruya became citizens of an independent nation that immediately became a member of the United Nations. This was the end of the of decolonisation period, and independence was granted to them by Australia, then governed by the Labor Party. The colonial period had been extremely short, just fifteen years. A further twenty-five have now passed since independence. Where do the Baruya now stand?

Since independence (1975–1995)

Several months before the proclamation of independence, Dick Lloyd, a missionary from the Summer Institute of Linguistics, who, from late 1951, had been the first European to live continuously among the Baruya and learn their language, returned with the first book printed in that language, a remarkable translation of the Book of Genesis. At the time only two of the small number of Baruya who knew how to read and write had become Christian, since in order to be baptised it was necessary for polygamous men to repudiate all but one wife. But repudiating a woman meant breaking an alliance with people to whom a man had given his own sister; it also changed drastically the status of the children of the woman concerned. The Baruya found this too difficult; they also did not really understand why the white missionaries from the various Protestant denominations — the Seventh Day Adventists, the Lutherans and the New Tribes Mission — fought among themselves to recruit them.

At that time the Lutheran mission, run by a German who had escaped from the German Democratic Republic, opened a trading post beside the mission. A sum of two hundred dollars was invested to purchase the usual range of goods: knives, rice, umbrellas, etc. When this first batch was sold, the money was reinvested to buy a second batch, and so on. At the end of the year, the missionary had $14,000 worth of cash and stock. He was criticised for running this flourishing business by the American missionary from the New Tribes Mission, who prided himself on living in poverty. True, the rate of profit was appreciable, but it was nothing compared with that of the large Australian commercial companies in the towns, Burns Philips and Steamships.

Fresh elections were held to elect the first parliament of the independent New Guinea. The Baruya voted successfully for a brilliant young man, Peter, a medical assistant who was a member of a traditionally hostile tribe, the Andje. They also provided him with a wife. Unfortunately Peter was killed three years later in an air crash, and his successor came from a tribe with which the Baruya traditionally had little contact.

After independence, increasing numbers of children were sent to the school, including girls, who, for the first time in the history of the Baruya, competed directly with the boys in learning to read, write, count and even run. Many young men went off to work on the plantations or sought employment in the towns. The older men remained in the village and continued to plant coffee. But much was now changing in the country. Many of the coastal plantations had been sold by their European owners, who were wary of the consequences of independence and left the country *en masse*. The plantations were bought up by the Big Men of the local tribes. The number of Europeans actually living in the country was dwindling. In the towns, insecurity and delinquency increased. Alcohol, which had formerly been reserved for the consumption of Whites or for the few natives allowed to enter their pubs, was now freely on sale.

The initiation ceremonies — which had never been discontinued among the Baruya during the colonial period, but had merely been held far from the eyes of the missionaries and the soldiers — increased in scale, albeit still without the rituals associated with war, which was now forbidden; and the practice of ritual homosexual relations began to decline. At the same time, the few Baruya who had studied and become policemen, nurses and teachers returned to take part in the initiation ceremonies. These were the very people who, twenty years earlier, had poured scorn on the customs of their ancestors. And it was one of them who in 1979 publicly explained to all the men of the tribe and the young initiates that the initiations had to be continued because strength was needed to resist the life of the towns and the lack of work or money; people had to depend on themselves. In my presence he shouted, 'We must find strength in our customs; we must base ourselves on what the Whites call culture [the word was spoken in English].'

Things continued to develop in this contradictory fashion, with the Baruya drawing on certain elements of their culture and abandoning others. They began to combine what they retained with ideas and practices from the West. Thus, in 1980, the Baruya decided to initiate new shamans and organise large-scale ceremonies, which are usually held every eight or ten years. There were few volunteers, since a person who becomes a shaman among the Baruya must remain in the tribe to protect it from attacks by evil spirits and to conduct the nightly struggle against the sorcerers of neighbouring tribes, who seek to lead the spirits of the Baruya astray or to devour their livers. The young men preferred to travel and they had less confidence than their elders in the powers of their shamans. Even the shamans themselves admitted that their powers had not been the same since the Whites had come. And yet a compromise was reached with European medicine. People attended the small medical post for the treatment of broken bones, wounds and infections. The shaman was consulted for internal ailments, which were signs of poisoning by means of sorcery.

That was the situation in 1986, when a problem unresolved during the colonial period suddenly resurfaced, a problem concerning some good coffee-growing land lying along a river. The Yuwarrunatche, neighbours and enemies of the Baruya, who had just lost a war and the land in question at the time Jim Sinclair arrived, decided to recover it by force of arms once they realised that the new State lacked the strength of the colonial administration. War broke out once more. The enemy tribe burned the Baruya village nearest to their border and fatally wounded a Baruya warrior with arrows; they shouted insults at the corpse, telling him to return to the land of his ancestors who had taken this land away from them. School closed down, and the villages were moved back to the mountain tops and surrounded by impenetrable stockades. The hospital and the airstrip could no longer be reached by the Baruya because of the proximity of their enemies, who maintained a permanent presence in the area. No aircraft would agree to land to load the Baruya's coffee. The road built by the colonial administration with the labour of the Baruya and their neighbors was cut by the latter and the bridges destroyed; the road became unusable after the first rainy season. A kind of involution then set in and continued until 1988.

Six or seven Baruya were killed in various battles, and four of their enemies, including their great fight-leader. But it was not the same kind of war as in the old days. Women and children were no longer killed, because that usually led to police intervention. Indeed the police came on two occasions by helicopter to arrest the 'ringleaders', but each time the villages were found empty, and the police merely burned down a few houses.

Finally, in 1988, although a genuine peace had not been established, a long truce set in. The airstrip became accessible once more, but the Baruya had drawn a lesson from the war and had started to build their own landing strip in 1987, in the vicinity of the village furthest away from their enemies, on a high mountain terrace. This strip became operational in 1990. In short, life began again, and the changes briefly interrupted by the war resumed with a new momentum. I shall now review some of these changes.

The latest changes

The Baruya planted more and more coffee, which is men's work. But the bulk of the subsequent work — harvesting, drying and hulling the coffee berries — is done by the women and young girls. Some men also perform this work though, those for whom coffee production and moneymaking have become a sort of passion. Several of them have already managed to save the equivalent of 500 to 1000 dollars. They have learned to sell at the right time and they use transistor radios to keep in touch with the coffee prices in Goroka, a town half an hour away by air. Until now they have done practically nothing with their money. In order to prevent it being stolen, the administration has advised them to place it in savings books, which it supplies. The money is then taken into town by the pilot of the administration plane.

After their experience with the cooperative, the Baruya have once again begun to band together and open small shops in which they resell at extremely high prices the usual range of goods — rice, soap, kerosene and matches — which they have flown in on the mission aircraft. But these businesses often go bankrupt, as the people working in the shops help themselves or give presents for which they do not pay. Increasingly the Baruya kill pigs in order to sell the meat, this at extremely high prices as well. The rule is to make as much money as possible, *makim bisnis.* The women too have entered the market economy. Almost every day a hundred or so of them come to sit near the medical centre, laying out in front of them several kilos of sweet potatoes and bananas and exchanging recent gossip while waiting for customers. Towards midday they return to their villages, most having sold nothing. They then eat what they had come to sell – which had not, in any case, been produced for sale. Economically these exchanges are marginal, but at the social and psychological levels they demonstrate a desire to imitate the Western world and even to become a part of it, if more in symbolic than in real terms.

It is this same desire to integrate that, I believe, explains a new phenomenon of major importance. In 1975 no more than two Baruya had been baptised. Since 1988, however, although there are no longer European missionaries in the region, *Haus Lotu,* churches made of wood and thatch, have been built in nearly all the villages. Many young people and a number of old women gather in these churches on Sundays. Someone who can read Pidgin English 'recites' the Bible and people sing in Pidgin or in Baruya, thanking God for having brought 'light and life' and asking him to 'forgive the sins of his creatures'. In 1988 I was shown long lists of the names of Baruya who were preparing to be baptised.[3] Among these recruits were many polygamous men. When I expressed astonishment, I was told that polygamists could now be baptised. I do not believe this is true, but the Baruya themselves think it is, and it seems to make their conversion to Christianity somewhat easier.

What is the explanation of this increasing desire for baptism? The Baruya do not seem really to understand the concept of sin, and their new Christian feelings do not prevent them from applauding when their enemies are killed, their villages burned or their pigs stolen. I see in this another aspect of their wish to become a part of the Western world, the world of their time. It is perhaps significant that the Baruya put on European dress when they go to pray, and that the women hide their breasts under a blouse bought in one of the local shops. Those preparing for baptism give much thought to the Christian name they are to receive: John, Samuel, Mary, and so on.

What has certainly changed most among the Baruya are the relations between men and women and between generations. Although the boys who remain in the villages are still initiated and live in the men's house, which they are supposed to leave only to go into the forest, avoiding all contact with women, they can now be seen walking around the village and talking to girls. Remarkably, the girls in one village have even put together a basketball team like the boys and practise on the same playing ground on the edge of the village. Jokes and glances are freely exchanged, something that would have been impossible five years ago.

That is where the Baruya stand forty years after that day when a white man leading a column of soldiers and bearers appeared on one of their mountain tops and planted his flag in the middle of their valley. Their society has not collapsed: it is still there, and the Baruya have even increased in number. But their life-style and ways of thinking have been transformed, turned upside down, and the process is irreversible. The Baruya have not submitted meekly to these changes. They have 'acted' and have been partly responsible for them, both the great shaman who sent his son to school and the orphan who became a mathematics teacher at the University of Port Moresby after having studied in Sydney, Melbourne and Auckland. But although they know how to adapt and thus to 'produce society', the Baruya no longer control the development of their own society. It is subject to enormous external forces that have penetrated and now direct it, forces that have come from the West and have already drawn the small society into the logic of the West's relentless expansion. But in the Pacific, 'the West' is no longer synonymous with Europe or the United States, for half the goods sold in New Guinea now come from Japan.

Conclusion

Let us briefly recapitulate the various aspects of these now irreversible processes of submission to the West and integration with it. The Baruya no longer produce their own tools and would no longer be able to make or use the old stone tools. They utilise a currency that is not their own and, in order to earn money, they must become either unskilled and poorly paid wage-labourers or small producers of coffee, which they do not consume and which others export to the world market.

The Baruya have become citizens of a State whose principles and models are of Western origin. Indeed it was the West that introduced them before granting independence to this artificially produced nation. Since independence, Australia has continued to provide a third of the budget of the new State, however this does not mean that the latter simply takes orders from its former colonial master.

But all this still sails way over the heads of the Baruya. We should note in passing that it is probably the existence of over 750 tribes of different sizes and speaking different languages — in a country of mountains and jungles where travel has always been extremely difficult — none of which had ever been able to establish its hegemony, that has made it possible to establish and maintain a parliamentary democracy. Elsewhere, in Africa and Asia, in places where one ethnic group wielded power over others before or after the period of European colonisation, many one-party states and puppet parliaments have grown up after independence.

But the very factors that facilitated the introduction of parliamentary democracy in New Guinea curb its effectiveness. The post-colonial State does not have the material and human resources necessary to maintain a universal presence and to enforce its laws. The tribes quickly realised this and have returned to the use of warfare to settle their problems with their neighbours, as in the good old days. The war between the Baruya and the Yuwarrunatche is an example of this general trend. The State is seen both as an abstract and remote power that is best avoided and as a mysterious near-inexhaustible source of money and various forms of assistance to be exploited as much as possible. Each tribe invokes its right to obtain as much as the others, and each attempts to obtain more than the others. The Baruya too have learned the rules of this game.

They are culturally subject to the West as well as being subordinate to it in economic and political terms. They learn to read and write in Pidgin, a colonial language composed of broken English and Malay, similar to the French and English Creoles spoken today by the black populations of the West Indies. Those who receive secondary or higher education must learn English, the only language that enables them — as it does us in France — to communicate with the rest of the world.

But the most important change is the general erosion and dismantling of the Baruya's innermost culture and the irremediable destruction of some of its components. This has happened in spite of the fact that many Baruya are proud of their customs and have not stood by passively or indifferently as they disappeared. Of all the forces acting on their society, two make *direct* attacks on their culture: the State, which prohibits war and assumes the right to dispense justice; and Christianity, which asserts that the sun and the moon are false gods, that all people are sinners, that the true religion is the religion of Christ, who died on the Cross to redeem the sins of people of all races and all colours. Like Islam and Buddhism, Christianity is a proselytising religion, and the Baruya will probably all be Christian in a few generations, espousing a form of third-world Christianity that may differ considerably from Western Christianity, but which still draws its inspiration from the latter's great eschatological visions and its symbols.

Some of these changes are welcomed by the Baruya themselves. They do not wish to see a renewal of constant, endemic warfare between themselves and their neighbours. But if war is no longer seen as a normal activity for men, for which they must be prepared from the time they are very young, and as an opportunity to become a 'Big Man', this means the collapse of some traditional values and of the traditional social hierarchy.

Furthermore, Baruya men no longer want to spend their entire lives in the two valleys where their ancestors lived and in the four or five others they used to visit at the risk of their lives. They like to travel by air, to stay away for several years, to play cards, to drive trucks. One of them even joined a Japanese factory ship. Two or three have married women from the coast, announcing that they would not be returning to the village and that the women who had been promised to them could be married off to other men.

But most importantly, there has been a major change in the deepest structure of Baruya society, the relations between men and women, a movement away from the traditional denial of women and the affirmation of male dominance. Not that these changes have been accepted without violence. Seven or eight women have been beaten to death or executed by husbands who could not tolerate the fact that they were no longer shown the respect and submission to which tradition entitled them. But the men today are less afraid of female pollution, and the women less afraid of the symbols of male superiority. A few young fathers can now be seen playing with their babies, even when those babies are girls. Previously the very idea would have made them spit in disgust and shame. One thing has not changed, however: marriage, which is still based on the direct exchange of two sisters between two men and two lineages. But the girls have an increasing say and are not forced to marry against their will.

That is my view of the forms and mechanisms involved in the Westernisation of a tribal society. For the Baruya, a white person is no longer a supernatural being but does remain a superior being, albeit one by whom, since decolonisation, they will no longer accept to be ordered around or whipped. But is it not, in one sense, the Whites themselves who, by granting independence, have denied themselves such liberties? And, on a more abstract level, is it not white religion that preaches that all men are equal before God?

Will these processes continue? Yes. Are they irreversible? Yes. Will they spread throughout the entire world? Probably, but here we must return to the idea that, although Westernisation will spread, its present three components will not spread with the same degree of success. Japan is today the most dynamic capitalist country, but it has achieved this without sacrificing either its political independence or the basis of its cultural identity. Indeed Japan was never a colony, and Christianity has not long been allowed to vie with Buddhism there. But the tiny Baruya society is as nothing alongside Japan, and there are hundreds of such societies.

I will make a prediction: The West's first triumph will be in Europe, where it will finally conquer Eastern Europe, a task begun in the sixteenth century, well before the advent of the communist regimes. It will also spread in the Orient and in Africa, in connection in this case with Japan and other Eastern countries. Must we join in the applause or tiptoe silently off stage? Why should silence be demanded of those in the West — not to mention the people of the Third world — who continue to believe that Christianity is not the only 'true' religion and that there is indeed no true religion; of those who see that political democracy does exist and welcome it, but know too that there is much to be done to extend social democracy and that nearly everything remains to be done to ensure that the economy and the wealth produced by capitalism, or appropriated by it, are shared out more fairly in the West itself and elsewhere? Why should we refuse to see these negative aspects?

They exist and they affect our lives. Why should we be resigned? Might it be because the end of history has arrived and we are at last living in the best of all possible worlds?

*   This text is an expanded version of a lecture given in Vienna on 13 June 1990, as part of the Wiener Vorlesung im Rathaus, under the title 'Wird der Westen das universelle Modell der Menscheit? Die vorindustriellen Gesellschaften zwischen Verënderunu und Auflösung'. An English translation of the lecture appeared in *The Age of Democracy. Democratic transition in the East and the South*, Basil Blackwell/Unesco, May 1991.

1   See Godelier (1982).

2   For the Baruya, the cassowary is not simply a game bird, it is a wild woman who wanders the forests of New Guinea. Women are strictly forbidden to eat its meat, which is reserved for young initiates and married men.

3   Most want to join the Lutheran church, but some prefer a recently arrived American denomination, The Church of Christ.

Chapter 2

'MY POOR BORDER DWELLERS'

(Yafar 1970—1995)

Bernard Juillerat

'Happiness and absurdity are sons of the same soil.'
Albert Camus, *The Myth of Sisyphus*

In memory of Sembos Wiy

When an anthropologist reaches 'his field', the group he has chosen to study is always in the midst of some crisis. In addition, he often arrives after everyone else (explorers, missionaries, recruiters, administrators, planters). As a rule, however, he is the first one to stop in the village for more than a few days. And above all, he is the first foreigner to pride himself on his lack of power: 'I am not a missionary or an administrator … I am only a man, nothing more', he tells anyone willing to listen, for fear of being taken for one of the 'bad guys'. People will not necessarily be glad to hear this, however, for while the local inhabitants do not like the intrusion of power, they often dream of the arrival of a certain form of wealth. And a wealthy, generous man is also powerful. But the ethnologist's means are limited, and regional development, whose rosy future is much touted by civil servants and local officials, requires an enormous investment of labour. No, true wealth is first of all the wealth of one's dreams, beginning with natural fertility to which the production of 'cargo' — the unlimited resources enjoyed by white people — seems linked. The problem is how to gain access to it, by the shortcut of the imaginary or by the circuitous route of reality.

The following pages present a few of the most striking features and events that gave each of my fieldtrips to the Yafar people of Papua New Guinea its distinctive stamp.[1]

1970: 'No gat rot'

When I first arrived in the Border Mountains, in 1970, it was the era of regular censuses, of the *kiap*'s (Australian patrol officers) speeches on a corner of the village common: speeches about the nation, about the Port Moresby House of Assembly (first elected in 1964), about voting by secret ballot, about the authority of the *kaunsol* [2] and the purpose of taxes, about keeping the village clean and the plans for building a road in the near future between the Sepik Loop and Vanimo on the north coast. In the evening, people would gather on the common around the radio each village had received from the Government; the men would huddle close and the women would stand back — for fear they might contaminate the radio with their periods and keep it from working, so the men of today recall with a hint of irony. But Australia's presence in this area dated only from the early 1960s, after the Protestant mission opened its airstrip in 1959. In 1962–63 Indonesia annexed the formerly Dutch western part of New Guinea, and a bilateral scientific expedition definitively established the location of the 141st meridian, which had been the map boundary for over a century. As they lived outside the Dutch enclaves situated on the eastern side of the border, the Yafar had been contacted by the Dutch administration and missionaries only once. In 1964, the Netherlands had founded a Catholic mission in Kamberatoro, in the former enclave of Jaffi, which was soon linked with Amanab by a motorcycle track. I was the last to arrive, but still after less than ten years of effective local colonisation. And the missionaries had practically never set foot among the Yafar, since the Catholics were too far away and the Protestants were too occupied with their Bible School in Amanab.

Labour recruiters, on the other hand, with the authorization of the government, had been busy, and fifteen Yafar had already been to the *tesin,*[3] a few had even signed up for a second two-year contract. In 1969, they were all still on the copra plantations on Gazelle Peninsula (New Britain), on New Ireland or on Buka Island; I saw the last two when they returned: tee-shirts, sandals, head gear and a ukelele. Indeed these were the last because the region was subsequently closed to recruiters in order to retain the local labour for the construction of the Sepik-Vanimo road. In contrast to the visiting *kiap's* account, the *boi* returning from the plantations told of the 'good' white bosses in Kavieng or Namatanai (New Ireland), who fed their workers well and took care of them when they were sick, and the 'bad' Whites in Buka, who gave Saturdays off, but made them work on Sundays and some evenings by torchlight; they told of the two dollars a week to buy cigarettes or a prostitute (the remainder of their wages was paid at the end of the contract), of the fights or the good relations between the different ethnic groups on the plantations. Worried about what fate held in store for them, a few of the first Amanab indentured labourers, who left in the early 1960s, had run away from Wewak during a stopover where they were made to do the most distasteful chores; some were captured, but others managed to make their way home, trekking for a month through the Torricelli Range, which was fortunately inhabited.[4] Such pathetic tales told by the elders are all that will feed the dreams of the younger brothers and sons of these semi-heroes, who had taken a plane, caught a glimpse of town with its supermarkets, and sailed on the ocean where, as Wiy used to say, 'the trees stop'. '*Mipela no gat rot*', 'we've got no road (to jobs)', no hope for the younger generation of escaping the workaday life of a subsistence economy: land-clearers and sago-eaters, pig-hunters and grub-gatherers, a horrifying infant mortality rate, endemic malaria and periodic epidemics of flu or tuberculosis, but for the oldest members of the group, there is also pride in living on one's own land where genealogies are reckoned in gardens, in sago palms planted by one's ancestors and in fishing rights along the narrow streams handed down from generation to generation. The only road in sight was the future one that the government was asking them to clear across their own territory, in exchange for money: picks and shovels were handed out.

The most valuable thing the *boi* (also called *pinis taim*, 'finish time') brought back from the plantations was their knowledge of Melanesian Pidgin (*tok pisin*), which they passed on to the younger generation; this is the only means of bridging the 750 different languages spoken in the country. At the time, no Yafar man over a certain age and none of the women spoke a word of *tok pisin*. Even today only the younger women are starting to use it. The Yafar who had stayed home knew nothing about the West; they were fascinated by my jungle boots, discovered their recorded voices and even their own faces in photos or in a mirror, and many were unaware that there was any such thing as writing. When they went to Amanab, they would travel in groups of five or six, for fear of sorcery in the territories they had to cross, in spite of the partially completed government road. The mail I sent and received was a complete mystery to them. No wonder then that the ethnographic investigation with its endlessly repeated questions irritated my interlocutors. My work was even boycotted for three months.

Aside from the *kiap*, the Yafar encountered the occasional army unit — national volunteers led by Australian officers. One day a section was camped near the village, and a helicopter dropped off a captain who had come to review the troops. The next day there was a parachute drop, and the Yafar children ran out with the soldiers into the bush to recover the boxes. For the next few weeks, every time the little Cessna from the Kamberatoro mission flew by in the distance, Waya — who will be introduced later — would point his finger in the direction of the aircraft and beckon towards the ground, as though to make something fall out of the sky, while enumerating: 'Fish, meat, tobacco, rice, sugar, biscuits...'

When I left the field on 10 June 1971, I gave my rifle to Wagif, my most valuable source of information, who thereby became the first Yafar *sut boi* (holder of a permit to hunt with a rifle), before going on to be elected councillor. Aside from several young men who were to escort me to Amanab, there was almost no one in the village when I left: my best 'friends' had not even come to shake my hand, and had disappeared into the forest at daybreak. Much later I came to understand that, more than indifference, what they were expressing was a feeling of abandonment, a certain shame at finding themselves alone once more, perhaps a reluctance to show their emotions. When an anthropologist shares his plate and his gun, he becomes, if not a source, then at least a symbol of plenty and well-being, withheld or contested, lost and found again.

1973: 'selfgavman'

In May 1973, the road was open as far as Aynokneri village, where I spent the night on the floor of an abandoned house after having shared a meal of rice and Japanese mackerel with my escort from Amanab. The next day, on Yafar land, I met teams of men busily clearing trees and levelling the ground. An atmosphere of good humour prevailed.

The two-year period of self-government that was to precede the granting of independence in 1975 had been announced and (barely) explained by the *kiap*. The Yafar, and many other groups in the area, reacted with a mixture of disinterest and fear. Not having experienced the abuses of colonisation in the area, the Amanab felt things could just as well go on as they were. What good was it to bring in poor Blacks in place of rich Whites who, even if they did not share their personal wealth, at least provided some temporary work at the district station. The evening discussions among the men smoking their acrid tobacco or chewing betel in the dim light often turned to their doubts, and to their fantasies, about this abstract entity called *selfgavman*, to which they felt the need to give a concrete and even human shape. Surprising rumours made the rounds of the region. The councillor from Ibagum, near Amanab, went about announcing that Selfgavman was going to come and seize all the food and tear out the sago palms. At one meeting on the road-construction site, he proclaimed that 'he' was in Vanimo and would be flying in tomorrow, in the shape of a tall, obese man with a huge belly — no doubt having grown fat on all that he took from others. Shortly afterwards, news came from Amanab that machines were going to level all the hills and make the forest into a wasteland of cut-down trees: Selfgavman again (in fact a Caterpillar used for the southern section of the road on the Sepik side).

At the same moment, the word 'independence' was spreading in various lexical forms and adding to the confusion. The expression *kisim indipendens* ('receive independence') lent itself to interpretation: what exactly were they going to receive? Wagif personally believed that the period of *selfgavman* would be followed by the return of the Whites, and was dismayed to learn that all European civil servants were to be definitively replaced by people from New Guinea.

In spite of such fears, internal solidarity operated. Differences were settled amicably, at worst by a verbal clash — and much waving of bare adz handles — in which men violently argued for the abandoning of their evil plants and respect for the government's 'law'. Thanks to Wagif's rifle and a few others,[5] no one could remember the Yafar ever having eaten so well. I had brought along a new rifle and a few boxes of cartridges (still available over the counter at the time), from which I gave Wagif a stock of 'pig-calibre' shells. Nor were the mediums idle either, but were often possessed by forest spirits, masters of game; evenings were interrupted by shouts from someone in a trance, followed by the feigned anger of the spirit, arrow drawn, then by long conversations between the nameless visiting spirit and the men, who would bring him food and betel in the hope of receiving more animals.

My notebook-cum-journal reflects my frustration each time people had undertaken some activity without informing me (fish-poisoning parties, planting rites, funeral in a neighbouring hamlet and so forth), moments which fortunately alternated with more fruitful days. One of these surprise events was the arrival of fifteen or so Sowanda, fairly distant neighbours and former enemies with whom the Yafar did not intermarry, but among whom their fathers once had exchange partners: first-hand observation of fear and shame behaviour on the part of the visitors — who had come bearing coconuts and yams that they had hoped to exchange for shorts and knives — of jokes at their expense by some of the hosts, of what it means to be non-kin. This was probably one of the last exchanges between the two groups. A short while later, some fifteen men, women and children from another hamlet filed in to receive a penicillin shot that I had promised them, to cure them of yaws, which was still endemic at the time.[6] To bolster each other's courage, they had all come together, for one syringe that had to be boiled between patients.

By the end of my stay, *selfgavman* had 'arrived', and the Yafar rarely mentioned it any more. For my part, I had managed to capture, on the short-wave band of my transistor radio, other, more remote events which made the 'hair-splitting of the ethnographic study' (to quote my journal) seem all the more petty: the American bombing of Phnom-Penh, the Yom-Kippur war, Three-Mile Island.

1976: the school and the last Yangis

When I returned, in February 1976, the Community School (the government-run primary school, where teaching was in English) that the Yafar and the government had been talking about since 1973, had just opened. A big clearing had been made and wooden buildings with leaf-thatched roofs stood in the middle. The largest held the first two classrooms, surmounted by the flag of independent Papua New Guinea with its yellow stars and bird of paradise. Closer to the road, a tiny roof and a corrugated metal cistern provided water for the *sik haus*, a tiny dispensary measuring a few square metres, where a *dokta boi* (three years of study on the coast) from the district had set out his boxes of chloroquine and dressings. A single prefabricated construction housed the headmaster and his family, brought in from the coast. Next door, Yafar 2 hamlet had not changed. It is there that I learned, upon arriving, that the important Yangis ritual was planned for April. No one had ever been willing to provide me with any details about this cult, but I happened to have brought along Alfred Gell's book, *Metamorphosis of the Cassowaries*, published the previous year, and which proposed an analysis of the same rite (Ida) performed by the Umeda, further to the north.

This was the high point of my six-month stay: I saw Yangis for the first and last time.[7] The Yafar themselves had not celebrated this rite for more than ten years and this was, to the best of my knowledge, the last performance. The period of relative prosperity that I had noted in 1973 continued, and each hamlet had the two rifles it was allowed. Endemic malnutrition had therefore declined, and it was this feeling of physical and social well-being that made it possible to celebrate the totemic cult, whose purpose, I was nevertheless told, was to foster fertility. Anxious about the prospect of celebrating this sacred rite — borrowed from their neighbours to the north several generations ago — and required to present visitors with garden produce and smoked meat, the Yafar could not conceive of taking such a risk in times of scarcity. The introduction of rifles had enabled them to resume the tradition.

But there was another determining factor of change at this ceremony: the presence of an outsider. The Yafar found themselves obliged, if not to include me in the actual process of worship, at least to give me a status, albeit marginal, but one which allowed me to go about my business of observing and, to a limited extent, of asking questions. The Masters of the totemic moieties thus had a two-fold task: to successfully negotiate with the spirits summoned so as ensure the efficacy of the ritual, and to keep an eye on me (exclude me or admit me, keep me away or tolerate me) as a potential 'spy' who might abscond with some of the primordial *hoofook* — the fertility principle, original substance and key notion of Yangis — or tell the women what I had learned. It was only during the public part of the ritual that I was given almost total freedom, since it was there that, after months of preparation in the immense wings of the forest, there was to be played out 'in the round' a piece of ritual theatre whose true meaning was carefully concealed beneath a luxuriance of symbols.

Such compromises with the ethnographer always eager for more information, but also capable of serving as a depository — through writing and recordings of images, speech and music — of a body of knowledge that the Yafar and other groups know is doomed to disappear in the near future are indicative of a situation of change, not to say crisis, that strikes to the very heart of cultural identity. A small society with no means of storing information is reduced to the paradox of telling an 'uninitiated' foreigner their ancestral secrets, secrets in which the young generation seems already to have lost interest. A salvage strategy on the part of the elders, for they have one generation at most in which to act, and not every group has an anthropologist standing by, microphone in hand. The request may even be formulated explicitly, as May would later do. But, without being fully conscious of his strategy, the informant can also make the first move and, little by little, reveal what normally should not have been divulged. This was the case of one man who, on many occasions, took pleasure in secretly bringing me what I had been looking for. I do not think it is a betrayal to reveal his name, Wiy, which I mean as a tribute to his tragic fate (see section '1991', below). His information was not always very reliable, and I had to do a good deal of cross-checking, but at the same time, he managed to let his 'betrayal'[8] be known by the community. He saw his challenge to the established order and to the primordial powers as a declaration of freedom. Immediately after the Yangis ceremony, he put me on the track of an interpretation, which was subsequently confirmed; however, he did this in the presence of a younger man, on whose face I could simultaneously read the extent to which this act was received as a transgression. On other occasions, Wiy secretly brought me a lump of red ochre, or a branch of leaves with bright red spots, both of which were supposed to be the blood of the primordial Great Mother; he insisted that I say nothing about this to anyone, predicting the death of his children if I did. But the next day, an adolescent was dropping transparent hints about this sacred object I had been given the previous day. Wiy had denounced himself, as good a way as any of winning a little prestige.

Through these anecdotes, we can see a change in the destination and the use of secrecy. At a time when a culture is crumbling under the impact of the glittering consumer society — but also under the pressure of the need to secure a bare minimum to eat — what good is a 'religious' secret that is thrown into question by the very tangible reality of 'cargo' and which soon will find no more receivers for its social transmission. What good is it — except to be transmitted elsewhere? Such knowledge can be perpetuated only if a certain ambivalence is maintained, with precisely these false precautions whose sole purpose is to preserve, for a little while, the very value that is in the process of being lost forever. But most Yafar were not this bold, I was going to say this lucid. For May, who that year became my chief interlocutor, things that were taboo could only be divulged in the absence of any witness, and then only by bits and pieces; for holding on to the impression that essential knowledge was still under his sole control was the price to pay for maintaining his status in the community. But I noticed that he, like Wiy, felt an irresistible urge to reveal something of what he knew, a desire in which the dread of symbolic loss and social shame mingled with the gratification of being chosen by the foreigner.

1978: *'blak nogut'*

With the Yangis ceremony, people forgot the various misadventures of national independence or the petty problems of parent-teacher relations. It was therefore only when I returned two years later that I realised the enormous disappointment with what people had already felt in 1973 were going to be the meagre times that would come with independence. In Amanab and elsewhere, the Australian administrative staff had all been replaced by indigenous civil servants. On the one hand, the exotic era of European patrol officers, sometimes accompanied by their wives, the times of the butterfly-hunting or penis-sheath-collecting *kiaps* who boasted of their life as cowboys back in Australia or of having just returned from the Viet-Nam war, were over. And on the other hand, the *blakpela kiap*, the 'black kiaps' had no money in the drawers of their administration and therefore no work to give out. They could barely, and then only irregularly, pay for maintenance on the Sepik—Vanimo road, which was constantly being cleared and overgrown again. And yet small chilli peppers were a booming crop; they were not hard to grow and once dried were easily carried to Amanab to be sold to the Administration. Even the women had fields.

The evening discussions reflected a dichotomy not so much between tradition and modernity as between the good old days of the Whites, who had money and 'gave work' and the present, when, in spite of unemployment, administrators still came from Amanab to collect taxes. These tirades invariably ended with '*blak nogut*' ('Blacks are no good', or perhaps '[the color] black is no good'),[9] followed by the expression of a desire that contained a lingering vestige of hope: 'the Whites must come back', which can be understood as 'white (the symbol of *hoofuk*) must be brought back'. Self-directed racism? Can one imagine an African saying anything of the like in the 1960s? What was I to do? Lecture them on the world economy? Explain the relation between an industrialised country and the Third World? Show them that the wealth of the past had indeed been taken away by the Whites (for example, the copra, which a few Yafar had helped produce and whose destination and use they had never known) and that what the Yafar thought they appreciated was only the crumbs of a cake eaten by others? The cargo conception of economic wealth blocked any rational understanding of this domain. In my own naïveté, I nevertheless tried to defend the notions of freedom and political autonomy — against my own 'colour' — taking the example of Africa, 'that immense country populated with Blacks like you', whom the bad Whites had once reduced to slavery. All to no avail: my audience always brought me back to their local concerns; for them, 'government' equalled their district administration. In the end, I became convinced that their view, for the time being at least, and their own interests could not be situated at any other level and that, in a sense, they were right.

One day it was announced that the *kiap* had come and was camped at the school to collect the taxes for the year (around 5 kinas per adult male).[10] But that day, all the Yafar were preparing to celebrate a rite for the spirits who controlled the game; this was to take place in Yafar 3, the hamlet furthest from the school. Taking me as a witness of the injustice done them, the men from my village decided to ignore the administration's presence and to perform the rite with their brothers of Yafar 3. At around five in the afternoon, a Tolai[11] presented himself at the entrance to the hamlet, alone (he had had the tact not to come with a policeman) and dripping with perspiration from having made the hour and a half walk separating the two villages under the sun of the 'big road'. I was in the ritual enclosure with the men who were getting ready for the night dance: somewhat their accomplice before this patrol officer — perfectly polite, as it happened — who made a little speech to these bad citizens, standing next to me as though to associate me with what he was about to say. He explained that Papua New Guinea was rid of the white colonisers and was about to enter a new era, that the people of New Guinea were now a single people, but that freedom was not easy — the Australians having withdrawn a good portion of their aid — and each citizen therefore had to make an effort by paying the tax. Although I agreed with his arguments, I felt uneasy at being 'taken hostage', even for a moment, by a government representative, and without realising it, I stepped back a pace, and the visitor noticed. In any event, his mission was successful, for to my stupefaction, nearly every man present reached into his netbag and took out here a tin box, there a plastic change-purse, and produced the required sum or whatever he had, in exchange for a receipt.

Although they were opposed to the government actions and not particularly interested in local development, the men never again spoke of organising another Yangis. Shortly after the 1976 ceremony, the Master of the Earth, in joint charge of the cult, died suddenly for no apparent reason; people explained this death by his intimate involvement in certain secret aspects of the rite. When I arrived in 1978, I found Now, my first teller of myths, mere skin and bones, and very weak; he died a few weeks later. I do not count the frequent infant deaths, which often went unnoted, as no one took the trouble to tell me about them.

This mission ended with my inviting May to come and see the ocean. When we got to Vanimo, where, thanks to an Australian friend, we were lodged in the most beautiful house in this provincial seat — the temporarily empty dwelling of the provincial commissioner — May did not even deign to glance at the 'big plane' parked on the airstrip (one of the last DC3s of the national civil fleet), climbed into the car I had rented from the Local Government Council as though he had been doing it all his life, but was awestruck by the ocean surging around his feet, then stirred to enthusiastic dreams at the spectacle of the wealth on display in the supermarket and even more by that of the thousands of coconut palms growing along the coast. All those coconuts rotting on the beach without anyone to plant them no doubt evoked for him some primordial time of abundance. In Wutung, a village on the Indonesian border, we visited a rock shelter containing some old bones still bearing traces of red ochre; May noted the similarity with Yafar customs, but did not notice one villager hesitate slightly before shaking his hand, a small incidence of coastal racism with respect to the 'bush kanaka' from the interior. Three days later he took the Cessna back to Amanab, while I was waiting for my flight to Port Moresby and on to France.

1981: 'we started to die'

When I arrived on 4 August 1981, the *big rot* was open for the first time as far as my house in Yafar 1, and I rode to the foot of the hill on the Local Government Council tractor. A few Yafar had heard the motor and were standing at the entrance to the village; among them was old Waya, morose but visibly glad to see me again. Here I would like to quote a passage from my journal, dated 10 August:

… I see Waya at the foot of a house. A sad reunion. His mourning for his wife is written on his face. He says to me: 'May came back from Vanimo after you left [in 1978] and we started to die.' A moment later he shows me the grave of Awan, his wife, in front of the house, he sits down as though still to keep her company. Next door I find my 1978 house in ruins: floor sagging, roof full of holes, walls torn down. '*Ol manki i stilim*' [the children have stolen everything]. Everything is gone except the cooking stove and the Roman scales. They put me in the *haus boi* [the adolescents' house], which the occupants turn over to me for three days, the time to build a new hut at the other end of the village. Everyone is downcast and/or sick. Ufwan [Waya's elder son] looks sullen or withdrawn, but he is above all feverish. [His wife] Amo is [temporarily] deaf and sick as well, she doesn't even hear me, I am told. Then I come upon Wagif, May's younger brother, leaning on a staff like an old man, face drawn, thin, his eyes are hard and his words bitter: 'I am very sick, I am going to die.' One would have taken him at his word to see him … Conversation with Wagif on the 4th of August: he rambles on to me about the Yafar's plight; I guess that he feels it to be bleak, hopeless, I see him anxious about the future. Suddenly he quotes the words of the *kiap* who had encouraged them to 'work hard' for the road. Wagif tells me that the road is the only way to change anything, to change life a little. All that spoken dramatically, brows knit and without a hint of a smile. I talk to him about the heveas he planted several years ago and which he let go to weeds. I talked to several other men about their small heveas fields, telling them it was the only saleable crop, the only stable market according to the administration. The road is fine, but there has to be something to use it for [the coast section did not yet exist]. The small chilli peppers [a prosperous crop in 1978] were finished, no more international market.

I found myself with my bundles, my boxes and suitcases in the *haus boi*. It had been raining for two days and the downpour would last another two. Everything depressed me those first days. The nine people dead, for the single hamlet, in barely three years, those who were sick, Wagif and his pessimism, the rain… May hasn't changed, even though Hwam [his first wife, in her 40s] was no longer living, died a year and a half ago. Wiy is still the same, the same ambiguous humor…

This afternoon, in the company of Yow and Kabyo [Ibniy's clan brothers], went to call on Ibniy [an elderly man, sick for over 6 months and living alone in his garden; one of my former 'informants']. Nice orchard-garden near the Yafar 2 road, a real house, two hearths, the door ajar. I see Ibniy, his face straining towards the visitor. He is naked, squatting in the middle of his house between the two hearths, one of which is full of glowing embers. He is nothing but skin and bones and is covered with dirt and *pukpuk* [dermatitis]. His face is puffy, and his feet and hands slightly swollen. Aside from that, he is talkative, speaks normally, but looks deeply unhappy. His eyes are watery. I think it is the smoke or an effect of his illness; Kabyo whispers to me that it is emotion. Behind him is a pile of sugar cane and a supply of red bananas. Three rusty cans brim with water. A ball of sago lies on a dry breadfruit leaf. I give him four tins of fish and some tobacco with newspaper to roll it in. All he has is an old can-opener that he doesn't know how to work. Kabyo and I demonstrate it on the first can. I ask him if he doesn't want to come back to the village, to his house. He seems to agree, though his brothers say that he is the one who wanted to isolate himself here and that he is ashamed of his condition. Yow laughs when I suggest that we take Ibniy back to the village: 'Em i no gat gutpela skin' [His body doesn't look healthy]. I leave, telling Ibniy that we are going to talk it over in the village and that

I will come back. He is overcome with emotion, holds out his hand and asks me to come back before I go home to my country.

In the village, people file through with fevers, deafness, coughs, asking for medicine … 'Ples bagarap, ples nogut' [The village is done for, no good]. The intention of May and his clan to found a new hamlet isn't very serious according to some [the future would prove the contrary].

Until 1978, Yafar was a community where a certain social harmony reigned, where rifles, chilli peppers and roadwork had changed a few things. Between 1979 and 1981, three events occurred which altered everything: an influenza (or tuberculosis) epidemic — no doubt another contribution from outside — which ran through the whole district and caused 25 deaths among adult Yafar (who number barely 200 individuals); the social conflicts sparked by these deaths attributed to sorcery and the subsequent onset of the break-up of the society, which finally occurred two years later; and lastly, the arrival from West Papua (Irian Jaya) of a hope that was as immense as it was frail, in the form of the Wes cargo cult.[12] To this must be added the ban on the sale of cartridges throughout the border region, a government concession to Indonesia in its fight against the Irianese independence movements, whose members had contacts on the Papua New Guinea side of the border; furthermore, any rifle brought in for repairs was seized. The era of bountiful hunts and sharing pig meat between houses was over. In 1986–87 the sale of arms and munitions was banned countrywide, following a rise in urban crime. Today bows and arrows, spears and traps have once again become the sole hunting techniques practised in Papua New Guinea.

The man who first told me that something was afoot, something hugely secret that I was to keep to myself, went on to inform me almost daily. Trust no longer reigned within the community, there were the followers of the cult and the sceptics: among the former was the main leader, a Yafar 3 man who had never had any power until then, the secondary leaders of the other two hamlets, as well as the youngest men, who periodically went to West Papua (Irian Jaya) to visit allied villages in search of information on Wes, the underground site alleged to contain the original 'cargo'. The few Yafar related by marriage to people in Indonesia were known as 'border-crossers', the legal term adopted by the government, in other words, people who had the right to cross the border for family reasons. The 'brothers-in-law' from the other side spoke Amanab, of course, but they used *bahasa indonesia* rather than *tok pisin*. These foreign kin were accustomed to seeing Indonesian soldiers rather than *kiap*, and the government stations in the region were the Senggi post, Waris (instead of Amanab), and Jayapura (rather than Vanimo or Wewak).

There was an odd atmosphere: men were constantly coming and going between the Yafar hamlets, holding secret meetings in the forest, but some nights they also organised public meetings, featuring inflamed speech-making with a view to preparing the moral restoration of the community that was indispensable to the advent of the millennium. Everyone was supposed publicly to exorcise personal and family disorders. Renouncing sorcery (embodied in the growing of certain magic plants) was the most pressing requirement. Then came marital discord, which gave some women — perhaps for the first time in Yafar history — the chance to speak out in public and to defend themselves or to accuse their spouse. The cult had triggered a wave of solidarity, which was greatly needed by the society as it had been brooding over suspicions of sorcery since the 1979 epidemic. Cult followers now greeted each other with a military salute, bringing their hand up to a non-existent cap. But we shouldn't be too prompt to smile at the mimicries of others. One day on my way alone to Yafar 3, I spotted the councillor, also the secondary leader of the cult, coming the other way; he was walking with his head down, no doubt lost in some millenarian daydream, and did not see me. When we found ourselves face to face on the narrow path, he spontaneously saluted me, although I was not regarded as a follower of the cult. And to my astonishment, I found myself returning his salute, in all earnestness, before we each continued on our way, without having spoken a word.

Prepared in secrecy, these expeditions to the villages on the Irian border, some ten hours' walk away, worried me greatly; for at the same time I read in the *Post Courier* — the Port Moresby daily I subscribed to — that the Indonesian army was sending reinforcements to the area to put down the Melanesian resistants from the OPM, who had recently been in the news.[13] The information that was whispered to me said that, in order to join Wes, cult members had to go to combat school, where they learned to fight with knives, bows or spears. I scented the amalgamation that some must have made, on the other side of the border, between a guerilla recruiting drive and the promise of cargo, between the 'prophets' claiming to know the secrets of Wes and the regional OMP leaders desirous of filling out their ranks.

Abandoning my promises to keep out of it, I explained my concerns, without witnesses, to the expedition member I felt most capable of understanding the gravity of the situation. It must be said that, at the time, the Yafar knew nothing about Irian Jaya and had barely heard of a country called Indonesia, which was only a day's walk from there. He promised to pass on my warnings and to look after the youngest boys, but added that, as far as he was concerned, he had had enough of planting bananas: 'Even if I die over there, I don't care.' This laconic response sums up the state of mind of certain men at the time: leave, get away from the confinement of the ancestral land, do anything, but somewhere else. A few adolescents left the school in Yafar 2 just before finishing their studies. This was a far cry from working on local development projects or weeding heveas plantations. Failing jobs in the towns or on PNG plantations, a small door seemed to be opening, if not on the millennium, then at least onto another life. A double-edged prospect, since the slightest contact, even peaceful and accidental, with members of the OPM, could mean years of prison in the Jayapura jails; alternatively, the Indonesian authorities sometimes welcomed PNG citizens with gifts and jobs on the Merauke—Jayapura road, under the watchful eye of the army.[14] Having indulged in numerous abuses over the years, the Indonesian army needed to touch up its image.

Following the departure of the first Yafar expedition to leave after my arrival, I sent a letter with a small party departing the next day to the person — I was not even sure he really existed — who was supposed to receive the Yafar at the other end, asking him to let them return home rather than involving them in a fight that was no doubt legitimate, but which wasn't theirs. An oral reply was sent back that was intended to be reassuring.

From that time on, I was accused, especially by the most fervent followers from Yafar 3, of meddling in what was none of my business and I was suspected of wanting to block their access to Wes. One evening I overheard a leader softly telling a few young men, who were drinking his words, that Europeans were nothing but *rabis man* ('rubbish men'). When I was more directly challenged, I was obliged to justify myself by saying that my sole concern was the danger the war in Irian Jaya presented for young Yafar men. The image of the White suddenly divested of his aura was linked to the widespread millenarian cliché that Europeans had simply stolen the cargo, which had originally been manufactured by now dead Melanesians. The Yafar were therefore under an obligation to re-appropriate the original *hoofuk*. Aside from the re-interpretation of local myths, the millenarian images I intercepted were often already familiar to me from my readings, including Biblically inspired prophecies, whereas the Yafar were still not Christianised and they had never heard a single verse of the Book of Revelations. A curious paradox: the Bible reached them in a reinterpreted form, not called by its name, unknown to the missionaries and via prophecies that had probably produced numerous conversions some two thousand years ago, in another part of the world. It has often been said that religions are born in times of crisis, in the form of messianic cults.

Rejection of everything that came from the government began with independence and now continued in the millenarian circles. Europeans were assimilated to the government, while discovery of the cargo and the resurrection of the dead were programmed for the other side of the border and in an insecure area. Sometimes the Yafar would catch wind of incidents that had occurred in other parts of their district, over issues they did not understand and which gave rise, among other things, to successive agreements signed between Port Moresby and Jakarta on joint control of the border zone. While the Indonesian army assumes the occasional right to pursue fleeing OPM members across the border, since 1990 they have official authorisation to organise 'civic' visits to border villages in PNG. I do not know if the Yafar benefited from this 'smiling operation'. Would it have reminded them of the visit, already far in the past, of the Indonesian bird-of-paradise hunters who, in the 1920s, had camped with them on friendly terms for several months?

Their disdain for the government received confirmation from an unexpected quarter. Complaints had been lodged with the Local Government Council about the district officer posted at Amanab. With the backing of the deputy from Amanab district, the Council voted to dismiss the officer and, the better to underscore the popular character of the decision, stirred up the population the day he was to take the plane. A few Yafar went to the landing strip, not forgetting to don their war gear, on instructions from the Council — bows and arrows in hand and blackened faces. When they came back, they declared with some pride: 'Dispela kiap em i nogut, mipela rausim em pinis' (This kiap was no good, we threw him out). Unwittingly, they were simply putting into practice the democratic principles chosen by the very government of which the undesirable officer in question had been the local representative.

The day before I left, some ten Yafar who had been absent for two weeks returned from the border deeply depressed. One of them admitted to me that they had been deceived and would not return. The Department of Agriculture agent from Amanab happened to be there, to check their hevea crop. I can still see the councillor, one of the cult leaders, who also held the traditional function of Master of the Earth, sitting at the foot of a coconut tree with his head in his hands, struggle to his feet to take the agent to his plot of land, which was overrun with weeds. For the Yafar, all was lost and everything — but what ? — had to be begun anew.

The next day, just as I was about to climb into the administration jeep that had come for me, old Waya, with his snow-white beard and still imbued with the aura of the valiant fighter he had been, with his natural authority and his inherited function of Master of the Sky and the Sun — he who had always joked with me without ever compromising himself by becoming the foreigner's 'informant' — suddenly burst into tears when I held out my hand. It was the tears of all the Yafar, of whom he felt himself somewhat the 'chief' or the emblem, that ran down his cheeks. When I returned five years later, I did not have the heart to visit his grave.

1986: 'mi winim pinis'

When we landed in Amanab in July 1986, I immediately noticed a new neighbourhood of wooden, leaf-thatched houses a short distance from the landing strip: one of the fifteen camps for refugees from Irian Jaya that lined the border from north to south. Of the some twelve thousand refugees having fled the Indonesian army's repression — northwards, following the failed capture of Jayapura by the OPM forces in February 1984 — more than a thousand lived in the overpopulated camp run by the Kamberatoro Catholic mission on the border.[15] In March 1985, the provincial Government had authorised the creation of a camp in Amanab, intended to relieve the one at Kamberatoro. When I arrived in Yafar — on foot since the road was once again impracticable — a new Pidgin word was making the rounds: *refujis*. But the Yafar did not seem directly concerned by the refugees' fate,[16] as they posed no threat to their lands or their safety.

Their main worry was for their own community, which had literally shattered, with some of the people coming together to form a new local group. The 1981 failure of the cargo cult had put an end to the emerging fraternity and had revived old tensions. After Waya's death, May became the new community leader, even though he was not recognised by everyone owing to a series of complex conflicts resulting from the 1979–80 epidemic. I also came to understand that the Waya of 1981 had been crying not only for his dead and the failure of the millenarian hope, but also over the loss of a battle, his final struggle with his younger clan brother May. The latent rivalry between the two big men,[17] although they belonged to two lineages of the same patriclan, had suddenly crystallised accusations of sorcery, in particular after the death of May's first wife. The break was consummated by the death of Waya's wife, in 1981, which logically May and his family were accused of having caused. After having gathered his lineage and other kinsmen and affines into a secret forest camp for almost two years, May had succeeded in founding a new hamlet as prescribed by the rules, that is respecting ritual and gaining the approval of the guardian spirits.[18] He finished the impassioned account of his battle with Waya by these words: 'When Waya heard that I had founded a new hamlet according to rule, not a word left his mouth, and he bowed his head: I had won (*mi winim pinis*)'. Waya's backers had stayed in the original hamlet (my former place of residence), while Yafar 2 had splintered into a multitude of tiny groups scattered around the forest, leaving the school and its staff by themselves. What had just happened corresponded exactly with the alternation between splitting and regrouping that had been described to me in my early investigations: history went on.

The Wes cult dissolved geographically, as it were, into a vast rumour running up and down the border. With the exception of a few nostalgics from Yafar 3, reality had covered over the dream, the awakening had reduced the feeling of absolute loss to one of a vanished illusion. Wagif no longer talked of going off to seek adventure and leaving his wife and children; he had just had twins, no doubt the first who had both been given a chance to live.[19] The sick man full of revolt of 1981 had given way to a good family man, almost happy in the new group that had been founded by his brother.

Three days after I arrived in May's new hamlet, an old Yafar companion, Bone, suddenly died coughing blood: I understood then that the epidemic had been tuberculosis, a disease introduced by Europeans and then unwittingly spread by the *boi* returning from the plantations. I can still see the Yafar men gathered in the middle of the village common where they had laid the naked body, washing it with banana stalks to bring out the scars left by the sorcerer's magic arrow. When they eventually identified the scar, among the many marks borne by the skin of a forest-dweller, each one in turn vented his anger at the unknown sorcerers who were killing them and going unpunished thanks to the government 'law', which banned reprisals, leaving them powerless and trapped between the crime and an imported law that did not recognise it as such. It was the occasion for the youngest to rehearse their rhetorical skills by taking up their elders' arguments against the invisible enemy.

That year I did not stay long with the Yafar because my mission was primarily to study a Waina-speaking group, the Sowanda, with whom the Yafar used to have exchange partnerships. I found the clan hamlets deserted and surrounded by tall stands of coconut palms that had been there for generations. The inhabitants preferred to live in the forest, in isolated 'second homes'; nevertheless, they kept up their village, as though to make their social structure visible to the naked eye. This double-residence system, which was probably also practised by the Yafar in former times, persists with no risk of splits precisely because everyone does not live together, and when internal conflicts break out, people merely go on living on their respective lands, as they normally do. There is neither fission nor fusion. It is social communication reduced to a minimum. And what isolation! Midway between the Sowanda and the Umeda, a clearing had been made and a future government-run school was under construction, ten years after the one in Yafar.[20]

When I came back from Sowanda, May resumed his assiduous visits (which had been going on since 1976), taking pleasure in murmuring into the microphone the secret versions of the myths or his interpretations on the openness or the closure of the subterranean world, home of the bad cannibal father. Switching between Amanab and Pidgin, he liked to replay the tape in order to put in a forgotten detail or to underscore certain vernacular expressions. It was at the end of this last mission that he asked me, when he died, to send his two sons the tapes he had just recorded; they were for him a condensation of the most important elements of his culture, something he could not yet transmit personally to his older sons, just on the threshold of marriage. The tape recording would keep his words in suspended animation until his children were ready to receive a paternal knowledge that was respected but already overtaken by history.

On each of my visits, the Yafar Pidgin had added new words. A few had to do with recent institutions, which deserve comment. First of all the word *yut* ('youth'), not only gave the young men an autonomous status with respect to their parents' generation, but designated groups of young bachelors who banded together into embryonic 'cooperatives' to cultivate common clearings, separate from the traditional gardens, where they produced items that they then sold in Amanab or to the school teachers in Yafar. The earnings were placed in a savings account at the new Amanab branch of the National Bank. The term *pati* ('party') designated the invitation issued by a village to a large number of people from the area — a break with the boundaries of kinship and an unprecedented extension of social relations — for a night of feasting and partying. Large quantities of food had to be prepared and cooked, in particular rice and canned goods, which supposes a substantial financial outlay, nevertheless possibly leading to a profit which would in turn be invested in another *pati*. The invitation was not free, and each diner had to buy his plate, indicated on a price tag (with reductions as the night wore on). In 1986, this new form of 'paying exchange' had just appeared among the southern and central Amanab; the Yafar had accepted invitations but had found the prices prohibitive. May saw this as an opportunity to increase his newly gained prestige as hamlet founder, but he was waiting to get together the sum needed to launch the operation. I left the area without ever having been to a *pati*, but in December 1987, I received a letter signed by May (written by Sembos, see below, section '1991') asking me for a contribution to the organisation of the first Yafar *pati*. With it was a budget amounting to 249 kinas![21] May explained that he was going to organise some intensive hunts ('with bows and arrows but with good dogs') to lay in a supply of smoked meat. I never learned whether or not the plan succeeded. Less interesting, from an anthropological point of view, the *kap ti* ('cup tea') was simply a kind of *danis* ('dance') organised by adolescents and children strumming guitars, beating on makeshift percussion instruments (the traditional drums being denied them for this purpose) and singing, until dawn, the same tune, inspired by the so-called Polynesian music played on the radio.[22]

What about Christianisation? The only effect I saw was that, when I returned in 1986, all the Yafar, men and women alike, had taken Christian names. Not through baptism, but on their own initiative, they had gotten their information from the missionary in Amanab. Where I had been accustomed to talking with Wagifs, Subwens, Kurays, I found Toms, Johns and one Clemens. In reality, however, these names were largely left on the shelf, and the Amanab names were normally used. At the same time, I learned that the Wamuru, an allied group living a short distance to the east, had 'officially' converted to Christianity under pressure from their councillor. A few young Yafar claimed to be willing to adopt the Christian faith (Protestantism) of their own accord. But they did not see any hurry (this was probably done sometime in the 1990s).

1991: 'dokta boi'

In 1989–1990, I visited the Banaro, in West Sepik, and did not return to the Yafar. However, since the mid-1980s, I had been corresponding with a young Yafar named Sembos, the son of Wiy (see above) and Afwey, who was finishing his nurse's training in Finschhafen. When I first arrived in Yafar, he was about five. In 1981, he finished the local primary school and, with one of May's sons, Kumul, was selected by the provincial Department of Education to go to the high school in Aitape, on the coast. Both boys completed four years of secondary school and came back to the village; but Sembos applied to train as a male nurse. A year later, he was sent to Finschhafen, on the northern coast, to a nursing school run by the Lutheran mission. And in December 1990, he returned to Amanab where he was to work at the health centre for a few months before being assigned to the dispensary in his own community. That is what he wanted: to come back and care for his own people, to convince them that illness and death could also be natural phenomena, and as a result to help put an end to accusations of sorcery, which had resumed, as he wrote me in September 1990: 'They [certain Yafar] are changing the modern way of life back to *tumbuna pasim* [the 'customs of the ancestors', an allusion to sorcery].' Furthermore, the mortality rate had once more begun to climb due to an epidemic of some sort: 'Yafar people are dying and the village is empty … starting from babies to adults.' Wagif had let him know that the Yafar were sick and were impatient for him to become the first *dokta boi* in whom they might have complete faith. Sembos in turn expressed his pride in being the first Yafar graduate and added: 'The time for me to graduate is coming and I am very happy that I will be going back to my home land to serve my poor border dwellers.' And as always, he signed: 'Pren bilong yu, Blak skin, Sembos Wiy.' His mention of the border says much about feeling marginal to the nation, forgotten by central government, stuck between a never-finished road and an increasingly militarised zone, symbol of an already forgotten millenarian dream.

Before telling the end of Sembos' story, I would like to come back to the Yafar attitude towards sickness and death. When I arrived in 1973, I noticed the absence of a man whom I knew well because he had helped with my inquiries on my first trip: Woy. I asked what had become of him and was told that he spent his nights in one of his garden clearings, a frequent practice with nothing surprising about it. It was only five days later that I had the presentiment that he must be at home, sick, and not leaving the house, and in fact that is where I found him, lying down, extremely thin, suffering from some disease that affected the lungs, his wife by his side. He admitted that no one came to see him even though he lived in the middle of the village: the result of shame. My antibiotics put him back on his feet and, one night — a sign of life — he was possessed by a spirit while some other mediums were in a trance outside. As he got to his feet for the first time, he fell from the house platform and it was a bloodied medium that rejoined the village community after months of silence. Time and time again the male nurse making his rounds of Yafar 3 found the houses shut, the sick holding their breath so as not to be discovered. I will not come back to Ibniy here, as I have already discussed his case (see above, section '1981').

One last example — though I was not there — is the death of Waya. To be sure, he was an old man. When I arrived in 1986, I asked about his passing away a few months earlier. I was told that he fell ill shortly after May had founded his new group; he stopped eating and within a few months grew very thin (like Ibniy, Woy or Now). Ashamed of his appearance, he asked to be moved to the forest; Wiy took me to see the shelter where he had gone on living for another few months: some palm fronds stuck in the ground at the foot of a tree ten minutes from the village, beside a path, not in a garden like Ibniy. His son, Ufwan, brought him sago every day and some other food until one day he found him dead. Symbolic categories are decidedly more powerful than family feelings and, anthropologist or not, it is hard to understand how the three children of this universally respected man could leave their father out in the cold of night and the rain, scarcely coming to see him and leaving him practically without food;[23] how a man of such prestige could be subjected to such general indifference. It was because a dying person is seen to be living on borrowed time, a future corpse, for the sick body is no longer that of a social person. It is on its way back to Nature, in a regressive movement in which withdrawal from the community implies inhumation in the primordial forest. People are waiting, during this liminal phase, for the body to have the good grace to step aside and allow the soul to resume its proper place between nature and society. Only then will the living once more speak with this spirit of the deceased, who has joined the anonymous ranks of the dead. The repression of the affects here appears in the form of an irrevocable renunciation, as the programmed consequence of a symbolic logic that has become part of society's law.

The sick person is isolated[24] only when his physical appearance — and not simply his condition — makes him 'ashamed' and when he knows that he is doomed. But through an identification with the sick, the shame affects both sides. It is because an emaciated body and dry skin are obvious signs of a loss of *hoofuk* that the person no longer deserves to live in society. If the person has lost his *hoofuk* it means that he has become nothing but a *roofuk* or an *arfêêg* (a term that by metaphor designates a corpse), a skin that is shed like that of a snake, which can only be destined to be discarded at the periphery; the centre, in other words the group and the village, must, on the contrary, rid itself of its *roofuk* in order to go on. This is a symbolic aspect upon which Sembos would no doubt have had to reflect.

Another form of resistance is the rejection of the caregivers, whom the sick person attempts to keep outside the group. A lack of faith in the medicine? No, for the Yafar always ask for medication for minor ailments. Lack of faith in the caregivers' knowledge or skills? Sometimes, in the case of young bush nurses. But the answer lies mainly elsewhere: in the anxiety of being transported to the health centre in Amanab or, worse, to the Vanimo hospital. To die anywhere but at home would be interpreted as an act of sorcery from 'outside' — from the groups in the Amanab area, for instance, or from other patients in the hospital — and not as a fatal outcome of the illness: disease does not kill, men do. Sembos would also have realised that the dispensary and its staff are identified with political power: the nurse is believed to have the right to retain you for long-term care, or to evacuate you to a better-equipped hospital without your consent. In this case, the patient is assimilated to the prisoner who is transferred to the coast (since the closing of the small Amanab jail in the 1970s). What is feared is not so much the acquisition of new services as the loss of that which made every individual a social being: the bond linking the person, even after death, with a group, a land and a history.

Let us now come back to Sembos, son of Wiy, from whom I had not heard since he left Findschhafen. It was not until January 1993 that I learned from a colleague in Port Moresby, who called Amanab, that, right after having started at the health centre, Sembos developed a bad cough. The diagnosis was 'TB', probably contracted on the coast. He was cared for in the same dispensary, but soon his parents — Wiy and Afwey — came to take him back to the village. The chief medical officer could not legally oppose their wishes, but Sembos — at his own request — returned some time later to continue his treatment. His family went back a second time and took him back to Yafar, against medical advice. He died there on 17 April 1991. Contaminated by their son, his father and mother died in turn, a few weeks later, and probably other members of the immediate family after them.

After seven years of study on the coast, he wanted to improve the lot of 'his people' as he was fond of calling them. But the *dokta boi* soon turned into a *sik man*. Imbued with a new status imported from the White world, he was going back to heal bodies and, so he believed, hatreds; but what he brought back was death. He believed he could change the traditional ideas about death, but he became their victim. Defeated, Sembos died like so many Yafar before him, on his own land and in the midst of his family, without medical care and presumed to have succumbed to the blows of human wickedness. Death is even more revolting when it is imputed to others. Whereas symbolic practices disappear so readily from cultural life, the desire to see things evolve remains imprisoned by a 'traditional' explanation that is rooted in a defensive manner of living one's relations with others, which is in turn fuelled by the culture: I can continue to believe in the spirits of the dead while, little by little, forgetting to worship them, I can perhaps forego revenge by physical or magical means on the person responsible for the death of someone close, but on this point I cannot remain silent, for speech is the only weapon still allowed. And it is this speech act, heavy with certainty and feeling, that creates divisions by becoming the coin of exchange of a negative reciprocity ever ready to spring to life.

I immediately wrote to May's son, Kumul, Sembos' former classmate and clan brother, asking him to help me count the dead and those who were still alive. I never received a reply: Yafar wasn't answering.

1995: 'Gol!'

At least not until one day in October 1995, when I received a letter from Kuray, who was an adolescent in 1970 and who had never been to school: he had obviously asked a school teacher to write the letter for him (in Pidgin). He did not answer my last messages or even mention them, nor did he say anything about the past tragedies; at best, he indicated the recent deaths of a few infants. One doesn't wake the dead. He was writing only to ask me to find a *bisnis man* in France who would buy the native gold (*gol*) from the Yafar at a better price than that paid by their government. Yet in the 1970s, a prospector had been sent out by the government to test the Yafar's land, and had concluded that there was no gold. Thus the Yafar's new horizon was none other than that which had inspired the hopes and the migration of so many Europeans to countless Eldorados, among which New Guinea. After all, is there any better symbol of hope and happiness, or any better symbol of disillusionment? Local gold had replaced foreign cargo.

1970–1995, twenty-five years that could be represented by a set of curves, were it not for the impossibility of summing up a slice of collective life in an academic diagram. The first line would be the natural curve of the health of the communities in the area; it has plainly deteriorated since the colonial period. The second line would be the curve of the region's history: migrations, land settlement, etc. The first of these factors triggered defensive reactions — attributions of sorcery — and in former times, offensive reactions as well —

avenging raids — which immediately destabilised the society and even permanently altered the organisation of the local groups. The second factor has almost ceased to be active today, since the land boundaries have been fixed definitively by the administration. With the period of Australian government, and then independence, new and just as fluctuating parameters mingled with the first: the opening of the national space, relations with the government and the regional council, education, the monetary economy, village development, the cargo cult, border problems, Christianisation, the generation gap. Confronted with these new elements, Yafar society has swung between rejection and enthusiasm, between dreams and harsh awakenings. The dilemma engendered by the opposition between millenarian hopes and necessarily slow, uneven development displays the typical profile of the projection of a combination of mythic and psychic images into the near future in order to mask a harsh reality that must constantly be tamed and softened. Since 1970, the Yafar's hopes, and therefore their happiness, have taken two forms: one due to a period of relative plenty within the bounds of self-sufficiency — 'the time of the rifles' — and the other engendered by the illusion of a new era yet to be created, seen at times as being against the Whites and the government, in the expectation of the millennium, and at times as being with them, in the hope that White knowledge, once obtained, would change life. These attempts led to a twofold failure.

The ebb and flow that characterise Yafar history, hopeful rises followed by sudden bitter declines, recall the myth of Sisyphus. When the hero climbed the mountain, his effort was one with his desire, as Albert Camus wrote, whereas the descent was like a 'respiration … that returns as surely as his misfortune'; the moment of an awakening that raises him 'above his fate'. In 1991, the Yafar Sisyphus once more stood at the foot of his mountain: one hand already on his boulder, he lifted his eyes towards the summit; and in 1995, we find him again bent to the ground, labouring to swirl the clay and the sand in his prospector's pan.

Footnotes

1   In the Border Mountains, Amanab District, West Sepik Province; see Juillerat (1996).
2   From 'councillors', elected by their village to the Local Government Council, established in Amanab in 1965.
3   From 'station', but with the general sense of 'urban area'.
4   See Juillerat (1979).
5   The administration would authorise no more than two guns per local group, as much in the interests of protecting animal life as for the sake of security.
6   The Vanimo doctor, Stephen Frankel, a future anthropologist, had taught me and fitted me out with the proper equipment, before personally visiting the Yafar on one of his medical rounds.
7   See Juillerat (1995) and Juillerat ed. (1992).
8   Supernatural punishments for revealing secrets involved essentially fertility: the indiscrete person would no longer find game; whereas the social penalties would take the form of revenge by sorcery on the individual or his children.
9   White is associated with the beginning state of things, whereas black is connected with maturity, just before decline.
10 At the time, one kina was worth around one Australian dollar.
11 The dominant ethnic group in the Rabaul area, in New Britain.
12 The name was a complete secret at the time, but became public knowledge and was openly used as of 1986 in the area of Amanab and beyond. I will not go into the content of the cult here; see Juillerat (1991, 1996, 2001a, 2001b).
13 'Organisasi Papua Merdeka': Organisation for the Independence of Papua or West Papua Movement. War had been brewing in Irian Jaya since the mid-1960s, but it did not erupt in the border zone until the end of the 1970s. In July-August 1981, the military command set up Operation 'Sapu Bersih' ('Clean Sweep'). See *Ethnies* (Survival International France), 3, 1985.
14 I want to make it clear that at no moment did the Yafar express the slightest interest in the OPM's struggle, or in its political or ideological interests. The only thing that held their attention was the promise of cargo. Later, I learned that they had never gone further than the Irianese border village where they had relatives.
15 The biggest camp was Black Water, near Vanimo.
16 Paias Wingti's government was at that time in the process of setting up a cooperative program with the UN High Commission for Refugees; until the end of 1985, the refugees were essentially dependent on aid from churches and NGOs.
17 I use the expression in its Pidgin sense of an elderly, influential man, and not in the anthropological sense of a prestigious man involved in ceremonial exchanges.
18 See Juillerat, 1996, Chap. 1.
19 In former times, the weaker twin would have been killed by the mother herself. The Yafar did not believe that a woman could nurse two children and still fulfill her economic duties.
20 Umeda had had a Catholic school from ex-Dutch New Guinea (taught in Pidgin) in the 1960s.
21 The list included rice, tinned fish, sugar, flour, powdered milk and chocolate, salt, oil and tobacco. Needless to say, I was unable to satisfy the request in its entirety.
22 Other Pidgin terms have also entered the language: *fri* (free), a word I myself had introduced in 1981 in my modest defence of independence, but which had also taken on the meaning of 'free of charge'; *bank*, a personalised institution 'giving' money for local development to 'good' men; *las* (?) *polis*, military police force or policeman traveling by helicopter and tracking notably Melanesians fleeing from West Papua to PNG.
23 To give good food to someone who is believed to be dying is regarded as wasteful.
24 When a sick man still has a wife to care for him, he remains in the village, but no one comes to see him. It also seems that women in the same state are not set out in the forest to die, but probably installed under the house, where they customarily give birth and menstruate.

Chapter 3

MEN'S HOUSES,
OTHER PEOPLE'S HOUSES

Philippe Peltier

Sepik art

In 1965, Anthony Forge published 'Art and Environment in the Sepik River'.[1] The article had an enormous impact. In it, Forge resolved one of the major problems that had been eating at anthropologists since they had become interested in works of art: the laconic — and even lack of — response on the part of local artists when questioned about their work. At best, a Sepik artist will explain to the poor anthropologist, in a curt phrase that brooks no appeal, that such a work represents simply a plant, an insect, a fish or reflections in the water. Any attempt to get more out of him is unfailingly countered by the argument that the pieces are made according to unchanging laws, 'because this is how our ancestors did it'. The refusal to comment is all the more disconcerting because the Sepik is one of the most prolific sources of artistic creation. Sepik villages are laid out around a Men's House, the facade of which is sometimes decorated with impressive paintings — as among the Abelam, where Forge worked — while the interior features a highly complex decor. Confronted with such evasive and stereotypic responses, Forge, and those who worked in the Sepik after him, wondered — and continue to wonder — whether each representation had a meaning and whether an iconological study might be envisaged. The question is unsettling for Westerners, who envisage art, at least in its classic forms, as a means of communication.

What Forge did was to demonstrate that art, and particularly that embodied by Men's Houses, is indeed a means of communication, but one that has its own rules. In view of the artists' obstinate silence and the absence of major myth cycles that would have facilitated an interpretation, he decided to analyse the myths he found and to compare them with those of neighbouring societies. He was thus able to demonstrate that, aside from their ritual uses, Men's Houses constituted a dormant world of symbols whose meaning could be detected in the mystification that consisted in convincing the women that these houses embodied a supernatural power.

The comparative study enabled Forge to show that, above and beyond the difference of architectural forms, similar modes of construction argued for a homogeneity of the representations, which have never been expressed in any form other than buildings and carvings. Men's Houses are thus another way of expressing representations of the world, they are 'a statement about … culture and society made in architectural terms'.[2] They are not amenable to discourse, but express the men's world without using words. He ends his article by showing that, whatever the forms and the symbolic references, the message is always the same: all speak of man's nature and his culture.

This idea, which is altogether classical for the Western mind where every architectural feature, and particularly the main structural elements, is supposed to reflect, on a series of different levels, the foundations of the social organisation — even if the meaning of these elements is never explicitly admitted or recognised — would become one of the obligatory passage points for all art analysis. The method used, and subsequently adopted by many researchers, was less classical.[3]

In the thirty years since Forge's work, the situation in the field has changed radically. In the 1950s, when Forge was conducting his Sepik study, the societies there had already undergone some modifications as a consequence of the war, but they were still living at their earlier pace. Modernity was not yet on the agenda. As the 1960s drew to a close, the forced march towards independence imposed by the colonial government induced a social and economic revolution. Men rose up preaching a return to ancestral ways; old ceremonies and initiations were revived and new buildings flourished.[4] This revival, in many cases undertaken to ward off a much-feared modernity, soon flagged in proportion to the hopes that had been aroused by the advent of a new society. Then, year in year out, villagers found themselves obliged to adapt to the modern world. Today, only a very few villages, like Palimbei, have managed to preserve their old atmosphere and the theatrical majesty of the Men's Houses. But the benches under these houses, where the men once spent so much of their time, now stand empty. And in the near future, Palimbei will probably suffer the same fate as the other villages: following the decline in population, the Men's Houses along the river have turned into modest buildings, sometimes even humble barn-like structures whose importance is apparent to the visitor only from the position at the centre of the village. There, as elsewhere, villagers have been forced to adapt to the laws of the market. Gradually the use of money — whose mysterious origin remains the object of much speculation — has superimposed itself on the traditional exchange values. Tourists, those strange beings who spend their time walking around with their hands in their pockets, have become the principal source of this money. Not only has it been necessary to organise, to rethink and to adapt *kastam*[5] especially for them, the villagers also needed to create those objects of which tourists were so fond, even if they bought all too few: *turist*, carvings or ornaments that often bore only a remote relation to the ancestral objects, but whose sale could represent a major portion of a family's income. It was for the tourists too that, in Angoram, Yentchan, Korogo — and perhaps soon in Kaningara — strange buildings were erected sprouting the new name of 'cultural centres'. These descendants of the Men's Houses are at the heart of a misunderstanding, however. For the tourists, they are the highest expression of local culture; for the locals, they are often merely a locale for the sale of souvenirs.

If one abides by Bateson's description of the Men's House — a place subjected to numerous taboos, a 'hot' place due to the violence and the murders necessary to its construction —[6] then there are no longer any Men's Houses in the Sepik. Or rather, there is every possibility: from those Houses that have survived in a world totally alien to the one in which they were built, to those that have been transformed until they are no more than skillfully decorated empty shells, to those that no longer exist, having disappeared altogether. But whether through adaptation or resistance, they show that their transformation was also a political tool that enabled societies to find a place in the modern world by playing on Western expectations: after all, isn't the Sepik synonymous with art and Men's Houses?

The Porapora region

To show this process of adaptation more clearly, we have taken the example of a small region located between the Lower Sepik, the Ramu and the Keram Rivers. It is known in the literature as Porapora. This region is inhabited by three linguistic groups — Aïon, Adjirab and Armé — who share a number of cultural features.[7] We will be dealing primarily with the Adjirab. This group lives in the centre of the region, on a territory bounded by the Ramu River to the east and, to the west, by the Keram, a tributary of the Sepik. The population is made up of exogamous matrilineal descent groups divided into moieties — in turn split into sub-moieties — and dispersed throughout the territory.[8] The territories and their use-rights are controlled by an older man, but, unlike the practise in the islands or in the Murik region,[9] there is no hereditary chief nor is there competition for an object that would ensure access to any kind of status or rank. Political power rests with a gerontocracy, the older men being obliged to redistribute to the younger ones the goods received in the course of exchanges. The production unit, however, is the household.

Until today this region was the object of very few studies.[10] All patrol reports since the Second World War mention its isolation. The difficulty of access, due to the frequent obstruction of canals by fallen trees and floating weeds or to the armada of mosquitoes that ensures that each passing canoe is a feast — and thus torture for the passengers — has ensured the region is not overrun with visitors. It was 'pacified' by the colonial forces in the early 1930s (no specific date can be established for lack of colonial archives). This belated pacification together with the presence of few missionaries — religious sects having had only a recent and superficial influence — has allowed the memory of the past to survive relatively intact. The situation is therefore not the same as that of other regions, even those close by: amnesia is not complete, as among the Banaro or in the coastal villages.[11]

Although the brand of ethnography that I practice comes under the heading of historical anthropology, the period when village life marched to the drum of 'tradition' is still partly with us, even if it is often evoked with ambiguous nostalgia.[12] I was therefore quite surprised to find, in spite of this isolation, on my first visit (1984) to one of the remoter villages of the region, one of the most thoroughly forgotten by the provincial government, the beginnings of an urban centre. There, between several hamlets, around the inevitable soccer field, proudly stood a church, a school and a small pavilion built for inter-village meetings. Oddly enough, whereas one might have expected a modern copy of colonial-style architecture, the new buildings were modelled on ... Men's Houses. Some young boys improvised a guided tour for us. Eagerly they directed our admiring gaze to the paintings, the carved posts and especially to the figures hung, in accordance with tradition, at the end of the crosspoles of the church roof. They saw nothing incongruous in this: such borrowing has a long history. From a Western viewpoint, it can be understood if one thinks of the propensity of Sepik cultures to import elements from neighbouring groups.[13] It can be understood, too, in the context of the movements that arose in the wake of independence when the young political leaders advocated a return to traditional culture. It becomes harder to explain, however, when one remembers that the transfer was carried out by elderly men trained in another tradition altogether. How and why did these men, in possession of knowledge and in charge of the new building program and its iconography, agree, even under strong pressure from outside, to adopt styles of construction and representation belonging to what were a priori antithetical worlds? How could men with modern convictions accept to represent *giaman god* [14] on the house of *papa god*? Through what irony of history had mutually alien buildings come to co-exist in forms that, even though they were only a distant echo of their original model, nevertheless bore it a strange resemblance?

If we are to analyse these transformations, we need to adapt our methods. While we remain strongly indebted to Forge's masterly work and accept that Men's Houses are indeed 'a statement about culture and society', the disappearance of the rituals and the numerous elements that were once a part of these Houses, and the absence of documents on the architecture of the Lower Ramu — the Adjirab's original home — make it impossible to construct a meaning this way, even if we resort to induction or comparison. I have therefore replaced the study of rituals by a comparison of the buildings as they now stand: the Men's Houses from the past with today's modern buildings; I have further replaced regional variations by a diachronic analysis of the transformations. Admittedly this method is not without its problems, the most important of which is the reconstruction of the state of the Houses at the time of pacification. I am aware of the limits inherent in this kind of reconstruction, but the example of Porapora is typical in that the opening up to the outside world — and the need felt by the groups to redefine themselves or to think their identity — did not arise with regard to the white world as represented by the rapid and transitory tourist trade, but with regard to specific enduring political and religious entities, which reduces the factors to familiar worlds. By proceeding in this way, I hope to show how these transformations, whether repeated or abandoned, resulted in the Adjirab adopting representations in which they attempted to associate events and structures. In other words, I am going to try to provide some insight into how the Adjirab acclimated their history and thus moved from traditional forms to new structures and ultimately came to demand their inclusion in the imagined chorus of those nations from which they receive, from time to time, the occasional muffled signal.

Construction and internal organisation of the Men's House

Even today the Men's Houses are the most imposing buildings in an Adjirab village. A great part of male social life goes on here: young bachelors and widowers live here, old men spend the better part of their time here. Here is where they sleep in the daytime, where they repair their arrows or spears for hunting or fishing; where they hold their informal meetings, discussing — far from the indiscreet ears of the women — sometimes the thousand tiny events that make up village life, sometimes news of the world that arrives belatedly and often distorted. Here too is where they gather when an illness calls for propitiatory rites or when political decisions must be taken that are vital to the life of the village.

At first glance, the Houses have a simple architecture: a roof over an unbroken expanse of floor. Closer scrutiny of a cross-section of the roof shows it is divided into two parts: at the front, an A-frame construction projecting beyond the front of the building and, at the back, an overhang resting laterally on the eave poles, which in turn lie on two rows of side posts, is supported in the centre by a ridge pole which itself rests on posts of an often impressive size. The entire construction is unified by a roof thatched with sago fronds attached to wooden slats. The roof proper is a complex construction. It is comprised of large rafter poles lashed at the top and bottom to the ridge pole and to the eave poles. These rafter poles in turn, by means of a system of vertical poles themselves resting on cross poles, hold the smaller rafters that receive the slats to which the thatching is attached. The flooring is made of unjoined planks laid crosswise over a series of joists supported on posts. These planks are fashioned by unrolling the trunk of a palm tree. The roof and the floor are structurally independent: each rests on its own system of posts.[15] All parts of the roof and the floor are lashed together, making the entire building highly flexible and therefore fairly resistant to earthquakes, which are frequent in the region.

The overhanging porch roof is a remarkable system, at once unusual, refined and complex. It is modelled on the spider's web, which makes it very resistant to high winds: two large poles crossed scissors-fashion rest on two scaffoldings that form a bracket supporting the entire structure. These diagonal poles receive a series of forces distributed by cross poles that are lashed together. The ends of all the large cross poles are carved with ancestor figures. From an architectonic standpoint, this overhang is separate from the back of the floor. The overhang and the roof are joined by the simple expedient of rafters lashed together in bundles of three and are covered by a single roof.

The difference in the principle of construction and particularly the independence of the two main elements would seem to indicate that these two parts were joined at a recent date. For the moment, I will simply say that the roof and the floor are initially constructed exclusively by the members of the descent group to which the house belongs. They are assisted by all their kinsmen, young and old, from near and far, and by their affines.[16] Next, often several months later, comes the second stage, in which the overhanging roof is erected under the supervision of their *adje*. An *adje* is an exchange partner from whom one receives and to whom one gives, formally and according to a strict rule of reciprocity, a certain number of items, among which used to feature yams and the bodies of men killed in war. Every elder of a descent group, and therefore in charge of a Men's House, is in an *adje* relationship with one of his counterparts. Each man has several potential *adje*, who belong to the different descent groups, but only one of these relationships is active and only the elders of a descent group can initiate exchanges with their *adje*. Apart from the occasions already mentioned, such exchanges can occur at any time, whenever a man so wishes: it is said that 'the road to the *adje* is always open'. The *adje* relationship is inherited through a naming system: it commemorates an earlier feat of arms and disappears if two *adje* become brothers-in-law. To finish the roof of a Men's House, an *adje* is obliged to have a tree felled; the trunk of this tree will be used to make the post that supports the end of the roof beam. This post is carved with the figures (totemic animals or heroes) of his own descent group. The setting of this post terminates the construction of the new House. On this occasion, the two groups exchange food— which will be returned with exactitude when the *adje* builds his own Men's House — and sing songs celebrating feats of arms, migrations and the number of enemy heads taken in war or on raids and exchanged by their ancestors.

In the course of this ceremony, the young boys from the descent group to which the House belongs hang from the projecting roof some of the objects and utensils used in previous festivals: food dishes, earthenware cooking pots, fish traps, fibre skirts, animal bones, torches that lit the night dances and so forth. The children of the House also have the right to lay hold of any of the goods in their own father's house without incurring opposition. Bows, arrows, assagais, adzes join the earlier trophies. Among these memorials are hung diamond-shaped or spherical wickerwork constructions representing, respectively, the web of the *akwemp* spider and the nest of the *agem* bees (both insects are especially feared because of their deadly sting). The considerable accumulation of objects gives an impression of wealth: it is a visible sign to visitors of the group's strength, of its capacity to organise exchanges and its power to reproduce itself. The hanging objects symbolically connect the women's world (the House mothers, responsible for a plentiful food supply and its preparation) with the men's (the fathers, whose role it is to protect and feed the children of the House).

This impression of wealth stands in stark contrast to the characteristic emptiness of the interior of today's House. All that it now contains are a few flutes and the belongings of its inhabitants or guests. Once carefully closed off, the House was the men's space *par excellence*, the place of their complicity with the ancestors, there where the most secret rituals were carried out. To protect this place from prying eyes, an enclosure was erected all around the house and behind the first side-posts. This fence delineated the strict separation between the space inside and the space covered by the overhanging roof. Inside, the House was divided into several areas whose boundaries were not physically evident. The first zone, immediately behind the front wall, was where the men slept in times of war or when ritual demanded their strict segregation from women. It is also where the young initiates lived during the time of their seclusion. Further on were the fireplaces, one or several; the men cooked their meals on these whenever taboos forbad their eating food made by their wives. Over these fireplaces stood structures comprised of several racks. The men would lie on the lowest — closest to the fire — when they were sick or needed to warm themselves or simply to escape the mosquitoes. On the upper trays, precious objects were placed in the smoke, which protected them from wood-eating insects. Some Men's Houses had large slit-gongs (usually two) the sides of which bore wooden carvings representing the spirits. These large drums were never shown in public, and their voices — those of the descent group's founding ancestors — were heard only at the most important ceremonies. To the left and right of these slit-gongs, enclosures made of fronds and leaves might be constructed for storing objects or masks. The further one penetrated into the House, the more powerful the objects found there. Along one wall were arranged the skull-stands. A few rare examples were collected in the 1950s and are now to be found in European collections.[17] These stands consisted of a post in the middle of which a cavity had been made to hold the skull. The shaft was carved, sometimes with simple rings or exceptionally with the representation of a human body. But the majority of these stands were not sculpted: all the care went into the skulls themselves, coated with red earth modelled into a face, the eyes suggested by shells. The red earth, obtained in the vicinity of Senaï,[18] was periodically smeared with vegetable oil so as to preserve the deep glossy finish of the face that was proof of its power and vitality. When a new stand was made, a head-shaped stone was placed inside the skull, though it would be hard to see in these stones an anthropomorphic shape and even more a set of 'ears', the feature determining the choice of the stone. These stones were even more important than the skull.[19] They were the invariable component of the object, which gave it its power. A house might have anywhere from five to seven skull-stands. Each was named for an ancestor. In front of these stands, on the floor, were placed skulls of wild pigs, crocodiles or marsupials.[20] All around the stand, sitting on shelves, hanging on the wall or suspended from the roof beams, were skulls, the trophies of head-hunting expeditions.[21] Finally, at the back of the house, behind the partition lined with the skull-stands, was a small room. This was the most secret part, where the most powerful figures were kept: probably wickerwork or wooden representations of the founding animals of the clans. These objects were brought out only on rare occasions, and were guarded by a few men, who were the only ones allowed to approach them.[22]

The problem of description

Like any description, the one we have just read is deceptive. It rests on partial data collected from those who, in their youth, had seen 'big' Houses, if by that we mean those that existed at the time of contact with the white world and which, in some cases, were still standing in the 1950s. Due to the absence of both visual and written archives, however, none of this information can be checked. Furthermore, memory has had time to winnow out what now appears to be fundamental from what can be considered anecdotal. And some elements have been blocked out, as they no longer played any role. Therefore, what counts today is no longer whatever each Men's House held, but the architecture itself, stripped of its inner trappings, which affirms the existence and the strength of a descent group. Paradoxically, the description of the earlier state in fact reflects the situation at the time of the study: it stresses what all Men's Houses had in common (mainly the construction principles, which probably did not vary from House to House) and sets aside the many discrepancies between them. In other words, it reduces all Men's Houses to a sort of ideal model common to all groups: the wealth of impressions, the multiplicity of references and the objects kept there have yielded, in recent times, to a certain aridity that overshadows the many variations that once made up the 'system' of Men's Houses.

Yet the study suggests that each Men's House was a complex world of its own, a testament to the individual history of each descent group. Its material wealth was made up of the many objects that comprised the group's memory. The identity of these objects yielded itself up only gradually and often through a casual phrase in a conversation that did not concern them directly. As our knowledge stands at present, they can be thought of simply as 'signs', traces, props indispensable to the remembering of events. They form groups, but no simple description can render their place or their function, and even less that which ties them together.

What was the relationship between the paintings on the inner walls or the inside of the overhang (or overhangs, since one might be built at both ends of the house), the masks, the personal belongings of an outstanding ancestor and the carved stones — extremely secret objects — kept inside a fibre framework covered with shells and embellished with an animal figure such as a dog or a crocodile?[23] For instance, the only Men's Houses that had paintings were those belonging to the group traditionally recognised as descending from the first founding ancestor to have appeared.[24] The masks belonged to the group which, with respect to its predecessor, occupied a symmetrical position in the dual organisation. Some of the signs formed specific categories, either because they could be reproduced and their possession was linked with a special fabrication skill (flutes fall into this category) or because they were objects that 'came with the elders' and were therefore irreplaceable. Objects once owned by warriors or remarkable ancestors came under this heading. Their special status probably explains why a few rare examples have been preserved to this day. Some, such as spears or shields, were associated with warfare. Others, such as lime gourds and spatulas, body ornaments or the small bags that elderly men used to wear around their neck and in which they kept 'precious' objects, were probably connected with magic and divination.

All of these objects are feared because they are imbued with a power that their owners can use. Many of these items were wrapped and concealed in enclosures woven from palm-fronds in the Men's Houses, where they bore witness to the history of the groups and secured their continued existence. Skull-stands too fell into this category. Their form varied with the descent group that owned them: some had tall carved posts and the head was coated with thin layers of earth; others were small tripods holding skulls that had been greatly enlarged by the many coatings of soil.[25] The first, concealed behind a screen when decorated with tall featherwork structures, were the only ones shown to the new initiates. The second were never decorated and could be seen at any time.

Each Men's House thus had its individuality, the singular product of the founding hero who, in creating it, had endowed it with a name and a personality, and had bequeathed it a certain number of 'signs'. Over the course of its history, it accumulated the traces of numerous events that enhanced its prestige, an indispensable asset for a society in which competition between groups is a major feature of social relations. So it was, then, that, behind a seemingly invariable architecture, Men's Houses displayed a multiplicity consonant with the logic of identity, where the unique and momentarily intangible character of each descent group was affirmed. For every Men's House was an ongoing process of reconstruction. Its prestige could be challenged at any moment, either after a war in which a portion of its goods was destroyed, or following a dispute in which the right to the possession of one object or another was denied. But colonisation eroded these specific features, and no new signs emerged to replace them. On the contrary, the invention of new signs or the introduction of new 'spirits' whose powers renewed the perpetually dwindling powers of the Men's Houses suddenly came to a halt. By putting a stop to the exchange circuits, colonisation signalled the decline of the Men's Houses. There was now nothing to arrest the inevitable progress of their entropy.

Given the disappearance of a large portion of this wealth, a study of the architectural structure is the solution of last resort. As we mentioned, the more-or-less two-speed transformation of the Men's Houses accentuates what the morphological analysis already suggested: the building is indeed comprised of two separate elements, each of which corresponds to a specific function. This bipartition is never openly asserted by the informants. The men of the descent group to which it belongs regard the House as a whole, as a structure whose overhanging roof is the sign, provided by the *adje*, that its existence is recognised. It would be unseemly for the *adje* to lay claim to this construction. In no case can he demand repayment or boast: the position of *adje* implies extreme urbanity and great reserve, which contrasts with the somewhat cocky attitude of the men in general. The difference between the two parts appears clearly only during the construction process or in certain exchanges.

Oral tradition, or rethinking an identity

To explain the different functions connected with the parts of the Men's House, the Adjirab turn to their oral tradition. Before presenting these texts, though, I would like to say two things. First, these texts, at least in their exoteric versions, never allude to the creation of Men's Houses or to any original model. And second, we will leave to one side the enormous problem of their symbolic interpretation. Not that the question is not fundamental, but the near complete disappearance of every representation makes it practically impossible to elucidate. Alternatively, we will retain from the oral tradition the passages to which the men refer explicitly when, in the course of the interviews, we talk about the relationship between the *adje* and the building's functions. These texts show that each part of the House originates at a different time and in a different place. They thus provide a key to the identity of the groups even as they enable us to understand how the Adjirab, by clever use of history, explain their place among the Lower Sepik cultures by way of the Men's Houses.

The first text is a song cycle (*anga*) that tells the story of the Adjirab groups. Or to be more precise, the text contains two song cycles, one for each moiety, in which each descent group recounts its own history. Each segment of the song relates a specific event, usually a war or the conquest of a territory. The verses are deliberately obscure, their meaning being known only to the oldest men, thus establishing their authority. These songs were performed for major events: return from a head-hunting expedition, opening of a House, end of mourning period — unfortunately the most frequent case today. On these occasions, the song may be interpreted in its entirety, each descent group presenting its segment, in chronological order. The complete performance takes from twelve to fourteen hours; but it can stretch over two days if a certain number of incidents are added which are often left out of ordinary performances. A fragment may also be performed in the event of a land dispute, by two or three men, in the course of the argument. In this case the performance takes only a few minutes.

Throughout the Sepik, these songs begin with an account of the way the world began.[26] This is the most secret part. Then they relate the origin of the moieties: how groups living in two villages along the Ramu were plunged into a shared adventure. At the outset, a man or a child of each moiety having died in mysterious circumstances is changed into a tree. The two trees grow on a bluff in the middle of the abandoned villages. In these trees live a number of families. Life is peaceful until one day a conflict arises. Each family sets upon one part of the tree, which succumbs to the blows and falls into the river. It drifts downstream until it reaches the sea, where it disappears. The now homeless families, having metaphorically killed their tutelary figure, flee the spot. They leave the two villages and disperse. Thus begins a time of wars and conquests, waged no longer on outside groups alone, but among the newly independent descent groups themselves. The fortunes and misfortunes of war threaten to undo alliances and territorial possessions. Even worse, certain descent groups, reduced to a handful of women, are taken in by more powerful groups, thus changing from one dual unit to another and undermining one of the major principles of equilibrium and the very existence of each unit. In the song cycles, or in certain portions that can be told, such changes and mobility are often portrayed by two female ancestor figures who roam vast expanses of land playing the savoury but dangerous game of encounter and massacre.

In the two origin stories, the tree is a metaphor for the Men's House: the latter is without any doubt the ancestor after whom it is named. To rebuild a Men's House is therefore to reiterate the act that begot the descent group, it is a way to reaffirm one's identity by celebrating the names of the founding hero and his epigones, represented by the skull-stands. It is they who demand the body of a man or a pig when they are thirsty; they who order wars or initiations. It was to quench their thirst that one of the most important rituals was performed: the giving of the blood of men killed to the enemy. After having been offered to the ancestors, the corpse was given to the *adje*. The *adje's* kin group could then consume them, before the heads, and these alone, carefully prepared, were returned and hung with the other trophies. The names of the dead and the events of the battle were made into songs, and these became part of the existing cycles. Corpses, ancestors, songs and territories therefore form a chain that confirms the links between land, community and ancestors — since the blood spilled onto the ground opens rights to this land. The identity of each descent group is thus founded not only by the sharing of ancestors, but also by the dead that are offered to them. The interior of the Men's House is therefore the place of the descent group *par excellence*, not only because it is there that they keep the representations of their ancestors, but because it is there — in the strict absence of any outsiders — that they also confirm the ties that bind them to these same ancestors. It is there that the certificates of ownership — the heads — are kept, in a chronological and spatial order ordained by oral tradition. Thus the Men's Houses multiply ancestor images: not only do they preserve their trace in the form of objects or skull-stands, they *are* the ancestors, whose exploits are recalled by each war. Within these Houses is re-enacted the alliance indispensable to the continuation of the group: the men feed the spirits who in turn feed the men.

The second text the Adjirab refer to when speaking of Men's Houses is the cycle that tells the story of Nduara and his younger brother, Emprung. Nduara is common to the whole Lower Sepik Valley, where he is known by various names: Mopul in Kambot, Andena in Murik, and so forth. Nduara is often depicted as an ambivalent character. In the Adjirab version, he is violent, but also the inventor of civilisation. He gives humans their staple food, sago, but sentences them to work for their living. He possesses marvellous decorations and magic powers, and he seduces all the women. Finally, he reinvents the Men's House, but uses it as an instrument of revenge. It is this last episode that interests us here. The myth tells how Nduara gets his younger brother to help him build his Men's House. He asks him to dig a big hole so as to erect the centre pole that is to support the roof beam. In reality, however, Nduara is planning to kill his brother. He wants revenge for a simple reason: Emprung not only seduced his wife, he proclaimed his victory by incising a design on her pubis. So the younger brother digs the hole, but his cunning is a match for Nduara's violence, and he makes a hiding place to one side of the hole. As he works, he chews betel nuts and collects the red juice in the halves of coconut shells. When Nduara suddenly stands the post upright, Emprung dives into his hiding place. The betel juice spurts out, and Nduara thinks he has been killed. Emprung makes his way through an underground passage to a garden belonging to his mother. She discovers him when she follows a bird that has stolen her mourning hood. She returns to the village with Emprung. They arrive on the day Nduara is to commemorate his brother's death and the inauguration of his new Men's House, a huge building decorated with paintings and carvings as no other building before it. Nduara's sister and his wife have prepared two fibre skirts for the occasion, one long and black (as a sign of mourning) and the other short and brightly colored. Nduara is infuriated by the return of his brother and pulls down the Men's House on top of all the inhabitants of the region, who are gathered there. Some are killed and turn into crocodiles, others manage to escape.

Like any literary text, these two myths are open-ended and can be interpreted in many ways. One way is to analyse the relations between the three main characters — the two brothers and their mother — of the story played out here between the House and the garden. The elder brother murders his adulterous younger brother. The latter returns to a female place of abundance (the garden) from which he emerges reborn. While he lounges in this garden, eating and attempting to repair the severed thread tying him to his mother, his elder brother founds the culture by completing the construction of the Men's House. Opposite the female world to which the hero regresses through his symbolic death, stands the male world; opposite the original state of plenty, the family gift, stands the world of the law.[27] Another interpretation sees the woman as the object of contention and the Men's House as the instrument of revenge. The two men clash over the possession of the woman, and the younger seems indeed to be the hero of the tale. As for the Men's House, intended as a tomb for Emprung and a monument to the glory of Nduara, it collapses, crushing the men who had come to take part in the inauguration, thus triggering the metamorphosis of two women, one into a bird, the other into a tortoise. All interpretations and commentaries are unanimous on this point: the Men's House is dedicated to war and to the law. But nowhere in this battle do the other men intervene. They are reduced to the role of hapless witnesses to the cosmic battle between two brothers. The law is overriding and is not to be questioned. The story of Nduara thus replays a moment of unity that is immediately destroyed by the violation of a taboo. To this extent, it re-enacts the story of the origin of the two parts. It shows that a Men's House is also — and above all — a story of the exchange of women. If women were admitted on a few very rare occasions, the House 'Mothers', on the other hand, were strictly forbidden entry.

More than the various episodes of the myth, it is the commentaries that reveal some unexpected aspects. First of all, Nduara is shown as a *tumbuna bilong namel*, a middle ancestor, not featuring in the genealogy, without a beginning or an end: he mysteriously vanishes — at least in the exoteric versions — after the fall of the House in Ombos. His sole mission thus seems to be to reinvent the Men's House by showing how to make the carvings and paintings. For the Houses on the Ramu, which are also the founding ancestor, are said to have no representations whatsoever. Nduara leaves a legacy of representations in his own image: without a beginning and without a past. Adjirab culture thus denies any borrowing from other societies; the story of Nduara sets the representations free of prior meaning. Each listener may play on any representation, or shift it around without having to worry that some story may have already given it a meaning and a status. This refusal to acknowledge a beginning goes hand in hand with the affirmation of locality: Nduara erects his house at Ombos. The site is still there. It lies on the way to the Sepik, and whenever a canoe passes over the former hearth, a silence infallibly descends on the passengers. For the river now covers the former site. Its course coincides with the orientation of the House: the overhang faced the coast, the back faced the mountains. There is nothing remarkable about the site itself, unless it is a rise that seems to indicate an old dwelling. But the choice of the site is not indifferent: it stands on the border between the Armé, Adjirab and Aïon groups. The commentaries add that those men not killed or changed into animals with the collapse of Nduara's house ran off in all directions, taking with them the carvings or the designs he had invented. Ever since, his shattered legacy lies dispersed over several regions: one sign is found in Murik, another in Sepik villages, still another in Aïon villages. The story of Nduara thus enables the Adjirab to affirm at the same time their particularities and their oneness with the local cultures. Lastly, another commentary,[28] less common it is true, reveals that Nduara had the idea of honoring his *adje* by building an overhanging roof. He simply added this new structure onto the existing building. This commentary confirms not only the architectonic independence of the two structures, but suggests that the *adje* relationship (or its formalisation in the building) is a more recent invention. At the same time, it shows that the overhang is connected with a function that is of a different nature than that governing the inside of the building. This link between form and function was confirmed on the occasion of a brief visit to the Banaro village of Toko, in 1987. The large Men's Houses had disappeared long ago, but when I asked about their form, people described a simple large building without an overhang. Seeing my astonishment, they told me: 'Here we do not have exchange partners as they do in Porapora.'

The oral tradition reflects two worlds that exist side by side: the song cycle that justifies dual organisation and assigns each group a place of origin, an itinerary and an order of precedence, is echoed by the Nduara cycle, of which we have given only a small fragment, relating the invention of culture, its emergence in the region and the formalisation — or perhaps the introduction — of a new form of social relations. The first period, when each Men's House was centred on the family, thus gives way to another period, in which the Men's Houses bear signs of relations within the society as a whole. These dual representations — the world of war and the world of culture, or more accurately the world of the ancestors and the world of alliances — are bodied forth in the two parts of the Men's House. These two complementary worlds are mutually exclusive and their respective spheres clearly delineated. The mutual exclusion stems from more than the simple fact that the overhang is built by the *adje*, and this is confirmed by a number of ethnographic features, in particular the fact that, during exchanges between two *adje*, any food that crosses a certain boundary (roughly the imaginary line running between the first side posts supporting the roof) ceases to belong to the recipient and must obligatorily be offered to the ancestors. Likewise, the bodies or the heads of enemies, mediums of exchange, are not the same substance when they are used inside the building as when they are used outside.

The edifice is thus divided according to very simple criteria: opposite the closed back end, where the objects founding the identity of the descent group are kept, stands the open front end, which is the site of exchanges between (at least) two descent groups. This complementarity and the exchanges that accompany it are an inevitable component of society. A descent group could not exist without another descent group with which to exchange. Each Men's House is a world that records and preserves, in a variety of forms, the traces left by a group as it competes with other groups while at the same time affirming its relations with them. As a consequence, the Men's Houses scattered over the Adjirab territory and belonging to the same moiety have more features in common than two Houses standing side by side but belonging to different moieties. Their differences might be signalled by architectural features — which are minimal — or by the type of objects stored inside. Membership in a genealogical entity here comes into competition with belonging to a territory. Yet the system is not conceptualised in terms of nested boxes, like Russian dolls, but as juxtaposed units: the rule of first born is superseded by that of first come to the soil.

From a local standpoint, to speak of Adjirab Men's Houses as an entity is a misnomer. And yet the Adjirab do have a representation of their Men's Houses that sums up all the features and opposes them to the other Houses of the region. It is these features (which supplant the individual characteristics of the descent groups) that are held to be specific to the Adjirab culture. The notion is probably recent. Like certain commentaries, it must have been formalised after colonisation, when the multiplicity of contacts with other cultures, from the Sepik or elsewhere, obliged the Adjirab to rethink their identity. Strikingly enough, it is the Nduara cycle that provided the framework. One can wonder to what extent the story of Babel may have served as a model. There is no way of verifying such a hypothesis, but like the tower raised to scale the heavens, the House in Ombos enabled the Adjirab to reassert their particularity and to explain that, over and above the multiplicity of signs and forms, there existed a greater geographic entity of which their culture is a part. Finally, the commentaries on the myth of Nduara provide a place of origin for those who had none, thus engineering an imperceptible passage from myth to history. For what we see here is indeed the invention of history, in the Western sense of the term: the passage from a local idiom to a broader ensemble.

Recent transformations: a church and a school in the shape of a Men's House

Some understanding of when and how the social transformations came about would illuminate many dark areas and permit a finer-grained analysis of the evolution of the Men's

Houses. But unfortunately, not a lot is known. The factors that, in part, protected Porapora — its remoteness and the difficulty of gaining entry to the villages — also favoured its fall into oblivion. The region was rarely visited by Australian patrols and their reports were extremely succinct; the earliest ones disappeared with the last world war. Under such conditions, any attempt to establish even the simplest chronology of the facts runs up against numerous obstacles: the scarcity of documents on the region makes it impossible for the fieldworker to recover lost or forgotten aspects; almost all the eye-witnesses have died, and those who are still living do not see any interest in reconstructing their past experience. Even were one to discover an orthodox reading of the past, one would have reason to wonder whether it might not have been recreated to fit the story.[29]

Confronted with these restrictions, my first task was therefore to try to determine a chronology. Once one has a rough sequence — often established by cross-checking testimonies — another problem crops up: the existence of two kinds of historical knowledge having often contradictory goals and logics.[30] Seen from the West, the history of social change in the area begins with the colonial period; seen from the village, however, this history is part of a long time-line and follows its own models. Seen from the West, history is a single strand; seen from the village, it is made up of a number of parallel strands. For example, a number of events have been appropriated by groups when they directly affected their own rights and customs. They were therefore incorporated into the songs celebrating the history of their ancestors. To this end, they were encoded so as to fit a prosody and a rhythm that made them easier to remember. Their translation does not fail to raise several problems of interpretation. The events themselves are told according to the rules of the genre: factual, descriptive, highly detailed, the story-line is often muddled, and the teller plays on images that draw their meaning from his own reference system. Finally, depending on the informant, there is often considerable variation: between full acceptance or total rejection of the Western world, there was probably a wide range of attitudes.[31] Some events are talked about and commented on freely, others are furtively acknowledged, without further commentary. The elements presented here are therefore partial and to a large degree stem from hypotheses. Because of the lack of documentation, they should by no means be taken for an ethno-historical study. They are based simply on what was perceived by the ethnologist and said by his informants concerning changes in the society some ten years after independence.

As in many places in the Sepik Basin, the history of the eruption of 'modernity' is marked by two turning points: the first was the ban on head-hunting, the condition *sine qua non* for pacification. The end of generalised warfare resulted in, among other things, a rapid transformation of the residence pattern. Formerly, each descent group had had its own Men's House, built a short distance from the village in order to preserve it from contact with the women and children. Each descent group lived together in a hamlet. Today's Adjirab village is a collection of hamlets whose population hovers around 300; the Men's Houses are built at one end of a cleared ground ringed with dwellings. It is not unusual for two historically linked descent groups to build a common Men's House.

The second turning point came in the early 1960s, with the end of the initiations and the exposition on the village common of the objects that used to be kept in the Men's

Houses, out of sight of the women. This display was accompanied by the conversion of younger generations to Christianity, but also by the purchase, by a few priests and unscrupulous merchants, of all the old objects. Within a short time, the Men's Houses were emptied of their objects, and thus of a large portion of their power and their character. But by the time the merchants and missionaries did what they did, the ground had already been prepared. Several Houses had been destroyed by bombardments of the valley in the Second World War; by an irony of history, the inhabitants of the Sepik watched the very White men who had forbidden them to make war engage in an act of massive destruction whose purpose has always escaped them. The Men's Houses were never rebuilt. No explanation was given for this refusal, though it is probable that the fires destroyed objects deemed to be irreplaceable. No doubt this was the sign that times had changed for good.

Several years passed. We have practically no information on the post-war years except that a strong cargo-movement appeared and rice-growing developed and was then all too quickly abandoned. Not living directly on the river, the Adjirab were not subjected to the hoards of tourists that thronged to the Sepik in the 1970s or to the economic development that hit the villages along the river or near the urban centres. All that reached them were the echoes of distant upheavals and those of the modernisation taking place in other parts of the province. Yet these were important years in historical terms. They marked the passage from one set of generations to the next, from those initiated and educated in an unchanged society to those who had gone to the *baible skul* (English 'Bible School'), and then on to Western-style high-schools.

Then came the end of the 1970s and Father Jünnemann. He began the construction of the church at Muruken. His building comes as no surprise: he was part of a two-pronged trend: the rediscovery of the 'traditions' by political leaders and the Church's application of the reforms recommended by Vatican II. Without the Bishop's permission and his logistical support, the building would not have been possible. The Church was beginning to change tactics: instead of rejecting all compromise with the devil, it now advocated getting to know the local customs and retaining those best suited to the praise of God's glory. The Roman Catholic Church of New Guinea, and the diocese of Wewak in particular, applied these divinely inspired changes with no less than religious fervor. After all, hadn't the Church, from the outset and in spite of the danger of drawing down the wrath of a hypersensitive hierarchy, implemented certain reforms advocated by a renascent Rome? 'Some missionaries have been enthusiastic about the use of indigenous motifs and styles in church architecture, music, vestment and ceremony.'[32] A church-raising in all its splendour was the ideal occasion for celebrating the glory of God. No means were spared. The posts and roof were made of local materials; but the paint, nails and certain components of the architecture were flown in by helicopter, as is the custom in New Guinea. A few architectural innovations were introduced: a system of trusses dispensed with the need for the centreposts that cut the line of sight, a row of windows was set into the outer walls to let in the light needed for the readings. Every surface was covered with paintings. The pangal[33] walls were painted on the outside with brightly coloured faces and on the inside with geometric designs. The side-posts and underside of the tie-beams were carved and painted with particular care. As a finishing touch, panels were fastened between the beams and the rafters. These featured semi-realistic paintings, some of which were inspired by Biblical themes taken from Western artworks seen in books. The altar, chairs, bishop's seat, confessional and baptismal font were all carved and painted as well. No surface was neglected. The worship of God, like worship of the spirits, brooks no approximations. Everything must conform to the desires and the traditions reinvented in this framework. As the perceptive psychologist he was, Father Jünnemann had understood that the success of the building and, as a consequence, of the implantation of the faith, depended on the success of the exchanges: in New Guinea anything perceived as boring loses some of its power. And so rice and canned goods appeared at each of the festivals that traditionally marked the end of one of the phases of construction: people still evoke these with emotion.

The result met every expectation. The church, which was a startling sight in this backwater, gave off an aura of wealth that might be the envy of certain Baroque monuments. It contrasted oddly with the little gray corrugated metal buildings along the Bien River. Everything was luxury and profusion. For the Adjirab, not only did the construction seal a new alliance, it also signalled the recognition of their culture by the very people who had combated it. This about-face of religious policy (the Church was one of the Adjirab's few points of contact with the outside world) must have seemed suspicious and even bewildering to some. There had to be something behind it. But it did open up new possibilities which, given the times, must be seized.

Jünnemann seems to have given the elders, even those who were not baptised, a great deal of latitude in determining the iconographic program. A number of men had in fact already taken part in the construction of the cathedral in Wewak, so building a church was no novelty for them. Nevertheless, a few guidelines as to symbolism and part of the program were in order. The program itself was simple. At the front of the church, the post — the one traditionally provided by the *adje* — was carved with the ancestor figures of all the descent groups. Inside the church, the side-posts and the beams carried the figures of mythical ancestors, executed according to tradition. A change was made in the two posts closest to the altar, however, as though the closer one drew to the sacred spot, the more the West regained its power: these bore two totally different figures. Black skinned, dressed in a loincloth, arms raised, they were accompanied by a bird with outspread wings. For the Western eye, there was no doubt as to their interpretation: they represented Christ, blackened by the tropical sun, with the Holy Spirit. Over the altar, that is on the side facing the apse, a painter had represented 'Revenge pursuing Crime', and facing the public, a naive figure that looked something like a devil but without his attributes. However, in spite of the clear break with traditional style and iconography, further investigation revealed that these two figures, far from being taken from religious history, belonged to the local past.

Why this ambiguity, this twin reading? The explanation lies, once again, in the past; it is based on an interplay of correspondences established early on by the missionaries themselves. To explain that, even though they might be black, headhunters and polygamous, Papuans were still like other men, they called upon representations of humanity's origins. Their demonstration was based on both the Bible and myths, which they had listened to attentively and collected.[34] Unfortunately, we will never know the reaction of the old Adjirab men on hearing the story of Adam and Eve for the first time or whether it was obvious for them to compare Biblical characters with those from their own tradition. But the analogy between certain passages enabled them in part to lay one text over the other. When this was not possible, the missionaries could easily explain that the Bible was a secret text that told the true hidden origin of things. This explanation also validated future changes, endowing them with a prophetic character not present in the myths.[35] From the meeting of the two traditions, sprang a new version of Genesis. Today it tells how, in the beginning, were Adam and Eve. This couple lived a holy life until one day Adam took a bite of the mango.[36] That was the beginning of problems for mankind, because there would be Blacks and Whites ever after, and for history, because things became less clear. For, while some agree to date the split between the two worlds back to this time, others favour a version centred on Noah's drunken sleep and the scandalous conduct of his son Ham. In the second version, the priests' influence is more directly apparent, reflecting an interpretation of the texts that was current in nineteenth-century scientific circles to account for the existence of black-skinned peoples. In any event, after these episodes, the fate of mankind was sealed: Blacks and Whites went their separate ways. Time passed. Fortunately for the white world, Christ came. Like Santa Claus, he brought with him the things that had vanished with the dawning of time: cars, radios, money, in sum all those items that make life so pleasant. Alas, blocked by incomprehensible forces, this wealth did not reach New Guinea. There men were left with nothing but their flutes and canoes. And that is how they missed their entry into the modern age.

This story shows how close we are to the cargo cults. The figure of Christ is associated with modern techniques and objects, with wealth. It would probably not take much to rekindle these cults, which were particularly powerful in the area throughout the 1950s. But once man's single origin had been established and the struggle between Blacks and Whites had been engaged under the august protection of the Church, events took a different course, divided into several once again hard-to-reconstruct stages, but which ultimately aimed to despoil the Men's Houses to the benefit of the new cults. If certain informants are to be believed, the most important stage was the 'transfer' of certain stones to Marienberg, accomplished by young men who held political responsibilities in the village.[37] At the time, they had not meant to dispose of the stones definitively, but to get them out of the immediate vicinity by entrusting them, together with other important items, to the missionaries and by limiting their power: there, on the hill dedicated to the Virgin Mary, shut away and guarded by a good shepherd, their effectiveness was supposed to dwindle. However, the missionaries put them up for sale, to the indignation of the very people who had sold them in the first place. The stones and objects reverted to the Whites, where they could no longer be controlled. When it came time to build the church,[38] history had to be reinterpreted to fit the new genealogy. To this end, as the carvings and their placing in the church show, the Adjirab played on the names common to both systems, replacing the ones with the others. Nothing could be simpler, since myth, history and the Bible all share the same fascination with names, places and travels. It was sufficient to look. Among Noah's descendants was the name Akab, which was none other than the secret name of the ancestor of the *aka* ('wild pig') descent group, the very one who had donated the land for the church. He was therefore represented on the last panel. Christ himself was depicted as a pregnant woman. The reason for this is not clear. His ability to perform miracles, but above all, to appear after death in different forms probably favoured this substitution: like mythical characters, Christ has the gift of ubiquity. Furthermore, he is an ambiguous figure because he did not marry.

In the course of these strange manipulations, the ancestor figures lost one of their old functions — that of protecting the group from outside attack, of overseeing their good conduct and morality — and acquired a new one: that of ensuring the continuity of history. This little game of Musical Chairs is not new to the society: to take a different name is to change groups or lineages, and thus to lay claim to a new position as well as sometimes to reinvent history. Here too the Adjirab were playing on their tradition.

From this standpoint, the church cannot be likened to a Men's House, but rather to a pantheon, one of whose functions is to weave ties between the old and the new, between here and there. The church is an abstract place, which establishes a genealogical chain for the benefit of all, while creating a distance between present-day individuals and their ancestors. Because of this, it stands at the opposite pole from the Men's Houses, which underscore the close, unshakeable ties between the living and the dead. In place of the plurality of the Men's Houses, the church establishes an *ecclesia*, whose fundamental characteristic is its unity, as though the entropy of the world had at last imposed its law, reducing the many Men's Houses to one.

This opposition can easily be read in the architectural elements of the church: it is transparent, open to one and all, where closure and taboos used to reign; it is decorated on the outside with thousands of figures, where the inside used to be painted with representations of the natural elements. At the prow is a post featuring all of the group's ancestors, where a single lineage used to be represented. Furthermore, it turns the world upside down, since where once sacrifices were offered to the ancestors, the church commemorates the sacrifice of one ancestor offered for all mankind. But above all, one feature indispensable to the Men's Houses will always be absent: the water holes scattered throughout the marshes that are home to the spirits of the descent groups and where the representations of the ancestors were buried. The church and the Men's House can therefore not be reduced to each other.

This new twist given to history by the church had enormous repercussions for the Men's Houses: dispossessed of their ancestor figures by modernity, they became mere abstractions, empty shells of limited symbolic value. The only reminder of their association with warfare were the ropes that told the score of the head-hunting expeditions and the cage-like structure woven from palm fronds hanging from the ceiling, which indicated the spot where the bodies taken in raids were once exposed. Their only function seems to come down to affirming the group's identity by means of the *adje* relationship. And now, this last remaining function, already badly eroded, is coming under severe attack. For several years now, it has been at the centre of a violent debate. The younger men condemn it as a dangerous institution, claiming that it reawakens old quarrels, appeals to the ancestors' spirits and encourages constant recourse to deadly magical practices. This accusation clearly shows that the dismissal of the ancestral spirits into the forest or their forced departure from Marienberg are perceived as having failed. The destruction — or sale— of the skull-stands did not suffice to drive them away or to circumvent their power. They still prowl the village.

Whenever something goes wrong, the young men immediately accuse the Men's Houses of being behind the disorders and the old men of keeping up an outmoded tradition that jeopardises the group's survival. This conflict stems from an episode of recent history. At the demand of the missionaries and with the complicity of certain elders, an entire age group was irrevocably excluded from the initiations, and more globally from traditional knowledge. With the end of initiations came the disappearance of the basis of political organisation and authority. From there it was only a short step to questioning the construction of the Men's Houses that founded the old men's authority and their momentary glory; and this step was gradually taken.

An irreversible evolution is thus taking shape, the last stage of which seems to be the end of the *adje* system. For the young people, however, things are somewhat more complicated. However anxious they may be to create a society free of sickness and death, and therefore dream of going back to the way things were, in the beginning, without sin and therefore without Men's Houses — which is why they condemn them — they are nonetheless the heirs of their past. They cannot ignore the system that underpins the land-distribution pattern and the relationships among descent groups. Obliged to compromise, whereas some would prefer to reject all concessions (the only way to ensure the success of their undertaking), young people are forced to acknowledge at least one of the functions of the Men's Houses, which is to express the identity of a descent group, thereby opening the door to all they contain. At least until now. For the generation gap is widening apace, not only because the old laws obliging the young to produce the wealth have disappeared, but because it is now they who are best equipped to cope with the modern world and to get the most out of it. Local schooling and, for some, continuing their education in the city, has given them an understanding of things that had totally escaped previous generations. And so the gerontocracy is gradually being replaced by the growing power of the younger generations.

Some time after the church was finished, the Muruken community, following a sinister affair of rivalry with neighbouring villages, decided to build their own school. This they did with mission aid. The new building was erected on one side of the soccer field, some distance from the church. With all the majesty of the Men's Houses, it too adopted the same form, but with a variant: both ends terminated in an overhanging roof decorated with all the elements required by tradition. The building housed several classrooms, which had been left without ornamentation. From the inside, the school seemed a model of sobriety compared with the church.

Whose idea was it to make a school in the image of the Men's Houses? Probably the first headmaster's. A native son of the village, he had become a teacher at the normal school in Wewak. There he was won over to the ideas of the Pangu Pati[39] and, upon returning to the village, worked — without much success — to revive the initiations and preserve the traditions. Nevertheless, he stated — too loudly and too strongly — that he did not believe in the ancestors' power or in magic. It seems that it was obvious to him that the school should be built on the lines of the Men's House: after all, in these societies didn't power rest on knowledge, and wasn't the new power therefore to be found in education? But from there to concluding that the school was perceived as the Western form of the Men's Houses and that the grades of school were the equivalent of initiation grades would be a naive step to take. It would be assuming an equivalence between Western education and initiation on the pretext that both are systems of education. Such an assimilation forgets rather quickly that initiations are reserved for men, are based on esoteric knowledge and, above all, form an introduction to the world of politics; whereas in Western education, knowledge is open to all, and politics plays only a minor role. Western schooling cannot be reduced, in either form or function, to a traditional system of knowledge. The deliberate and much vaunted shifting of the architectural forms was possible only because these forms had lost much of their original meaning: in the school building, these forms and representations no longer bear witness to a body of knowledge, they now proclaim an identity. The traditional world has been so rejected and made so abstract that its representations now have only a very general value. The problem is no longer one of filiation, but of a still vague set of ideas gravitating around an emerging definition of Adjirab identity. For the moment, however, the forms that have been shamelessly adopted and applied denote a process of folklorisation for which the school is the most widely chosen vehicle, busily engaging students in the manufacture of traditional articles devoid of any utility (coconut-shell eye-glasses) or converted to a new use (sacks for washing sago made into book bags).

The construction of the school thus marked the end of a trend that began with the Western invasion of this remote corner of swampland. The three buildings cited (the modern Men's House, the church and the school) illustrate three phases of this transformation. After a period during which the old system withstood the shock of contact with the white world, then another during which the church became a way, through filiation, of discovering a past, thus reestablishing a link with an original state of society, the school seems to be one of the final manifestations of the transmigration of forms that is now nearly exhausted. Efficacy has yielded to claims for identity.

Between 1987 and 1992, the old decrepit school was torn down. Today all that is left is a slit-gong once used to call the children in the morning and two tall poles on which, following a ritual practised in all schools, the national flag was raised at the start of the school-day. The church was destroyed in 1992. Its posts lie on the ground, useless but carefully stacked. Another page has been turned, and with it, modernity has driven its wedge a little deeper: in place of the old-fashioned traditional school stands one of those soul-less buildings for which the modern age has such a gift, with its corrugated roof and gray walls. A present from the local government shortly before the general elections, it bears no trace of the past; instead, it shows all the signs of a break yet to be completed.

Footnotes
1   See Forge (1965: 23–31).
2   See Forge (1965: 29).
3   Especially the Anglo-Saxons, among whom Gell (1975), Tuzin (1980), Bowden (1983), O'Hanlon (1992). For a discussion of the relationship between art and identity, see also Hanson and Hanson (1990).
4   On the role of Australian advisers in this revival as well as in the construction of Men's Houses, see Beier (1976). The reader may also consult Tuzin (1980) and several articles published in *Sepik Heritage* (Lutkehaus *et al.* eds., 1990).

5   See Schindlbeck (1990) and Schmid (1990).

6   Bateson (1971: 134).

7   Laycock recognises four linguistic groups. He mentions, effectively, Gorovu, spoken by the people of Bosmun and the language of Kambot. The groups retained here are those given by the Adjirab people themselves. For them, Bosmun is a remote place, as is the village of Kambot, though they once often warred with the latter. The language of the Armé people may be a dialect of Adjirab, but is perhaps closer to Banaro. We have separated the two here for ethnographic reasons. The Armé group settled this region long ago, but was pushed back by the Adjirab at a relatively recent date. A number of their traditions (mortuary and marriage rites) are radically different from those practised by the Adjirab groups. Laycock (1973) calls the Adjirab, Adjora. Curiously, this name is rejected by the region's inhabitants. The name Adjirab is said to mean 'the good eel place' (*djir:* 'eel', *ab:* 'good')

8   Properly speaking, these descent groups are exogamous units. All claim to descend from a single apical ancestor, although the genealogical link is not direct. Marriages are made by sister exchange or by preferential cross-cousin marriage. Residence is uxorilocal. Each descent group lived in its own part of the territory. This usually comprised a tract of swamp, a tract of sago plantation and a tract of forest where gardens were cleared in the dry season. Each descent group also belonged to a totemic unit that was divided into halves and sub-halves, following a classical dual system.

9   See Lipset (1990).

10 There are only two studies on Porapora: Schwab (1970) and Huppertz (1977).

11 The only recent work on a region bordering the Adjirab is B. Juillerat's study on the Banaro (Juillerat, 1993). The Banaro live on the banks of the Middle Keram. Although they are neighbours of the Adjirab, contact between the two groups has been infrequent. Nevertheless, they share a portion of their history. One Adjirab descent group took refuge along the Keram, where they planted fields of sago palms. The Banaro still recognise the rights of certain Adjirab groups in these fields. A number of the inhabitants of Yar village are descended from a group from Ombos (or, according to information collected by Juillerat, from Ogomania), who fled, probably at the beginning of this century following a war, and settled on the Keram (Juillerat, 1993: 80).

12 See Juillerat (1993: 33–34).

13 A propensity amply demonstrated in M. Mead's work (see Mead, 1938).

14 The Pigdin term used by churchmen to designate 'idols'. The word-for-word translation is 'false gods'.

15 Readers interested in a more extensive comparison of the construction principles may consult the drawings made by Wallace and Ruth Ruff for the houses in the Sepik (Ruff and Ruff, 1980, 1990) and by Christian Coiffier for those more specifically on the Middle Sepik (Coiffier, 1990). The initial drawing of the Agur house in Armada was done by Gérard Clavé, in July 1987. Upon his return, a study of the structures and the drawings was carried out under his and Pierre Jacquot's direction by the third-year students of the Environment department of the Institut d'Arts Visuels d'Orléans. I would like to take this opportunity to thank them all.

16 Unlike Banaro practice, each House belongs to a single descent group. This group may be aided by other groups of the same kind from the same sub-moiety (therefore having the same totem) if they are too few in number to build their own House.

17 Principally in one German missionary museum, see Huppertz (1997).

18 The Senaï site is of cultural importance. It was on the outskirts of the present-day village that the mango grew which gave rise to one dual unit, see below.

19 It must be remembered that the Adjirab territory is swampy and has no stones. Their very scarcity makes them valuable. All the stones had therefore to be imported, but we have very little information as to their sources. They probably came from the hill region, but some may have been exchanged, in villages on the coast, for skulls or children.

20 Photographs of these displays can be found in Höltker (1966) or Hauser-Schäublin (1989: 355, ill. 97). The Men's House in the photo is from a neighbouring region, however: very slight but real differences may have existed. The construction of the Bosmun Men's House together with part of the opening ceremony is described by Höltker (1966). The Bosmun site, too, is of cultural importance. The village is presently occupied by a population with whom the Adjirab claim not to have any dealings. Relations with Bosmun, though rare, were nevertheless not exceptional. From the standpoint of form, the Men's Houses look much alike.

21	The custom reported by Father Lehner of hanging bones from trees has been strongly deplored by the older men of the village. Nevertheless, it did exist in other areas. What Lehner saw in the village of Pinam must therefore be regarded as an exception corresponding to a particularly turbulent moment in its history.

22	In spite of my questions, I never received any explicit information about them. Höltker (1966) also mentions a wickerwork figure kept in this room. In 1987, in Pinam, in the Men's House that was still standing at the time, this room contained a series of carved characters that had disappeared a few years later. Bernard Juillerat describes the Banaro Men's House (Juillerat, 1993: 130–132). The same components are found there, with a few variants that are not without their importance. Can the geographical distribution of the figures kept in the back room be used to determine a culture area characteristic of this region or must we be content with broader criteria? The question will be left open for the moment. Nevertheless, I must point out that the architecture of the Men's Houses in this area is radically different from that found on the Middle Sepik. There the space is divided into top and bottom, whereas on the Lower Sepik the division is front/back (Schuster, 1985: 24–25). We may suppose that this variation reflects different functions — and different symbolic representations.

23	Object MNAO 66-12-14, in the Musée National des Arts d'Afrique et d'Océanie, is to my knowledge the last exemplar of these hoods. These were objects having a similar shape and appearance, but much larger. They represented the founding ancestors of certain descent groups.

24	The documentation provided by old photographs poses a problem. As far as I know, no systematic record was ever made of all the Men's Houses in a region. It is possible therefore that, following a widespread habit of travellers, the first photographers took pictures of the Houses that struck them because of their size or their decoration, ignoring the simpler buildings and so condemning them to oblivion. This approach distorts any reading we might make of the material culture in general and of Men's Houses in particular.

25	One of these heads is conserved in Basel's ethnographic museum. The wooden stand has been lost (destroyed by insects while the object was in Marienberg). It carries the catalogue number Vb 14 399.

26	For a complete study of one of these songs, see Jürg Wassman's (1991) remarkable work.

27	This interpretation follows B. Juillerat's work, which sees the Oedipal conflict as the key to the explanation. On this subject, and on Yafar myths whose themes resemble those of the Nduara myth, see Juillerat, 1991, esp. Ch. 1 and 2.

28	I heard this only once, but from the lips of the oldest men. They gave this commentary considerable importance.

29	See Strathern (1974).

30	See Gewertz (1983: 12ff).

31	This remark, made by Bernard Juillerat concerning the Banaro, applies equally to Porapora (Juillerat, 1993: 34).

32	See Taylor-Hubert (1990: 209).

33	Pangal — the base of the sago palm which, once flattened into a thin layer, prepared and dried, is painted.

34	One of the few articles published on Porapora is a set of myths collected in the 1950s by one of the priests living in Marienberg and who, for several months, was in charge of this region that had long been the preserve of Father Lehner (see Schwab, 1970).

35	See Jeudy-Ballini (1988: 242).

36	A number of uncertainties surround the status of this mango, some of which, via an alternative route, connect with the question that worried Medieval Christian Europe: was there sexuality in Paradise?

37	According to the same version, these stones disappeared in the forest.

38	After the 'revocation of the *tambaran*' (see Juillerat, 1993), in other words after the abandoning of traditional religion under the impact of missionary activity and the dismissal of the spirits (Pidgin: *tambaran*) that used to be summoned up in the Men's Houses. The Banaro use the term to designate both the spirits worshipped in the Men's Houses and the objects they inhabit. The ritual alternated between calling the *tambaran* (to come and live among men) and dismissing them to the forest (1993: 123 f). In the late 1930s, pressed by the missionaries, the *tambaran* returned to the forest for good. I did not collect any specific information on the circumstances of this revocation.

39	One plank of the political platform of the Pangu Pati, founded by Michael Somare, the first Prime Minister of independent New Guinea, was defence of local traditions and cultures. The party is strong in East Sepik province.

Chapter 4

CARGO CULT OR SIN CULT?

A Melanesian rite to better God

Monique Jeudy-Ballini

'It takes a very long time to become a true sinner. It's not something you achieve just like that. Hard work and good health are two conditions, but even then nothing is certain. Let's say one has to have the right aptitude. All this takes a long time to attain'

Jorn Riel. Le récit qui donne un beau visage

'Without the trade store there would be no Anglican god'

A Maring pundit (quoted in Lipuma 1988: 88)

The Sulka of New Britain (Papua New Guinea) often refer to the past, using the stereotypical missionary expression, as 'the time of darkness', that era of ignorance and error which came to an end when Christianisation ushered in the 'time of light'. Yet the fact that some people speak of themselves as those who *both* follow the customs of the ancestors *and* keep the Ten Commandments shows that, in certain contexts, light is not necessarily the opposite of darkness. Borne along by a constant current of recomposition and totalisation, Sulka thought strives to maintain a necessary but non-dichotomous relationship between the two terms. I showed this in an article published in 1988 based on the analysis of a myth legitimising the practice of a certain rite.[1] I will offer here a closer examination of the modalities of this same rite.

The Sulka number over 3500 and are divided into three main groups living several days' walk apart in the eastern part of the island of New Britain. The vitality of the exchange relations and the constant flow of persons between the separated communities account for the cultural homogeneity that prevails in spite of the fairly contrasted sociological environments. Living essentially on the products of their own gardens, the Sulka also earn a little money by selling the copra or the cacao produced on small family plots. Salaried work in town or on the large commercial farms, another possible source of income, attracts only a small number of young men and then for a length of time that does not as a rule seem to exceed three or four years.

Situated on the shore of Wide Bay, some twelve hours by boat from the provincial capital, Rabaul, the original territory, today home to the largest population, was evangelised around 1930 by Catholic missionaries from the Sacred Heart congregation. Twenty years earlier, the first church in the Sulka area had been built by the same congregation among another section of the population in the region of Mope, in the north-eastern part of Gazelle Peninsula. In contrast to some previous experiences in New Britain, these missionaries encountered no notable hostility on the part of the Sulka. With no direct competition until recently, in particular before the Seventh Day Adventists began to overshadow them, their principal and only detractors were the members of what they long denounced as a 'cargo cult'.

This so-called 'cargo-cult' began spreading a few decades ago among the Wide Bay Sulka by way of their Mengen neighbours, gaining the surrounding localities as well (Sohr, Kol, Tomuip, Baining). Although it has attracted large numbers of Mengen, only a minority of the present-day Sulka population are members and they are congregated in a single village. The movement is known as the Pomio Kivung Group,[2] a name that has never been replaced by a vernacular equivalent. Its literal meaning is 'Pomio Meeting Group' (from the Pidgin *kivung*: 'meeting' — Pomio being the name of a Mengen village). Like the Church, it was to this movement too, that the local administration alluded every time it wanted to denounce a 'cargo cult' in the area. The question of the activities associated with the Kivung Group is an extremely sensitive subject and is generally met with silence or reticence, since those who belong will not let those who do not belong talk about it, and those who do not belong seize the pretext of being outsiders to justify their inability to talk about it.

In the analysis of the way this movement functions, I will dwell in particular on two aspects: the very specific interpretation of the notion of 'sin' that underpins cult-members' activities, and the meaning of the path travelled by the money given during the rites which is seen as having a major instrumental role.

Custom revisited

Feeding the ancestors and redeeming sins

In its present form, the cult's members, among other obligations make twice-weekly food offerings to the spirits of the dead and monetary contributions to 'redeem sins'. 'Sin' or 'offence' (Pidgin, *pekato*; Sulka, *kermatnek*) is minimally defined as any violation of the Ten Commandments and the self-imposed renunciation of 'bad magic', chewing betel, or failing to accomplish ritual duties. Subject to 'redemption' are not only the sins of Kivung members, but also the presumed sins of those who remain outside the movement, Sulka or non-Sulka, living or dead. The amounts given individually range from a few toeia to one kina or more,[3] according to the gravity of the sins to be redeemed, which is appraised by the participant. In the coded language of the group's members, the rite is referred to as 'washing' (*orop*), which is instrumentalised by the money, compared by the movement leader to soap that 'takes away the ugly skin and reveals the good skin'.

As a sort of extension of this 'washing' of persons, the members of the Kivung also take on the upkeep of the cemetery grounds so that, as one of them explains, the dirt and the diseases present in the soil cannot harm the deceased. Since the colonial administration's prohibition on exposing corpses and celebrating second funerals, all dead must be buried in the village graveyard. The shrub-lined clearing in which they rest is entirely free of weeds, with no material indication to mark the gravesites. Cleaning consists of sweeping the ground and removing the weeds that have come up since the previous week. This civic service, which in theory is incumbent on the entire village community, is performed exclusively by the movement, which thereby secures a monopoly on relations with the dead.[4]

On a ceremonial site next to the cemetery where the food and money offerings are brought twice a week, stands a house known to all as the Ancestors' House. It is framed by two written lists: towards the back wall, engraved on a board planted in the ground, is the list of the names of all those buried in the cemetery; near the front wall, a list of Roman numerals refers to the Ten Commandments. These numerals are disposed on a wood carving representing Moses with the Tablets of the Law. The whole display rests on a traditional club. At the base of this club or wedged among the branches of a nearby tree is an empty can, for the coins that people will come, one by one, to deposit, in an amount known to each alone, for the redemption of sins.

Built on the lines of the traditional dwellings, the Ancestors' House is typically covered by a roof of thick vegetal thatch that comes down to the ground and keeps out all light. The only opening is a low narrow doorway that one must stoop to pass through; there are no windows. Except for the one village that is home to the Kivung movement, this type of construction has completely disappeared from the Sulka area. People today say that the dark houses gave their residents somewhere to flee to and thus provided them with a chance to escape any assailants that might come — as their eyes would be unaccustomed to the sudden darkness and they could not see them. Architecture of this type is currently interpreted today as referring to the ignorance that, until the advent of Christianisation, kept the ancestors under the sway of murder and fear. The Ancestors' House is thus plunged into inner shadows that implicitly recall the obscurity of mind prevailing in the 'time of darkness'. At the same time, the Ancestors' House, as the site of a rite purportedly based on the strict observation of God's commandments, attests by its presence next to the cemetery that 'light' has indeed come to the land of the Sulka.

The twice-weekly offerings made by the movement members must include both food and money. The foods differ slightly from the villagers' ordinary fare, and generally consist of what are regarded as the best varieties of tubers, rarely eaten or cultivated fruits like pineapples, store-bought rice or canned meats. Prepared in a nearby hut that serves as a kitchen, the food is taken into the Ancestors' House, where dishes and cutlery are set out — utensils which the Sulka, whether or not they are members of the movement, hardly ever use for eating. The food is dished onto the plates for the spirits of the dead, who are thought to come and eat its *nunu* ('spirit', 'image', 'duplicate', 'reflection'). After an hour or two, the food left by the spirits of the dead (the food minus its *nunu* and therefore 'cold') is taken out of the House, and then divided up and eaten by the members of the movement.[5]

The funds collected are periodically turned over to the Mengen responsible for the general management of the movement and who centralise, not only the Sulka's money, but that of the other Kivung subgroups in the neighbouring populations. Once a year, all the takings are

deposited in an account opened in the name of the Pomio Kivung Group, at a bank in the
provincial capital. In 1967, a total of A$ 40,000 was collected.[6] A document drawn up by the
group's treasurer for the period from 1975 to 1986, concerning the whole movement, indicated
a sum of nearly 300,000 kinas.[7] This money, invested in constructing a medical post and
school, health and administrative facilities on the grounds of a village located in Mengen
territory, heralded, according to the leader of the Sulka movement, the advent of the first 'town
born from the money of the Ten Commandments'.[8]

Food and money are connected by a relation that is both continuous and
discontinuous. The bond of continuity accounts for the fact that one cannot be given
without the other. This link further appears in the fact that the money is deposited in an
empty tin can, thereby replacing the food that previously filled the recipient. Unlike food,
however, money can be deposited only outside the Ancestors' House, it was explained to me,
so as not to defile the House by introducing into it the sins the money was paid to redeem.
The difference in the way the two types of offering are handled suggests a discontinuity
between money, which falls into the province of sin, and food, which does not. In fact, food
is so far removed from the idea of sin that there was a time when the members of the Kivung
Group grew most of it in gardens worked in common which they called *paradiso*.[9]

'This is not a cargo cult'

The name 'cargo cult', used by missionaries and government agents to stigmatise Kivung
activities, is violently contested by the movement itself. The group's objection can best be
understood as the rejection of a clearly pejorative label.[10] On the occasion of a Sunday
homily in which he had used the term once too often, a Catholic missionary was publicly
reprimanded by the movement's leader:

> Father, plenty of times you've talked about cargo cults. Do you see cargo cult here? Where
> is there cargo cult? Who cares about cargo cults? Where is there cargo cult? Do you see
> cargo cult? Shut your mouth. You don't know. Me, I know custom. It isn't your custom,
> it's my custom. People do like they think. You can't stop someone thinking. Now suppose
> I say, 'Stop saying mass!' Can you do it? Can you do it? Suppose I say: 'It's finished, you
> don't say mass any more.' Can you do that?

This diatribe persuaded the missionary to drop the subject, an obligation to keep silent that
he justified (to the anthropologist) by the fear of seeing his Sunday congregation decline. In
short, the Kivung was willing to hear what the Church had to say only once the Church had
heard its injunction to keep quiet.

The same speaker claimed he did not know exactly what the mission or the
administration meant by 'cargo cult'. To know about this, he would indeed have had to
engage in the cult! Nevertheless, it was clear to him that this term implied an opposition
between Kivung ritual and work, and thus contained an accusation of passivity — following
an interpretation found in other New Guinea societies.[11] He therefore seized every available
occasion to repeat that the members of Kivung were not content to simply 'stand idly by'.
Several times he had given the masks he made for ceremonies the provocative name of

'Cargo Cult'. When he cried out this name on the dancing ground, as is the custom at ceremonies, he had, he said, the jubilant feeling of defying his detractors. He imagined that those who were 'always talking [to him] about cargo cult, cargo cult, cargo cult', must then say to themselves: 'This man, all the time we are talking to him about cargo cult, and yet he put work into that!' Indeed, everyone knew that making a mask was *wok* ('work'; Sulka, *eha*). And it was clear that a man capable of doing such 'work' could not be suspected of idleness, no more than one who went to the trouble of raising pigs. He himself raised pigs and, as a way of recalling that this was indeed 'work', his herd from time to time boasted an animal that bore the name of Cargo Cult.

Custom as a divine commandment

If it is not a cargo cult, the reason is that it partakes of 'work', and thus embodies custom itself.

'We work because we know that things cannot happen by themselves,' the same speaker told me, as a way of indicating that this was nothing unusual.

> Today we remember: the great men of old, the ancestors of our great men and their ancestors worked at this. And that is what has come back today. People, at the mission and in other places, are fighting this custom. But whose custom is it? I have been sent to court for this … But it's my thing, it's the custom of my ancestors … It isn't for something new that I am sent like that to court. It's something from before that the ancestors worked at.

As a rule, when the Sulka say 'work' (*eha*) they are referring to the cultivation of gardens and the raising of pigs that are fed with produce from these gardens. At the same time, as is often the case in Melanesia,[12] the term covers the whole notion of performing a ritual. Inappropriate, for instance, for wage-labour on plantations, the notion of 'work' properly applies to the definition of an initiation, a marriage or a mourning ritual. Described as an act of remembrance or fidelity, 'work' consists of doing today as the ancestors did in the past, the legitimisation of each act depending on the retrospective attribution of a precedent to it.

To recall that 'work' partakes, by definition, of 'custom' is to say that what is done is right because it is not new. 'It was not invented just recently', declared one follower of a messianic movement in another province, thus denying any connection with a cargo cult.[13] It is also on their claim to continuity with the past that the Kivung Group members base their legitimacy, thereby putting History on their side. Thus detractors cannot incriminate them without calling all of History into doubt.

Perceived as forgetting, as ignorance, error, deviation, infidelity, and even treachery, discontinuity — or difference in general — appears as a disqualifier.[14] So that those who, like the mission or the administration, denounce Kivung activities, condemn ancestral practices or want to impose their own changes implicitly discredit themselves. It could be said — literally — that they do not know what they are talking about.

Yet continuity and discontinuity are exclusive of each other only in a perspective that assumes their mutual incompatibility. In opposition to this viewpoint, which is that of the

Church and the administration, the Kivung 'works' to impose another conception of history in which continuity answers for discontinuity, where fidelity to what was is conceived as fidelity to what is supposed to be. This is true of the Kivung practice of offering food to the dead, presented by the movement leader as an ancient Sulka funeral rite. This 'custom', he asserted:

> ... the ancestors used to work at it. We had forgotten it and I brought it back. Suppose I did not do this work, there would be no more Ten Commandments. It was the Ten Commandments that said to me 'Do this work!'

The Ten Commandments are taken literally as orders, injunctions commanding the members of the movement to 'work', in other words to work at continuity by reviving the rituals performed by the ancestors. In short, they are an injunction to remember, to be faithful to 'custom', which is thus provided with an origin and a legitimacy rooted in the Bible. The Bible prescribes this fidelity, whereas the mission, like the administration, condemns and combats it. To 'work' therefore means to be placed in the predicament of disobeying the mission in order to obey God's commandments. It is impossible to do one without doing the other, and so the 'custom' in question puts the Church in contradiction with the Bible.

The call to keep the commandments accounts for the need to carry on the 'work' of the ancestors, and vice versa, the 'work' accounts for their survival. ('If I didn't do this 'work', there would be no more commandments.') 'Ancestral custom' and the divine commandments are linked: preservation of the commandments rests on observance of 'custom', and the perpetuation of 'custom' depends on keeping the commandments. One could say that in a way 'custom' ranks as a divine commandment.[15]

Working and knowing

The movement leader observed with some acrimony: 'Everybody knows the Ten Commandments, but nobody does the work of the Ten Commandments.' The excellence on which the Kivung members pride themselves stems from the fact that theirs is the only practice that involves both 'knowing' and 'working'; they are the only ones, as opposed to 'everybody else', the living (outside the movement) but also to the dead.

About the ancestors, the movement leader said in substance that they already kept the Ten Commandments, but without knowing it. They too, he argued, believed, for example, that one must not kill or steal; they too upheld the principle of neighbourly love through the institution of the former *taven*, village heads or 'fathers' who looked after their co-residents. Thus, like the Kivung 'custom', the Christian commandments 'are not something new', as one of the Sacred Heart missionaries was told by the Sulka as early as 1913:

> An old man, E Rougua, more than 70 years of age, with grey hair and a long grey beard, without a tooth in his mouth, and supporting himself with a stick... told me in substance : You need not tell us that we should take good care of our relatives (4th commandment), that we should not kill anybody (5th commandment), that we should not commit

adultery (6th commandment), that we should not steal (7th commandment), that we should not lie (8th commandment).

These things, he said, are not new to us; we are fully aware of them although we act against them frequently. I am an old man now. When I was a boy, I was taught these lessons by my relatives who had not learned them from any white man, but knew them all by themselves. For at that time they had as yet no knowledge of people with a white skin ; they had not seen any, and still less had come in contact with them.[16]

Let me mention that, while for the Sulka members of the Pomio Kivung Group the divine commandments may not have been 'something new' with respect to ancestral practice, for the missionaries themselves, the tribe's religion or morality did not appear entirely new either. The remarks made by the missionary Carl Laufer, who saw the Sulka founding hero as a local version of the Supreme Being and implicitly regarded the Sulka as Christians in fact if not in name, could in this sense be regarded as a Kivung-style discourse.[17]

According to today's movement members, the ancestors were unaware that, by respecting custom, they were actually keeping God's commands. One can thus infer that the ancestors were in a position to violate the Ten Commandments without knowing it. They were unaware that, when they performed acts condemned by custom, they were actually sinning; similarly, they were unaware of what was wrong with certain traditional techniques such as sorcery or love magic. In short, while the 'time of darkness' that preceded evangelisation lasted, men were constantly sinning without knowing it. Then 'light' came, and they discovered they had been sinners.

In this respect, the dawning of 'light' together with the Biblical commandments was the advent of the rule, but a rule that was laid out as such, a *written* rule, which henceforth enabled one to commit acts classified as transgressions... and to know it. In this rule, it would seem that the element discriminating between darkness and light was less the commandments' negative definition of what constituted a transgression than the fact that, while the rule did not prevent the offence, it henceforth forbade ignorance. The first commandment could thus be said to read 'Thou shalt know'.[18]

Symmetrically to the ancestors, who did the 'work', that is kept the Ten Commandments but without knowing it, the Sulka outside the Kivung Group are today denigrated as those who do nothing but pray, that is who know, but do not work. By not 'working', as an applied knowledge of the Ten Commandments enjoins them to, by therefore not following the 'custom of the ancestors' who used to 'work', they are committing a sin.

The ancestors and the non-Kivung living share the same inability to establish a continuity between knowing and 'working': when they work they do not know it ; and when they know, they do not work. The ancestors and the living not affiliated to the Kivung also have in common the fact that they do not redeem the sins they commit. What neither group does, the members of the Kivung undertake to do for them. Today the money given *for* the ancestors by those who claim to be 'following the custom of the ancestors' (the Kivung members) must therefore redeem two kinds of sins: sins defined as a breach of the divine commandments and sins stemming from the failure to redeem sins. In other words, the money is meant to redeem the fact that the ancestors followed their custom instead of following the divine commandments and abstaining, for instance, from killing or practising sorcery; and

> the fact that the ancestors did not redeem their observance of custom, that is, they did not redeem the sins they (inevitably) committed by following it.

Those who follow the 'custom of the ancestors' must therefore give money to redeem the fact that the ancestors followed the 'custom of the ancestors'.

The cult of excellence

The opposition stressed by the Kivung between 'knowing' and 'working' is also drawn between praying and paying. To be sure, the same speaker concedes with respect to Sulka outside the group, 'the others, too, pray to God for their offences, but they don't give any money. So what can God do with all those offences?' The condemned discontinuity between praying and paying contrasts two ways of relating to God: an internalised mode (prayer) asking God to give, and an externalised mode (payment), asking him to receive. Knowing and working, praying and paying: the Kivung movement refuses the separation of these terms, and treats it as a sin. This sin, committed by the ancestors, is likewise committed by all those living outside the movement, and resides in the fundamentally ineffective character of their relationship with the deity.

When they 'worked', in other words when they kept the commandments but without knowing it, the ancestors were working, but in vain, since their work was not dedicated to God and was therefore of no value as a sacrifice. Likewise, today those outside the movement who know the commandments but do not keep them, who pray to God but do not give money, who thus abstain from paying with either their person or from their pockets (in other words, who abstain from making any sacrifice whatever), can never hope to have any sway over the deity.

Just as they declare themselves the only ones who combine 'knowing' and 'working', the members of the Kivung also claim to be the only ones to combine prayer and sacrifice, asking and giving. They are, quite unmetaphorically, the only ones to pay a price for praying to God, which is also a way of designating themselves as the only ones capable of rendering God's power effective. It can be said that here 'work' is to knowledge as money is to prayer: a sacrifice necessary to move the deity to make use of its power, the implication being that nothing God does to benefit people can ever be free of charge. Paying with one's time by 'working' or paying with one's wealth by giving money keeps the knowledge or the request from being in vain. In the terms of the quotation above, that is what is supposed to force God to 'do something' with the offences people pray for him to redeem. The religious concern of the Kivung Group here should be understood as a concern with effectiveness, which bears on the ability of its members to move God to action.[19]

The sacrificial dimension believed by its own members to distinguish the Kivung movement is also what, from the viewpoint of non-members, defines the conditions of membership. Of the Kivung members, they say, for instance, that they were forced to give up all their magic, the 'bad' magic (for killing), but also the 'good' magic (for seducing and healing); that they destroyed their personal weapons; that they continually impoverish themselves by the amount of money they pay to redeem sins; that this poverty drives them to hire themselves out to white planters; that their self-imposed prohibition on betel chewing exposes their mouth to all sorts of infections and makes it stink. Seen as disarmed, both literally and figuratively, by all these deprivations that weaken them (leaving them vulnerable to sorcery and disease), they are further suspected of depending on persons outside the movement who in exchange for payment ensure them the benefit of their own magic.[20] From the viewpoint of non-believers, who claim the movement is the product of a 'dream' and denounce the illusion kept up by its members, the constant sacrifices made by these members are no doubt one of the few things whose reality and truth are undeniable; and all the less deniable as it is the extent of these sacrifices that is advanced to explain non-membership (the fact that one has either left or refused to join).

Echoing what is said outside the movement about their vulnerability, Kivung members implicitly show the full measure of their sacrifices when they describe the hostility they encounter because of their membership (risk of being poisoned, murdered, etc.). The leader of the Sulka movement often terminated our conversations by referring to his fear of talking. The constant feeling of insecurity of which he spoke took him one step closer to the 'custom of the ancestors' that he prided himself on observing, since the ever-present fear of murder is believed to have characterised the 'time of darkness'.

The value of sacrifice resides in the twin aspects of the offering: that of paying for the gifts one has given the deity with a deficit of 'strength'. Having become better Christians through the means they adopt to compel God to make use of his power, the members of the movement themselves enjoy all the more power because they consent to weaken, deprive, expose themselves — to sickness or misfortune. Defenceless, weaponless, and for that very reason in a position of strength: perhaps this is the meaning of the club which, in the carving erected near the Ancestors' House, supports the representation of Moses and the Tablets of the Law. The condition of the effectiveness of the gift, and its price, is the weakening it implies for the person, a weakening that can sometimes go as far as that peculiar state of frailty the Sulka assimilate to madness, or to the total loss of strength that spells death.

Among the members of the Kivung, there was a man whose slight mental derangement was thus attributed to sorcery on the part of persons hostile to the movement. A few weeks before he died, in 1985, it was to this same type of activity that the leader of the Sulka movement ascribed the illness that was to end his life. Two previous deaths in the Kivung Group had been imputed to the same causes by its members. It may be that these interpretations were more an attempt to ascribe an operative meaning to these events than a quest for a cause. It was an attempt to salvage misfortune by giving it a dedicatory, sacrificial value: death sent from outside as the price of membership in the movement thus partakes, a posteriori, of an offering.[21]

In the same system of gift and debt, this could be regarded as a Melanesian illustration of the analysis carried out by Charles Fredrikson in Portugal, showing how the transformation of misfortunes into aggressions victimising the woman in the *serra* at the same time provides her with a virtually inexhaustible fund of sacrificial credit that she can invest in her relations with the saints.[22]

Gifts of objects and gifts of oneself: these two modalities of the offering, each implying the other, are the vehicle for the sacrifice the Kivung members make of their 'strength'. The sacrifice here conditions the capacity to render God powerful, in other words effective. The excellence of the movement is defined as knowledge applied to bettering God. Rather than a sign of blessing or divine approval, the prosperity awaited is a mark of the Kivung's power to constrain the divinity. But more specifically, what is this constraint and what is this prosperity?

The fecundity of sin

Among the Kaliai of New Britain, people sometimes say that God changes into a devil so as to 'test the moral fibre of his subjects'.[23] The Sulka in the Kivung Group have a different version of this divine ambivalence: God was hampered by Adam and Eve's chastity because it prevented the earth from being populated. So he decided to turn himself into a serpent. Then the former catechist who was telling this story drew the obvious conclusion: 'Without sin the earth would still be uninhabited.'

Sin therefore was doubly responsible for the origin of humanity. First as a principle of life: no sin, no people. And second, as an ontological principle: in order not to sin, remarked in substance the Sulka leader of the Kivung movement, you would have to be dumb, blind and without hands (because I have a mouth, I lie; because I have eyes, I covet; because I have hands, I kill, I steal, etc.). One might as well say people are no longer supposed to be human; one might as well say, therefore, that it is the vocation of the members of the human body to be instruments of sin.

In the beginning, sin was a sign both of the humanity of mankind (having eyes to covet with, a mouth to lie with, etc.) and of its divinity, namely: God's will that they become sinners. If the serpent tempter is indeed an avatar of the deity, as this version of the Fall has it, then sinning is tantamount to doing the will or the desire of God.[24] Each time a person sins, he is showing his allegiance to God, he is acting as God's debtor. And in so doing, he puts God in his own debt.

Sin is thus a means of putting the deity in one's debt; a double process, in fact, since it consists, for humans, of doing what God wants by sinning, and then proceeding to 'redeem' the sins committed according to his will. It should be noted that this logic of indebtedness cannot be attributed to a specifically Kivung ideology, since it can also be found in other ritual contexts. This is the case, for example, of the practice known as 'paying/compensating for the desire' (*enkim/srim ka svil*), which obliges the organiser of a ceremony — the 'father of the feast' — to make a gift to every member of the audience who has expressed his admiration or his emotion — the actual word used is his 'desire' — for the beauty of a mask, a song or a dance.[25] However the expression of 'desire', which is assumed to be the outcome of the magic performed by the organiser of the ceremony, represents nothing other than the fulfillment of his own desire that the audience become 'desiring'. The desire of the one is thus satisfied by the 'desire' of the other, and is attested by the gift that must obligatorily be forthcoming from the 'father of the feast'.[26] Thus, whether he be human or divine, the being whose desire one fulfills thereby incurs a debt that he is obliged to repay.

However, even if sin is the expression of God's desire and an indication of one's allegiance, sin alone can never signify sin, in other words prove allegiance. Sin requires a ritual in order to exist as such. Specifically, the money paid by the members of the Kivung certifies the reality of the sins. It does this so successfully, moreover, that it cannot be introduced into the Ancestors' House for fear of defiling it. The money paid certifies the reality of the sins just as, for example, in other ritual contexts the brideprice or the funeral payment certifies the reality of the marriage or the mourning. Potentially omnipresent in all mankind, sin is not fulfilled as the divine will until it is redeemed. It has only an ostentatory or a dedicatory reality. Unredeemed sin, the sins of the ancestors or of people outside the Kivung, does not constitute a statement of the relation to God. It is, in a sense, an act devoid of intentionality, of which one may ask whether it still deserves to be called a sin.

Sin does not have an autonomous existence in the sense that it could be associated with specific behaviours denoted as guilty. It saturates virtually all human conduct, but acquires true relevance only within a relation, the one the Kivung ritual establishes between two acts, of which one is always a gift of money. 'No sins, no money', said the leader of the movement. One would be tempted to say 'no money, no sin'.

In this sense, as much no doubt as a means of wiping out offences, the monetary redemption of sins represents a way of bringing the sins into existence. Redeeming sins means first of all causing them to be. The monetary payment whereby sin is in this way ritually manufactured can thus be understood as a way of compelling others to become sinners. No money, no sin, as we have said. By paying for all, for the dead and for those living outside the movement, the Kivung methodically ensures the growth and multiplication of the number of sinners.

If the money paid indeed certifies the reality of the sins, it thereby certifies the reality of the debt. God cannot deny the existence of that for which a payment has been made, any more than men in society can do so. The payment here is a gift that retrospectively turns each sin into a debt owed. God, incapable of denying the existence of the debt, must then reimburse this debt to humans. Within the Kivung, sin can be defined in this way: acts the redemption of which compels God to create prosperity. While it is an expression of divine power, prosperity also appears as a sign of men's power over the power of God.[27]

'No sins, no money', declared the leader of the movement, almost as if he were setting the conditions of a tit for tat. Absence of sin is sterile, the corollary being the absence of prosperity. For, while sin lies at the origin of humanity, it also lies at the origin of human economic development. It is this development that is announced by the first 'town born from the money of the Ten Commandments' — in this case, the town born from the commandments that were violated, since kept commandments do not generate payments of money.

The fecundity of sin is inexhaustible, as the movement leader said: 'There is always some sin to be redeemed.' This assertion indicates that there is always some sin that has not been redeemed, and that one is a sinner for not having redeemed it. The Kivung member is defined ontologically as a perpetual debtor who can never repay all his debts, whereby he also gains the means to establish himself as a perpetual creditor. The obligation, and with it the promise of prosperity, are infinite since the debt is indelible.

The wages of sin and the creation of debts

On the art of governing sins … and those who govern

The sums collected — the wages of sin — are centralised by the Mengen and deposited in a bank account held by the Kivung Group; the declared recipient is the national government, of which the money is said to be the 'head' (*ka lpek*) or the 'picture' (*ka kaunun*).[28] Lacking the resources to ensure the economic development of the whole country, according to the Sulka leader of the movement, this government is forced to restrict aid to those localities to which it feels it is under obligation: for example the home locality of the Kivung, from which it has received earlier material support.[29] This government aid — which would be no more than a reciprocal contribution to counterbalance the sums paid in by the movement members — should take the form of roads, airports, bridges, stores, office buildings and other installations.

Yet, far from being an end in itself, the construction of these facilities, seen by the Kivung as so many indicators of economic development, is regarded as representing only the first stage of a much more ambitious plan. These external signs of prosperity are designed to whet the economic appetites of the Whites,[30] who would then let flow the financial and industrial investments they have been witholding from the indigenous populations. The sharing of resources would then be a time for sharing in white people's knowledge, considered to be the origin of these resources. Partaking in their knowledge would at last enable the Sulka to understand why they had been so long refused access to it. The project of creating a 'town' and thus setting up Western civilisation as an icon aims at learning the secret reasons that have kept the Sulka at a distance from it. Much more than aspiration to the abundance of the Whites or to equality with them, often mentioned in the ethnographic literature, it could be that aspiration to knowledge is among the principal issues involved in the Kivung movement.

By displaying their prosperity as one dangles a lure, it seems the members of the Kivung are basing their strategy on the idea that, as the French say, 'One lends only to the rich'. This view of matters undermines to some degree the classical anthropological interpretation, which postulates a unilateral desire on the part of Melanesians for Western goods and sees this desire as one of the principal driving forces driving messianic movements. The view as seen from the Kivung suggests that it is above all the idea the Sulka have of white people's cupidity for Melanesians' resources which commends this strategy to the movement. If creating a 'town' may be one of those imitative strategies observed elsewhere in Melanesia,[31] perhaps the mimicry in question expresses not so much desire for a foreign way of life as a means of addressing white Europeans, using the only language they are presumed to understand.

Observations on movements in other populations suggest, however, that the Melanesians' desire is not self-evident. They note, for example, the absence of millenarian expectations or the patent lack of interest in products from the West.[32] This is also suggested by studies questioning the pertinence of the distinction between subjects and objects in Melanesian societies,[33] or showing the transformed meanings and values given products exogenous to these societies.[34] Accepting that Melanesians are not necessarily envy ridden should, from this point of view, prompt us to examine our own projection of envy, in other words to ask ourselves what drives us to assume the desirability of whatever our societies produce. The idea that Whites' avidity for the local resources may be a relevant fact for Melanesians seems to have attracted little attention. It is as though it were of no importance that the colonisation, the alienation of lands, the predatory activity of gold prospectors, bird-of-paradise hunters, 'blackbirders' or other recruiters of labour or soldiers during the war, like the exploitation of forests and mineral resources today, were and are activities of Whites in Melanesia, never of Melanesians in the West.[35]

Another interpretation of the Whites' rapacity is conceivable, however. In terms of the ideology of desire discussed above, the rapacity thought of by the cult members as being the product of a ritual construction might refer to their own desire of exciting the cupidity of the Whites. Thus this cupidity, rather than constituting the motive of the subjugation of the Melanesians by the Whites, as was the case under colonial rule, would instead manifest the subjection of the Whites to the action of the movement and demonstrate the ultimate superiority of the knowledge wielded by the Kivung. Thus the capacity of the movement to control history would be visible even in the intrusion of foreign powers into the region.

The relationship the Kivung Group strives to establish with the national government by assuming the role of money-giver partakes of the logic of debt which underpins all social relations in Melanesia, and particularly all exchange relations. But its specificity lies in achieving this by 'hijacking' the relationship with another government authority: the agency charged with managing the province.[36]

The opposition implicitly posited by the Kivung between national and provincial governments appears to be based on three main factors:

— the fact that the historical founder of the movement as well as its present leader (both non-Sulka) are members of the national parliament, whereas the provincial parliament has never had a Kivung group member;[37]

— the fact that the national government represents one and all, the whole independent country in its relation with 'white people's countries'; the provincial government, on the other hand is a mere subsidiary of the former and is accused, in addition, of being a Tolai vassal;

— the fact that the national government neither demands nor represses, unlike the provincial government, which is persuaded that it is periodically owed money (taxes) and which places its repressive system at the service of the administration. For Kivung members, who refuse to pay the provincial tax, the judicial 'persecutions' carried out by this administration are a recurrent subject of protest. The local Church, in the person of the missionaries who urge people to pay their taxes and who condemn the Kivung movement, is also a part of the system of repression.

The Kivung's decision to turn over the collection to the national government, by contrast, sheds some light on their refusal to pay the annual provincial tax. It can be interpreted as an attempt to substitute a fertile far-reaching relationship for a local relation judged to be unsatisfactory and non-productive.[38] Paying one's taxes, paying what is owed is a very poor relationship — and an impoverishing one as well. For two reasons: it precludes the reversibility of roles, since those who pay and those who receive are always respectively the same; and not only can the money paid out never appear as a gift, but it cannot even rank as a claim, because nothing is ever forthcoming to counterbalance it. The money received by the provincial government is seen as being invested solely on behalf of the Tolai, with no positive fallout for the Sulka. As long as taxes go to this government, denounced as a 'Tolai government' because it counts a majority of Tolai, things will never, it is claimed, be otherwise.

The members of the Kivung movement refuse to pay the taxes assessed by the provincial government because they have already paid the national government — which in fact has not asked them for anything. Indebted to one institution, they deny this debt by placing the other institution in the position of being their debtor.

This type of relationship, in which one is able to exercise compelling force precisely because one has given something the receiver never asked for but which will oblige him to reciprocate, corresponds to the Sulka definition of the relation of 'solidarity' known as *mokpom* (literally: 'to hold each other').[39] This is a long-term bond, since it can theoretically be passed on from one generation to the next; this mutual obligation, in which each in turn is creditor and debtor, is the opposite of the momentary relation of 'aid' or 'loan' (*a tol*) instigated by satisfying a request and ending shortly thereafter with the repayment of the loan.

The Kivung strategy consists of so contriving it that the acquittal of the debt (paying their taxes) amounts to a claim. It thereby implies transforming an obligatory gift (the tax) into a voluntary gift, in other words turning something owed into a gift and a gift into a debt by playing one government against the other. In this way, the Kivung's debt to the provincial government becomes the nation's debt to the Kivung.

For the members of the movement, who are debtors of one government because they have chosen to be creditors of the other, the reimbursement demanded by the province indirectly gives its full importance to the credit extended to the national government. The impossibility of avoiding debt (taxes), heightened by its aggravation (fines, lawsuits, prison sentences), accounts for the fact that the members of the movement have no choice but to make the best of their misfortune, since they cannot avoid it.

The interest of misfortune

Judicial persecutions, hostility from outsiders, insecurity, new debts, the various ills by which the Kivung claims to be beset are a measure of the sacrifices made on behalf of the national government; at the same time as they give the refusal its demarcative value. We are better than the others because, in order to obey God's commandments, we disobey both the provincial government and the Church; we are better because we pay the national government, and pay the full price, or twice the price: the monetary price and the price of misfortune.

These misfortunes cannot be entirely unfortunate, however, since they are imbued with an operative value, with a sacrificial meaning. One former catechist and Kivung member asserted that Hell was not something to be feared after death because it was what people were already living here on earth. And it is precisely because one lives through Hell during one's lifetime that one no longer has to fear it afterwards — since living consists, if I may sum up his viewpoint, in paying in advance. Members of the Kivung, as we have seen, pay with zeal. The sacrifice contained in these repeated payments (of their goods and their person) can be viewed as a total rejection of any gratuitousness, beginning with gratuitous misfortune. Sacrifice is in this sense the capacity to produce misfortune for oneself for the purpose of rejecting the gratuitousness of misfortune. A sign of excellence because it is a sign of belonging, misfortune as defined by the Kivung is also a sign of sin. The movement's durability relies precisely on this ambivalence, as we shall see.

From the movement leader's affirmation that 'there is always some sin that needs redeeming', we inferred earlier that there was always some sin one was guilty of having failed to redeem. The perpetuity of the debt, the fact that there is 'always some sin that needs redeeming', corresponds to a dimension of the Kivung that fits the definition of what, in a different context, Charles Fredrikson analysed as an 'etiology of failure'.[40] It is to this debt, to this neglected redemption that the members of the Kivung attribute retrospectively any failure. One anecdote illustrates this nicely: a man, apparently on his own initiative and shortly after joining the movement, spent the night in the village graveyard beseeching the spirits of the dead to show themselves. But in vain. For all he gained from his long wait for a miracle was, in addition to a cold, the suspicion of the other members, who promptly interpreted the absence of results as the sign of some sin he had failed to redeem and which was now preventing the spirits from coming forward.

Among the Sulka, this type of explanation of failure is not peculiar to the Kivung movement. It can be found, for example, in the content of one male initiation rite that involved repeated applications of manganese earth (*a ket*) to the teeth and exposing them to the heat of a fire. At length, a sort of shiny black lacquer formed that could last several years. The success of this ordeal, described as long and painful, was subject to one precondition: that the novices 'reveal' their past 'offences' or 'failings'. Today people say that admission of these 'offences' (*kermatnek*), having to do for example with murders, thefts, illicit sexual relations, was not sanctioned by any particular punishment, but that whatever the novices neglected or forgot to confess, 'the *ket* would reveal it'. Failing the test constituted this 'revelation': the earth would not adhere to the teeth, or would chip off, leaving uneven black splotches. The novices were then enjoined to reveal what they had been keeping back before renewing the ordeal which, if they had told all, would this time be successful.[41]

In the teeth-blackening ritual (no longer performed) as in Kivung practice, the question of 'offense' is couched less in terms of moral content than in terms of power, that is in terms of an operative, manipulative relation to knowledge. An offense is whatever jeopardizes the effectiveness of the rite. Rather than implying something sanctionable, it implies something that sanctions. Sin, in other words, is not evil itself, it is whatever renders the rite inoperative. Everything that in daily life is experienced as failure therefore signifies the presence of sin. Wounded game that escapes, a fruitless fishing expedition, a clumsy accident, for example, are all warnings, all calls to order.

If collective prosperity is proof that sins have indeed been redeemed, as the emblematic 'town born from the money of the Ten Commandments' shows, individual misfortune or failure, conversely, reveals failure to redeem:

> If I don't pay for that day I didn't work, that day I didn't give food or didn't clean up the graveyard, or for a work of the Ten Commandments I didn't do, if I don't redeem that, the dead will get cross. There will come a time when the ax will cut me, or I will fall out of a tree, or a flood will carry me away... For that thing I didn't make amends for, a mark like that will appear.

Misfortune or failure — which reveals sin — is itself a sin. It is the original sin that founds and federates the Kivung society, which resides in the failure to redeem sins. The same speaker observed later: 'My money watches over me', 'money is my guardian' (*kwa mani kamtot mang dok*).

The effectiveness of the movement, achieved through reiterated sacrifices for the redemption of sins, cannot manifest itself immediately. The definition of Kivung practice as 'work' arises precisely from the idea that 'things cannot go fast'. The person who made this remark observed in substance that, when you plant a taro, you have 'to wait before you can harvest anything'. And he added, alluding to the movement's detractors — no doubt as a way of turning their presumption of irrationality against them: 'They would like everything to go fast. Their idea is: "I work today, today I see."'[42]

Nor can the effectiveness of the movement be visible at the individual level for each of its members. The lonely night-long vigil for the miracle in the graveyard could only result in disappointment. Only failure can manifest itself in a proximate and immediate fashion to the individual. The effectiveness of the sacrifice can never manifest itself this way. It establishes a spatial distance, the space between the Ancestors' House in the Sulka village and the 'town born of the Ten Commandments' in Mengen country; and it is deferred in time, disjoined as it were from the act of depositing a coin in a tin can. Failure, with its higher visibility quotient, in fact argues for renewed allegiance to the Kivung movement.

Ascribed to a manifestation of the spirits of the dead, individual misfortunes or failures which punish the non-redemption of sins amount, in a sense, to negative miracles. Nothing of the like could indeed ever happen to someone outside the movement. The spirits take no interest in such people, the movement leader insists, for 'the dead are only concerned with men who give them food'. Refusing to join the Kivung, members believe, does not engender any reprisals. Failure to redeem sins, or to make offerings to the spirits is thought to have adverse consequences only for movement members, not for those outside.[43] Exteriority is of course no protection against misfortune, but the misfortunes that may befall a non-believer are not attributed (by the members of the Kivung) to the spirits. Since the spirits punish only those they care about, the capacity to be punished implicitly claimed by the members of the Kivung appears almost meritorious. Expression of a relationship with the dead, price of membership in the group, tribute paid to excellence, misfortune thus imbued with punitive value is therefore not entirely misfortune for members of the group. In this way it differs from the kind of misfortune that, outside the Kivung, is precisely nothing more than misfortune.

The profitability of the movement

The problem of accounting for the durability of messianic movements, in view of the inevitable disappointments they must engender, has received several responses in the literature, as Mondher Kilani has shown;[44] their diversity is related to the degree of strategic irrationality or rationality attributed to the movements. Kivung practice among the Sulka would suggest that the movement derives its staying power from its unquestionable profitability. A major contribution in this regard resides in the demonstration of the bond between the local dimension (the Ancestors' House in Sulka territory) and the supra-local dimension (the 'town' in the Mengen region). This relation is conceptualised by means of another, between money paid and investment made, between depositing a coin and building a 'town'. The Kivung is profitable because it enables its members to conceptualise the relation between the redemption of sins and the advent of prosperity. The money that redeems sins is the same as that which gives rise to towns. Redeeming sins betters people because it makes them prosperous. The symbolic and the economic are thought in the same terms, and the movement's profitability is predicated essentially on the refusal to disjoin them.

Its cost-effectiveness is thus based on the means employed by the Kivung Group to demonstrate their superiority to those who reason in terms of a supposed opposition between 'real' (what is effective, true) and 'imaginary' (what is inoperative, erroneous). To the non-believers who disparage the movement as nothing but an illusion, the existence of the 'town' provides concrete evidence of their own illusion. With its health and administrative facilities, it is a testimonial to secularism and accountability where some charge the movement with superstition. To the local authorities, it manifests their inability to exercise authority, therefore their ineffectiveness. In by-passing the government responsible for managing the province, the members of the Kivung act to relieve it of the functions it is to exercise in the future economic development of their region. In so doing, they place the very authority that oppresses them for failing to fulfill their obligations (refusing to pay the provincial tax) in a situation of failing to respect its own obligations.

In response to those who accuse the Kivung rite of being part of the 'dark' pagan past, they claim to be best Christians. The religious discourse of the mission is taken literally. Appropriately demetaphorised, the divine commandments become orders, the redemption of sins is accomplished in monetary terms, and the 'time of darkness' is recreated in the dark interior of the Ancestors' House. Indeed there can be no better Christians than these apostles of tradition, for to demetaphorise, when it comes to redeeming sins, is to act in accordance with the customary practices of payment consisting of making a gift in kind (a valuable and/or food) 'to compensate for' (*srim*), 'to drive out' (*pet*) or 'to finish' (*rum*) the harm (anger, shame or suffering) caused someone.

The Mengen claim that part of the money collected by the Kivung movement is turned over by the movement to the local Catholic mission.[45] From the standpoint of the mission, which is in need of money and regularly appeals to the faithful through fund-raising drives, the best Christians should therefore also be defined as those whose sins help build churches. No doubt, the God the Kivung strives to better will recognise His own.

Addenda

a)   Since this article was written, a trip to New Britain, in 1994, enabled me to gather some more information on the Kivung movement. I did not incorporate the new material into the text because it would have called for new and substantial developments. I will therefore limit myself to the following brief indications. In the Mengen area, the 'town born from the money of the Ten Commandments' has acquired some new facilities. The Kivung has established its headquarters in this 'town' now endowed with shops, a wharf and a jail, which is said to be always empty and whose usefulness in such a setting would seem to reside in the demonstration of its

perfect uselessness. A large house for receiving visitors has been built on the model of
the (extinct) Men's Houses erected until several decades ago for the celebration of
second funerals. The interest on bank accounts is used for disaster aid in the name of
solidarity with affected areas in New Guinea and in the rest of the world (via the
National Appeal Committee). It is also from this interest that the sums contributed to
the Catholic mission are drawn. It should be noted incidentally that, for some of the
Sulka in the movement, membership in the Pomio Kivung Group does not exclude the
possibility of belonging to fundamentalist movements like the Seventh Day Adventist
Church.

b)   *Extracts from the* Post Courier *on-line, dated 1st and 31st January 2000 :*
'The East New Britain governor [the leader of the movement] has openly challenged
the Church to excommunicate him and other Kivung members. The problem came to
head during a talkback show on the provincial radio […] in which Catholic priests […]
branded the association a 'cult movement' which was involved in activities not
considered to be Christian-Like. [They] claimed that the group was nothing more than
a cargo cult movement which made false promises to the people and prospered on their
ignorance. […]
[They] said the association was involved in practises which included its members
digging up skeletal remains of dead relatives from bush cemeteries and re-burying them
in a cemetery close to the association's headquarters and then leaving food next to the
graves.
[In his reply, the governor] branded the priests liars and the Catholic Church as a
hypocrite which practised the very things that it has branded as immoral and
unchristian-like. He called on the priests and the church to explain if their digging up
the remains of a catechist who died over 50 years and keep his bones in a casket at a
church on the Gazelle Peninsula, was different to what they practised. 'I am not
criticising, I am just making comparison.' [The governor] laughed loudly…
[He] said members showed their respect for the dead by inviting them for a meal and if
other cultures practiced that, there was nothing wrong if they did the same. He said:
'The Japanese do it, the Chinese people and the Taiwanese do it, the Asian countries do
it. If the Church is condemning us, will they condemn those cultures too?' […]
Speaking in Tok Pisin [the governor] said it was funny the Catholic Church should talk
about the issue of the association followers contributions, when that very Church
collected money from its members each Sunday. [He] said that the Catholic Church
had not right to prevent the association from adopting the 10 Commandments.'

Footnotes

1   See Jeudy-Ballini (1988). The material presented here was collected among the Sulka of New Britain between 1980 and 1988, in the course of three missions conducted with the financial support of the Centre National de la Recherche Scientifique. Matters relating to the Kivung movement were extremely sensitive issues to discuss with my informants, owing to the acute reticence and tension aroused by their very mention. I owe the bulk of the material presented here to 'my father', Petrus Mangil, a member of Milim village and leader of the movement in the Sulka area until his death, who divulged the information on the condition that it would never get back to his country. I would be grateful to those who read this to enable me to keep this promise.

The analysis I propose was nurtured by several months of exchanges with Charles Fredrikson (from the Anthropology of Portugal group at the École des Hautes Études en Sciences Sociales, Paris). His work, in particular on debt, renunciation, sacrifice and misfortune, as well as his critical comments on my handling of the Sulka material were a privileged source of inspiration. To this unfailingly attentive and stimulating partner in dialogue, I would like here to express my gratitude.

2   For recent analyses of the Kivung movement among the Mengen and the Baining, the reader may consult respectively Trompf (1990) and Whitehouse (1996).

3   The kina, the national currency, is divided into 100 toeia. At the time, the annual tax paid by a woman was around K2.

4   This cleaning up is also described as one of the ritual activities performed in other populations (Ryan 1969; Strathern 1979/1980). Note that the maintenance of cemeteries was formerly an obligation imposed by the German colonial administration and placed under the supervision of health officers. On their patrols, these health officers would punish (with the help of the police — *luluai*) the men of the village whose cemeteries were not kept up. Before the Kivung decided to take over this task, it was the local doctor's job to see that the villagers did the work.

5   One man who did not belong to the movement claimed that, once the ancestors had eaten the *nunu*, the food was 'like ice'. Nevertheless, those outside the movement, who never miss a chance, understand this 'cold' to mean much more prosaically the effect of the time elapsed between the cooking and the eating, thus jeering at those who are credulous enough to think they are eating what was not eaten by the spirits, whereas in reality they are eating the leftovers of rodents and other marauders that managed to sneak into the House.

6   See Panoff (1969: 2244).

7   Given the fluctuation of the national currency, and the absence of an official exchange rate, it is hard to give a precise equivalent for this sum. An estimate can be made from the fact that, in 1986, one kina was worth around two US dollars. According to Guilhem Maistre, who worked with one Mengen subgroup, various sources mentioned, in 1991, the remarkable sum of 4.5 million kinas (Maistre 1994: 29).

8   Built with imported materials (Fibrociment, corrugated metal), the facilities in question are no different from those built for similar uses in the other towns of the area. At the time the study was carried out, there were no particular restrictions on access to these facilities for non-Mengen or people from outside the Kivung.

9   This is the only instance of the term or the notion of 'paradise' I encountered in connection with Kivung activities.

10 See Hermann (1992).

11 Hermann (1992).

12 See for instance Jorgensen (1991), Kempf (1992), or Josephidès (1985 : 135).

13 See Hermann (1992: 65).

14 I have shown this elsewhere, when discussing cultural otherness, condemned by the Sulka because they regard it as forgetting, as a loss. This is the case, for instance, of the otherness of their Baining neighbours, seen as infidels of a sort, as Sulkas who have forgotten to remain what they are (Jeudy-Ballini 1988).

15 It might be the eleventh commandment, as the sculpture beside the cemetery suggests, by the inversion of the roman numerals for the number nine, carved as XI instead of IX. On the use of the concept of 'custom' as 'anticipating past', as Roy Wagner (1969) puts it, the reader may refer to Keesing and Tonkinson eds. (1982).

16 See Joseph Meier (1945: 34). 'I already knew all that', one Orokaiva leader of the 'Taro' cult replied when a missionary explained the 'broad lines of the Christian doctrine' (Worsley 1977: 72).

17 See Laufer (1955: 55–56). Laufer's writings about the Baining contain another even more striking illustration, in which the missionary strives to show how each of the Ten Commandments has its counterpart

in one of the major principles governing what he calls 'tribal morality' (Laufer 1946/1949: 524–525). On missionaries' appropriation of local representations, see Jeudy-Ballini (1998 and 2002a).

18 I will not attempt here to analyse the general ideology of the rule, violations and amends in Sulka society. Nevertheless, it would be worthwhile asking whether awareness or knowledge of the 'offence' does not precisely create the 'offence'. Speaking of adultery, for example, the Sulka say that it is reprehensible only if it becomes public knowledge. But my data do not allow me to decide the extent to which this principle might apply to other forms of transgression.

19 One could object that all religions are a way of mobilising God. For the Kivung, however, the meaning of the 'work' performed in the movement is based on the postulate that there are some religious practices that do not mobilise anyone (praying without giving any money, for instance).

20 The speaker who mentioned this point claimed that, by giving up their own magic, the movement members had deprived themselves of 'strength' (*ka selpak*) and that they henceforth had to 'pay' people outside to recover enough of it, for instance, to be able to win over a future spouse. Using the same distinction between 'good' and 'bad' magics, while modifying their content slightly, the leader of the Kivung Group said that members had only given up their 'bad' magics, under which heading he placed love magic because it might encourage stealing someone else's husband or wife.

21 This remark is in line with Andrew Strathern's reading of the deaths that occurred in a cult in the New Guinea Highlands: 'I gained a strong impression, although no-one would say so, that these deaths were interpreted as a necessary sacrifice before the ghosts would release the money' (1979/1980: 166).

22 See Fredrikson (1994).

23 See Lattas (1992b: 46).

24 In Sulka, the same word, *ka svil*, means 'desire' and 'will'.

25 See Jeudy-Ballini (1999).

26 The nature of the present varies and is usually left to the discretion of the organiser. It can be bits of cloth, string bags, ornaments, taro cuttings, small objects or coins, for example. Equivalent practices can be found in other societies, in New Britain (Dark 1983; Maschio 1995), New Guinea (Strathern and Strathern 1971) or the Trobriand Islands (Weiner 1976). See Jeudy-Ballini (1999 and forthcoming).

27 On prosperity as an expression of divine power, see Lipuma (1988: 88) : '…from the Maring perspective, the essence of being a Christian, indeed the power and authority of Jesus Christ is his worshippers' access to rice and fish. The food distributed by the Church is not an added benefit to Christianity but its heart and soul. As one pundit put it: 'without the trade store there would be no anglican God'.'

28 With respect to the 'image' (*nunu*, referring for instance to a reflection in the water) and understood as a sort of immaterial duplicate of a being or a thing, the *kaunun* picture designates, in Sulka, the figurative and materialised representation of this being or thing (a woodcarving, for instance).

29 It is not possible within the scope of this article to discuss the geopolitical aspects of the movement, even though they are crucial. Let me simply say that the 'locality' in this case covers several districts around Pomio (in Mengen country) and includes essentially, besides the Mengen and the Tomuip involved in the movement, only a fraction of the Sulka population. The rest of the population living in the Mope region, together with the Baining and the Tolai, belong to another district. The idea of secession from the latter has been raised by the Kivung Group, which sees this as one possible means of throwing off what it regards as a Tolai yoke.

30 *O Kaer*, in vernacular, *ol waetskin*, in neo-Melanesian pidgin : literally 'Whites'. When I use the essentialising term 'Whites', it should be viewed as a translation of the vernacular and pidgin words.

31 See Lattas (1992b).

32 See Ryan (1969), Billings (1983), Kilani (1983), Hermann (1992), Kempf(1992). A. Strathern mentions the natives' yearning for wealth which, once in their possession, would put them on an equal footing with the Whites. At the same time, he remarks: 'if the economic acquisition of cargo was truly an important aim in the cult, one might have expected at least a faltering in the enthusiasm if the cargo was not forthcoming. Unfortunately, we cannot be sure at this point, for it seems that the cult was forcibly halted before the practitioners had reached any stage of disillusionment. There is some problem here' (1971a: 261).

33 See Iteanu (1990), Breton (2002).

34 See Sahlins (1992b).

35 Judging by the ulterior motives attributed to them in certain provinces of Papua New Guinea, it is to be feared that ethnologists may sometimes be counted among the predators, as may be tourists and film-makers (Coiffier 1991, Errington and Gewertz 1989).

36 Endowed with an independent government since 1975, Papua New Guinea is divided into 19 provinces, each with its own governing body. The Sulka, like the Mengen, the Baining, the Tomuip and the Tolai, live in East New Britain Province.

37 The present leader of the Kivung Group was re-elected to the national parliament in 1991 (Maistre 1994).

38 An analogous principle, but underpinned by different means, appears to be at work in the New Hanover 'Johnson Cult', described by Dorothy Billings (1983).

39 See Jeudy-Ballini (2002b, 2004).

40 See Fredrikson (1991).

41 Like the magical practices that the Sulka say 'go cold' (have no effect) as soon as they are revealed, it is as though the simple fact of naming the 'offences' made them lose their power. But the same revelation that, in the case of magic, accounts for the failure of the rite is, in the case of initiation, the condition of its effectiveness. And for the same reasons. Revelation (magic) or admission (initiation): each time, speech acts externalise the powers, thus supposing a distancing and a consequent dwindling of these (beneficial or harmful) powers.

42 This notion of gradual development runs counter to the analyses that establish a correlation between Melanesian expectations and temporal discontinuity (McDowell 1988; Kempf, 1992; Errington, 1974).

43 This can be seen as a case of 'etiology of failure' as well as an indirect illustration of the protective powers attributed to non-belief (Fredrikson 1991 and 1994; Jeudy-Ballini 1991 and 1998). For the Sulka, these same powers, also attributed to ignorance and exteriority, account, for instance, for the fact that evil spirits cannot harm those who, because they are uninformed or strangers to the area, are unaware of the risk they run (Jeudy-Ballini 2002a).

44 See Kilani (1983).

45 See Maistre (1994). This piece of information, not mentioned by the Sulka at the time of the ethnographic study (1980-1988), has since been confirmed by them (see *Addenda*).

Chapter 5

HUMAN SACRIFICE AND
CARGO CULT IN NEW IRELAND

Brigitte Derlon

On central New Ireland's Lelet plateau, with its broken relief rising to an altitude of 1200 metres, four villages are home to some 500 persons from the Mandak linguistic group: this is the last remaining population of mountain-dwellers on the island. During my stay, from 1983 to 1984,[1] several informants told me that, before the missionaries' arrival, at the beginning of the century in other words, one clan in a coastal Mandak village at the base of the plateau sacrificed a succession of young children in the hope of obtaining European goods. If I spontaneously believed in the existence of this cargo cult — which featured themes common to a number of similar movements — conversely, I did not lend credence to the child murders. I had never heard of human sacrifices being attested in the framework of millenarian movements in this part of the world, and the fact that the victims mentioned by these mountain-dwellers were children — whose murder is spontaneously repellant — made me to think that these sacrifices were merely the echo of old rumors rehashed by missionaries and administrators concerning the 'abominable' practices of the cargo cults. By repeating these false rumours, I told myself at the time, the plateau Mandak were probably trying to dissociate themselves from the Mandak groups on the coast. Since unfavourable weather and the imminence of the celebration of some rituals in the mountains had made me put off and finally abandon my plans to visit the village in question, which was hard to reach from the plateau, my information on this cult unfortunately remains limited to these brief snatches.

Nevertheless, in spite of the incomplete and indirect nature of my sources, I would like to show, in the present text written several years after the fieldwork, how analysis of the traditional human sacrifices practised in New Ireland on the occasion of funerals — a custom of which I was aware at the time but whose reflection I had not recognised in the cargo cult — actually lends credence to the existence of these child sacrifices. Such sacrifices most probably attested the New Irelanders' desire to acquire rights to the goods and secrets possessed by Europeans. In support of this hypothesis, to which I will return in the final section devoted to the cargo cult, I will examine first of all the material on traditional sacrifices, which leads us to explore certain features of the land-holding system, the representations associated with filiation in these matrilineal societies and rights in the famous *malanggan* objects. After which, we will be prepared to understand the surprising role of human sacrifice as a way of obtaining European manufactured goods. To my knowledge, this role does not yet feature in the inventory of the variants of the Melanesian cargo cult.

Foreign influences

The Bismark Archipelago, of which New Britain and New Ireland are two of the principal islands, suffered the painful effects of European mercantile interest and proselytism at an early date, both manifesting themselves in the 1870s. English and German merchant vessels in search of trepangs and copra crossed those of the first labour recruiters, working at the time for the sugar-cane plantations in the remote Pacific, while new Wesleyan converts (Methodists), originally from Fiji, were beginning to evangelise the local populations.

In 1881, ten trading stations had already opened at the northern end of New Ireland and on the small nearby islands, a region that, with its dense coconut-palm cover, natural harbour and no lack of spots to drop anchor seemed an ideal location to merchants and traders.[2] In spite of repeated attacks on the ships and the trading posts, followed by punitive expeditions and ending notably in the death of eleven white people between 1881 and 1895,[3] the almost total disappearance of the stone axe, observed in the north of New Ireland from the late 1880s,[4] indicates that the local populations had quickly begun to trade with Europeans on a massive scale. At the end of the nineteenth century, certain northern villages were, it seems, bulging with goods from the West, following a spate of competitive trading which in the space of a few years sparked a 300 per cent increase in the going price for copra.[5] The villagers even sold Europeans specially produced carvings, bearing strange designs unrelated to those dictated by tradition;[6] some of these probably even stand in our museums and are held to represent genuine manifestations of *malanggan* art.

Often using a combination of subterfuge and violence to fill their ships with cheap and easily exploited labour, the recruiters for plantations in Queensland, Fiji or Samoa enrolled some 2,500 inhabitants of the Bismark Archipelago in 1883 alone,[7] one year before the annexation of the archipelago and northeast New Guinea by Germany. With the plantation economy developing apace in these newly conquered regions, and notably in New Ireland where it is estimated that an area of 6,000 hectares (a quarter of which was already planted) was designated for the exploitation of copra in 1905,[8] measures were taken by the colonial administration to facilitate the recruitment of New Irelanders for plantations throughout the German protectorate. The pacification of the island, achieved between 1900 and 1904, together with the completion in 1902, thanks to the forced labour of the local populations, of 200 miles of road along the eastern coast, from Kavieng (the administrative capital set up on the northern tip of the island), enabled recruiters to circulate easily and without fear throughout the most populous area of New Ireland. The forced relocation of inlanders to the coast was imposed as much to establish the *pax germanica* as to increase the potential labour supply on the littoral. Villages thus gradually disappeared from the mountains, except for those on Lelet plateau, which were more difficult to control because of their altitude and their distance from the coast. Last of all, the creation of a head tax, to be paid in marks, forced many New Irelanders to sign on with the local plantation. In 1906, one third of the workforce of the entire German protectorate came from New Ireland alone.[9] In certain districts (Kavieng and Namatanai) up to 70 per cent of the active male population had worked for at least three years on European-run plantations.[10] The figures show a horrifying mortality rate among recruits: between 1887 and 1907, 40 per cent of those working in northern New Ireland died before the end of their contract.[11]

In 1875, some ten years ahead of the Catholics from the Sacred Heart Mission, the first Wesleyan missionaries landed at the southern end of New Ireland, opposite the Duke of York Islands. After having sailed around to various villages on this part of the island, whose narrow, broken coastal plain is sparsely populated, the Methodists concentrated their efforts on the northern half, already controlled by the merchants and traders, and temporarily confined the Catholic missionaries to the south, with the help of the 'zoning law' enacted in 1891 by the German administration. Although the Methodist implantation was facilitated by the number and the non-European origin of their catechists, it was not until the first decade of the twentieth century that the well-devised distribution of their mission posts — first along the east coast and then on the west coast of the northern half of the island — ensured their regular presence in a majority of the villages.[12] Still slight at the turn of the century, the impact of the two denominations on traditional customs and beliefs was truly making itself felt by 1910.

The intense contact with Europeans had dramatic effects. The massive displacement of the young men of New Ireland, recruited to work on plantations throughout the protectorate, emptied certain villages of the better part of their vital resources and blocked the transmission of traditions between generations.[13] Diseases introduced by the Europeans (dysentery, smallpox, sexually transmitted diseases) aggravated the death toll and contributed to lowering the birth rate below the replacement threshold.[14] This resulted in so sharp a drop in the population that by 1907 the German administration realized that its labour pool, so vital for the economic interests of its colonies, was in danger of drying up, and grew alarmed.[15] In the same year, a highly pessimistic account[16] reported that the population of New Ireland was dying out and had abandoned a number of its traditional customs, about which it would soon no longer be possible to obtain information.

Human sacrifice

Traditional sacrifice of the wife or child of the deceased

Even before the contact situation gave rise to cargo movements — including the Mandak cult that my informants on Lelet plateau associated with child sacrifices — ritual killings that could be assimilated to sacrifices existed in New Ireland. Various sources concerning a period before 1910 indicate that the death of a man could lead to the sacrifice of his wife and/or child, which was carried out by the victim's own matriclan or matrilineage. Such sacrifices are attested for the linguistic groups located on either side of the Mandak area, namely the Kara and Nalik to the north, the Barok to the south and the people of the Tabar Islands off the east coast of New Ireland.

In the Barok area, where the meaningful social unit is the lineage, only the child was killed in the event of a sacrifice at the death of the father. The New Irelander pastor, Linge, originally from this linguistic area, evokes this old custom in his memoirs. He tells how a member of the widow's lineage, usually her brother, would quickly take one of the couple's children and beat it to death. He suggested that the victim, killed without warning the mother, could be either male or female, and writes that the half-sister born from the first marriage of his mother was sacrificed this way upon the death of her father.[17] In 1974, Jessep, a Canadian anthropologist, collected seven cases of earlier child sacrifices from informants in three Barok villages.[18] Except for one case — in which a little girl was handed over by her older brothers to their cross cousin (their father's sister's son) to be strangled by him — the child's killing is always ascribed to a member of its own lineage; and in the only two cases mentioning the identity of the sacrificed child (of which the one cited above is an exception), the victim is presented as being a girl and the youngest child of the deceased.

In the other areas mentioned, it was the wife of the deceased who was sacrificed. A German area administrator reports that, in the early twentieth century, in one region on the east coast of the Kara zone, the wife was almost always strangled by a close male relative at the death of her husband.[19] Without noting the frequency of this phenomenon, a member of the 1907–1909 German naval expedition states that, in the Nalik area, the execution by strangling fell to the brother or the son of the victim.[20] Groves, who spent some time in the Tabar Islands in 1933, after this practice had already disappeared, reports that it was the real or classificatory brother of the young widow who took her life.[21] Two sources of information on the Kara area mention, not the murder but the suicide of the wife upon the death of her husband. They indicate that the women of Mangai village were often driven or forced to kill themselves by their own clan.[22] The Hungarian Birò, who stopped over in New Ireland in 1900, writes that the women of Kara could at that time commit suicide either by throwing themselves off a cliff, hanging themselves or having themselves strangled by a friend who was not a kinsman. He adds that women with a child at the breast were strangled and that only women with older children could choose whether to live or to die.[23]

In other words, it would seem that the way wives died ranged from suicide more or less of their own free will to forced suicide close to pure and simple murder, and that being strangled to death by a member of their matriclan — apparently the most frequent form of death — could be done with their consent or under constraint. A man's authority over his sister and her children explains the fact that, in most cases, the killing of the deceased's wife, in the north of the Mandak area, and of his child, in the south, were done by the victim's brother and mother's brother, respectively. Among the Lelet Mandak, for example, it is the brother who receives and distributes to his own lineage the brideprice given for his sister, and who fulfills her social obligations to her husband's clan on her behalf. If his sister's sexual conduct is mentioned in his presence, he will feel ashamed and will wash away this shame by a gift of pig meat; formerly he would have felt obliged to strangle her or to compel her to commit suicide if she had violated any prohibitions whose transgression was punishable by death. The mother's brother, in turn, is responsible in particular for seeing that his nieces and nephews make proper use of the things associated with their common descent group (land, knowledge of magic and ritual).

Human life for land rights

When stated by the authors who have reported the existence of the phenomenon, the reasons for sacrificing the wife or child of the deceased seem at first glance surprising. They have to do with the desire to acquire rights in the land owned by the deceased husband's or father's descent group (with two exceptions that will be mentioned later). Groves notes that, in the Tabar Islands,

> [i]n former times, by killing their sister, own or classificatory, upon the occasion of the death of her husband, male members of the woman's *ti-i-ti* [lineage] acquired rights in the land and coconuts of the *ti-i-ti* of the deceased husband.[24]

The following is also reported concerning the old customs of the Kara village of Mangai:

> That land shortage must at one time have been acute is suggested by the custom of *kiut*, whereby a woman and her descendants gained rights to the land of her husband if she committed suicide upon his death. Her clan, one informant said, often urged or even forced her to do this. Two ancient ladies were making use of rights gained in this way. There is no evidence of land shortage today.[25]

Jessep's detailed 1974 study of land tenure in the northern Barok area shed a bit of light on the circumstances that might induce a descent group to sacrifice one of its members in order to obtain land rights. In the two of the seven cases of child sacrifice for which Jessep's informants added that the victim was a small girl, the child's mother, who had borne several children, did not come from the village of her husband, on whose family lands she was living.[26] As the right to use the land of the spouse's or father's lineage was limited to their lifetime and as a person could not live in a village if he or she did not have the right to use the land of one of its lineages, this woman and her children would have been obliged, upon the death of their husband and father, to return to the village where their own lineage had its land. The sacrificed child, who won for its own lineage permanent rights in the land of its father's group, thus allowed its mother and siblings to go on living where they had resided until then and enabled its lineage to establish itself in this village, of which it became a resident. It was this last point, the integration of a lineage into a village from which it did not come, that Jessep's informants stressed.[27] In the second of the two cases, in addition to the life of the child, a pig was given to the lineage of the deceased father; the lineage, which was dying out, in turn gave not a small portion but the totality of its territory to the lineage of the sacrificed child.

> Kaleleang lineage came to Kono in this way. A big man of Kono named Nabua, of Ngeat Karamane lineage, married a woman of Komalabuo [another Barok village] named Gatin, of Kaleleang lineage, and she came to Kono and lived with him on the land called Ion. She had five children, and when Nabua died, Kaleleang decided to kill the youngest (a girl), and both bodies were buried together in one hole.

... This was ... to get the ground Ion, so that the ground would now belong to
Kaleleang. It was this way — the little girl was a sufficient payment, so the ground no
longer belonged to Karamane; because Kaleleang blood had fallen, it bought this ground,
and so Kaleleang now lived at Ion.

... Gogo Tare lineage came originally from Lihir Island [off the southeast coast of
New Ireland], but has been at Karu now for many years. A woman of this lineage named
De married a man named Baun of Gono Wutumsisi lineage of Karu, and they lived at
Karu. De had two twin sons, Bubumasang and Gutingbulut, and then a girl named Bero.
When Baum died, the twins sent Bero (by arrangement) to Baun's sister's son, who
strangled her and she was then buried with her father. Also, the twins killed a pig worth
ten strings of shell money and gave it to the nephew. The nephew then stood up and
promised all the land [of the father's lineage] to the twins, and this land has belonged to
Gogo Tare ever since.

... The two lineages agreed, and Wutumsisi lineage thought it better that the land
went to the children (rather than to other lineages of Gono clan), because Wutumsisi was
becoming extinct [in the Barok area, the land of an extinct lineage usually goes to the
lineage that organises the funerals of the last to die in the moribund group, with priority
given to lineages belonging to the same clan as the extinct lineage]. If Wutumsisi had still
been strong they [the members of this lineage] would not agreed, or they would only have
given a little bit of land.[28]

Four other cases were reported to Jessep by an influential man from a lineage named Satele,
on whose land a river flows through the Barok village of Kanam. This man summed up the
way land transactions were carried out in exchange for the sacrifice of children upon the
death of their father and pointed to the four sections of the river that his own lineage had
formerly given to four other lineages in this type of transaction.

If I die, and I have land, and my child's lineage kills my child, and buries it with me in the
same hole, then the child's lineage wins some of my land. Look at the river at Kanam —
the section of river near the bridge is known as Arugage, and it belongs to Nalagos
Kolonobo lineage because, before, a Kolonobo child was buried with its Satele [the
speaker's lineage] father; Satele had agreed with this beforehand, that Kolonobo would
win the water.

The next section is called Anatabilong, and it belongs to Laudagon clan, since a
Laudagon child was buried with a Satele man. So with the next bit, called Abuang — it
went to Nalagos Kunuraba-Usagale lineage; and then the part called Aunaneino, which is
a cave frequented by eels, went to a Nalagos lineage ...

These sections of the river could be fenced off, and fish and eels caught with
poisonous roots. The rest of the river, going inland, still belongs to Satele.[29]

The shortage that led these lineages to sacrifice children upon the death of their father was
not the result, as in the preceding cases, of not having any land at all where they were
immigrants (following a marriage that did not respect the preference for village endogamy),
but of a lack of access to a fishing spot on their own territory.[30]

In the two quotations above, Jessep's informants speak of an agreement between the deceased father's lineage and that of the child: the small victim was probably not killed until its father's lineage had agreed beforehand to give up a small piece of territory in exchange for this human life. In other words, these human sacrifices could not be used to compel the father's lineage to grant land rights, and probably only a lineage that had a big territory and was on good terms with the lineage of its male member's wife and children would agree to the proposed transaction.

Two bodies, one grave

Decided and carried out by a member of the victim's own descent group and used by this group as a means of winning rights to a piece of land owned by the deceased's group, wife and child sacrifices had yet another feature in common: they were followed by funeral rites that doubly violated the rules usually governing funerals. First of all, whereas in New Ireland every person is supposed in principle to be buried in the graveyard of the male enclosure of his/her descent group (matriclan or matrilineage), even if the person lived far from clan lands, the sacrificed person — woman or child — was buried in the male enclosure of the descent group of her deceased husband or of the child's deceased father. It is true that there were other exceptions to this rule,[31] but its violation following a sacrifice performed at the death of a man is the only instance of a descent group, in this case that of the person sacrificed, *freely choosing* to bury one of its members in alien ground rather than in its own land. Secondly, the deceased man and the sacrificed victim were buried in the same grave or burned on the same pyre, whereas two persons having died the same day and belonging to the same male enclosure were always buried separately (except for a woman who died in childbirth and her dead child).

As for child sacrifices in the Barok area, all of Jessep's informants said that the bodies of the father and child were buried in the same grave; one of them indicated that a member of the child's lineage would place it in the hole with the father (see three preceding quotations). This detail is also found in Linge's work, who underscores the importance of the shared grave. Not only did the New Irelander pastor entitle the paragraph describing child sacrifices, 'The burying of a child with its father', he seems to make these exceptional funeral arrangements the very goal of the sacrifice, when, at the beginning of his book, he speaks of 'the killing of a child to be buried with its father' (Linge, 1932:11).[32]

> *The burying of a child with its father.*[33] If a man of a different [clan] is married to a woman of my [clan], 'Kobanis Ulurag', and she bears him a son or a daughter and he dies before her, then a man of my [clan], usually an uncle, will quickly take one of his children and beat it to death, and take it to the grave and bury it in the same grave with the father … They did this to my own sister, Inmale.[34]

The only reference to funerals following the sacrifice of wives are in Birò's notes on the Kara area. These indicate that the wife's body, together with a child at the breast, were burned on the same pyre as the husband and father, and that the bones left after cremation were gathered up and kept in one reliquary basket. These notes also tell that, in this linguistic area and probably throughout the northern half of New Ireland — as far as but excluding Barok — where figures called *malanggan* were made for the ceremonies marking the end of the funeral rites, the deceased and the person or persons sacrificed (one or two wives, wife and infant) were commemorated by a single *malanggan* carving showing them as superposed figures or heads. This is the only known exception to the rule that only members of the same descent group can be commemorated by the same *malanggan* object. Without giving a reason for sacrificing the wife of the deceased — or, as a matter of fact, a child at the breast — Birò writes:

> The corpses of adults are cremated on funeral pyres. Wife and child of married males are incinerated with the deceased. These are first strangled, a task performed by a stranger and not by one of the kinspeople. However, wives follow their husband into death only if they are childless or have but a child at the breast. If the child is older, the wife may choose: if she does not wish to survive her bereavement, she can commit her child to the care of relatives and jump from a high rock, hang herself or have herself strangled by some friend so requested.
>
> … The bones of incinerated corpses are placed in special baskets; after adding boiled food to the bones, the baskets are fastened with strings and suspended in the hut of the deceased.
>
> … After adding fresh food to the skeletal remains, the baskets containing them are carried to the appointed place on the day fixed for the ceremony [*malanggan*] … The baskets with the bones, facing the spectators, are suspended from pegs, and there is beneath each basket a carved figure [a *malanggan* carving] which represents the departed.
>
> … Collective carvings, i.e. superimposed figures or merely heads, are placed before baskets which contain the bones of several persons cremated together: a husband with one or two wives or a father and mother with their infant child.[35]

Apparently the sacrificed individual who thus won his/her descent group perennial rights in the land of the deceased husband's/father's group was, exceptionally, identified with this group. This identification was the will of both groups involved in the transaction: that of the victim, who would kill or urge the victim to kill herself so that the wife or child might follow the man into death, into the grave or onto the pyre; and the deceased's group, who agreed to bury the victim's corpse in its own burial ground, and, when the sacrifice occurred in the *malanggan* diffusion zone, to later make a single funeral figure for the departed couple.

Was there a connection between this symbolic identification of the sacrificed individual with the deceased husband or father and the transfer of land from the group of the latter to that of the former? Why were only sacrifices of the deceased's wife or child recognised as a means of gaining land? In the name of what logic did the deceased man's descent group give a piece of its land to the group of his sacrificed wife or child? Some elements of the answer will be provided by exploring the way the people of New Ireland view their social relations and manage their land-holdings.

Filiation, sacrifice and land rights

Conception, filiation and land-holding

In the Mandak and Barok areas, which have been the subject of recent detailed anthropological studies, theories about conception acknowledge the father's role, by no means minimising it as is sometimes the case in matrilineal societies; instead, they assign him a primordial function. In the Mandak area, he is considered to be solely responsible for making the embryo's substance, its body matter, while the mother's role is restricted to that of a nurturing container for the unborn child.[36] In the Barok area, where the child is thought to be formed by the mixing of the father's and the mother's substances,[37] the most detailed representations, collected in the south of this linguistic area, specify that the semen, emitted after several episodes of intercourse, reveals the woman's procreative capacities by turning her vaginal secretions into 'good blood', which, by closing the uterus where it gathers (as opposed to the 'bad' menstrual blood that runs out), works in conjunction with the semen to form the embryo.[38]

Although they stem from notably different views of conception, similar metaphors are used to express the relations between individuals and groups in the two linguistic areas. Each exogamous social unit (matrimoiety, matriclan, matrilineage) sees itself as a 'maternal container' for its members, in the image of what a mother is for her unborn child, and thinks of itself, in the image of the father initiating the act of conception, as the origin of life for the social unit that gave it its women.[39] The child is called the 'blood' of its father and his descent group; children born of the same father or of real brothers are said to be of the 'same blood'; and a clan or a lineage calls itself the 'blood' of another social unit if, in a previous generation, at least one woman from this clan or lineage married a member of the other unit and there are surviving descendants in the maternal line. A special term, identical in both linguistic areas, designates the child of a male member of the descent group.[40] People always show respect and deference when speaking of those to whom they owe their 'blood' and who, through the male act of procreation, passed on to them a substance that bridged the boundaries of their respective social units.[41]

These 'blood' ties between father and children, which therefore extend to their respective groups, give rise to transfers of wealth and knowledge. In addition to the food and daily care, the father gives his children in particular the bulk of the education that will enable them to become accomplished adults in every area of social life. He can transmit to them the elements of the esoteric knowledge and magic that are not the exclusive property of the descent groups, and it is the father who provides his sons with part or the total amount of the brideprices for the wives he chooses for them.[42] In the Mandak area and the northern Barok area, the sum total of that which is received from the father, starting with his 'blood' at conception, creates a debt for the children and their descent group, which is collectively repaid at the death of the father by the gift of a pig presented at his funeral.[43] Acknowledgement of the patrilateral ties is also expressed in the land-holding system, which will now be outlined.[44]

The rights the land-holding group (the matriclan on Lelet plateau in the Mandak area or the matrilineage in the Barok area) exercises over its territory are justified by the fact that their land contains the birthplace of the group, a spot associated with the presence of a supernatural being that often manifests itself as an animal.[45] The site and the entity are merged linguistically in a single term: *masalai*, in neo-Melanesian. Alongside these primordial rights, every group can also gain secondary rights in the land of another group, providing they have furnished one or another of the compensations set by tradition. In the case of individuals, all own primary and inalienable use-rights in the land of their descent group, as well as secondary use-rights in the land of their father's group and that of their spouse; these rights are acquired without compensation and can be exercised respectively for their father's lifetime and for the duration of their marriage.[46] But if certain compensations are given, an individual can acquire other secondary rights, perennial or life-long (i.e. transmitted or not to descendants) in lands that do not belong to his/her group. Let us take a closer look at these secondary rights, some of which are, as I have said, group rights and others individual rights, with a stress on the role played by patrifiliation.

Traditionally, when a man died, his children could extend the use-rights (initially limited to the father's lifetime) they enjoyed in the land of their paternal clan, which they frequently did. This life-long use-right was obtained in exchange for an enormous pig presented at the father's funeral. When a descent group was thus dying out, the lineage (Barok area) or the clan (Mandak area) of the children of one of the last male members could acquire perennial rights to the entire territory on condition of assuming financial responsibility (pigs, shell money, taros) and performing the funeral rites for the last to die.[47]

In point of fact, any person on good terms with a descent group might procure a life-long use-right in pieces of its land if he gave a pig when this group was celebrating a funeral. Likewise, when a land-holding group died out (a clan at Lelet, a lineage among the Barok), groups other than those of the children of the male members of the group in question could tender for perennial rights to the entire territory of the moribund group, and thus offer to perform the funeral rites for its last members. For instance, on Lelet plateau (where, whenever several groups declared themselves, that of one of the children of the members of the dying clan always prevailed), this opportunity could be seized by a clan whose territory adjoined that of the dying clan, whereas in the Barok area, it would be a lineage from the same clan as the dying lineage or one of the lineages with which it had married.[48]

To acquire perennial rights to another group's land, a matriclan or a matrilineage was not compelled to wait until one of its counterparts was dying out. A large sum paid in strings of shell money[49] could persuade a group to cede this type of right to pieces of its territory. Alternatively, land transfer was sometimes the indirect consequence of a killing — and not the direct result of the sacrifice of a child. Jessep writes that, in the Barok zone, a lineage could give a piece of land in compensation for the life of a warrior from an allied lineage killed on its territory by their common enemy, and that a lineage responsible for a homicide would do the same thing to compensate the victim's lineage.[50] When I mentioned this at Lelet, all my informants said was that, in order to restore peace between various groups after a killing, the clan on whose land 'the blood had fallen' sometimes gave pieces of land to the victim's clan, whether or not the killer was one of its members.[51]

On the other hand, only the descent groups of the children of the male members of a clan or a lineage could make use of human sacrifice to gain a perennial right to a piece of this clan or lineage territory, since, in the Barok area, the only form of human sacrifice practised was that of the child upon its father's death. It is possible to think that this means of acquiring land was also in force in the Mandak area because, notably, of the strong similarity between the land-holding systems in the two neighbouring linguistic areas. The extreme reticence of the Lelet inhabitants to talk about practices of which they are ashamed after over 50 years of Christianisation may well explain the silences and the denials that greeted my questions on this custom.[52]

The logic of sacrifice

In light of the foregoing, several hypotheses can be formulated concerning the logic behind the gain of a piece of land for the murder of a child. It could first of all be considered that, as in the case of the gift of land stemming from the killing of a warrior, the father's descent group compensated the life of the sacrificed child by giving a piece of its land to the child's group. Yet it is hard to understand why the father's descent group would be willing to compensate a life they themselves had not taken,[53] and of someone who had never done anything that might make it worth compensating his or her group, unlike a warrior who had given his life to defend the territory of an allied group.

Following another line of analysis, we see that, like most compensations for rights to the land of another group, the killing of a child can be understood as an exceptional type of contribution to the funeral rites of a member of a group giving up pieces of its territory. It is conceivable that, instead of giving a pig as compensation for everything the father had transmitted to his children during his lifetime, and perhaps making a present of an additional animal to enable the children to gain life-long use-rights in the land of their father's group, the children's own descent group would offer the life and corpse of the youngest child. In reply to this more valuable gift (one human life in place of one or two pigs), the father's descent group would have responded by granting the children's group perennial use-rights to part of its land.

The hypothesis that the killing of the child was at the same time 'a dramatic way of symbolising the children's indebtedness' to their father and a way of paying off the debt, as Jessep puts it,[54] is quite correct, as confirmed by the Barok themselves. Several of the Canadian anthropologist's informants attributed to this killing the double function of repaying the children's debt to their father and enabling the lineage of the mother and the surviving children, living as immigrants in the deceased's village, to acquire a piece of his group's land.[55] The New Irelander pastor, Linge, on the other hand, does not link this custom with winning land but explains it as a way 'to return the love and care of the father toward his children', and claims that descent groups that have intermarried practise such child sacrifices as a form of deferred reciprocity.[56]

Should we therefore consider, as we might be tempted to do, that granting the children's group right to a piece of land belonging to their deceased father's group was explained uniquely by a concern to maintain a balance between the groups, with the gift counterbalancing the repayment of the children's debt — the sacrifice of the youngest — that was greater than the usual amount, set at one pig? I do not think so. First of all, it would not explain why the children's group, if it wanted to repay its debt with a supplement and win, in return, an unusual favour from the deceased father's group — namely a perennial right in their land — could not have given a certain number of pigs, for instance, instead of the child's life. And secondly, the hypothesis does not account for the exceptional symbolic identification of the sacrificed child with its father, which appears clearly in their funeral rites.

To my mind, the reasons for burying the child in the male enclosure of its father's group, and especially in the same grave as its father, should be sought in the maternal metaphors associated with the clan and with its male enclosure. According to Wagner, the Barok 'depict the image of group membership through the containment of the body in the mother's womb, and eventually in the ground of the group's territory',[57] and the male enclosure as 'a perfect image of containment … [that] could be likened to a womb containing … the dead'.[58] Likewise, the Lelet Mandak associate the image of the corpses absorbed by the ground of the group's male enclosure with the image of the foetus in its mother's womb; in Pinikindu, a Mandak village on the coast, the term for the stone wall surrounding the male enclosure comes, notably, from the word 'womb'.[59] The metaphorical gestation of the corpses in the group's land thus echoes the representation of the clan as a 'maternal container' for its members. In this perspective, might not the grave in which the corpses of the father and his sacrificed child are deposited be regarded as a symbolic womb encompassing their two bodies? In this case, one might therefore suppose that the child, the fruit of the same womb-container as its father, was 'reborn' in death as a member of its father's group?[60] It was in order to be buried with its father, as Linge wrote, or as I would say, in order to be affiliated to its father's descent group through the symbolism of the shared grave, that the child would have been sacrificed by a member of its own lineage.

This interpretation of the funeral rites following a child murder as a post mortem change of social affiliation has the advantage of providing a plausible explanation for the transfer of a piece of land from the father's group to that of the sacrificed child. People's primary use-rights in their clan land are seen as transmissible, upon their death, to their descendants in the maternal line. In this sense, they are distinct from the life-long use-rights a person may acquire in a land held by a different group, which cannot be transmitted within the person's own descent group. If the father's group was willing to consider the sacrificed child as one of its own — as I have postulated — then it was only correct to give it an automatic right to a piece of the group's land identical to that of the other members, namely a perennial right that could be transmitted to the child's maternal kin from generation to generation. Although the sacrificed child changed its social affiliation, it kept its maternal kin, whom it could not repudiate, and it is to them, in particular to the mother, that the rights would go: those rights that the child had acquired in death to the land of its paternal group. The result is the a priori paradoxical but logical situation in which, following the sacrifice of a child, persons (mother, siblings and their descendants) could make use of rights in the land of another descent group as maternal kin of one of its members: the sacrificed child, now a member of its father's group. The use-rights exercised by the maternal kin of the sacrificed child, rights in a piece of land held by the lineage of which the child had become a member in death, could be assimilated to perennial rights gained by their group and transmissible within this group from one generation to the next.

Giving back the 'blood'

But why ever did the father's lineage agree to a transaction that deprived it of a bit of its land in exchange for the membership of a dead child? Most likely because, by seeing to it that the child followed its father in death and into the grave, the victim's lineage acknowledged a debt in a radical, spectacular and dramatic manner: this child, and any surviving siblings — therefore part of the members of the lineage — owed their 'blood' (in other words, their entire substance for the Mandak; or that part of their substance produced by the semen which sets off the process of conception, for the Barok), the origin of their life and part of the wealth, goods and advantages they have enjoyed, to the deceased man. Thus, instead of being reimbursed by a pig (in other words, by an item having an economic value and functioning as a substitute for the substance, the care and the goods and advantages received from the father), the children's debt to their father was repaid by simply giving back the bodily substance of one of the children in the form of the child's corpse, placed by its lineage in the father's grave, and by the post mortem affiliation of this child to its paternal lineage. What the father's lineage recovered, exceptionally, by the sacrifice of the child, was part of the 'blood', of the substance that its male members give, through the act of procreation, to the lineages of their wives and which never goes to nourish their own group.

As I understand it, the logic underpinning these child sacrifices suggests that they represent the extreme form of acknowledgment of the patrilateral ties which are characterised by the sharing of 'blood', since this was the only instance (not connected with compensations for dead warriors) in which a descent group agreed to cede a piece of its land to another group without financial compensation, and it only ceded this property to the descent group of the child of one of its male members. But these child sacrifices at the same time expressed the limits of these patrilateral ties insofar as it was only the affiliation of the sacrificed child to its father's descent group, and therefore the transformation of this 'blood' into a clan tie, that justified the transfer of property from the father's group to that of the child.

A similar logic probably operated in the sacrifice of the wife upon the death of her husband, a custom followed in northern New Ireland and in the Tabar Islands. Providing, of course, that the conception theories — ill known for these societies — also assigned the primary role to the father and that these sacrifices were practised only when the couple had children, or failing that when the deceased man's clan could nonetheless think of itself as a 'blood-giver' with respect to the wife's clan, owing to other fruitful unions between the two groups. In this case, one could envisage that the mother's bodily substance, given as a corpse, might substitute for that of the child, whose life was spared, and that, by adopting her husband's social identity, she repaid in a spectacular manner, the 'blood" debt of her clan. The idea that the sacrificed woman thus became a member of her husband's clan seems to be corroborated by Biró's notes, mentioned above: not only was a single *malanggan* object carved and displayed for the two members of the couple, as though they effectively belonged to the same clan, but the fact that the husband's clan gave food to the skeletal remains of the couple contained in the basket exhibited at the foot of the carving can be interpreted as an acknowledgment of the clan's maternal role as 'nurturing container' with respect to the victim, who is assimilated to one of its members. Furthermore, if it is a reflection of the commentaries provided by the people of New Ireland, the astonishing statement by Billings and Peterson, already quoted, that 'a woman and her descendants gained rights to the land of her husband if she committed suicide upon his death', points in the direction of my interpretation, according to which the maternal kin of the victim, in this case the wife, would inherit the land rights she had effectively acquired in death, by virtue of her affiliation to the deceased man's group.

Land rights and rights in *malanggan* objects

Traditionally, human sacrifices, whose analysis will enable us to make sense of those that, from what my informants say, were performed in the setting of the Mandak cargo cult, were not done only with a view to obtaining land. They could also occur in conjunction with *malanggan* objects and ceremonies.[61] We are now going to take a rapid look at the second of these, which we need to assess in order to understand the cargo cult.

In the past, in the northern half of New Ireland and on the small nearby islands as far as but excluding the Barok area, the rites marking the end of the funeral cycle revolved around the manufacture, display and destruction of one or several wood carvings or wickerwork pieces belonging to the mixed class of *malanggan* objects. These included statues, poles and friezes representing a variety of elements ranging from the deceased to the solar and lunar entities responsible for creation. The class of *malanggan* was divided into a multitude of types, subtypes and (in some regions) families of types. Before the disappearance of many *malanggan*, each matriclan on Lelet plateau controlled at least one subtype of these objects; each subtype had its own motifs, sometimes its own form as well as specific rites and then differed from the other generic suborders held by the other clans. Linked, similarly to the territory, with the clan's emergence and identity, *malanggan* patterns were governed by a system of laws modelled on that of land-holding.

Like the clan territory, a space held by a clan and worked by individuals in the form of temporary clearings, a *malanggan* subtype was a pattern held by a clan and individually exploited in the form of ephemeral material objects that were destroyed at the end of the ceremony during which they had been manufactured. Just as only someone who had a use-right in a piece of land was entitled to occupy and work it, so only someone who had a use-right in the *malanggan* pattern could commission copies to be made in view of commemorating departed close kinsmen. Unlike the corresponding land use-rights, though, the right to use a *malanggan* pattern was not a birth-right for all members of the controlling clan, but was transmitted uniquely to certain young members, both male and female, thus establishing certain social distinctions within the group. That being said, like land-rights, these use-rights were transmitted without payment from one generation to the next within the clan, and were characterised by transmission in the maternal line to the descendants of their beneficiaries. A person, child or adult, who did not belong to the clan holding a given *malanggan* pattern could acquire the right to use it in exchange for the present of a pig on the occasion of a funeral; like life-long use-rights in the land of another group acquired in exchange for the same compensation, this limited right — authorising a person to make a single copy of the *malanggan* subtype concerned — could not be passed on to descendants in the maternal line and therefore could not become a perennial right for the person's group.

Finally there were transfers of the control of a *malanggan* pattern from one clan to another (all members of the clan holding the use-rights to this pattern would renounce them simultaneously), and these were obtained in exchange for the same compensations as transfers of control over land: namely in exchange for conducting the funeral rites for the last members of a dying clan, or in exchange for an important sum of traditional shell money.[62]

The similar management of land and *malanggan* suggests that the sacrifice of the wife and/or child upon a man's death — a recognised way of transferring a land-holding, which is attested in different linguistic groups in the *malanggan* diffusion zone — could also enable the victim's clan to acquire rights to the model of a subtype of *malanggan* initially held by the husband's or father's clan.

Before analysing a document that corroborates this hypothesis, it needs to be clear that every right in a subtype of *malanggan* entails a corpus of knowledge, and that transfers of rights between individuals and groups were also transfers of knowledge. On Lelet plateau, the male individual who held a use-right in a *malanggan* subtype was duty-bound to have a thorough knowledge of the pattern, in other words, to have the mental representation of all the invariable motifs which, featuring on each of the copies made, justified their classification in a given generic order and suborder. He also knew the technical and magical secrets that often went with the making of the individual copies of each pattern, and the specific rites that marked each stage of their manufacture, their display and their destruction. Because he possessed this knowledge, the person could guide the craftsman he had commissioned to make one or several copies of the pattern, and he was also equipped to conduct the different stages of the *malanggan* ceremony in which he would thus exploit his right of use. The origin myth attached to the *malanggan* subtype, symbolic equivalent of the sacred birthplace of the clan — which justified the control exercised over the territory around it — was, in all likelihood, transmitted only to those clan members who controlled the pattern. Women were supposed be ignorant of the material existence of *malanggan* objects, and the manufacture, display and destruction of these pieces unfolded far from their eyes, in the male enclosure concealed by a tall fence made of leafy branches. The women were instructed uniquely in the specific female rites (dances, ritual distribution of food, etc.) connected with the *malanggan* subtype in which they acquired a right of use. This right, exploited on their behalf by their male clansmen, as a rule their brothers, enabled them, like the men, to fulfill the social obligations connected with the commemoration of their dead.

Transmission of use-rights to the model of a *malanggan* subtype took place between individuals and always at the end of a ceremony in which the person ceding the right had commissioned a copy of the subtype in question. Prior to the hand-over, the male beneficiary of the right had received permission to remain in the hut where the craftsman was making the object and to be present at each stage of the ritual — even the most secret ones — so as to acquire all of the technical, magical and ritual knowledge necessary. It was while the object was briefly displayed in the male enclosure, before an all-male audience, that the person who had commissioned it announced the identity of the individual who had previously given him the right to reproduce this *malanggan* subtype, and proclaimed the name of the person or persons to whom he had transmitted his own knowledge and whom he officially declared to be the new holders of a right to use the pattern. When the receiver of the right was not a member of the clan holding the pattern, it was publicly stipulated that his right was limited, that is restricted to the manufacture of a single copy and that the right was not transmissible to other members of his clan. This rule did not apply when the ceremony was the setting for a transfer between clans. In this case, the beneficiary of the right, as a member of the clan officially designated as the new holder of the *malanggan*, received full rights, with no restrictions on the number of copies and transmissible to his descendants in the maternal line.

A human life for rights to a *malanggan*

We now come to the story of a transmission of rights to a *malanggan* pattern. The events occurred at the end of the nineteenth century in a village on the west coast of the Kara area, and were reported to Küchler in 1983. The story tells how a clan, Moromuna, 'got right to Malangan by killing one of its women and giving her to Moromaf',[63] another clan considered to have originated the *malanggan* known in the region:

> 'Kumaut of Morokomaf sub-clan [Moromaf clan] was married to a woman of Moromuna clan. … Kumaut taught his knowledge about the images of *Malangan* to his children. Since the clan Moromuna had not bought the images received, a fight broke out between the clans. To make a truce, the clan Moromuna after the death of Kumaut killed one of its own women, the wife of Kumaut called Pururau. The blood of Pururau paid for the *Malangan* and the land taken by Kumaut's children.[64]

On Lelet plateau, when a man exploited his use-right in the pattern of a *malanggan* subtype held by his clan and commissioned one or several copies to be made during a funeral ceremony, his child would often give a pig (provided by his maternal uncle) on the occasion of these rites so that his father would initiate him into the secrets of this *malanggan* and give him the right to make a copy at a later time. In the story set down by Küchler, it would seem that the children did not hand over any compensation for the knowledge their father had passed on to them, which probably concerned several patterns of *malanggan* subtypes controlled by his clan. Even if one can imagine the father not daring publicly to introduce his children as the new holders of a use-right in these *malanggan* whereas they had not made prior compensation, their illicit knowledge could materially enable them in the future to order the manufacture of these subtypes. Furthermore, there was no guarantee that the children, perhaps emboldened by their father's transgression and by his manifest disregard for the interests of his own clan, would not be tempted to have several copies made of each pattern and to transmit what they knew to their own matrilateral descendants. This, I believe, explains the anger of the father's clan and the fight that broke out between the two clans. Peace was restored when, upon the death of the father, his wife was sacrificed and given to her husband's clan by her own clan group. In all likelihood, her own group in turn received control over the patterns of the *malanggan* subtype whose secret knowledge had been unlawfully revealed to the children. As maternal kinsmen of a member of their father's clan — in this case the mother, who had in death become a member of this clan — it was henceforth normal for the children to have acquired, without compensation, the knowledge associated with this clan's *malanggan* patterns and to exercise a non-restrictive and transmissible right of use.

And it is probably because, in death, the wife was affiliated to her deceased husband's clan that the children, by virtue of this sacrifice, received control both over several *malanggan* patterns held by their father's clan and over a bit of its territory, as the last sentence in the passage from Küchler seems to suggest. In effect, while not everyone necessarily enjoyed use-rights in a *malanggan* pattern controlled by his clan, everyone did, by birth, have use-rights in the clan territory. When the wife or child of a deceased man was sacrificed in order to obtain a piece of land, the victim's post mortem membership in the deceased's clan did not justify the victim or his/her descendants acquiring use-rights in a *malanggan* held by this clan. Conversely, however, when the same sacrifice was made in order to obtain rights to a *malanggan* held by the deceased's clan, the affiliation of the victim to the latter's clan automatically implied that both the victim and his/her matrilateral descendants received use-rights in a piece of this clan's territory.

The similar management of clan territories and *malanggan* patterns strongly suggests that human sacrifice was not restricted to resolving conflicts arising from infringement of the rules governing the transfer of *mananggan* rights between members of different clans. Let us suppose that several members of the same clan live as immigrants in a village relatively far from their homeland. If none has the right to use a *malanggan* pattern held by their clan, their matrilateral descendants have every chance of being deprived as well: they live too far, both geographically and affectively, from any members of their clan who might give them such rights. Gaining control of a *malanggan* subtype is the only way for this little group to dispose of a full right of use to a *malanggan* with no restrictions on the number of copies that can be made and with transmission to their maternal descendants. Since the distance from their clan precludes any hope that it will make an effort to get together the considerable financial resources needed to buy a *malanggan* pattern, all they can do is wait for the husband of one of their women to die and then resort to human sacrifice. As indicated above, this solution has the advantage of also procuring them control over a piece of the dead man's clan territory. There is every reason to believe that, during the funeral ceremony in which a single *malanggan* object was made to commemorate the sacrificed individual and her deceased husband or father, the members of the victim's clan were initiated into the knowledge relating to the *malanggan* pattern in question. These clansmen were in the position of maternal kin of a member of the clan holding this *malanggan*, in other words, the victim, affiliated in death to the clan of her husband or father. They received, gratuitously, an unrestricted right of use in this model which they could pass on to their descendants; they thus became co-responsible for controlling this model, a control henceforth exercised by their clan group. It is likely that only a clan holding several *malanggan* subtype models would be willing to divest itself of one of them in exchange for the sacrifice — and thus membership in their group — of a person belonging to the clan of the wife of one if its own male members.

White people's malanggan

The site of the cargo cult

Equipped with an analysis and interpretation of traditional human sacrifices, we can now return to my informants' reports of this clan that sacrificed children in view of obtaining white wealth.

This particular cargo cult arose in a coastal Mandak village called Mesi, and, from what the Lelet Mandak said, lasted several years before expiring in the space of a few months under the influence of the first missionary. According to Threlfall,[65] Mesi was the first village on the central west coast to be visited, in 1907, by a group of evangelisers, and the missionary who chose to live there died at the end of the same year. This cargo cult, probably extinguished by the end of 1907, may have arisen four years earlier. In effect, 1903 was a catastrophic year, marked by a terrible famine following a long period of drought; it is therefore easy to imagine how desirable European commodities, mainly foodstuffs, must have appeared to the famished population, whose gardens were ravaged and who were reduced to living on the plants and berries they could find in the wild.[66]

When the evangelisers arrived in Mesi in 1907 — twenty years after the first Wesleyan missionaries set foot in New Ireland — the villagers had a very bad reputation with white people because of their warlike ways and the recent killing of several merchants. These evangelists themselves barely escaped being killed and eaten, if we are to believe the accounts of their first contacts with the villagers.[67] At this time there was a great difference between the populations of the northern part of the island and the long alluvial plain along the northern half of the coast, on the one hand, and the west-coast populations, on the other hand. The first region had been heavily settled by merchants, planters, labour recruiters, colonial administrators and missionaries. Decimated by disease and cruelly exploited by the colonists, these populations paid a high price for their access to European goods. Alternatively, the population of the west coast, who lived in an area difficult to reach by land and ill controlled by the colonial administration, had only a recent and episodic experience of trade with Europeans, even though some villages had been visited by merchant vessels and labour recruiters.

Far from being just another Mandak village, Mesi is a mythico-religious centre: closely associated with fertility, it was particularly well suited to the emergence of a cargo-type movement. According to beliefs still alive on Lelet plateau, the two rivers that empty into the sea to the north of the village define the boundaries of a sacred space called Katandan Moroa, the chosen home of Moroa, the male entity identified with the sun. Regarded as having presided over the original creation of all things that are pleasing and beneficial to mankind, including *malanggan* objects, pigs and shell money, Moroa is the male procreative principle behind natural fertility. He is also ultimately responsible for the fecundation of women: the semen of their sexual partners cannot take effect if Moroa has not at the same time deposited his own supernatural semen in their womb. Near Katandan Moroa lies the territory of Sepka, which belongs to the lunar entity, Sigirigum. Endowed with an ambivalent sexual identity, Sigirigum is Moroa's wife and his female counterpart in representations having to do with natural and human fertility: it is she who triggers menstruation and who, in the last instance, is instrumental in stopping the flow following fecundation, and therefore responsible for gestation. On the shore of Moroa's territory is a spring (*lemetla*) which serves as the entrance to the underground world of the dead, Kantimum, ruled by the solar entity. The ghosts of deceased humans live there in an atmosphere of fertility, plenty and harmony that the fertility-rite experts are able to produce temporarily in the world of the living by re-enacting the sexual encounter of the solar and lunar entities, Moroa and Sigirigum, using the sacred stones they procure in Katandan Moroa. It is also on the outskirts of Mesi, in a place called Lukun (from *loronkun*, 'taro') that Sigirigum, at the command of her solar husband, took on the appearance of Nirut, an old woman with a hump planted in taros, in order to introduce these tubers to young humans.

'Giving a corpse for the white people's *malanggan*'

The story told me by one informant featured a striking expression. Under the direction of a Mesi villager known as Lupalau, the Lurumbi clan, of which he was a member, sacrificed a succession of toddlers, 'so that all its members might become the *lavaunpanga* of a white people's *malanggan*'. Formed from the verb —*un*, 'to acquire, obtain', and the adverb *panga*, 'all, everything', and therefore meaning literally, 'those who acquire all things for themselves', *lavaunpanga* is a term used specifically to designate those individuals — children or adults — who were initiated into the secret knowledge concerning a subtype of *malanggan* object and who thereby became the official assignees of a use-right to the pattern. Although my informant did not tell me that the aim of the Lurumbi clan was to obtain 'control over the white people's *malanggan*' — or according to the vernacular expression, to obtain 'the skeleton of the *malanggan*' — the formulation nevertheless suggests that this was in fact the case. In effect, only control over a *malanggan* ensured the clan that many of its members could be given the right to make copies. The same informant added that a finger of the sacrificed child was given to the parents, who were told that 'the *malanggan* had eaten the child'. Then he added: 'it was the clan's duty to give the *malanggan* a *lau* so that all its members might become the *lavaunpanga* of the *malanggan*.' *Lau* designates both the corpse and the spirit of the deceased when death was the result of murder, an accident or suicide.[68] Thus the Lurumbi clan killed one of its very young members and fed its corpse to what it regarded as a 'white people's *malanggan*' in the hope of acquiring control of the *malanggan* in question.

This 'white people's *malanggan*' was a shark called *lembebanan* or *labanambe*, whose belly was full of merchandise and books that Moroa, the solar entity behind these creations, had originally sent to the black people by way of the dead, but which had been diverted from their true destination by white men. *Lembebanan* and *labanambe* are formed from the word *lanaanan*, 'food', a term found in the expression *levenpangaanan* (literally: 'all foods'), which designates manufactured European products, also called 'cargo' in neo-Melanesian, and from the syllable —*mbe*— part of the root of the words *lembeve* and *lembele*, meaning respectively 'shark' and 'womb'. As ritual esoteric language typically uses words from everyday language minus their last syllable, the two names given equally to this curious shark probably played on the ambiguity of the two words. The Mandak representation of 'food' as something every individual receives free of change from their nurturing container, respectively their mother and their clan group, could be the source of this image of merchandise contained in a womb. Such an image would express the vision of 'cargo' as goods rightfully belonging to the inhabitants of New Ireland by virtue of a sort of maternal descent reckoning from Moroa to themselves.

As for the choice of the shark as the womb-like container of cargo, it can be explained by the importance of this animal for the coastal populations that catch it, fishing from their frail canoes with bait and a lasso attached to the end of a board. There are myths that tell how Moroa created sharks and taught them to let themselves be caught by men, providing these had kept a series of taboos before setting out to fish; to men, Moroa taught the ritual and magical techniques necessary for catching the sharks.[69] In other words, like the cargo initially intended for the inhabitants of New Ireland, the shark was created by Moroa so that people might catch and eat it. Expert shark-catchers recognise several types, some of which cannot be caught by humans and have only a spiritual form that shows up as a shadow in the water;[70] this seems to be the type that served as a model for the *lembebanan* or *labananmbe*.

Mythic representations and dualism

One myth connected with the cargo cult and presenting a number of analogies with more traditional myths explains how the white people robbed the black people of the goods Moroa sent them. I will summarise the story as it was told to me:

> Long ago, a black man and a white man, who were cross cousins and ghosts of the dead, found themselves inside the *lembebanam*. The white man worked for the black man who was the boss of the *lembebanam*. Nevertheless, the black man did not know how to make the cargo Moroa had given him together with books, telling him to give it all to the black people, to those who were alive. One day, the two cross cousins came out of the shark to wash themselves in the sea. The white man suggested a game to the black man: they would take turns diving in the deep water to see who could stay down the longest. The white man went first, and came up after a long time. When it was the black man's turn to dive, the white man seized the occasion to go back into the *lembebanan* and run off with it. It is in the books contained in the *lembebanan* that white people, those who were alive, learned to make cargo.

In certain traditional esoteric myths unknown to the women, which tell of episodes of creation, Moroa and Sigirigum, the sun and the moon, are both presented as male characters. They address each other using the kinship term for same-sex cross cousins, and each is responsible for the humans belonging to one of the two dual units of which they are also the emblems.[71] In these myths, Sigirigum takes the role of the bad hero responsible for foolish creations such as raising rats, using liana for strings of shell money or using inedible nuts that he chews with the wrong leaves soaked not in lime but in secretions from his wife's vagina. So that he himself and the humans in his charge may gain the benefit of Moroa's intelligent creations — including raising pigs, using real shell money and chewing areca nuts with lime — Sigirigum plays a little trick, inviting Moroa to a celebration where he offers him rats, liana and inedible nuts. As his cross cousin hoped, Moroa is compelled to reciprocate, and throws a celebration at which he gives Sigirigum and his group of humans genuine nice things, enjoyed until then only by the half of humanity for which he was responsible.

In the myth associated with the cargo cult, the black man and the white man, like Moroa and Sigirigum, are regarded as cross cousins and each acts on behalf of one half of humanity: black humans and white humans. One might have expected traditional myths to urge the people of New Ireland to compare themselves with the members of the dual unit led by Sigirigum; in effect these myths mention an initial imbalance between the two halves, owing to the lunar entity's inability to make good creations, and they speak of the desire of this entity to procure for the humans in his charge the superior goods owned by the other half. But it is the white people who take on this role. The idea frequently found in Melanesian cargo and millenarian movements that the dead, who act here as go-betweens for Moroa, were supposed to deliver the cargo to the black people alone, effectively makes it possible to place white people in an initially inferior position (clearly expressed in the myth by the white man's subordination to the black man, an inverted reflection of the situation experienced by the New Irelanders at the time) and to attribute to them the desire to procure goods meant for others by the superior will of the creator entity. As Sigirugum did to Moroa, the white man tricks the black in order to get what he wants. But whereas, in the old myths, the two halves are made equal by means of a subterfuge — based on the expectation of reciprocity — as well as by an exchange in which Moroa is invited to give Sigirigum — at the latter's instigation — the genuine things he had created, the opposite imbalance arises between black and white: the trick enables the white people to steal the goods and knowledge the sovereign solar entity intended to reserve for black people, ever after kept in their state of unknowing.

On the one hand, the followers of the cult regarded the cargo and the books containing the secrets of their manufacture as Moroa's creations, intended for the people of New Ireland but usurped by white people. In this, they were showing more than a simple desire for European manufactured products; they were manifesting a deeply rooted will to restore a vision of the world in which the almighty solar entity had created expressly for them all things that were pleasant for humans. This vision was severely shaken by the arrival of the Europeans, exclusive owners of these ever-so-enviable new items. On the other hand, they saw these same goods as symbolic of both white people's identity and their specificity as attested by the identification of the shark that contained them with a *malanggan*. This association between cargo, books and a *malanggan* was no doubt facilitated by the fact that the local populations never saw the production phase of manufactured goods. White people could therefore be suspected of behaving like the clan fashioning copies of its *malanggan*, hidden behind a high fence of vegetation erected around the male enclosure and forbidding entry to all outsiders in order to protect the secrets, techniques and magic spells connected with their production.

Offering a sacrifice to white people
But let us come back to my informants' account of the conduct of the cargo cult. Having killed the child, the Lurumbi clan would suspend the corpse from a ritual post erected in Katandan Moroa, beside the spring known as Legepkevi, the source of one of the two rivers

bounding this sacred place. This ritual post, *laramba*, traditionally appeared in certain rites marking the closure of the funeral cycle in which the table placed at the foot of the post was used to display the food (taros and pig meat) before it was distributed. It was also used when, following illicit sexual relations between two persons (from the same dual unit or guilty of an adulterous relationship that had become known), the mutually offended clans, as a peace gesture, offered each other the respective bodies.[72] Each clan killed the clan member who had violated custom, made a *laramba*, which it set up in the other hamlet, suspended the victim from the top of the post, then buried the body that had been likewise presented to it, in its own graveyard. The *laramba*, then, the name of which comes from the verb 'to give', was thus used to display the food or the cadaver given by one group to another. The two aspects, it seems to me, are conjoined in the ritual post used in the cargo cult. The sacrificed child displayed on the post was said to be 'fed to the white people's *malanggan*' and therefore seen as a form of food, at the same time as it was probably seen as a corpse presented to the Europeans so that they might bury it in their own ground, as in the traditional sacrifice where the child was given to the lineage of its father and buried with him.

The Lurumbi clan would then wait for the *lembebanan*, the shark, to swim up to the Legepkevi spring from the sea or the world of the dead (depending on the version), and deposit, on the table at the base of the ritual post, the merchandise and the books it carried in its belly. A taboo placed on this spring ensured the clan that no outsider could benefit from these goods. The *lembebanan* would indeed arrive, but it would deliver only part of its cargo, namely the merchandise. When this had been exhausted by the cult members who, without the books, could not manufacture the goods themselves, another child would be sacrificed. Each sacrifice, which was followed by the arrival of the *lembebanan* and the delivery of the merchandise but not the books, therefore bore witness to the partial failure of the preceding one.

Before being killed, I was told, the child was fed in Katandan Moroa on the foodstuffs formerly procured by the *lembebanan*, some of which were put by for the purpose. It is worth noting that the sacrificed victim was fed on the contents of the *lembebanan*, the 'white people's *malanggan*', before being killed and 'fed' to this *malanggan*, as the parents were told when they were presented with the child's severed finger. This two-way nourishing relationship, which joins the sacrificed child with the instrument of the whiteman's identity (the shark filled with merchandise and books, seen as their *malanggan*), may echo the image of the child nourished by the contents of the nurturing womb that is its mother, and the image of the corpse which nourishes the graveyard of its clan where it is buried, two representations that are associated with the notion of membership in a clan.[73] In this case, we would have here a symbolic short-cut expressing the following thinking: the members of the cult wanted the sacrificed child to be affiliated in death to the group — here white people — whose *malanggan* it was to win for its own clan.

As we saw earlier, this was traditionally the only way an exchange could enable a clan to win control of a *malanggan* initially held by another group and to be taught the knowledge indispensable to the manufacture and ritual display of the copies which could not be transmitted either under force or outside a ritual funeral setting. It was therefore entirely in line with this tradition that a clan from Mesi seems to have tried to exchange the life and the social identity of several of its very young members for the technical and magical ability to procure European manufactured articles.

I will add one last argument in support of my hypothesis. Traditionally the clan which, in return for the sacrifice of one of its members, received control of a land or a *malanggan* belonging to another clan, necessarily got it from a clan to which it had given one of its women, since it was only a man's wife or child that was sacrificed upon his death. Now it happens that New Irelanders did give women to white men. The women of New Ireland were highly prized by the colonists, who took them as concubines or used them as prostitutes; and many children were born of these unions. The fact that Europeans had fathered children raised by New Irelanders may have promoted the idea among the latter that they were indebted to these white men who had given them their 'blood', and that by foregoing for their own benefit the life and social identity of some of their children, they might both pay off this debt and acquire rightful control of European goods. Furthermore, nothing prevents us supposing that one of the merchants killed by Mesi villagers before the arrival of the first missionaries may have had a child with a Lurumbi woman, and that the first child sacrifice was performed following this death, prompted by the dramatic food shortages that plagued New Ireland in 1903: this situation is indeed comparable to a total lack of land or *malanggan*, which can drive a clan to traditional human sacrifice.

Insofar as only a clan holding several *malanggan* subtypes would probably agree to forfeit control of one of them, it is likely that the cult followers were seeking, not to deprive Europeans of their control over the production of merchandise, but merely to ensure their own source of the production of these goods, separate from that of white people. They were probably not aiming at a new inversion of the imbalance between Black and White mentioned in the cargo myth, but at establishing through exchange a true balance between these two halves of humanity, and therefore a parity comparable to that reigning in traditional myths between the dual units following the exchanges between Moroa and Sigirigum. In other words, like so many of these movements, this cargo cult seems to have reflected the deep-seated desire of its members to deal with Europeans on an equal footing.[74]

The association of merchandise and books with a 'white people's *malanggan*', the pivot of the cult and source of its original features — in particular recourse to child sacrifice and the desire for the victims to be affiliated in death to the white people's group — left a remarkable reminder: the Mandak verb for writing ('I write': *anamalanggan* [75]) is itself formed from the word *malanggan*.

Footnotes

1 During a 16-month ethnographic study funded by a DGRST research fellowship.

2 See Lomas (1981: 6–7).

3 See Schnee (1904), quoted by Lomas (1981: 6).

4 See Parkinson (1907: 287) and Finsch (1914: 245, note), quoted by Lomas (1981: 7).

5 See Boluminski (1904: 134), quoted by Lomas (1981: 8).

6 See Bodrogi (1967: 76), who has translated and published the notes taken by his compatriot, L. Birò, in New Ireland in 1900, in the course of a voyage made for the purpose of collecting *malanggan* objects for the Budapest ethnographic museum.

7 See Schnee (1904: 59), quoted by Panoff (1979: 163).

8 See J. Reynolds, 'New Ireland District', *Encyclopedia of Papua New Guinea*, ed. by P. Ryan (Melbourne, 1972), vol. 2: 847–859; quoted by Lomas (1981: 13).

9 Panoff (1979: 163).

10 Hahl Report dated 4 October 1913 (RKA-Reiches Kolonialamt — 2313, Bobine G. 8486, National Library of Australia, Canberra, quoted by Panoff (1976: 164).

11 Hahl Report dated 4 September 1904 (RKA-Reiches Kolonialamt — 2309, Bobine G. 8495, National Library of Australia, Canberra, quoted by Panoff (1979: 166).

12 The information on the history of Methodist missions in New Ireland is taken from Threlfall (1975).

13 When, in 1903, Parkinson (1927 [1907]: 522) expressed his surprise at not finding any masks in the Tanga Islands (off the southeastern coast of New Ireland) where they once abounded, he was told that they were no longer made because the young men were away from their natal village and could no longer be initiated into the secrets of mask-making.

14 See Scragg (1957).

15 Chinnery (1929: 46–47).

16 Parkinson (1926 [1907]: 524).

17 Linge (1932: 11, 50).

18 Jessep (1977: 203–214).

19 Boluminski (1904: 28).

20 Walden and Nevermann (1940: 13).

21 Groves (1934–35: 352–353).

22 Billings and Peterson (1967: 26).

23 See Birò's notes, published by his fellow-countryman, Bodrogi (1967: 64).

24 Groves (1934–35: 352–353).

25 Billings and Peterson (1967: 26).

26 This remark in no way implies a connection between the mother's foreign origin and the fact that the child sacrificed is female; these are simply the two cases on which Jessep's informants were most forthcoming.

27 Note that these cases, reported by Jessep's informants, occurred before the turn of the twentieth century, in Kono and Karu villages.

28 Jessep (1977: 206–207).

29 Jessep (1977: 209).

30 If human sacrifices seem to have been traditionally restricted to rare cases of lack of land or fishing zones, it is likely that, before bringing them to a halt, colonisation, through the plantation system, first increased their rate. In the Barok and Mandak areas, and probably in the other linguistic areas as well, whose land-tenure systems are still little known, trees, which are grown by the men, belong to the man who plants them. If a man has planted trees — usually banana palms — on the land of his wife's or children's descent group, the latter is supposed to tear them up upon his death because they are not its property. (The trees the man has planted on the ground of his own descent group belong to his maternal kinsmen who make the largest material contribution on the occasion of his funeral.) The exploitation of copra, instigated by merchants and planters, suddenly made coconut palms very valuable; but these are slow-growing trees that only begin producing years after they have been planted. In order to continue, after a man's death, to exploit the coconuts he has planted uniquely on the ground of his descent group (otherwise they would be torn up at his death), his wife and children have no alternative but to acquire permanent rights to the land on which the

trees are growing. While human sacrifice was not the only means of gaining rights to a piece of land belonging to another descent group, it did have the advantage of not depriving the group practising it of part of its wealth. That is probably why W. C. Groves mentioned that killing the wife enabled the group to gain rights to the coconuts of her late husband's lineage, and why F. Boluminski noted the frequent sacrifices of wives in north New Ireland (in the vicinity of Lauan village), which was an early centre of intensive copra production. Furthermore, the German administration probably increased the number of human sacrifices by forcing the inland villagers to move to villages on the coast, where they found themselves in the situation of immigrants.

31   On Lelet plateau, for instance, the man in charge of one of his clan's male enclosures and anxious to win prestige by organising funerals, would, in exchange for payment, accept the bodies of the refugees he had admitted to his hamlet. Upon occasion he would also use his authority to perform the funeral of his own wife, turning a deaf ear to the demands of her clan, who wanted to take the body back to their own group's male enclosure.

32   Linge (1932: 11).

33   Italics in Linge.

34   Linge (1932: 50).

35   Birò, quoted by Bodrogi (1967: 64, 66).

36   See Clay (1977: 31), Derlon (1997a: 57, 345 and 2002a: 232–233).

37   Jessep (1977: 68-69).

38   Wagner (1986: 62).

39   See Clay (1977: 5–6, 32–41), Wagner (1986: xvi–xviii, 49–50, 89, 146–175 and 1988: 57–58), Derlon (1997a: 347 and 2002a: 234).

40   See Clay (1977: 39–40), Jessep (1977: 69–70), Wagner (1986: 62–63), Derlon (1997a: 57, 345 and 2002a: 232–233).

41   See Clay (1977: 67–71), Wagner (1986: xvii, 64–65), Derlon (1997a: 347, note 3 and 2002a: 232–233).

42   See Clay (1977: 64–66, 107–108), Jessep (1977: 65, 261), Wagner (1986: 56, 63, 171, 197–213), Derlon (1997a: 305 and 2002a: 217).

43   See Clay (1977: 116), Jessep (1977: 71, 235–238), Derlon (1997a: 57, 166, 177 and 2002a: 223).

44   For a detailed analysis of the land-holding system on Lelet plateau, see Derlon (1997a: 319–337 and 2002a: 221–226).

45   See Jessep (1977: 157–202), Derlon (1997a: 320–326 and 2002a: 222–223).

46   See Jessep (1977: 149–150), Derlon (1997a: 327 and 2002a: 222).

47   See Jessep (1977: 233–285), Derlon (1997a: 333–334 and 2002a:225).

48   See Jessep (1977: 233–285). It was always the entire territory of the moribund clan that was at stake; the territory was not shared if several groups were candidates: there was only one winner.

49   See Jessep (1977: 313–315), Derlon (1997a: 332–333 and 2002a: 225).

50   See Jessep (1977: 214–232).

51   This could mean that, when a person had been killed and found on a land, the clan to which it belonged was often suspected and would prefer to cede a piece of its territory as compensation rather than suffer the revenge of the victim's clan.

52   Under the leadership of Ben Lenturut, bishop of New Ireland and himself a native of Lelet plateau, the United Church was infiltrated in 1972 by several ecstatic movements known as 'Holy Spirit Movements' (See Derlon 2002a, 2002b). These were an outgrowth of evangelical and fundamentalist sects characterised by an extremely dogmatic and puritanical approach to Christianity (See Barr 1983). In the 1980s, this new trend in the United Church was very strong at Lelet, where the most fervent members came from the 20—30 year-olds who had attended school. Impressed by the local pastor's sermons, which presented their pagan past as the work of Satan, and by the young people's clear disdain for traditional customs, my privileged informants, all elderly, refused for over a year to acknowledge that some of them were still using human skulls or that the young boys used to be circumcised during certain types of *malanggan* rites. Their refusal to admit that their ancestors once practised child sacrifice is therefore easily explained, and all the more because I was too hasty in ceasing to question them on the subject, perhaps unconsciously happy with their negative replies.

53   In the 1970s, as shown by a land dispute reported by Jessep (1977: 208), it was this inability to understand why they should have had to pay for the life of a child they had not killed that one Barok lineage used as an

argument for demanding and obtaining payment for the pieces of land used by a lineage that had once sacrificed one of its young members. While the true logic behind this acquisition of land in exchange for the sacrifice of a child now escaped the villagers, they had nevertheless grasped the fact that it could not be simply compensation for homicide.

54 Jessep (1977: 213).

55 Jessep (1977: 206–207).

56 Linge (1932: 50).

57 Wagner (1987: 58).

58 Wagner (1986: 153–154).

59 Clay (1977: 156).

60 On Lelet plateau, bodies used to be buried in a foetal position, in a log-lined vertical grave, which suggests that the father and his child rested like two foetuses in the same grave.

61 Cf. Küchler (1987, 1988, 1992) and Derlon (1990, 1997a, 1997b).

62 For details on the parallels between land rights and *malanggan* rights, as well as the ways and means of their transfer between individuals and groups, see Derlon (1994 and 1997a).

63 Küchler (1983: 72).

64 Küchler (1983: 73).

65 In his history of the Methodist Church in the New Guinea island region (1975: 80).

66 The 1903 drought is mentioned by Linge (1932: 16).

67 Threlfall (1975: 80).

68 Note that the name Lupalau itself, which my informants used when speaking of the Lurumbi clansman, instigator of the cargo cult, is built on the word *lau* and therefore could be a nickname given as a reminder of his role in the human sacrifices linked with this cult.

69 See Köhnke (1974: 15–16) and Brouwer (1983: 57–58).

70 Brouwer (1983: 57–58).

71 See Derlon (1998).

72 Or the cadavers of two other persons — a man and a woman — used as substitutes if the guilty individuals were too important to be sacrificed by their respective clans.

73 See Wagner (1986: 153–154 and 1987: 58).

74 See Derlon (2002b) for information on the way the Mandak today envisage some of their relations with Westerners.

75 The prefix ana- acts as the personal pronoun 'I'.

PART TWO

Chapter 6

IN AUSTRALIA, IT'S 'ABORIGINAL' WITH A CAPITAL 'A'

Aboriginality, politics and identity[1]

Barbara Glowczewski

Sometime in the 1960s, for both ethical and political reasons, the term 'Aboriginal' and 'Aboriginal' began to be written with a capital 'A', thus becoming an ethnonym; it applied to the descendants of the first inhabitants of the Australian continent, some 500 groups speaking different languages and designated — even now — by different names.[2] Today, Aboriginal groups have not only different languages and cultural backgrounds, but different histories as well — reserves, separation of children from parents, mixed descent — all of which has put more or less distance between them and their heritage. And yet many still claim that there is such a thing as an 'Aboriginality' which unites everyone under the same identity, even if not everyone can agree on its definition.

Sociologists and anthropologists generally concur that this is an ongoing process in which they themselves have a part.[3] Nevertheless official and private discourses offer contradictory versions of this identity:[4] on the one hand, an identity of continuity, based on language, religious beliefs and practices, and pre-contact world-vision and life-style; on the other hand, an identity of resistance, aimed at the revision of contact history, valorisation of national identity symbolised by a flag, land-rights, denunciation of bad living conditions, analyses in terms of exclusion and exploitation. While some calls to resistance have gone out from the cities to tribal communities countrywide, the emergence of pan-Aboriginality is also accompanied by new affirmations of singular identities partly defined by tradition. In other words: all Aboriginals insist on their Aboriginality, but rather than advancing this claim by opposition to non-Aboriginals as a political entity, Aboriginal people affirm themselves as different from their other Aboriginal neighbours. It is as if pan-Aboriginality itself were prompting the emergence of these identity singularities, as if the process of anthropological and social heterogenisation were part and parcel of political uniformisation.

The various federal, state and regional governments regularly create royal commissions, make recommendations and pass laws and budget priorities in an attempt to find solutions for all Aboriginal descendants. It is the government that says who is legally an Aboriginal person, how he can claim his rights and what is supposed to promote Aboriginality; and it continues to enlist more and more public servants and consultants to do this — including Aboriginal people. Yet, despite this élite participation in the constant elaboration of indigenous policy and programs, the population concerned insists on the differences of interests and opinions within the Aboriginal community, and on the need for negotiations with the 'rank and file', and not only with appointed or elected representatives. Over the course of their long struggle for the right to exist and to manage their own affairs, recognition of an initial sovereignty, which would confirm once and for all the Aboriginal peoples' original ownership of the land, has become a question of principle. In the 1970s and 1980s, a committee of non-Aboriginals and the National Aboriginal Conference (NAC), an ex-body of nationally elected Aboriginal representatives, militated for a treaty with the federal government. But many Aboriginals proved to be reticent about the idea, arguing primarily that no one body was qualified to sign on behalf of all groups concerned. Nevertheless, the idea of a treaty became a popular symbol, in particular due to a song by the Aboriginal rock band, Yothu Yindi. The 1988 bicentennial celebrations held out hope for a solution. At the Aboriginal Festival in Barunga, the Prime Minister confirmed the relevance of the issue and the necessity of negotiating a treaty or a compact aimed at 'reconciliation'.

After the bicentennial, the idea of reconciliation supplanted that of a treaty, which had been rejected by all opposition parties, who saw the two-nation distinction as a threat to Australian unity. A council for reconciliation was created in September 1991, with both Aboriginal and non-Aboriginal members. A year later, its task turned out to be highly topical. For the first time in Australian history, a native community won a Supreme Court decision, recognising their native title on lands: this was the 'Mabo case', and it concerned a group of Torres Strait Islanders. The situation was tossed about in the local and national media, and aroused bad feelings and incomprehension among non-Aboriginals, who took increasingly hostile and open positions: racist declarations, alarmist appeals, and even the constitution of defence committees to counter what was felt to be a threat. Yet these first Australians now constitute less than two per cent of the population; just what kind of threat could they pose? The Mabo verdict should enable other Torres Strait Islanders and Australian Aboriginals to command recognition of their native title; but the concrete application of such titles remains to be determined: according to some politicians, 80 per cent of Australia could be subject to such claims. What power do the Aboriginals stand to gain by winning recognition as native land-owners? No one really knows. Except that they would become inevitable partners in most decisions involving development. In this context, Aboriginality is synonymous with a destiny rooted in the land, in the name of ancestral ties, and engaged in an alliance with the nation's future. This would be the philosophical rewards of a bond with the land traditionally defined as eternally present.

Aboriginality: *body* versus *spirit*

Aboriginality as a pan-Australian identity is a post-contact construction with respect to non-Aboriginals, whereas 'nativeness', as an ethnic identity, has always been the very basis of the cohesion of every Aboriginal group, through theories of conception and kinship, the organisation of society and marriage, the domain of economic survival and the religious system. It is politically correct, in today's social sciences as well as in political movements against racism and for universal equality of civil rights, to criticise all essentialist arguments attempting to justify ethnic differences or make distinctions between peoples on the basis of racial characteristics: i.e. biological and genetic transmission, and references to blood or to skin colour. In other words, anything having to do with the body or with innate features is now taboo. It is preferable to explain differences by non-corporeal and acquired criteria, such as culture, or the length of time a group has occupied a territory conferring native or assimilated migrant status.

For indigenous peoples, however, the notions of innate and acquired, like those of body and spirit, are inseparable insofar as the definition of what is innate and of the place of the body is cultural. Without this discourse, their culture loses a major mode of transmission. In everyday life, popular discourses on the transmission of physical features and on body marks have become more important than ever and increasingly sought after, whether as expressions of ethnic tensions or in the paramedical domain. Popular essentialism, like various indigenous theories, is not based on innate transmission alone, however, but also on the notion of contagion or pollution from outside substances, where an individual's body is thought of as reflecting the health of the society as a whole. The same logic operates in everyday racism, which abusively amalgamates a people's identity with the ills afflicting certain of its members. In this context, criticism of essentialism should include two aspects that are often neglected: first, the ideological effects of the West's depreciation of innate features as opposed to acquired ones; and second, the specificity and the place in discourses on identity of indigenous essentialistic theories. In Australia — as in many other Oceanic societies — essentialism has proved to be inseparable from a certain relationship with the environment, which differentiates people according to the natural species with which they identify.[5]

Conception and transmission: how totemic and linguistic identities are distributed

For nearly a century, anthropologists have been fascinated by Aboriginal theories of conception. The theme is well known: traditionally, Aboriginals did not attribute conception to copulation but to a spirit-child's entry into the uterus; this conception was announced in a dream to the father, mother or a close kinsman. (I will not go into the question of whether or not Aboriginals were aware of the connection between copulation and conception.) For decades, whenever the question has been put to them, they have replied time and again that there is no child without a spirit-child. In other words, the human being is something other than the result of what we call biological transmission. We could also say that there is no body without a spirit, and that this spirit comes from somewhere else than the body of the father or the mother.

What we are interested in here is the status of this 'somewhere else' and how it links a human being 'from the inside' with his ancestors. For this contains a paradox: the spirit transmits certain 'essences' that are going to identify the child in its spirit and its flesh with certain kinsmen, but also with certain natural species or phenomena, and with a land. Anthropologists customarily call this spiritual and physical link a 'totem'; in Australia it is known as a 'Dreaming'. Here again the many debates on whether or not totemism is a manufactured concept tend to obscure the fundamental reality: while there is no general definition of totemism, the term 'totem', and even more specifically 'Dreaming', tend to translate highly complex indigenous concepts which differ from group to group. Although we lack a standard definition or even an adequate translation of singular concepts, we must nevertheless attempt to understand what they say about the body and the spirit that is different from Western conceptions. In the present case, they say that the identity of each person is founded on an exterior agency which internally links the person to ancestors, animals, plants and so forth, and to places.

In the case of physical transmission, the development of the foetus, which is animated by a spirit-child that comes from the land — it can be a tree, a rock, a water hole — reacts to all outside substances that enter the mother's body. Therefore all Aboriginal groups traditionally imposed dietary taboos on a woman during pregnancy, forbidding her to eat various foods believed to be dangerous to the child. Some taboos lasted as long as the mother breast-fed the child, as her milk was also thought to be capable of transmitting harmful substances. The following example was recorded in the Kimberley in the 1930s: the mother could not eat honey received in exchange for pearl-shells, for pearl-shells being associated with Kaleru, the Rainbow Serpent, giver of spirit-children, might harm the child or make the mother sick.[6]

There are many indigenous theories about contagion through contact with substances, but I will not go into them here. I will simply add that, in addition to food, the semen transmitted to a pregnant woman during sexual intercourse was also believed by some groups to contribute to the child's development. Whatever physical likeness the child bore to the father or mother, however, was attributed to the Dreaming, to the totemic essence; people who had the same Dreaming were also supposed to share certain physical traits stemming from their spiritual affinity with a particular species. These characteristics may be different for men and women. For instance, among the Warlpiri, I found that Opossum clan men have a particular foot shape which recall this animal, while the women's lips become black when black plums are in season: the 'Plum' is a female totem associated with the Opossum.[7] Commonly, too, a child may have a birthmark, explained by the circumstances in which its spirit entered the mother's body. For instance, an infant may have a mark where his father shot the kangaroo that was the child's spirit before it was born. Over and above the complex symbolic elaborations each Aboriginal culture has developed in its own language, all theories about the process of conception and gestation stress one fact. The body and its substances, blood in particular, carry essences that go beyond the purely human dimension, although they are also what gives each person his human nature, his singularity, and identifies him with a place that will enroll this individual in the collective identity of the group that is tied to the same land as well as in the broader identity of all those who speak the same language.

The shared language itself is believed to come from the ancestors, for the spoken word comes from the Dreaming. For the Warlpiri, in particular, it is the spirit-child that transmits the power of speech. It has been pointed out that, for the original groups from the Western Desert that migrated northwards (south of the Kimberley) — now the majority of the Aboriginal populations, known as Wolmeri (Walmadgeri, Walmajarri), Julbaridja (Yulparija) or Wonggadjunga (Wangkajunga) — the notion of human being covered first of all those who recognised each other as *djandu*, nearby groups speaking the same language, and extended outwards to the *ngai*, distant neighbours having different languages and customs but with whom there were direct or indirect exchanges of objects or rituals.[8] Beyond this horizon, even if objects and rituals circulated, the more-or-less 'human' status of people was debatable. The notion of *djandu* is found in different desert languages. The same study shows that the terms Walmadgeri and Yulbarija were both used by the northern river peoples to designate those in the south, but when they became local culture markers, they were also adopted by new migrants from the desert.[9]

There is a general tendency throughout Australia to use different terms, depending on whether one is designating a group from the inside or the outside. For example, northwestern peoples usually call the desert peoples to the east (Central Australia) Waringari, Warmalla or Woneiga. These same groups, however, differentiate each other by the language they speak (Warlpiri, Aranda, etc.): in reality, Warlpiri use the terms Warmalla and Woneiga (Warnayaka) to designate dialectal variations that characterise Warlpiri associated with the lands on the far western edge of the tribal territory. With colonisation, certain terms came to circumscribe expanding local identities, such as Walmajari in the Kimberley, or Warlpiri, Pintupi or Pitjantjatjarra in Central Australia. What should be remembered from all this is that traditional ethnic designation was based on local proximity and the ability, if not to speak the same language, then at least to understand each other in spite of differences. The borders between 'tribal' identities were fluid and were redefined with each new alliance that brought the various intra- or extra-tribal groups into contact for the purpose of exchanging goods and rituals. Marriages tended to be contracted within the linguistic unit, although from time to time union with outside groups would renew or inaugurate alliances between the contracting parties.

Kinship and ritual: how mythic filiations and alliances are reproduced

I have shown elsewhere that the Warlpiri and their neighbours apply the term 'human being', Yapa, to all those, whatever their language, who identify each other using the same classificatory kinship system or certain equivalences.[10] Of course identification assumes encounters and alliances. But the particularity of this system of communication is that the alliances are based primarily on shared rituals before being grounded in marriage; they are founded on the sharing of certain non-human ancestors, often designated by totemic names. More specifically, it is the route travelled by these ancestors, known as a 'Dreaming', that connects one group's places to those of another, that endows them with this common, shared identity designated by the Dreaming which goes with it: Kangaroo Dreaming, Goanna Dreaming, Emu Dreaming, Yam Dreaming, Rain Dreaming, and so on. Some of these routes are more than a thousand kilometres long and run through the territories of different language groups: the ritual cycles and objects associated with the different places are also transmitted, eventually returning to their starting point enriched with new mythic episodes and rituals. Celebration of these connections by the local groups constantly renews the ties of classificatory and totemic kinship. This is not to say that the groups at either end of the chain necessarily know each other or even recognise their kinship, but that, in each place, identities are thus recomposed.

But classificatory 'kin' is by no means synonymous with consanguinity: various anthropologists have stressed this point all too often forgotten by theoreticians. Traditional Aboriginal people speak of these relations as their 'skin', as opposed to our notion of blood, but others also speak of 'flesh' or 'body'; so to say someone is of the same 'flesh' explicitly designates an essence of the Dreaming that is shared by all members of a group, an essence that is both external and internal, corporeal and spiritual, and which is usually also a totem. The notion of being one 'body' or one 'skin', on the other hand, refers I think to the surface marked or penetrated by this essence which inhabits the body on a continuous basis (in the case of a small group) or temporarily (in the case of a bigger group) when it is painted on the body with ritual designs.

This is not the place to explore the complex connections between inside and outside that can be found at every level of ritual life, as well as in gender relations.[11] Nor am I going to attempt an explanation of the classificatory kinship systems: the complexity of the Australian models is a constant source of wonder for mathematicians. But there is one fundamental rule that should be retained: traditional Aboriginal societies had a kinship system that, in many cases, divided the group into two, four or eight categories. The members of the same category regarded each other as 'brothers' and called those in another category by another kin term. This system does not use ranked classes but alternative roles: during any ritual, everyone in the same category automatically receives the same role; this role changes for the whole category when the context changes, in another ritual, for example. This applies to initiations, funerals and totemic rituals. In each case, it is the position of 'brother', 'father', 'mother', 'spouse', 'mother- or father-in-law', and so on, with respect to the initiate, the deceased or the ancestor celebrated, that determines the role the person plays. Thus both kinsmen and direct allies are placed in a category of classificatory kinship. There is no room here for outsiders, unless they are identified with a classificatory category and thus become 'kin' in their own right.

The articulation of this form of kinship, which is still used in those communities and towns where Aboriginal groups have kept ritual alive, brings us back to the initial question of essences. A child is identified by its spirit-child with one or more Dreamings, as well as with a place. But it is the rituals that enable close kin to situate a child in a filiation which, according to the group, will give it the essence it will share with its father's line, its mother's line or with another group. Through these rituals, the child will acquire, in addition to its — let us say 'biological' or 'adoptive' — parents, yet other 'fathers' and 'mothers', together with as many potential classificatory kinsmen and allies as there are people present in a given context. This kind of generalised kinship does not encompass everyone as sharing the same essence, however. Instead, it defines a conjunction of Dreamings for each person, with the associated stories, rituals and places, for which the child will be responsible, together with a group of brothers within a broader category of 'skin brothers'. Rituals constantly reaffirm these singular filiations shared between a group of people, non-human ancestors and specific places by consolidating the alliances that maintain these singular ties between all the allies. Aboriginal people call this in English 'The Law'. 'Following the Law' means first of all being initiated: passing certain tests, receiving the secrets revealed to one sex or the other, and being at the same time affiliated to one group and allied with another. Both a man and a woman are duty-bound to follow and celebrate certain Laws: the term Law designates the ritual cycles that distinguish the various groups, but these can also be transmitted from one group to another.

The circulation of Laws strengthens kinship and alliance links while affirming the differences of identity. Since the 1970s, however, the southern Kimberley has been experiencing a 'Walmadgerisation', owing to the fact that the Walmadjeri (Walmajarri) desert groups have brought their Laws to the decimated groups of Fitzroy.[12] How have the Laws of one linguistic group come to supplant those of another? This can be explained by three partially linked factors: some decimated groups have been prevented from celebrating their respective Laws; they have also totally or partially lost their language; and there has been increasing intermarriage between different groups. In regions with more than a century of colonial contact behind them, many people are now of mixed ancestry, not only mixed Aboriginal and European descent, but also mixed with Asian indentured labour working in the pearl-shell industry. Aboriginals of the Kimberley have developed numerous strategies to cope with this situation. Despite the reserves and the near century-long ban on free travel, increasing numbers of rituals have circulated between coastal groups, and the western and the central deserts. Motorised vehicles have enabled tribes to extend their links with other far-away groups; some have changed kinship systems and the organisation of their rituals; new funeral rites have developed to include people of mixed descent and adapt the various changes brought in by the European settlers.[13]

The result of the accelerated circulation of the rituals and their accompanying myths was not a uniformity of beliefs, but the inclusion of various local versions in a new mythico-historical continuity that sometimes gave rise to messianic-type cults.[14] The exchange roads travelled by the objects and the rituals, which covered northwestern Australia and spanned the entire desert in pre-contact times, as well as the routes followed by the stories that linked the groups into a long chain, took on a different dimension. Increasingly Aboriginals on the move had the opportunity to compare local versions. In the 1950s, Petri had noticed that the coastal and the desert groups held certain pre-human ancestors known by different names to be equivalent: for instance, the Wanji peoples, who moved from the coast to the desert, are supposed to have brought with them the first Laws on the continent, while for all the desert groups, the Dingari are the first to have performed initiations.[15] Another myth runs in the opposite direction, crossing part of Central Australia and the whole Kimberley; this is the Two-Men Dreaming, also known as Watikutjarra Dreaming.[16] Stories about Rainbow Serpent, Kangaroo or Dingo link other groups. Through this recognition of common Ancestral Beings, the desert groups, who have maintained their Laws, are seen by certain groups in the north, who have lost their own Laws, as custodians of the ancestrality and the authenticity of a Dreaming order in the regions where, for various reasons, these Laws have been abandoned; on the other hand, ancestral heroes from the northern coastal regions continue to attest the power of these lands in certain desert cults.

People have always adopted ceremonies from neighbouring groups, but replacing one's own ceremonies by new ones means a partial change of identity, which introduces different levels. In the Kimberley, coastal or river groups, who identify with their locality and their original language, insist at the same time on their differences and on the fact that, by virtue of a given Law, they are all the same or the same as the desert peoples. There are also families who do not participate in any ceremony, but believe that Aboriginal identity should be marked on the body of their boys through some aspect of the ritual initiation common to most northern and desert groups. Some therefore send their sons to be initiated in a group speaking a different language, while others have them circumcised in the hospital. In this case, interestingly enough, circumcision is no longer the sign of affiliation to a local group and of alliance with others, it has become a physical indication of pan-Aboriginality. Others still, faithful to the Christian injunction, do not practice circumcision, but found their Aboriginal identity on a different base.

Mixed descent and separation: how the ban on mixing the colours provided a pretext for taking the children away

At the time of the first European contacts, many Aboriginal people regarded white skin as the sign of a ghost. Europeans were therefore often thought to be spirits of dead persons. Nevertheless, the first children of mixed descent born with light skin were not identified with a European father. Their skin colour was explained by the indigenous theory of contamination by substances: for instance the mother must have eaten too much flour. This remark can be understood in another way, though: as meaning that the ingestion of food imported by white settlers marked the onset of a disorder in the transmission of substances or essences, in other words, identities. In the same vein, among the Worora of the northwest, the men were reported to complain that their dreams had become too 'heavy' since they had been working on the cattle stations: they dreamed of too many things from the white people's world and there was no room left to dream of spirit-children; this was the explanation they offered for the near sterility of their group.[17] In Arnhem Land, in the 1970s, on the other hand, many women found themselves with more than four children; the unusual numbers were blamed on the fact that white people had sunk too many wells, which attracted spirit-children. These examples indicate that Aboriginal people do not view conception as a matter of biological transmission, but instead always as a relationship with the environment: the confrontation of the Aboriginals' world with that of white people had altered the circulation of essences.

The way Aboriginals look on people of mixed descent has varied with the region and in reaction to colonial policy, which was obsessed with preventing the mixing of colours. Until recently, administrators and settlers spoke of 'full-blood', 'half-caste', 'quadroons' and so forth. Based on the idea that Aboriginals do not have recessive genes in the colour of their skin, the notion of a racial 'whitening' was developed. 'Half-caste' girls were separated from their families to be married to 'quadroon' boys, so that their daughters might be married to even lighter boys, until every trace of Aboriginal ancestry had vanished. In this process, the men were not to be married to a lighter girl. The theory, put into practice by the welfare services, is not without its similarities with Nazi racial rules stipulating that an Aryan woman would be permanently defiled by a single sexual relation with a Jewish man. This idea was based on the theory of impregnation that all of a woman's children would be marked by her first sexual relation. At the turn of the century, Bischofs, a German Pallotine Father in charge of the Aboriginal mission at Beagle Bay in the Kimberley, expounded on this theory in a text devoted to the Aboriginals of the northwest coast.[18] He devoted over a page to the idea that, if an Aboriginal woman had intercourse only once with an Asian, all children born thereafter would be of mixed blood. As Chief Protector of the Aboriginals of the northwest, he therefore urged that Aboriginals be kept away from both Europeans and Asians: mixed unions were regarded as a crime, and Aboriginal women surprised with Asians were charged with prostitution and either jailed or sent to a mission. Children born of unions with Asians or Europeans were taken away from their parents.

Many life-stories tell of the strategies used to shield mixed-descent children from the segregationist policy: they were hidden from passing patrols, or even rubbed with charcoal to hide their light skin. Today many Aboriginals are looking for their lost families. For years they were refused access to the colonial archives, but now an Aboriginal organisation has been created to assist them in their search. Numerous reports indicate that Aboriginal men and women in the north did not necessarily see these short-lived unions with Europeans or Asians as a bad thing. In the Broome region, affairs between Aboriginal women and fishermen from Malaysia or the Philippines are often presented as love stories. Maddock[19] reports that, in Arnhem Land, Aboriginals did not reject half-castes, but they did make fun of them and called them 'dogs' if they refused to take part in ceremonies. Unlike European settlers, Asians were not generally feared because they did no harm; instead, they brought 'good things', like curry and opium. On the northern coast, 'yellowfella' designated people of mixed Aboriginal and European or Asian descent and their descendants. On the west coast, the expression 'coloured' was employed more explicitly for people of mixed Aboriginal and Asian descent who had developed their own community after two or three generations. Following the Second World War, many Asians were sent back to their own countries in accordance with the 'White Australia' policy; their descendants, raised by their families or in the centres reserved for people of mixed descent, were assimilated by the administration to the other Aboriginals, unless the 'whitening' policy gave them European status.

Like the administration, Aboriginals on the reserves continued for a long time to use the expressions 'full-blood' and 'half-caste'. But these terms indicated a difference of status having less to do with skin colour than with a way of life: half-caste tended to refer to Aboriginals, whether or not of mixed descent, who lived in town or in the white people's world. Urban militants have denounced the use of both terms and for a time used the expression 'part-Aboriginal' for people of mixed descent. Later it was decided that all persons of Aboriginal descent, whatever the shade of their skin, could identify as 'Aboriginal' and be given this status.

Jordan writes that this insistence on an Aboriginal identity stems in part from the fact that, after having been depreciated by Europeans for decades, it once again took on a positive value after the referendum granting Australian citizenship to all Aboriginal people and giving them various social advantages, such as scholarships or, more recently, the possibility of obtaining a lease to live on a land.[20] With the new laws, many families that had maintained their 'coloured' status (as descendants of Asian settlers) to protect themselves from the discrimination against Aboriginal people began to claim their Aboriginality, and the term 'coloured' has fallen into disuse. Some people were even unaware of their Aboriginal background, kept from them by their adoptive families. The latest census figures, however, show that the majority of Aboriginal people are now proud of their roots. Although all descendants of Aboriginals are now officially recognised as Aboriginal in all government reports and brochures concerning them, it is still not unusual for the opposition 'full-blood/half-caste' to resurface at the first sign of discord within Aboriginal organisations or even in families. Nevertheless, with the valorisation of Aboriginality, the opposition does not have the same meaning. The mention of blood does not refer to some purported racial purity but to a way of thinking: anyone who seems to betray the Aboriginal cause will be accused of being 'half-caste'; but 'full-blood' can also be used as an insult, suggesting the incapacity to understand the new issues of Aboriginality.

The desert and northern Aboriginal peoples who have survived European contact have tended, for the past twenty years, to define their way of living as following two Laws, generally opposing everything that came from the 'blackfella' to the rules imposed by the 'whitefella'. The Warlpiri thus use the term *yapa* (humans) for all Aboriginal people — even the coloured people they now see on television. This is contrasted to Kardiya, which is used for 'Europeans', as non-Aboriginal Australians usually call themselves. Although the opposition between the two Laws is expressed in terms of colour — black *versus* white — as well as in terms of relations of power, I believe it also reflects acknowledgment of the impossibility of any traditional alliance, as this would require that the partners' idea of self have a common foundation. This is a directly cognitive issue: it is not so much a question of same skin colour as of sharing a certain way of thinking, which for traditional Aboriginal people is directly linked to the environment and to the reinterpretation of myths and rituals.

Defining identity in terms of locality, language, totemic essence (Dreamings), classificatory kinship or ritual life (the Law) raises the question of the relationship between these identities as Aboriginal points of view and our Western categories, which, to put it schematically, oppose the identity of the self (in psychology or psychoanalysis) and cultural identity (in anthropology and classical sociology). I believe that this dichotomy does not exist in traditional Aboriginal societies. Not, as some suggest, because the notion of self is purely social, the individual being identified with society as a whole, but because society is entirely grounded in a notion of the self that defines each individual as involved in a network of identifications and self-references. These vary according to the context, but remain based on socialised internalisations of something external that is found in all manifestations of the cosmos (people, places, animals, plants, wind, rain, etc.): the notion of Dreaming, which permeates these cultures, partakes of this kind of internalisation. In a context of relative social disintegration, particularly in urban communities, Aboriginal identity, at the family or even the purely individual levels, is often based on certain characteristics which reveal a link with the traditional notion of self:[21] attachment to places and development of local Kriols, importance of extended kinship networks and duties of assistance, search for direct links between transgressions of some Law by Aboriginals and natural catastrophes or accidents, confirmation of paranormal powers to kill or cure, visions or dreams containing messages or stimulating creativity, and above all interpretation of signs attributing a totemic and localised spirit-child to a newborn infant.

Aboriginality: *culture* versus *policy*

> Aboriginal spirituality is the core part of being Aboriginal. There is a need to push for Aboriginal Spirituality (capital S) being recognised as an established philosophy by educational authorities, religious groups (…). Aboriginal Spirituality gives everyone, from infancy to old age, a sense of 'who I am'. It is Aboriginal Identity (capital I). It is respect for Elders, caring and sharing for each other and a strong connection and love of the land. Aboriginal Spirituality should be nationally registered as an Aboriginal Religion, and as such, given the recognition and status to which other recognised religions have privilege. Resources should be made available to teach Dreamtime stories to non-Aboriginals and those Aboriginals who were removed from their cultural heritage in infancy or as children. Aboriginal children should be given Aboriginal names at birth to reinforce their Aboriginality.

The above passage sums up the recommendations made by a delegation of Aboriginal women to a conference on the theme of 'Safe keeping: women's business'.[22] After decades of anthropological discussions on the religious or non-religious status of Aboriginal spirituality and at a time when deconstructionist tendencies are blaming traditional cultural references for freezing Aboriginality in an ideal and nostalgic image of a mythical Dreamtime, it is interesting that the same elements are asserted by Aboriginal people, women in this instance, as the basis of a religion that should be made official like any other and as the very foundation of Aboriginal identity. Yet it is clear from various analyses that many young — or not so young — Aboriginals, who insist on their Aboriginal identity, do not rely on religious beliefs or may even reject them. On the other hand, the call for 'caring and sharing', here used to define their religion, also frequently serves as a secular statement of Aboriginal identity. Aboriginal health organisations, among others, advance the formula to oppose risk-taking and deviant behaviours (alcohol abuse, domestic violence, etc.).

Aboriginal spirituality, it must be remembered, is part and parcel of a relation to the land. And it so happens that land claims top the list of political demands. Justification of Aboriginal peoples' claims as the original occupants of the land are based on peoples' spiritual association with places and their responsibilities as custodians. Even when these responsibilities are not longer exercised, it is with reference to the past culture as heritage that Australian law recognises the protection of Aboriginal sites. In other words, 'religion' has become synonymous with 'culture', not necessarily in the way it was traditionally practised, but in a way it can be acceptable to national, and now international, norms, such as the status of recognised religions, schooling, the art market or legislation designed to confirm the ancestral link between Aboriginals and the land.

Between the land and God:
how Christian Churches negotiate
with the principles of Aboriginal spirituality

The debate over the connection between religion and ethnic identity is reminiscent of the question of Jewish identity: to what extent can a person be considered Jewish if he or she does not practise or even believe?[23] The answer depends on the branch of Judaism. Since a person is Jewish by ancestry, and more specifically through the maternal line, all that is needed for some is to acknowledge one's Jewishness and to be acknowledged by the others (which brings us back to the ethnic questions raised in the first part of this chapter). For others, being Jewish is inseparable from living a Jewish life style, which implies religious practice and the physical inscription it commands for boys (circumcision); this idea is also found in certain Aboriginal groups, as I mentioned earlier. In either case, Aboriginal or Jewish, the religious arguments — unlike Christianity, Islam or Buddhism — have one point in common: it is inconceivable that adopting the Jewish religion or Aboriginal spirituality is enough to make a person a Jew or an Aboriginal. Knowledge, or even practices like circumcision, cannot confer this identity. The reason for this inconceivability differs in the two cases at one level at least. Judaism is a collective and historical destiny, and a sign of a people's specificity; it is transmitted through both essence and culture. It is this memory, passed from one generation to the next in what tends to be an endogamous community, that founds the group's 'authenticity', whereas the majority of the Jewish people lives in exile (even though for some the return to the land of Israel is a necessity). Aboriginal religion lies both in the individual and in a network of connections between individuals and their respective lands and myths. But this network does not include all Aboriginal people nor does it cover the entire territory of Australia, either historically or geographically. Each individual exists only because he or she embodies ancestral spirits of the land, those celebrated in ritual life; in other words, spirituality is inseparable from the notion of person and place. From a traditionalist point of view, Aboriginal people who deny the link between the individual, the spirit and the land have 'lost' the knowledge of their link. But it is still present, not only through their ancestors, but in their very being, because there is no person without a territorialised spirit.

Does this mean that non-autochthonous people are without a spirit? A text by Stanner carries the title, 'White Man Got No Dreaming', according to the expression used by many Aboriginals, for whom 'lacking Dreaming' is the sign of not being Aboriginal.[24] In various parts of Australia, it has been reported that, when non-Aboriginals live for a long time with Aboriginals, their children born in that place are given a Dreaming, the sign of their implantation. Some Aboriginals also consider that Christianity — or rather the story of the Bible and of Christ — are the white people's Dreaming. Nevertheless, most of them note a fundamental difference: Australian Dreamings are rooted in the land, whereas this European Dreaming claims to be everywhere and nowhere. In reaction, some groups in the Kimberley suggest that Noah's ark has its secret place in the Australian desert and will save them from a new flood.[25] Similarly, Jesus (Jinimin) showed himself to some Woneiga (Warlpiri) in Central Australia: he had a black and white skin, and announced that Aboriginal people will have a white skin once they win their fight against the Europeans; he promised to protect their culture, which he took with him into the sky in the form of two cults — Wanadjarra and Worgaia — which have since spread through the Australian West.[26] The differences in the way Dreamtime Beings and the Christian God are linked to the land invite us to rethink the whole question of 'monotheism'.

Aboriginal people who have not abandoned the beliefs of their ancestors often take a theological approach to Christianity.[27] The aim of their reflection is not strictly religious, however. Just as the ancestral religion was inseparable from the social and political organisation, especially the distribution of land rights enabling the people to live, so today's spiritual reflection is concerned to define the 'place' of Aboriginal people in Australian society through the respect of their land rights in an economic environment of development (urbanisation, mining, cattle stations, etc.). In other words, while Aboriginal spirituality defines Aboriginal identity, it is also a political statement. Tony Swain has defined the Warlpiri's idea of the Christian God as the 'ghost of space': he opposes the Aboriginal notion of place to that of space, an encompassing notion alien to the Aboriginal mind, which thinks in terms of relations between places but not of a spatial continuum encompassing them.[28] He shows that this notion was more or less included in, or rather seen as assimilable to, an alliance between Dreamtime Beings and space, between the Warlpiri and God. The aim of this alliance was for God to 'learn the Warlpiri's language' (from the translation of the Bible into Warlpiri) so that he would understand and recognise their relation to place, thus enabling his representatives on earth — especially the governments — to do likewise and give Aboriginals back their ancestral lands. Translations of the Bible, encouraged by several Christian groups, help preserve local languages, but not without the risk of transposing indigenous spiritual concepts. Adaptation of traditional elements to celebrate the Christian message (song rhythms, boomerang percussion, body painting or the painting of objects, use of dreams) has also given rise to indigenous churches with their own cults.

On the initiative of Christian groups, an exhibition was held in 1990, entitled 'Aboriginal Art and Spirituality'.[29] Religious paintings from various Aboriginal communities were displayed; the few Biblical themes represented were surrounded by a majority of works featuring itineraries and places from ancestral Dreamings. Mainstream Churches, contrary to most of the new evangelical sects, tend to promote the spiritual importance of attachment to the land. A manifesto on land rights was published by the Catholic Commission for Justice and Peace of the Australian Council of Churches,[30] and the World Council of Churches also came out in favour of land rights.[31] In January 1988, the Australian Heads of Churches, in a declaration entitled 'Towards Reconciliation in Australian Society', called on Parliament to formally recognise Aboriginal prehistory and the continuing importance of its heritage; the counsellor for Aboriginal affairs to the Catholic bishops submitted a project to all political parties for negotiation of the terms of a 'compact'. After discussion with all the parties, the term 'reconciliation' was adopted.

The Australian Churches have taken sides in the debate, but this does not mean they are leading the Aboriginal movement, or, as in other parts of Oceania, that Christians have provided activists with political training or even raised their indigenist consciousness. Although Pat Dodson, of Yawuru-Djugun descent and ex-Chairman of the Council for 'reconciliation' set up by the government in 1991, trained for the priesthood, his kinsmen had him initiated immediately after his ordination, and when he took up the political struggle after law school, he left his religious functions. In fact, Aboriginal activism has often developed in reaction to mission schooling.

The impossible alliance:
how conversion and allowances contribute
to neutralising attempts at self-determination

Christian conversion, with its various syncretisms, allows some groups to maintain their tribal identity, but the Churches can also have the opposite effect, channelling former local and linguistic singularities into a uniform Christian evolution.[32] Conversion to Christianity was often violently imposed in the missions, which took children away from their parents to raise and teach them in mission schools. Native languages were frequently undermined. The marriages organised by missionaries were purposely conceived to oppose polygamy and the large age difference between the spouses inherent in traditional marriage by bestowal. By opposing the marriage prescriptions, the missions destroyed the social cohesion of the traditional alliances. And by forbidding the performance of certain rituals that once marked the life-cycle, they weakened the models for becoming an adult and threw traditional sexual roles into question. Finally, by refusing to recognise European or Asian paternity, they prevented the emergence of new family structures.[33] The paternalism practised by the missions into the 1960s has been strongly criticised. In a way, the inability of many communities to manage their own affairs under the new structures of authority is directly related to decades of infantilisation. Destitution of the father's authority in particular led to a rise in the number of matrifocal homes, leaving the men without authority and drowning in grog.[34] For lack of family models, many young people, boys and girls alike, succumbed to alcohol. Christians found an ideal source of converts among the young or older drinkers, who had resisted conversion until then. For many Aboriginals, being a Christian became synonymous with 'no grog and no gambling', in other words with fighting the financially irresponsible attitude entailed in playing cards and drinking and thus ignoring the family's needs.[35]

The very notion of an evil inherent in humanity is fundamentally alien to the Aboriginal way of thinking; nevertheless for Christian Aboriginals, the concept becomes a means of exploring the evil introduced by the European settlers.[36] In this new distribution of powers, many Aboriginals see Christianity as the only way to protect themselves from the harmful effects of contact — alcohol, violence, disintegration of society or new sexually transmissible diseases. Some charismatic movements hold up 'healing' as proof of the power of Christianity. In April 1993, a gathering was organised at Halls Creek to show the Aboriginals invited from far and wide the lame being made to walk and the blind recovering their sight. Such a display of Christian 'power' does not necessarily invalidate the powers of the Dreaming, though. Instead, it becomes one of the recognised magical principles that legitimises Europe as a conqueror against whom all indigenous powers must be mobilised. For instance, today most funerals are celebrated by the Christian Church with a religious service and burial in the cemetery. But they are also the occasion for huge community gatherings at which kin and allies, who have often travelled hundreds of kilometres, perform the traditional rituals to find the culprit.[37] It is the power of the Dreaming that is believed to bring about the punishment. In the same vein, the northern Aboriginals tell a story, in demonstration of their Law, of some workers drowned during the construction of a dam: the site should not have been disturbed because it was the home of a dangerous serpent ancestor-spirit that lived in the sacred rock.

Is the alliance of Christianity and Aboriginal spirituality compatible with the existence of two separate laws, the Dreaming and the Australian government seen as being connected with the Bible? This is by no means clear if we consider the exclusive character of Christianity as well as that of Western economics and politics represented by the Australian government. The same question arises when traditional elements receive their only official recognition from Western institutions like art, schools and the justice system. By showing certain images of Aboriginals yesterday and today, indigenous writers, artists, musicians or film-makers participate in the promotion of Aboriginality and in defining this concept according to international cultural norms. The introduction of an Aboriginal school curriculum and bilingual programs has perverse effects as well, however. The dynamism and creativity of oral literature is thus threatened by the purported 'authenticity' of the written versions of myths, which are often desacralised in the process and even made into stories for children instead of remaining knowledge acquired in the course of initiation into adulthood. A young Aboriginal boy, who was a brilliant student at the Broome school and had been initiated according to tradition by the Bard people, maintained that the teachings of the bush did not belong in school. The concern to keep the two laws separate can also be seen in the way the elders insist on keeping their secrets, even if it means withdrawing some books from the shops. Some even refuse to transmit their knowledge to the following generations, perhaps to prevent it from being dissolved in the generalised mediatisation. This might explain why some elders have abandoned their traditional functions and have taken to drinking out of solidarity with the younger men.

A series of so-called 'Captain Cook' myths, from north Australia, tells the story of European contact. Comparing versions, Maddock has found some recurring themes such as that of white men offering gifts that are rejected by the Aboriginals or that of white men stealing from the Aboriginals.[38] In the stories about the Macasans, who traveled to the north coast every season before the arrival of the European settlers, the interaction is more ambiguous: when the Aboriginals try to accept the gifts, the exchange doesn't work.

In no case was there an attempt on either side at a balanced alliance. The elders in Broome tell of a treasure buried in a particular spot in the present-day town: they say it is a 'will and legacy' left to the Yawuru, the traditional custodians of the region, by the first European navigators. According to the official history of Australia, the first to land on this shore, in 1699, were the Dutch captain, William Dampier, and his crew. However the linguist Von Brandenstein has recently suggested that, in the sixteenth century, the Portuguese established a secret colony slightly further north and cut a road as far as the present-day town of Broome; in contrast to the violence that followed the arrival of the English settlers, relations between the Aboriginals and the Portuguese were quite peaceful. One sequence of Walungarri, an important ritual performed in the Kimberley, shows a dance evoking the gift of wine and tobacco to the Aboriginals by the Europeans (were they the Portuguese?) as well as a grand celebration held by the latter upon arriving. Dampier, on the other hand, was unable to communicate with the natives of what is now Broome, and ultimately fired on them. So is alliance with the order imposed by the settlers possible or not?

Since Aboriginal people began receiving money, in the form of wages, allowances, pensions or mining royalties — which only dates from the late 1960s — they have often been accused of 'throwing it away' on cards or alcohol, or of running down the cars or the houses given to them by development programs. The latest militant slogans urge rejecting the image of Aboriginal people as victims in favour of a successful image. But many families of Aboriginal men or women who have broken into politics or achieved renown as international artists (painters, film-makers, rock musicians) find it hard, in spite of their success and newfound resources, to escape the pressure of their surroundings and being sucked into 'fourth-world' living conditions. In these circumstances, Aboriginal culture is perceived as more profitable to the non-Aboriginal dealers than to the artists themselves. Could this be a replay (or demonstration) of the 'Captain Cook' myth, where white men have their gifts systematically rejected by the Aboriginals and at the same time go on stealing from them? Is it possible to think in terms of reconciliation when there has never been an alliance? Alliance by definition supposes that each partner retains his differences, not only culturally but also and above all socially, which means keeping power of decision to manage one's own affairs. But all non-Aboriginal gifts (money, food and other consumer goods or equipment), and even the Australian laws, continue to have a perverse effect. They either destroy or assimilate, or, more subtly, do not leave room for self-determination.

Some non-Aboriginals complain of racism in reverse, which might be explained in the following way: day in, day out, Aboriginal people are confronted with a bureaucratic machine that constantly frustrates their attempts at self-determination. They can therefore only regard with suspicion any non-Aboriginal they identify with this dominant order which excludes them by stigmatising them and at the same time alienates them while purportedly trying to seduce them. But this climate of suspicion and rejection is not restricted to relations between Aboriginals and non-Aboriginals; it can often be observed between Aboriginal family groups living in close proximity. In such conflicts, one group or individual typically accuses the other of making 'bad' alliances with non-Aboriginals, or of being like 'coconuts', black on the outside but white inside. When someone is highly successful, the accusation is that they are too different to have a legitimate place with the others (the insinuation being that the accused are not genuine Aboriginals and should not be there).

Such accusations burden everyday life with tensions and conflicts, and highlight the breakdown of the traditional approaches to conflict resolution that used to enable different groups of people to cohabit seasonally on the same spot. But they also show that the massive cohabitation imposed in communities and towns is now a permanent phenomenon. Because new self-management structures are lacking, the indigenous population has grown increasingly dependent on a bureaucratic welfare system which spawns its own contradictions. But it is also possible to see these conflicts in a positive light, insofar as they call for new forms of reconciliation and oblige all parties to constantly define themselves, thus reinforcing local singularities. In the process, the conflicts become a site for the construction of a multifaceted Aboriginality, one to which each party, through its involvement with a community, is required to contribute.

Reconciliation and decentralisation: how policy makers and bureaucrats fight over Aboriginal status

> The policy of assimilation means that *all Aboriginals and descendants of Aboriginals* are expected to attain the same manner of living as other Australians, and to live as members of a single Australian community enjoying the same rights and privileges, accepting the same customs and influenced by the same beliefs, hopes and loyalty as other Australians.[39]

Aboriginal legislation can be divided into roughly four phases. Between 1829 and 1936, in reaction to the violence committed on Aboriginals by the settlers — sexual abuse, killings, enslavement[40] — the government set in place legislation based on a policy of 'protection'. Its purpose was to segregate Aboriginals from the European Australian society by providing them with ration depots when they were driven off their lands by settlers. Gradually control of the population movements legitimised the arrangements with the settlers, allotting them free Aboriginal labour on the cattle stations or sending the Aboriginals away to work at missions or on reserves.

The Native Administration Act of 1936 marked the beginning of the 'assimilation policy', based on the idea of racial 'whitening' and imposing specific regulations on 'quadroons' (see above). Until the 1960s, census figures divided Aboriginals of mixed descent into different categories: they were not considered 'Aboriginals' if they exhibited 'positive' characteristics, in the light of their character and the standard of their intelligence, according to a law passed in South Australia (1939 Act). People of mixed descent could gain citizenship rights by applying for a certificate of exemption if they could show proof of good conduct and had severed relations with their tribe; this was the only way of gaining access to paid employment and sending their children to school without separating them from the family. By forbidding Aboriginal people from different categories to mix, the policy of assimilation merely justified a form of apartheid that was already operating in public places. Until the 1960s, the Broome movie theatre had separate seating for each category as defined by the colour of their skin: white, Asian, half-caste, and full-blood. The Native Welfare Act of 1963 systematised segregation by denying Aboriginal status to whoever had a quarter or less Aboriginal ancestry.[41]

The 1967 referendum giving all Aboriginal people the same rights as other Australian citizens marked the start of the policy of 'integration', bitterly summed up by many Aboriginals as the right to get drunk. The obligation of equal pay resulted in the dismissal of the Aboriginal workforce from the cattle stations rather than their integration. A population without work or a place to live was suddenly forced to take refuge in reserves or on the outskirts of towns. It was then that the government threw its 'White Australia' policy into question by admitting migrants first from the Mediterranean countries and then from Asia. The notion of a multicultural Australia, with its cocktail of ethnic immigrants, placed Aboriginal peoples in the context of the specificity of their own culture, as a minority sharing a common identity. Aboriginal status was extended to all people descending from an Aboriginal ancestor, whatever their other ancestry. While this new attitude helped promote the idea of Aboriginality, it exacerbated the opposition between those living in reserves and those living in towns. New problems were created that were further complicated by contradictions between federal legislation and the state laws which gave Aboriginal people different rights according to their region. A federal law, for example, allowed Aboriginal people to apply for native title providing their lands were on 'vacant Crown land'; but this law was valid only for the Northern Territory (Aboriginal Land Rights Act, 1976), the other states having rejected it. Western Australia has the 'Western Australian Aboriginal Heritage Act, 1972', which protects registered sacred sites; but the state only gives a 99-year lease on reserve lands. A complementary law, the Community Services Act of 1972, was passed with a view to community development on the reserves or in towns of this state.

Since the 1970s, official Australian policy has shifted from 'integration' to 'self-determination' and 'self-management'.[42] Although these promises reflect Aboriginal peoples' desire to manage their own affairs, the bureaucratic complications created by the measures actually set in place have led many activists and anthropologists to conclude that they were a failure.[43] In 1985, the National Aboriginal Conference (NAC), an independent group of Aboriginal advisors to the Federal Minister of Aboriginal Affairs, a consultative body without any real power but having a radical impact, was dissolved and replaced by the Aboriginal Development Commission (ADC), a body of Aboriginal public servants disposing of a budget to promote community development and to buy land for Aboriginals. In 1990, the federal government overhauled its Aboriginal services and replaced both the ADC and the old Department of Aboriginal Affairs with what was intended to be a decentralised administration, the Aboriginal and Torres Strait Islanders Commission (ATSIC), formed of a federal hierarchy with appointed members and regional councils with elected members. Its mandate was economic development. Interestingly, the name juxtaposes the term 'Aboriginal' with the expression 'Torres Strait Islanders'. The latter are distinguished from Aboriginals because they have occupied a territory — the islands off the northeast coast of Australia — for a shorter time and because they are related to the Melanesian peoples. But the indigenist policy includes them as native peoples.[44] The ATSIC allocates federal budget resources for the Aboriginals and Torres Strait Islanders to the different services concerned with them (development, health, housing, etc.), but it is constantly accused of being too centralised and not giving enough power to its regional councils, or of not taking local needs into account.

It was in this context of bureaucratic weight that the High Court verdict was handed down in 1992 in favour of a group of Torres Strait Islanders claiming native title on Murray Island. This was the famous 'Mabo case', after the name of one of the plaintiffs. 'Mabo' was a landmark because it invalidated for the first time the formerly legal notion of Australia as *terra nullius* and recognised the general principle of 'native title' predating colonisation. The question now is how to recognise other claims to such titles, and what rights do they confer? The Prime Minister suggested creating a special court to decide the claims of different groups. But at a conference held in 1993 with the Premiers of the six states, the proposal was almost unanimously rejected, especially by the Premier of Western Australia, who felt not that the decision should lie with each state government but that recognition of native title would threaten the economy, in particular that it would frighten away foreign investors. Prime Minister Keating replied that recognition of native title applied only to land presently occupied by Aboriginal groups and that this could only facilitate negotiations with investors, especially the mining companies. A year later, a heated debate still divided much of Australia, and in 1997 the situation was at a standstill. The Native Title Act of 1993 was passed at the federal level, creating, among other things, a system of courts. But some states passed their own legislation allowing them to review or even overturn this process. Aboriginal people were caught in the middle. Nevertheless, alongside certain radicals who challenged the system by demanding native title to the entire town of Canberra, there are also communities that have already negotiated agreements with mining companies or tour operators.

The real solution, it seems to me, is not to oppose the interests of Aboriginals to those of the nation as a whole, but to see how, as the traditional owners of the land, Aboriginal people can participate in the decisions relative to development so as to benefit not only on an individual basis, but also to give their community something more to look forward to than soon joining the so-called 'fourth world'. After decades of control and welfare, it is clear than money and services are not enough. For many Aboriginals, who call pensions (for children, the aged and unemployed) 'sitting down money', what they need is to be able to 'stand up' with dignity, and that is only possible through a complete social restructuration, implying recognition of their links with the land and development decided by themselves.

Some Aboriginals hold long-term leases on the land, especially in the Kimberley, where by the mid-1990's 51 per cent of the land used for cattle stations was in Aboriginal hands. This recent evolution was possible because the stations were abandoned by the settlers when the cattle industry went into decline. From the viewpoint of Aboriginal people, running these stations enables them to survive, an example of a two-speed economy which provides enough for them though seeming unprofitable to non-Aboriginals. Many Australians feel that separate development for Aboriginals is synonymous with apartheid[45] and that Aboriginal special services and rights give them an advantage over other Australians,[46] an attitude echoed by the rejection of the idea of 'native title'. Yet, in view of the failure of the 'assimilation' or 'integration' policies, it is clear that both precolonial and colonial history have given Aboriginal people needs that are different from those of other Australians or immigrants, but which also differ according to whether or not an Aboriginal group has been alienated from its land.

A challenge to anthropology: legitimising indigenous status to obtain land rights

Native Title to particular land ... its incidents, and the persons entitled thereto are ascertained to the laws and customs of the indigenous people who, by those laws and customs, have a connection with the land. It is immaterial that the laws and customs have undergone some change since the Crown acquired sovereignty provided the general nature of the connection between the indigenous people and the land remains.

Membership of the indigenous people depends on biological descent from the indigenous people and on mutual recognition of a particular person's membership by that person and by the elders or other persons enjoying traditional authority among those people. Native title to an area of land which a clan or group is entitled to enjoy under the

> laws and customs of an indigenous people is extinguished if the clan or group, by ceasing
> to acknowledge those laws, and (so far as practicable) observe those customs, loses its
> connection with the land or on the death of the last of the members of the group or clan.

This is the definition of native title given by Justice Brennan, one of the judges in the Mabo
case. But another judge, Toohey, founded native title not on observation of custom, but on
the plaintiff's argument of 'occupation of the land since 1788', not necessarily with constant
presence but regular visits proving 'possession'. According to the lawyers who have
commented on these judgments,[47] if this criterion is accepted for attribution of Aboriginal
titles, it becomes possible to claim a land without having to prove current practise of customs
but merely by justifying occupation of the land at the time of colonisation. The Supreme
Court also ruled that a title is extinguished when the land is used for permanent public
establishments such as roads. But contrary to the legislation in the Northern Territory, which
restricts claims to 'vacant' lands, native title can be claimed on national or maritime park
lands. The status has not been defined for land sold to private parties or under lease — most
cattle or fishing enterprises — or when development activities such as mining, tourism and
so forth have been started on them. The different questions of compensation also remain to
be settled. In the Northern Territory, the land handed back under the 1976 Land Rights Act
gave the Aboriginal owners a right of veto over future development as well as a right to
royalties (4 per cent maximum) on profits from mining. Most of the mining companies,
however, backed by some local governments, refuse to generalise this system to pending
native title claims.

Given the knotty legal situation, many lawyers and anthropologists have been recruited
to define the local content of eventual native titles. Aboriginals themselves disagree over the
question of traditional inheritance rights. With the transmission of land, for instance, what
should be the rule: traditional descent reckoning, patrilineal, matrilineal, or some other? Or
should the colonial history be taken into account and right to land given to all descendants?
In the 1970s, at the time of the first land claims in the Northern Territory, some
anthropologists criticised the systematisation of unilineal transmission and the notion of
patrilocality. In the Western Desert, for example, links with the land are determined
primarily by the individual's conception Dreaming (totem, see above), which often differs
from the father's Dreaming. Even in the Central Desert groups, who follow a patrilineal
pattern of transmission, land ownership is inseparable from other ritual land rights held by
the matrikin or other allies. As for the groups on the northwestern coast of the Kimberley, I
am currently working with the oral history and analysis of the ritual system of custodianship
of the Dreamings (partially maintained) to show that the traditional land-holding system
was highly complex and in fact incompatible with generalised patrilocality.[48]

The current interest in providing an anthropological definition of the content of native
titles highlights the importance of this moment of Australian history when indigenous
people are consolidating their Aboriginality, not as a shared political ideology, but as a force
of local cohesion, locality by locality.[49] More important than the similarities visible in these
approaches, though, is the fact that localisation carries with it a singularisation of identities
which implies both continuity with local ancestral heritage and creation of new social

structures. This continuity is affirmed, as can be seen in the many Aboriginal initiatives, through the maintenance or renewal of ceremonies, the creation of cultural festivals or the reconstitution of local history. The new structures are evident in the many new Aboriginal associations: tribal or family corporations for the purpose of resettling lands or negotiating their participation in the development of towns or national parks, women's groups, resource centres, and so on. As Myrna Tonkinson writes:

> While Aboriginality is developing as a political force, local and regional Aboriginal identities continue to have salience and provide, though not exclusively, some of the content of Aboriginality. And there are reciprocal influences on local attitudes. The two forms of identity help sustain each other and are therefore likely to coexist well into the future.[50]

This polarization between local identities and a pan-Aboriginal identity is, in my view, a particularly dynamic element in the creation of new alliances with local powers (ruling structures like the shire) or non-Aboriginal interested parties (like developers). These alliances bring both autonomy and support, owing to the political alliances contracted at the national level, which involve not only Australian interests but also a form of international solidarity with indigenous groups from other parts of the world.[51] In its 1993 public report on the Mabo decision, the Commission for Reconciliation underscored, for example, treaties concluded by other governments: New Zealand with the Maoris and Canada with the Indians.

In the past decade, militant groups themselves have developed exchanges with other indigenous peoples, both political — at the United Nations — and political-cultural — the Festival of the Pacific, held in Townsville in 1990 and in the Cook Islands in 1992. Local delegations travelled to these manifestations taking with them both the specificity of their regional heritage — dancing and traditional art forms — and new forms of individual creativity — plastic arts, literature, theatre, cinema or music. National recognition of these artists and the recent fame of some Aboriginal sport champions no doubt helps to promote a respect for Aboriginal culture that makes them symbols of a new political force. Not only Aboriginals who have remained close to their land, their language and their customs but those, too, who have been dispossessed of these are increasingly coming to identify with this many-sided Aboriginality.

Footnotes

1   A shorter version of this text has already been published in English under the title 'All One but Different' — Aboriginality: National Identity versus Local Diversification in Australia', Chapter 14 in Jürg Wassman (ed.), *Pacific Answers to Western Hegemony — Cultural Practices of Identity Construction.* Oxford: Berg International: 335–354, 1998 (from a panel of the ESFO symposium held in Basel, 1994).

2   In the mid 1990's the French edition of Hachette encyclopedia recognised the Australian use of the term as a proper noun. Many in France, unaware of the etymological origin of the term 'Aborigène' ('ab', from the origin), pronounce it 'Arborigènes', perhaps associating these first Australians with tree-dwellers (tree = *arbre* in French)?

3   Beckett ed. (1988); Thiele ed. (1991).

4   Keefe (1988).

5   In one work devoted to identity in the South Pacific (Linnekin and Poyer 1990), the authors raised the question of the relevance in these societies of the Western opposition between Mendel's genetic theory and Lamark's transmission of acquired characteristics: Watson (1990: 39) notes that culturally inherited ethnic differences persist only when a people identifies with its land.

6   Kaberry (1939: 169). These pearl-shells circulated as wealth transmitted by both women and men, although they were used as ritual objects exclusively by men, when they would go into the desert to perform rain-making ceremonies. Among coastal groups, they were hung on the pubic tassels by both the boys, as a sign of their initiation stage, and by girls as a sign of virginity.

7   Glowczewski (1989).

8   Kolig (1977).

9   Kolig (1977).

10 Glowczewski (1991).

11 Glowczewski (1991).

12 Akerman (1979). Recent fieldwork by the author in the region (Glowczewski 1999, 2001) demonstrates more complex phenomena, for instance the spread of the didjeridu, a NE musical instrument, or the cultural revival of some groups of mixed descent, and the reappropriation of indigenous data recorded in the past.

13 Kolig (1989).

14 Glowczewski (1983), Koepping (1988).

15 Editor's annotations to the writings of E.A. Worms (1972).

16 Glowczewski (1998a)

17 Lommel (1950).

18 Bischofs (1908).

19 Maddock (1977).

20 Jordan (1988).

21 Keen (1988).

22 'Australian Indigenous Women and Museums', National Conference, 6–8 March 1993, Adelaide.

23 The South Australian Jewish community officially backs the Aboriginal peoples by lending their support to an oral history project. Other ethnic minorities have also spoken out for recognition of Aboriginal rights in the name of their own religious denominations, for instance the Armenian Apostolic Church or the Greek Orthodox Church.

24 Stanner (1979).

25 Kolig (1988).

26 Petri and Odermann (1988 [1964]).

27 Mowaljarlai and Malnic (1993)

28 Glowczewski (1996) for a discussion of Swain's thesis (Swain 1988).

29 Crumlin (1991).

30 'Land Rights — A Christian Perspective', prepared for the 'Churches Task Force on Aboriginal Land Rights', set up by the Australian Council of Churches (Catholic Commission for Justice and Peace), Derek Carne, 1980.

31 'Justice for Aboriginal Australians', report of the World Council of Churches, 'Team Visit to the Aboriginals, June 15 to July 3, 1981', for the 'Program to Combat Racism', Geneva.

32 Swain and Rose (1988).
33 Some people of mixed Aboriginal and Malay or Indonesian descent were in contact with the Muslim religion, which, like the Aboriginal religion, was rapidly opposed by the Christian Churches: the children were taken away from their parents and forced to convert.
34 Hunter (1993).
35 Goodale (1987) suggested, following an unpublished paper by McKnight, that, for some Aboriginal groups, card-playing was a way of redistributing resources, something like the traditional hunting ethic. But this redistribution was (is) disturbed when the winners spent all their money on grog or on paying the fines of those jailed for drunkenness, upsetting the social and physical health of the entire community (Hunter 1993).
36 Rose (1988).
37 For example, a hairstring rope is passed around and, when it shakes, it is believed to indicate the person(s) responsible for the death.
38 Maddock (1988).
39 Myrna Tonkinson emphasises in italics 'all Aboriginals and part-Aboriginals are expected' and adds: 'The 1965 Native Welfare Conference modified the wording: 'the policy of assimilation seeks that all persons of Aboriginal descent will choose to attain a similar manner of living to that of other Australians' (Reynolds 1972: 175, emphasis added)' (M. Tonkinson 1990: 213).
40 For example, the organised enslavement (blackbirding) in the northwest of men, women and children by pearl-masters, who made them dive for pearl-shells.
41 M. Tonkinson (1990). The policy of assimilation founded Australian citizenship on an Anglo-Saxon model which excluded all immigrants supposed to be non-assimilable: Asians, Mediterranean peoples and Jews. After the Second World War, the immigration service received confidential instructions indicating the physical characteristics — specially skin colour — to be taken into consideration for refusing applications. When Australia agreed to accept war orphans, it was stipulated in writing that they were not to be of Jewish descent.
42 'Our Future Our Selves', Report of the Aboriginal and Torres Strait Islander Community Council, Management and Resources, House of Representatives Standing Committee on Aboriginal Affairs, August, 1990.
43 Tonkinson and Howard (1990), Hunter (1993).
44 The same evolution can be observed in the case of the Australian Institute for Aboriginal Studies in Canberra, renamed the Australian Institute for Aboriginal and Torres Strait Islander Studies.
45 Kolig (1973).
46 M. Tonkinson (1990).
47 Declaration by Brown and O'Donnel (1992), consulted in unpublished papers giving no further reference.
48 Glowczewski (1998b).
49 Some Aboriginal activists have suggested adopting a local term, 'Koori', to refer not only to the Aboriginal peoples of the southeast, but also for all Aboriginal peoples of Australia and their descendants of mixed ancestry. The use of 'Koori' has been well accepted in the southeast, but not in other regions, where local groups prefer to use their own names, for example, Nyoongar, in the southwest includes the people of the region of the town of Perth.
50 M. Tonkinson (1990: 215); see also Glowczewski (2004).
51 This solidarity with minority groups goes hand in hand, especially among young people, with identification with a 'black' culture, often carried by popular music from Australia or overseas.

Chapter 7

'MIPELA WAN BILAS'

*Identity and sociocultural
variability among the
Anga of Papua New Guinea*[1]

Pierre Lemonnier

It is not unusual today to belittle or even to reject out of hand that pillar of ethnography, the comparative approach. Among the practices regarded as particularly futile is the use of models, suspected of being a mere reflection of anthropologists' *a prioris*, especially when these models are built from data gathered many years before.[2] Taking the opposite tack, the present article defends the virtues of a comparative ethnological approach that uses *comparable* sociological entities. In other words, I intend to show how an anthropology of *nuances* focuses on assemblages of sociological phenomena whose regularity, simple presence or distortions in space or time make it possible both to characterise the sociocultural identity of a given population and to envisage the structural or the historical transformations it has undergone.

I have taken the example of the Anga tribes of Papua New Guinea, or rather the Anga *culture*. This sociological entity is considered to be homogeneous to a degree such that any micro-variations observed lead to defining specific social logics, and understanding the presence or absence of these logics in other parts of New Guinea or the rest of the world leads to better knowledge of the ways societies operate and evolve. First of all, I will lay out the ethnographic landscape as described in the different studies conducted among these groups by some ten anthropologists since the mid-1930s. Particular attention is given to the way the singularities identified in each area of social reality consolidate and confirm each other so that systems of compatibilities appear whose variants reveal the mutual implication of structural logics and functional dynamics. In this respect, the contrast between Anga forms of social organisation and those found in two other regions of New Guinea — the southern coastal societies and the Highlands Big Men groups — is enlightening. Then I will give a brief account of the way the members of one Anga society, the Ankave, represent to themselves the various sociocultural assemblages with which they deal, and how they produce and reproduce their identity and their differences. Finally, using this example, I will attempt to show how monographs and comparative studies can complement each other; in the course of this demonstration, I will underscore the sectors of anthropological research that would be excluded by a study carried out at the local level alone.

Anga culture: about unity in diversity

Why speak of an Anga 'culture' in the first place? Why consider that this set of New Guinea Highlands populations exhibits specific sociocultural features which make them a good subject both for study in their own right, insofar as they form a whole, and for comparison with other sociocultural sets? In short, what is the nature of the *homogeneity* observed in the twelve Anga linguistic groups, and what is the nature of the *heterogeneity* that appears when they are compared with other populations, of New Guinea in particular?

Their specific homogeneity can be appraised in two ways: first of all, certain sociocultural realities — such as language and material culture — are so original that they are in themselves enough to distinguish the Anga from the other cultural groups of New Guinea; and second and above all, one finds in these groups certain mutually reinforcing sets of traits of social organisation and of representations whose specific combination is enough to set the Anga apart from other societies in New Guinea.

Language

The Anga are the direct descendants of a population of non-Austronesian speakers who settled the Menyamya region several thousand years ago (Bhatia, pers. com.); today, numbering some 70,000, they are dispersed over a territory of 140 by 130 kilometres comprised of steep mountainous terrain at the intersection of three provinces of the independent State of Papua New Guinea: Eastern Highlands, Gulf and Morobe. Driven by that passion for differentiation so typical of societies in New Guinea,[3] as well as — probably but how can one be sure? — by demographic growth incompatible with the resources of the Menyamya valley, which were decreasing as the forest cover regressed,[4] part of this population left its original home and gradually spread from valley to valley until there were finally some forty tribes or local groups speaking ten mutually unintelligible languages.[5]

In terms of both their syntax and their vocabulary, the Anga languages form a relatively homogeneous family, whereas they bear very little or no resemblance to other languages of New Guinea, even those that are geographically close.[6] According to the Swadesh test (which measures the relative closeness of a hundred common words), the proximity between the Anga languages themselves ranges from 21 to 75 per cent, whereas they share at most 3 to 5 per cent of their vocabulary with any other geographically close language. Bilingualism is limited to villages and hamlets located near a border with another Anga group.[7] It may have become more frequent after the Australian-imposed peace, thereby favouring mobility between groups, but it is certain that at least a handful of people spoke the language of the trading partners or affines they visited from time to time.

Worldwide many examples of imperfectly congruent cultural and linguistic areas can be found. In the case of the Anga, however, a strong coincidence between language and culture exists on two levels. The Anga linguistic family as it has just been defined correlates closely with representations and practices which will be shown in this article to constitute one vast homogeneous culture with regard to the whole of Papua New Guinea. It is possible to further divide the Anga tribes into several continuous sets that share similar technical practices, social organisation and systems of representation, and which, in the majority of cases, correspond precisely to the different Anga languages (see below).[8] For instance, the Baruya language is spoken by the members of five tribes, each of which has its own territory and political organisation.[9] Likewise, marriage, residence pattern, cooperation in performing tasks, initiations, male domination, warfare and land-holding, take similar forms in all these Baruya-speaking tribes and, in most cases, contrast with those found in neighbouring groups.

Sometimes two Anga groups speak different languages but have very similar social organisations — the case of the Baruya and the Simbari, two geographically close groups whose vocabularies also show the greatest degree of similarity (65 per cent); the reverse is not found, however: in the present state of our knowledge,[10] the sociocultural heterogeneity observed between same-language tribes is always much less than that observed between one linguistic group and another. For example, at the far western edge of the Anga territory, the small lowland groups living along the Vailala River have, at first glance, very similar patterns of territorial occupation and use. Whether one takes the Sambia, the Ankave, the Ivori or the Lohiki, their low population density, their mobility, their dispersed residential pattern or the relative importance of hunting and gathering compared with horticulture, all contrast with the way the members of these same groups live at higher altitudes. And yet, beyond these apparent similarities, each small lowland community is sociologically much closer to the other members of its own linguistic group, with which it shares a political organisation, kinship system, world view and male-initiation system, than with other semi-nomadic groups which are geographically close but belong to a different Anga group.

The number of tribes thus speaking a given Anga language *and* having the same social organisation and system of representations varies from one (among the Ankave, Ivori, Lohiki) to more than a half dozen (the Menye and the Kapau-Kamea): it is roughly proportional to the number of people who speak each Anga language, which ranges from fewer than a thousand (Ankave, Ivori, Lohiki) to tens of thousands (more than 15,000 for the Menye and more than 30,000 for the Kapau-Kamea).

To sum up: language is a primary criterion of sameness and difference for the Anga, based on an evaluation of relative similarities or differences. Any Anga language bears more resemblance to any other Anga language than to a non-Anga language, whether or not the latter is geographically close. For the sake of simplicity, I will use the term 'Anga culture' for the set of all tribes speaking an Anga language, keeping in mind that each Anga language corresponds to one or several tribes which make up a subset of this culture, with its own characteristics. These will now be examined.[11]

Material culture

All Anga are horticulturalists, in other words farmers working small fields (0.1–2.5 ha) — referred to as 'gardens' in the literature because of the large number of species grown and the individual attention given each plant — cleared for the most part in the forest. Tubers (taros and sweet potatoes) ensure the bulk of the diet, but large quantities of sugar cane, bananas and leafy vegetables are also produced.[12] Everyone also raises pigs (in reality domesticated wild pigs, *Sus scrofa papuensis*). Hunting plays a marginal role in the diet, but game (marsupials, wild pig, cassowary) occupies a fundamental place in initiation rituals and exchanges (particularly between affines). Compared with other parts of the island, the intensity of Anga horticulture and husbandry is middling. For instance, the Anga do not dig their gardens, make compost, or use manure or mounding, practices which in other areas are designed to produce the large quantities of tubers needed to feed their bigger herds.[13] Nevertheless, although these negative features of Anga farming go hand in hand with the absence of large numbers of animals and therefore with the lack of any developed system of ceremonial exchanges involving pigs, they do not suffice to characterise a particular sociocultural grouping.

There are, however, some techniques which are peculiar to the Anga.[14] This is the case of several objects (bee-hive shaped dwellings set on low pilings, men's grass skirts made of thick layers of flattened aquatic plants, a belt incorporating two cassowary femurs marking the groin, eel-traps), and at least one complex practice, the production of salt from a plant. Alongside these specifically Angan artifacts or practices, there are many other technical features that can be found in other New Guinea groups (or in other parts of the world); but their *simultaneous* presence tells us we are among the Anga. For instance, many human groups shave the top of the head almost entirely, leaving only a topknot; likewise clubs with a stone head in the shape of a ball, a disc, a star or a pineapple are frequent in New Guinea. But a man wearing this haircut *and* carrying such a club is sure to be an Anga. The same conclusion can be drawn upon seeing a person wearing a barkcloth cape and a grass skirt as described above, or strips of cowrie shells and plaited stalks of orchids across his chest and standing in front of a bee-hive-shaped house, and so on. Not only are these elements of material culture found in one form or another in all Anga groups, they are rigorously absent from neighbouring societies. And *vice versa*, several traditional techniques found in neighbouring groups are not used by the Anga. In the northwestern part of their territory, for example, just across the Lamari River, people sleep on headrests, the men's houses have a centre post, men braid long artificial locks into their hair, and so on. Furthermore, in the case of all these objects and practices, there is no intermediary situation. Clearly, material culture is one of the areas in which the Anga and their neighbours inscribe their identity: and use of the technical features described above disappears *de facto* as soon as one steps outside the Anga territory.

Of course the Anga share a host of techniques with other groups in New Guinea: their way of making fire, use of the adze and digging stick, use of bows and arrows, use of bamboo as a container, and so forth. The important point is that several objects and even entire techniques are either peculiar to them or radically unknown to them, and that these technical peculiarities or these absences are observed in all Anga linguistic groups. In themselves this assemblage of technical features — which have no functional significance here — does not say a lot about Anga social organisation in general.[15] There is no question of reverting here to nineteenth-century German evolutionism and characterising a population by an assortment of objects for which some *a posteriori* meaning has been imagined, I simply want to point out a second type of cultural production — techniques — which, like language, have features that, by their very existence, differentiate the Anga from the other populations of New Guinea: for instance, a wrapped bar of Anga salt looks like nothing else on earth.

By their simple presence (or absence) — that is what we are talking about and not the relative frequency of a phenomenon — the vocabulary items or the techniques just discussed are cultural features which set the Anga apart from any other population in New Guinea. In addition, the groups delineated in this way happen in this case to be rigorously identical. Nevertheless, even though there are links between language and techniques, among the Anga as elsewhere,[16] this particular coincidence in the mapping of two kinds of sociological phenomena does not imply any particular relation between them.[17] Very little is known of the history and the internal consistency of Anga languages or techniques, although specialists may one day succeed in restoring them. This perfect coincidence merely tells the outside observer that, at least two areas — Anga thinking and their practices — show a pronounced degree of homogeneity and originality which clearly distinguish the Anga from the other populations of the island. We shall see that these same groups are also set apart by the overall form and logic of their social organisations.

The Anga in the New Guinea setting

Although no systematic study has yet been devoted to the internal consistency of the Anga's languages or their technical acts,[18] we do have comparative studies and regional overviews of the social organisations of New Guinea which show both the Anga's specificity and their place within the broader set of Melanesian systems. Of course, many of the features of social organisation found among the Anga are present in other groups as well. Take, for example, various aspects of the kinship system (e.g. sister-exchange), representations of attacks on the body (by invisible spirits and so forth), land-holding (reversion of right of use to the descendants of the original clearer), political organisation (power linked with success in war) or male—female relations (role of initiations in the reproduction of male domination). Conversely, certain practices are less developed among the Anga than in other Melanesian societies, or are totally unknown. Of course, *each of these practices is not meaningful in itself, but as a component of a particular social logic.* Maurice Godelier was the first to underscore this consistency, following his analysis of a northern Anga group, the Baruya.[19] This strictly Angan configuration — which defines Great Men societies — is opposed both to the basic configuration of Big Men systems, illustrated by the majority of Highlands societies,[20] and to that found in the coastal groups of southern New Guinea.[21] As we shall see, alternating comparison and analysis of each of these three types of social logic will enable us both to develop general models that contrast these logics *and* to refine our understanding of Anga social organisation itself.

Via Big Men: discovering Great Men
The ethnology of the central Highlands tribes of what is today the independent State of Papua New Guinea, who most resemble the Anga in terms of their environment and forms

of agriculture and husbandry, underlines the place of ceremonial exchanges of wealth and the political status of the organisers of these exchanges, generally referred to as 'Big Men'. When one of these events is to be held, the members of a group (often a clan or a local group, but sometimes a whole tribe) are mobilised more or less regularly in view of presenting gifts of various goods to the representatives of another group. The latter reciprocates at some later time by in turn giving to those who created this obligation an equal or greater quantity of the same items of wealth. In the eastern Highlands, such exchanges entail small amounts of goods and take place during the performance of fertility cults and male initiations.[22] In the west, on the other hand, considerable quantities of wealth are manipulated, and their ostentatious distribution to the guests is the focal point of these encounters, whose relative success or failure reflects on the reputation of the groups present and affects the quality of their relations until the return exchange, usually several years later.

The primary aim is to gather at the most opportune time a sufficient amount of wealth: especially pigs (which will be given live or in the form of meat and fat), but also valuable shells, feathers or cosmetic oils. In preparation for these events, whose success provides the basis of their prestige and their political foundation, the Big Men of each clan or tribe enlist their dependents, who may be kinsmen, neighbours, refugees to whom they give land or young men they are helping to marry by providing part of the bridewealth.

Full-blown ceremonial exchanges are the most visible expression of an original complex of social relations in which several of the most characteristic features of these societies are combined and interwoven. In fact, on the occasion of such events, all manner of personal gifts are made at the time as a group receives a collective gift. For, if a Big Man speaks and acts on behalf of his followers, those who helped him amass the wealth also give some of the items to guests with whom they have a personal relationship: affines, maternal kin, members of a clan or a lineage on whom they themselves have inflicted losses in battle which must be compensated. As a number of studies have shown, it is because the same items of wealth (essentially pigs and shells) are used in the various types of ceremonial gift-giving that these can take place simultaneously.[23] In particular, payment of bridewealth and gifts accompanying the growth of children or payment of homicide compensation belong to the same exchange sphere as the intergroup ceremonial prestations. In other words, the animals or the shells received on the occasion of a marriage may be used in turn for personal or collective gifts of another order. Since intergroup exchanges are always in some way connected with the processes of compensating for killings by which peace is established and preserved, it is in the end the possibility of considering pigs[24] as a substitute for a life which lies at the heart of these ceremonial exchange systems.[25]

But equating pig meat with human life is only a necessary condition for these simultaneous ceremonial prestations. If intergroup exchanges occupy a central place in group life and embody such a range of social relations, it is also because various political, matrimonial, economic and other institutions assume forms that are not only mutually compatible but mutually reinforcing. In a Big Men society, peacemaking and peacekeeping procedures, intergroup competition and marriage are all features of social reality involving the manipulation of wealth by Big Men; and the social relations they activate or the prestige they procure in one area have repercussions on the other areas of social life. Therefore the Big

Man's characteristic skill at manipulating wealth is as useful to him in making peace as it is in organising the ceremonial exchanges proper; and from his success in ending conflicts, he reaps the prestige he uses to attract the followers who aid him in his economic ventures. Another particularity of these societies: in many circumstances, relations between individuals or between groups give rise to activities that fuel both the mechanisms of ceremonial exchanges and the Big Men's strategies. For example, young men seeking a wife, refugees or the unfortunate outcastes known in the literature as 'rubbish men', all those who receive help from a Big Man generally reciprocate by raising pigs for him.[26] Likewise, the enemy or ally who receives a homicide compensation[27] often goes on to become an affine as well as an exchange partner and rival. Big Men are richer than the common man: they have more wives, who combine their labour to raise a bigger herd; their greater number of marriages also means that these men have more affines (who are privileged exchange partners) and therefore find it easier to obtain wealth or to cause it to circulate.

Visibly at every turn there is a web of actors and social relations which translates into a circulation of wealth orchestrated by Big Men. These converging and mutually reinforcing behaviours and institutions, all of which come into play in intergroup ceremonial exchanges, constitute a social logic specific to the Highlands.[28] Activation of the principles of social organisation discussed above does not always yield as tightly woven, coherent a fabric of personal and group relations as that found in the Big Men Societies in the western part of the region (the most representative), but everywhere: 1) compensations for life and death generally take the form of gifts of wealth; 2) political power is based on skill in negotiating peace, organising intergroup exchanges and building up a following of dependents; and 3) the pig exchanges mobilise the minds, energies and hopes of individuals and groups alike.

Although the Anga share some similarities with the central Highlands groups, the two models contrast radically. Comparing the central Highlands pattern with his analysis of Baruya social organisation, Godelier saw that the links between the various areas of social reality that made Big Men societies so original involved the very features that were absent or altogether marginal in Anga groups, namely: regular ceremonial exchanges between groups, political power bound up with the manipulation of wealth, and systematic use of pigs in the gifts accompanying marriage or compensation for the life of warriors killed in battle.

By way of contrast, in a Great Men society, the group is mobilised by war and male initiations.[29] Around these two events revolve three main hierarchies which structure the life of the society: the ranking of Great Men among themselves (masters of the initiations and great warriors; sometimes great shamans); the subordination of all women to the men as a group; the authority of the oldest men over first-stage initiates. At the centre of this system of institutions and social relations stands, in the mind of every Anga — albeit to a varying degree — the idea that women's sexuality is detrimental to men, that it saps their warlike spirit and therefore jeopardizes the survival of the group. The initiations give the men physical and moral strength; it is also in this framework that they are taught the practical knowledge which enables them to compensate for this dangerous state of affairs. And at the same time, these rituals found and regularly confirm male domination.

It is therefore entirely logical that the figures exercising positions of direct responsibility in initiations or warfare should be those who, because they were born into a particular lineage (masters of the initiations) or owing to their personal talents (great warriors or shamans) rise above other men. Intra- or intergroup exchanges of wealth are very limited. The only collective ceremonies of this kind are feasts at which a tribe or a local group presents itself with cooked vegetable foods and game at the same time as it honours new initiates. Yet 'wealth' (shells and vegetal salt) is not absent from other exchanges; but given the limited circulation, and above all as we shall see below, given the relative compartmentalisation of prestations, the absence of intergroup relations based on the giving of wealth does not leave room for an organiser of exchanges like the Big Man.

This schema varies from one Anga linguistic group to another, but the relations between the political sphere, male—female relations, warfare and initiations are in all events those described above. For example, Pascale Bonnemère's analysis of the Ankave case shows that the elements brought into play and enacted during male initiations vary with the local theories about how children are made and grow.[30] Ritualised homosexuality — fellatio practiced by the initiates on the older boys — for example is found only where semen is regarded as the primary substance needed for a child's conception and growth in the uterus. These theories in turn affect the way the men block out their own use of female substances or powers in the course of the initiations to re-engender the young boys and turn them into adult warriors. Likewise, any role ascribed to women in the making of a human being or an adult man appears to have a direct correlation with their status in the society.[31]

The war/initiations/male domination complex is obviously not the only one whose social organisation turns out to have important variants when Anga societies are compared. But it is striking that, for each area examined so far, it is *the same* elements that are combined differently from one group to another. We have seen this to be true for the variants in the form and content of male initiations, which faithfully reflect the (different) theories about the production of human beings. A similar situation appears in the connections the Anga make between sickness, attacks on the body and preservation of the social order. All groups in this set share the idea that, with a few exceptions, individual bodily dysfunction results from harmful actions performed by another person or by a spirit following some behaviour that has upset the social order. But the correspondence established between the various types of attack on the body, sickness or symptoms, and the particular sociological context varies from group to group according precisely to those features which oppose their ways of maintaining good relations — i.e. relations deemed normal and desirable — between kin and neighbours. Whether or not the carriers of disease are manipulated by magical means in order to weaken the opponent — if they are, the pathogenic agents extracted from the patient's body are systematically directed towards enemy territory[32] — determines whether or not the shamans take part in making war, which in turn alters their political role as well as the way they acquire their powers.[33] Furthermore, within the local group, the contexts and forms of aggression on the body (sorcery or attack by invisible spirits) reinforce the rules of good conduct, which are precisely those that distinguish a group. For example, among the Ankave, these practices and the resulting sicknesses remind everyone of the necessity of not neglecting the exchanges and the sharing of food and objects around which the life of the society is built. Baruya sorcery, on the other hand, stresses an implicit reference to cooperation in tasks and in sister-exchange.[34]

It is the existence of variations affecting *limited* sets of elements (like theories of conception and growth, initiations, or invisible actions on the body and their disease-carrying agents and how these relate to maintaining social harmony), *together* with the fact that they intervene in the framework of specific and always identical social patterns (the making of warriors out of range of the women's debilitating influence, punishment of deviant behaviour by sickness) which justify speaking of *one* culture, an original set of institutions, practices and representations around which each Anga group has developed its own specificities. By comparing the monographs on these societies, it is possible gradually to define the overarching structure, the framework common to all their social organisations, and at the same time to identify the areas and ways in which these are dissimilar, and the extent of their differences.

Reassessing the role of wealth among the Anga

The multiplication of ethnographic studies on the Anga had one noteworthy result, which was to confront the Great Men model of society, elaborated by Maurice Godelier from his own work with the Baruya, with the data gathered in other groups. We have seen that, in Anga societies as a whole, the principal hierarchies are, first, the distinction between Great Men and the rest of the male population and, second, men's domination of women. None of these societies holds intergroup feasts, and the manipulation of wealth does not provide a base for political power. Power here lies with the men in charge of a complex of institutions in which are tightly interwoven war and the mechanism of initiations by which the men preserve and reproduce their fighting abilities while at the same time keeping the women, and to a lesser extent the young initiates, in a position of inferiority.

The main result of these comparative studies on the Anga is that, in each tribe, we find that core of relations which Godelier showed to be central, consistent and endowed with a social 'logic'. More specifically, whatever variants we found offered no indication that male initiations were not *regularly* to be designated as a crucial institution in these societies, ensuring each time the two main functions underscored by Godelier: 'constructing a collective force of all the men, held together within their generation by a bond stronger than anything that could divide them', but also with respect to women, presented as 'a constant source of danger for men and especially a danger for the reproduction of the society as such'.[35] It could be added that, at the same time as the men themselves ensure that the bodies of the young men emerge matured and hardened from a complex process that protects them from women's harmful powers — a process nonetheless based on female procreative powers — they also equip the initiate's mind and at the same time that of all the men, to withstand that other threat to the warrior: terror of the enemy. Male initiations are a school of courage, constantly teaching the warrior both endurance and mastery of his own fear.[36]

Comparative Anga ethnography also confirms the absence of that central pillar of the *Big Man complex*: political power based on the manipulation of wealth. More broadly speaking, it confirms the opposition between the world of Great Men and that of Big Men, in which 'the role of wealth in relations within a society ... seems to lessen the necessity of constructing male domination through ... the initiations'.[37] Conversely, Godelier's hypothesis of a connection between initiations and marriage by sister-exchange without bridewealth[38] must no doubt be abandoned. Most Anga groups do indeed practise a form of marriage involving the obligation to make gifts of wealth to the wife-givers, notably in the form of bridewealth, and this is done without the slightest emphasis on sister-exchange.[39] Nevertheless, all these societies have Great Men who fit the Baruya prototype trait for trait, and all place male initiations at the top of their list of collective events. At the same time, intergroup exchanges of wealth are not found in any group. In other words, if the Anga situation is counter-proof that, without generalised circulation of wealth, there is no room for Big Men,[40] conversely it shows just as categorically that marriage with bridewealth in the totality of cases is by no means inconsistent with a Great Man system.[41] Perhaps there is some particularity of northern Angan initiations (Baruya, Sambia) — for example ritualised homosexuality — that is in some way connected with the dominant mode of marriage in these societies, which is sister-exchange. But the male initiations themselves, as they are generally performed by the Anga, do not appear to be linked to any particular type of marriage. Likewise, it is no longer possible to consider that the small scale of the exchanges of wealth among the Anga stems from the fact that 'the production of kinship relations is not based on the accumulation of material wealth [and that there is therefore] little inducement to produce such items of wealth, especially pigs'.[42] The ethnography shows two factors at work here: a scale or threshold effect when it comes to the respective *quantities* of wealth manipulated by Big Men, and a phenomenon of *quality*, since the very way this wealth is used plays a crucial role.

In all Anga groups, marriage alliances include a series of gifts to the bride's people: game, pig meat, labour. Where the dominant form is direct or deferred sister-exchange, gifts of wealth are not directly involved. In particular, no bridewealth is given. But this does not mean wealth is absent from the ceremonies marking the stages of the life cycle. In Baruya groups, for example, even two generations after a marriage for which a woman was not given in return, and in spite of the birth of many daughters and granddaughters to the couple, the descendants of the original bride's paternal and maternal kin demand a compensating gift of wealth from the wife-takers' lineage. An identical payment — comprised of strings of cowrie shells, vegetal salt, barkcloth capes and, today, Papua New Guinea currency, but never including pig meat — must be paid when, following a marriage by 'sister'-exchange, one of the women has borne many more children than the other. In other words, even in a group where sister-exchange is central, wealth plays a potential role in marriage.[43]

Among the Ankave, whose form of marriage involves bridewealth, the payment is presented as compensation for the body of the bride, for the labour she will provide and for the children she will bear; the emphasis is on the (relative) break with her paternal group and on the affiliation of her children to her husband's group.[44] The other shell-gifts are made at the time of a boy's initiation, after a death and in compensation for a killing following a feud or at the conclusion of peace with the enemy. The point common to all these gifts of shells is that they occur in extremely *well-defined* contexts. A specific context usually calls for a specific type of shell. The pearl-shell a maternal uncle gives his newly initiated nephew is the only possible response (*potije* gift) to the pig killed for him earlier in compensation for having been struck at the same time as his nephew during the initiations (*sɔmoe'* gift): the *sɔmoe'* must be a whole pig (that has been killed) and the corresponding counter-gift must be a pearl-shell. Likewise, the brideprice (*abɔxɔ' nɔguɔ'*, lit.: money for the woman) is paid to the bride's paternal kin in the form of strings of cowrie shells invariably placed on top of the haunches of pig meat for the maternal kin. Compensation for a killed warrior must be composed of an assortment of shells, but must never include any game or pig meat. In each case, the circumstances of the gift, its direction and the kind of object given are very clearly defined. Interestingly, these exchanges involving shells reproduce a feature common to all Ankave ceremonial gift-exchanges, even those having nothing to do with wealth. For instance, the gift presented to the maternal kin of a woman who is pregnant for the first time can only be comprised of pig meat; the gifts given the cross-cousins of the deceased at the ceremony concluding a mourning period are smoked eels, and so forth.

Ultimately, analysis of the Anga's uses of wealth and particularly its circulation in the prestations marking the life-cycle stages reveals the extreme *compartmentalisation* of the exchanges in which these goods feature. Unlike the world of Big Men, where pigs are regarded as a sort of universal equivalent that can be used in a great number of gifts and transactions, the Anga exchange many kinds of 'objects', and in most cases one kind cannot be substituted for another: a gift of game cannot be replaced by a gift of shells, and a shell cannot replace a piece of pig meat. Animal meat is generally used to compensate the care given to the body and its growth, while shells repay a group for the loss of one of its members. Even shells have narrowly defined uses; often a particular circumstance calls for a particular kind of shell. The 'commercial' sphere allows certain substitutions: for example, vegetal salt functions as a currency, in other words as a universal equivalent, among the Baruya.[45] Likewise, the Ankave seem always to have purchased pig meat with cowrie shells. But the possibility of substituting one kind of goods for another is strictly limited to such economic relations.

Compared with a society like the Baruya, where the predominant marriage pattern is the two-way exchange of women, Big Men societies are characterised, as I have said, by a single sphere of exchange in which marriage and all manner of compensation processes involve the transfer of wealth. But with respect to other Anga groups which exchange wealth for women — and in general to compensate human lives — the circulation of wealth in Big Men systems is distinguished by decompartmentalised exchanges: goods of a same type or those that are direct substitutes for each other (e.g. pigs and shells) are used indifferently for a great variety of gifts. In Big Men societies what is given and the circumstances of the gift are still clearly set out, but the bulk of the gifts are comprised of pigs — either living or in the form of cooked meat.[46]

Such compartmentalisation of exchanges is typical of Anga societies (and by extension, of Great Men societies) and functions as a curb on large-scale movements of wealth. The use of shells or vegetal salt to compensate the life of warriors killed in battle is another. By excluding pigs from the goods used to indemnify a group following a killing, the Anga also preclude any possibility of prolonging the peacemaking ceremonies by a peaceful form of rivalry based on the exchange of pigs.[47] Finally, the limited importance of pigs in Angan exchanges goes hand in hand with a minimum use of 'financing', which is so central to the prestations and politico-economic strategies of Big Men.

Wealth and Great Men: reassessing the model

The foregoing close-up of the way the Anga manipulate wealth helps to refine the opposition between Great Men and Big Men on one of the axes defined by Godelier, but it accounts only in part for the forms of exchange and the place of politics in Anga society. There are known cases of groups in southern New Guinea that make a limited use of pigs in their compensation procedures (marriage, homicide, peacemaking), but which have gone on to develop competitive exchanges of *vegetable goods*; and these exchanges are explicitly presented as substitutes for armed violence. Yet owing to the absence of 'financing', which is in turn linked to the absence of pigs in these ceremonies, there are no Big Men in these societies.[48] In other words, although analysis of the Anga's use of wealth shows how they differ from Big Men societies, it says nothing about the absence of linkage between politics and the exchanges which, together with a particular way of associating war and male-female relations through the initiations, globally characterise the world of Great Men. Once again it is the confrontation of Anga ethnology with other types of societies in New Guinea — and I use the much-disparaged word, 'type', deliberately — that enables us better to circumscribe the areas of social reality and the relations which underpin the specificity of Great Men systems as illustrative of specific social logics.

Compared with the Big Men societies of the western Papua New Guinea Highlands and with the societies on the southern coast of the big island, the Anga are distinguished first of all by the *absence of intergroup ceremonial exchanges*, something anthropology might legitimately be expected to account for. The societies on the southern coast of New Guinea are ample proof that the nature of the goods available for such exchanges does not in itself explain their absence: just as the members of these societies vie perfectly well to outgive each other in vegetable goods, so the Anga have no lack of game or cultivated plants whose exchange could *a priori* give rise to rivalry, not to mention pigs, which could easily be raised more intensively given the potential of their environment and their agriculture. Therefore what needs to be explained is the absence of intergroup exchanges themselves.

To do justice to this question would exceed the scope of the present article. But it is possible to posit that this absence depends not so much on a single factor as on several features of Anga social structures which are mutually reinforcing, in other words, on a coherent set of practices and representations that leaves no room for such exchanges.[49] In the first place, all Anga groups have food-giving ceremonies, planned in advance and requiring additional labour on the part of individuals and the group: these are the feasts marking the end of the initiations. At these times, the whole community, usually a valley or an entire tribe,[50] gives tubers (and often game) to the initiates and their 'sponsors'. When this ceremonial food has been distributed, most of the other people present consume the leftover meat and the piles of tubers that have been baked for the occasion. Anga ceremonial exchanges are therefore inward-looking, with the communities actually making gifts of food to themselves.

Of course this characteristic is not in itself inconsistent with intergroup exchanges; but it may be comparable to a tendency observed on the southern coast of New Guinea, where cooperative events are associated with the reproduction of the group as a group, and particularly with regard to external enemies. Are the importance of these common initiations and their relation to war incompatible with all peaceful relations with the outside, in other words with enemies? Could it be that, for some reason, each group of societies in New Guinea chooses to engage in a *limited* number of collective events: war and intergroup exchanges for Big Men societies, war and initiations for the Great Men? The south coast groups showed that this is not so, since, in addition to their intense practise of a warlike activity (headhunting), they also organised male initiations and intergroup exchanges. Nevertheless, these societies did not seem to have had masters of rituals, that is forms of political power based on the monopoly of access to the invisible, in this particular context. Power accrued first of all to the great warriors — who were often mediums as well — and then to the owners of gardening magic, whose talents qualified them for second place as organisers of the ceremonial exchanges of vegetable goods.[51] The determining factor seems therefore to be the *number of sites in which political power can be exercised.*

In New Guinea, before the upheavals wrought by contact with the outside world, the four areas of life in which political activity might be rooted were warfare, monopoly of access to the invisible, initiations and ceremonial exchanges. These areas could overlap, but for some reason, the rule seems to have been that, in a given society all four were rarely developed at the same time. The Anga political arena was dominated by the great warriors and the masters of the initiations, as though no room remained for a third form of political power connected, for instance, with the creation of economic exchanges. To this must be added the rigidity, even the ranking,[52] of the political positions in Anga societies: for instance, the great warrior's power falls dormant for the duration of the male initiations; and *vice versa*, the master of the initiations barely has the right to voice an opinion outside the male rituals. The areas of political life are clearly segregated, both by sector (war, initiations) and by period of activity, and nothing argues for the existence of any political rivalry centred on the organisation of ceremonial exchanges.

No one feature of social organisation just discussed seems sufficiently determining in itself to exclude all possibility of peaceful intergroup exchanges among the Anga. But everything suggests that this characteristic of Anga societies arises from the conjunction of these features and their mutual reinforcement, which is altogether real; for every feature mentioned relates directly to the link between war and initiations that is central to the collective undertakings of these groups and which affects (or used to affect) even the most humble features of daily life.

Anga identity: 'mipela wan bilas'

First man

This survey of Anga culture would be incomplete without a rapid discussion of the way the Anga represent and experience their membership in a particular tribe as well as their inclusion in a much broader ethnic group. It is one thing to show how comparison between the Anga ethnography and that of other groups in New Guinea enables us to define the salient features of Great Men societies, and by means of successive contrasts, to refine the social logics that demarcate the island's vast sociocultural groupings. But how do the Anga themselves define and reproduce various sociological units? How does each Anga group perceive the other neighbouring or more remote groups? In short, how do they explicitly or implicitly determine their own identity?

Until the 1950s or 1960s — and even today in the case of the most isolated groups — the members of an Anga tribe knew very little about the world beyond the ridges and streams bounding their territory. Sporadic visits were made to the neighbouring valleys,[53] where there were enemies, trading partners or affines, but more remote hamlets were known only from hearsay. Even today, aside from a few politicians or administrators, only ethnologists and linguists know the exact tribal make-up and the geography of what we call the 'Anga' ethnic group.[54] Many Anga know that there used to be an *Anga balus* ('the Anga airplane', in Tok Pisin; it flew in the 1980s) or that an all-province Anga Development Authority, created in the late 1970s, oversees Anga community rural development. But for most Anga people, awareness of an Angan entity distinct from other peoples of Papua New Guinea came only after the Australian government imposed its peace, which made it possible for Angans to travel without having to fear for their lives. Only when they began to leave to work on the plantations (between 1955 and 1975, as a rule) did the Anga realise that their neighbours were not the only ones who wore grass skirts, barkcloth capes and body ornaments very similar to their own, or that those who wore these same *bilas* were only a small portion of humanity.

All Angans were nevertheless conscious of belonging to an overarching set of tribes, which they saw as including between a third and half of the groups we ethnologists now know to comprise the Anga culture. This set was *de facto* identified with *all* humanity. For each tribe, this inclusion in a larger unit was (and still is) legible in the relations with other Anga tribes — who spoke different languages and had different customs — but also and above all in a *common* history, several episodes of which often form the basis of the initiation rituals.[55] In particular, every linguistic group situates its beginnings and *those of the whole community of 'wan bilas'* somewhere around Menyamya, usually near a cliff a few kilometres west of the present-day Menyamya administrative post.[56] Each tribe surrounds the location and the name of the hole from which humans emerged — in this instance the Anga, but some informants have no qualms about adding Europeans — with utmost secrecy, even though they know they share these secrets with other Angans. The origin myths say that the first man to come into our world — the 'middle' world for the Ankave, who will serve here as our example — gave those who followed him — the respective ancestors of the different linguistic groups — their language and their body ornaments, before each set out on the long trail that eventually led them to their present-day territory. Several of these myths also tell how the bones of one of these first men were shared out among all the groups and were made into the awls used to pierce the septums of the boy initiates. In one version of the Ankave myth, for example, the man whose bones played this crucial role was put to death 'because he had no name' — a radical as well as spectacular way of reserving human status for the Anga alone![57] From his blood sprang the red cordylines that generation after generation of Ankave have cut and used to mark out and decorate the sacred enclosures where they initiate the boys and which they then replant near the house of the master of the initiations. The blood also soaked into the ground where it had spilled, and this earth is magically preserved in a bamboo tube and rubbed on the initiates' bodies. The man's spirit showed the first master of the initiations how to make the young boys grow and make them strong.[58] This 'history' belongs to the Anga groups twice over, for it is found in the origin myths of several groups, and the content itself refers to a common origin. It thus both creates a bond between the Ankave and the other Anga groups and, through the use or the sharing of objects or substances that go back to mythic times, it binds men together, diachronically (from the time the Ankave appeared on earth and learned to turn boys into adult men) and synchronically (among all the initiates of a given group).[59] The Ankave bone-awl is only one component of their *oxemɔxɔ*', a magic bundle whose powers are activated by the masters of the initiations when it comes time for the rituals. The *oxemɔxɔ*', too, appeared when the Anga emerged from the ground, so that, in the event one of these objects was destroyed, they were able to procure one from a neighbouring group. One last example of the Anga's common past evoked in the initiations: in one of the 'lessons' taught Ankave initiates, the origin of the rituals is explicitly associated with the appearance on earth of the Ankave tribe and the other Anga groups.

Reference to this common past is made in one form or another in every group, especially during the initiations. For J. Mimica, in the Iqwaye ceremonies during the male rituals, 'every boy ... enacts the stages of primordial creation of the first men'[60] that occurred at Kokwayakawa, which is none other than the Baruya's Bravegareubaramandeuc, the Sambia's Kokoyoko and the Ankave's Obixwa.[61] Periodically the Baruya go to the site of their origins to pick the magic leaves required for their masculine rites.[62]

The male initiations are not the only time their shared origin plays a role in Ankave ritual life. At mourning ceremonies, they sing dirges recalling the stages of their slow migration through territories that now belong to other groups. In an entirely different domain, the spells recited silently before setting a trap evoke the overcrowded men's houses in the groups with whom the Ankave lived in some distant past, a way of encouraging the masters of wild game to let them capture many animals. It is also the opinion that different clans, and thus the linguistic groups in which they prevail, have over the course of their mythic history acquired distinctive traits: one clan climbed up a tall column of smoke into the sky to get bananas and sugar cane; another is associated with the origin of the moon and fire, or initiations; others still brought humans dirges, barkcloth capes, vegetal salt and so forth. At the tribal level, the members of certain clans specialise in specific functions or tasks, either because they are recognized as having a particular aptitude — the Baruya have warrior and shaman clans[63] — or because they have inherited a ritual object and/or specific knowledge — the case of the masters of the initiations in all groups. Possession of such an object may be traced back to the beginning of time (the case of the Baruya *kwaimatnie*, given by Sun and Moon before today's humans ever saw the light of day)[64] or to the original distribution of languages, body ornaments and ritual instruments. But possession is also the outcome of historical processes that have led various clans (sometimes lineages) of the same tribe to specialise in certain tasks which they perform at given points in the male initiations.[65]

This history of the sharing out of a symbolic activity, or if one prefers of setting in place a complementary functioning of clans and tribes, anchors part of the Anga political order in a remote past. Besides the ranking of Great Men discussed above,[66] it institutes the initiations, sets their content and justifies the segregation of women from what is seen as crucial knowledge. At the same time, however, this history also stresses the wholeness of Anga culture as well as the specificity of the various social units that comprise it. In other words, regular reference to a mythical past held to be common to all Anga — of which each tribe obviously has its own version — is also a prime component of the identity of each linguistic group (read: cultural subset) and of each tribe, but also of each Anga clan. We will now see that knowledge of the *individual* history of each tribe plays a similar role.

Us and the others: building a tribal identity

Each tribe identifies with a specific past comprised of migrations, natural catastrophes, wars and peaces, or marriage alliances. Being a member of a tribe means subscribing to its past as its members imagine it at a given moment; it means adopting a large portion of the friends, enemies, trials or heroic ancestors of all those, in one or several valleys, who consider they have a territory to defend in common and who work together to reproduce their physical existence and their social order.[67] This past itself defines an identity: for instance, 'we' are those who are willing to go to war against or alongside those that our tribal history designates (even temporarily) as enemies or friends. Or again, taking the lower-ranking social units such as the clans in a given territory: 'we' are those whom our ancestors led to a given valley or hamlet in a more or less recent past.[68]

All members of a tribe hold in common various cultural representations and social institutions, which they also share with the members of the other tribes that make up their linguistic group. For example, they acknowledge having a particular way of dealing with their dead, of managing the forest, of initiating their children or of acquiring a spouse. Like the more immediately visible identity markers — 'costumes' and body ornaments, type of house, bows or arrows and so forth[69] — these practices and their corresponding representations are seen as distinguishing elements of a cultural (and linguistic) community. The distinctive features of each group may be listed in response to the ethnographer's questions, but they are also spontaneously forthcoming when the Anga talk about their neighbours. Sometimes, when telling war stories or when on a trading expedition or a 'patrol' with some missionary, government official or ethnologist, someone will inspect a tree or a fruit and explain its use (or the fact that this is unknown). Or, as the Ankave do, recall that a frightful war followed by large-scale migration was triggered by some women who had made fun of the grass skirts worn by the neighbours invited to their male initiations. But the points that elicit the most comment invariably involve whole sectors of the social organisation. The Ankave say:

> — With the Kamea, it is the women who squeeze the red
>   pandanus seeds!
> — The Iweto do not beat the drums when they mourn.
> — You know, with the Menye, its people who eat men,
>   not the *ombɔ'* [spirits]!

The most startling case — at any rate the most stupefying to hear — is no doubt the remarks made by the first Ankave man to visit the Baruya (to work on the Marawaka airstrip in the

1970s). Two things and only two had struck him: 1) the Baruya exchanged their sisters in marriage without giving bridewealth; and 2) Baruya women's septums were pierced. In other words, an Ankave traveller immediately puts his finger on two sociological phenomena — forms of marriage and the existence of female initiations — that occupy a prime position among those ethnologists identify and comment on for pages, if they do any travelling at all between groups (preferably on foot, but it can be in their minds, in their colleagues' books).

Sharing a history and recognising sociological specificities are obviously not the only elements that go into a tribe's identity. This history is constantly being reproduced (and transformed) through various collective practices.[70] Taking the Ankave as our example once again, three events are (or were) capable of drawing the bulk of the population of the three valleys that form the tribe's territory: first-stage initiations, war and final mourning rites. The male ceremonies alternated between the two principal Ankave valleys, with the specialists of each local group collaborating for the occasion.[71] As is often the case, what is periodically reconstituted during the initiations is the entire edifice of the tribe.[72] The unity of the tribe is also expressed in another area that is less tangible, but which indisputably concerns the whole Ankave group: that is the existence of a terrifying community of invisible man-eating spirits harboured and guided by humans (*ombɔ'*). These spirits periodically gang up on a given local group, even though their dwelling places are dispersed around the four corners of the territory.

The initiations, the ceremonies closing a mourning period, even when the *ombɔ'* from a neighbouring valley come to lend their colleagues a hand (or rather a 'tooth'), are all occasions for a division of labor which illuminates the complementarity of various members of the tribe: everyone takes part in the same event by performing complementary tasks, either all together or in turn. This is true for the masters of the initiations, who are responsible for whole ceremonies or specific ritual operations, but also help their colleagues in all circumstances, at least when the different Ankave valleys are at peace with each other. It is also the case when certain warriors from one local group support their cousins in border fights or when *ombɔ'* cross the mountains in the night to devour the corpse of a victim one of them has killed by magic.[73] It is true as well when an Ankave man goes to sing and beat the hour-glass drums for the ceremonies marking the end of mourning for a distant kinsman in a local community other than his own.

In all these circumstances, the battle, the rite or the ceremony is the more-or-less direct manifestation of a set of representations specific to a given culture (in this case the Ankave linguistic and cultural subset). But these individual events always concern a given community — the whole tribe or only the members of one of its constituent local groups, depending on the case. The simple act of excluding some of the other members of the group defines a social unit, resembling the others in structure or the meaning of the rites, exchanges or meetings it organises, but unique in the identity of those who participate. The evil deeds of a man-eating spirit, the warrior's zeal, the presence of a mourner, or the knowledge of a master of the initiations, each makes its contribution to a collective event, alternately as privileged actor or organiser (a specialist) and then as spectator or ordinary participant. The way these alternating collaborations contribute to the cohesion and the expression of the tribe's group identity varies,[74] but each time, they give rise to a mixture of sharing and complementarity of the type that underlies the distribution of the ritual objects among the different linguistic groups or clans of a tribe.

The informant, the comparatist and the model

Syntheses that attempt to distinguish Big Men and Great Men systems using a system of relations between a few social practices favour certain orders of phenomena at the expense of other *a priori* just-as-worthwhile features of the group under examination. So why all the fuss about such typologies. There are three reasons.

First because, far from simply 'fishing' for some sociological features to bolster up a foregone conclusion — a frequent criticism of comparative models[75] — the syntheses advanced for New Guinea begin with a study of the most salient institutions and social practices — presented as such by the informants themselves — in the groups studied.

Next, because the practices whose interrelations and consistency are confirmed by anthropological models in view of comparing contrasting forms of social organisation are not only those that mark stages in the collective life of these communities, but also those that serve to distinguish them from their neighbours and to construct and reproduce, year in year out, their social and cultural world: initiations, male-female relations, warfare, attacks by man-eating spirits, and so on.

Last of all, *these models take into account the greatest number of variables conjointly* (exchanges, marriage, the political sphere, male-female relations, use of the natural environment, war, peace) and relate them to each other in a meaningful way. They indicate which phenomena are linked, in each set of societies (Big Men and Great Men societies), and the nature of the relations between them. These relations obviously take a particular form in each group. For instance, among the Anga, as we have seen, where the particularities of the war/initiations/male domination complex have repercussions on the women's status, on the content and unfolding of the initiations, or on cooperation in performing tasks, the representation of the person is not identical in all groups, far from it. Nevertheless, the relations that are crystallised in the initiations and which form their foundation are connected in every case with gender relations, with incompatibilities of state between male and female bodies, with the ways they mature, with the need men have to block out the fact of using female powers to produce warriors on their own, and so forth. Each ethnographic reality is just as particular in Big Men societies. Even in New Guinea's Western Highlands province, where these figures come closest to the ideal-type described in the models, a study of the identity and the role of those taking part in exchanges (as givers or receivers), of the forms of marriage, the site of competition or even the nature of the groups participating reveals profound differences.[76] But in every case, the concrete societies accurately illustrate the model relations between marriage, homicide, compensation, intergroup competition or the organisation of exchanges. In other words, whatever their diversity, all so-called Big Men societies fit the general model established twenty-five years ago, and this model is opposed, as described above, to all forms of Anga social organisation inasmuch as these groups are Great Men societies corresponding rigorously to Godelier's model, even though each fits in its own way.

It can never be sufficiently stressed that the practices retained in these models mobilise the thoughts and actions of the members of these societies on an everyday basis. Thus, in spite of thirty to sixty years of 'contacts' with the outside world, exchanges, enemies, man-eating spirits and even, until very recently, the initiations still constantly occupy the thoughts of all Anga people. Likewise, in Big Men societies, preparations for ceremonial exchanges were and are still central to group life, especially when the resulting succession of 'alternating disequilibrium'[77] is the peaceful version of the eternal intergroup rivalries. Andrew Strathern explains that, unlike the new activities stemming from the market economy, the missions or the State, ceremonial exchanges are one of the key institutions which enable the Melpa to preserve their social identity with respect to the non-Melpa world.[78] In addition, the crucial character of the institutions and representations retained by the models has been emphasised in all monographs, whatever the date of the study or the author's school of thought. This answers another frequent charge that ethnologists and their informants are themselves incapable of appreciating the distance between an earlier state of the cultural systems they describe and their contemporary form, and notably of apprehending the changes that have occurred in the wake of the Western invasion.[79]

The logics described in the anthropological models make no claim to account for all specificities of the societies concerned or to reduce individual geniuses to a common essence. This would be futile, for each population has a social structure, techniques and symbolic systems whose richness and ultimate coherence can be fully expressed only by a monographic study. It would take several books to describe how the members of different and sometimes cross-cutting sociological units (tribe, valley, clan, lineage, valley local group) produce, exchange, share, celebrate or fight 'together'; how their feelings of loyalty shift with the context; and notably how the range of contexts itself changed after the monumental event of the Highlanders' discovery of the existence of white people. In particular, we would need to understand why certain of these 'focal institutions' that A. Strathern talks about gradually take a backseat in some groups, while they remain crucial for another group that is neither more nor less open to the outside.[80]

The multiplication of new situations — or if one prefers, the acceleration of history — favours comparative research. Though it would be good to consider the extent of the changes, which may vary in magnitude according to whether they are studied in the decades immediately following 'contact' or in a society that has suffered from more than a century of colonial violence. But unless he or she is working in a society that has been deeply transformed by indentured labour, the State, missions and the market — in which case the definition of a sociocultural identity can become an issue of knowledge and power — even the most experienced and tenacious ethnologist will never get even the most 'inward-looking' informants to systematically compare their way of life with those of other groups in their area. Undeniably, the Ankave man mentioned earlier put his finger on a fundamental point when he spontaneously contrasted Baruya marriage or initiations with the practices of his own group; but he knows *nothing* about the Anga groups on just the other side of the territory whose queer practices strike him. And systematic comparison of Anga cannibalism or study of the various bases of political power in New Guinea are the least of his worries.

An extremely meticulous monographic approach is indispensable for constructing and refining models; conversely, these models lead to further exploration of their particular ethnographic spheres in each society studied. Nevertheless, while continual feedback between the two approaches appears as necessary for the elaboration of models as it is for the refinement of monographs, it is important to remember that the two are complementary: it is not a case of either/or. The comparative models summarised in this article describe sociocultural sets that resemble each other in the way various features of their social organisations form *systems*; these features are as invisible for someone living in the society as they are striking for someone looking on. No doubt the models offer a 'simplified' vision of these societies and the logics — in the sense of coherent associations — we think we see at work; but 'simplified' does not mean 'distorted'. All societies in which Big Men (or respectively Great Men) have been identified correspond, without forcing, approximating or twisting the ethnographic data, to the syntheses constructed to account for them. It is clear, for instance, that many societies in New Guinea have neither Big Men nor Great Men.[81] But among the groups usually considered to be Big Men societies (Melpa, Enga, Mendi, etc.), not one corresponds merely 'somewhat' or 'roughly' to the model described at the beginning of this article. All display the entire set of *general* characteristics set out in the model. The same goes for the Great Men societies, whose typical social logics are illustrated by all Anga groups.

Comparing these models with each other, or with those of other New Guinea social systems, means trying to select which components in a consistent set of sociocultural practices, institutions and representations, are likely to change when one shifts one's mental gaze from one set of societies to another. It also means attempting to circumscribe the structural, functional or historical conditions — insofar as such a distinction can be made — of these transformations. In short, it means seizing the opportunity to understand the diversity of tiny portions of humankind that can reasonably be compared. Such an endeavour remains, at least for the author of these lines, the aim and the justification of anthropology.

Footnotes

1   *Mipela wan bilas*: 'we who have the same body decorations', in *Tok Pisin* (also called neo-Melanesian or Melanesian Pidgin). Spoken for over a hundred and twenty years now, Tok Pisin began as a trading language, based on English (85 per cent of the vocabulary). Today it is the *lingua franca* of nearly two million people, and is in the process of becoming a Creole in its own right, since many children are now raised directly in this language (see e.g. Kulick 1992).

2   E.g. Bensa (1996), Biersack (1991), Carrier (ed. 1992), Hays (1993), Mitchell (1994), to mention only recent publications on Oceania.

3   Kulick (1992: 2).

4   Thirty km long and between 5 and 10 km in width, the Tauri River valley is today an immense expanse of grassland extending above and below Menyamya; one must go up the side valleys to find the rainforest, which is sometimes now confined to the ridges.

5   Until recently, there were still twelve: in addition to Kawatcha, which was spoken by a scant 30 people at the beginning of the 1970s, according to Lloyd (1973: 79) and which seemed to me to be on the brink of extinction in 1980; at the same time the Ameye language had apparently only one native speaker left, a man I encountered among the Langimar. The Kamasa could not be located this trip. On the western edge of the Anga territory, several other groups are mentioned as having had their own language which died out within living memory.

6   See Foley (1992), Lloyd (1973).

7   Little is known about bilingualism along the borders with non-Anga groups. Owing to absence of contacts, bilingualism did not exist in the western part of their territory, which was separated from the Pawaian groups by several days' walk through a remote no-man's land. In the south, where 'Kukukuku' (Anga) raids terrorised the coastal populations, the few peaceful relations that existed were strictly commercial. Little documentation is available on the situation in the northern and western parts of the territory, but judging from the relations observed today between Baruya and Youndouyé or between Sambia and Fore, for example, bilingualism was extremely rare. Likewise, in the early 1980s, northwestern groups (Watchakes, Jeghuje, Langimar) had only episodic contacts with the Markham Valley tribes (Lemonnier, n.d.).

8   Three possible exceptions come to mind: 'Yagwoia' speakers are split into two non-adjoining groups (Yeghuje and Iqwaye); we will leave it to the ethnologists who have already described them (H. Fischer and J. Mimica, respectively) to detail their sociological similarities and differences. Likewise, the apparent homogeneity preliminary studies have indicated among the Kapau (known as Kamea in the southern and western parts of their occupation zone) may be only an illusion. S. Bamford's work (1997) is a first step towards improving our knowledge of the tribes that comprise this linguistic group, which happens to be the largest. A third exception could be the two Langimar- (or Angaataha-) speaking groups, today separated by more than a day's walk and located on either side of a Kapau enclave; as far as I can judge, however, the (incomplete) information I obtained in Benula (in the west) cross-checks completely with the data collected by B. Blackwood among the 'Manki' in the east (Blackwood 1978: 17).

9   The Baruya proper, but also the Youwarrounatche, Wantekia, Andje and Usarumpia.

10 See note 7 above.

11 For the distinction between culture, tribe and society, see two extremely clear texts by M. Godelier (1973: 93–131 and 1985: 159–165).

12 Anga horticulture has been described by Blackwood (1940), Bonnemère (1996), Bourke (1980), Lemonnier (1982, 2000) and Lory (1982).

13 In the western Highlands, it is not unusual for half of the sweet potato crop to be used to feed pigs, which may number up to several hundred per square kilometre.

14 By 'technique', I mean both intellectual and material means of acting on matter (for techniques as social productions, see Lemonnier 1992).

15 Like any other material culture, the Anga's presents itself on the whole as a system. In other words, some of the elements employed in technical behaviours (raw materials, means of working, energies, gestures, skills and knowledge), and often entire technical activities (agriculture and husbandry, ways of building house walls and garden enclosures, use of plant fibres for making string, barkcloth, grass skirts, carrying bags, etc.) connect together into systems of relations in which functional dependence, symbolic processes and social logics are tightly interwoven. Yet only parts of these systems have been explored as yet (e.g. for the Anga, see Lemonnier, 1986), and, with the exception of totally original activities like the production of vegetal salt, it is still not possible to list a series of operations or a combination of techniques specific to *all* Anga groups and to them alone. For example, there is nothing to indicate that building a specifically Angan house or trap involves any original way of working the wood or the bark. In these examples, the only clear specificity is the final assembling, visible in the finished object.

16 This can be seen, for example, in the technical vocabulary, but also in indigenous representations and classifications of elements (materials, tools, agents, etc.) and of the results of technical action (Lemonnier 1993a). In particular, language is one of our rare gateways to the representations of the elementary means of action on matter (see, for example, the unsurpassed article by Lefébure 1978).

17 Which would have to be limited to a given technique: e.g. one might imagine that a certain verb form in Anga corresponded to a strictly Angan technique. But this does not imply any overall correspondence. It should be remembered that Haudricout showed that even the congruency between words and things is very imperfect (1942; see also Haudricourt and Delamarre 1955).

18 At least not for the Anga as a whole. Nevertheless see Healey (1981), for their languages; and Fetchko (1972) and Lemonnier (1986), for their material culture.

19 Unless otherwise indicated, the expression 'Anga group', which I will use from here on, refers to one of the sets of Anga tribes having the same language, identical techniques and, as we will see later, the same social organisation.

20 See Godelier (1982), Lemonnier (1990).

21 See Knauft (1993), Lemonnier (1993b).

22 See, e.g. Read (1952), Feil (1987: 199–214), Lemonnier (1990: 81–85).

23 See Godelier (1982), Modjeska (1982), Strathern (1982).

24 The pig, its meat, fat and blood, are considered to be substitutes for or tokens of life. But since pigs and shells are interchangeable, the latter can fulfill the same functions as equivalents of human life.

25 See Lemonnier (1990, 1993b).

26 See e.g. Panoff (1985), Strathern (1971b: 200–208).

27 Allies who do not receive compensation for their people killed are potential enemies.

28 Whatever Hays (1993) may say; he maintains that 'Highlands' is nothing more than a 'fuzzy set' completely lacking in consistency or anthropological interest.

29 For Great Men societies, see Godelier (1982). The terms Big Man and Great Man have become standard usage. They refer to two different political statuses and forms of social organisation *sui generis*. As far as ethnographers know today, the only Great Men societies are the thirty or forty tribes characterised by the Anga language and culture, whereas Big Men societies are found in several large cultural sets of the New Guinea Highlands. When speaking of warfare, the ethnographic present refers to the period before the *pax australiana*, even though the 1982–1988 war between the Baruya and the Youwarrounatche, and the regular skirmishes between the Menye and their neighbours constitute notable exceptions.

30 Bonnemère (1998).

31 Bonnemère (1996; ed. 2004).

32 See Lory (1981–1982), for the Baruya.

33 Lemonnier (1992).

34 Lemonnier (1998a).

35 Godelier (1992: 19–20).

36 Herdt (1987: 25–27) has rightly stressed this other feature of Anga societies, which was the perpetual climate of insecurity stemming from the constant threat of enemy attack and the fear this generated.

37 Godelier (1990: 86).

38 Godelier (1982: 271, 1990: 86, 1992: 19–20).

39 These groups are the Ankave, Ivori, Kapau-Kamea, Langimar, Lohiki, Menye, and Watchakes. Nowadays the Sambia too practise a form of marriage involving gifts of wealth (Herdt, pers. com.).

40 Godelier (1982), Modjeska (1982), A. Strathern (1982).

41 Several Anga groups practice marriage with bridewealth payments on a very small scale, alongside the dominant practice of sister-exchange (see Godelier 1982: 50–56 for the Baruya, but this is true of the Watchakes as well). The groups mentioned earlier practice *only* marriage with bridewealth.

42 Godelier (1982: 271).

43 A crucial point, but one I will not go into here: these payments, which are explicitly regarded as compensation for children, are *not* required when the couples formed by an exchange of sisters have gotten along well, helping each other with their gardens and giving each other pieces of pig meat when the occasion arose. This indicates an indirect but indisputable equivalence between life (children born to the union), work (collaboration between the brothers-in-law), pigs (shared meat) and wealth (given as compensation). If we recall the roundabout ways by which the coastal societies of southern New Guinea too calculate equivalences between women and wealth in a general context of direct exchange (Lemonnier 2002), we have enough reasons to pursue investigation into the conditions in which New Guinea societies establish or fail to establish some equivalences that have crucial consequences.

44 Bonnemère (1996: 168–172).

45 Godelier (1969).

46 For instance, in Melpa marriage, a distinction is made between the 'pig for public distribution', the 'pigs for the house' and the 'pig for the girl's vagina' (Strathern and Strathern 1969: 147–156). The same is true for the Tombema-Enga (Feil 1981: 66). Unless I am mistaken, the ethnography does not mention a particular term for the numerous items of wealth, aside from the pigs given for a marriage (e.g. Brown 1969).

47 Lemonnier (1990).

48 For a discussion of how the various elements whose association constitutes the essence of Big Men societies are disjoined in southern New Guinea, see Lemonnier (1993b: 140–146; 1995).

49 This does not mean individual factors do not play any part at all. For instance, it seems indeed that, in New Guinea, peaceful competition in 'economic' exchanges involves primarily locally produced goods (pigs and yams), whereas pearl-shells, which can be used in all Anga groups as the equivalent of a warrior's life, are the result of a business transaction, a brave one, to be sure — the journey is long and sometimes through enemy territory — but one not visibly involving local labour.

50 Apparently it is only in certain Kapau groups that male initiations are limited to the one hamlet (personal work in Aseki during 1980).

51 Lemonnier (1993b: 138–139).

52 Godelier (1996: 153–172).

53 Or rather to certain neighbouring valleys. In 1993, nearly half the Ankave *men* in Ikundi had never been to the valley immediately north of their territory, the home of their traditional enemies, and nine out of ten had never visited the most distant Ankave hamlet, although it was less than three days' walk away. Almost none of them had ever seen the Vailala River, which bounds their territory on the west, and although all were familiar with Menyamya (the closest administrative post, two days' walk away), three quarters had never been to an important mission located less than an hour's drive north of Menyamya. The women's movements were even more restricted.

54 'Anga' is a name invented by white people to replace the term 'Kukukuku' (or Kukakuka), whose meaning in the various Anga languages that use it varies, but is usually pejorative (Lloyd 1973: 67–68; Blackwood 1978: 6–8).

55 We understood 'common' history to mean the history shared by the groups with which each tribe recognises ties, and not that of the whole set of what are today defined as Anga groups. Similarly, for the Melpa, a prototypical Big Men society, 'the history of a group … is decisively bound up with the history of its *moka* [ceremonial exchanges] transactions, and each *moka* is both an expression and a redirection of that history' (Strathern 1991: 209; see also Ballard 1995).

56 Lemonnier (1981: 46).

57 In one form or another, the tendency to identify one's own group with humanity is found in all groups (however we do not know if this is true around the perimetre of the Anga territory). The Iqwaye regard some Anga as less human than others, less human than themselves, in any event (Mimica 1981: 56–59). In the same vein, the Baruya regard themselves as better than their neighbours, whose skin is darker because they live farther from the sun (Godelier 1982).

58 For more on these points, see Bonnemère (1996: 252–253).

59 The death of the man who brought order to the first humans was therefore necessary in order to obtain the bones used to pierce the boys' septums. The Ankave see this operation as killing the initiates, before they can carry out the procedures by which they transform their bodies so as to re-engender them as adult warriors, according to Bonnemère's interpretation of these rituals (Bonnemère 1998).

60 Mimica (1981: 51).

61 Godelier (1982: 22), Mimica (1981: 58).

62 Godelier (1982: 148).

63 Godelier (1982: 162–163).

64 Godelier (1982: 136).

65 See, e.g. Godelier (1982: 135ff). Among the Ankave, it is the two largest clans that are responsible for the initiations.

66 I will not go into this here. Instead, see e.g. Godelier (1982: 135ff).

67 'A tribe is therefore a provisional combination of a certain number of kinship groups in one territory. Tribes come and go…' (Godelier 1985: 163).

68 In reality several clans appear, in name at least, in several Anga linguistic groups at once. The Anga were, and in most cases still are, unaware of this, so that it has no sociological impact on their daily lives (this is obviously not the case for Anga history, by which I mean the one that remains to be written by historians). Here I am talking about those social units that are functionally recognised as clans on the local level.

69 See Lemonnier (1984, 1987).

70 These practices are not frozen: they change with the historical evolution of the groups in question (splits and mergers, escapes to another territory, etc.). Again, see Godelier (1985: 163–165). What I have written here about tribal identity is also valid for the reproduction of the identity of a valley or a local group.

71 These men, called *i'pan'nə' xənej'* ('mothers of the initiates'), are the custodians of the sacred *oxeməxə'* ('man-fight/anger'); this is also the name of the red cordylines mentioned above, which must be present for the ceremony to take place.

72 Now that there is less need for warriors, and that tensions have arisen between valleys, it is the unity of each valley that is produced. Nevertheless, there is some nostalgia about the collaboration of earlier times, whose disappearance is felt as a threat to the group's security.

73 Unlike ordinary humans, *ombə'* are very fast, travelling underground or along invisible pathways made of long strings of shells (for more on *ombə'*, see Lemonnier 1992, 1998b).

74 Contrary to the situation created when sacred objects are held by only a few clans (Godelier 1982: 134–157), alternating participation in mourning ceremonies, for instance, does not imply a political hierarchy.

75 For example, A. Bensa (1996: 42–43) speaks of ethnological monographs in which 'the analysis cuts the material (the 'data') ... to fit the meanings it wants', and whose 'dim light ... results essentially from systematically taking the data out of context'. Or Hays (1993: 48) denounces studies guilty of 'imposing a priori a grid of traits to demarcate a 'region'.' Note that these authors, who are objecting on principle, are simply assuming all comparative work to be stupid and lacking in rigour, whereas the only receivable criticism on this subject would be a case-by-case demonstration of the inanity of the comparisons proposed or of the inexactitude of the supporting ethnographic data.

76 Lemonnier (1990: 156–157).

77 Strathern (1971b: 11).

78 'The new activities do not in themselves constitute relationships between persons in the Melpa social system. They are all activities oriented towards others: other people, *other structures*. By preserving *moka*, and certain associate key institutions, notably bridewealth payments, the Melpa have retained a sphere for their own continuous history, which acts as a filter in respect of the outside' (Strathern 1991: 211; italics added).

79 When it comes to Oceanic ethnography, some even venture to suggest that Big Men are a colonial product resulting notably from the devaluation of shell money following the massive imports of shells by gold prospectors and administrators (Hays ed. 1992: 12; 1993: 147). It is pointed out that, as a consequence, the exchanges were modified in 1940 and 1950 (Hughes 1978: 316). This is true. But it must be remembered that the first ethnographic accounts we have of the Mount Hagen Big Men go back to 1934 (the arrival of Vicedom), which is a year or so after contact (April 1933). Can it be seriously maintained that the observations of Vicedom, or those of Strauss (who arrived in 1936) describe a radically new situation? Or that A. Strathern was incapable of accurately documenting the changes that had occurred in Melpa society since it had opened up to the rest of the world? Even Knauft (1993: 8), whose remarkable survey of the southern coastal societies of New Guinea shows the interest of a rigorous comparative approach, does not hesitate to write: 'It is all too easy to find polar contrasts between regions for which primary accounts were gathered at different times and/or with different ethnographic and theoretical agendas.' Not only is there nothing 'easy' about looking for strong correlations between social practices, but as soon as two or three societies are involved, the comparative approach becomes a brainteaser in which the researcher spends the bulk of his time chasing after counter-examples to support his hypotheses and rejecting those thus invalidated.

80 Sister-exchange without payment of bridewealth remains the predominant form of marriage among the Baruya, while bridewealth payments have become common among their Sambia neighbours (Herdt, pers. com.). In another sphere, that of vernacular architecture, some groups have rigidly maintained the shapes and techniques observed at contact, while others quickly adopt architectural elements seen elsewhere; but for the moment this contrast remains unexplained (nevertheless, see Coudart's hypotheses, 1994).

81 This is demonstrated by several authors in Strathern and Godelier eds. (1991).

Chapter 8

WHY SHOULD EVERYONE HAVE A DIFFERENT NAME?

Clan and gender identity among the Ankave-Anga of Papua New Guinea

Pascale Bonnemère

A side from a few well-known pioneering studies,[1] it has been only in the last fifteen years that there has been a research boom in the anthropology of personhood, attesting new interest in the ideas members of all societies have about individual identity. This area of anthropology is concerned with the ways each culture goes about defining the person, its primary object of study being the discourses and practices surrounding the personal attributes recognised by the society: body, name(s), spirit(s), emotions, personality, physical features and so on.

Alongside its principal aim, such research has also added to our knowledge of the systems of representations and ritual practices societies have built up around individuals and the important events of their life cycles, and has led to theoretical advances in the analysis of kinship systems and of the sociocultural constructions of gender difference.[2]

Research on representations of the individual and the person in New Guinea has focused on those in which the body occupies a prominent place. For the time being, there is little need to ask ourselves whether this is a theoretical a priori or an ethnographic reality; rather, we must note that, in spite of the predominance of analyses of what the men and women in this part of the world have to say about the conception, constitution, growth, care and decline of the human body, there is no lack of researcher on other, less physical components of the person.[3] Having appeared in isolation and over a long period, these articles have had less impact; nevertheless, today they are still regarded as fundamental, and some predict (at least in their titles) that interest in the mere body is on the verge of disappearing.[4]

In the 1970s and 1980s, personal names attracted the interest of few Melanesianists, although they were studied by many European specialists. The latter were attempting to alter a tradition of anthroponymic research which, in Europe, was rooted in philosophy and history, and based on the classification of names rather than individuals, and on the history of these names.[5] From the outset, the New Guinea studies, on the other hand, adopted an anthropological approach aimed at 'identifying the rules of name bestowal followed by a society, the principles determining how one classifies individuals by naming them … and the laws governing the naming *system*'.[6] Working on the hypothesis that 'anthroponyms are never simply conventional terms that are interchangeable or meaningless',[7] anthropological analysis aims to discover how the society enrolls its individual members in socially defined groups, how these individuals are classified and 'allotted a position'.[8]

In the following, I will analyse how name forms are typically constructed and used by the Ankave-Anga of Papua New Guinea. I further hope to show that the study of personal names provides a means of understanding some of the rules governing social organisation as well as an access to the principles underlying the construction of sexual identity.

The Ankave

The Ankave occupy three densely forested valleys to the southwest of a mountain chain running the width of the island of New Guinea from east to west. Some one thousand in number, they belong to a set of twelve Anga linguistic groups which speak related languages, share certain cultural features (absence of Big Men, male initiations, asymmetry between the sexes, absence of inequality among the men), and have an oral history that attests a common origin.[9]

As primarily horticulturalists, the Ankave grow taros, bananas, sugar cane and sweet potatoes in gardens cleared in the forest. They also raise a few pigs, hunt, trap eels for ceremonial needs and gather a wide variety of leaves and fruits in the forest. For this purpose, each family regularly builds a temporary shelter several hours' walk from the hamlet containing their main house. There some gather and prepare the fruits of the *Pangium edule* and the breadfruit tree, both of which grow in the lowest-lying parts of the territory; others make barkcloth capes from the *Ficus*; and others yet manufacture eel traps. As a result, Ankave hamlets are occupied only intermittently throughout the year. To this mobility orchestrated by the appearance of the various forest fruits and the need for clothing and game, must be added frequent changes of residence. Thus, even though settlements may be permanent, there is a periodical rotation of their occupants.

The Ankave are divided into exogamous patrilineal clans,[10] and residence is usually patrivirilocal. That being said, affinal relations provide the possibility of access to additional lands and enable the Ankave to satisfy their penchant for mobility. A man who takes a wife must pay monetary compensation to her family. The woman is chosen, insofar as this is possible (see note 10), outside the husband's own clan, among the categories of women who are not forbidden to him. For the marriage rules are expressed in the form of taboos, the most strict being the prohibition on marriage between two individuals related in the maternal line, by virtue of the belief that blood is transmitted exclusively by the mother.

Relations between men and women are marked by complementarity. This can be seen in the majority of ritual and subsistence activities as well as in the representations of the person. Thus the theories of human conception and growth, like the steps of the male initiations, all reveal the conjunction of substances and of the male and female agents needed to make individuals and to bring their body to maturity. Generally speaking, the body is the primary material that must be acted on so as to ensure that every person grows and stays in good health.

Seen in this context, the person's name does not seem to be an essential attribute of individual identity;[11] and the fact that several people can have the same name merely confirms this impression. Furthermore, when addressing someone, the Ankave much prefer to use kin terms, or what I call *petits noms* — an expression that has been translated here by J. Mimica's term, 'names of endearment' — which everyone shares with other members of the society (see below). Ultimately, then, we will see that an Ankave's name has less to do with personal identity than with the position he or she occupies in certain social groups and within a set of siblings.

Bestowing a name and contexts of usage

The Ankave do not look on the moment of birth as a fitting time to name children; they do not receive a name until they begin to crawl, or even after they have taken their first steps.[12] This applies only to the firstborn, however; the younger children are given the name of their same-sex elder sibling to which is simply added a suffix indicating their birth order.[13] Thus, even though a baby is not given a personal name until it is several months old — since its spirit (dƏngƏ') must first manifest itself —[14] the community knows the baby's future name as soon as it is born. The qualifiers indicating the order of birth within a set of same-sex siblings are also the names of the fingers of the hand, and are placed after the principal component.

Personal names are usually given once and for all; normally people do not change names over their lifetime; in fact, name changes are very rare among the Ankave,[15] whereas in three other societies of the same Anga set — the Baruya, Sambia and Menye — initiation means a new name.[16] Once a person has children, he or she can be called by a teknonym, which means literally 'so and so's father or mother', in this case therefore related with an identity arising from filiation.[17] The teknonym never completely replaces the personal name acquired in childhood, but it can be used as a term of reference as well as address.

A child's parents talk over and choose the name together, taking into account their own clans but sometimes also reaching back to those of their matrilineal or patrilineal ancestors. Among the Baruya, on the other hand, 'a name is never inherited through the maternal line'.[18] Other members of the Ankave child's family may also give their opinion when the name is being chosen. For instance, one man of around fifty expressed the wish that his nephew's name include his own, which was the clan name of an ancestor (FFM), and that his niece be named after a river located on the territory of a valley their father had left to go and live with his wife's family in another valley. It is clear that, in asking that his younger brother's children be given these names, he was seeking to perpetuate the memory of their original valley. In this specific case, the individual becomes the depository of the memory of a group with which he is connected, and the name becomes much more than a simple individual identity marker.

In rare cases, the choice is made by only one of the child's parents. Some, usually female, names refer to an event that occurred either during the birth (birth of the child deep in the forest, a birdcall heard just after the birth), or during the marsupial hunt organised by the men in the days immediately following the birth. The mother, in the first case, or the father, in the second, relates what happened and suggests naming the little girl after the event in question.

When addressing each other, the Ankave prefer to use kin terms rather than personal names.[19] Personal names are really used as terms of address only between people who have no kinship ties, not even classificatory ones.[20] On the other hand, they are often used in addressing children, even though there are specific terms, but which are *de facto* rarely used: *nge'wə'* is used for infants, irrespective of their sex; *iwe*, for little boys and *mie'j'* for little girls;[21] *i'pa'nə* can be used to address a young boy who has completed the first-stage of initiation (notably piercing of the septum). The equivalent term for girls who have reached puberty but are not married is *a'pijə'*, but I have never heard it used as a term of address. Later, women are called by their name, by a kin term, or by the teknonym, 'so and so's mother'. The terms designating second- and third-stage initiates — *Səmazinə'* and *Səwangə'* respectively — are used only in reference. An old man, or simply a third-stage (which is the last) initiate is called *xwojangə'*. In all events, personal names are normally employed when two people are talking about a third person.

How are Ankave names constructed?

There are several rules for constructing Ankave personal names. In general, it can be said that they are composed of one or two what I call 'principal' components. These refer to a clan, a toponym, some natural element or to an event connected with the child's birth. Usually in second position come components referring to birth order, skin pigmentation, a 'name of endearment' or a physical or social trait. The fact that personal names can draw on so many registers has as an almost inevitable corollary: the unlimited number of second components. This phenomenon, common in New Guinea, is also found among the Palawan of the Philippines, but is completely alien to the Jivaro of Amazonia, for example.[22]

One of the general characteristics of the Ankave naming system is that men's and women's personal names are constructed on different patterns.

Men's names

The prevailing rule for composing the personal names given to male infants could be described as 'bilateral'. This 'bilaterality principle' operates on several levels. The vast majority of all male names (94.4 per cent)[23] have two principal components. Within this set, 90.7 per cent refer to clan names and of these, the majority (55 per cent) mention both the father's and the mother's clan. In this case, the name of the father's clan usually comes first (78 per cent of the time). Note that, when speaking of the members of the Idzadze clan, who sometimes intermarry,[24] the synonym Erauje is often used. Someone whose parents both belong to this clan can therefore be called Idzadze Erauje or Erauje Idzadze.[25]

Analysis shows that, when a person's name does not make reference to both parents' clans, the Ankave try to mention in a relatively well-balanced manner ancestral clans in both the maternal and paternal lines. For example, when the first component of a man's name is the name of the maternal clan of a agnatic male ancestor, the second refers in over half the cases (51.7 per cent) to the mother's clan. Conversely, when the first component is the clan name of a maternal female ancestor, the second always mentions the father's clan. But several names follow a more complex logic: when the first component is the name of a cross-line male ancestor (MFM, MFFM, or FMFM), the second part of the name refers either to the father's clan (68.7 per cent) or to the maternal clan of a male agnate. It is therefore difficult to affirm that in this case too there has been an effort to balance the references to the patrilateral and matrilateral clans.

To give an idea of the variety encountered in the composition of male names, here are a few examples: In the case of Oti dzadze (Otɔ Idzadze), the father is an Idzadze and the mother's father's mother is a clan Otɔ woman.[26] Witɔ Toradze received the name of his mother's father's mother's clan (Witɔ) followed by that of his father's mother (Toradze). Jaderotɔ bears the name of his paternal great grandfather's mother's clan. Omɔrɔ Erauje's father was a clan Omɔrɔ man and his maternal grandmother an Idzadze.

In all events, there is a principle operating at the different levels of analysis which tends to emphasise in a complementary manner both of a male individual's affiliations; this concern for bilaterality appears in the structure of the names — usually two juxtaposed principal components — as well as in the clan affiliations chosen for mention. The only potential limit on the latter is the Ankave's knowledge of the genealogy of the individual receiving the name. Indeed it seems that any ancestral clan can be chosen to feature in the name given, which means that it is impossible to deduce with absolute certainty a man's own clan by looking at his name.

In fact there is even a fair risk of error, since, first of all, only 55 per cent of the names composed of two components refer to either parent's clan and, second, the order of the two components cannot be regarded as immutable, even if the name of the father's clan usually comes first (78 per cent of cases). In this respect, it must be said that, when both of a man's parents belong to the same clan and his name is comprised of two components referring to this clan, informants invariably affirm that the first component corresponds to the father's clan name. Likewise, when a man in the same situation bears a name containing only one clan term, the second being of another type, informants always say that the first name designates the father's clan.

I would like to end this analysis of men's names by attempting to see which configurations are not represented by concrete cases. Given the wide choice available to the Ankave for constructing personal names, it is my guess that the systematic omissions mean something. For example, in single-component names, the mother's clan is never explicitly mentioned; it appears only indirectly in the form of 'names of endearment'.

To sum up: men's personal names are constructed on a bilateral pattern with a patrilineal bias, but which nevertheless tends to strike a balance between the two lineages linking an individual with a set of ancestors. This in turn suggests that, for the Ankave culture, this sort of equilibrium is crucial in defining the identity of the male individual.

Women's names

Contrary to men's names, those bestowed on little girls plainly follow a principle of unilaterality, which can also be found on several levels. The majority of female personal names[27] have only one component (66.7 per cent), and the remaining third are not constructed on the dominant male pattern of two clan references. This unilaterality is clearly skewed towards the father's clan: when a woman's name contains a descriptive term making indirect reference to a clan (toponyms and endearment names), in 99 per cent of the cases it is to the paternal clan.[28]

Analysis of the configurations not retained confirms the patrilineally biased unilateral model, since no woman's name mentions two clans or contains two indirect clan references. Likewise, there is no personal female name in which a clan name is juxtaposed with an indirect reference to a clan. All these omissions indicate that female-name structure is governed by a strong unilateral bias. Furthermore, in single-component names, the mother's clan never appears and even indirect references to her clan are rare, which again confirms that women's names place the emphasis on patrilineal descent reckoning.

When attempting to assess the possible significance of the position of the terms in two-component female names, it appears first position is always occupied by the component more strongly marked by clan membership: for instance, in order of frequency, we find a clan name followed by a toponym or a name of endearment, or one of the latter followed by what I call a 'neutral' qualifier (see below). These configurations show that position is important in the construction of personal names; this can be seen in the fact that the two components of a name are not interchangeable and that the first always conveys more information about the person's genealogy than the second. Furthermore, there is no reason a priori that the same should not be true for men's names. In this case, the first component might thus correspond to the more important affiliation; which would explain the fact that the father's clan is usually mentioned first and that, when both parents come from the same clan, informants always maintain that the first component refers to the paternal clan.

In all personal names, whether male or female, the qualifiers I call 'neutral' are those that contain no clan reference whatsoever. These can be divided into six categories. The first contains a component referring to skin colour (*wɔ'a' /wiej'* or *bɔri*); it always appears in second position and can in no case be the only component of a personal name.[29] This qualifier is used in men's names as well as in women's. The second category refers to the person's size, and appears uniquely in women's names, whether they are comprised of one or two components. Note that these two categories refer to the physical appearance of the person, a practice encountered elsewhere in New Guinea.[30]

The third category contains those names referring to an event that occurred at the time of birth or during the marsupial hunt immediately afterwards. This practice is also attested for the Daribi and the Wiru of Papua New Guinea, as well as in the Fiji Islands.[31] Such references are usually found in single-component names. The fourth category contains components that refer to the individual's personal history: being an only child, for instance, or having lost her father just before birth.[32]

Reference to a plant or an animal in the natural environment is a fifth type of 'neutral' qualifier, found only in female names. Such references to the natural world are restricted, *de facto* and for reasons unknown, to a bird (*ingə' obe*) and two species of areca palm (*nə̃ ngijə' wondi* and *wamondi*). The sixth and final category is an arbitrary collection of terms that did not fit into any of the preceding groups, but which always occur in second position, notably following the name of a bird and usually concerning some detail of its behaviour.

In sum, none of the 'neutral' qualifiers makes explicit or implicit reference to a clan, but this does not make them a homogeneous group. Some evoke a social fact (something that happened at the time of birth or during the hunt that provides the marsupials presented to every woman who has just given birth, or a family trait), others mention more personal realities (a physical trait, skin colour).[33]

Of the components containing an indirect clan reference, almost all (35 out of 36) are toponyms referring to rivers, settlements, or mountains located on the girl's father's clan territory. Since 83.7 per cent of female personal names contain a clan reference in one form or another, and 99 per cent of these are to the father's clan, it is usually possible to guess the woman's clan from her name, providing one knows the location of each clan's territories, and every Ankave does.

Therefore, however paradoxical this statement may seem, it is as though the Ankave regarded women's names as one of the privileged vehicles of patrilineal descent reckoning. One can imagine this as a way of referring to patrilineal descent where the physical constitution of the person says nothing about such a rule, since it is women alone who ensure the sharing and continuity of a vital bodily substance generation after generation, which is their blood.[34]

Symmetry and asymmetry in male and female personal names

We have seen that Ankave men's and women's names are constructed according to fundamentally different rules. The first follow in the majority a bilateral pattern, while two thirds of the second have only one component. Next, male names refer more often to clans, while female names use a great variety of qualifiers, including neutral terms, as the principal component. Another important difference has to do with the nature of the references. Men's names favour the genealogical, temporal dimension, with many references to the clans of remote ancestors. In women's names, the spatial dimension predominates, together with a different form of temporality focusing on events.

What conclusions can be drawn from these differences? As a hypothesis, I would make a connection between the Ankave's apparent desire to use men's names to mark the continuity between an individual and certain often remote paternal or maternal ancestors and the historical place of the alliances the two now-dominant clans had to conclude with the autochthonous clans in order to settle on the territories that are now theirs. It was in effect by intermarriage with the local clans (Toradze, Angə̃rə̃) that the members of the immigrant Ngudze and Idzadze clans were able to take up definitive residence on the territories of these local clans. In this case, the men's names would in a way testify to a time when women were of capital importance for the establishment — and the survival — of these refugee clans. If we accept this postulate, we could go on to reason that the balanced use of the names of matri- and patrilineal ancestors in the construction of male names could be traced to the same desire to acknowledge the crucial role of the allied clans in the very life of the group. We would still need to explain the absence of this same balance in the composition of female names, however. All I can say at present is that, unlike men, women usually leave their natal group when they marry. Embedding their clan affiliation in the woman's name is a way of recalling who is to receive the marriage payments and part of the gifts in kind that accompany her transfer to another group.[35] By doing this, patrilineal descent is once again expressed, since the identity of those receiving the bulk (70 per cent) of the various gifts — all members of the bride's father's clan — is one of the elements that allows us to define the Ankave kinship system as patrilineal.[36]

Nevertheless, the important differences between the structures of male and female names should not be allowed to overshadow their many formal similarities. In both cases the indication of birth order is treated as a suffix and placed after the principal component(s). Likewise, single-component names never contain a direct reference to the mother's clan, and in two-component names, two indirect clan references or the name of the mother's clan plus a 'neutral' qualifier are never found side by side in either men's or women's names.

To end this short comparison of male and female personal names, let us take another look at the system used in naming siblings. The set consisting of the brothers' names and that of the sisters' are usually treated separately. To take an example: the oldest child of Ngudze Idzadze and Tǝmnǝkǝ wie'j', a boy, is called Idze Erauje; the second child, a girl, is Sawi; the third, a boy, Idze Erauje Akwiye (Idze Erauje 'second'); the fourth, a boy, is called Idze Erauje Padzǝrwa ('third'); and the fifth, a girl, Sawi Akwaej (Sawi 'second'). Generally speaking, the two naming systems are unconnected, as though each set of same-sex siblings formed an uninterrupted series.

Half-siblings, or children born of the same woman and different men who are brothers or cousins (as often happens under levirate), are considered to be one continuous series of siblings, and the birth-order qualifiers in their names follow, even though they do not have the same father.[37] Consequently it appears that, in the naming system, real cross-siblings are treated as being separated by a greater distance than classificatory same-sex siblings; a bit as though shared gender entailed a greater degree of sameness than shared filiation. In other words, in this naming system, a set of boys — or girls — having the same mother and fathers from the same lineage, or having the same father and mothers from different clans is a unified set, while the set of the names of the boys and the girls born to the same parents is a mixed set. This implies that, for the Ankave, the distance between the sexes is greater than that between persons of the same sex belonging to only partially linked genealogical groups.

If we now look at the construction of gender identity using what we have learned about personal names, we cannot help seeing that the logic behind boys' and that behind girls' names follow distinctly different lines of reasoning. These differences suggest that Ankave representations of men's and women's social identity, as embodied in the name, are radically disjoined. Thus, just as the theories of procreation and the continuity of generations establish the respective functions of each gender in the process of human reproduction, so too the components of a person's name are chosen as a function of the representations of the principles supposed to govern men's and women's incorporation into a social set of genealogically linked individuals as well as their inscription in a geographical setting appropriated by the clans into which the population is divided. Zonabend formulated this reality nicely when she wrote: 'In names are embedded the many facets of social reality.'[38]

It also seems that there is no connection between an Ankave individual's physical appearance and his or her social attributes: in the event, personal names do not reflect representations of the individual's bodily composition.[39] Nevertheless, it is the women who bind individuals together through the transmission of blood, and it is in their names that patrilineal descent reckoning appears most clearly.

Names of endearment

When the Ankave are eating together, giving each other areca nuts or sharing the latest news around a fire, and a younger close relation joins them, it would be altogether unfitting to address him or her by his or her personal name. The proper term of address in these circumstances is what I call in French the *petit nom*, or 'name of endearment'. Endearment names are affectionate expressions whose forms and use contexts obey strict rules. They are invariably the names of wild or cultivated plants: for instance a member of the ginger or the balsam family or a cultivar of sweet potato, banana or pandanus. All the men whose mothers belong to the same clan are addressed by the same term(s).[40] Likewise, women whose mothers are from the same clan answer to one (or more) term(s) corresponding to other plants. Names of endearment are constructed according to two criteria, then: mother's clan and gender.

The contexts in which these terms of address are used are characterised by good humour, friendliness,[41] affection, all of which cannot be experienced in certain relations with kin or neighbours. Roughly speaking, the marital relationship is excluded, as is that between affines of different generations. More generally, the person using the endearment name is always older than or the same age as the person addressed. But the latter is obliged to reply in the same vein, therefore using the endearment name of the other person, whatever his or her age.

Both the construction of these endearment names and the circumstances of their use indicate that they are one of the manifestations of the relationship linking each individual with his or her mother, characterised by affection, the sharing of food and protection. These are terms of address that every individual has in common with many others of the same sex. Like the personal name, but even more obviously, the endearment name cannot be regarded as a means of expressing and conveying a strictly individual identity.

When the winds of change rise …

Although they are still very isolated due both to the nature of their environment and to administrative factors, the Ankave are increasingly subjected to contact with missionary groups. The Lutheran Church, whose services are two days' walk away, periodically sends an evangelist to teach those who so wish the rudiments of reading and writing using the New Testament published in Tok Pisin (Melanesian Pidgin). His role is also to baptise these 'converts', a ritual whose simultaneous consequences are the risk of catching cold from being plunged into the icy waters of the nearest stream and the acquisition of a new name. Naturally these names are taken from the only book they have ever held. And needless to say, the names are immediately altered to fit the specificities of the Ankave language so that the name of the Biblical figure is sometimes hard to deduce from the local pronunciation.

The adoption and use of such a name in everyday life is far from established practice; nevertheless, when we first visited the Ankave in 1987, no one would ever call someone by their Christian name; when we went back in 1994, this had become possible, though infrequent. Such changes notwithstanding, there is no child who has not been given a name constructed according to the rules described in this article on the pretext that the evangelist of the moment had already given them a Christian name. Today kin terms and endearment names still hold sway.

It seems highly likely that, when the Ankave anthroponymic system does begin to change, one of the specificities of this system, homonymy, will play a prominent role.[42] It is clear that this basic principle does not prevent taking a Christian name. The fact that several people may be called John, Rebecca or Abraham in no way disrupts the naming habits the Ankave inherited from their ancestors, since many villages often have two Idzadze Ngudze or two Ikundi wie'j'. That being said, recent experience shows that these habits run little risk of being abandoned for Biblical names, if only because the latter do not easily lend themselves to application of the rules for naming siblings, which is the second major feature of the Ankave anthroponymic system.

Footnotes

1   See Mauss (1938), Lévi-Strauss (1962).

2   Bromberger (1982: 113).

3   See Glasse (1987), Ryan (1958), Strathern (1970), Harrison (1985), Wagner (1972).

4   See, e.g. Martin (1992).

5   For more details, see Bromberger (1982: 104), Brutti (1993: 3–7), Zonabend (1980: 9).

6   Bromberger (1982: 103; see also note 3).

7   Zonabend (1980: 18).

8   Lévi-Strauss (1962: 248; English translation, p. 187).

9   See Pierre Lemonnier's article, this volume.

10 Certain demographic phenomena nevertheless make it difficult to respect exogamy in every clan. Some members of the Idzadze clan, notably, which accounts for 50 per cent of the total population, find it hard to avoid intermarriage.

11 The same is true among the Orokaiva (Iteanu 1990: 38). On the other hand, among the Manambu, studied by Simon Harrison, 'the basic elements of a person's social identity at Atavip are, first of all, his name, and secondly his paternity and matrifiliation' (Harrison 1990: 57). Likewise, the German missionary, Hermann Strauss, fascinated with the culture and language of the people now known as the Melpa, with whom he lived for many years both before and after the Second World War, writes: 'The name of a person, or of any object … encapsulates his being and soul — indeed the name *is* the person or thing' (Strauss 1990: 168).

12 See also Blackwood (1978: 116).

13 The same practice — giving what Mimica calls 'names of endearment' — is found among the Iqwaye (Mimica 1981: 40).

14 The word *dɔngɔ'* is used in various but closely related contexts. It designates first of all the life-breath, the act of breathing, life, being alive; but in a less physical sense it also means spirit, mind, thought, consciousness, will, memory.

15 Recently two such cases arose: one young man changed his name because the one he had been given was not constructed properly; it referred to a clan with which neither his mother nor his father had any connection, even searching back through their respective genealogies. A small boy was also given a new name because the one he had 'would have kept him from growing'. This comment provides a rare glimpse of a link between a person's name and their physical integrity.

16 See respectively, Godelier (1992: 6), Herdt (1987: 157), Lemonnier, personal communication.

17 Something J. Turner wrote about a Fijian group applies here to the Ankave: 'While personal names in this culture identify persons in terms of their positions within a system of descent groups, teknonymy labels persons in terms of their relationship to other persons' (Turner 1991: 15).

18 Godelier (1992: 7).

19 In contrast, the Kaluli, who live near Mount Bosavi, 'usually address kinsmen … by their personal names. Kaluli use kin terms mainly for formal greetings at ceremonial occasions or when one person wishes to stress his link to another in order to secure a request ('Brother, give me some tobacco.')' (Schieffelin 1976: 58). We will see below that, in the same circumstances, an Ankave will almost invariably use the 'name of endearment'.

20 This situation rarely arises in small populations.

21 These two terms correspond to the kin terms for the category 'child'.

22 See respectively, Iteanu (1990: 38), Macdonald (1977: 93) and Taylor (1993: 659).

23 These percentages were calculated on the basis of the names of all people living in the Suowi valley in the summer of 1990. Of a total of 153 males, the names of only 125 could be analysed, as 15 were infants or very young boys who had not yet been named and the names of 13 others contained a term whose meaning was doubtful or unknown.

24 See note 10.

25 Although informants do not comment on this point, the sound of the name is often altered slightly, notably by elision, so as to distinguish individuals who would otherwise have identical names: Erau Madze for Erauje Omadze, Ngwi PatSe for Ngudze PatSe, Erwa Madze for Erwatɔ Omadze or Erwati dzadze for Erwatɔ Idzadze.

26 Today extinct, the Otə clan was related to the Idzadze and located in the most isolated valley of the Ankave territory. As the child of two Idzadze, Oti dzadze had every chance of being named Idzadze Erauje or Erauje Idzadze, two extremely common names. The reference to the Otə was probably brought in to avoid adding to the already large number of men bearing this name. (See also note 25.)

27 Here too percentages were calculated on the basis of the names of all people living in the Suowi valley in the summer of 1990. Out of a total of 155 female inhabitants, only 123 had names that could be analysed: 20 were infants or little girls who had not yet received a name, 10 names contained a term whose meaning was doubtful or unknown, and two women were from neighbouring tribes.

28 In a recent article, Mimica analyses the Iqwaye system of personal names, which turns out to be similar to the Ankave's, but much more standardized. In the Iqwaye system, the 'matri-name … is only a component of male names. Women have only patri-names' (1991: 84).

29 But one can address or refer to a person simply as 'wə'a' ('the light-skinned one'), in particular when there is very little ambiguity as to the person's identity. Likewise, one can speak of 'nane bəri'), the 'dark-skinned older sister'.

30 See Glasse (1987: 203), Wagner (1972: 87).

31 See Wagner (1972: 88) and Strathern (1970: 62). For Fiji, see Turner (1991: 11).

32 See also Wagner (1972: 89).

33 Some of these 'neutral' qualifiers seem to me closer to the nicknames analysed by F. Zonabend in the Burgundian village of Minot. In this case, 'the nickname evokes either a specific moral or physical behaviour, or a striking event in the person's life' (1977: 269).

34 Bonnemère (1996: 227–228).

35 R. Wagner says much the same about the Daribi's tendency — found among the Ankave as well — to name women after paternal rather than maternal kin (1972: 100–101).

36 Bonnemère (1996: 362–363).

37 But the rule of naming the set of brothers separately from the set of sisters applies here, too.

38 Zonabend (1980: 17).

39 J. Mimica is of a different opinion when it comes to the Iqwaye: 'The man's and woman's own patrilineal group name, the patri-name, refers to their bodily interiority, specifically the bones. The man's mother's patrilineal group name, his matri-name, refers to his bodily exteriority the flesh' (1991: 84). One wonders in passing why female names do not receive the same treatment.

40 For each clan there exists, in effect, a set of equivalent terms from which one can choose.

41 The friendly feelings surrounding the use of endearment names recall the Melpa practice of sharing a food and deciding to use the food-name as a term of address between the two persons involved (A. Strathern 1977: 504).

42 It is this particular feature of the Ankave naming system that I chose to evoke in the title of my article: the Ankave do not feel the need to give each person a different name. Interestingly enough, this practice is strictly avoided in other societies (see esp. Taylor 1993: 659).

Chapter 9

OF ATOLLS AND GARDENS

An attempt at participant ethno-archaeology in Tuamotu[1]

Jean-Michel Chazine

In the middle of the Pacific Ocean lies the Tuamotu Archipelago, with its seventy-five atolls sprinkled over an area larger than that of Europe, forming a fragmented set of islands long settled by human populations in spite of the extreme climatic and ecological constraints constantly impinging on their relations with the environment. This string of low-lying islands is strikingly different from its French Polynesian neighbours, and it is precisely these differences which make it a distinct object of study. It is a complex space, comprised of tiny individualised territories in a vast expanse of sea: a few thousand square kilometres of land scattered over nearly two million square kilometres of water!

It was therefore interesting, with reference to the general Pacific atoll system, for us to look at some of the Tuamotu atolls and to analyse, from a chronological perspective, the interrelations between the detectable climatic and environmental variations, and the past and present adaptability of their occupants. Yet, as we will see, the implementation of this general study produced some wholly unexpected results. The researchers' program, which consisted in rehabilitating the former cultivation-pits was subsequently, and unbeknown to the researchers themselves, diverted from its original purpose by those for whom it was meant before being in turn re-appropriated by them.

Conditions of the study

The general study first of all undertook to collect geo-morphological data on the coral substratum, which were completed by a few datings that made it possible to circumscribe past variations in sea level. With what is known about the average growth rate of the outer reef, we were able to show, first of all, that the emergence of lands allowing continuous theoretical human occupation seems to have occurred, in Tuamotu, no earlier than 500 AD.

It so happens that this period corresponds exactly — with the exception of the Marquesas Islands, which had been occupied for several centuries by then — to the general occupation phase of the eastern Pacific.

The parallel anthropological study carried out on a few specific atolls where ethno-archaeological excavations and studies on ancient occupation sites had already been conducted, consisted in establishing correlations with the environment as it changed over time. It was interesting to see whether certain criteria of habitability, deduced from the sites and/or remains of settlements, could also at a later time be compared — or even correlated in view of classifying the atolls — with the categories normally used by geographers.

While the more-or-less continuous human occupation of a space is clearly and primarily dependent on the food resources available to its occupants, these resources are locally just as dependent on those provided or allowed by the environment as on those resulting from the techniques of exploitation and enhancement employed by the inhabitants.[2] It was possible to think that, in such small spaces, the reconstruction of the human occupation process, one of the basic aims of archaeology, would be incomparably easier. And too, in these relatively closed yet interlinking little areas, modern depredations seem not to have done much harm for the moment.

Although the islanders are still largely dependent on their environment, the evolution of this environment or of the contingencies to which the inhabitants are subjected is harder to detect, especially for 'prehistoric' times, in other words for this part of the world: before the Europeans arrived.[3] Here, too, however it was important to make good use of one of the anthropological particularities of Oceania, namely the vigorous 'oral tradition', which had long been directly proportional to the social vitality of a place and which, in spite of everything, made it possible to preserve a large amount of knowledge. Even though this oral tradition is now somewhat corrupted, and in some cases obsolete, and even though its 'depth' is limited to three generations at best — when it comes to technical information and material culture — the remains have nevertheless proven to be consistent and determining enough to be validly used.

Although limited, collective or even individual memory is still an indispensable support and guidepost. The example of the renewed interest in modern-day *tahua* (healers also acting on the supernatural as well), who cleverly manipulate cultural information and its present-day transpositions, shows how easily new uses, chronological short-cuts and syncretic creations are accepted by popular consensus. In the minds of elderly Paumotu, the past is amalgamated and lost in an often idealised 'in former times' or 'once upon a time', which sometimes include the twentieth century. It is therefore necessary to factor in this recently introduced neo-cultural background noise.[4]

The atolls

Atolls are what remains of old volcanoes when the mechanisms of erosion, subsidence, eustanism, deformation of the lithosphere and sea-level fluctuations have taken their toll; they are circumscribed by living coral reef, which has gradually reduced them to rings a few dozen kilometres around and projecting a scant few metres above the water.[5]

The reference curve of the average fluctuation in sea level that has gradually been established indicates a regular drop of some sixty centimetres over the last 1500 years, in other words, since 450 AD. However, present or very recent observations suggest a reversal of the process (on the order of one centimetre per year), the causes of which are still under debate (greenhouse effect, El Niño, earth's natural cycle, for instance), has been under way for several decades at least. This means that any direct correlation between age, outer-reef growth, average sea level and systematic habitability of the atolls remains to be defined, at least for those periods in which sustained human population was feasible. Nevertheless it also proves that, with the exception of the observation time scales, there is quite a bit of room for uncertainty between the deductions that can be made from the geo-morphological observations alone and their actual effects on the island populations. This uncertainty is further amplified if we take into account the extreme variability in the evolution of the purely human contingencies. In fact, it turns out that the distribution of the archaeological traces of human activity presently observed does not reflect the apparent 'natural' occupation capacities of these islands and, in any event, does not seem to be connected with the sudden disappearance of specific plant or animal species.[6]

The Tuamotu archipelago was discovered in 1521 by Quiros, but did not receive further noticeable European visits — if one excepts Roogeveen in 1721 — until the end of the eighteenth century. Here were the last uninhabited islands, not only in the Eastern Pacific, but in the entire world. This explains why these lands were seldom noted by nineteenth-century observers in their journals and logs. It is true that the fluid and relatively 'discreet' way these lands were controlled or used by their inhabitants did not fit the known patterns of the time, and thus led to the conclusion of an absence of appropriation or technical culture there. And so the idealised picture of the Polynesian 'king of the sea, Viking of the South Seas' grew up and spread, and continued down to our time.

Upon further investigation, the reality of this space proved to be more complex, and, although the occupation of these low-lying islands remained a visual paradox, in reality it exhibited all the logical and rational features of societies which, in order to survive, are obliged to be closely attuned to their environment, especially when it is such a small, limited and fragile one. These features largely determine the way humans occupy their space, which, aside from a few variations, shows little differentiation from one island to another. The people who gradually settled these islands did so in identical fashion, but each time the variations in local parametres — the sea, lagoons, winds — generated a few additional differences.

Agricultural practices and cultivation-pits

Viewed from the open sea, these tiny rings of greenery seem to be entirely covered in a dense forest of palm trees, broken only here and there by nearly desertified spaces. In 1835, Darwin had already remarked that the ocean and the dry land seemed in these places to be locked in constant struggle and that it seemed astonishing that such a meagre barrier was not instantaneously destroyed by the mighty and relentless surge of this immense ocean (Darwin, 1842)

At close range, in spite of the traditional clichés about atolls, blue lagoons and swaying palms, the coconut groves shrink, covering large areas only there where they are truly exploited. Elsewhere a specific vegetation comprised not only of bushes but also trees is once again developing normally and expansively. Introduction of the coconut palm and its generalised diffusion date back no further than the first half of the nineteenth century, but they considerably altered the appearance of these islands, as well as deeply transforming their ecological and human structures.

With resources, an appearance, a population and a habitat that were sometimes very different from those of other southern and central Oceanic societies, and occupying a fragile space whose precarious and clearly inadequate potentialities were preoccupying, this group of islands was in a sense placed in 'cultural quarantine'. And yet, paradoxically, the marine resources of Tuamotu were those most systematically exploited for (mother-of-pearl) pearl-shells, sea cucumbers and whale hunting. Coconut planting by Europeans — missionaries, traders and administrators — aside from the fact that it generated the beginnings of a market economy, was designed by the new arrivals to compensate for the cultural and agricultural deficiencies of these lands, until then apparently uncultivated, by endowing them with a visible economic utility. As the basis of an evermore artificial economy, coconut plantations had from the outset a considerable impact on the subsequent evolution of these islands, and therefore on the reconstruction of their past. In a few words, systematically bringing under cultivation communally held lands obliged families and their lineages to define in legal and sometimes contradictory terms, the boundaries of certain plots inasmuch as they procured an income or speculative means of monetary exchange that did not correspond, either economically or culturally, to former traditional practices or needs. The administrative 'districts' formed from the ancestral *matakainanga*[7] (domains formerly belonging to a family group that managed marriages and the land, and which were carefully marked out and regulated in space and time), were consequently occupied intensely only during the annual *rahui* season (the institutionalised communal phase of exploitation), the rest of the time being left almost completely deserted.

Previous generalised occupation of the coral ring is attested by many remains of ceremonial structures used for both socio-religious functions and land management. Such appropriation markers indicate, almost by omission, that these 'sea-faring' fishermen also tended to their dry-land territory. In fact they often even practised (their own) forms of organised exploitation of the vegetable resources. The techniques used and their production coincide with the characteristic criteria of horticulture, and that is the word used from the outset to describe the practices of Oceanic peoples, even if they are also often akin to simple forms of agriculture.

A bibliographical search turns up very few descriptions of these growing practices and, as earlier archaeological and ethno-historical investigations mention them only in passing, it was not until we made some direct field observations[8] that they took on a strategic dimension. A few missionary journals mentioned that 'the islanders dug holes for growing tubers the size of a champagne cork'[9] or that they 'buried roots in the ground and some time later came back to gather the product'.[10] Sometimes these 'holes' became 'pits'[11] in which it was possible actually to grow food crops.

In 1930, the ethno-archaeologist, K.P. Emory, conducted a preliminary and quasi-systematic ethnographic study of the material culture of the Tuamotu islands; it was accompanied by extensive archaeological explorations. At this time Emory inspected a few of these cultivation pits, some of which were still in use. To these, as well as to the corresponding tools, he devoted a few lines of technical description: the first, and until recently, the only references in all the available ethno-archaeological literature.[12] Nevertheless these pits, tangible, concrete, precise components of material culture, whose size is determinant for their quantification potential, never became the object of an individual study. In fact, nearly the same is true of the general study of agrarian remains in the Pacific Ocean.

Found almost everywhere and covering from a hundred or so square metres to several hectares, cultivation-pits are more or less regularly distributed around the inner rim of the atolls. The exploitation techniques that have been pieced together thanks to earlier descriptions are now well known.[13] Briefly, these are large pits dug down to the surface of the water table; the evacuated earth pitched up around the perimeter reaches a height of from two to eight metres, forming a succession of steep hummocks.[14] The adjective 'brackish' often associated with their use stems above all from the usual consequences of the abandonment of the pits owing to the establishment of the *rahui* in districts remote from the village.[15] To the eye, these cultivation-pits are the most numerous, common and in fact largest elementary remains of pre-European human occupation of Tuamotu, and of the atolls of the South Pacific in general. They are a characteristic feature of a true agrarian architecture in any rural landscape, and reconstruction of their food-producing potential attests to the important role they played.

In addition to systematically measuring the shape and area of over a thousand pits, we were able to reconstruct the old techniques by collecting the know-how of a few elderly persons on different atolls who were eye-witnesses or themselves possessors of ancestral knowledge. We where thus able to establish a different image of the old ways of occupying these low-lying islands. Today, monoculture of the coconut tree together with widespread dependency on government and metropolitan handouts have almost totally eradicated the food resources derived from agriculture and the knowledge that went with them.

An experiment in transplanting the past

In view of this almost general loss of know-how and the dramatic dietary deficiencies observed, the discovery, by true ethno-archaeological investigation, of an important autochthonous food-producing potential prompted us to try out these methods. The data we collected provided detailed descriptions of the succession of operations as well as the yields obtained, justifying our decision to get involved and make practical use of the disconnected pieces of information. Piecing together knowledge freshly rediscovered and then reconstituted, in part thanks to the tattered memories of a few elderly inhabitants and in part owing to techniques of investigation borrowed from the human sciences and agronomy, represents a dynamic and stimulating challenge.

The switch from research findings, from the 'scientific' sphere, to their concrete application sanctioned by future users is a transformation rarely attempted, not only for ethical, but also purely practical and structural reasons. In the present case, the stakes were even higher because the justification for such an experiment was based on a largely bygone past. In reality it was the simple fact of taking into consideration all the archaeological, historical, environmental, and then sociocultural and agronomical data that, little by little, gave rise to — and defined — the idea of attempting such an experiment, in which separate disciplines appeared effectively to complement each other. Indeed, one of ethno-archaeology's favourite areas of application and expression is precisely Oceania. By combining agro-pedological and geo-morphological observations with the ethnographic data, we were able to define a 'virtual' reality that objectively lay in the past, but which lent itself at the same time to a new genesis. The only real unknown — although we had already had a glimpse of it as well — was 'quite simply' how the population was going to accept this sort of cultural transplant, a veritable technological 'auto-intra transfer'!

We envisaged the experiment first of all as a trial run, taking advantage of the interest, charisma and efficiency of a former village leader; and afterwards as a more global agro-cultural restoration campaign, using audio-visual techniques and mediations whenever possible. For the territorial government, this was also an experiment in verifying the true developmental possibilities of the French Polynesian atolls and could help provide an answer to the economic and social concerns of which they are the object.

Today islanders' truly rural activity is reduced to its simplest expression: upkeep of the coconut groves is rudimentary at best, if not non-existent. Although it is hard work, the harvest is more akin to gleaning or simple gathering. Spread over the year, these operations occupy only part of the time. And in any event, income is ensured by an artificial subsidy system known as 'equalisation', which has nothing in common with the true world price of copra (on the order of one tenth the subsidy level). It appears increasingly clear that this set of measures is a simple socio-economic formula to combat the depopulation of the atolls. But the measures are also limited to exclusively economic or purely financial operations. No alternative involving a minimum level of food production has ever been envisaged or suggested. Aside from the anarchical channels of 'unauthorised' enrichment, observed in a few pearl-shell farms, the sociocultural fabric is in a state of almost total disrepair.

Once we had proof that the Paumotu's ancestors knew how, under well-defined conditions, to cultivate, improve, renew and settle their garden plots here, and that they produced enough food to satisfy their needs, we set up a program to rehabilitate a few old cultivation-pits on one atoll, with the gradual support of a few cultivators and local leaders. Roughly speaking, this program[xvi] featured a series of attempts at restoring cultivation-pits that had stood abandoned for over a century, and planting them with both traditional and recently imported food-species. The trials were to be carried out and observed over a period of at least two years.

The program got off to a good start, but soon bogged down, at least with respect to the calendar we had drawn up, due to delays in releasing the funds. Fortunately, the parallel program of demonstrations and audio-visual displays enabled us, in spite of everything, to maintain a climate of patient if not completely favourable expectation on the part of the population and the persons more specifically involved.

The village community had seemed at once quite interested and quite apathetic. The innovative side of the project, linking tradition closely with development, was attractive to certain villagers, but the historical void separating them from this tradition was still a very real handicap. Moreover, so many Europeans had already come promising them the moon, advocating one technique after another, that they preferred to quietly wait and see.

Because of both technical and human difficulties encountered on the experimental island, two other locations had to be and were chosen, and this was at the request of their occupants. The new locations presented the advantage of being closer to the village and being the sites of fairly polyvalent activities: rudimentary gathering of copra, but also of seashells for necklaces and various kinds of fishing. Each was under the direction of an active, enterprising and efficient family head backed by a united kin group. After an observation phase of nearly two years — described by some as inactivity — these leaders began to show an interest, based on the content of the agricultural or food-producing possibilities they themselves had assessed. This interest, which had grown almost on its own, also contrasted sharply with the concerns expressed by others, based essentially on the amount of money they anticipated in return for their co-operation.

As the program unfolded, one negative parameter gradually took on an unexpected importance. The thick layer of rich vegetal matter at the bottom of a number of pits was already home to a great many *tupa* crabs (*Cardisoma carnifex*), which initially made serious inroads on the sites' production capacity. The *tupa* ravaged the few taro plants that were left after the initial planting, so that we did not have enough shoots to replant the area planned and, above all, this created problems with the administrative regulations. In the beginning, the plants matured without any noteworthy intervention or difficulty. But as soon as the *tupa* discovered the shoots, it took them only a few days to do serious damage. So a way to combat this unexpected predator had to be organised. Since the generalised abandonment of the coconut groves that had covered between 80 and 90 per cent of the atoll area, the crabs had proliferated quite rapidly in the wet zones and therefore particularly in the abandoned cultivation-pits. The soil, which already favoured organic and biological activity, was quickly adopted by these nearly omnivorous crabs. The earlier regulatory systems, such as the widespread human consumption of these animals, had completely disappeared. Even worse, such was the amnesia and the ignorance, that many people were convinced that the crabs had never been eaten because they are dangerous. This idea, contradicted by old descriptions, comes from the fact that the accumulation of all manner of refuse, in the island agglomerations that have grown up since the second half of the nineteenth century, effectively made the *tupa* unfit for human consumption. But wherever the population density, and therefore the amount of refuse produced, is not excessive, their content can be assimilated, and they are indeed edible and eaten. This is true in many archipelagos as well as in the other South Pacific atolls.

Obtaining taro shoots, a problem that arose in the first trials, was another obstacle. Despite the presence, in the early stages, of a market gardener from the Austral Islands — he had set up after the 1983 cyclones — willing to sell us his own shoots, their number fell far short of the hundreds we needed. Those we procured from a farmer in Tahiti could not be shipped owing to the strict application of a phytosanitary regulation theoretically designed to protect the Tuamotu atolls, as the fumigation normally and obligatorily done on site by no means guaranteed plants would not be infected with certain diseases. Further information and analyses showed that the near totality of the islands of French Polynesia were already contaminated. But as the phytosanitary services could not guarantee that the shoots were innocuous, their transfer from island to island was not authorised. The difficulties involved in finding another source that met the phytosanitary and technical requirements meant that our only sources of supply were the residual shoots and those produced in our own pits.[17] Nevertheless, these parameters were an instructive indicator, for they gave a good idea of the time needed to plant the tens of thousands of square metres exploited, which were certainly close to the parameters regulating the size of the growing pits in former times.

These problems notwithstanding, I later discovered that a dozen households in the village had, of their own accord, begun very quietly reconstituting small vegetable gardens in which taros accounted for a large portion of the produce. The little study we did and the videos we taped at the time showed that some of these 'secret' gardens had been going for over a year and that some were even in their third production cycle.

Our experimental program — which in my opinion had had a few hiccups — had in fact taken hold elsewhere and of its own accord, independently of us, since we knew nothing about it. This was in large part due to the video sessions we had organized on several occasions at the town hall. The relatively detailed technical and comparative information provided at these showings assuaged people's doubts and hesitations, and prompted them to carry out their own, almost clandestine, experiments. So as to avoid the 'shame' attendant in this rural world on quitting or failing, each household preferred to keep their own experiment a secret. Initially the undertaking proceeded discreetly. Then, as the results proved positive, the plants were gradually displayed. In time, the front yards, usually restricted to ornamental plants, were transformed by these new family vegetable plots, which, little by little, overflowed their backyard enclosures and began to expose themselves to passing glances.

A few personal innovations in the techniques of plant preparation or composting had been imagined and tried out by some, revealing to us at the same time, behind the individualization processes, the mechanics by which techniques and know-how are personally appropriated. Last of all, it should be noted that, for those attempts that were crowned with success, the master gardener's display sometimes took on an ostentatious character, showing an additional degree of skill that enhanced their standing in the eyes of the community.

Conclusion

Beyond the successive difficulties, which are after all part of any experiment in development, the attitude changes or the initiatives on the part of a few people offer food for thought. The experiment shows that the successful introduction of an outside element into a functioning system has, at the very least, to answer to contingencies that are often much more complex than — or entirely different from — those one would have thought, whether one is dealing with people, nature or their common environment. Secondly, it is interesting to see that, while people reacted in terms of individual motivation, the determining factors turned out to be the technical and comparative details to which the population has full access.

In the case of our program, originally developed on the basis of ethno-archaeological observations and reconstitutions, but specifically adapted to the rural environment and subsequently to the area of agronomy, it is interesting to note that, even though it was diverted and slowed down by external problems, it nevertheless went ahead, not only unbeknown to me, but in a space that had not been anticipated.

The challenge of 'trying to revive the past' in order to demonstrate that, even in a small, isolated enclave, it not only held potential but provided a precise answer to certain needs was accepted and at the same time diverted. The very targets of the program, adopting a prudent, circumspect pedagogical attitude, appropriated the experiment, and they did it in a much simpler way than we had expected. The productivity and yields of the gardens they could make for themselves became very clear to them as soon as the advantages could be isolated and identified. Once they had acquired the necessary techniques, their individual approaches both united and differentiated them.

To be sure, the simple technological, and even economic, demonstration is only the first step, a necessary one, but not sufficient in itself. For such an undertaking to succeed, it must then fit into the cultural fabric, into the pathways and spaces conceivable by the community it addresses, and then go on to achieve true autonomy.

The way this appropriation took place, in Ana'a atoll particularly, as well as the requests arriving today from other atolls, are conclusive and comforting. They teach us that it is not enough to propose examples of development bolstered by an arsenal of irrefutable technical and economic arguments for them to be accepted. Sociocultural regulators intervene and by creating an obstacle here, a limit to excesses there, can sometimes also become amplifiers.

The entirely unforeseen fight against the taro-eating crabs also shows how chains of ecological regulation are constantly at work. Changes to the occupation conditions of the atolls combined with eating habits constantly raise new problems, the ones flowing from the others. One of the specificities of the rural world and of agronomy is having to take this into account. Many plans and experiments motivated solely by the logic of technical or economic rationality have foundered because such social and environmental parameters were ignored.

The exemplary situation of the Tuamotu Archipelago shows that the inertia of the past exists: one can complain about it or put it to use. All evolution, be it environmental, human or social, has a 'history' which literally cannot be circumvented. By taking this history into account, the Tuamotuans will be able to move towards an optimal and autonomous recovery of their own potentialities.

This project was originally intended as a local demonstration of the agronomic capacities of the atoll soils; unbeknown to us, however, it spread to a good number of households as soon as proven techniques were put to use demonstrating its success. What had been programmed for at best the medium or the long term took hold in other places, in other ways and faster than we had planned. By reestablishing a dynamic, active connection with their past, the Paumotu not only rediscovered part of their roots, they gave new value to a past that could also become a legitimate source of pride.

Footnotes

1   This article is based in particular on work carried out during different missions conducted by CORDET and FIDES (MEDETOM) and then within the ATP (Centre National de la Recherche Scientifique) project, 'For a history of the environment and natural phenomena'.

2   In an environment like that of the low-lying Tuamotu islands, the impact of, first of all the open sea, then the lagoons on the emerged land, although synchronous with human presence, do not respect the same variable orders of magnitude. Even though the decisive parameter of sea level acts on a scale of thousands of years — while it is only a few decades for the shell fish and fish (benthic and halieutic) populations — the corresponding time scale of human populations is a mere few centuries, by approximately two-hundred-year chunks. Finding the smallest common multiple for observing these respective time scales is therefore the challenge that this particular space obliges us to make. The ecological parameters are so tightly intertwined with those governing the tiny human groups occupying this space that there is no choice but to try to understand them in a complementary fashion.

3   The evolutionary gradient visible from archaeological data and ethno-historical observations seems to have remained relatively stable in these islands from the first landings down to continuous occupation. Aside from a few cases, whether in the high or the low-lying islands, successive technical changes, the key to establishing prehistoric ethnological chronologies, are almost impossible to isolate. We still do not know exactly the range of uses to which the basic materials found on an atoll were put. These are restricted to coral or shells hardened by calcification, to bone or mother-of-pearl, to name only the hard materials capable of lasting any amount of time in an exclusively chalky soil. Under the best possible conditions of preservation, in a dry, airless place, the lifetime of plants and organic material is at best little more than a hundred years.

4   This explains why, in many cases, aside from collecting ethnographic information on the past or its present-day remains, archaeological methods will be needed to identify and order certain phases of activity. In particular, the periods before European arrival, which was recent in this part of the world, have been forgotten.

5   In principle there are several parameters which determine whether or not people can settle for short or long periods of time: whether or not the vertical deformation of the lithosphere and the fluctuations in the sea level, climatic and volcanic cataclysms, evolution of the madrepores, the pedology and the flora enable the coral rim — especially on the reef — to afford a minimum of protection against the onslaught of the sea, thus allowing the formation of soils necessary to the implantation of the different life forms. No human settlement of any kind can become stable until this transformation is sufficiently advanced.

6   For the sake of comparison: the floral dynamic observed on most of the atolls since the 1983 cyclones accounts for a buried paleohumus enriched horizon. The intensity of this dynamic is such that not only has it withstood the episodic cyclones, it also corresponds to a reappearance of the state that existed prior to the transformations of the nineteenth and twentieth centuries, appearing even beneath refuse-strewn and sterile soils. The generalised presence of at least one paleosoil can be explained in part by the recently named 'endo-updwelling geothermic' phenomenon, which explains the occasional welling up of certain biochemical nutrients through the porous coral substratum (Rougerie and Wuathy, 1986); this phenomenon naturally promotes a certain development in the vegetation.

7   The present-day administrative districts coincide roughly with the space of the former *matakainanga*.

8   See Chazine (1977).

9   See Montiton (1874).

10 See Fierens (1873).

11 See Moerenhout (1937), Lucett (1854).

12 See Emory (1975).

13 See Chazine (1985, 1988, 1991, 1992, 1993, 1996, 1999).

14 The average visible depth ranges from 2.5m to 4m, depending on the pit; this corresponds to the average stable level of the underlying freshwater, a freshwater lens, which is linked to the volume of rainwater trapped after percolating through the substratum under the coral ring.

15 Another frequent reason is ignorance of the limited thickness of the pod of freshwater (see note 14) that floats on the surface of the brine (following the Ghyben-Hertzberg principle). If the excavation is too deep, the pit goes through the thin layer of freshwater and you wind up with brine or brackish water.

16 See Chazine (1985).

17 These therefore had a lower theoretical rate of reproduction and proliferation.

PART THREE

Chapter 10

FOOD AND WEALTH

Ceremonial objects as signs
of identity in Tonga and in Wallis*

Françoise Douaire-Marsaudon

It was primarily the objects used in ceremonial exchanges by the Samoans and the Maori which provided Mauss, in his essay, *The Gift*, with the opportunity to discuss the system of ritual gift-exchange found in Polynesia.[1] Since this essay, Mauss has become an obligatory reference on the question, a bit like a tradition which has grown up and now dictates that any discussion of Polynesian ceremonial exchanges must begin with Samoa and/or the Maori.[2] The present article suggests a shift of focus to other parts of Polynesia: the societies of Tonga and Wallis. Two types of ceremonial objects will be studied, food and wealth, together with the representations associated with them in the thinking of the societies I have selected.[3]

Through a presentation of these objects and the logics they entail, I would like to show that they are in fact privileged emblems of a group's identity. I will use material taken from contemporary case studies, but I will also call on some historical sources. A fairly striking consistency will also appear between past and present, in terms of the nature of the gifts as well as the forms of the exchanges. However we will also have to inquire into the appearance of objects and practices which seem to have little to do with tradition.

In both Tonga and Wallis, the objects used in ritual exchanges fall into two clear-cut categories: food, or *kai*, which is comprised essentially of pork and tubers; and non-edible valuables, called *koloa*, 'items of value' or 'riches, wealth', a term that designates primarily mats, barkcloth fabric (*ngatu*) and coconut oil.[4] The terms *kai* (food) and *koloa* (wealth, riches) denote the same objects in both societies. Two additional features should also be underscored. Generally speaking, and in spite of further shadings that will be added in the course of this discussion, both categories — *kai* and *koloa* — are strongly gendered, insofar as the ceremonial foods are produced, baked or cooked and presented by men, while the 'riches' are prepared, manufactured and presented by women. Finally, these objects are produced and given by groups, though both the nature and the composition of the donor groups are subject to change.[5]

To facilitate the analysis, *kai* and *koloa* will initially be dealt with separately.

Kai, or food, the men's gift

Polynesian gift-exchange ceremonies are striking both for the quantity of food collected and distributed, and for the ostentation with which this accumulation and distribution are carried out. In Tonga and in Wallis, at the time of large *katoanga*,[6] tens and even hundreds of baskets filled with food are neatly lined up on the *mala'e*.[7] These baskets usually accompany offerings composed of piles of raw yams (including *Dioscorea alata*), taros (including *Colocasia esculenta*) or *kapé* (*Alocasia macrorrhiza*), topped with a large cooked pig and a number of mats and lengths of barkcloth, or *ngatu*. When the *kava* ceremony is nearly completed, the total number of piles and baskets is cried out together with the contents of the baskets and the name of the village or the group that has given the offerings.

The examples of *katoanga* given here were deliberately chosen from different time periods. Here is the description of a *katoanga* held at the end of the nineteenth century, in Tonga, for the jubilee of a missionary:

> At the signal, a voice rang out, first enumerating the piles of foodstuffs. This is essential in Tongan etiquette... In addition to the masses of *kava*, the official crier counted out one hundred and sixty-seven baskets of yams. Each basket held between ten and fifteen of the size of our large beets; one hundred and seventy-five roasted pigs, three of which weighed perhaps three hundred pounds; two hundred and eighty-four baskets of *faikakai* ['cakes' made from the flour of tubers and coconut milk], the islanders' favourite treat which is not disdained by Whites either, each basket containing some twenty pounds; one hundred three-pound loaves of bread; many varieties of fish. Everything was piled with attention to symmetry and, at intervals, on tall poles, pieces of coloured fabric flew like flags on festive ships.[8]

We are fortunate in having the description of a large *kataonga* that was held in Tonga at the very beginning of the nineteenth century for the lifting of an eight-month-long taboo imposed on pig, chicken and coconut. One of the privileges of a Polynesian chief, and not the least, used to be the right to taboo whatever food items he chose for as long as he decided. Violation of such taboos was supposed to entail not only physical punishment if it was discovered, but also supernatural reprisals: a sickness that would 'eat' your insides until you died, fitting retribution for someone who had ventured to eat tabooed food. The man who witnessed this lifting of the taboo, Mariner, reckoned that a little more than 400 large pigs had been killed, and 3,000 yams brought. First of all, some 20 pigs and around 500 yams were set aside to be presented as an offering near the graves of the Tu'i Tonga, the former paramount chiefs of Tonga. Mariner recounts that this food was left standing for several days before being distributed, in a state of more than dubious freshness, to the lower classes. The remaining quantity was divided into four lots, each comprising some 500 yams and 100 or so pigs. These shares were given to: 1) the Tu'i Tonga; 2) the gods (i.e. their priests); 3) the *hau* (the 'temporal' king), who immediately shared them with his chiefs and warriors; 4) the highest-ranking chiefs. With the exception of the Tu'i Tonga's share, these items were then redistributed according to the chiefs' ranks, from the top to the bottom of the social ladder, 'till every man in the island gets at least a mouthful of pork and yam'.[9]

We see that, with the exception of the portion reserved for the Tu'i Tonga, the rest is redistributed by order of rank. These public distributions are thus a means of enabling one immediately to 'visualise' the social body, of reminding everyone, and perhaps of confirming, that it is based on rules and an ordering necessary to the maintenance of good order. Which of course does not prevent rivalries — enabling an ambitious man to win a place in this order; such rivalries, as we shall see, can also find expression in the accumulation of ceremonial gifts.

The third example of ceremonial gift-giving is taken from a 1989 field study done in the village of Taoa, in Tonga.[10] That year, Prince Tupouto'a decided to go to Vava'u, in part to celebrate his birthday, on May 4th, and in part to attend the Wesleyan Church Conference, which was to be held the same day. Forewarned, the whole village began buzzing like a huge beehive well before the day set for the festivities. The men had cultivated the Prince's plot and planted it with the best variety of yam, which used to be reserved for chiefs (*kahokaho*).[11] The women took shifts in the communal house to manufacture a long piece of barkcloth and a large mat. For the day, fifty-three *pola*, a kind of portable 'table', had been planned, each of which would bear three or four small baked pigs, tubers (yams, sweet potatoes, taros), chicken, fish, *lu*, *faikakai*, and sometimes fruit juice or even cigarettes.[12] These *pola* were for the meals of the guests who had been invited to both the Wesleyan Church Conference and the Prince's birthday. When the guests had eaten their fill, the leftovers would be, as was the custom, shared out and redistributed among the village kin groups. Note that, besides the oven food, the villagers presented the Prince with a mat and barkcloth made by the women, as well as two live pigs, one big and one medium-sized,[13] together with some one hundred raw yams (in addition to those grown for him).[14]

Here are a few figures to indicate the quantity of food given at three *katoaga*[15] held on the *mala'e* in Wallis, between November 1988 and January 1989.

— The 150th anniversary of the arrival of the Marist missionaries (20 November 1988):
    32 large pigs
    74 medium-sized and small pigs
    76 baskets of cooked tubers[16]
    12 piles of raw tubers (*kape*)[17]
— Marriage of the king's grandson to the senator's daughter
    (23 December 1988); the king's gifts to the senator:
    10 large pigs
    56 small or medium-sized pigs
    56 baskets of tubers
— Installation of the new deputy, Kamilo Gata (17 January 1989):
    17 large pigs
    48 small and medium-sized pigs
    60 baskets of cooked tubers
    2 piles of raw *kape* and yams.[18]

A rapid calculation reveals that the quantity of meat presented during these three *katoaga* comes to approximately fourteen tons! The bulk of the food was presented to the guests participating in the *kava* ceremony. The piles made up of raw tubers surmounted by a large pig were given to either the beneficiaries of the ceremony, for example the new deputy (the third *katoaga*) or the high-ranking guests (the king, the bishop, the ministers). The baskets containing cooked tubers topped with a medium-sized or a small pig were usually distributed to the guests, once the pigs had been cut up.

During all the *katoaga* preparations I saw — arranging the piles, lining up the baskets, raising the poles decked with *manu* (the Wallisian equivalent of *pareo* in Tahiti), and so forth — a joyous hubbub invariably reigned on the *mala'e*, though not free from rivalry between the donor groups: for instance, in Wallis, between the three districts (Hahake, Hihifo and Mua), or between villages. For the first *katoaga* cited above, the presentation was made by the village, and one had only to 'hear' the silence that fell as each village's gift was called out. At stake in these events is the prestige of each village, but also of each Wallisian who, on this occasion, identifies with his village. I add that, during the three *katoaga*, the food publicly presented and enumerated was not eaten there, but taken home and shared out to the members of each kin group (*kaiga*). Although it was not possible to verify this, all my informants concurred in saying that a great number of people in Wallis ate pork on those days.

But the sharing of food also serves to *re-create* an order disturbed by an event such as a birth, a marriage or even more, a death. One such 're-ordering' occurred in a fairly striking manner in Tonga, on the occasion of the funeral of Taoa's village chief, Maka.[xix] Here is the list of the food prepared by the chief's widow and the villagers of Taoa, which was subsequently distributed and eaten on site by the villagers and their guests (whose number fluctuated between 50 and 350):

> 8 large pigs (*puaka hula*)
> 11 medium-sized pigs[20]
> 1 horse (*hoosi*)
> 4 cows (*pulu*)
> 2 tins of corned-beef weighing 20 kg each
> 2 boxes of mutton chops (*sipi*) weighing 20 kg each[21]
> some 100 baskets containing taro, *kape* manioc and yams.

The men of the village killed and cut up the animals, scraped the tubers, made the ovens and watched over them. The women prepared the poultry, the *lu* and the *faikakai*.[22] For the duration of the five-day funeral, the village did nothing but prepare food from dawn to dark. As I said, the food was given first of all to the guests. When they had eaten their fill, it was the villagers' turn to eat and then to divide up the leftovers. The amount of food, and of meat in particular, consumed over the five days was considerably greater than everyday fare.[23] For the villagers of Taoa, this was a time to do their *fatongia* to their village chief. The term, which means both 'duty' and 'fee', designates in fact everything an inferior owes to a superior in terms of family, social, domestic or political hierarchy. Finally, according to my informants, during these five days, the whole village worked as a single kin group, a single *kainga*, united around the mortal remains of their chief.

A comparison can be made between this funeral of a Tongan chief and the installation ceremony for the deputy for Wallis, however different the circumstances may be. It can be considered, for instance, that, in the case of the second ritual, the presentation, sharing and consumption of food constituted an event designed to bring the effervescent election campaign to a close and to underscore, for the space of the ritual, a somewhat shaken social peace. These distributions of foodstuffs also, at least temporarily, created relations between people (divided in this case along political lines) who habitually clashed or ignored each other. The installation of the deputy according to tradition, in particular with distribution of food — and *kava* of course — is a good example of the adaptation of 'custom' to a modern-day event. Perhaps it would even be better to speak of custom appropriating a modern-day event.

Piling up, distributing and destroying food — since it is perishable, it is eaten — are also designed to make clear to everyone who is who: in effect, a chief accumulates and distributes more than an ordinary man. His wealth and his liberality are measured first of all in food. But a chief is also someone to be fed. In the Tongan myth relating the origin of *kava*, a couple too poor to fulfill their obligations to the Tu'i Tonga sacrificed their leprous daughter to him. The mark of absolute poverty is not to be able to give an *'umu* containing both tubers and a pig to one's chief.[24] What is true for the poorest couple is also true for each chief, from the bottom to the top of the Tongan social pyramid: each must make gifts to his hierarchical superior, and first of all gifts of food, if he wants to *maintain his rank*. Furthermore, the chief himself is very often a big eater, and *embonpoint* is a sign of rank.

In the societies of Tonga and Wallis, the chief is still seen as the mediator between humans and the powers above, spirits of the ancestors or god. It is the chief's *mana* that is believed to make the crops grow in the ground. In Tonga, villagers receive their plot of land from the prince; however when they offer him presents, when they fulfill their *fatongia*, they do not see it as an exchange of 'land for tribute' but as a relation of indebtedness: the ceremonial gifts are presented to the prince in token of gratitude not so much for the land as for past and future harvests. It used to be that the chief's *mana* — and especially that of the paramount chief, the Tu'i Tonga — was believed to cause the crops to grow from the land, but also babies in their mother's womb. Today the growth of babies *in utero* is believed to be the work of the Christian god. Yet it is not unusual for Taoa villagers to send the prince a basket of yams when the birth of a child in the village is announced. In Wallis, a poor harvest is still today interpreted as a sign that the chief has lost his *mana*. If the breadfruit trees do not yield, if the yam harvest is meagre, if the sows produce small litters, the chiefs, or at least the village chiefs, are held responsible for these failures, and are promptly dismissed![25] There is thus a relationship between the supernatural, the chief and product of the land.[26] The chief must bear witness to this relationship, especially by his generosity: 'To be hospitable is to follow in the footsteps of one's ancestral god, by whose agency the earth originally gave forth its fruits and the sea its fish.'[27]

Myths ensure a detailed account of the nature of the relationship between such items and the supernatural. In Tonga, most products of the land come from the gods. The chiefs' yam (the *kahokaho*) was stolen from the gods of Pulotu (the Tongan paradise) by a Tongan spirit woman. The shark sprang from the sacrifice of the goddess Hina. The coconut palm grew from the spot where Hina buried the head of her lover, a serpent-god.[28] The most-valued foodstuffs came into existence through defying the gods or through a sacrifice, which enabled these items to be transposed from the supernatural to the human realm. In this light, food constitutes a sort of link with the divine.

Koloa *or wealth, the women's gift*

In addition to food, a number of objects were traditionally considered to possess exceptional value and therefore to be appropriate for ceremonial giving. Before discussing more specifically women's wealth, *koloa*, we need to take stock of the items covered by this term.

The objects formerly regarded as precious are the following:

1) mats, barkcloth, coconut oil[29]
2) decorated baskets, combs, chiefly decorations
3) clubs, lances, canoes, incised and carved whale teeth, wooden headrests, *kava* bowls or *tano'a*

This break-down into three categories can be explained by the following reasons: all the objects in the first category are manufactured by women only, but intended for men and women alike. They used to circulate among commoners as well as among chiefs, even if not the same objects were involved in the two cases. These objects ranked explicitly as valuables, as 'treasure', as their name, *koloa*, indicates. Once given, these objects could be redistributed. However, some, the most precious, used to belong only to chiefs; these were kept and transmitted as heirlooms.

The objects in the second category used to be manufactured exclusively by women of high rank. They could be given to men or to women, but they always circulated among the chiefly families. It seems that, as a rule, once given, they were no longer redistributed, but kept and passed down. Nevertheless, according to one old source, noble women made them into a 'sort of trade'.[30] With the exception of the baskets, these objects are no longer made.

The objects in the third category were manufactured exclusively by men and intended for men. Those who manufactured them were craftsmen (*tufunga*) working in the service of chiefs; their job was precisely to make these objects either for the chief's own use or for him to give to other chiefs. These objects were probably not redistributed once they had been given, but were kept and passed down as heirlooms, particularly the whale teeth, because they were so rare. Today such objects are produced primarily for the tourist trade.

There is an obvious similarity between the objects in the second and the third categories: all are chiefly objects which circulate only among the aristocracy. They are given, then kept and transmitted rather than being redistributed. They are also sometimes exchanged.

But the objects explicitly ranked as wealth, or *koloa*, are above all those in the first category; coconut oil, mats and barkcloth (made from the *hiapo* or paper mulberry, *Broussonetia papyrifera*). These objects have a number of functions. They are at once profane objects, everyday objects, precious objects symbolically overcharged and a 'currency'. They are used in ceremonial and in commercial exchanges.[31] They can be a medium of payment.[32] They can also be hoarded and transmitted as heirlooms. But while the material base of each of these functions is the same, the objects which are utilised and/or exchanged are not strictly the same as those which are kept. Those which are kept and transmitted are more precious than the rest. We are going to see that, alongside those objects that circulate regularly, there are what Annette Weiner calls 'inalienable possessions', which are stored.[33]

When they talk about *koloa*, wealth, today's Tongas and Wallisians visualise above all mats, barkcloth and coconut oil. In Tonga, the term was given at the beginning of the nineteenth century as the equivalent of 'riches, property, anything of value'.[34] The dictionary compiled by the Marist missionaries translates it as 'richesses, tout objet précieux, ce qu'on possède'.[35] Churchward's dictionary lists the following meanings: 'goods, wealth, riches, possessions; what one values; cargo, store, shop, produce (of a country)'.[36]

Barkcloth, mats and coconut oil are items whose manufacture requires the use of procedures ranging from the extremely simple to the highly sophisticated.[37] The production sometimes also entails the use of rituals, as in the case of the black tapas.[38]

As ceremonial exchange objects, *koloa* appear in two contexts: rites of passage and chiefly ceremonies. In the rites of passage — birth, marriage and death, and formerly circumcision and onset of menses — *koloa* can have several different functions. Some *koloa* are not exchanged but are closely connected with the body of the beneficiary(ies) of the ceremony. The skin of the newborn child, of the young spouses and of the deceased is rubbed with coconut oil. The baby is presented to the mother's and the father's people lying on a little bed comprised of barkcloth and a mat. During the ceremonial exchanges, the young couple sits on a seat made of one or several rolls of barkcloth and one or several mats rolled together, which later serves as the bridal bed. The body of the deceased is exposed on a 'mattress' made of a length of barkcloth and one or several mats, before being buried rolled in one (or several) pieces of barkcloth and one or several mats, and then covered with more mats. The coconut oil, barkcloth and mat are placed on the body in that order.

Most *koloa* enter the gift/counter-gift system and are exchanged between kin groups. They are always presented *together with* food, *kai*, the men's gift, with which they form a *whole*. The two *kainga*, that of the groom and that of the bride, in the case of a marriage, the paternal *kainga* and the maternal *kainga* in the case of a birth or a death, exchange gifts of *kai* and *koloa*. To give an idea of the way these exchanges are conducted, here are three examples, all connected with marriage. The first took place in Tonga, at the beginning of the twentieth century:[39]

> When the bridegroom and his people arrived at the place where the bride and her people waited, the gifts from the groom's relatives were presented to the bride's, being deposited before the house in two lines running parallel to the house front. The line closer to the house consisted of manufactured articles (*koloa*) such as tapa and mats furnished by the women of the bridegroom's people. The outer line consisted of oven (food) gifts and kava called *ngaue* (work) furnished by the men of the bridegroom's people.[40]

What is interesting here is the joint presentation of the women's goods, *koloa*, and the men's goods, the food gifts, which Gifford tells us are called *ngaue*, a term meaning 'work' or 'effort'.

The second example, again from Tonga, is given by Collocott and also dates from the beginning of the twentieth century. The scene takes place after the gifts have been deposited in front of the house where the marriage ceremony is to take place (in Tonga this is usually the house of the father of the groom).

> The house is filled with women connected with the bride, no men are there, their place is with the food, which is their especial care. Presently a woman is called from the house. She approaches the bride, assists her to rise, and leads her by the hand into the house, where the women divest her of her clothes. … This clothing had been provided by the bride's family and will subsequently fall to the share of the bridegroom's people. She is then arrayed in clothing, inferior in quality and quantity to that taken from her but still good, provided by the bridegroom and led forth again to her mother's lap [the two spouses in effect sit on the knees of their respective 'male mothers', in other words their maternal uncle] but presently another woman is called from the house to come and lead her in. Again, she is undressed and clothed afresh in raiment given by the husband. The clothing taken from her on this second occasion is for the bride's people.

According to Collocott, this scene can be repeated several times if the bridegroom is sufficiently rich, but usually twice is enough. Collocott's description goes on to show the bridegroom being in turn subjected to the same changes of clothing.[41]

Here now is the last example. It is a description of a marriage which took place in 1988 in Wallis, between the king's grandson and the senator's daughter, at which I was present:

> The bride arrived on the royal *mala'e* dressed in a European-style wedding gown of white lace. After the church service, the royal *kava* ceremony took place. While the *kava* was being prepared, the bride was led into the garden, behind the royal palace. There the women of her people removed her white dress (given by the king, thus by the groom's people) and dressed her in an impressive quantity of fabrics of all kinds, particularly velvet and satin, for which Wallisians have a high regard. Thus arrayed, the young bride returned before the palace and sat down. The preparation of the *kava* continued, as did the speeches. After some ten minutes, the young woman was led away again. This time it was the king's women relatives — her husband's people — who undressed her, then powdered her with *lega* (saffron powder) and finally dressed her in an enormous quantity of barkcloth, even more than the first time. The bride then returned to take her seat, with some difficulty given the quantity and the weight of the cloth she was wearing. Into her hair had been inserted a number of banknotes, some 100,000 Francs CFP (the equivalent of 1100 dollars at the time). When she had been installed, she was served the first bowl of *kava*. After the ceremony, the couple left for the senator's house, where the bride was undressed by her women relatives and the cloth gifts shared out among the members of her group.

Once again, in spite of the introduction of money, there is a striking continuity, on the one hand, between Tonga and Wallis, and, on the other, between the beginning of the twentieth century and today. In the last two cases described, it is clear that the 'undressers' keep their booty. The gifts are exchanged here by the agency of the recipients' bodies, those bodies which don the *koloa* and transmit them from one kin group to the other.

It is also noteworthy that the groom's people gave visibly more than the bride's. The reason for this is that the groom is a relative of the king, whereas the bride is a relative of the senator. By virtue of his high rank, the king — and his kin group (*kainga*) — has a duty to show more generosity than the senator and his *kainga*. All gifts are exchanged in public, and the days following these ritual exchanges will be spent discussing them. It must also be said that even with commoner families, the exchanges of gifts ostensibly take place between the *kainga* involved and that here too the group's status is taken into account. In effect, in Wallis, where the principle of seniority is particularly important, if either of the spouses is an eldest child, his or her family has an obligation to show more generosity than the other.

Generally speaking, when it comes to marriage, whoever is called 'father' oversees the sharing and distribution of the food. For the distribution of the *koloa*, in each of the kin groups involved — that of the bride or the groom — the task usually falls to the father's sister. This is almost systematic in Tonga, where the *mehekitanga* (paternal aunt) — or her proxy — always occupies the place of honour and, before beginning the distribution, takes her share, usually the finest piece.[42]

The ceremonies concerned with hierarchy — bestowal of titles, visits, homecomings, chiefly rites of passage — give rise to large-scale *kataonga*; these presentations of ceremonial gifts take place on the chief's *mala'e*. The gifts are brought by the chief's *kainga*, in other words his subjects. The gifts are solemnly enumerated and counted before being distributed. If for one reason or another, the meeting involves two chiefs, they exchange gifts furnished by their respective *kainga*.

As one observer at the beginning of the twentieth century remarked: 'the amount of cloth and mats collected are indications of the wealth and station of the families'.[43] Today the presentation of *koloa*, whether on the occasion of a rite of passage or a great chiefly *katoanga*, still represents a public display of the wealth and status of the groups involved.

Nowadays, in chiefly families, despite the equalising influence of Christianity, these purportedly non-competitive exchanges can abruptly spill over into frantic rivalry between two families, particularly on the occasion of a marriage, and ultimately empty the houses of both family heads. The rivalry for family status is so strong in *koloa* exchanges, especially in Tonga, that, when the social distance between two families is too great, the future newlyweds often prefer to elope to the capital and get married on their own, with the blessing of the poorer family.[44] Gift objects are thus one way for each of the groups involved in an exchange to decipher the wealth and station of the other groups. But gift-giving is also, at least insofar as kin groups are concerned, a way of challenging the respective rank of those concerned. Woe to him who does not maintain his rank; glory to him who enhances it! As one inhabitant of Wallis pointed out, even for the most critical individuals, it is very hard not to yield to the pressure to give, and to the ensuing incitement to outgive.

Finally, *koloa* are also hoarded, accumulated like 'treasure'. In fact that is the exact translation of the word *koloa*. In past times, in Tonga, the rarest, the finest, in a word, the most precious *koloa* were manufactured by groups of women under the direction of women from the aristocracy. Like the objects manufactured by artisans and reserved for the chiefs of a noble *kainga*, these *koloa* were regarded as the property of the chief's sister, or more precisely of her *kainga*, and constituted her 'treasure', or better the family treasure. Each aristocratic *kainga* thus owned a certain number of fine mats and *ngatu*, some of which were very old, very worn, but extremely prestigious.

> Each lineage seems to have a duty with a presiding priest who had in charge the *fakafaanga* or precious and sacred possessions of its god. Part of the *fakafaanga* were fine mats which constituted a form of wealth.[45]

The most precious pieces of Tongan barkcloth were 'embossed'. The blocks, *kupesi*, used to produce the design were made following a pattern that was forbidden to replicate outside the *kainga* and which constituted the family seal. Only noble families had the right to own and use the blocks, which were passed on from one generation to the next.[46] Even today the chiefly barkcloth fabrics are called *ngatu 'eiki* (literally: 'aristocratic barkcloth'), a name which distinguishes them from ordinary tapas.[47] These *koloa* were indeed, as Mauss says, ' precious articles, talismans, emblems'.[48]

As for the mats, the biggest and finest were reserved for the chiefs. Each also had a 'name', given by the original design which indicated they belonged to a particular noble *kainga*.[49] Thus the words of one missionary speaking of the fine mats of Samoa can also be applied to the *ngatu* and the mats of Tonga:

> Among the mats … there were three categories: ordinary ones, sacred ones and illustrious ones. The latter are renowned: people know where they come from, where they are from and who is the great chief who, by wearing them, attached to them an indelible memory of honour. However shredded and worn they may be, they are nevertheless held in great esteem. The experts in the science of mats, the d'Hozier of the area, know the name and the history of the famous mats, for each has a name. Without needing to examine them, they will tell you what they are worth. These illustrious mats are brought out only on important ceremonial occasions.[50]

It is these *koloa*, to the exclusion of the others, that come close to the Maori *taonga* described by Mauss. It is they which are, in this author's words, 'strongly linked to the person, the clan, and the earth … They are the vehicle for its *mana*, its magical, religious and spiritual force.'[51] According to Gifford, in Tonga, the centrepiece of the family 'treasure', the *fakafaanga* comprised in particular of fine mats, was a special mat which was treated as the shrine of the 'clan' spirit or god.[52]

These particular *koloa,* unlike the rest, are 'known', as are their owners. They are at once 'wealth' and 'signs of wealth'. The chief's treasure is there to testify to the number of his subjects, to the number of persons in his *kainga*. This is precisely why these *koloa* are not distributed outside the *kainga* but transmitted and/or given to a prominent member of the kin group, who will transmit them in turn. On this point, our analysis of the Tongan material is perfectly consistent with the paradox of 'keeping-while-giving' so brilliantly developed by A. Wiener[53]: certain *koloa* are kept, while others are exchanged; and it is not the same ones which are kept or exchanged. The most valuable, those that bear the family name or blazon, circulate only within the confines of the kin group, whereas the others circulate between groups. Of course a high-ranking chief must also be able to distribute an impressive quantity of mats and *ngatu,* selected from among those manufactured for exchange. It is therefore the totality of what is known as *koloa* which, among the aristocracy constituted and still constitutes the family property, its reserves or its treasure. In speaking of this set of valuable objects, some of which are kept and others given, one could also use M. Godelier's expression, 'keeping-for-giving',[54] which goes further than Weiner's 'keeping-while-giving'.[55]

Gifford tells us that, when a chief died, part of this property was distributed by the deceased's paternal aunt or by his sister, but another part, the *koloa kelekele,* was buried with the body.[56] It was thus possible to accumulate *koloa* over a lifetime, sometimes through personal merit. But how?

In Tonga, all *koloa* used to be controlled by the women of high rank, who supervised and directed the women's work. They had authority over all the *koloa* manufactured by the women under them and disposed of the items as they wished, including more less making a commerce of them.[57] 'Commoner' women had to ask their permission to use these *koloa,* which it is unthinkable that they could do without, given the role they play in rites of passage.

The accumulation of *koloa* was therefore probably exclusively a matter for chiefly families. For these, one means of accumulation was marriage. High-ranking chiefs were polygamous, and marriage strategies took into account the potential *koloa* wealth of the bride-to-be. But *koloa* could also be won in war. During the early nineteenth-century civil wars, chiefs would capture women and share them out for the explicit reason that they would be able to manufacture *koloa.*[58] Furthermore, each fortress or village taken was systematically pillaged primarily for the purpose of taking spoils of *koloa.*[59]

Amorous feats were also a good means of appropriating *koloa. Mana'ia* were young men whose romantic exploits enabled them to collect *kie taupo'ou,* or virginity mats. A great number of mats raised the standing not only of the interested party, but of his whole kin group, giving rise to veritable strategies for accumulating these mats on the part of the *kainga.*[60] Here too a connection with the divine appears: these *mana'ia* were thought to posses a god-given power (*mana*) which enabled them to attract women and therefore wealth. But it can also be said that these *koloa,* these riches, as representations, are supposed to produce or create wealth. On one hand, they are accumulated wealth, treasure, on the other, they are signs of wealth and power, insofar as they also testify to the number of the chief's subjects, who work for him. Finally, they are also believed in themselves to attract wealth and power. As Mauss shows in the case of the Kwakiutl coppers, these hoarded objects are 'mingled together as regards use and effect'.[61] He who amasses great numbers of *koloa* possesses *mana,* and since these *koloa* are themselves *mana,* they are believed to attract more *koloa.* As far as mental representations go, in any case, *koloa* function as a kind of capital.[62]

I must stress here a fundamental aspect of gift-exchange in Polynesia: if, as I attempted to show, chiefly groups used to have strategies for accumulating *koloa,* it is because competition for power *in terms of 'wealth'* was indeed a reality; in this case, and on this specific point, gift-giving, and least in Tonga and in Wallis, would be of the same order as potlatch.[63] In Tonga, for example — before the nineteenth-century constitution froze it into a British-type system — the traditional socio-political hierarchy was based on a system of titles (*ha'a*) of great vitality, which bore witness to the political history of Tonga; some titles grew in prestige while others fell into disuse; some lineages even 'captured' titles.[64] Competition for rank thus remained open and constituted one of the principal driving forces of Tongan history. This rivalry was carried on by war, of course, but in times of peace, also by competition in terms of (high-ranking) wives and 'riches'.

Today the groups of women (*kautaha*) who, in Tonga, manufacture the *koloa* function on a much more democratic basis than they used to,[65] and commoner women now control their own production of mats and tapas, even though ownership of the blocks (*kupesi*) continues to be restricted. In the Tongan village of Taoa, when the village women manufacture a length of barkcloth for the crown prince, Tupouto'a, they use a special block with original designs, which is kept by the wife of the village chief (*pule kolo*). In principle, this block may be used only in the manufacture of barkcloth for the prince and his family. In reality, however, I observed that certain women in Taoa had received permission to use the prince's block and owned a roll of barkcloth bearing his 'arms'.[66] These fabrics are used as prestigious gifts to be presented, for example, to foreign visitors. As in the past, marriage and the birth of the first child are occasions for a couple to accumulate *koloa*.

In Tonga, even the poorest women, once she is married, must have at least one roll of barkcloth (*ngatu*). Not to have one's stock of *ngatu* is degrading. All the women in Tonga told me the same thing, even the youngest. It is the essential item of a dowry: 'When you get married, if you don't have at least one roll of barkcloth, of *ngatu*, it means you're poorer than poor, it's worse than if you didn't have a roll of toilet paper', one informant told me. The same kind of representation is found in Wallis; a family that 'has any self-respect', rich or poor, has to have at least one roll of barkcloth and a few mats, so as, explicitly, to meet one's ceremonial obligations; otherwise 'you are a nobody'. Note that barkcloth is usually manufactured by groups of ten or so women who are either relatives of the person for whom the fabric is being made or neighbours.[67] In this context, too, the idea prevails that in order to have a large quantity of fine barkcloth, you must have a gift for gathering, a quality that raises you above other mortals. Of course, in Tonga as in Wallis, when a person is unable to manufacture their own stock of barkcloth and mats, they buy them.[68]

The relationship between these gift objects and the basis of identity, including its most individual aspect, is clear here: these objects serve not only to link one group to another into a vast network of social relations, but also to enable an individual to acquire his or her place in this network and to become 'somebody'.

As we have seen, the *koloa* distributed in ceremonies are always accompanied by food, *kai*, produced by men and presented raw and/or cooked by them in the ground oven. This contradicts what Linnekin writes of ceremonial exchanges in Samoa, where men's goods are exchanged for women's goods[69]: 'The normative structure of exchange events, the archetype of which is marriage exchange, is that *toga* are exchanged for *'oloa*.'[70] In Tonga and in Wallis, each group gives a set of gifts comprised both of men's and women's goods.[71] Moreover, this is perfectly consistent with the cognatic organisation of these *kainga*, where both male and female lineages are taken into account.[72] In other words, gift exchange is an indication not only of the wealth and station of the exchanging groups, but of the respective skills of the men and women who comprise them.

Food and wealth: 'the origin of things'

Can we now go a bit further with the elucidation of the symbolic charge with which *kai* and *koloa* are invested? It must be kept in mind that the ultimate objective of the food and wealth, over and beyond the means employed to procure them, is first and foremost to fulfill one's ceremonial obligations on the occasion of rites of passage with respect to those who are *kainga* or to those of higher rank. It is possible, therefore that, when one groups presents *kai* or *koloa* to another group or to a chief, it is representing itself in both its productive and its reproductive capacities. The idea I am defending here is not a logic along the lines of 'a pig is the equivalent of a man' or 'a mat is the equivalent of a woman'; instead, I am arguing that food and wealth, ceremonial objects *par excellence*, are more than simply substitutes for persons, they are a way of over-representing the men and women of a group, of re-presenting them *with something added*, something their material, physical presence does not possess. To better explain this, I will turn to the system of representations of the life cycle.

In the representations of the life cycle in Tonga as in Wallis, the person's bodily sheath is thought to come both from the transmission of the parents' bodily substances *and* from the food consumed over the course of one's life. In Tonga as in Wallis, food played — and continues to play — a decisive role in 'making' a child: the child's flesh results from a series of transformations, one of which consists in changing the products of the land from their 'raw' state to 'cooked' — men's work *par excellence* — before they go on to be transformed by the maternal substances after being eaten.[73] Sharing food grown on the same land and baked in the same oven is also believed to make non-kin into kin.[74] Following this line of thinking, the ceremonial food gifts, produced and cooked by men, commoners, would represent not only, materially, the work (*ngaue*) done by the men of the group, they would also be the sign of these same men's reproductive capacities: even if these men do not 'grow' the crops in the earth or the children in the women's womb — creative processes which are the sole purview of chiefs, they still have their own part in perpetuating the group.

On the other hand, *koloa*, as we have seen, are valuables produced by the women of a *kainga* in view of being given and/or kept (in the past exclusively by noble women, today by the kin group concerned). But their symbolic value, too, appears to be connected with the representations of the life cycle. Several indications, listed below, have led me to this conclusion: First of all, the application of the three elements, coconut oil, barkcloth and mat, on the recipient's body, in that order, on the occasion of rites of passage, whether birth, marriage or death. In Tonga, when nobles marry, the couple sits on a large roll of barkcloth fabric, the components of which are gendered: 'The male *kumi hoko* and the female *kumi kupu* are folded together and rolled up into a single very large bale to serve as a seat for the wedding couple.'[75] In the past, one of the mats that had comprised the deathbed was once again spread out after the funeral and watched over by the family; they would wait until an insect lit on it as the sign that the deceased had passed on into another life.[76] Last of all, equally significant is the presence, in the shrines of the gods or the deified ancestors who existed before Christianisation, of such objects as a whale's tooth or a piece of wood or a weapon, objects which, when they had been rubbed with coconut oil and turmeric powder, then dressed in a piece of barkcloth (*feta'aki*) were believed to house the god.[77]

All these examples of rituals, many of which disappeared with the arrival of Christianity, suggest that the representations of *koloa* were linked first of all to the conception of the continuity of the *kainga*. In the rites of passage, the overlaying on the body of the oil, then the barkcloth, then the mat could represent 'skins' within which the mysterious alchemy of life is created or perpetuated or recreated, *just as it occurs inside the woman's womb*. The roll comprised of the mat and the *ngatu* is called *fala'aofi*, the term *'aofi* meaning at once 'hollow', 'inside' and 'to shield someone as with one's body'.[78] In this case, coconut oil, barkcloth and mats would represent, in addition to material goods regarded as wealth, capacities for giving or perpetuating life.

If such is the case, the very concrete set of items comprised of tubers, one or several pigs and a roll of *koloa* (barkcloth and mat) would be not only the fruit of labour — or a work — but also *signs of the promises of life embodied by the men and women of a group*. Food and riches, *kai* and *koloa*, would be the very expression of the *kainga*, which is therefore conceived as a group 'in the making', an entity engaged in intergenerational continuity.[79]

In this event, as Mauss said, when one exchanges objects ceremonially, it is 'because one is giving and returning 'respects' … Yet it is also because by giving one is giving *oneself*'.[80] This is even the only way of giving oneself, momentarily, to others. But at the same time, because these ceremonial objects are also a promise of life, they symbolically go beyond their producers, men and women, and inscribe them in a chain of generations, a filiation, in short in a duration.

The competition between *kainga* thus becomes understandable, as one group seeks to prove that it is stronger, more powerful than the other. This competition, expressed in 'exterior' signs of wealth, is itself merely the sign of another rivalry, that which opposes the groups in terms of their numbers, present and to come. Today, in large-scale *katoanga*, the gifts are still enumerated by a crier: this is to show the size of the 'people' (*kainga*) of the high-ranking chief in question. Which brings us back to the Polynesian notion of *mana*: *mana* is the capacity to accumulate and distribute, but this capacity is measured first of all by the number of people the chief can gather around himself. And it is precisely the gifts of *kai* and *koloa* which represent these capacities.[81]

In traditional Tongan society, the production of gifts of *kai* and *koloa* was supposed to result from cooperation between the chief of the *kainga* and his people. His subjects would provide the physical and material labour of preparing the ground and its produce; the job of the chief was to infuse the process of production with the life-force of his *mana*.[82] Study of the great biannual *'inasi* ritual — found in similar forms in Wallis and throughout Polynesia — shows the position each person was supposed to occupy in the work of reproducing the social body as a whole: during the ten days of the ritual, from the far ends of the archipelago to the royal *mala'e*, all Tongans, from the humblest commoner to the highest-ranking chief, would flock to present the first fruits of their harvest to the Tu'i Tonga and to his sister, the Tu'i Tonga Fefine, the living earthly representatives of the bisexual deity, Hikuleo, who provided the products of the land and the sea.[83] It is the force that flows from the gods, *mana*, which causes the fruits of the land to grow and multiply, and each chief, at his own level, possesses a share of this force, which he uses for the benefit of all. The *kai* and the *koloa* contain a share, *'eiki*, a value received from the chief and which makes them part of the supernatural, divine world to which the chiefs themselves are linked. The sacrifice of the first fruits, called *polopolo* in both Tonga and Wallis, is not a gift made to the chief in the hope of receiving something in return: in the form of a portion — this is the literal meaning of the word *'inasi* — meant to be a minimal share, it is a symbolic restitution of everything the Tongans have received from the gods through the agency of their chiefs; and at the same time, it is the sign of the indelible debt they have contracted vis-à-vis the latter.

Today the Tu'i Tonga and the Tu'i Tonga Fefine are no more, and the missionaries have relegated the god Hikuleo to the rank of shameful accessory to paganism; a whole section of the old socio-cosmic representations vanished with the advent of Christianity. Still, what is one to make of the answer I received on several occasion from my village informants when I asked them why they gave gifts to the chief: 'It is out of gratitude!'? How is this answer to be understood if not by placing it in a reasoning identical to that exposed above: a chief's subjects do not give him gifts in order to receive something from him; they are giving the chief back a portion, regarded as minimal, of what he has given them. They are thus, today as yesterday, in a relationship of permanent indebtedness to the chief, which provides the basis, generation after generation, of their mutual relations.[84]

In guise of a preliminary conclusion, I would like to advance the idea that the ceremonial gift objects of food and 'riches', in the societies of Tonga and Wallis, serve as strong identity markers because they are connected with the divine, with the 'origin of things', as M. Godelier puts it.[85] But another reason is that food and wealth are also the signs of promises of life, in other words, the token of the future of a kin group as well as of the society as a whole. In this sense, they reveal another paradox — different from Weiner's 'keeping-while-giving' or Godelier's 'keeping-for-giving'[86] — since native thinking attributes them a twofold function: that of transcending history by being the token of a perpetual contract, and that of implementing history by providing a group or a community with the material and conceptual means to inscribe itself in the duration of time.

Metamorphoses of the ceremonial gift

As we have seen, the ceremonial objects of Tonga and Wallis are identical. They are given and/or exchanged in almost identical forms and for almost identical purposes. Furthermore, there is remarkable consistency over time as far as both the objects themselves and their representations go. When one knows that the societies of Tonga and of Wallis have undergone and are still experiencing profound religious, economic, social and historical upheavals,[87] the 'historical weight' of these objects and their representations can seem surprising. In any case, it provides a major indication of the staying power of certain identity markers. But it also raises other questions: at what point do the transformations of a society become so great that these markers disappear? Is anthropology equipped to detect — let alone prevent — these moments of identity loss?

The reader will have noticed that other objects than those we have just discussed appear in the ceremonial exchanges of both Tonga and Wallis. This is true in the case of food, of corned-beef or mutton chops, which clearly have nothing to do with custom. It is also true, among the *koloa*, of *manu*, of cotton, of satin and other fabrics. It is true in Wallis of the *kava papalangi* or the 'White people's *kava*', in other words whisky, which is a suitable present for a visiting White to give to customary chiefs.

These objects, even though they are not indigenous products, are clearly imbued, within and by ritual, with a value and a function identical to those of the traditional objects of ceremonial exchange.[88] The same is true of whisky, even if its effects on the body are different from those of traditional *kava*. Finally, as we shall see, it is also true for money, at least when it was first introduced. In Tonga, money appears in the large-scale *kataonga* alongside the other gifts, from the end of the nineteenth century,[89] where it is generally presented with the *koloa*, that is *by the women*, which might seem surprising given that currency, at this time, generally came into a family via male labour.[90] Even before the introduction of money, however, it seems that *koloa* served as legal tender: according to a missionary writing at the end of the nineteenth century, 'before the importation of money, mats were almost the only coin of exchange'.[91]

It is possible that, if, in the ritual context, money was spontaneously classified as *koloa*, it is because it fulfilled, at least when first introduced, the same kinds of functions as indigenous 'riches'. One of the *katoanga* in Wallis described above shows a bride whose hairdo was garnished with banknotes. There too it could be said that the function of this public display of money is no different from that of the other objects, at least in this ritual context. We thus have new objects, objects from the modern Western world, but which have been first taken over and then integrated into the gift-giving rituals on an equal footing with those objects hallowed by tradition.

However, objects from the modern world are not always simply new. Sometimes they bring with them practices which break sharply with the vocation of the traditional gift. Examples can be found in both Tonga and Wallis, but they are perhaps more flagrant in Wallis insofar as its society seems to have been made more vulnerable by the changes it has experienced; unlike Tonga, the society of Wallis does not enjoy the advantage of numbers (6,000 inhabitants in Wallis, 100,000 in Tonga), and above all it is totally dependent on a foreign state.[92]

But let us begin with Tonga. We have seen that, in Taoa village, relations between a noble chief and his land-holders are governed by the notion of long-term exchanges dictated by a debt, a debt of 'honour', as the villagers say. The chief is seen as the dispenser of land and of the fruits of this land: he grants his people tracts of his domain and, as mediator between god and men, he is the guarantor of future harvests. The land-holders carry out their *fatongia*; they cultivate the prince's yam plot and present him with an offering of ceremonial gifts at various times of the year. This set of gifts and counter-gifts probably provided a model for relations which still prevails. However, in the last few years, due to a surge in the population, Tonga has seen a serious land shortage.[93] In connection with this problem, a wholly new set of practices has appeared and developed. Today certain nobles grant plots of land to people in exchange for what in the West would be regarded as a substantial bribe; I hasten to add that this practice is entirely unlawful. As the villagers see it, however, things are considerably more ambiguous. In effect, some class the 'money-for-land' transaction under ceremonial gifts, given from time immemorial by a person to their hierarchical superior: the gifts used to be in kind, now they are in the form of money. Even though Tongan informants claim to share this view, at the same time they measure the perverse effects of the situation: on the one hand, the amount of money given for the same piece of land rises significantly each year and, on the other, particularly, the use of money considerably reinforces the inequality of land-holders before access to land.[94] Furthermore, noble families, especially those in the business world, increasingly tend to restrict the sphere of those with whom one was traditionally supposed to show generosity to the family circle: relatives, subjects or 'clients'.[95]

In Wallis, as our informants saw it, particularly those most politically engaged, the traditional chiefly families, on the one hand, and the Catholic mission, on the other, are today the best institutional representatives of Wallisian identity, particularly with respect to the French administration. But at the same time, some members of these families or of the mission are seen as sorcerer's apprentices whose actions sometimes jeopardise this same identity. They are for instance criticised for the use of 'envelopes', a practice which appeared a few years ago and is becoming current. Today among the ceremonial gifts made to the church or to chiefs on the occasion of rites of passage or public *katoanga* feature sums of money, presented alongside the other gifts, but in an envelope. The problem here is not that money figures among the gifts, but that this money is presented in a sealed envelope, hidden from sight and thus not subject to the usual social control; in sum it has neither colour nor odour, and therefore could be — and is — kept for one's personal use (put in the bank) instead of being redistributed.

This practice is a complete break with tradition and should be compared with another, also new, procedure. Today possession of a food freezer enables its owner to keep pork, whereas in the past, this same item used to be, by definition, the first in need of redistribution. The reproach addressed to the traditional chiefs is that, without being clearly aware of it, they are transforming the system of customary gifts by placing it in the service of non-indigenous practices. By perverting the practice of gift-giving — by making the gift a means of personal enrichment — they are betraying the custom that they are in principle charged with representing and defending. It is obvious that these practices mark a change which affects the value system of these societies. One informant summed it up in the following way: 'A fellow's value used to be measured by what he gave away, today it is measured by what he keeps.' Behind the modification of the relationship between people and objects stands the alteration of relations between people themselves.

Such observations about ceremonial objects, in Tonga as well as in Wallis, nevertheless allow us to shade this somewhat trenchant opinion. The oddest thing, perhaps, is that these two behaviours — amassing to give away or amassing to keep — do not function as two terms of an alternative but exist side by side, as values, within the same society, though in different spheres. One can even wonder why money, a universal equivalent introduced decades ago, has not finally replaced the traditional ceremonial gift objects. As we have seen, money indeed features among these gifts either among the gift objects or alongside them, but not instead of them. Without being a financial specialist, it can be said that, since money is by definition anonymous and interchangeable, it cannot represent a person, neither a man, nor a woman, nor a group.[96] It can therefore not replace such objects as food and wealth, since their characteristic feature is precisely that they are the sign of a group and provide its members with identity markers. It should also be noted that 'riches', *koloa*, function as a means of identification beyond the borders of each country, at least in Polynesia. When a

Wallisian goes to Futuna, to Samoa or to Tonga, or even to Tahiti, the best passport, in his view, is still a length of barkcloth carefully rolled up in a mat and accompanied, if possible, by a basket of food.[97] Finally, one last remark: today it is increasingly common for gift objects to be bought with money. Nevertheless, their immediate function remains unchanged: to be exchanged in the traditional gift-giving circuit.[98]

Food and wealth as ceremonial gift objects appear, in the societies of Tonga and Wallis, as identity markers. Bound up with representations of the life cycle, these objects bring into play the entire network of relations — between groups, genders, individuals or hierarchies — which forms the basis of the social order. At the same time, the incursion of either new gift objects or new ways of giving attests to new ways of thinking these social relations. This leads me to remark on two things: first of all on the longevity of customary objects and the traditional practices of gift-giving — that obstinate tendency to last which constitutes the strength of things; and second, on the simultaneous transformation of the paradigm of the relations between people and objects — in other words, between people.

This long-lasting (temporal) journey of ceremonial objects and traditional gift-giving practices in societies otherwise undergoing decisive mutations is surely a testimony to the health of their identity markers. And more perhaps? For instance, the sign that, in the present case, the ambient cultural homogenisation has reached one of its limits? Today such a conclusion is still premature.

Footnotes

*   The field material used in this article was collected during a study (November 1988–June 1989) made possible by a grant from the Fyssen Foundation and the support of the CNRS (GDR 116 ITSO). I would like to express my gratitude to both institutions. My thanks also to Paul van der Grijp for his careful reading of the manuscript.

1   See Mauss (1990:8ff).

2   See Linnekin (1991b) and Weiner (1992). The latter's demonstration is also based on the case of Hawaii.

3   Tonga is an archipelago of 169 islands, with a total of 100,000 inhabitants. It is the only independent Polynesian kingdom that subsists today. Wallis (Uvéa) is an island some 125 km square, to the northwest of Tonga; it has a population of 6,000. The country is headed by a king, the *Lavelua*. In 1961, Wallis was combined with the island of Futuna into the overseas territory of Wallis and Futuna. History has created numerous bonds between the Tonga and Wallis. Besides the fact that the two were originally (1000 BC) settled by Polynesians from the same stock, the island of Wallis was conquered and for a large part colonised by Tongans in the 15th century. The Wallisians threw off this domination at the end of the 17th century, but maintained close ties with Tonga until the arrival of French Catholic missionaries (1837), who cut off exterior contacts for fear of Protestant influence. Today, while the inhabitants of Tonga and Wallis are firmly attached to their specificity, they speak nearly identical languages and recognise common origins, traditions and customs (see Douaire-Marsaudon 1998a).

4   No doubt the ceremonial drink, *kava*, should be added as a third category. But since *kava* is associated particularly with chiefly rituals and therefore entails implications other than those of gifts of *kai* and *koloa*, I chose to leave this subject to one side.

5 Agnatic or uterine kin group, descent group, the subjects of a chief, the village, etc. For both societies, in each of these settings, the group in question is called the *kainga*, a term whose broadest meaning is 'relatives' or 'family'.

6 Public presentation of ceremonial gifts.

7 Public ground reserved for ceremonial gatherings.

8 See Monfat (1893: 439).

9 For the full description, see Martin (1981: 94–96).

10 Taoa village is located in the Vava'u archipelago to the north of Tonga. Situated in the hereditary domain of crown prince Tupouto'a, it has some 450 inhabitants, most of whom are his tenants. Prince Tupouto'a does not live in the village, but in the capital. In the prince's absence, authority is exercised by a commoner chief (*pule kolo*).

11 This plot is cultivated every three years. When the prince is absent, baskets of yams are sent to him by boat.

12 *Lu* are bundles of banana leaves tied up into a packet containing various delicacies prepared by the women, such as pieces of meat or fish in coconut milk, with taro leaves. *Faikakai* is a kind of cake made of wheat flour (formerly flour from tubers) and coconut milk cooked with sugarcane and wrapped in banana leaves. The bundles of *lu* and *faikalai* are laid in the ground oven, covered and cooked along with the other contents.

13 A large pig weighs between 100 and 150 kgs, sometimes more; a medium-sized one, between 50 and 100 kgs.

14 The two live pigs were bought with the money collected from the 'tables' or *pola* each of which usually seated relatives.

15 In Wallis, the term is spelled differently.

16 The content of these baskets is the same as that indicated in the preceding text, namely: between 10 and 15 yams, depending on their size, per basket and about the same number of *kape*; the number of taros ranges between 18 and 25.

17 The piles measured 2m in length by 1m in width by 1.5m in height.

18 The piles measured, respectively: 11.5m long by 1m wide by 1.5m high, and 4.5m long by 2m wide by 1.5m high.

19 This was the *pule pulo*, the commoner chief, as opposed to prince Tupouto'a, the noble chief.

20 In fact, while the *'uma* were being prepared, I saw that some small pigs had also been killed, which had been brought by family or *'api*, but I was unable to count them.

21 These boxes contained frozen mutton chops from New Zealand.

22 See above.

23 Some three tons of meat were distributed over the five-day funeral. Everyday fare consists above all of tubers (taro, *kape* and manioc) accompanied by either products from the lagoon or canned fish (bought in village shops, *fakekoloa*).

24 The same idea of the sign of absolute poverty is contained in not having a roll of barkcloth fabric, an essential item of women's goods (see below).

25 After discussion, the villagers go to the village chief and explain that they no longer want him; the adults of the village then proceed to nominate a new chief, whose name is submitted for approval to the customary hierarchy, in particular to the king. This can happen to any chief, including the king. Everything depends on the seriousness and the extent of the damage. In Tonga, the deposition of a noble chief by his tenants is inconceivable; if their harvests are poor, they have only themselves to blame.

26 This is a widespread notion in Polynesia. Here is what Firth has to say about Tikopia: 'He [the chief] is considered to be able through his relations with his ancestors and gods to control natural fertility, health and economic conditions in the interests of his dependants. Material evidence of his powers is given in native belief by the condition of the weather, of crops, of fish and of sick persons whom he attempts to cure' (1940: 490).

27 See Bell (1931: 131).

28 On these various myths, see Gifford (1924: 155–64 and 181–84).

29 For a detailed study of Tongan barkcloth, see Kooijman (1972: 297–314). For women's production in general, the most complete historical source is Martin (1817: 337ff, 1981: 365–68). See also Tamahori (1963), Kaeppler (1971, 1974 and 1978); Kirch (1984), Bataille-Benguigui (1985), Douaire-Marsaudon (1986) and James (1988a, 1988b). For changes in the production of material culture in Tonga, see van der Grijp (1993b).

30 See Martin (1981: 297).

31 Tongans exchanged their *koloa* and particularly, it seems, their barkcloth fabric (*ngatu*) for valuable products from other archipelagos: fine mats from Samoa, wooden objects from Fiji (weapons, *kava* bowls, headrests; see on this subject Kaeppler 1978: 246–52). Each group of islands had its 'specialty', which was renowned and which made these objects much prized, precious, within a space that extended well beyond the boundaries of each island or archipelago.

32 At the time of a funeral, or after a birth, a number of *koloa* are also used to pay for the services of a specialist, for example the *ha'a tufunga*, who, in Tonga, organises the funeral ceremonies for members of chiefly families (Gifford 1929: 198). Likewise, *koloa* can also be given to the midwife or, sometimes, to the priest.

33 See Weiner (1992).

34 See Martin (1981: 424).

35 See *Missions maristes* (1890: 165).

36 See Churchward (1959: 270). The term *koloa* is sometimes combined with another particle, as in *falekoloa* (lit. 'house of *koloa*'), which designates village grocery stores. The expression *angakoloa* applies to someone who seems to have a 'natural' gift for accumulating wealth (Churchward 1959: 10).

37 The oil is still made for daily bodily use in all Tongan families. The mats are used for sitting or sleeping. In former times they were used as sails; some were waterproof and worn by men at sea. The coarsest mats still cover house floors or are hung across the entrance in cold weather (Martin 1981: 367). The finest are used to make the *ta'ovala*, the belt worn over one's clothing when going outside. Barkcloth is less used as a household product than it once was, having been replaced by cotton; but white (*tutu*), undyed tapa used to be worn as everyday apparel. Hung vertically, it still divides the *fale* into separate rooms. At the beginning of the 20th century, it also served as a periodical napkin (Gifford 1929: 187).

38 See Tamahori (1963: 67-68), Kooijman (1972: 306). 'In early times, the women had to refrain from sexual intercourse for two days before starting to make the dye.... By custom, women who prepare this dye do not leave their special house until all the work is finished, sleeping during the day and working by night. During this time they do not bath and their food is brought to them' (Tamahori *ibid*.).

39 This is not the place to describe the entire marriage ceremony, simply the exchange of gifts.

40 See Gifford (1929: 192).

41 For the whole ceremony, see Collocott (1923: 222–23).

42 On the importance of the brother/sister relationship in Tonga, see Douaire-Marsaudon (1993, 1996b, 1998a, 2002a, 2002b, 2002c). It should also be noted that a share of these *koloa* is kept out of the exchanges and given to the young people as a sort of dowry; but all testimonies agree that it is important first of all to give each one what they have given, attempting to balance the exchanges between the kin groups. In other words, the young couple may end up with a very small share in spite of the quantities exchanged.

43 See Collocott (1923: 222).

44 See Marcus (1979: 87).

45 See Gifford (1929: 317).

46 See Kooijman (1972: 314, 319).

47 See Kooijman (1972: 331).

48 Mauss (1990: 10).

49 See Gailey (1980), James (1988a, 1988b).

50 See Monfat (1890: 145).

51 Mauss (1990: 51).

52 See Gifford (1929 317). It is possible that this mat-shrine is also what Gifford called *falaui*, of which he says that it was 'a mat that is called by a name and used as a god' (Gifford 1929: 241).

53 See Weiner (1992).

54 See Godelier (1994: 90, 1996: 50–53).

55 It must be said that the ceremonial objects which circulate between groups are not, properly speaking, guaranteed by a store of highly valuable objects as is the case with the gold standard for money. But the symbolic value of the objects given by a donor group is, in effect, based on the group's standing, which is itself expressed and in a certain manner, guaranteed by the family 'treasure'.

56 See Gifford (1929: 181).

57 See Martin (1981: 297, 368).

58 See Martin (1981: 138–39).
59 See Gifford (1929: 215).
60 See Collocott (1923: 228).
61 Mauss (1990: 45).
62 No trace is to be found in the sources of a conception similar to that of the New Zealand Maoris, for whom, according to Mauss, gift objects are inhabited by a spirit, *hau*, which makes them want to return to where they came from. The term exists in Tonga and Wallis, but it generally designates the temporal aspect of the king's function, which he exercises physically and militarily. In Tonga, the term *hau* also designates a champion, someone who is victorious because of his physical strength, which comes from the gods (or the ancestors).
63 Godelier (1999: 159). Godelier recalls that, for Mauss, potlatch 'disappears' from Polynesia because the hierarchy had become fixed ('the clans have definitively become hierarchised'), thus paralysing all or some of the competition, one of the essential conditions of potlatch being 'the instability of a hierarchy'. This is forgetting that Polynesian hierarchies did not become definitive before contact with the West — the case in Hawaii, Tahiti and Tonga — before that, competition for power was almost an institution, as N. Gunson so well demonstrates in his article on leadership in Polynesia (1979). As far as Tonga is concerned, while the same hierarchy tended to turn into a caste system, rivalry for power was accentuated by the fact that the number of young nobles was on the rise at the end of the 18th century.
64 See Bott (1981: 41ff).
65 See Kooijman (1972: 319–20), Douaire-Marsaudon (1986: 189–90).
66 In this case the barkcloth also bears the indication *koe sisi o Tupouto'a*, which means 'this is the garland — the pattern — of Tupouto'a'.
67 See Bataille-Benguigui (1985) and Douaire-Marsaudon (1986).
68 This is true, for example, of certain women in Tonga who live in the capital. In Wallis, families are accustomed to buying their barkcloth from Futuna: this is the *siapo*, renowned yesterday as today for its delicate patterns (on the *siapo* from Futuna, see Chevron 1841: 32).
69 Note that, on the occasion of a marriage, there are, alongside goods exchanged *between* the kin groups, others which constitute a sort of dowry for the bride and the groom. The groom is expected to contribute 'men's' goods: land, (live) pigs, etc. And the bride is supposed to bring women's goods: mats, tapas, coconut oil. But since these objects constitute the estate of the new household, one can hardly speak of 'exchange' of women's goods 'for' men's goods. Likewise, in both Tonga and Wallis, one can still trade a roll of barkcloth for a pig and vice versa. In this context, a female object is exchanged for a male object, but this transaction is neither the 'standard structure of exchange', nor, in any case, 'the archetype of marriage exchange'. This kind of exchange is practiced 1) in view of obtaining something one needs; or 2) because one does not have the necessary currency. It is therefore barter, which can eventually enable a person to obtain money. But in no case can it be termed an exchange of ceremonial gifts.
70 See Linnekin (1991b: 3). For Samoa, following Mauss (1990: 8–10) many authors, among whom Mead (1930: 73–74), Shore (1982: 203–204) and Linnekin (1991b: 2) class women's productions — tapa, coconut oil and mats —as *'ie toga* and men's productions — canoes and tools — as well as European products — commodities and money — as *'oloa*. This is an inversion of terms with respect to Tonga. Nevertheless, recent observations would seem to indicate that the traditional Samoan model was actually quite similar to that of Tonga, down to the vocabulary (Tcherkézoff, personal communication).
71 This is true of Futuna, too, as well as of Puka-Puka (the Cook Islands, see Hecht 1977: 191) and Rotuma (J. Rensel and A. Howard, personal communication). To the best of my knowledge, the two contexts in which men's products are exchanged for women's products are the following: when a boy is officially courting a girl and gives a *kava* in her honour: 'The boy usually prepares an *'umu* (small piglet and some yams) for the girl who recipocates with a *mohenga* (lit. 'bed'; barkcloth and mats)' (Rogers 1975: 399); and in ritual exchanges between brother and sister. These exchanges take place in the privacy of the domestic setting.
72 According to G. Milner, in Samoa today, the groom's family gives a sum of money (*'oloa*) to the bride's family, who is responsible for providing the food for the feast (1966: 164).
73 See Douaire-Marsaudon (1993: 488, 1998a).
74 The same type of conceptions are found in Samoa (see Tcherkézoff 1992b: 3), and in Hawaii: 'The term for adoption is *hanai*, 'to feed': one becomes a child of another by nurture. So likewise, to be long supported by

the food of a given land is to become *kama'aina*, a 'child of the land'. In both cases, kinship is the sharing of substance through eating' (Sahlins 1992a: 199).

75 See Kooijman (1972: 321), see also Tamahori (1963: 162).

76 See Gifford (1929: 328).

77 We could mention other rituals in which *koloa* are clearly connected with the life cycle. The umbilical cord ritual is still performed today: when a girl is born, her umbilical cord is usually buried under a *hiapo*, a paper mulberry (*Broussonetia papyrifera*) for the explicit purpose of making her into a good producer of barkcloth. Tongan oral tradition tells that, when a young chief sets off for other islands, his mother rubs him with coconut oil and gives him a new *ta'ovala* (fine mat). The same stories speak of the virginity mat, *kie taupo'ou*, that girls used to give to their first lover.

78 See *Missions maristes* (1890: 34).

79 Food and wealth, it should be recalled, are accompanied in many rituals by the ceremonial drink known as *kava* (an extract of the root of a pepper, *Piper methysticum*). If one accepts the theory — which I have defended elsewhere — that *kava* roots are a substitute for ancestral bones, it is clear that *kai, kava* and *koloa*, are, in the context of gift-exchange rituals, the expression of all those who make up the *kainga*: ancestors, the living and their descendants (Douaire-Marsaudon 1993: 766ff, 1996a, 1998a: chap. 18, 1998b, 2001).

80 Mauss (1990: 46; author's emphasis).

81 C. Gailey classifies *koloa* by opposition to men's productions. According to her theory, women's productions, including children, are conceptualised as *koloa*, therefore as valuable goods, while men's productions are classed as *ngaue*, meaning 'work'; this is supposed to be proof of the lesser value ascribed to men's productions (Gailey 1987: 105ff). Yet it must be borne in mind that, in Polynesia, gender difference is cross-cut by differences in rank, which are not gender based. *Koloa* are regarded as valuable goods, but certain men's items like weapons, canoes or incised whale-teeth enjoy the same reputation. Alongside fine mats, a 'treasure', *fakafaanga* would also contain particularly valuable weapons (Gifford 1929: 318).

82 For the different forms and values of the respective services of the dominant and dominated parties in 'the reproduction of society', see Godelier (1994).

83 See Douaire-Marsaudon (1993: 813ff). Today the *'inasi* ritual has been replaced by a large-scale demonstration of agricultural prowess some aspects of which are reminiscent of the past (see Bataille-Benguigui 1976).

84 For Mauss, the Polynesian gift and counter-gift system is not the same thing as potlatch because 'the element of usury in the reciprocal service rendered is lacking' (Mauss 1990: 88, n. 9), which explains in part the fact that these exchanges are not agonistic (*ibid.*:7). Everything depends on what is considered to be provided as service and counter-service. In Polynesia, the chief's service has an undeniably usurious character because it is inconceivable that his tenants could ever extinguish the debt they owe him. Here too the example of the ceremonial exchanges of goods in Samoa may have led Mauss to this conclusion, contrary to what seems to be the lesson of the same exchanges in Tonga and Wallis, where they seem to be of an agonistic nature.

85 See Godelier (1999).

86 See Weiner (1992) and Godelier (1994: 902, 1999: 33).

87 For economic and political changes in Tonga, see van der Grijp (1993a, 1993b, 1997, 2004), Benguigui (1989) and the article by Bataille-Benguigui and Benguigui in the present volume, Chap. 11.

88 See Sahlins (1992b).

89 See Monfat (1893: 441, 445, 447).

90 See Gailey (1980).

91 See Monfat (1893: 441). Note that the word 'mats' is used by the missionary as a generic term clearly designating both mats and barkcloth (*ibid*).

92 One of many examples of the problems of identity raised by such dependence; up until 1989 — the time of my last trip — French was taught to the children of Wallis just as it was to French children, as a mother tongue. Whereas in the majority of homes Wallisian is still spoken.

93 In principle and according to constitutional law, every man of 16 years and older has the right to use the land, called *'api*. In reality, today a little over 60 per cent of the men in Tonga do not have their reglementary plot.

94 See van der Grijp (1993a: 246).

95 See Marcus (1980).

96 This was the case when a Greek city-state or a medieval seigneury struck coin. It is the case even today with modern States. It will become less and less true with the advent of a currency such as the pan-European Euro, and perhaps even more with the development of electronic payment.

97 But the foodbasket — often composed of yams — is forbidden on planes.

98 Once they enter the traditional gift circuit, these objects can be given over and over, but to my knowledge they do not leave the circuit again to be exchanged for money.

Chapter 11

IDENTITY AT STAKE IN THE PRESENT-DAY KINGDOM OF TONGA[1]

Marie-Claire Bataille and Georges Benguigui

Every human society must resolve at least two fundamental questions: first, how to live together and second, how to survive together, that is, in particular, how to produce together. We are among those who think these are separate questions, and will concern ourselves here with only the first. To inquire into how to go about living together ultimately comes down to inquiring into the ways of managing the conflicts inherent in any society. Obviously a strongly hierarchical traditional society does not manage internal conflicts in the same way as a liberal Western society.

We will attempt to address one aspect of the problem which is relatively frequent in what we are accustomed to call third-world countries, namely the passage from a traditional hierarchical society to a liberal society in which democracy is held to be the political ideal. Rapidly, to borrow Max Weber's distinction between charismatic traditional authority and legal-rational authority, we will distinguish, on the one hand, a society in which potential conflicts between social groups are downplayed or even suppressed by traditional authority and, on the other hand, a so-called liberal democratic society, accustomed to settle its conflicts by majority rule, notably through elected representation.

Beyond this very important matter of political democracy, the aspiration to a new way of managing society and its conflicts, we would like to elucidate the issue of identity at stake in these new political conflicts, for we feel strongly that a traditional regime cannot be reduced, for example, to a simple hierarchical organisation, or democracy to majority rule alone. Traditional regime or democracy refer to specific conceptions of society and therefore to different social identities.

Political conflict, conflict of identity

For our study of the issue of identity underlying the passage from a traditional society to a liberal democratic form, we will take the example of the last independent Polynesian kingdom still in existence, the Kingdom of Tonga.[2] Tonga is well known in anthropological literature for two basic reasons. The first has to do with its kinship system, the second with its strongly ranked social stratification, and it is this second point which interests here. Furthermore, when we speak of Tongan tradition or traditional Tongan society, it must be kept in mind that we are talking about a neo-tradition set in place in the course of the 1870s, a combination of an earlier original tradition and elements of western culture. G. Marcus suggests calling this neo-tradition a 'compromise culture'.[3]

Several authors[4] over the last few years have taken an interest in the evolution of in Tonga's political situation, emphasising the rise of an important current of opposition which calls itself the 'Pro-Democracy' movement. And it is true that we have seen a prodigious evolution in this area since the 1980s, reflected, for example, in the emergence of a vigorous press as well as by the opposition's spectacular results in the legislative elections following an unusually bitter campaign.

In many instances, the above authors stress the tradition/democracy opposition and as a rule assimilate the idea of democracy to modernity. However, beyond the political battle, what interests here is the conflict surrounding identity. We postulate that, in Tonga today, by means of the political conflicts obviously connected with the essential evolutions in society — in terms of social stratification and the economy — another debate is being conducted, another conflict. This debate, this conflict bear on the question of identity. The question is, what does it mean to be Tongan today, what shape should the collective future of Tongan society take? The question is, since we are talking about identity, what should the relationship to the other be, which in turn raises the question of nationalism, perhaps even of xenophobia. We will see that, contrary to what one might expect, this debate is not simply about an opposition between tradition and democracy, even if it does have something to do with this, too. We will note that the staunchly avowed partisans of democracy are also defenders of tradition, or at least of some aspects and vice versa, that some of the fiercest partisans of the royal family are active modernisers. In other words, the present political debate reveals a typology of attitudes based on a cross between a democracy/royalty dimension, on the one hand, and a tradition/modernity dimension, on the other; between a democracy/royalty dimension and an economic development/non-development dimension.[5]

The birth of democratic claims

It must first of all be said that, when it comes to theory, Western-style democracy is often associated with individualism: for instance, in principle each elector goes into the voting booth alone, and there makes his decision and marks his choice. Certain authors have even assimilated the democratic process to the operation of the market. Thus some partisans of democracy in Tonga claim that the first elements of democracy were introduced in Tongan society, at the end of a difficult civil war, by King Tupou I, the direct ancestor of the present king, as well as by missionaries in the second half of the nineteenth century. But whether it was the King or the Wesleyan missionaries who lent him their support and aid, the seeds of democracy are supposed to have been sown insofar as freedoms and elements of individualism were set in place by the granting of a constitution and by the new Christian religion. In passing, it should be noted that Tonga has one of the world's oldest constitutions and that, unlike those of most of the other South Pacific countries, drawn up in a context of anti-colonial struggle, Tonga's Constitution was bestowed on the people from above, by the king.

It is perhaps paradoxical to defend the idea of the seeds of democracy having been sowed by Tupou I, so little is Tongan royalty inclined to democratic ideas, but this paradox is only superficial. To be sure, King Tupou I instituted a genuine State, eminently centralised and hierarchically ordered, in which the king is, even today, invested with considerable powers, the like of which are enjoyed by no contemporary head of State except in totalitarian dictatorships. In addition, to replace the relatively numerous and flexible former chiefs, the King created a narrow, rigidly defined nobility, endowed with important revenues (from land-holdings through something like a fief system) and broadly defined rights. This political system, playing on words, calls itself a Constitutional Monarchy, but it bears no more than a surface resemblance to a liberal social regime. Nevertheless, it must be recognised that King Tupou I also established an embryonic democracy and favoured the appearance of the first signs of individualism. King Tupou's 1875 Constitution, the bulk of which is still in force, replaced the old system of customary law. In his speech, presenting the Constitution to Parliament, the king declared:

> The form of our government in the days past was that my rule was absolute, and that my wish was law and that I chose who should belong to the Parliament and that I could please myself to create chiefs and alter titles. But that, it appears to me, was a sign of darkness and now a new era has come to Tonga — an era of light — it is my wish to grant a Constitution and to carry on my duties in accordance with it.[6]

He in effect instituted a rule of law, a State where, at least in principle, no one is above the law, which already implies a certain form of equality. And indeed, for example, the royal government was found guilty several times after having been taken to court by its citizens.

It is also important to point out that, of the three parts into which the Constitution is divided, the first is a declaration of rights. This declaration has thirty-two articles guaranteeing, in particular, the equality of everyone before the law,[7] chiefs or commoners, Tongans or foreigners, as well as personal freedom, freedom of speech, of worship and of the press. It provides for a Parliament, one that is far from being a model of democracy[8] to say the least, but which has the merit of still allowing the expression of differing opinions. It grants the right to vote to all men, whereas previously commoners played strictly no role in political life.[9] At the same time, the declaration that all land belonged to the king and therefore could not be sold, as well as the institution of the right of every man over the age of sixteen to the enjoyment of a piece of land which could be passed on to the eldest son, signified a considerable break with collective life, a break with the traditional organisation into groups of households headed by a chief. This in turn led to the gradual constitution of a nation of individual small 'land-owners'.

Severe criticisms, bearing essentially on the failure to respect civil equality or on the separation of powers, were made of the Constitution. On several occasions one of the most knowledgeable people in this area, the historian Sione Latukefu, voiced the opinion that it was non-democratic because systems based on chiefs are by their very essence non-democratic. It nevertheless remains that the texts decreed by King Tupou I — reduction of the chiefs' powers, abolition of serfdom, creation of courts of law, land reform, elections, etc. — even if not always applied in full, sowed seeds of equality and individualism, at least in the minds of some. To be sure, these seeds would take time to sprout, but they would at least have had the great merit of having existed.

Although they rapidly threw their support behind those in power so as to have an easier time establishing themselves upon their arrival in the nineteenth century, the Churches clearly worked in the same direction, sowing their own seeds of equality and individualism. The first of these was the declaration that all men are equal before God, granting each Tongan a soul and thus the possibility of going to heaven, depending on each individual's efforts. In traditional religion, only the chiefs had the right to an afterlife, and upon dying would go to the world beyond, Pulotu. In addition, the Churches constructed their own hierarchies in parallel to the traditional ranks, and the religious leaders may sometimes have appeared as rival authorities to the classical chiefs. Thus the Churches today are a means of social advancement and participate in the growth of the new middle classes. Later we will see the crucial role played by these Churches in the debate on democracy and identity.

These seeds, sown at the end of the nineteenth century, sprouted and grew only upon activation of certain powerful factors, which contributed to the flowering of democratic claims. They began to sprout notably with Tonga's entry into a capitalist market economy and its transmutation into a consumer society, with all this represents in terms of individual enterprise[10] and 'keeping up with the Joneses'. In a newly fledged capitalist country, to be an entrepreneur is first of all to be individualistic, as opposed to community-minded, and this means claiming one's place in the sun. The demand increases as soon as the entrepreneur becomes aware of the place he occupies in the economic life and development of the country. The advent of the nuclear family has also encouraged individualism, which is favourable to democratic claims. As one manager said to us, 'I work so my children can have butter on their bread in the morning, the extended family comes afterwards'. Three other factors must also be taken into account. These are education, emigration and the changes in the social structure.

Tonga is a third-world country where education is valued in the extreme, and has been since the arrival of the missionaries at the end of the nineteenth century.[11] Speaking about education, the same King Tupou I declared:

> See what knowledge has done for the white man! See what ignorance has done for the men of this land! Is it that white men are born more wise? Is it that they are naturally more capable than others? No: but they have obtained knowledge...[12]

Thus the kingdom of Tonga has a very high level of schooling and education, which is fairly rare in the third world. A veritable education boom is now underway, even if some aspects have drawn criticism. One of the reasons often given in justification of internal migration to the capital is that is where the best schools are. A high proportion of Tongan families send their children abroad for the same reason. Many Tongans attend foreign universities, quite often in countries with a liberal political tradition, where they discover Western democracy. To this must be added the existence of a secondary school and a micro-university, both private, neither Church nor State affiliated, which is most exceptional in Tonga. The two establishments, created by F. Helu — an astonishing figure whose essential reference is Periclean Greece — the objective of which is to develop critical thinking, have played a striking role in the birth of the democratic spirit owing to the uncontested intellectual reputation of their founder.[13] The latter is one of the very few Tongans familiar with both traditional and Western cultures. Perhaps the common people's remarkable thirst for knowledge has some connection with their will to outdo the chiefs and nobles.[14]

Alongside education, the role of emigration in the emergence of the debate on democracy is worth noting. Since the 1960s–1970s, Tonga has become a land of emigrants, and its principal export is now labour. This was once part of an explicit government policy, conceived as a safety valve for demographic pressure.[15] Moreover, this policy was supported by the mainstream Churches. There are no official statistics on emigration, but estimates vary between 35,000 and 50,000 for the number of Tongans living outside the country.[16] Whatever the true figure, it is high if one remembers that the population of the archipelago is only some 100,000 inhabitants. Although it is impossible to arrive at a very accurate evaluation, the sums of money and the various goods these emigrants send back to their families in Tonga represent the country's primary source of revenue. Since the vast majority of emigrants live in liberal democracies (New Zealand, Australia, the United States), it is not surprising that democratic ideas also filter back through this channel. Tongans living abroad have their own press, which can also be found in Tonga. They have kept up solid ties with their homeland through the family network and return to Tonga, in not negligible numbers, to vacation or attend social events such as weddings, funerals, the anniversary of the founding of some institution (school, church, etc.).

Lastly, the social structure, which Tupou I had worked to stabilise and perpetuate, has considerably evolved towards a broad diversification. Under this king, things were relatively simple: there was a steep pyramid with the royal family at the top, then a limited number of titled nobles, spokesmen for the nobility, and finally the common people, most of whom worked the land. For a variety of reasons we will not go into here, the mass of commoners grew in complexity, spawning new social classes (bourgeoisie, middle classes, big farmers, etc.), even though peasants remained the largest social group.[17] Intellectuals made their appearance. Today this very important modification of the social structure has produced a diversity of opinion in the country which is not usually encountered in a traditional society.

The democracy debate

At first the debate on democracy was not easy to spot. One simply observed that the political discussions in the 'kava clubs'[18] were taking on more importance, that certain intellectuals attempted to bring problems of Tongan society into the discussion. In particular, they broadcast a radio program critical of the government. The program would be silenced by an authoritarian decision of the same government in 1985,[19] and one of its principal broadcasters, 'Akilisi Pohiva, a National Education teacher, would be purely and simply fired.[20] In 1986, following these events, the program was replaced by a modest bimestrial newsletter, *Kele'a*, the primary aim of which was to denounce corruption, excesses and mismanagement within the State.[21] It is noteworthy that the newsletter's four founders were all teachers or ex-teachers having attended universities abroad. Subsequently, three of the four were to be elected to Parliament as People's Representatives. Although this institution was not truly a place for legislative innovation or a real means of monitoring government activity, it would serve as a sounding board for *Kele'a* campaigns, and all the more effectively as some of the parliamentary debates were broadcast on radio. Little by little, with the election of some of its leaders, the significance of the newsletter's campaigns would evolve, and the periodical would become the rallying point for the most committed members of the opposition. Then would come a shift from simple denunciation of excesses and corruption to open demands for the right to monitor government activity and for accountability.

'Akilisi Pohiva, who had become one of the main opposition leaders, justified this demand, arguing in substance: the monarchy as it stood was fairly adequate in the context of a subsistence economy since in this case accountability is not a real problem; but in a money economy, taxpayers have a right to expect of a responsible government services in exchange for their taxes and an accounting of the use of public funds. In his own words: 'the cornerstone of a money market economy is that there must be accountability.'[22] But these demands struck at the very heart of tradition. This was in itself a scandal, a sacrilege even, in a society as strongly hierarchical as Tonga's. It effectively meant that the elected representatives of the people could demand accounts of the ministers, nobles for the most part (and some members of the royal family to boot), appointed for life by the king as he pleased, and accountable to him alone. It was tantamount to challenging the king himself. The sacrilegious aspect of this claim can be seen only if one knows that, according to tradition, the present king unites in his own person three royal lines, the most ancient of which is of divine origin, the first ruler having been born, according to the creation myth, from the union of a mortal woman with a god. The Speaker of the House expressed his personal feelings about this veritable scandal for the traditionally minded when he said, in 1989: 'What I have noticed during these last three years is that People's Representatives have upped themselves and they are looking down on chiefs and Ministers.'[23] In this context, the demand to oversee ministerial activities has little chance of succeeding. In effect, while the law indeed stipulates that the Parliament can impeach a minister, the cases in which this can be done are highly circumscribed. Furthermore, as the elected People's Representatives can in no case form a parliamentary majority, owing to the constitutional provisions (see note 7), this procedure is entirely theoretical and the government cannot be censured in reality, except in very rare cases.

The final step in the democratic debate was taken at a massive Convention held in the capital of the country, Nuku'alofa, in November 1992, on the Tongan Constitution and Democracy. In the course of this convention, nearly all of Tonga's intellectuals, those living locally or abroad, spoke, as did many pastors and priests. This new stage produced the idea of a new Constitution, one which would reduce the royal function to the same role as that of the British or the Dutch rulers. F. Helu declared, in particular: 'The Tongan monarch should be apolitical as is the British monarch.'[24] This was nearly *lèse-majesté*, a radical challenge to tradition, to the 'Tongan Way' (*faka Tonga*), even if the democrats took care not to speak in these terms.

There would be a split within the opposition. For a number of the active critics of corruption and the excessive salaries paid Members of Parliament, who agreed on the need to monitor government activities, this was going too far. They considered that it mattered not so much to change the Constitution as to apply it in full. Such was, for example, the position of a well-known People's Representative, Laki Niu. This New Zealand-educated lawyer had been a very active member of the opposition. Yet, as a committed royalist,[25] he had long considered that the main problem was to apply the Constitution decreed by King Tupou I as it should be, and not to overhaul it. He added that a democratic system built on a foreign model would result in dissention: 'My concern is that if Tonga becomes a democratic society, only the wealthy people will be able to get into Parliament and not necessarily the men of principle.'[26] In the end, Laki Niu ran against the 'Pro-Democracy' candidates in the 1993 legislative elections.

Kele'a, the most radical opposition paper, was not the only publication that took a stand in favour of the democratic claims. *Matangi Tonga*, a highly professional magazine, clearly indicated its leanings, but in far more circumspect terms. Here are few of its editorial comments. In September 1989, the editorial ended on the following note: 'There is no doubt we need a Parliament, where good virtue prevails, which has the power to rule, a Parliament of the people, for the people and by the people.' In January 1991, the editorialist wrote: 'Tyranny by the Tongan government is becoming a major obstruction to the administration of justice and the making of laws in this country.'

The debate on Tongan identity

The passport affair

At first glance, the opposition's exigencies can be read as classic demands for the democratisation of the political system, advanced primarily by the up-and-coming middle classes. On the whole, this opposition claims to be peaceful, even seeking, it says, to avoid the explosion that is inevitable if the government refuses to move on reform. To be sure this aspect clearly exists. Yet we feel it is essential to look behind this public debate and see another, hidden, debate which concerns this time the identity of the Tongan people.

From this standpoint, it is important to note that the most successful opposition campaign,[27] the most followed, the one which provoked the greatest repercussions and had the most decisive impact, was their objection to the sale of passports, which clearly posed the question of national identity. In 1982, the Tongan government decided to raise revenues by selling passports to people in a precarious situation, such for example as the Chinese of Hong Kong or Imelda Marcos. The sale of these various categories of passport — hence at different prices — brought in millions of dollars.[28] Yet it is impossible to ascertain exactly how much they earned because, instead of being included in the State budget, these millions were deposited in a US bank and are supposed to be used as needed for Tonga's 'development budget'.

In an interview with a New Zealand television channel, the King justified this practice by his fear of seeing these very special revenues eaten up by salary rises for government employees. This cannot fail to surprise, given that no important decision concerning the government can be taken without the King's approval.

The sale of passports was felt, by the bulk of the population, to be scandalous and unworthy. As Papiloa Foiaki, a well-known businesswoman and former People's Representative expressed it: 'It is an arrow in the heart of people.'[29] The sales triggered very strong reactions, essentially for two reasons. The first has to do with the fact that this income was actually controlled by the King himself, it was kept secret and was therefore impossible to monitor. It was even said that it was the royal family's pocket money. The second, and by far the most important, is that people felt it was the very identity of the Tongan people that had been sold.

It is the fear of losing this identity that is essential here, and it is stated explicitly. For instance, people are frightened by foreigners who want to settle permanently in Tonga.[30] One reader writing to the *Times of Tonga* in April 1991 expressed a typical reaction, saying that the sale of passports makes them look like madmen, giving whoever has enough money *carte blanche* to their country, with the possibility to control the nation and throw them out. In the same newspaper, Futa Helu, the director of Atenisi, the institution mentioned above, had written a few months earlier that at no time would Tongans be servants of these foreigners as is the case for a great number of Fijians, who now work for the Indians. The influential magazine, *Matangi Tonga*, whose professionalism and moderation we have already cited, expressed concern about these sales as early as 1987, voicing the opinion that the question of national identity had become akin to putting a 'made in Tonga' label on an export or 'transformed in Tonga' on an item for re-export. In the January–February 1991 issue, the magazine returns to this subject in its editorial, 'Tonga has sold its soul': 'Citizenship is something that Tongans were brought up to consider as a birthright and something to be proud of. It is not something you buy … Tongan citizenship as a commercial product is hard to come to terms with …' The editorial sums up general opinion if one judges by the number of signatures on three petitions or by the size of the demonstration, organised on 8 March 1991, against such passport sales. Some two thousand people, a very large number considering Tonga's very small population, fell in behind the leaders of the political opposition as well as those of the two principal Churches of the country, the official Methodist Church and the Catholic Church. The government was obliged to acknowledge the sale of passports to be unlawful. In effect, just before the beginning of the proceedings instituted by one of the opposition leaders, the government was forced to convene the Parliament in an emergency session, something extremely rare in Tonga's history, which reports only two such sessions, both in very specific contexts.[31] This time the purpose was to modify the Constitution and to regularise the naturalisation of several hundreds of people.

Identity and democracy

In the present case, it was the partisans of change who most clearly expressed their attachment to Tongan identity. Yet this sentiment is often accompanied by fairly clear elements of xenophobia, notably on the part of the most active People's Representatives in Parliament or on the staff of *Kele'a*, which ran the headline in its June 1992 issue: 'The Chinese and the Indians are going to outnumber us; call a halt before it's too late'. Among the most influential avowed supporters of democracy are some who go a step further and explicitly defend certain aspects of tradition precisely because these seem to them to be a part of Tongan identity. This is the case, for instance, of Epeli Hau'ofa, a sociology professor at the University of the South Pacific in Suva (Fiji) and a writer known in particular for a collection of humorous short stories about Tonga and economic development.[32] In one of his political exposés, after having given the reasons he felt underlay the decline of the aristocracy and the rise of democratic aspirations in spite of absolute monarchy, E. Hau'ofa went on to say that, in his view, the nobles should be maintained in their function as reminders of the past and symbols of Tongan identity: 'In saying what I have said, I did not wish to write the aristocracy off, far from it … They are the foci of our culture and identity as single people, as well as being the signposts of our historical continuity as a nation.'[33]

Another example: Futu Helu, a particularly listened-to intellectual and fierce partisan of democracy, is also one of the best connoisseurs of Tongan tradition, which he teaches. Significantly, F. Helu always wears the *tupenu*, the traditional wrap-around, never trousers. On a somewhat different note, Anna Taufe'ulungaki, deputy director of Education and doctor of linguistics from the University of Birmingham, declared:

> We are in grave danger of losing our identity as Tongans. We have been too preoccupied with Western values and priorities. Money is all. Many chiefs don't recognise their full responsibilities to their own people. Even the language is at risk. There are certain values and ideas that are uniquely Tongan and can only be expressed in the Tongan language. Lose that and what are we? Cultural loss-makers like the Welsh.[34]

Several times she comes back vehemently to the importance of the Tongan language for the preservation of Tongan culture. Like the *Matangi Tonga* editorialist, she speaks of Tongan identity as the 'soul of a nation'. It was also an elected representative of the people, V. Fukofuka, one of the founding members of *Kele'a*, who sponsored a bill stipulating that the Tongan language must be the basic language used between government employees … and that knowledge of the Tongan language must be a prerequisite for employment by the government.

Obviously other partisans of democracy do not share these positions and do not defend traditional values. We can read, for example, in the *Matangi Tonga* editorial for March–April 1991, that tradition must not be allowed to hobble innovation, even if the culture is rooted in the past, that one must embrace the future and not be afraid of bilingualism, even if the rejected pieces of tradition end up in museums and history manuals. Some even make direct attacks on this tradition, usually in the name of Christian values and democracy. One such attack was launched in public, in 1974, at a seminar held under the auspices of the Tonga Council of Churches. Several participants had expressed sometimes very severe criticisms, based on Biblical references, of the land-holding system, which is extremely favourable to the nobles. In its closing resolution, the seminar declared: In the Bible, obligations went from the rich to the poor, from the person who had land to the person who did not own any, from the powerful to the powerless. Most obligations in our Tongan community go in the opposite direction.[35]

Among the most active critics of tradition is the Catholic Bishop of Tonga, Monsignor Finau, who died in October 1993 at the early age of 59. He aimed vigorous criticism at corruption in State offices and in the ranks of Parliament; he was also an active defender of democracy in the name of the Gospel. For instance, in October 1989, apropos of the spectacular parlementarians' walkout by the People's Representatives, he declared:[36] 'The historic walkout of September 1989 is a prophetic call for changes in Tonga's Constitution ...' In January 1991, the Bishop pronounced the present political system 'simply ridiculous'. Furthermore, he was persuaded that, if the people of Tonga were invited to choose between traditional values and Christian values, they would choose the first, which explains his running battle against many aspects of traditional culture. He added that there 'there is a huge discrepancy between our culture and the teachings of Christ'. On many other occasions and concerning a variety of practices, the Bishop spoke out clearly against tradition, explaining that these were no longer Old Testament times but those of the New Testament. In his February 1989 editorial for the Catholic monthly *Taumu'a Lelei*, the Bishop challenged the 'Tongan Way' (*faka Tonga*) which consists in spending considerable sums of money on visits by Church leaders or important people. In March 1989, at a tourism convention, the Bishop once more declared in substance: when we are in fear of losing our identity as Tongans, we must answer a few questions: Are we afraid of losing our privileged position? Are we afraid of our moral decline? Perhaps we are afraid of justice? Perhaps it is the fear of becoming slaves to the dollar? It could also be the fear of seeing our own people truly develop.[37] In his last editorial for *Taumu'a Lelei*, published shortly after his death, he asked once more: 'Are we for Christ or for our own culture?' The Bishop's behaviour was so irritating to some that the King ventured to call him a 'Marxist', producing considerable shockwaves felt well beyond Catholic circles. The Crown Prince, on the other hand, had called him a 'representative of a foreign power', namely, the Vatican.

Another example of violent political criticism in the name of Christian values came from a Tongan Methodist theologian living in Australia who, at the Convention on the Tongan Constitution and Democracy, mentioned above, declared: 'The Constitution does not satisfy the philosophical, ethical, or theological standards appropriate to a society which could, in the fullest sense, describe itself as Christian.' By the same token, it is important to note that the highly respected Reverend 'Amanaki Havea, then president of the official Methodist Church, the King's Church, declared in 1990 that he believed in the separation of State and Church as institutions which are independent of each other but which can be one in God. This rings much like an abandonment of the King by his own Church, if one remembers that, in the modern history of Tonga, Church and State have been very closely intertwined,[38] and that most of the incidents in the history of the Churches of Tonga can be read in a political light. Reverend 'Amenaki Havea played a considerable role in what concerns us here. He was head of the Pacific Theological College in Suva (Fiji), a multi-denominational Protestant institution which developed a doctrine relatively close to Catholic liberation theology.[39] Lastly, the first president of the 'Pro-Democracy' movement was a Catholic priest, and the vice president, a pastor of the official Methodist Church. These were not just any priest or any pastor, since each was the editor of his own Church's monthly.

The passport affair is not the only place where the identity debate appears. It can be seen in other areas as well. The partisans of the system in place, the royalists, defend the institutional status quo in the name of tradition. They might be thought to be acting out of self-interest, since those royalists taking part in the public debate have every interest in maintaining the status quo which means the preservation of their often considerable privileges. Even if this were true though, it does not explain everything involved in the choice of an argumentation based on tradition. There are other arguments are as well: since the end of the civil war at the close of the nineteenth century, rulers have been engaged in building a genuine State which managed to preserve — Tonga is the unique case in the South Pacific — a minimum of national integrity during the colonial era;[40] the present king has worked determinedly for the country's economic development and, if one compares with the neighbouring countries, for example Western Samoa, Tonga comes out well; the royal family has afforded Tonga a long period of stability, and so on.

Of course these arguments are sometimes used by the royalists, but more often their rhetoric is grounded on tradition, proving that, in their view, arguments based on this tradition are not only the most legitimate, they are also the most effective. Incidences of this tradition-based anti-democratic argumentation are countless. We will mention in particular the government's rebroadcast, on the eve of the 1993 elections, of a speech by the late Queen Salote Tupou II, the much-revered mother of the present king, urging respect for tradition. Briefly the argument goes that the status quo should be maintained in the name the traditional identity of the Tongan people and of national unity, everything else being regarded as bad because it is alien to the tradition of the country. As an example, we will cite a comment made by the noble Fusitu'a concerning one *fono*.[41] 'There are new alien elements which seek to separate the people from the chiefs and from the legislative assembly, despite the fact that they form a single body'; it should be understood that, by alien, he means Tongans educated abroad to progressive ideas. Likewise, in a speech before the Parliament, the Finance Minister declared that political parties create dissension. Fortunately, he added, Tongans usually return from abroad without this contagious political virus that comes from the West, one of the signs — indicating that some have nonetheless been contaminated — being the wearing of trousers in place of the traditional *tupenu*.

The idea that democracy creates dissension while tradition maintains social cohesion crops up frequently in royalist speeches. Here is yet another example. In 1992, the noble Fusitu'a, appointed 'Speaker of the House' by the King, declared in front of the overseas conference of the League for Freedom and Democracy (formerly an international anti-communist movement), that freedom was more important than democracy and that Lincoln's definition of democracy was outdated, and he went on to say that the existence of political parties led to the domination of the weak by the strong.[42] Another noble, Malupo, defended the status quo in the name of maintaining the 'traditional values of respect, love and peaceableness'. He added: 'We are still at peace only because we still ask things of each other.'

However it is the King himself who expresses the clearest opinion on the subject. In an interview granted in January 1990, he rejected the idea of a democratic government because, he said, it would allow communism, or a dictatorship, to seize power in Tonga. Above all he stresses that the objective of Tonga's government is to work with all Tongans, without opposition, that the kind of government provided for by the Constitution is government by consensus, and finally that 'the guardian of popular leadership is the King not the Parliament'. The logical outcome of all this is that, for some royalists, a political party would be envisageable and legitimate only if it were powerful enough to rally a very large majority of the population favourable to the royal family. This explains at least in part the attempt to put together a political party (which was to be termed 'Christian democrat'), on the eve of the February 1993 legislative elections, when the government convened the eleven principal religious denominations in Tonga.[43] Needless to add, the government met with a polite refusal from most of the Churches, which considered the government proposition manipulative and ill-timed.[44]

Democracy and development

Since we have said that there are democrats who are also traditionalists — and conversely — we are now going to show that being a democrat does not necessarily mean being in favour of rapid economic development, and vice versa. This is particularly clear in the case of the King. Since he mounted the throne over twenty-five years ago, the King has done everything in his power to implement a dynamic policy of economic development (including encouraging emigration to ease demographic pressure). In reality, progressist royalists are busily sawing at the branch on which they are sitting.

They are caught up in a basic contradiction: the King wants both progress and tradition. I. Campbell taxed the King with having brought with him to the throne the seeds of political instability insofar as he was a modernising radical.[45] When the King attempts, at all costs, to ensure development by opening-up the country, favouring emigration, developing education and tourism, inviting foreign capital and international aid, liberalising the economy, etc., he is contributing to the dismantling of tradition. It must be added that several members of the royal family, beginning with the King himself, are setting the example. They involve themselves, sometimes ostentatiously, in business ventures, but in so doing, they undermine their traditional royal status. By going into business, they are behaving like everyone else, like the common people, even if they gain economic power. Papiloa Foliaki, the businesswoman mentioned above, expresses a widely held opinion when she says: 'Commercialism and tradition are now in conflict, even in the monarchy itself. In commerce everyone is the same. Ordinary people are saying, 'If the monarchy is doing what we are doing, what are we to do? What is behind our royalty any more?'[46]

Other royalists, on the contrary, even among those most favourable to evolution of the political system, are worried to see Tongans turning into clones of Western civilization. This is the case of Langi Hu'akavameiliku, who holds several ministerial portfolios, among which that of Deputy Prime Minister, and who, on the one hand, some time ago submitted several projects to the King for constitutional reform and, on the other hand, declared at the thirty-first South

Pacific Conference held in Tonga: 'Even among ourselves, we don't know whether we are equal or Pacific people or clones of the facade of Western society.'[47] In October 1993, Langi Hu'akavameiliku came back to the subject in an interview given to *Matangi Tonga*, replying that it was crucial for Tonga to think about what kind of development is achievable, which could be undertaken according to Tonga's own criteria, and not a Western-style development; but he added: 'I want to be a modern man and a Tongan, not a modern man who happens to live in Tonga … we hope that whatever we do, we will still maintain our Tongan identity, our government and the Monarchy.'[48]

In the opposition camp, it is highly significant that the leader, 'Akilisi Pohiva, is for slow-paced economic development. For him, rapid economic development supposes calling on foreigners who would then come to dominate and destroy Tongan society. It is therefore necessary to envisage slowing down the economic-development program and not trying to do like everyone else. The appeal to nationalism is even clearer when he adds: 'What should be done now is to make the Tongan people angry, tell them something like, that the Indians are going to come and destroy them, something that will make them sit up and be proud of themselves.'[49] True, Pohiva can evoke one of the most famous phrases of King Tupou I, spoken at the proclamation of the Constitution on 4 November 1875; '*Tonga ma'a Tonga*', which is usually construed as 'Tonga for the Tongans', carrying national overtones, whereas , strictly speaking, it could also be understood as 'all Tongans for Tonga'. To put it another way, here Pohiva is appealing to an old-style, somewhat prickly nationalism. As can be seen, one can be a staunch supporter of democracy and at the same time be wary of economic development, once again in the name of Tonga and the identity of the Tongan people.

Conclusion

We have tried to show that, in the context of the growing invasion of a small third-world country by Western values, one cannot be content to analyse political battles in terms of political sociology alone. Behind these very real and sometimes bitter political struggles, over defence or undoing privileges and which are by no means to be denied, lies a highly charged issue of identity. The stakes are all the more vital because a small country like Tonga has extremely limited resources, whatever the area considered. To take only one example: can a written literature be produced today in the Tongan language by such a small population completely encircled by an Anglo-Saxon material and moral culture? And in fact this literature is practically non-existent.

In our countries, it is becoming fashionable to complain about the loss of identity signposts and to laugh it off. The question of identity nonetheless exists, and it is the source of many difficulties. We should not be surprised then that the issue of identity, as we have attempted to describe it in contemporary Tonga through the ongoing political battles, appears fragmented and sometimes vague. Indeed has identity, wherever it may be, ever been something totally homogeneous, stable and non-contradictory? One has only to recall here something Lévi-Strauss said in his seminar on identity: '[Societies] split [identity] into a multitude of components the synthesis of which, for each culture, though in different terms, poses a problem.'[50] Wherever it may be, major periods of transition often produce constellations, even variegated patchworks, composed of old and new, and one of these constellations ultimately prevails when one period has finally given way to another.

Footnotes

1 This text was written in 1995. Since then, there have been new events and some changes in the actors. Nevertheless, the relationship we have tried to present between identity, tradition and democracy remains for the most part unchanged.

2 Tonga is an archipelago in the southern hemisphere, situated between 15° and 23° lat. s. and 173° and 175° long. w., not far from Fiji and Samoa. It is comprised of 170 islands, 36 of which are inhabited by a total of some 100,000 persons.

3 See Marcus (1977).

4 See, e.g., Hill (1991), Campbell (1992).

5 The issue of Tongan identity also involves nationalism (sometimes xenophobia) and tradition, but the two are so often intertwined in the argumentation that it is hard to sort them out, for, as we have already said, we are not dealing with a tradition but with a neo-tradition which exhibits a nationalistic aspect.

6 Quoted in Latukefu (1975: 41).

7 In fact, the Constitution contradicts itself on this point since there are areas in which the principle of equality before the law — between nobles and commoners — is not recognised.

8 The Parliament is a legislative body comprised of the twelve ministers and governors, all appointed by the king and accountable to him only, of twelve nobles elected by the thirty nobles of the realm and of nine representatives elected by the people. On important questions, the ministers and nobles almost always vote as a bloc.

9 As everywhere, women would not gain this right until much later, in 1951, through a constitutional amendment (Act n° 15, 1951).

10 As an example of development of the entrepreneurial spirit, we can cite the widespread fascination with the cash-cropping of pumpkins for Japan. Production rose from 1,088 tons in 1988 to some 18,000 tons in 1993 (see Grijp, n.d.).

11 The first school was set up in 1829 by missionaries. Primary education was made compulsory in 1846, and since 1974 the age for leaving school has been raised to 14.

12 Quoted in Latukefu (1974: 75).

13 Both establishments are named 'Atenisi', the Tongan form of the word 'Athens'.

14 A. Taufe'unlugaki, the deputy director of Education points out that the use of English is also an equaliser, enabling people to circumvent the special vocabulary used with nobles. Thus MPs often speak in English during pauses in a parliamentary session.

15 Tonga's population in 1921 was 23,759, and in 1986 it was 95,649.

16 See Bataille-Benguigui (1991: 231–238).

17 See Benguigui (1989). In passing, it should be noted that, contrary to the previsions of the Constitution, the number of men over the age of 16 not having been allotted land is considerable and on the rise.

18 Kava, made from the root of a pepper plant (*Piper methysticum*), is the traditional drink reserved for men in Polynesia. It is drunk on ceremonial occasions. Both its preparation and its consumption are the object of a rigorous codification accompanied by an order of precedence. It is also consumed informally, notably in cafés commonly called 'kava clubs'.

19 There is only one radio station in Tonga and it is State owned.

20 This teacher would later have the Tongan government condemned for unfair dismissal (verdict rendered in May 1988).

21 It seems that *Kele'a*, an often pamphleteering newsletter, is now deeply in debt following a series of lost libel cases. The magazine *Islands Business Pacific*, in its February 1994 issue, mentions debts amounting to US $ 44,000.

22 In *Matangi Tonga*, March 1990. *Matangi Tonga* is the only genuine magazine in Tonga. Launched in November 1986, shortly after *Kele'a*, it is trimestrial.

23 To understand this remark, one must recall the importance attributed by both tradition and the law, to respect for nobles. For instance, there is a law, not applied today but not abrogated either, which stipulates: 'It shall be unlawful to pass any of the nobles on horseback or in any vehicle without stopping until the noble has passed and saluting by raising the hand' (Town Regulation Act, section 13).

24 See Helu (1992).

25 An example of his royalist stand, even before his break with the opposition: 'it is unlawful in law to criticise the king or to judge him, and I firmly support this' (*Times of Tonga*, 11 April 1911).

26 Laki Niu was publically accused of corruption by the leader of the opposition, A. Pohiva (pers. com. from A. Pohiva, August 1993).

27 Among the very important campaigns waged by the *Kele'a* group, we can cite those against the astonishing stipends MPs award themselves or those against tax reform.

28 In the past few years, these prices could be as high as US$50,000.

29 See Bain (1993: 167).

30 This fear of foreigners has a long history. Article 3 of the 1875 Constitution forbid the importing of Chinese labour. The article was modified in 1912, extending the ban to all Asian workers, with very few exceptions.

31 The first was in 1915, during the First World War, the second, in 1982, after hurricane Isaac.

32 See Hau'ofa (1983).

33 See Hau'ofa (1993). Friends of Hau'ofa's democratic camp sharply criticised this position.

34 See Bain (1993: 116).

35 See Tonga Council of Churches, 'Land and Migration', Nuku'alofa, 1975.

36 Most People's Representatives had walked out of the Parliament for 2 weeks in protest against the disdain they felt the government and the nobles showed them.

37 In the May 1989 issue of *Matangi Tonga*.

38 S. Latukefu's book, *Church and State in Tonga*, sheds particular light on the subject (Latukefu 1974). Note that in the arms of Tonga, the two olive branches represent the union of Church and State, as does the motto: 'God and Tonga are my inheritance.'

39 Nevertheless, the official Methodist Church is divided over the positions taken by Reverend Havea. For instance, at the Church's last annual assembly, in 1993, the delegates from the outlying islands moved against the political articles published in the Church monthly.

40 Tonga is the only State in the South Pacific never to have been directly colonised, it was merely declared a protectorate from 1900 to 1970.

41 The Tongan *fono* is a meeting convened by the person in authority in view of expressing his wishes. It is different from the Samoan *fono* which usually permits an exchange of views.

42 This noble declared to the Tongan News Association in 1991 that freedom of the press did not exist anywhere in the world, not in Tonga, in the United States or Australia or New Zealand … and that media owners had their own means of censoring news that might not be good for them.

43 This government attempt was paradoxical insofar as, on several occasions, different ministers had complained about the Churches' meddling in politics.

44 Pers. com. from Mgr. Finau, August 1993. Certain Churches are nevertheless staunch supporters of the status quo.

45 See Campbell (1992: 79).

46 See Bain (1993: 167).

47 Quoted by K. James in the newspaper *Contemporary Pacific* (see James 1993). It should also be noted that the Education Ministry has left Tonga's school system in a deplorable state for many years.

48 See too the editorial in the April 1994 issue of *Matangi Tonga*: 'Democracy yes; free enterprise, yes; but at the same time we should not allow the process of change to alienate Tongans in their own country.'

49 In the March 1990 issue of *Matangi Tonga*.

50 See Lévi-Strauss (ed. 1977: 11).

Chapter 12

CULTURE, NATION, SOCIETY

Secondary change and fundamental transformations in Western Samoa

Towards a model for the study of cultural dynamics

Serge Tcherkézoff

The belief that we can observe and translate the identity of a culture directly is no doubt an illusion. At first everything we see seems to speak of a certain cultural identity simply because everything seems alien to the outside observer and therefore to call for new categories. In these conditions how can we classify the material without projecting onto it what is, a priori for our culture, an alien culture? Secondly, no society is exempt from the effects of history and daily changes. But to speak of transformations — in the diachronic sense — is no easier. How can anthropologists integrate this dimension when they often spend only a few years 'in the field'. Furthermore, depending on the observer's distance, close up — say an individual or a life-history — or further away — for instance a system of obligatory social relations (taboos, laws) — the periodicity of change and its logic will appear very different. So what distance should we favour?

When the object of study readily lends itself to projection, the solution is not to tell ourselves that we will achieve greater objectivity by paying greater attention. This would be another illusion, only confirming our projections as we went. The solution is to state our conditions and methodological choices clearly so as to enable the observer to make a preliminary choice. Some ethnocentric projection is inevitable because the observer does not stand 'above' the human societies that provide the material for observation; he is an integral part of society. But he will make use of that which at least serves the manner in which anthropology initially defines its ethical position with respect to the other.

As far as I am concerned, this choice is dictated by a general conception of the 'comparative' relationship implied when an observer, in the name of social science — and therefore in the name of the Western value known as 'universalism' — attempts to translate the reality, however mobile, of a particular society and therefore the reality of a concrete local totality.[1] To speak of identity and of changes in this identity supposes accepting the idea that societies and cultures exist, and that each constitutes a particular reality. Universalism is at the same time a necessity on the ethical level and an obstacle when it comes to talking directly about a concrete reality, which every 'society' (whether remote or Western) is. I have therefore chosen to define the idea of a particular society in contrast to the logic implied in the universalistic idea of humankind. The latter reasons in terms of a group considered as a collection of elements, *prior to being considered as a collectivity* defined as to their nature, such that each element ('human being') represents in the same manner the entire set ('humankind'). I posit, on the contrary, that the characteristic feature of an individual society is first of all the phenomenon by which all individuals express and practise their *belonging* to a single *whole*, the latter being narrower than the set of all human beings: 'we are…', 'I do this because my ancestors did it…', and so forth.

To speak of belonging to the same 'whole' is to speak of a *hierarchical* system, for here precisely we are no longer in a logic of the collection: one can be seen to belong because one occupies one or more *ranks* which, though not meaningful in themselves, immediately take on meaning when placed in a context, in other words in relation to other positions occupied at the same moment by other individuals. Rank is the different possibility each person has to represent to a certain extent the whole for the others. Hierarchy is a global phenomenon: there is always a difference between two ranks, between two positions involved in belonging to the same whole (two identical positions would mean a single belonging, a single social subject.[2]) Defined in this way, the notion can be applied to even the most 'egalitarian' societies, those 'without (centralised) power', and so on, for I am not talking about the kind of inequality in which the difference precedes the relation. I am talking about the fact that all of the individuals belong to one space, conceived as a unified place, but in which all positions are different.

An eloquent visual example of this is the way people throughout Western Polynesia arrange themselves when they come together in a socially recognised group: they form into circle — Samoans speak of a 'sacred circle' (*alofi sa*). This figure is well suited to showing a single belonging: each person sits around the circumference and at the same distance from the centre, which is the place of the divine.[3] Yet the circle is oriented, simultaneously and contrary to the geometry we are familiar with, by axes of value which divide the circumference into clearly differentiated arcs. Within these arcs, each point is different from the next. In Samoa, these points are represented by the posts that hold up the conical roof of the ceremonial house, itself comprised of a circular base, a circle of posts and a roof, with no internal partitions.

A social system, and therefore a system of belonging to a whole and therefore a hierarchical system, can be identified by the fact that it is a system of prohibitions sharing a single belief about the content of and the reasons for these prohibitions, but operating on a graduated scale: the highest ranks are those carrying the greatest number of prohibitions.

Prohibitions affect the way the highest ranking person enters into contact with those of lower rank, for instance the caste system in India, or the way those of lower rank come into contact with the highest-ranking person: this is the Polynesian taboo.

In this methodological perspective, the major transformation marking the passage from one period of identity to another is one which modifies the system's rules for belonging — in this case I will speak of 'fundamental transformation'. The social revolution is a type-case; for Europe, one has only to think of 1789 or 1917. In the case of Samoa, things are not that simple. Whether before or after Christianization (roughly 1830–1860), before, during or after the colonial period (1899–1962), before or after introduction of the modern school system of the 1950s (patterned, but only partially, on the European model), the system of belonging remained by and large unchanged. Briefly, since we will be coming back to the subject, we are talking about the '*matai* (title) system', the *faamatai*: a hierarchy of ancestral names associated with lands. These names, known as '*matai* names' (*o suafa o matai*), define 'family' groups (*aiga*): all those affiliated with this kind of name and who display this attachment. These names are transmitted in the same way as the aristocratic titles; hence the fact that the anthropological literature speaks of 'titles',[4] the term used by Samoans when speaking English; but in Samoan, they speak of '*matai* names'. The name is carried by the person who has been elected and formally invested with the name by the family, *aiga*, and who then becomes the *matai* of the family; I will use this term (the literature uses chief, high chief, title-holder). These are not 'aristocratic' titles, however, since all families in Samoa, without exception, are *aiga* defined around such a name; the 'chiefs' are family heads, and no one is left out because everyone belongs to at least one family.

This is a properly social phenomenon. Such names do not simply form a mythic stock which harks back to the history of each family. At every generation, they form a global, country-wide hierarchy — the official order of all ancestral names — made visible, enacted and verbally expressed by the *matai*, all those individuals invested with one of these names. The *matai* make numerous decisions concerning everyone; but because their authority is exercised on behalf of the ancestors they personify, the result is that, at each generation, a hierarchy is recomposed which forms the basis of the whole social organisation governing families, the village, land-holding and politics. Samoa is famous throughout the South Pacific for their enduring '*matai* system'.[5] Of course we will see that there have been many secondary changes — those not affecting the principles of the system. We will also see that, since 1990, in other words very recently, there has been a deep-seated modification of the system of political representation which may pave the way for a fundamental transformation. But in the meantime the long-term identity remains unchanged: the hierarchical logic is still the same, as are the forms of social belonging which make up this hierarchy.

We therefore need a more complete model which takes account of secondary changes.[6] These cannot be left to one side because they are the gateway for the event, however tenuous, which may later work its way into the whole, eventually laying the groundwork for the fundamental transformations that will affect the first level of the configuration, that is the system of belonging.[7] In any event, observation demands this complement. It is clear that everything we observe is not only the hierarchical fact of belonging and the ways it is enacted, however complex and varied these may be, as in the case of the system of Polynesian titles. Individuals also do a host of other things, which appear to be something else because they are no longer explained by the hierarchy and even sometimes seem to run counter to it. We must pay close attention to these contexts, for they provide a ready entry for new elements and change. But because they are not central to the phenomena of belonging, they more often escape the attention of the interested parties: these are areas in which people acknowledge that things 'just happen', either by chance or because they are felt to be inherent properties of people and things.

We will return to this in the second part of the article, devoted to the question of change. For the moment, however, let us turn to the question of identity.

Identity: the sacred circle

Although I will keep the singular of this term, since I am talking about contemporary identity, the kind I observed, I will distinguish three categories, based respectively on the Samoan culture, on the existence of a national State, Western Samoa, and last, on the social system which brings all people together into a single hierarchical system of belonging, the '*matai* system'. In each case, we will find the figure of the circle, which organises the system of belonging and so maintains the feeling of identity.

Cultural identity: faaSamoa

In the South Pacific, east of Wallis and Futuna (French territory), northwest of the Fiji islands, southeast of Tuvalu, north of the islands of Tonga (each of these three names designates at once an archipelago, a cultural identity and an independent State) lies a group of islands whose some 200,000 inhabitants, whenever they happen to meet coming from different villages and islands, all use strictly the same language, the same way of greeting each other, of inviting everyone to sit down in a circle to talk, eat and so forth. Even more astonishing, they immediately or rapidly agree on the order of precedence, even if the meeting is impromptu: the seating order in the house where they meet, the speaking order, the order in which drink and food are served,[8] etc. If someone from outside the archipelago is present, he will always hear the same cultural discourse of 'us' versus 'you' in response to his questions: 'Here we do things this way.' In this discourse, the term that accompanies the 'our way' of doing this or that is *faaSamoa*,[9] 'the Samoan way'.

There is thus an awareness of a Samoan cultural identity. A very strong awareness, in fact; Samoans are constantly glorifying the *faaSamoa*; yet another phenomenon famous throughout the South Pacific.[10] This observation about awareness of an identity is amply confirmed in the immigrant communities which have left these little Pacific States to find work in Australia, New Zealand, or on the West Coast of the United States and in the American state of Hawaii. There too one hears the same discourse whenever people meet who recognise themselves in the *faaSamoa*, which means whenever they come from this group of islands we can thus designate as the archipelago and the culture area of the 'Samoan islands'.[11]

To this mutual recognition by insiders ('our *faaSamoa*') must be added the attitude shared towards outsiders, those who, by their origin and their inability to understand Samoan, show that they do not come from this circular world where the way of life is the *faaSamoa* but where the language too is the *faaSamoa*, for this is also the word — there is no other way of saying it — Samoans use to qualify their language with respect to other languages.

Their neighbours, first of all, have been known from time immemorial and feature frequently in the war legends and the genealogies tracing marriages between high-ranking families: the immediate neighbours are Fiji and Tonga. They, too, are 'humans', *tagata*, and therefore products of the same Creator, Tagaloa-a-Lagi, the traditional chief god of this region;[12] but their way of life and language are the *faaFiti* (Fijian) and the *faaToga* (Tongan). Categories of broader regional identity, such as 'Polynesian' or 'Pacific islander', and the 'Pacific Way' are still infrequent, outside intellectual and government circles that is. Beyond that, Samoans used to know nothing through their own tradition, since it told them that the 'world' (*lalolagi*, 'that which lies beneath the sky') was bounded by the celestial vault (the *lagi*, in fact several layers of curved heavens, the dwellings of the gods). Recent history has introduced them to *Tama uli*, 'black boys', some hundreds of Melanesian workers imported by a few European settlers in the nineteenth century; however, these workers, who have all but disappeared today and whom many young people have never encountered as a group, were not really 'human' in the social sense.[13] History has also introduced Samoans to the *Tama seina*, 'Chinese boys', another group of indentured labourers imported in the twentieth century. Here history took a different course. Asians numbered a few thousand, intermarriage was frequent, a Chinese business quarter grew up in Apia; but the New Zealand government forcibly repatriated many in the name of a concern typical of the time (the 1920s), the preservation of the 'purity' of the Samoan 'race'.[14] The merchant quarter still exists, but its population is heavily mixed; there are also a number of merchant families of mixed blood and a few mixed-blood children in Samoan families in the villages. All these families speak Samoan in the home; the children one notices here or there are the same as other children, even if it is known that their grandfather was one of those workers; and the only teasing that can be heard among children is the phrase *mata seina*, 'Chinese eyes'.[15]

Last of all there is the Papalagi, the European, the first foreigner to land on the shores of these islands (if one excepts Fijians and Tongans). The term Papalagi which designates this foreigner is still in use today. It is the common word, pronounced without a thought as to its possible etymology which, if accurate, still indicates the huge distance, in cosmological terms, that Samoans attributed to the original home of this newcomer: he is the one from the confines of the celestial circle.[16] To be sure, his quasi-divine status is considerably diminished, but the European remains a special, problematic being. He is lauded because he belongs to the people who brought the 'good word' — and Christianity, at least what it became when it was adopted by the Samoans, is today one of the things Samoans refer to as being part of their tradition; he is admired (but that is all) for his technological achievements; but he is almost scorned for his inability to live in 'society' (what Samoans call *nuu*) and to understand the 'social' facts of others (personal notes). This image of the Papalagi is even more pejorative in the mouth of intellectuals or politicians (at least those in power until the mid-1980s),[17] who see him as a plunderer of cultural treasures (he collects data and then publishes 'absurdities about our way of life, our politics, the grammar of our language') and as someone who has no social values, an 'individualist' (in the ordinary sense of the word), and so forth.

Comment

On the question of cultural plunder, this acerbic criticism clearly comes from a few intellectual or academic circles. The example often cited by these Samoans is Margaret Mead's book on adolescence in Samoa (1928) which many regard as a tissue of 'lies' (*pepelo*).

Concerning the criticism of European social life and Europeans' inability to understand what a 'society' is about, that is a life organised in the manner of a *nuu* (village in the sense of a set of those who belong, see below), the view is much more widespread and each person has a more-or-less shaded opinion. Everyone — and not only intellectuals and politicians — thinks he knows all about life in Europe (by hearsay: the accounts of many emigrants), whereas, in the early 1980s, the date of my first stay, tourism was non-existent (if one excepts the Australian cruise ships that stopped to allow their passengers to spend a day or two in the capital and its two main hotels, with spectacles featuring local songs and dances). I witnessed, in various villages, the swarms of children observing with a mixture of curiosity and fear the event created by the arrival of a *Papalagi* (the fear came from the fact that mothers often use the image of the *Papalagi* as an ogre to threaten a disobedient child that, if he was not good, she will send for one).

Many things have changed in fifteen years, accelerating rapidly after 1987: electrification, a road system, construction of several hotels, launch of a campaign advertising Polynesian traditions ('Samoa: the cradle of Polynesia') aimed at bringing in tourists, mainly from Australia and New Zealand, but also from the United States and even Europe, where Western Samoa has opened an embassy in Brussels (see below); and recently relying heavily on brochures offering attractive financial conditions to foreign investors.[18]

The islands of Samoa thus constitute a homogeneous cultural area, even if their geography and history present some discontinuities. Proceeding from east to west, we find the small cluster of the three islands of Mana'a, the narrow but very long island of Tutuila with its once-important port of Pago Pago,[19] then further west, a group of two large islands (each over 70 km in length), with an area (nearly 3,000 km² for these two alone) and a population (160,000 inhabitants) which makes them the largest territorial group in terms of emerged surface and population in Polynesia:[20] Upolu, also with a sheltered port that has recently turned into a regular town (Apia), Savaii, and two little islands located between the larger ones, Apolima and Manono. The tales of war and the genealogies say that Manua ruled all these islands several centuries ago, which means that everyone would have acknowledged the genealogical supremacy of this group's principal *matai* chief title, the *Tui Manua*. At the time of contact this was no longer the case, and the important chiefs of Upolu, Manono and Savaii dominated and frequently waged war on a local scale. Nevertheless, cultural unity persisted, even in the absence of a single, centralised power, with thousands of different *matai* chiefs and ten or so great chiefs around whom the others rallied and to whom they lent their support in the form of food (cultivating gardens, fishing) and warriors.

By a fluke of European colonial policy (the division decided in Berlin in 1899), the eastern islands (Tutuila and the little Manua group) became — and remain today — an 'unincorporated' American territory,[21] while the western islands came under German control. The latter had been independent until the end of the nineteenth century, but they experienced the gradual establishment of a small population of European settlers (5 per cent of the total population at the start of the twentieth century), who developed the town of Apia, at the north end of Upolu, into a trading post and the headquarters of the various 'consuls' created by the European sub-groups (Germans, English and Americans). Between 1899 and 1914, the islands were a German colony, but the administration hardly had the time to establish a different social organisation. When war broke out, the United Kingdom asked New Zealand to land in Samoa and to retire the German flag: this was done without a struggle, since, in military terms, the German garrison was inexistent. Between 1921 and 1962, the League of Nations (and then the United Nations) placed these islands under New Zealand administration. But this was only a 'mandate' (later a 'Trusteeship') and New Zealand had no plans for a settlement colony. It simply set up a central administration, which had little effect on village organisation, and public schools alongside the already well-established Mission school system.[22] In 1962, these islands became an independent State, the first post-colonial State in the South Pacific: Western Samoa.

The administrative division into two Samoas, the State of Western Samoa (pop. 160,000) and the American territory of eastern Samoa (pop. 36,000) had no effect on the cultural unity, which is fully evident today. Indeed, the kinship networks still extend over both Samoas. At life-cycle ceremonies and for every funeral, all living members of this family network (*aiga*), which can run into hundreds of individuals and in all cases at least a few dozen, try to be present.[23] People are therefore constantly meeting and travelling. Contacts between family members within each of the two Samoas are even more frequent on family occasions, to which must be added travel between the village and the administrative centre (Pago Pago for American Samoa and Apia for Western Samoa), and trips into town to sell their garden produce.[24]

The Samoan language is a vehicle for this constant renewal of community feelings and therefore common identity; while some words may change and new expressions appear owing to modernisation and Westernisation, these changes quickly spread. It must be stressed that, in both Samoas, the Samoan language, the language transmitted by the ancestors, is still spoken by everyone and, in the case of older people, it is often the only language spoken. In Western Samoa, the Samoan language comes first in every setting; in elementary school, on the radio, in the newspapers, in government offices, in Parliament, practically the only language heard or read is Samoan; official documents, however, are bilingual.

Comment

The story could have been very different. After public schooling was expanded by the New Zealand government (the percentage of children in full-time education was already high thanks to the Mission), there was a manifest desire to make English the language of education and therefore that of administration as well. But the New Zealand period did not last long enough: mandate in 1921, creation of a number of schools in the 1930s and 1940s and, at the beginning of the 1950s, the sentiment of imminent independence and therefore room made for the Samoan *cadres*. The years immediately preceding

independence also saw the return of the first scholarship winners (awarded by New
Zealand and the Commonwealth), who had left to attend university, who had been able
to achieve a Masters degree and even go on to earn a PhD in New Zealand with post-
doctoral work in the United States or Europe. The most famous is no doubt Aiono Dr.
Fanaafi Le Tagaloa, Foundation Professor at the National University and Samoa's first
Ph.D. (obtained in London), appointed upon her return Vice-Director and then Director
of National Education, the first Samoan to hold this office. She and others, highly
sensitised (by their travels) to the problem of cultural unity and the preservation of the
language — in particular in light of the disastrous situation of New Zealand's Maoris —
became ardent advocates of the complete Samoanisation of elementary education and the
administration, and at the same time proposed lexical rules for integrating new notions,
based on Samoan words. The wager paid off, and today the Samoan language is used by
everybody, young and old, farmers and the Prime Minister, as the everyday tongue as well
as the language of ceremony.[25]

National identity: *Samoa i sisifo* ('West Samoa')

I will restrict myself here to Western Samoa, which I know best.[26] Over the last two
centuries — and for longer according to legend — the stakes involved in the *matai* titles as
well as the wars seem to have ratified a certain estrangement between the archipelago's
western group and its eastern islands. In the west, three or four great names made the history
of pre-colonial warfare and held the key posts in the 'native' administration, under New
Zealand's rule, with a view to preparing for independence.

'O le Ao o le Malo': the head(s) of State

The absence of a single power, mentioned above, was so firmly entrenched in people's minds
that it had a consequence that was no doubt unique in the world. In the consultations
leading up to independence,[27] a Constitution was drafted along European lines, which
provided for a parliament (members to be elected by each district: approx. 40), a cabinet
(headed by a prime minister), chosen from among the members of Parliament, and a head of
State (who was also to be chosen from the body of MP's by election and for a period of five
years). But an exception was made to these rules, by constitutional amendment because of
the joint presence of two great '*matai*' names (Malietoa and Tupua Tamasese), which had
dominated the history of warfare in the eighteenth and nineteenth centuries, had played an
important role in relations with the Missions and with the foreign business community, and
then had occupied the most important positions in local government under New Zealand's
rule. Clearly these two names — and therefore the *matai* who bore them — must hold the
supreme office. First of all, it was obvious that the head of State must be a *matai*. The spirit
of the Constitution combined the Western idea of democratic political representation with
the traditional notion of rank, based on the *matai* system: all members of Parliament would
be *matai*. Secondly, to choose one over the other would deeply divide the country. Therefore
Malietoa Tanumafili II and Tupua Tamasese Meaole were *both* appointed heads of State,
jointly, simultaneously and for life. When one died, the other would continue in office until
he too passed away. Only then would the five-year mandate system come into force. Today,

one of the men has died and the other (Malietoa) continues to exercise the charge of head of State, which gives rise to another no doubt unique phenomenon: [in 2004] Malietoa has been head of State for an uninterrupted period of forty-two years! The rest of the system operates as provided in the Constitution, except that the relationship between the idea of the traditional *matai* chief and the voting system set up to elect a parliament has turned out to be awkward, and today holds new dangers, as we will see.

This to us astonishing but altogether Samoan decision shows that the idea of *malo* 'government' (see below) does not stand above the *matai* system. In the *matai* system, rivalry between men of similar rank is usually resolved according to hierarchy. But when the contest occurs at the very top, there remains only one solution, which is extreme: war. That is why one of the first acts of the German colonial government was to create a supreme court of law with the power to decide all matters relating to *matai* titles. This was an essential tool in eliminating traditional warfare. At the time, the high-court German judge could easily decide, rightly or wrongly. Today the situation is more complex because the judges themselves are Samoans; but this Land and Title Court continues to play a very important role in the life of the country.[28] When the present head of State (Malietoa) dies, the rivalry between the descendants of the two names (Malietoa and Tupua) will flare up again, but the wars of the nineteenth century are now too far away, and the question will be decided by election. A noteworthy fact: much of this election will be decided outside Parliament, when the extended Malietoa family (which numbers into the thousands) will already have to choose among their members the successor to the title of Malietoa *matai*. Most political rivals since independence (except for the newcomers in the last government) are *matai* whose genealogy dates far back and therefore connects at some point with that of the present Malietoa, one of the oldest families in the country; they are therefore 'heirs to the name' and are eligible to carry the title. The one who is finally vested with the title by the extended family will, as it were, be already chosen for the country's highest office — at least if the national identity we are talking about remains unchanged; if, on the other hand, the future were to show that the *matai* system is no longer the site of all decision-making, including political deliberations, then we would have to conclude that a fundamental transformation is underway.

It is thus not around *one* man or *one* political function that the country builds and lives out its unity, but rather around a number of such men and functions. To explain their order and the fact that, for example, it was impossible to take Tupua without Malietoa, or vice versa, we need to turn again to the ideas governing the *matai* system. It was because these two men were or are among the greatest *matai* that they were dealt with in this manner. It is because the Constitution on the whole is based on a combination of democratic ideas about representation and on the *matai* system that it looks so odd to our Western eyes and, also, that it so effectively ensures a national identity by carrying over into the political institution the fact that a *matai* is a *sacred* representative (in him lives the ancestor who bore the name which became the title passed down in the family), but one who is chosen *democratically* and can be dismissed (theoretically all members of the family are eligible to stand for election). The *matai* represents the family; together with other *matai*, he represents the village; finally, some of them represent the district. It is enough to look at the linchpin of the whole system as defined by the Constitution: to be a member of Parliament (and therefore eventually of the government or even head of State), one must be a *matai*. Only *matai* can be elected. It must immediately be added: today there are nearly 15,000 *matai* for a population of 160,000; this is therefore no oligarchy closed in upon itself.[29]

'O le Malo': the government

All Samoans one encounters, without exception, are proud of belonging to their country and take true pleasure in repeating the terms that identify them as a nation and a State: *O le Malo Tutoatasi o Samoa i sisifo* (as it appeared until the end of the 1980s on every Samoan's passport). This country has a 'government', it is a country, a 'State'; that is the content of the term *Malo*, which designates the established power, the oneness of authority (a district is *itumalo*, 'one face or one side of power'). In the ordinary sense, the term also designates 'victory' or the 'victor, winner' (in war, in rhetorical competitions). It also means 'guest', which says much about the Samoan duty of hospitality and the welcome extended to the outsider who is the guest of a Samoan family. Lastly, this country is 'independent' (*tutoatasi*; it 'stands [up] by itself'). Many know that it was the first independent State in the South Pacific. And the national holiday, in early June, which commemorates the independence of *Samoa i sisifo* ('West Samoa'), always gives rise to an immense expression of rejoicing in which all villages participate with huge parades and artistic or sporting competitions held on the big ceremonial ground of Apia.

It is not without significance that the government is called the *Malo*. This means that it is the 'winner' (formerly in war, today in the elections), but it also means that, on its own, it would not constitute a level of identity were it not totally immersed in the *matai* system. For alone, all it represents is ' strength', *malosi*. But the country is not founded on 'strength', but on 'God', according to the national motto and the Constitution; and here God is the pinnacle of the *matai* system, both its origin and its reference, the Christian God having taken over the role once played by Tagaloa, the demiurge of Western Polynesia. This comment on the manner of designating the government thus touches on the problem of elections (see below): if the *malo* (and thus politics) were to be separated from the *matai* system, there would be a risk of fundamental transformation.[30]

As an independent *Malo*, this country has its own 'dignity' and 'place in the order of the world' (*mamalu*). It also has its own 'sanctity' (*paia*), for as the national motto says and the Constitution confirms, this country is 'founded upon God'. Thus every law, every order, every written indication of a legal nature — such as the price of tickets posted in a city bus — is introduced by formulas such as: 'in the name of the dignity and the sanctity of this country, it is forbidden to…, it is permitted …, the prices are…', and so on. This central reference to 'God' (*O le Atua*) does not stem from the fact that some Mission managed to identify itself with the idea of government. On the contrary, a man who chooses to be a minister or a priest cannot be a *matai* or, if he holds the title, he must give it up. There is a continuity here with the preceding central divine figure, Tagaloa-a-lagi, who was both the pinnacle and the origin of the *matai*. Indeed the oldest title names descend from God, but they have in turn created other names.

This brings us back to the *matai* system, as does the expression for 'country': *atunuu*. When a Samoan, speaking of this State of Western Samoa, says it is his country, or when, as an emigrant in a distant land, he sings of his nostalgia for his 'dear country' (*o lou atunuu pele*), he always uses the word *atunuu*, which signifies literally a 'deployment of social groups' — and observation shows that these groups are ordered by the logic of the *matai* system. *Atu* is a term indicating a direction considered from the standpoint of the speaker and moving away from him. Dictionaries usually translate *Nuu* as 'village', and Samoa is effectively a 'country of villages'; there are some 350 of them. Everybody lives in a village (Apia, the capital, is itself a grouping of juxtaposed villages) in the sense that their name, their family and their land are defined as the component parts of a village. There is no larger physical reality. A village is a set (represented as a circle) of relatively closely grouped houses (more accurately, sites where a *matai* name originated) and their surrounding lands, sometimes extending out a great distance, which are in part the lands of each founding house of a name and in part village lands worked in common or not yet allocated. In various places, often invisible to the inexperienced eye, the lands of one village stop, and those of another begin. The district is an electoral division and the Member of Parliament is a village *matai*, like all *matai*.

There are other words for the village as a place to live or an occupied area. Significantly, though, these are seldom used, and it is the word *nuu* that one hears over and over. The village is designated as a *nuu* in the sense that a village is first of all a set of different social groups, each of which is itself a *nuu*. A village is the assemblage of four *nuu*: the group of the village *matai*, the group of the daughters and sisters of the *matai*, the group of the sons and finally the group of the wives.[31] Each of these groups operates according to a clear set of rules and — essential for our discussion — is modelled on the *nuu* of the *matai*. Cooperation among these four groups accounts for a good share of village life.

Social identity: *aganuu* (faaSamoa)

O le faamatai: the title system

When a Samoan talks about his society in English, he does not differentiate between 'culture' and 'society', and, as is the habit in Anglo-American, he will even speak more often of 'culture'. But if he is asked, still in English, to characterise his 'culture' in Samoan, once it is clear that the subject is the *faaSamoa* (as opposed to the *faaToga*, for instance, or the *faaPapalagi*, the Tongan way of life and language or those of the Europeans), once it is clear that it is not a question of the history of his 'country', *atunuu*, he will say that 'the essence or the nature of Samoan culture is…': what follows is usually a list of taboos and duties surrounding the *matai* system and religion, introduced by the phrase: *o le aganuu faaSamoa…*'. The term *aganuu*, the dictionary translation of 'custom', seems to be only another vocabulary item of the discourse on culture. But, like the concept 'country' (*atunuu*), the word 'custom' (*aganuu*) refers to the unit of social organisation, the *nuu*, meaning both the groups that make up the village (each of which meets in a circle) and the whole village as these groups taken together. Furthermore, the first root (*aga*) means 'the essence or the nature' of something, in the sense of 'the true place (of this thing) in the overall order of the world', its meaning at all levels, and so on. In short, custom, that order of things which is the *faaSamoa* (but the term is not obligatory because we are no longer speaking with reference to the neighbour or the outsider, we are speaking of the essence of the *faaSamoa*, we are speaking from the inside) is 'the essence of the phenomenon represented by the *nuu*', *aganuu*. But the *nuu* is the realisation, in the organisation of the society, of the order established by the *matai* system.[32] Here I will stress two points: the organisation of the *nuu* is the *matai* system, it is a *system* based on belonging and not a stratification in the village society; secondly, no Samoan is left out of this system of belonging.

The *faamatai* (from now on I will use this term because it is shorter than its translation: 'the system of *matai* [names]') is, for everyone, the social system of belonging. Every person, in every social situation (therefore subjected to at least one prohibition and one obligation, and usually to several) acts (in accordance or in conscious and deliberate contradiction) with reference to a 'place' (*tulaga, nofo*) that he sees himself as occupying with respect to the others present in this situation. We observe that the representation of this place always refers to the place occupied by the *matai* name with which this person is linked, with respect to the other village *matai* names within the 'circle' of these names, the '*nuu* of the *matai*'. The *faamatai* is therefore not 'the group of chiefly families', it is not only the *matai*, the individual 'chiefs': it is the fact that everything entailed in being part of society is *faa-matai*, 'guided by the *matai* phenomenon':[33] the representation of the sacred order of the ancestors' names throughout the country — a fluctuating representation at this level, but very clear at the level of each district and each village taken in isolation.

Everyone thus has in mind the circle of the *matai* of his village, and determines his own position with respect to his peers as though the interaction were homologous to that of the *matai* names from which everyone descends.

We have already seen that the '*matai* name' is the name of a memorable ancestor who has founded a family in the sense of having left the memory of a specific genealogy and a history of great and small events, often connected with wars, which is passed on. In Samoa, every person belongs to a 'family' (*aiga*) and often to several, and each *aiga* is something like a culture group, defined around the preservation of one or several ancestral names. There is therefore no such thing as a person who is not linked to at least one *matai* name, and when we see that reference to the place occupied by this name guides all personal interaction, it becomes clear that we are dealing with the most inclusive system of belonging.

The name of an ancestor becomes a *matai* name (*suafa o matai*), a title as the literature has grown accustomed to calling it, if this name has authority over a land: a land that has been connected with the name since time immemorial, or which was given to this ancestor by another *matai* who had authority over this land, often in token of a service rendered in time of war. Today as yesterday a *matai* can still create a *matai* name and give this new name a land over which his own name had authority. In this ideology, where the continuity between the gods, the ancestors and men is uninterrputed, men have always behaved towards each other as (they imagine) the gods behave towards them. The great *matai* names come down from the gods (they originate in the cosmogony), others can be traced back to another *matai* name (which originally created them).[34]

The name has a founding house (*maota*), and this house becomes the home of the *matai* and those he wants to gather around himself once he has been invested by the extended family. The name must always be carried by someone in order to stay 'alive'. The person invested with the name is therefore called the '*matai* of the family' (*o le matai o le aiga*). After a number of generations, the extended family (*aiga*) thus created is defined as follows: is considered to be a member any person, even living at the other end of the archipelago (people are scattered far and wide by marriage), who can (and wishes to) state any genealogical link (paternal, maternal or by adoption) with any of the *matai* who has succeeded to this name (and whose connection is known and accepted by the other members). He thereby becomes 'an heir to the name' (*suli*), he can take his place in the 'extended family circle' (*aiga potopoto*) which meets whenever there is a decision to be made concerning the whole family — and he can be a candidate to this name when the incumbent *matai* ceases to exercise his charge and a successor must be chosen.

Comment

Two distinctions need to be added:

1) The extended family circle which elects the new *matai* is divided into those who descend, through male or female links, from a son or a brother of the founding *matai* (or from the one who is the reference for the succession in question), who are called the 'male children' and who are eligible to succeed, and those who descend from a daughter or a sister of a *matai*, who are called the 'female children',[35] and who are supposed to 'know', by divine communication, who among the 'male children' will make a 'good' *matai*. This fundamental dichotomy no longer operates in a number of families, where all lines have become sources of potential candidates; this is the beginning of a deep-seated change which must be linked with the others which tend to diminish the operation and the efficacy of the social division of labour between 'brother' and 'sister' lines on behalf of an image of mankind closer to the Western conception, in which there are only men and women (see below). Among other things, this produces a feeling of equality between the lines descending from a woman and those descending from a man, hence the claim that each should 'have a turn' at choosing from their own line the person who will bear the title of *matai*.

2) For a candidate to be *eligible*, it must be possible to say: 'Look how well he has served (*tautua*) his family all these years!', which means that the person (man or woman) is not merely a genealogical heir, but that he or she has actually participated regularly in the life of the group and that they have demonstrated their 'generosity' (*alofa*), since 'service' consists chiefly in doing all one can to help collect and prepare the goods to be given in the exchanges between families (exchanges which are constantly cropping up and which make village life), but also to cook and do other jobs for the *matai* and his immediate family.

It should be noted that the charge of the *matai* can cease to be fulfilled; this can happen for three reasons: the death of the *matai*, an illness which renders him incapable of performing his duties — the *matai* then announces that he wants to hand on his title to another — finally a series of acts judged reprehensible by the family as a whole — the 'family circle' meets to decide to rescind the person's right to carry the name. For in Samoa, whatever is done by consensus can also be undone by it.

Consensus

This point must be stressed. The *matai* is always chosen by consensus, obtained if need be by exhausting those who were not initially agreed, after several days of meeting and discussion. Of course some voices carry more weight than others, but the person's rank simply makes his speech more persuasive. In the *aiga* family, there is no voting, no system which might give some the right to vote and not others, or which might make some votes count double, and so forth. And as long as any opposition is voiced, the discussion must go on, for any choice imposed by the majority would, people say, in the months or the years to come, only lead to dissention and even violence.

Of course any consensus is arrived at more or less by force. But those who are listening to the debate, on behalf of whom the discussion is held, and those who are even present in the persons speaking, are the ancestors, beginning with the founding ancestor whose name is the reason for the discussion. Therefore, it is what is said aloud, in public, that matters. Once all expressed arguments have been exhausted, the persistence of any unvoiced opposition is something else, which does not prevent everyone from drinking the ceremonial drink from the same bowl (*kava*, the drink of the gods and the ancestors). The union approved by the ancestors can no longer be undone. It is something like giving one's word, even reluctantly, in an honour system. It is not easy to go back on one's word and if one does, one immediately leaves the domain of discussion and crosses over to the side of violence. Decision by consensus is a very strong decision, for to subsequently go against it, one is compelled immediately to opt for violence (not to mention the dread of breaking an agreement witnessed by the ancestors: the person will fall sick before they have time to consider how to use violence). This is the ideology that presided and continues to preside at every Samoan discussion in a 'sacred circle', whether at the family or the village level; it is therefore fundamental. It is thus easy to conceive that the introduction of a system operating by majority vote would change many things.[36]

'O le nuu': the village

This set of names connected with a founding land might merely constitute a group of families living side by side, an inert list of family names and lands. To this, however, must immediately be added the village dimension, at least in the sense of *nuu*. As we know, Samoa is a network of villages ('country': *atunuu*), and its custom is 'the essence of the *nuu*' (*aganuu*). This dimension is present from the outset because a land is always a 'village land'. It is located in the territory of the village, which means that certain decisions can have a considerable impact on the way this land is used. Even if the land holds a founding house — and in this event nothing and no one can annul it, it is an ancestral site and the ancestor is believed to be buried there — the village can expel the people who occupy it. The village cannot change the name which has title to the land, but it has every right over the individuals who live on a land belonging to the circle of village lands. These rights used to include the power to put someone to death or to banish them. Today they still include banishment, a sentence which can be pronounced against an individual, against a *matai*, or against several individuals, even a whole extended family, living on this family's village land. One can see the limits arising from this system. Not only is there no such thing as private ownership of the land, but the village can sever the tie that links individuals to their ancestral right to use a land, with the typically Samoan distinction between, on the one hand, the principle of ancestrality, which is off limits: this land remains X's land, and if those living there are banished, other members of the family, living in another village, can move onto it; and, on the other hand, the individual: this person is entirely subject to the consensual decisions of the group to which they belong, namely, first of all the extended family circle, which can expel one of its members, and then the village circle, which has authority over the families and the persons that comprise them.

How can a village decision be imposed on a family? Because every family is part of a circle of which it is only one component: the circle of the village families. Every family is a group that reproduces itself around the preservation of a name which must 'live' and therefore must be carried on. This name is connected with a land; both are basic components of the social circle formed by the village. The village *nuu* is nothing other than a circle of *aiga*, a circle of *matai* names (which range from ten to more than fifty) together with their associated lands. To say that the village can dictate the way a family uses its land is simply to say that a family always lives with other families, in a circle, and that, in the event of serious misconduct, the whole circle can decide to expel this family, which is only one component of the circle, just as the extended family 'meeting in a circle' (*aiga potopoto*) can decide to banish one of its members — in the same way as it must decide which of the individuals in this circle will be the family's next *matai*.

Every Samoan belongs to a sacred circle at every level. Outside the circle he ceases to exist. The individual does not exist if he has no 'family circle' (the literal translation of *aiga potopoto*) to belong to. The family (his place of origin) does not exist if it is not inscribed at the territorial level in a village circle (*nuu, nuu o matai*). If this kind of belonging is not in place, the individual cannot sit down in a house because every house represents a circle of belonging; in this event, he is without a house, which is inconceivable in the Samoan culture; he must be able to sit down, and know what post to lean against when his family meets, the two being synonymous: when a person 'belongs', he knows at what 'place' in the circle he belongs. The same is true at the village level: the *matai* of a family could not sit down with other *matai*, he would not know what post to sit against when the circle of the *matai* (*nuu o matai*) met to decide village affairs.

This strong sense of belonging, this security in one's identity comes at a cost, as the following anecdote shows. Curiously — something that might seem surprising in a Polynesian system — Samoan society has sometimes been judged by Europeans, determined at the start of the century to see the spirit of enterprise emerging and developing there, as conveying 'communist' values, a lamentation repeated in other terms by the more recent New Zealand administration and today by development experts sent to advise Samoa in exchange for international aid and loans.[37] It is true that the communist ideal and the sacred principle of so-called 'traditional' societies share the fact that they leave no room for purely individual decisions, *at least at this level*; a person is first a member of a group, which, in the Samoan culture, is represented by the shape and the idea of a 'circle'.

Comment

The phrase 'at this level' is not a matter of pure form: the personal decision against the group or with no reference to the group, is not something taken within the circle of identity: it is not taken *at this level* — but it does indeed exist. A very large portion of the things that affect the life of every Samoan originate outside the sacred circles of belonging. Nevertheless, our concern for method compels us to work outwards from the circle and not the inverse. The observer can perceive these things happening outside the circles on condition that he regard them, methodologically speaking, as 'level-2' phenomena, which should be understood by opposition to the phenomena of 'level 1'(the relations of belonging; see below, the section on change). For what makes these phenomena 'Samoan' for us is not, or not only, their apparently universalistic content ('the individual'), but the fact that they are experienced by Samoans as things that do not belong to any of their 'circles'. Once we step into the circle (as observers), what we see going on outside it becomes culturally specific, instead of being immediately bound up in the projections of our own categories ('the individual as opposed to society'). We will mention some of these facts when we discuss change, because this 'level 2' is the level that is spontaneously open to the introduction of new elements. Here we find political strategy, the competitive relationship to objects, private ownership, sporting activity (but not the results of this activity) or, in former times, warfare (but likewise not the outcome of war); for during the time of the 'action' *fai* (sport, war, work, travel), a circle of identity must ensure the *tapuai*, 'communication with the divine realm', and it is only the encompassing of the former by the latter which produces a tangible result; in Samoa, people say that the outcome of a sporting event is the fruit of the spectators' *tapuai* (their union — *feagaiga* — with God) and not the result of the players' action, or rather it is the result of their action insofar as the action is itself the product of the spectators' *tapuai*.[38]

In Samoa, one is thus a member of a circle: the assembled family (*aiga potopoto*), one of the *nuu* of the village, and on a more conceptual level, the circle of villages, the one that makes up the district or the one that makes up the whole archipelago. A family name is always part of a system of names, which is, in its broad rules, in the way it defines for all Samoans the quality of being a Samoan person, the *faamatai*. But the system can best be seen at work in the village community, and Samoa is thus primarily a set of several hundreds of circles of names. In each village, the circle of these names is called the *nuu o matai*, the *nuu* of the *matai*. It is manifested in the regular meetings of the village *matai* (*fono o matai*, or simply *fono*). They meet in one of the village founding houses; in some cases it is always the same house, that of the name of the village's greatest and most ancient *matai*, and in some cases they meet in a different house each time, to honour several *matai* names. All of these houses are, physically, a circle of posts holding up a huge, more-or-less conical roof. The *matai* sit on the floor (a stone pavement covered with a layer of coral and then a layer of mats), cross-legged and leaning against a post. No post is the same as any other, and the seating order around the circle of posts is an instantaneous representation of the hierarchy of names. This hierarchy is historico-legendary and is inscribed in a series of statements which relate the origin of the village and the hierarchy of its *matai* names.

Even today these phrases are used in greeting whenever one *matai* meets another. *Matai* greet each other through the intermediary of their ancestors, as it were, as though each actually was the founding ancestor of the *matai* name he bears, and had just relived a condensed version of this ancestor's history.[39] But that is what each *matai* is: not only does he bear the ancestor's name, he 'is' this ancestor, from the day he is invested with the name until the day he dies or the family decides to take it away from him.[40] This is visible, for example, in the way children, even very little ones, address their father — which surprises the visitor. Even the day before his selection, they called him 'Pita' (from Peter) or 'Siva' (from a compound name beginning with the word for 'dance', *siva*) and so forth, using 'his birth name' (the equivalent of our first name). They would use this name in all situations where a European child would say 'Daddy'; in Samoa, kin terms of address do not exist; only the proper names are used. In short, the day before, they called him 'Pita'. This morning, the bestowal ceremony took place and, of course, the children had known for quite some time that their father was going to receive the title '*Fonomalii*' (for example) and become the *matai* of the family. That very evening, without a hint of hesitation in their voice, they are calling their father by his new name: 'Fono!' (the *matai* name was Fonomalii, but all names, ordinary ones or *matai* names, are shortened in address; the first part is kept or, more rarely, the last).

Beyond the village, there is no social identity which operates on a continuous basis.[41] The hierarchy of *matai* names, however, is used country-wide in the following manner. First of all, as we have seen, when *matai* from different villages meet, they exchange greetings using formulas which sum up the genealogical history of their villages (these are condensations, but it can still take several minutes to utter them because they are made up of several statements which describe the principal names of the sacred circle and their history). However each one recites the history of the other: 'Welcome to you who… (comes from village X)', 'Thanks to you who… (comes from village Y)'. In other words, a good *matai* knows the basic history of the names of between a hundred and three hundred villages and, even if two *matai* are meeting for the first time, once they have exchanged names, each usually knows what village the other comes from and the rank his name holds within his village. The exchange of the formulas which summarise the village's history merely confirms this knowledge and creates a more intimate relationship, after which conversation can commence.

To sum up: a *matai* is at home anywhere in Samoa. In a less ceremonial manner and with reduced verbal exchange, the same holds for anyone, once they have told each other what village and family (and therefore what *matai* name) they come from. The fact that a *matai* is at home in any village, in short, that the hierarchy of the *matai* system is universal for a Samoan, is further shown by the following rule: when a family holds a bestowal ceremony for a *matai*, if the village concerned is of course participating (the new *matai* is in the circle of names which makes up this village and to which the name being bestowed belongs), any *matai* passing through can also join in the ceremony and the accompanying exchanges. Once he has entered the house, he will expect to receive little or much, in accordance with the greatness of his name.

Comment

A 'great' name is, in sum, an ancient name, which thus appears in numerous genealogical histories of various names in the country, and therefore one which many people know. Being an ancient name, it is at the centre of a far-flung kinship network. The older the name, the more lines are connected with one or another of the *matai* who has carried this name and who is remembered; this makes it possible to gather more things for exchanges and thus to affirm, confirm or even enhance the rank of this name. In the long run, these fluctuations can affect the hierarchical position within the village, and the *matai* will claim a different post to lean against the next time the village *matai* circle meets.[42]

The *faamatai* is thus at the same time a hierarchy that can be observed daily in the village and an ideology of belonging to a system which for everyone defines 'Samoa'. To be 'Samoan' is always to be able, through the agency of the *matai* name one carries or to which one is linked, to establish a status orientation ('respect' — *faaaloalo*) in relation to anyone one encounters anywhere in the country.

Let us now go back to the beginning and finish this point. Each person has a place in relation with that of the *matai* name to which he or she is linked. A village *nuu* is first of all, as we have seen, the circle of *matai* — which is the circle of *matai* names, the circle of the deceased ancestors, the latter personified by the *matai* (in the sense, this time, of the person bearing the name). This is the village council, which decides everything, by consensus. But the *nuu* is also the *nuu* of the 'daughters of *matai*', that is to say, all of the women related by blood to the *matai* names of the village. They have their own meetings, their own ceremonies, and their internal hierarchy is modelled on that of the *matai* names. The same holds to a certain extent for the third *nuu*, that of the 'sons of *matai*', which is comprised of the men in the village who are not *matai* at the time in question. Last of all, it is true, but with even greater nuances, of the 'wives of *matai*', whose group is structured by the hierarchy of their husband's *matai* names.[43] It should be added that a woman's membership in the *matai* system is always governed more by her blood ties than by marriage. These wives, who do not really belong to their husband's *nuu*, are, in their home village, full members of the *nuu* of the 'daughters of *matai*' of their respective villages, and they reactualise this membership if they divorce or are widowed, and even each time they return to their village alone, which they do frequently. Distances are never very great, and Samoans have a notable habit of visiting and travelling, by virtue of their tradition of *malaga*. Today the word has come to designate any 'journey', even personal trips, but until the1940s, it meant that a whole village went to pay a visit to another, with ceremonies and competitive dancing, singing and wrestling, which went on for several days (during which time marriage plans were also drawn up). Old people say that these *malaga* were a frequent occurrence. It was the principal opportunity to celebrate and to 'get away'. In Samoa, 'home' is the village, which is an exogamous unit, even though not everyone is necessarily related. The importance of the *malaga* tradition can be ascribed to the fact that marriages are contracted between villages.[44]

Because of this, every man and woman, *matai* or not, carries around a mental image of the hierarchy of *matai* names which constitutes his or her ideological reference in relations with others. That is the *matai* system; it is at the heart of the *faaSamoa* which identifies the Samoan culture area, and that is why it organises the Samoan identity into a series of connected and concentric circles: those of the families and those of the village, and less frequently, those of the districts and those of each island: finally, and on a more imaginary plane, those of each of the two Samoas, and even of the entire Samoan culture area, a circle which would exist if all the *matai* of the two Samoas, western and eastern, were to assemble and meet together.

Change

'Tradition/modernity'

By following our initial choice of method, which attempted to discover the system of belonging, we have caught a glimpse, however brief, of the values behind the Samoan identity: the *matai* system (*faamatai*), system of ancestral names which have become ranked titles; the *faaSamoa*, 'the way of life and speech proper to Samoa' and claimed as such by Samoans; the *atunuu* ('country') and the *aganuu* ('custom'), in the sense of the deeply ingrained nature of the village group hierarchically organised in a circle, by order of rank of the ancestral names. These values give a densely textured picture of Samoan identity as it can be observed today, as Samoans themselves see it and live it in practice.

It would be tempting to end our portrait of identity here. Though it is clear that each of the foregoing paragraphs, each of the sentences, even, calls for a detailed development, even restricting ourselves to a list of features, as we have done, we can say that the picture is relatively complete. The representation of 'us' held by each Samoan is the complex of memberships in the *aiga* family and the village *nuu*, conveyed through the system of ancestral *matai* names connected with a land.

Must the sociocultural changes now be weighed, so to speak, in terms of the degree of resistance offered by the various elements glimpsed up to this point? This is the usual naive 'tradition vs. modernity' approach. It is true that the constituent elements of identity which can be seen today are also found in older people's evocations of the 1920s to 1940s, and even in the nineteenth-century accounts written by the missionaries and administrators of the time.[45] One therefore gets the impression that little changed over the nineteenth and twentieth centuries. More accurately, one could think that nothing is known about pre-Christian Samoa (before 1830), but that historically documented Samoa and present-day Samoa are astonishingly close to us; thus, everything relating to Christianity — such as it has become in Samoa — is claimed by today's Samoans as their tradition, as their 'custom' (*aganuu*) ever since 'the darkness gave way to the light'. And one would award them 'first prize overall' for conservatism and resistance to Western acculturation, at any rate since the 1830s.

Indeed, in the explicit Samoan discourse, the relationship between 'tradition' (the *faaSamoa*) and 'modernity' (the *faaPapalagi*, the 'Papalagi or European way') is clearly weighted in favour of the former. This pair of terms comes to mean the custom of a specific society, 'Samoa' versus the Europeans' custom — it is no longer a society — as it is perceived by Samoans in its global dimension: currency, the market, individualism, etc.

It should be noted in passing that, unlike other South Pacific peoples, in Papua New Guinea for instance, whose vision of inherent European otherness would include, alongside Christianity, human rights and democracy,[46] Samoans see each of these latter values as an area of their own identity, moreover an area in which they feel themselves to be closer to the truth than today's Europeans (whom they see in Samoa and especially whom they observed in New Zealand or Australia when working as immigrant labourers). They go to church regularly and see that Europeans do not. They point out that, in their *matai* system, all 'men' have equal 'dignity' — *mamalu* (however, they say it is the *matai* names who enjoy the dignity, not the living) — whereas Europeans let their own people starve in the streets — something that never happens in Samoa and is even unthinkable; on this subject, people explain to foreign visitors that, in Samoa, 'you only have to know two words: *faamolemole* ('please') and *faafetai* ('thank you'), to always find a house to stay in and a meal to share'. These words belong to the vocabulary of relation, 'respect' (*faaaloalo*), and make it possible to locate a hierarchical relationship on the circumference of a circle, in sum to integrate the asker; whereas, as emigrant Samoans have remarked, the same words used by Europeans by no means prevent, in certain cases, the person being left on his own, the relationship being limited to acts of (Christian or public) 'charity'. Finally, some Samoans consider that European-style democracy (*faaPapalagi*, expressed in Samoan by the English word 'democracy'), that is majority rule, is a source of inequality and conflict compared with Samoan-style democracy (which they call *temokalasi*, the Samoan phonetic transcription of the English word), which appeals to 'consensus' in the sense already discussed.

To say of someone's action or personality that they are *faaPapalagi* ('European-like'), or worse yet, *fiaPapalagi* ('deliberately wanting to mimic the Europeans') was and still is a grave insult, a cause for resentment and conflict. To tell someone that he has forgotten the *faaSamoa*, the rules of custom, is just as serious. Banishment, and therefore temporary loss of membership in one's village and *nuu* group, still constitutes very harsh punishment, owing to the ensuing shame, even if it is only a social death (and localised, since a person immediately finds other relatives in another *nuu* to take him/her in). It is therefore almost impossible to find someone who acts with total disregard for the constraints of the *faamatai*.

Yet everyone would have only to cancel their contributions to the family exchanges, and of course a certain new population, chiefly young wage-earners from town, is sometimes tempted to do just this. Some are duplicitous, attempting to conceal a (small) portion of their salary from their parents, but no one ever goes the whole way. In reality, no one could, unless they were to emigrate to another country, and even then, they would have to shun the Samoan community. The only persons or families who manage capitalist-style accumulation to any extent, instead of putting everything into the exchanges, are the 'half' families (*afakasi*) in and around the town (a small fraction of the population). And even here, while they manage it on the European or Chinese side of their tradition (a male ancestor who was among the traders who arrived in the nineteenth century), it is possible because, at the same time, this monetary policy gives them liquid cash and enables them to distinguish themselves, sporadically but spectacularly, by massive contributions to the exchanges. No 'half' merchant family in Samoa is totally cut off from the *faamatai* — they would go broke within a month. Moreover, the European or Chinese ancestor or his children have often become *matai* by receiving a *matai* name from the family of their wife or their mother.

Much could be said about the use of the *faamatai* today in the new contexts of politics or business. But the details simply re-confirm the permanence and the importance of the components of Samoan identity discussed above. Far from eliminating these elements, the new contexts provide fresh fields for their exercise.

Here we touch on yet another dimension. These new contexts arose precisely because their appearance did not imply a flagrant contradiction with the *faamatai* and did not threaten to suppress it — below, in the section on religion, we will see this major particularity of Samoan history. But once they have arisen, they create new elements of identity which mingle with those already present, and the latter are induced to change — imperceptibly at first, but in a way that may have an impact later on. And we move towards a fundamental transformation if these changes, situated from the outset at the first level of the configuration or working their way up to that level through the dynamics of change, thereby induce an insuperable contradiction. This is what we will look at now.

At the same time, we will continue to examine Samoan identity by observing the secondary levels open to change. Describing the secondary levels of the socio-cultural configuration (what I will call 'level 2') means pursuing our study of identity. Of course the observer will notice a host of things in addition to those which constitute the system of belonging ('level 1'). And it is important not to neglect this area, for it is precisely here that change is constantly making inroads. Any attempt to talk about this level immediately demands a definition of the period of identity and the sequence of these periods. Here identity and change are closely intertwined.

Why does change creep in here? For these are levels which elude, if not the awareness of the interested parties, at least the main focus of their attention in terms of causal explanations. At this level not everything needs to be explained or connected to everything else. One no longer has the feeling that a change in one element will trigger the modification of all the others; for here things are no longer part of a sacred circle, they are much less interdependent. And because these levels are no longer defined by the key-value of belonging and are no longer organised by the logic of the circle, they may have no conceptualisation in the local language.

Furthermore, we are talking about phenomena which the observer perceives even if the informants' explicit discourse makes no mention of them. As a consequence, identification of these areas partially reflects the observer's own cultural and professional preoccupations. It depends to a large extent on the latter's standpoint, and, for instance, there is no way to be sure that the inventory of these areas is exhaustive. It also depends on the observer's sensitivity to the indications of belonging under study and which will have been identified as the first level of the configuration. For it is especially there, where the observed phenomena subsequently appear to contradict the level-1 data, that he will stop, even involuntarily, and try to understand these paradoxes.

This itinerary is part of the method imposed by the comparative approach.[47] In order to avoid identifying by pure ('ethnocentric') projection the contexts in which we think we recognise familiar phenomena, we must set them against the backdrop of the system of belonging in which we initially sought the specificity of the society. This preliminary research — translating the system of belonging — is particular, and the method rests on a very precise dictionary: the logic of the possibilities of the hierarchy, that is to say the logic of whole/part relations which alone enable us to model a system of belonging. But the only direct basis for the translation of the other contexts is our projections: here or there we see 'power', the 'economy', 'conflict', 'domination', and so forth. How can we express the 'Samoan-ness' of these phenomena? What makes them 'Samoan' in our eyes? How can we say something more or else than our already well-established definitions of these domains? By finding a contrast, by observing how, for Samoans, these are things experienced outside their circles of identity. The example of violence springs to mind. If we address the subject directly, all we obtain are trivialities about 'human nature'. If we observe how the fact of standing outside the circle allows a process of violence to be set in motion, we have taken a step towards translating the specificity of the Samoan culture. We will return to this subject when we come to the sphere of politics.

I personally have observed the following sets of contradictory phenomena:

— a highly individualistic and violent relationship with a portion of the invisible beings people believe in, namely *aitu* spirits; whereas relations with the divine are governed entirely by the *faamatai* system, and direct relations between the individual and God, as in Western Christianity, do not exist;

— a highly egocentric and/or competitive attitude in certain relationships which appeared to me to come under the *faamatai*; also the observation of this attitude, rapidly giving way to violence, in the relation to certain objects and to the fraught idea of possession; whereas the first observations tend to dwell on the constantly stressed values of staying 'in one's place' in the hierarchy, and on the values of sharing and collective ownership only, ownership by the *aiga* family as such and therefore under the management of the *matai* (what an early twentieth-century German administrator called communism 'Samoan style')[48];

— the constitution and evolution, within the notion of political representation by consensus, of an area of electoral strategy which recently gave rise to a huge debate in Samoa about the relationship between politics and the values of the *faamatai*, when certain government measures pointed out a number of contradictions at level 1.

These categories are clearly predictable, for all I did was to be sensitive to the major domains that my own culture taught me to identify: religion, economics, politics. The difference with the usual method is that, having made an effort to avoid these divisions in the first part of the study, I then used them to deduce these categories from my initial observations, which dealt with precisely that which appears to be indivisible because it is a 'total' social fact, in this case the *faamatai* with all it entails. This gives us the means to measure, as it were, the intensity of past or ongoing change by measuring the degree of contradiction that is beginning to build up in the way the new phenomenon was or is being integrated at level 2, and especially in the way it then does or does not work its way, with or without contradiction, up to level 1.[49]

The faamatai and religion

The realm of the divine and the spirits
Samoans' attitude towards the *aitu* — we will call them 'spirits' — claims our attention: it is a combative relationship. People are wary of them, for they are like thieves or assassins,

concealed, ready to strike from behind, to steal a soul, to silently attack a night-time walker, to don the appearance of a relative or a friend and to lead to his or her death whoever is unfortunate enough to let themselves be deceived. Spirits are the chief cause of illness. Everyone believes in spirits, even pastors (all church personnel has been Samoan for a century). When anger and sorrow overwhelm somebody weeping over their sick child, people go for their machetes and, standing there in the dark, call on the spirits to come and fight. Spirits are connected with a place, especially the spirits of the dead, those of the legendary as well as the recent past. For the most part, a spirit is a 'night-time' being, on the side of death, the forest and the open sea. Anything that is 'dark' and 'hidden' can harbour a spirit.

Alternatively, the relationship with God (O Le Atua: 'the God') is like the relationship with the family *matai*: communion around the circle (*faatasi*: 'together') and 'respect' (*faaaloalo*). God is the source of society, of the whole *nuu* organisation, of the *faamatai*. People address him as a group: the evening family prayer, the Sunday village prayer. People take their place with respect to others, in the house or in the church, according to their rank in the *faamatai*. They make offerings (in church) which are announced publicly at the end of the service and which, like the distribution of the kava, provide an image of the family rankings in the village at that moment: a person who is 'great' is supposed to give more, and if he cannot … it is because he is no longer as great as he was thought to be. God is 'light', on the side of 'day' and life, on the side of the village. People pray to God at home and in church, just as they prayed to the old god inside the house and on the central village ground. Every house is a potential temple, as is the entire village.

If we consider the literature on Oceania and its linguistic history, nowhere do we find such a strong, clear-cut dichotomy as here. The *aitu* and the *atua* are mixed together in the missionary accounts;[50] and according to one comparative study, the most that can be said is that within the cosmological space, the *atua* are placed further away or higher than the *aitu*.[51] What happened? First of all, it is clear that the new god has taken the place of the old one: the entire system of prayer and relation with the *faamatai* remains unchanged. And secondly, the relationship between light and darkness (the conditions of prayer, the fire offering, etc.) is still the central dogma.[52]

Nevertheless, one important change has entered the picture. This relationship is also used to represent a new temporal dichotomy: the Christian era is the time of 'light', the Samoans say; that is why, they add, the preceding era was the time of 'darkness'. Formerly 'night', today 'light'. Therefore, as they say as well, formerly there were only spirits. The study shows that everyone knows numerous stories from their grandparents about how their own grandparents, etc. had dealings with one spirit or another; in a word, belief in spirits has by no means disappeared, even if, without our being able to ascertain the exact extent, it is clear that some modalities of this belief have changed. Alternatively, the vast majority of Samoans are unable even to name the figures of the pre-Christian pantheon, although it reigned until the middle of the nineteenth century, including the name Tagaloa.[53] Today, in the time of light, spirits are defined as being antinomic to the time and the light of day, and they come out almost exclusively at night (when they can unleash their fury). The representation of the past, bolstered by this new dichotomy God/spirits, therefore supports the idea that formerly there was no 'God', only 'spirits'. The ultimate consequence of this reformulation of the past being: men themselves used to be 'half-man, half-spirit'.[54]

We may, without undue risk, judge that, as everywhere else in Polynesia, the old system was quite the reverse: a seamless hierarchy running from the principal creator god(s), their multiple forms which appeared at various times and places, to local spirits, wandering souls, humans created by the gods, humans born from the union of a mortal and a god, and finally, to ordinary humans. Myth told that nothingness (*Leai*) had preceded the Sky (*Lagi*) and that Night (*Po*) had come before the Light-of-Day (*Ao*), and everyone drew their conclusions: life — therefore society — consequently required constant ritual work so that Day might keep Night at bay while wresting away a portion of the sacred so that life might be reproduced (encompassment): cooking, tattooing, marriage, bestowal of a *matai* name, etc. all cooperated in transforming the raw into the cooked, darkness into light, the sacred powers of death into powers of life. Today this universe has become much more static: during the day we are with God, and this relationship is conducted through speech; at night we must fear the spirits. God is pure goodness, the spirits are incapable of anything but evil, and are basically stand-ins for the Devil (*Tevolo*).[55]

The boundaries of change

Has this change led to a fundamental transformation? It seems not. The appearance of a dichotomic and static perspective on history has not altered the social system of belonging. Partaking of 'daytime' (physically or symbolically), the relationship with God is as it ever was and transits through the *faamatai*, encompassing as it were, the personal, combative relationship with the spirits: in the 'daytime' it is not mentioned. When a spirit takes action (illness, etc.), means exist today as they did yesterday to root out the evil with the help of healers and to reinstate the supremacy of light. In daily life as in ceremonial practice, the relationship between God and the spirits, in other words, the relationship between life and death, is as it has always been: the social labour of the *faamatai* guarantees the first and consequently maintains the second at a lower level, where evil prevails only at times and in spaces bounded by the first domain[56]

To be sure, the sources of life are now seen as being located directly on the side of 'light' (God), whereas formerly, they were transferred (and transformed) by working on the sacred domain of 'night'. That is why, for instance, God is today considered to be the source, the foundation and the supreme head of the whole *faamatai*, and the investiture of the *matai* has more to do with all that than with tattooing (formerly an essential feature, as an operation which imprinted on the body the 'blackness' of the sacred powers of 'night' — whereas today tattooing has become a simple distinctive sign of rank: a *matai* 'should be tattooed', but no one knows why, or explanations are sought in the area of outstanding physical feats, in this case the endurance required to withstand this long, painful operation). But the result is basically the same when it comes to the *matai's* authority and his role as representative of the family group.[57]

The real boundary between contemporary Samoa and a fundamental transformation is that of the point in time when the relationship with God would no longer be mediated by the *faamatai* but would become a wholly individual matter, either due to a change in the religious system or to the disappearance, for other reasons, of the *faamatai* itself. There is no sign of this, however; God was even placed in the preamble to the Constitution drawn up at the time of independence, in 1962,[58] and he likewise features in the national motto: 'Samoa' the *atunuu*, and therefore the *nuu* therefore the *faamatai*, 'is founded upon God' (*Faavai i le Atua Samoa*).

But the horizon is not unclouded for all that. It is clear that the *faamatai* and the main Church have to a certain extent drifted under the influence of the London Missionary Society: bureaucratisation, monopolisation, social stratification are present in part of the system — or at least if the complaints voiced by certain village pastors are to be believed. It is therefore not surprising that a good number of Samoans lend a willing ear to the discourse of the new Churches, arriving from the United States in particular, which denounce the hypocrisy of the mainstream Churches' administrative machinery, urging a cleansing of the institution as well as of the soul. The problem is that these new Churches have relatively little connection with the *faamatai* and consequently encourage an individual relationship between God and the believer's soul. Today [early 1990s], in some families, even those of 'great' *matai*, the parents may go to the traditional church, while some of their children (in the 25-year-old bracket) reject this practice and join, sometimes even militate in, Youth for Christ and other similar groups.

To be sure, the plurality of denominations is not new in Samoa, since from the start there were the Protestants from the London Missionary Society, the Methodists and the Catholics, who were rapidly joined by the Mormons and, in lesser numbers, the Seventh-Day Adventists.[59] The strategic use of this multiplicity within the family and the village is well known. Each time a family quarrel of any importance breaks out, one fraction may decide to change Churches: one way of saying, of course we are still part of the family, but we are pulling back on a secondary level. A decision of this kind does not throw the family and the village system into question because it takes place on the level of competition and strategies; just as, at the village level this time, Samoa is known throughout the South Pacific for the rivalry between neighbouring villages to have the biggest and newest church building. All of which means that this country of 160,000 inhabitants is divided into over 300 villages and prays in more than 1,000 churches. But this multiplicity adds nothing that might contradict the first level, that on which God is the foundation of the *faamatai*, and therefore the foundation of the village and the family. Alternatively, an individual relationship with religion which would short-circuit the *faamatai* would rapidly lead to a fundamental transformation. No such upheaval is visible for the moment, but the question should be posed nevertheless, in view of the movement to join the new Churches.

Let us now look at the other aspect of change: the fact that the new God has supplanted the old one has visibly not created a fundamental transformation, since the *faamatai* remains in place — there seem to be no profound differences between the present situation (familiar to those of fifty and over) and that described by the first travellers and missionaries (but their accounts are too superficial for us to say absolutely). How are we to understand this? By looking at the issue of prohibitions and then at the figure of the pastor.

Continuity of prohibitions

The missionaries were of course eager to stamp out the worship of Tagaloa and the village gods. But there was not much of a battle[60] since the main taboos lay elsewhere, in the *faamatai* underpinning the ranking system, and these were not abolished. The family temples were the founding-houses of the *matai* names, in which, morning and evening, the *matai* called together the family circle and prayed to the deity.[61] These houses are still standing, since they are simply family dwellings (at least in the case of the 'great house' surrounded by other smaller houses, which is used by the *matai* and/or his guests). People continued to call upon God and, moreover, kept the same name for him: *O le Atua*, since the missionaries had taken over the term to designate the God of the Bible. People continued to ask this god for the good things men have always asked of the gods. What was added was Bible reading, but since the Bible spoke for the most part about *alofa* (according to the translation of the Biblical 'love') the values of the *faamatai* were maintained (see below on *alofa*). The village temples, on the other hand, were *malae* (cf. the Tahitian *marae*), not like those in Tahiti or Hawaii, which were a stone-paved platform with posts and standing stones representing the gods, but simply a ground (ideally circular) at the centre of the village: a space watched over by the deity (it is the Samoans who say this), whose votive posts are the founding houses which encircle it and whose references are the village ancestors, with their names forever enthroned in the ceremonial definition of the village recited each time two *matai* from different villages meet. Thus the taboos were not abolished, nor was the *faamatai* undermined in any fundamental way.

One fact clearly played a crucial role: the missionaries were so bent on succeeding that they went to the trouble of learning the language and translating the Bible (all in 10 years).[62] The two key-words of the relationship with the deity (*atua*, 'god' and *alofa*, the 'sympathetic' relationship between the gods and men, between the ancestors transformed into *matai* names and men, between a *matai* and the people of his family, between an elder and a younger member of the family, etc.) were thus unchanged. As the way these concepts were invoked was itself not changed in any fundamental way (so clearly was it linked to the *faamatai*, which was not abolished), no fundamental ideological transformation ultimately occurred.

The temples remained standing because they were houses, the old concepts were left intact. But what about the objects? It seems there were very few cult objects; thus here too there was no reason to throw a quantity of material symbols onto the fire. But above all, the chief symbol of the Samoan cult was the genealogy inscribed in memory, which links the living and the hereafter. A genealogy is not an object that can be seized and thrown into the fire. It is highly significant that it was — and still is — surrounded by very strong taboos, as are all cult objects, except that Samoan taboos apply to the way and the circumstances in which a genealogy is to be recited aloud, in front of others. It is highly significant, too, that, when the Samoans learned to write and when many *matai* felt the need to set down part of the family history in notebooks, a series of unverifiable rumours sprang up concerning unexplained losses, forgotten hiding places and purported thefts of these notebooks, as is the case elsewhere, in Africa for example, of fetishes or the regalia of sacred chiefs. Today as yesterday, these rumours are still making the rounds of the villages.

Pastor, sisters and wives:
from integration to fundamental transformation

The pastor 'as a sister'

The new god obviously did not come alone. There were his messengers, in this case the Protestant pastors from the London Missionary Society, who made their way from eastern Polynesia (Tahiti) westwards, arriving in Samoa in 1830. In a certain fashion, it was with the pastor as with his God: he was immediately promoted to level 1, just as Jehova took the place of Tagaloa. But he could not pre-empt the spot previously occupied by the traditional priest. The traditional priest was the *matai* himself. It was he who led the family in prayer and who made the offerings. This can still be seen today: the *matai* indicates the order of prayer, distributes the roles (the words of forgiveness, thanks, petition), chooses the hymns. Knowing the Bible is just as necessary for a *matai* as knowing the ceremonial formulas for the main Samoan villages and the genealogies. In other words, the contradiction was present from the outset. Either the new personnel replaced the old and brought down the *faamatai*, for the pastors were not 'heirs' (*suli*) to the *matai* names, and the society changed completely. But the missionaries lacked the means: they were only a few individuals as against 30,000 inhabitants, all supporters of the *faamatai*.[63] Or the pastor took up a position that was already defined in the system but not one corresponding to the function of priest: one in which his presence did not eliminate the role of the *matai*. The insertion which turned out no doubt to be the least contradictory was to identify with the *matai's* 'sister'. The sister (the person and/or a representative who may be male, of the line descended from the sister or the daughter of the first ancestor) is also believed to be in spiritual relation with the deity and with the ancestors of the *aiga* family, in this way playing a role in the choice of the successor to the title of *matai*; sometimes 'she' even plays a priestly role, as at the *matai's* funeral. According to the legend known by everybody or almost in Samoa, the *matai* who dominated the politics of the district where the missionary boat landed, and who was busy waging a war, adopted this new god (the legend also says he had had a vision prophesying a new god who would bring him victory — which came true) and declared to the missionaries that henceforth they would be 'as' a sister [line] (*faafeagaiga*) with respect to his *matai* name, and therefore with regard to his people (family, village and district).[64]

Since the new god was adopted, and the *matai's* supremacy in war and politics obviously contributed to the spread of this new religion throughout the district, the only way this new element could relate to the *faamatai* was by integration (otherwise they would have been in total contradiction from the start and have prompted a struggle between the Mission and the *faamatai*). The pastor, too, was therefore integrated and became 'as a sister' (to the village). This expression became his official title, the honourary term of address: *O le Faafeagaiga.*

But the parallel goes further. Just as the new god did not come alone but with the antithetical pairs: 'god/devil, good/evil', and just as he introduced into the heart of the representations of historical time a moral dichotomy between good and evil, between god and the spirits-and-the-devil, the pastor too was not alone — he was married — and the pastoral couple introduced into the heart of the representations of the village *nuu* the idea of a social dichotomy between the sexes. Paradoxically, the consequences of this implant were more serious in the long run than the diachronic projection of the Night/Day opposition — these have been neglected in the analyses of the history and anthropology of contact in Samoa. For the moment, these consequences still affect only the second level, but contradiction with the first level is nearing breaking point. Let us take a closer look.

The pastor and the married couple

The typical Protestant church staff is a couple: the pastor and his wife. The ideology the couple would try to establish in the village was that of a world organised by complementarity between 'men's and women's tasks'. Furthermore Protestants as well as Catholics developed the new idea of the sanctity of the marriage bond.

Here, too, a serious historical study remains to be done, but the broad lines are already apparent. We can see from Missionary reports how the pastor's wife took over the education of the village women in matters of homemaking, housekeeping, health, dress (they imposed long, high-necked dresses), thus creating the idea and the phenomenon of a unified group of 'women' that had not previously existed as such. This affirmation is supported by the conflicts which can still be observed, and those recounted time and again by older people, between the organisation of the village into *nuu* groups (the *matai*, their daughters, their sons and, separately, their wives) and an organisation into male and female halves. These halves were activated through para-religious groups (choirs, Christian youth groups) and, especially, by the development in each village, with the arrival of administrators from New Zealand, of 'women's committees' for health care (since 1918) whose attributions and will to control more and more affairs grew apace (personal notes). This development, encouraged by the medical sector, was possible only because the ideology of a male/female dichotomy had already been instilled and because the Mission had already established a division of labour along these lines.[65] One has only to read the memoirs of one of the very first missionaries, George Turner, who arrived around 1840:[66]

> I was appointed to a district on the south side of Upolu... I took up my abode in the centre of the district. Daily attendance at the children's school, a class in the afternoon for the young men... a weekly lecture in some part of the district; a day spent entirely with my teachers and preachers; a prayer-meeting on Saturday afternoon; preaching three times, visiting the Sabbath-school... a meeting of the church members for prayer and exhortation once a month; the administration of the Lord's Supper on the first Sabbath of the month; and a monthly missionary prayer-meeting; — these were among my principal duties during my first year of missionary life in Samoa. Mrs Turner had a meeting once a week with the women of the district, took a class at the Sunday-school, and had also a daily class of girls.[67]

In view of the immensity of the task that lay before them, Turner and the other missionaries saw the urgency of having local teachers, and in 1844 they created the Samoan Missionary Seminary in Malua, which quickly gained fame throughout the South Pacific. It graduated — and continues to graduate — all the Samoan missionaries who set out to evangelise other countries and all the pastors working in Samoa. Today, when a boy graduates from high-school with a high grade-point average, he asks himself whether he should apply to the State college or go to Malua (which has a four-year program) to become a pastor. Both paths are regarded as prestigious (and promise a lucrative occupation in the end). From its beginnings, the seminary made marriage an important factor in the selection of candidates. Let us listen again to Turner:

> Marriage prevents admission to many of our home colleges; it is not so at our Samoan Mission Seminary. If we have the choice of two we reject the single man, and admit the married couple, for the simple reason that the wife needs education as well as her husband, and, when instructed, is a great blessing to her sex in the village where he may be called to labour. 'We want a young man who has a wife that can teach our wives and daughters something', is sometimes the adjunct to an application for a village pastor.[68]

Life at Malua was modelled on village life (the students had a garden and grew what they needed to feed themselves), with the addition of course of classes and prayers:

> Wednesday is what we call our industrial day, and until two o'clock, is specially devoted to improvements about the premises … while the young men are at work in the early part of the day, I have embraced the opportunity of having a class with their wifes. The main instruction of them, of course, devolves on the ladies.[69]

What was the consequence of the creation of a 'women's unit'? This was something new: either it was created from nothing, or, which comes down to the same thing, it consisted in moving a conception up to the first ideological level which had until then belonged to level 2.[70] From the outset, the result was a vague double system within the village organisation. For some decisions, the *nuu* groups can still be seen operating, and the 'village daughters' still enjoy their full sacred authority owing to the fact that they are both the 'treasure' and the spiritual link of the *matai* name with the deity and the origin of things. The wives do not participate, but each of them possesses this same authority in her own village when she goes home.[71] For other matters, there is a tendency for the 'women's committee', whether it is a formal body or not, to decide: in this case, it is primarily a question of age, and an older woman (even an in-married wife) will have authority over a younger 'village daughter'. In sum, a certain configuration of the pastoral presence paved the way for the later encounter with the New Zealand administration's health programs and prompted the creation of 'women's committees'. These committees reinforced an awareness of the existence of women as a group, a fundamentally new category in Samoan culture at the *faamatai* level (which recognised *matai*, their sisters or daughters, their brothers and their wives, in this order of value and reciprocal determination).

This awareness was quickly affirmed. As early as 1852, the missionaries decided that the living of the village teacher (the pastors trained by the missionaries) should be provided entirely by the villages (in the beginning, London headquarters had subsidised them). Of course the villages furnished the pastor with bed and board, and the texts tell us just how constant and abundant the gifts of food were. But for the rest (everything that required imported objects and therefore money), help had to come from London. From the outset, the missionaries had accustomed the Samoans to making a special contribution, in May, to the Missionary Society (the gifts were sent to headquarters). They also instilled the habit of making the same kind of gift to the pastor, again once a year, this time at the beginning of the year. As often happened in those years, the *matai* wanted to organise the missionaries' decisions by local decree and to impose fines on those who failed to attend church, for example; Turner tells how he spent his time trying to make the *matai* understand that whatever was obtained by obligation would not be right, and that they must not confuse their 'legislative' powers with 'religion', where everyone is 'at liberty to search the Scriptures and worship God'.[72] In the discussions where the Samoans were not very happy about having to make a second annual contribution (to which the missionaries replied that the Bible teaches the duty of reciprocity; the teacher works for them, he brings them the word of God, he teaches, and, as Turner says, 'the man who does *their* work should be paid by *them*'), Turner tells how the *matai* suggested that 'the *women* pay the teacher one year, and the *men* the next, and so on alternating', a proposition the missionaries obviously did not accept.[73]

The new female identity thus created had difficulty reconciling the two previously sharply opposed components. On the one hand, there was the woman as heterosexual partner (*fafine*) and, on the other, the 'village daughter' (*teine, tamaitai*) whose body was 'responsible' for her family's *matai* name and who never mingled her village identity with her life as a married woman, and even less with her life as a sexual being.[74] When this identity encountered another, more recent innovation, salaried work (a still very limited sector), it gave rise to the figure of the female employee (office worker, shop attendant) who is clearly subject to unequal treatment (salary, ambiguous attitudes, even sexual harassment) by her superior, usually a male. The latter plays heavily on the ambiguity of the new figure. Normally he should act very shy, reserved if not retiring in the presence of a woman regarded as a 'village daughter' (*tamaitai*). As this is hardly compatible with the needs of the modern workplace — or rather as today's work is not done within the logic of the *nuu* sacred circle — he tends to privilege the other aspect, that of *fafine*. Such is the outcome of the contradiction inherent in this composite figure, which mingles elements from levels one (*teine, tamaitai*) and two (*fafine*). For the time being the transition is in progress, and the urban setting in which men and women relate is facing a serious challenge from which anything can emerge, including the installation of a cruel inequality that Samoan women have never yet encountered. Another striking result is that, around the small town, around the women in the workplace, a population of women and their friends is growing up which, for the first time, feels it has its word to say in national political life. This fringe of the population weighed heavily in the referendum (see below) which recently led to the partial introduction of universal suffrage (insofar as it was more particularly the peri-urban population that participated in 1990 vote).

The other outcome, the new image of the married couple, has for the moment produced far fewer contradictions, owing to a combination of circumstances. Because tradition dictates that the spouse must be found in a village other than one's own — this rule is still seldom infringed — because the reasons for this rule have to do with the non-sexual image of the woman in her own village (all her life she remains a 'village' daughter, a daughter of a *matai* name and therefore a daughter of the village circle of *matai* names), the couple's public life, to put it succinctly, is in the image of a brother—sister pair: surrounded by taboos on the verbal expression and the gestual demonstration of anything that might suggest a sexual relationship. By promoting the sanctity of marriage, the Mission assuredly altered the practice of serial marriages — a high-ranking man might carry on marital relationships with several women, each of whom lived in a different village, but it seems these relations were successive rather than concomitant, with the possibility of backtracking (personal notes). But it did not evacuate the highly valued central image of the brother–sister pair. We thus see that peoples' present-day representation of the village — which includes this new dimension of the distinctive men/women opposition — did not destroy, on this point at least, the idea that, in any one village, these men and these women are first of all (in public, in the 'daytime') like brothers and sisters. To be sure, the high value placed on the couple in terms of 'man/woman' led to a certain confusion between the wives and the daughters of the village as far as the organisation of community decisions was concerned, and that is a radically new phenomenon. But for the time being, when it comes to this new category of 'women' in the village, the prevailing image is still that of the woman-as-sister (which is no longer true in the world of salaried work).

Here, too, we can see the boundary between a secondary change and fundamental transformation. Extrapolating retroactively, we can say that, prior to the Mission, there was a primary level at which men and women were defined with respect to each other, through reference to the *matai* name: the women were the daughters of this name, the men were defined first of all as their brothers (and the man designated to carry the name and become *matai* was chosen by the supernatural will of his elder sister: she somehow 'knew' that this brother was best qualified to reincarnate the ancestor). At another level, men and women were viewed as sexual partners, and the woman was the so-called 'weak' member of this relationship. Today in the villages the first level still prevails over the second. Were this tendency to be reversed, the woman would be reduced to the role of sexual object, which would rapidly annihilate the *faamatai* by abolishing the principal area of prohibitions (connected with the body and especially sexuality) applying to the daughters of the *matai* name and enabling this name to maintain a rank and therefore its 'life' in the circle of village names.

But when the first level meets with Christianity, it sometimes presents a universal aspect: a 'human race', *tagata* under the eye of a universal god, but which is made up of brothers and sisters only, at least when these beings are precisely under the eye of God, in other words in the social and cosmological 'daytime' (visible, etc.) — for 'at night', relationships change. This leads adolescents in particular to feel they are living in a strange, difficult world, where open seduction remains forbidden, but where part of the social domain which created and maintained these taboos (the village as *nuu*) is disappearing, in particular the young peoples' integration in these respective *nuu* groups, under the eye of the *matai* and away from the wives. Increasingly young people feel themselves to be human beings of the two sexes (men and women: *tagata*) and no longer members of the *nuu* (non-*matai* men gathered in their *nuu* called 'the strength of the village' and the 'village daughters' — *tamaitai*); but they are still immersed in the ideology, very much alive in their parents, of a world governed by the *faamatai*, and therefore a world of 'brothers/sisters', a world that can be breached only in the absence of watchful eyes (at 'night'). Hence both the many possibilities of sexual misconduct and, almost inevitably, a harsh awakening upon return to the light of 'day': public shaming in front of the whole village, serious psychological crises, sometimes suicides, or the salvation of emigration when possible.

Another unforeseen consequence of the pastor's new status concerns the circulation of money and, although timidly for the moment, the emergence of a social group which for the first time is not the product of the *faamatai*. If the village is big enough, the pastor can become rich. The weekly gifts are marked by competition on the part of the various families of the village with respect to the 'sister of the village'. Of course, like all Samoans, the pastor and his family put a portion of these gifts back into circulation in ceremonial exchanges. Nevertheless, it is striking to see that a number of men (and a few women) who today voice modern opinions on economics and politics (see below) are the children of pastors: their relation to the *faamatai* was less restrictive (part of their identity was formed in their nuclear families since a pastor's family is somewhat set apart from the pastor's genealogical extended family), and their relatively comfortable lives gave them greater access to books, scholarships, imported goods and foreign travel.[75]

The *faamatai* and the economic sphere

As I indicated at the outset, what strikes the observer here is the duality of people's behaviour towards what we call 'things': some subscribe to an ideology of consensual sharing and others to rampant egotism.

Before going any further, I would like to recall my method. I am not going to draw up a checklist of what, for us, comes under the heading of 'economy' and then look at Samoa to see what items are present. This would replace comparative analysis with a run-of-the mill ethnocentrism. Instead, I will confront two conceptions: ours, which talks about 'things', 'goods', their 'market' value etc., and the Samoan perception, but apprehended first with respect to the *faamatai* and then stepping back from it. In the *faamatai*, the site where genealogical relationships are perpetuated, everything is somehow seen in terms of relations, nothing in terms of things. An initial comparison with our mode of perception immediately pinpoints the matter of land: for us in the West, it is a commodity, but for Samoans, it is a *matai* name; it is alienable for us (it can be bought and sold), it is inalienable for them. Next we notice that a number of other things (what we call 'things') are not connected with the *faamatai*. This time it is our perspective — the continuation of a search corresponding to our category 'thing' — which leads us to perceive these phenomena, whereas Samoans do not elaborate any ideological system concerning them. Having come to this point and looking back to where we started, we are surprised: the Samoan attitude towards things is anything but a demonstration of *faamatai*-style sociability.

Because this second aspect gives no hint of a fundamental transformation in the making, we will evoke it first, before coming back to the things governed by the *faamatai*: land and houses, where the boundary that would signal such a transformation is, on the contrary, very close. This is another paradox. Things that are new, introduced, dazzling signs of European industrial culture are massively present in Samoa and are the object of bitter competition — yet they give no sign of provoking fundamental transformation. Alternatively, that which has been present from the dawn of time, namely the bond with the land, manifests a will to change, at least if one listens to the official government line — and it is the government itself which claims to want to hasten this change.

New objects

In Samoa, new objects, from carpenter's tools to cars, from electric refrigerators to radios, clothing and jewellry, clearly fall under the heading of private property. At the village level, there is no general authority over these objects: they belong to a family and the relationship with them stops there. Very clearly the notion of family in this case no longer refers to the extended family defined by the *matai* name, *aiga*, but to the 'household' (but still called *aiga* in Samoan), composed of a couple and their married children (those who have stayed at home), grandchildren, a couple of which one member is closely related to the *matai* name, to which may be added brothers or sisters of each of the spouses with their young or married children. And even at the household level, it must again be said that the object belongs to the person who bought or received it. The capacity to possess money, the position of receiver on occasions when gifts are given, all clearly mean that valuable objects come under the authority of the elders. But even in this case, people do not say 'the radio belongs to the household of couple X'; they say: 'It's X's radio (naming the head of house)'. At most one can say that an older person can easily ask a younger person to use an object that belongs to him/her, even if it remains more a request than an order.

In this area, Samoans are Western industry's dream consumers — or would be if they had the means to satisfy all their desires. If one were to believe what they say or do as soon as they have a little money, they would buy more than their houses can hold. To be sure, few Samoans have salaried jobs, but money circulates throughout the country in ceremonial exchanges, coming into the system from those who give money instead of fine mats or pigs: salaried workers, emigrants who return home for festivities, take part in all of the ceremonies involving a member of their extended family (life-cycle rituals, but also the bestowal of a new *matai*, the construction of a 'large house' *fale tele* or a church: in these three cases, the whole village participates), and finally relatives living in eastern Samoa (or 'American' Samoa, as Samoans also call it), who, unlike their cousins in the west, are almost all salaried, in American dollars (they sometimes go so far as to give a television or even a used car).[76]

The goods people are most interested in are motor vehicles, radios, televisions, colourful clothes, perfume, tools, refrigerators. The motor vehicle is a status symbol: it is much used to transport relatives, neighbours, friends. In Samoa, people are constantly visiting from village to village owing to the far-flung kinship network. A hundred years ago they would go on foot or navigate along the coast, using long, wide-bodied rowboats. But the distances are great: to get from the east coast of the island of Upolu to the western side of Savaii, one must cover 150 kilometres of land as the crow flies (and therefore much more by the winding roads), not counting the boat-crossing. Today [early 1990s] people use the bus or the car, for those families which own one (inter-island travel is by ferry). The number of cars is growing fast: traffic jams in Apia, completely inconceivable even ten years ago, have become common in the town centre — which recently was obliged to put in traffic lights, a curiosity for some time … and a source of accidents, as the old tacit rules of right-of-way mingle with the new colour code.

The radio has long been a common household item, and every house has one. This is, it should be said in passing, an essential tool of Samoan democracy: Parliamentary debates are broadcast in their entirety, in real time, and are closely followed in all villages. Not because people are fascinated with all that is said — some debates on foreign policy or municipal sanitation are even somewhat obscure for some villagers — but because everyone knows the names of all members of Parliament (they are all *matai*) and because debate on the floor is a rhetorical contest exactly like those that take place in the 'village councils' (*fono*); the Parliament is also called *Fono*: it is 'the country's *fono*'. Verbal jousting in Parliament employs the same rhetorical figures, the same stock metaphors drawn from legend and myth, from stories of village foundations … and from the Bible. When Parliament is in session, each village discusses the daily parliamentary 'victories' and 'defeats' of this *matai* or that. In addition to this aspect, when it comes to debates on questions of general interest (taxes, etc.), people listen to and comment on the content as much as the form. Television on the other hand has long been used to watch programs from American Samoa, re-runs of Americas serials: all children are familiar with *Days of Our Lives* or *Charlie's Angels*. More recently, Western Samoa has undertaken its own programming, and the present government consistently uses this new tool to broadcast, during the news, a number of what come down to party-political speeches. But this is all too recent for us to be able to measure the consequences.

There is no need to go into detail about the Samoans' taste for perfume, well known throughout Polynesia, where, by virtue of ancient beliefs whose content is no longer even formulated (the 'light', the radiance and the fragrance of the chief's sacred power [*mana*]), men and women are eager to acquire bright colours and perfume bottles of all sorts. Last of all, men — and women, it should be stressed — buy, whenever possible, tools (for cutting wood, doing mechanical jobs, etc.) foremost of which is the lawnmower! There is a basic opposition in Samoan cosmology between the head, the front or the centre, and the back. For instance, the front of every house must face the centre of the village and/or the road: it is the noble part. Every household is proud of their well-kept front yard: an impeccable lawn (the children's first chore in the morning is to pick up the leaves, cigarette butts and whatever else the wind has deposited during the night), relentlessly mowed, or the carefully spread and renewed white sand, or the small, carefully swept corals.

In short, after working on the plantation, in the late afternoon, before prayers (held at sunset: the division between *Ao* and *Po*, both material and cosmological day and night), it is not unusual to see a Samoan use his state-of-the-art gas-powered lawn mower just received from his New Zealand cousins, then open his refrigerator and take out a glass of soda that has been chilling, turn on his TV to listen to the popular program already broadcast on radio announcing the deaths, births and marriages sent in daily by families so that everyone in the country, primarily far-flung relatives, is immediately informed (and can set about preparing the objects they will need to bring to the ceremony) and finally put on his flowered shirt, and after having perfumed himself, take his car to visit a female relative a few villages down the road in order to arrange for a number of fine mats for the upcoming wedding.[77]

Every object mentioned in this account of the end of a day is considered private property (except for the fine mats). If a neighbour, or even a cousin (from a different household), wants to borrow or use one of these items, he will spontaneously propose money or another object in return. That is not surprising, you may say; it is a bit like that in the West, where these items come from. But what is surprising, or rather what gives one the impression of observing something specifically Samoan, is seeing this type of individualistic, commercial relationship taking place between people who have accustomed the observer to seeing and thinking of everything in terms of a group sharing everything around a circle according to a unanimously respected hierarchy. When, using the method we set out, one has *first of all* observed the *faamatai*, with its obligations of mutual aid and reciprocity in conducting ceremonies and the exchanges that go with them, where people manipulate food (including bread and corned beef), pigs and fine mats, one is somewhat taken aback to hear that the same individuals find it perfectly normal to pay to borrow a lawn mower or to be driven into town.

The other aspect that comes as a great surprise to the visitor is the fact that this presence of Western goods and services as well as the way people relate to them seems never to conflict with any aspect of the sphere of the *faamatai*. It is simply a different matter. The same people who, when it comes to buying or using these objects, vie with each other, count every penny, never lend without something in return, and know how to convey the idea that 'What's mine is mine', assiduously fulfill all the obligations pertaining to family and village solidarity with the acts of 'respect' required between younger and older members of the *nuu* (*aganuu, faamatai*). It is also instructive to see that Samoans are astonished that we should be surprised their compartmentalising these attitudes. For them there is nothing unusual in this since the two domains are completely separate.

Objects: a movable boundary

This distinction makes us realise that the boundary for the possession and utilisation of these objects — a limit which, if it were to be exceeded, would lead to a fundamental transformation — is hard to imagine. Seeing the behaviour of the Samoans who, though still in the minority, amass all these objects, one tells oneself that, even the day the whole country keeps its food in the refrigerator, replaces its machetes with lawn mowers and drives around in cars, nothing will have changed. This sounds like a pretty bold prediction, but it is meant to reflect a conviction I felt strongly during my fieldwork. Because the intrusion of these objects in no way affects the *faamatai* (or any of its corollaries), the secondary changes introduced by these objects will remain secondary.

One very clear sign is the way Samoan houses fill up with these objects without any change resulting in their structure and use. Even a house with a television and a refrigerator remains first and foremost a temple and a place for formal meetings in the sight of God. If people are watching television, and guests arrive from another village, they immediately switch off the program, and everyone sits down in a circle on the ground and declaims the long sequence of formulas necessary to lift the taboo on entry and the opposition distinguishing people from different villages so they may become a group united at a higher level: the sacred formulas relating the foundation of each village are exchanged. The day someone says: 'Wait, my soap opera isn't over!', the society I am describing will no longer exist; but for the moment, such an attitude (in an adult) is unthinkable. However cluttered a house may be, it is always organised so as to leave a large circular space clear, unfurnished, so that a meeting can take place at any moment. The day a notion of comfortable furnishings takes precedence over the rules of circle meetings, this too will mean that the society in question is no longer the same. For the moment there is no sign of anything of this kind either.

The foregoing analysis is obviously restricted to the way objects are used. However, we know all too well that one item, the television, can itself be a messenger of many new things. When all Samoan TV showed were American serials, which amused everyone because their world seemed so strange and unreal, the impact on everyday social conduct was zero. Now that TV is on the way to becoming a tool of power in local political struggles, many things may change, and in the near future. Moreover, another recent item is creating problems. The price of VCRs has dropped in the last few years, as we all know, and emigrants now bring back or send home this kind of material. All of a sudden, more and more video shops have opened up, and they sell everything. The magic of the cinema (the theatre, the screen, the size of the pictures), everything that helped create a distance and make the film an unreal world with respect to Samoa, has disappeared: to those who watch videos as they would a documentary, everything seems 'true', like a book — at least this is the attitude I thought I perceived. If this is indeed the case, then the impact of videos may well be of an altogether different nature.

Whatever may come of this unclear future, the material world of today's Samoans is unsettling; not particularly for them of course, but for the visitor. At first he does not feel as if he is in a foreign country. So many things are familiar; just as, seeing the churches, he feels as though he is in a European village. But gradually a feeling of unfamiliarity sets in. There are far too many churches for it to be 'like home'; it is the same Bible, but one quickly has to admit that the organisation of the service shows more concern for local *faamatai* hierarchy than for the soul's salvation. And those familiar objects all divided into two categories that have nothing to do with each other. White bread, tinned fish or corned beef (but not the other items) and the packages of hardtack (big hard biscuits that keep forever) are given, returned, given again, like fine mats, in the course of ceremonies.[78] They belong to the ceremonial circuit. But other foods and household items are not objects of exchange. We could continue in the same vein for attitudes in the home, at work, etc. For the Western visitor, the impression is one of constant oscillation: hardly has it entered his head that, on this point, Samoans are 'like us', always have been or have become acculturated, than he encounters another element which abruptly puts them at the other end of the scale of cultural variations.

Houses and land

The objects we have been discussing until now are privately owned. This is visible from the way individuals express ownership and lending and borrowing. Simple observation of the language itself provides the framework for their classification. The possessive adjectives and pronouns used with these objects are from the *-a-* group: 'my', is *la'u*, 'your', *lau*, 'his/her', *sau*, etc. There is another group of possessives, however, indicated by *-o-*: *lo'u, lou, sou,* etc. The distinction is common to all Polynesian languages, extending even to the Austronesian family.[79] It opposes objects whose owner is the cause of the owning (the *-a-* group) to those whose owner is not the cause of the owning (group *-o-*).[80] In the latter group, Samoan places the different notions of the *faamatai* ('my *matai* title', 'my family', 'my village', 'my custom'), etc., parts of the body ('my head', etc.) and kin terms ('my father', 'my cousin', etc.), which, in view of the way the rule is stated, comes as no surprise: it is not the incumbent *matai* who is at the origin of the possession of his title, it is not individual who created his body.[81] But in this same group one also finds land and houses. In effect, many people in the South Pacific take for it granted that 'the land owns the people' and not the other way around.[82]

The formula holds for both land and houses. When a Samoan talks about 'his' house, he means: the house of his family, the house of his ancestors. The house is not privately owned — it is fact inalienable. Every house stands on a family land — yet no land is privately owned either (see below for the nuances). A family land belongs to the *matai* name, to the founding ancestor, as it were. But he himself received it from the gods or from another *matai*. Ultimately everything can be traced back to the divine, the only element that is the origin and the cause of ownership. Houses therefore always belong to an *aiga* family. And the word for 'house', *fale* refers not so much to the roof and walls as to the relationship between those who live there and the ancestors, manifested by the fact that these people were able to bring (the building materials of) a house to this place.

Let us examine the first kind of house, called *fale Samoa*, the 'Samoan house'. To be sure, there are several types of house, from the 'large house' *fale tele,* the founding house and the like, also called 'house for guests', down to the little huts built over the stone oven, and in between, the houses lodging the various family-households that make up the local residential core of the extended family.[83] The first are big and round, the second small and round, the third are oval, or in more recent times, rectangular. But all are comprised of a foundation of large stones in between which are driven hardwood posts, regularly spaced around the circular, elliptical or (more recently) the rectangular perimeter of the foundation; these posts support a roof which too is conical, elliptical or four-sided, made of thatch (coconut palms or sugar cane leaves) or (more recently) corrugated metal.

With the exception of the more recent corrugated metal, which appears to be gaining ground [and became generalized after the two hurricanes of the early 1990s], the building materials are taken from the family land and thus belong to this land. Significantly, in the nineteenth century, when a couple married, the gifts from the boy's family might include, not only food (pigs, taros), but also the necessary building materials for a house (the hardwood posts, which were difficult to obtain, and the roof, by far the most delicate component), as opposed to the goods given by the woman's people, consisting of fine mats and tapas. The missionaries tell how these pieces were transported: the house, which was a wedding gift, could be dismantled and moved[84] and yet it was inalienable.

In short, the 'house', both a building and a social unit, is not a privately owned commodity. The obvious origin of a fundamental transformation would be that it become private property, something conceivable only if the land itself were to become alienable. This is, however, not the case (see below).

New houses

It would seem that a new element has crept innocently enough into the picture: imported materials. By virtue of the non-contradictory character (vis-à-vis the *faamatai*) of purchased privately owned objects, as we have seen, building materials were imported early on and rapidly adopted, the houses built by the nineteenth-century European settlers serving as a model. Corrugated metal replaced thatch because it lasted longer (people discovered only later that it provides poor insulation from the heat, but since Samoan houses do not have walls, the air still circulates). Until then nothing seems to have changed. But this opened the way for new materials: brick, cinderblock, concrete. Some families began building Samoan houses with a foundation and sometimes even pillars made of cement, then 'papalagi houses', with walls made of wood and even cinderblocks — while keeping the interior architecture which allowed them to regard the house as the site of a sacred circle that could be activated anytime a meeting was held there: rooms were added on to one side or a second story was built, but on the ground floor, at the centre of the house, a large room stood empty.

Two consequences resulted. First of all, the house became immovable — whereas the traditional house was considered to be moveable (see note above: the posts were merely wedged between the stones, and the roof could be transported like an overturned boat). Of course the founding site (of the *matai* name) was fixed; even when it is rebuilt, the founding house remains in (approximately) the same place; but in theory the family *matai* can decide (if the family meeting attended by most of the members upholds the decision) to banish a given household, or a household can decide to move in with another set of relatives. The second consequence was that the fixed house becomes charged with private investment (the building materials) which, following the logic already outlined in the case of private goods, belongs to an owner and therefore must follow him. But clearly a cinderblock house cannot be dismantled. This unforeseen consequence, this intrusion of the privately owned object into the context of the 'house' (*fale*) has raised the possibility of an altogether new strategy.

In the last fifteen years, small house-owners have begun to display a new attitude: households have started enclosing the land (which is becoming then more like a garden) surrounding the permanent house, thus creating in the middle of the — theoretically indivisible — extended family land a semi-private space. They continue to say that the land comprising this space is inalienable, but the fence now makes it hard for the authority of the family council headed by the *matai* to have a say in the way the land is used. Quite naturally those who act in this way consider it normal for all or some of their children to live in this house, but therefore also on this land, after their death. This is obviously what happens and used to happen in general, except that the ideology of the former succession was entirely different. The *matai*, representing the will of all, *did not forbid* X's children to remain on the land that their father had occupied and cultivated, for these children seemed, like their father, to be people who 'cared about the extended family (*tausi le aiga*)', people who showed they never forgot the rules of solidarity. But the reasoning has changed. The idea is now developing that the children will stay 'because their father paid for the cement to build the house', which as one can easily guess, gives the heirs less encouragement to remember their debt to the family group. Wherever this occurs (especially in the villages surrounding the town), one can already see the solidarity customary in family exchanges coming unravelled, with each household trying to do as little as possible; for each has begun to think of its own perpetuation, and not necessarily in terms of the continuation of the extended family (that of the *matai* name, and therefore the idea that one must give as much as possible in the exchanges which, vis-à-vis the other families, are supposed to assert the 'life' of the family name, of the *matai* name).

Just as the TV and the VCR, a priori privately owned objects, furtively introduce a new dimension through the content of their images, the building materials which, in the form of a sack of cement, seem as remote from anything to do with the *faamatai* as a mechanic's tool box, can permeate an object at the heart of the *faamatai* — the house — and open the way for a possible fundamental transformation in the notion of ownership.

Land: public, family and private

The foregoing description has already taken us to the heart of the land problem. We saw a tendency to establish a private relationship with a plot of land. This is patently in contradiction with the traditional status — still in force — of family lands. But certain aspects resemble the case of the four per cent of the land fallen under private law during the colonial period and of the sixteen per cent of the land which constitutes the public domain. I will be brief here, as the reader can find more detailed information in an earlier study I made of this question.[85]

From the standpoint of the *faamatai*, all land is family land. The land that makes up the world is the *lalolagi*, 'that which is under the sky', and God is its sole owner. Of this expanse, the inhabitable growing lands (which in Samoa include even very steep mountain slopes to which taro and banana trees cling) are *fanua*, a word which also designates the placenta. No more needs to be said: throughout Oceania, people consider that they were brought into the world by the land (which owns them).[86] From the coast to the ridges of the mountains occupying the interior of every island in Samoa, the land belongs first and foremost to the village, under the authority of the *nuu*, and therefore of the council of the *matai* of the *nuu*. What is not under cultivation now, will be some day; what was, no longer is or is resting in fallow. The bulk of local land is comprised of family lands, each under the authority of the family *matai*, stretching outwards from the founding house, down towards the sea and up the mountainside (the village council can always decide that a plot should be cultivated in common, if only in preparation for a large-scale exchange in which this village will compete with another). The village has authority over the people who live in it, but it cannot unmake what makes it: it is a circle of names, these names are ancestors' names as well as land titles, thus the *nuu* is a circle of family land-holdings.

Before the Europeans arrived, one hundred per cent of the lands were family lands (*fanua o aiga*). The *matai* has the authority to accept the arrival of new relatives or people who thus become 'adopted' members of the family (*aiga fai*). In the nineteenth century, here as elsewhere, Europeans would contract to occupy a plot and build a house or a store. The European thought he was 'buying' the land when he handed over objects or money. The *matai* thought he was granting an adoption, an unlimited right of use (but which could be revoked by family consensus). Some later *matai* probably understood the meaning of buying

and agreed to transactions for which they had not received the corresponding authority —
since it did not exist. All of this transpired in a context of endemic warfare between districts
(end of the nineteenth century), in other words between 'great' *matai* who were in part
manipulated by factions of the small European trading-community. The latter was seeking a
foreign power to take Samoa on as a colony, but was torn internally by conflicting wills,
some favouring Germany, others England, yet others the United States. During this period,
the search was on for money, in particular for the purchase of arms.

Fortunately these purchases of land were few, while others were invalidated by
Germany when Samoa finally fell to its lot, not out of a philanthropic concern for the people
of Polynesia, but because the aim of the colonial power was to develop profitable coconut
plantations rather than to divide up the territory into small plots for individual settlers. The
short German presence (1898–1914) was not enough to fulfill the plan for large-scale
exploitation. When New Zealand was granted Western Samoa in 'mandate', four per cent of
the land had been recognised by the Germans as privately owned and remained so (even
today these lands, most of which are located close to town, can be bought and sold); sixteen
per cent of the lands, corresponding to the German plantations, were confiscated and frozen
as 'Crown lands', then at independence, they became public lands. The rest (80 per cent)
remained under control of the *faamatai*, which made Samoa an almost unique case in
contemporary Polynesia.

It is clear that, if these lands were ever to come under private ownership, the whole
faamatai would collapse. Samoans do everything required by the *faamatai* because — they
say in many ways — this participation is what builds and maintains their feeling of being 'at
home' when they are in their house and on their land. The same sentiment is expressed in its
negative version: 'If I no longer take part in the exchanges, in the name of what could I stay
on this land?' In a system where there is no private property, permanence is manifested by
belonging: by giving, one constantly reaffirms: 'I belong to this name, therefore to this land!'
No one is saying here that life in a society still firmly governed by the *faamatai* is better or
worse than in a society governed by private ownership. What is important is that the status
of the land is the basis of everything. That is the boundary between change and fundamental
transformation.

Do we see any such transformation on the horizon? Perhaps. It happens that the
present government [of the early 1990s] is very concerned with bringing in money to make
up for the drop in remittances from Samoans working abroad (who suffer from a high rate of
unemployment in their host countries and whose children, born abroad and hoping to enter
the job market there, are less inclined to give everything they earn to their relatives back
home), has repeatedly called for more investment and has clearly said that Parliament should
consider changing the status of the land so as to enable investors to buy or rent property.[87]
Meanwhile, the government, which at the beginning of independence used public lands (the
16 per cent inherited from the German period) for state farms, is now dividing these lands
into plots to rent to Samoan families (on very long leases), which considerably augments
private land-holding and social inequality: these families use the lands for commercial-type
plantations, and only the well-off (already involved in trade) have the means to pay the rent
and use a vehicle to work these lands.

The *faamatai* and politics
The vote

This point could take a whole chapter on its own, so I must be content with an allusive treatment. The problem has to do with the way the idea of political representation, introduced by European influence, made its way into the *faamatai*.

Before independence, the sacred decision-making circles were held at the level of a family, a village and a group of villages. In each of these cases, the *matai* represented his own people. He was chosen by his people and could be dismissed by them.[88] The 'family circle' (*aiga potopoto*) met and made what one can call a 'democratic' choice, since everyone could participate and voice their opinion. This was a special kind of democracy, however, since the final decision was reached, not by vote, but by consensus, a very specific type of unanimity in which, to be sure some opinions carried more weight than others, but where in the end each person, by consent or tacitly accepted constraint (while awaiting a better occasion to impose his own viewpoint), communed in the decision by the ritual consumption of *kava*, with the ancestors and God as witnesses. We have seen the process.[89] The *matai* thus chosen was the consensual representative of the whole group. In the village council (*fono*), decisions were reached in the same way. Everything seems to indicate that Samoans were unaware of the very idea of decision by majority vote.

When, at independence, God was placed at the head of the Constitution and the village *fono* was taken as a model for the country's *Fono* — the Parliament — it was obvious to the members of the Constituent Assembly that, to be a member of Parliament, one had to be a *matai*. Only those who had already undergone a preliminary selection giving them the capacity to represent a group could claim to represent an even larger group. The member of Parliament would represent a district (the country was divided into some forty districts, following old boundary lines, with the addition of a few new ones), and therefore a group of villages, and therefore a group of *aiga* families, each of which was already represented at the local level by its respective *matai*. Naturally enough, even if it seemed shocking to the outside observer who saw it as the chiefs exercising a hold over the people, it was decided that only *matai* would be eligible to vote and to stand for parliamentary election.

The preservation of this tradition was accompanied by a new element, however. The foreign experts helping draft the Constitution had the idea of including the possibility of electing members of Parliament by a majority of the votes expressed.[90] It must be said here that the practice of voting, apparently unknown before the arrival of Europeans, was clearly demonstrated to the Samoans as it operated in the predominantly European trading community which made up the town of Apia and which elected 'consuls'. Majority rule was also the practice in the missionaries' assemblies where, in the early days (1840s–1850s), decisions about the work of the Mission were taken by consultation among the ten or so missionaries living in Samoa. The 'native teachers' looked on but did not participate.[91] Last of all, at the time of independence, it was recognised that a number of the new State's citizens of foreign extraction, Europeans or Chinese, were living as individuals (often on the 4 per cent or private lands), and could not legitimately be represented by a *matai*. A list of 'individual voters' was created for them, who would designate their members of Parliament by a simple majority of votes expressed (in the same proportion as the rest of population).

From the outset, voting was a part of political life and went with the citizenship extended to the descendants of the foreigners who had been settling in Samoa since the start of the nineteenth century. Everyone was a Samoan citizen, but the Constitution had created two lists of voters, the 'individuals' (a few thousands) and the 'districts' (in which only the *matai* were eligible to vote and to stand for election).[92]

Since the possibility of voting existed, it was put to use in the district parliamentary elections, few in the beginning, but rapidly spreading to the majority of districts. In effect the status of the member of Parliament was ambiguous. On the one hand, he was going to sit in the 'country's *fono*', and this national sacred circle must obviously reproduce the rules governing the regional *fonos*: choice by consensus, as is proper when the higher beings (the ancestors) guarantee and witness every decision — to distinguish a 'winner' (*malo*) by majority vote indicates a war-like logic, a logic of the *malo*, which does not befit the circumstances. On the other hand, even though Samoa was a new State, it was adopting a 'government' that bore the name of *Malo*. Samoans had long known what a *Malo* government was: it was the government of the nineteenth-century consuls, that of the German governor, of the New Zealand administrator, who each time would appoint a council of *matai* but only in an advisory capacity. But the logic of the *Malo* admits a procedure which distinguishes winners from losers. With regard to the district, putting a choice to the vote was considered to be 'ugly'. Only consensus should be used. But people already knew that going to Parliament meant following a path of 'power' (*pule*) — the MP was called *faipule*.[93] Soon there were enough *matai* who considered it a good thing to stand for parliamentary election, even if X was already an MP and had every chance of being designated by consensus due to the fact that his *matai* name, for instance, was the greatest (the oldest) in the district. It was good to run against him because this was competition for 'power' (*pule*) and not only for 'sacred dignity' (*mamalu*) and seats around the 'sacred circle' (*alofi sa*) of the district *matai*.

In short, in the space of a few years, choice by consensus became rarer as the surge in the number of candidates made it necessary to proceed by vote. The worm was now in the fruit, from the point of view of the *faamatai*. An ideological element that had been clearly placed on the second level — voting was accepted for the few thousand 'individual' voters — had become mingled with elements from the first level: choosing among the *matai*. For the individual voters, the duty to vote for the number of members of Parliament allotted to them was a fact which in no way undermined the *faamatai*. In the first place, this population represented only a small portion of the country's total inhabitants. And in the second place, the distinction between this group of foreign extraction, which voted by universal suffrage, and the districts, in which only the *matai* were eligible to vote and to stand for election, was situated at a level which was not primary to the definition of the country. It lay at a secondary level, and these differences resolved into unity: everyone was a citizen of the new State. At independence, the full-blooded Samoans, people of mixed blood and the European residents who so desired all became 'Samoans'. Now, on the contrary, the vote is no longer a secondary element, since it enters into the very way the *matai*-member of Parliament is designated.

This designation is henceforth inscribed in both the traditional logic of the *faamatai* and in that of the *Malo*, the second being in a certain fashion included in the first: the *Malo* is constructed by a meeting of the *matai* and therefore by the *faamatai*. But the logic of the *Malo* has introduced into this construction an element of its own (the logic of 'winning') which is borrowed from a different world: that of majority rule.

Side effects and possible fundamental transformations
One might think that none of this makes much difference. And that is effectively what everyone thought at the time. But the presence of voting at the heart of the system soon produced other repercussions. In a matter of some fifteen years, the state of mind changed from one in which the district elected the man who seemed 'worthy' (*mamalu*) to represent it, even if it was necessary to decide among a small number of candidates, to a different mentality in which ambitious men eager to sit in Parliament declared their candidacy and thought about how to win the election at any price. But those *matai* had retained their traditional prerogatives. One of these stipulates that a *matai* can always create another *matai* name and give it to a relative (or an adopted son) together with a land from the territory governed by the extended family of which he is *matai*. Creations of this type proliferated, especially in the year before an election, each candidate thus attempting to create a pool of voters. Every new *matai* thus created was one more elector and, reciprocity *oblige*, his voice was a vote for the candidate in question. Of course many of these creations were unlawful in the sense that no land was really given and no one waited for the new title to be registered by the Land and Title Court (which can take a long time because the job of this court is precisely to hold hearings and inquests to verify the validity and the authenticity of this new title).

In the mid-1980s, two consequences appeared simultaneously. First, the number of *matai* created in this manner soared, and second, a new generation of *matai* entered Parliament. Many of these new men wanted to break with the traditional views, which they felt to be backward looking, and open the country to exchanges with the outside. These MPs were much more attuned to foreign opinion, which continued to voice surprise that Samoa, together with Tonga, was still run by an 'oligarchy'. Owing to a variety of circumstances, the government managed to squeak through a referendum in which it proposed taking a step towards universal suffrage. As of 1990, all adults over the age of twenty-one are eligible to vote in parliamentary elections; but the right to stand for election by universal suffrage is still restricted to *matai*.

The referendum and its consequences sparked an immense, countrywide debate, which [was] still running [in 1992–1994]. The opinions expressed indicate that, for some, the move towards partial universal suffrage, which confirms the supremacy of the vote over consensus, has not crossed any boundary line which might lead to overturning the *faaSamoa*. Better still, those who hold these opinions and who back this change consider themselves the true defenders of the *faamatai*: they claim to have struck at the root of what they regard as the disastrous trend threatening to make the *matai* name an object of electoral manoeuvring, which would rapidly have ended in everyone, or nearly everyone, being a *matai*.

Their opponents remark ironically that this trend would have produced the same result as the referendum: with everyone a *matai*, everyone would be an elector. The jest was only half true, however. By virtue of the distinction between the brother's and the sister's roles within the *faamatai*, the traditional view holds that the role of *matai* should be filled by a man rather than a woman, for that is where the 'work of the family' is done, whereas the women (those related by blood) are supposed to be in close communication with the divine, to 'know' the right decisions to make, and to thus advise their 'brother', who will promulgate and actualise these decisions.[94] The doubling of the number of *matai* concerned the men in particular. Consequently, when the government proposed the referendum, a notable proportion of women favoured a 'yes' to universal suffrage.[95]

More seriously, opponents of universal suffrage evoked the very grave long-term consequences that could result from breaking the constitutive link between the sphere of government and politics (in short: the *Malo*), and that of the *faamatai*. Paradoxically people also brandished the idea that democracy would be diminished and social inequalities increased.

The first point gave rise to discussions in the village *fonos* and the newspapers. Those in favour of universal suffrage obviously cited the history of Western democracy: what could be more egalitarian than the principle of 'one person, one vote'? But those in favour of the 1962 Constitution pointed to an often overlooked aspect: democratic supervision of the elected official. Because the *matai* is democratically chosen by his family — and above all because they can dismiss him at any moment — he is held in check by the principles of the overall system: family, village, etc. As he carries out his parliamentary duties, makes his decisions, he will have in mind the traditional values. Members of Parliament elected by universal suffrage, on the contrary, will develop the ideology that put them there: a distinction between their political duties, for the duration of a legislative mandate — during which only Parliament can remove them, in the event of serious misconduct — and their role as family *matai*. The sentiment of belonging will no longer attach to their family and through it, to the entire *faamatai*, but to the Parliament as a 'political' site, to the 'political class', as we say in the West, and therefore to two entirely new groupings with respect to the ideological principles of Samoan culture: daily town life and the political parties.[96]

To conclude on this point, I will quote something that is said not altogether in jest. Those who deplore everything that contributes to separating politics from the *faamatai* say mischievously that their language supports their view; when the word 'politic' is transcribed into Samoan, it becomes *polokiki*, a word play suggesting that politics is like football (*polo*, a Samoan word taken from 'ball' and *kiki* from the verb 'to kick').[97] The image expresses the fear that politics may grow as far from the *faamatai* as the result of a Western football game from the supporters' desire to win: however much they call upon the gods, the outcome depends on what the players do on the field. But this is not the Samoan conception of things. Samoans consider that what the players do on the field would be useless without the 'sacred circle' of supporters who come to watch their team play; this follows the same thinking as the traditional distinction between the respective roles of brother and sister. We have already stressed the importance of the pair of notions *tapuai/fai* (communication with the divine/action): the second is nothing without the first. The outcome of the game depends on the players' action inasmuch as the action itself is the product of the supporters' *tapuai*. This *tapuai* is much more than a prayer: it thinks into existence the 'sacred circle' indispensable to any action; when this happens, the players are no longer alone on the field, they are part of a whole (their families, their village, God). This is what the relationship between the *Malo* and the *faamatai* should be, people say. When the two drift apart, when the *Malo* is no longer encompassed within the *faamatai* — for that is what we are talking about — but becomes a simple distinction between independent sets of principles, the *Malo* is no longer anything but *polokiki*. Here at the same time we have a definition of the boundary line, summed up in a play on words. If this transmutation of the *Malo* into *polokiki* were to become general and permanent, Samoa would without a doubt undergo a fundamental transformation.

The second aspect must also be inventoried: opponents of the new system fear an increase in the inequalities between urban and rural settings. One of the dynamics involved has just been mentioned: the possible emergence of a political class. Today most members of Parliament are city dwellers, at least part time, and have acquired daily habits which every day estrange them a little more from life in the village. Another dimension of the problem resides in the areas of law and policing. In the Constitution, the High Court obviously has supreme authority. And the authority of the police extends throughout the country. But in reality, the village authority claims its autonomy in the name of tradition: the council of the *matai* is the supreme local legislative and judicial authority, and its orders are carried out, if need be, by the group which functions as a police force: the *nuu* of the village sons (the men who are not *matai*). The result is a subtle sharing of powers. If the crime has been punished and compensated in the village according to customary law (payment of the homicide price, for example, in fine mats, etc.), it must still be judged by the system provided by the Constitution, and therefore by the court, in town; but the court will tend to reduce the sentence substantially. And if a village has to call in the police, it is because the local forces of order have failed, which brings considerable shame on the village in the eyes of the country at large. In reality, one practically never sees a policeman outside the capital, Apia. Samoans say that 'the village police force is the *matai* system', the '*faamatai*'. Nevertheless, the sentences pronounced by the village *matai* are normally restricted to fines or banishment — which is already a very powerful system. Violence is unlawful, in the name of Constitutional law: the *matai* cannot order that X's house be burned or that the culprit be killed. Nevertheless it sometimes happens that, in the case of events of this kind, it is rumoured that the violence was ordered by the *matai of the village*: the latter may be arrested, but they are usually released for lack of evidence[98].

The same tension can be found in the Land and Title Court, which registers *matai* titles and settles disputes over successions. Traditionally there was no authority above the *faamatai*. In the event of a dispute (between lines for the succession to a *matai* name, between villages or districts when the conflict spread), there was no alternative but war to determine a winner (*malo*) and establish a 'power zone' (*itumalo*). The use of 'force' (*malosi*) reorganised things, but afterwards the representation still used the same standard of genealogical justification. This is the familiar logic of Polynesian *mana*: If X wins, it is really because he had more *mana*, and therefore he was genealogically superior; force merely upholds the principles of the *faamatai*.[99]

An initial change was introduced by the German colonists, who sought, on the one hand, to eliminate occasions for local warfare and, on the other, to exert as much control as possible over the succession to titles so that the lands would not be snatched up by small settlers (this was not in order to defend the Samoan people as such, but because, as I have said, there were plans to develop large-scale plantations controlled by the German firm DHPG). And so the Land and Title Court was created, which constituted a sort of central *fono*,[100] while taking care to stress their attachment to the values of the *faamatai*. The German judge, E. Schultz, claimed to be a specialist on Samoan customs — and in fact he did publish a number of distinguished academic articles in Germany — and he surrounded himself with *matai* of renown. The Court had the final word in disputes and officially registered the election of every *matai* in the country. Apparently the system worked, and continues to do so: for the time being, everyone considers that, even though this court is an instrument of the *Malo*, it nevertheless corresponds to the principles of the *faamatai* and acts as their safeguard.

Expressed in the form of a multi-level model, the general ideology still seems to be the following. At the first level, the *faamatai* encompasses the *Malo*: the members of Parliament, the members of the government, the judges of the Land and Title Court are all *matai*, 'true *matai*', imbued with the principles of the *faamatai*. The two domains are identical. The contradictory aspect (the use of force, the notion of winning by force) is subordinate. In point of fact, Samoa has been astonishingly peaceful since the start of the twentieth century, with no army and a police force limited primarily to urban areas. At the second level, the *Malo* wields its authority: Samoa is a State, justice is a matter for the central power, and even the *faamatai* is under its authority: a title must be ratified by the Court. But this court does not operate in contradiction with the *faamatai*: the judges decide by virtue of a 'genealogical knowledge' (obviously including every kind of discussion and manipulation imaginable, but which remain on the genealogical level), not on the order of a political power.

This ranking of principles[101] indicates that it is at the same time the boundary line beyond which a fundamental transformation would be produced: the day a *matai* title could be registered or invalidated in the name of the reigning political power, according to an ideology of *polokiki*. This is the turn of events feared by today's opponents of the introduction and extension of universal suffrage in parliamentary elections. It is not the observer's place to decide whether or not this fear is founded. But it is his place to identify the boundary beyond which sociocultural dynamism could spill over into fundamental transformation. In the case of the political sphere, the limit is the inversion of the relationship between *Malo* and *faamatai*.

As can be guessed from these few examples, the issue of democracy is not as simple as the notion might suggest. For one thing, the Samoan paradox is no paradox at all when it asserts, by the voice of the partisans of the *faamatai*, that a system of political representation founded on customary chiefs can be a stronger guarantee of democracy than Western-style democracy itself. But to understand this, we must let go of our idea of 'chief' and look closely at the social reality of the Samoan *matai*, as we have attempted to do in this chapter. The *matai* want to be to the government, the *faamatai* wants to be to the *Malo* what the spectators are to their rugby team when two villages meet: the source of the action, by the fact of sitting down 'in a circle' and communicating with the divine (*tapuai*), thus gaining genuine 'understanding' (word base on the word 'light'. When this hierarchy deteriorates, all that is left is football, *polokiki*. And to continue the play on words: in Samoan, supporters of the *faamatai* distinguish between 'Samoan-style democracy', which they call *temokalasi faaSamoa* (consensual decision by virtue of the 'knowledge' gained by those in whom the ancestors live, the *matai* sitting down in a circle), and 'Western-style democracy', which they call 'democracy *faaPapalagi*'.

But in this play on words, a good part of the country's future also comes into play. Recently the pro-*faamatai* faction tried to bring the government before an international court of appeal on the grounds that the 1990 referendum on universal suffrage was unconstitutional. This initiative may astonish the Western observer. History seems to be repeating itself, as it were. Just as the German creation of the Land and Title Court, at the beginning of the twentieth century, was an accepted transformation, with the role of war in the *faamatai* being replaced by judicial procedure, so present-day opponents prefer to appeal to a court rather than to take up arms. Quite clearly the use of force to ensure the victory of the *faamatai* (in the event to overturn the 1990 referendum on universal suffrage), when one discusses this possibility with some of those in opposition, is rejected, 'because it would go against the principles of the *faamatai*', and they add, 'it's no good trying to defend a principle by its opposite'. It is even astonishing for a Westerner to see the extent to which fierce political antagonisms have not led to violence, and in guise of a conclusion, we can perhaps advance a generalisation.

The period of its identity that presently characterises Samoa, which we have been discussing since the beginning of the chapter and which has been taking shape ever since Samoans adopted Christianity as 'their tradition', will perhaps be judged an exception with regard to the overall history of Samoa. Perhaps it is only a parenthesis, a century of peace between the violence of the pre-colonial wars, when the idea of *malo* was the armed branch of the *faamatai*, and a new violence that is sometimes evoked of late, a violence which might spring from these new sites that elude the authority of the *faamatai*. First of all, the beginnings of urban violence, as gradually part of the town of Apia is no longer perceived as forming one or several *nuu*. And then violence on the part of a central power increasingly anxious to assert its authority as it distances itself from certain requirements of the *faamatai*. For instance, there is talk of arming the police — they do not presently carry weapons; there is talk of training soldiers with the aid of a few experts from Australia or New Zealand in order to create a small army; and, for the first time, in 1994, when a peaceful march on Parliament was announced by the opposition, one member of Parliament threatened to call in the New Zealand army.

Meanwhile, however, this peaceful interlude is well worth noting and reporting. It has been possible because traditional warfare, the tool of the *faamatai*, has been replaced by a combination of *faamatai* and *Malo*, traditional family chiefs and a national government, one example of which is the Land and Title Court; just like this other example of the central justice system, which takes into account the way villages have already dealt with the crime brought before the court. This interlude will last as long as the combination does not tilt towards an inequality that would introduce the logic of 'winning' by *malo*.[102] It will be remembered that the official term for Government also means 'victory', *malo*, conveying a logic of warfare in which one side is the 'winner', *malo*; a logic of inequality. This interlude holds a lesson in hierarchical compromise between tradition and acculturation, between social organisation and political power, between thought and action (*tapuai/fai*). Is this the exception, that of a small State in the South Pacific, with a unique history, one that has nothing to teach us? I do not think so. Rather, it should be seen as the fruit of a combination of the sacred and power spheres, which is not basically new, but which, when put into action in a community of 160,000 people, offers an interesting, more clear-cut formulation to the visitor interested in comparison.[103]

Footnotes

1   See Tcherkézoff (1993b).

2   See Tcherkézoff (1983, 1989, 1994a).

3   In Samoa this is the place of the *ava*, the drink of the gods (what in the literature on Oceania is called '*kava*'): the only man allowed to circulate in this central space is the bearer of the single bowl from which each in turn will take a drink.

4   Modern anthropological literature on Samoa is almost entirely in English.

5   See Davidson (1967), Buck (1930), Gilson (1970), Krämer (1902), Keesing and Keesing (1956).

6   The term 'secondary' in no way means quantitatively less important. I am talking about a secondary level of the model used to translate the ethnographic observations, secondary with respect to the choice to give pride of place among the constituent elements of identity to the system of belonging.

7   Sometimes the fundamental transformation is triggered by an external factor, as was the case of the European arrival (Tcherkézoff 2004). But it can also result from an internal evolution (see below, the land-holding and political systems).

8   See Tcherkézoff (2003a: chapter 2).

9   For the Samoan terms, I have used the official transcription, which is different from that used by non-Samoan linguists, grammarians and lexicographers (glottal stops and vowel lengths are not indicated).

10 See Buck (1930), Freeman (1983), Holmes (1987), and personal notes (comments by visitors from other South Pacific countries overheard during the 1983 Pacific Games, held in Apia).

11 Samoans themselves occasionally use this expression when the conversation (or the song) is in English.

12 Today (and since the mid-nineteenth century) he has been replaced by the missionary God, but the new god inherited many features of the first.

13 For the history of the importation and presence of people from Melanesia, and for the Samoans' attitude towards these 'black' men, see Meleisea (1980).

14 The history of the Chinese in Samoa obviously parallels that of the Melanesians, but the outcome is different, for far more workers were imported (never exceeding 2 200 present at one time, however, in other words 6 per cent of the Samoan population), the importation lasted longer and their relations with small-scale private European commerce were more frequent and closer. On the history of multi-culturalism in Samoa, see Tcherkézoff (2000c).

15 Children of Chinese extraction, with the exception of a more pronounced eye fold, almost always look on the whole like full-blooded Samoans.

16 One of the first missionaries, present in the 1840s, who made a detailed study of the language and helped translate the Bible, held that the word would have meant 'bursting through the sky' (Turner 1861: 9). [This view is shared by many Samoans, but in fact the idea of 'bursting through' is not part of the etymology; see Tcherkézoff (1999b); the reference to the 'sky' is more acceptable, even if it could have been a new folk etymology from early nineteenth century (Tcherkézoff 2003b). In any case, certain links between the Polynesian cosmological Sky and the supposed origin of the Europeans have been inferred by many Polynesian at the time of early encounters (Tcherkézoff 2004: chapter 9).]

17 Afterwards the government personnel changed, and the neo-traditionalist attitude, a certain wariness of trade with Europeans and tourism, gave way to an open-armed welcome to compensate the economic deficit (high unemployment among Samoans having emigrated to New Zealand and elsewhere whose remittances accounted for a quarter of the national budget), but also because the new personnel had a more universalistic ideology, paid more attention to development advisors and had a certain confidence in Western expertise (see Tcherkézoff 1992b, 2003a: chapter 3).

18 See Tcherkézoff (1992b). On Mead's book, see Tcherkézoff (2001a, 2001b).

19 Ideally situated half-way on the long passage between the United States and Australia, the well-sheltered port of Pago Pago was a supply stop for the great ships and then an American military base, now long closed (the Japanese had been expected to land during World War Two, but they did not get as far as Samoa).

20 Along with the 'French Polynesia' group, but the latter is not culturally homogeneous. The eastern group of islands (Manua and Tutuila) is much smaller.

21 The currency and the passport are American, but the inhabitants do not vote in American presidential elections, the group is not a state of the Union and they have their own parliament and governor. Nevertheless they do elect a representative to the American Congress.

22 The Mission, established in 1830, evangelised the whole population in the space of 30 years and rapidly became a local Church with an all-Samoan personnel. The Theological Seminary was known throughout the Pacific, and the 'teachers' trained there themselves soon struck out as missionaries to the westward islands (Tuvalu and Melanesia: Vanuatu, New Guinea, etc.).

23 The same sentiment possesses those who have emigrated (40,000 to New Zealand) and the airline connecting Samoa and New Zealand has a high rate of filled seats. From the economic standpoint, this is a severe and constant drain on emigrants' salaries.

24 Because it is a long trip (from the western tip of Savaii to Apia took two days by bus and boat, until the coastal roads around each island were recently paved, thus shortening travel time), villagers would come to town for several days, sleeping at the home of relatives or simply behind their stall on the floor of the (covered) market. (These long trips were no doubt instrumental in shaping a microcosmic social organisation inside the bus, where one finds a condensed version of the fabric of village social relations: see Tcherkézoff 1995b, 2003a: chapter 5.)

25 However the importance of English in secondary education — the sciences are taught in English — entails in part yet another selection: it is easier for those whose families have access to English (government employees, merchants) to complete their studies; this new division is also found in the opposition between town and country; nevertheless, teachers are quite hostile to any form of social class inequality (this hostility is a general feature of Samoan ideology; see Tcherkézoff 2003a: chapters 5–6 on the opposition between inequality and traditional hierarchy) and go to great lengths to help those who have less facility.

26 And when I use the shortened form, 'Samoa', I will also be referring to the western archipelago, which became a German colony in 1899, then a mandate of New Zealand until its independence in 1962.

27 Tensions ran high, and there was even an uprising resulting in several deaths at the end of the 1920s (see Field 1991). The story is a complicated one because the local merchant bourgeoisie played an important role in opposing New Zealand's economic supervision. This was not a struggle for national liberation, though, since New Zealand's administrative presence was more or less limited to the towns and their environs, and to the education and health sectors. In the 1950s, preparation for independence was a relatively cooperative effort and in any case a peaceful one. The Constituent Assembly included a large representation of the country's *matai* as well as two *papalagi* advisors representing Australia and New Zealand, one of whom was a well-known historian, J.W. Davidson, founder of the 'school' that studied Pacific colonial history from the colonised people's standpoint (see Davidson 1967).

28 See Meleisea (1987), Meleisea and Meleisea (1987).

29 For details and the evolution of the figures, see Tcherkézoff (2003a: chapter 3) and, for the nineteenth-century transformations (2000a, 2000b).

30 That is why the recent initiative (1990) in favour of universal suffrage stopped half-way: everyone was to be an elector but only the *matai* would be eligible. We will return to this point.

31 This is patent in the field study, but has not been remarked, except by Aiono, who made a point of it (see Aiono 1984, 1986, 1992 and a series of lectures given in Marseille in May 1994 at the Ecole des Hautes Etudes en Sciences Sociales). Without mentioning these *nuu* groups, Meleisea, writing in English, rightly

notes that *nuu* is more a 'polity' than a 'village' (see Meleisea 1987). See below note 43 for the nuances: the wives' group is not truly a *nuu*.

32 Samoans also say outright that the characteristic feature of their custom is the *faamatai*, the '*matai* system'. But this response is more typical of intellectuals, who spontaneously compare with foreign social systems 'without *matai*'. I am interested here in the fact that, even from a purely insider viewpoint, the order of things is *aganuu*. Each time someone wants to justify an obligation or a prohibition to a younger person, not to an outsider, they invoke the *aganuu* 'imperative'.

33 For the Samoans who put the word in writing, it is an institution and, as in English usage, they sometimes capitalise it (*Faamatai*). But the term designates first of all the set of social principles which stem from the system of belonging constituted by the transmission and reproduction of the *matai* names. For Samoans, it is the functional equivalent of our reference to 'democracy' or 'equality'. Everything connected with social relations flows from, or at least, people say, *should* flow from the *faamatai*, from the 'spirit of mataism' (to use a local English neologism). Furthermore, in the current political debate, *faamatai* can also mean an embryonic political party or all the individual *matai* taken together. Recently, in reaction to certain tendencies of the present government (this note was written in 1994), several *matai* created an association to preserve and promote the values underlying the system of belonging constituted by the transmission of the *matai* names. They called it 'Faaiganuu Faamatai' or simply 'Faamatai'; its leitmotiv is the defence of the consensus made possible by the traditional practice of the sacred circle, in contrast to the decisions obtained by majority of votes expressed (Hon. Le Tagaloa Leota P., pers. com.); see below the section on consensus; see the magazine *Poliata Samoa* (n°1, Dec. 1994), published in Apia, which includes pictures of the Hawaiian trip organised by the association; the outcome was the proposal to create an Alliance of Pacific Cultures (see 'Introduction', this vol.). It should be noted in passing that the word *Faiganuu*, like *nuu*, is the basis of a word meaning 'association, organised group' (*fai*: to do, make; *-ga*, noun suffix); the Samoan village, in the sense of *nuu*, is a 'social organisation' first, and only afterwards a geographical site.

34 It may be that, in pre-Mission times, there was a distance between *matai* names regarded as *paia*, 'sacred-divine' (which had the right to this title, according to certain informants) and others not qualified as such (is it because they were sufficiently recent for the memory of their creation by another *matai* to have been preserved?) (see Tcherkézoff 2000a, 2000b). Today, and since the mid-nineteenth century, it seems, the term *paia* is applied only to religion (and to the country, since 'Samoa is founded upon God'): 'Samoa' is *paia*, God's 'name' is *paia* (*O le Suafa Paia*) and the Bible is the 'sacred-divine book', *O le Tusi Paia* (but the church building is *falesa*: 'house' = *fale*, 'sacred, forbidden' = *sa*; the term *sa* was and is still used for all prohibitions having to do with the family, the village, the State or religion).

35 In both cases, the term 'child' is the one used by a female speaker, the *aiga* family seems therefore to be feminine; the oldest families, who claim divine origin, descend from women who became pregnant through the magical action of a god who had assumed an animal or a human shape.

36 We will see that this is exactly what happened in the parliamentary elections, which introduces the possibility of a fundamental transformation.

37 See Meleisea (1987: 60), who cites, among others, the remarks of the first German governor, in 1900, Solf, who, three years later, was to create the Land and Title Court (see above, note 28). What Solf called 'communism' was the idea that 'individual ownership' cannot emerge in a system where the 'local authorities' (the *matai*) decide for the individual, even in matters of 'personal welfare' and 'economic development'. The same terms are used today [early 1990s] by the Asian Development Bank (ADB) and certain new Samoan civil servants to describe an ongoing debate over private ownership (Tcherkézoff 2003a: chapter 3) . One might think that this ideology would have led Solf to lose interest in the *faamatai* or to attempt to do away with it. Here again we find the same balance of power as that encountered by the missionaries in 1830. Compared to the Samoan population, there were never more than a handful of Europeans, even during the German colonial period, and foreign powers never discovered any particular form of wealth in Samoa that might justify military occupation. So they were obliged to get along with the *faamatai*. Furthermore, Solf firmly believed that the only future for the country lay in large-scale coconut plantations (this was why Germany agreed to take possession of these few islands; since 1857, the Hambourg firm Godeffroy, later replaced by the firm Deutches Handel und Plantagen Gesellschaft, had been earning ever-increasing profits from copra). On this point, he opposed the expansion of small-scale independent planters and tightly reined in the 'purchase' of land by private parties. In the same line of reasoning, he sought to control or to arrive at

what he judged to be a 'rational organisation' of the succession to the *matai* titles, and therefore to control those who received the authority to manage the lands and, thereby, the authority to grant more-or-less unlimited right of use to a given colonist 'buyer'. For Solf, such control was a means of guiding the economic future (plantations) of the country rather than allowing small-scale free-enterprise to develop. Let me add that purchases by small-scale colonists had already been checked by the Berlin commission after 1889, for the same reasons.

38 For this anthropological method of building an ethnography in levels, see Tcherkézoff (2003a: 445–494). This *tapuai / fai* distinction touches on a conception central to the whole Samoan culture, which applies to any task, any action (from fishing to waging war, from playing a sport to driving a car; see Tcherkézoff 2003a: chapter 5), and which defines the relationship between power and religion; for instance, the *matai* 'makes power', but it is the family circle which 'makes *tapuai*', and it is the women–as–sisters (of the *matai* name) who best represent this *tapuai* bond with the divine. All aspects of experienced or imagined sexuality are also on the side of *fai* action. In Samoa, sexuality is strictly limited to a conception in terms of *fai* action; it lies outside the sphere of identity-relations, outside the sphere of human relations referring to a shared identity and inscribed around the circumference of the family and village circles — the humans sitting around these circles are all each other's 'brothers-and-sisters' (see Tcherkézoff 1992a, 1993a, 1999a, 2003a: chapters 7-8, n.d.1).

39 Marshall Sahlins has already reported this use of the 'heroic I' in Oceania and elsewhere, where the teller relives in a historical present the story of the hero (his ancestor) so vividly that not only is the action narrated in the present, but the subject of the action becomes no longer 'he' but 'I' (see Sahlins 1987: 47).

40 Throughout this section I intentionally stress the *faamatai* as a system of ancestor worship and the *aiga* as a cult group articulated around a genealogy, in order to correct the image usually conveyed by the literature of an aristocratic society with a system of chiefly families. But notions which, expressed in this way, look like 'religious' concepts can very well be part of the social morphology and even furnish the fundamental scaffolding for the whole social organisation (we once would have said that they 'can function as an "infrastructure"'; see Godelier 1978) — the Indian caste system is there as proof (see Dumont 1966; Tcherkézoff 1994b, Part Two).

41 A little shading is in order here. A number of great *matai* names are linked with a territory in several villages (as a result of past wars, marriage strategies) and are the source of numerous other *matai* names whose founding house stands in these villages. Succession to these great names requires that the representatives of all these villages meet together. Furthermore, since the beginning of the twentieth century, there is, over and above the village, the *malo*, the government, as I have already said, but this *malo* theoretically is not above the *faamatai* (see above, section on national identity; also notes 28 and 30). Until now it has not had authority over the *faamatai* when it comes to titles, but this may come about if a separate political class grows up (see below). Meanwhile, the contradiction already exists in the area of criminal law (see below).

42 Or, in the other direction, he may be made to feel that he would do better to sit here rather than there, and the principal *matai* of the moment will tell the bearer of the kava bowl to serve this *matai* after having served others who used to be brought their kava after the *matai* in question. One may wonder whether the disappearance of the qualification 'sacred-divine', *paia*, for certain *matai* names (if indeed it did exist as such) did not exacerbate the rivalry and fluctuation. The notion of a 'great' name (significantly this is almost always expressed in Samoan with an added English qualifier: 'high chief'), which often refers to the two or three principal *matai* of the village (who bear the 'founding' names and sit against the most esteemed posts), designates merely, when the discussion takes place at the country-wide level, names with a very old genealogy (going back over fifteen or twenty successive *matai*). Furthermore, the few names resulting from more recent wars and, in part, from the post-contact era, are 'great' and even 'very great' names', and have received (no one knows precisely when) a special qualifier (*Tama a Aiga*, 'the children of the families [of Samoa]'). A number of *matai* challenge these qualifiers, maintaining that this supreme status is recent, at least in the case of certain names, and that the 'founding' families of Samoa are, in any event, other names (See Aiono 1992 for examples, and So'o 1996 for an historical study of the Tama Aiga complex).

43 Here a number of explanations would be needed. First of all, some people say that 'the two village *nuu*' are the *matai* and the daughters (and sisters, and aunts, etc.): *nuu o matai ma nuu o tamaitai*. The third group is also constituent of the *nuu*, but it is rarely called 'the *nuu* of ... (the boys, etc.)': it is called 'the strength of the village', in the service of the two other *nuu*, their *matai* and their sisters and paternal aunts. The fourth group

is a complicated affair. First of all, this group is a constituent part of the village inasmuch as these women carry on collective activities, but for some, this does not make it a *nuu* because wives are not members of the village (in the sense of members of the 'circle' of *matai* names). And secondly, the discussion concerns only the wives of *matai*, for the rest, the wives of non-*matai*, do not form an official group but are integrated into their husband's household (if the couple lives with his parents, which is far from always being the case when the husband is, precisely, not a *matai*), where they do many of the chores (the same may be symmetrically true if the couple goes to live with the wife's family, the non-*matai* husband may be given the heaviest household chores to do; see Tcherkézoff n.d.1).

44 This touches on the fundamental opposition between the Samoan representation of gender categories between the woman from the village (a 'sister') and the woman-as-wife (see Schoeffel 1978, 1995; Shore 1981; Tcherkézoff *op. cit.* see above note 38).

45 For more on this period, see the bibliography in Freeman 1983 (which lists the most important titles), or for the specialist in search of more complete information, Pereira 1983. [The very first accounts of the 'circular' form of Samoan villages and houses date back to 1787, with the arrival of the Lapérouse expedition: Tcherkézoff (2004: 45 note 22).

46 See M. Godelier (this vol., Chap 1).

47 See above, notes 6 and 38.

48 See above, note 37.

49 The movement thus begins in the expected way. But surprises can crop up, such as, for example, when to the relationship between the *faamatai* and religion (or economy, politics), is added an unexpected relationship between the *faamatai* and gender categories: any distinction between the genders is in contradiction with the *faamatai* since, in the latter, social position is independent of the person's gender, even if, in fact, huge statistical majorities appear, such as the fact that 90 per cent of the *matai* are men.

50 See Turner (1884) and Stair (1897).

51 See Cain (1979), Monberg 1991. According to Aiono, the pre-Christian demiurge of Samoa, Tagaloa, was invoked as an *atua*; which is what one would expect in view of the relationship Cain's comparison (1979) seems to indicate: the *aitu* are more or less 'over there', while the *atua* are more or less 'up above'; Tagaloa inhabited the sky, the local *aitu* spirits inhabited and still inhabit the villages or its outskirts, or the forest, or the sea.

52 I base my remarks on comparison between the present-day situation and missionary reports (see Pereira 1983 for a bibliography) as well as on Aiono's opinion (com. pers.), who, as a child, heard her grandparents talk about prayer practices and use words which were a legacy of the pre-Christian era. What has not changed in the way of praying is this: people pray at transitional moments, between day and night (at dusk and dawn), between the cosmological Day and Night; people pray in the home, making the sacred circle, and therefore organising the seating and speaking orders (for petitioning God, for giving thanks, for starting a hymn then taken up by the group) such that the relationship with God goes through the group hierarchy: younger–elder– *matai*–God, affines–consanguines–*matai*–God, sister–brother–*matai*–God, and so on; the gas lamp has replaced the fire that once burned at the centre of the house and which was part of the offering — which consisted in making the flame shoot up, *fanaafi* (Turner 1861: 166: '*A flaming fire* was the regular evening offering to the gods, as the family bowed the head, and the fathers prayed for prosperity'; Aiono Dr. Fanaafi, personal communication; see Aiono 1996 and Aiono-Le Tagaloa 2003) — but people have kept the same arrangement, the same gestures and the idea that 'light' rises up to God (and in post-contact times, that 'light' keeps the spirits away). On the whole, the Samoan religious discourse is still much more aligned on the opposition night/day (with a few changes in the nature of this opposition, see below) than on oppositions familiar to Western Christianity (between Good and Evil or between life 'on earth' and life in the 'hereafter', between 'body' and 'soul', between the material and the spiritual, etc.).

53 Everyone is familiar with the name because it is also a *matai* name; but few know that it used to designate the pre-Christian creator (*Tagaloa-a-Lagi*: Tagaloa-in-the-sky).

54 Man, *tagata*, was created by God: that is what the Bible says, and that is also what the pre-Christian myths say about Tagaloa (Turner 1884). The myths have been forgotten. The first myth, on the other hand, presupposes God's presence and therefore already the time of light. Through a sort of anachronistic compromise, the pre-light men were thus represented as both 'men' — since Samoa existed before the arrival of Christianity (see below, the Samoan representation of this arrival) — and 'spirits': *afa tagata afa aitu* (*afa*: 'half').

55 On the pre-Christian system, see Tcherkézoff (2003a: chapter 1; 2004: chapter 9). Once it was decided (probably by the missionaries) that the word *agaga* would designate the 'soul', spirits were also called 'bad souls' — *agaga leaga* with some ambiguity as to the term *leaga* which still exists today: sometimes it means 'bad', as in a discourse infused with moralism imported from the West, and sometimes it retains its initial meaning: 'that which is not of the order of things of the Daytime world': *le-aga*; likewise, *agaga* could be a redoubling of *aga*1: 'that which defines the essence of' the being or the thing one is talking about; 'its place in the order of the Daytime world'. The missionary, Turner, points out that the concept of *agaga* already existed and designated a spiritual principle of the individual, which, at the time of death, left the body for the Island-of-the-Dead, Pulotu; he proposes the etymology: verb stem *aga* 2, 'to go or to come' (Turner 1884: 16), which is most certainly an erroneous etymology, for the word *aga*2 means something more like 'to confront, to go towards, to challenge, defy', and its redoubling carries the connotation of 'rebellion' (see Milner 1996:8).

56 The case of Samoa is therefore different from the 'syncretism' practised in French Polynesia (see the case of the Australes, in Babadzan 1982: 246ff).

57 One little-known aspect of this change concerns male sexuality, which was and still is of the 'night' (here as elsewhere in Polynesia, see Grépin 1995, 2001). The connotation of value remains, but the user's guide has been lost (the powers of Night, *Po*, wild powers which must be tamed so they may serve the group). Hence the dichotomy felt by adolescent males, who are given to understand that it is good to 'spill their seed', and at the same time that sexual intercourse belongs to the 'nocturnal', 'bad' realm when it occurs outside marriage (which is entirely on the side of 'daytime or light'). Generally speaking, the effect of this dichotomy, induced by the integration of Christianity and its local adaptations, had a far greater impact on the representations of gender, sexuality, etc., than on those of the hierarchy of social positions as related to ancestral names in the *faamatai* (see below for marriage and the status of women).

58 'In the Holy Name of God, The Almighty, The Ever Loving,
Whereas sovereignty over the Universe belongs to the Omnipresent God alone, and the authority to be exercised by the people of Western Samoa within the limits prescribed by His commandments is a sacred heritage
Whereas the Leaders of Western Samoa have declared that Western Samoa should be an Independent State based on Christian principles and Samoan custom and tradition … we the people of Western Samoa give ourselves this Constitution.'

59 The London Missionary Society (today the Congregational Christian Church of Western Samoa) is the largest (50 per cent of all Church members), but it is loosing membership. The other Churches present from the outset are the Catholic Church (25 per cent) and the Methodist Church (15 per cent). These three Churches have always worked through the *matai* system and are therefore regarded as 'traditional' by the new Churches. A fourth, more recent but well-established Church is the Mormons (8 per cent), followed by the Seventh-Day Adventists (3 per cent). The last two are something of middle-of-the-roaders in the *faamatai*/individualism.

60 There is yet another circumstance. The missionaries had been preceded by various European adventurers, some of whom had established their authority (and guaranteed they would be well fed) by preaching a 'new' religion and waving the Bible. And, as throughout Polynesia, one idea was already central to the culture: the gods are former 'chiefs', the living chiefs have the *mana* (mystical power) once possessed by their ancestors, the victorious chiefs always come from somewhere else (another district, another island), and therefore it is always good and even desirable to integrate a god who comes from somewhere else. The power demonstrated by certain objects and knowledge in the possession of the Europeans helped accredit the power of the god they preached (see Turner 1861: 11; for other South Pacific examples, see Sahlins 1987: 37–38).

61 See Turner (1861: 145–146).

62 The New Testament was translated, verified and printed in 1850 (Turner 1861: 76-77).

63 Turner, writing around 1860, gives the figure of 35,000 (Turner 1861: 3), which, if accurate, would mean that, until the 1920s, the population remained stable (See HWS: 133; Meleisea 1987: 121) or rose by only 20 per cent (percentage of the deaths during the1918 influenza epidemic; cf. HWS, *op. cit.*), as the 1921 census shows a population of 33,000 Samoans. It is true that the intensive health programs did not get under way until somewhere around this time. Samoa was fortunate in that the Mission did not arrive in the baggage of an army in search of a 'new world' to conquer. And that luck held, since Samoa has never been occupied by a

colonial army (with the exception of the period during the short-lived Mau uprising against New Zealand mandate; see Field 1991). It should also be kept in mind that the number of missionaries never exceeded ten for the entire country.

64 This was Malietoa Vainupo (of the 'Malietoa' title, which is the title of the present head of State; see above, the section on national identity). For the legend, see Meleisea 1987: 13. The familiar part of the legend concerns the prophesy and the presence of Malietoa. Alternatively, the gift of the term *feagaiga* and the creation of the title *Faafeagaiga* are not as widely known (Aiono, pers. com.); today everyone knows and uses the honourific title *Faafeagaiga* for the pastor, but no one seems to know where it came from.

65 See (Schoeffel 1979, Chaps. 9–10).

66 Turner worked in Samoa from 1840 to 1859. The first missionaries, Williams and Barff, arrived in 1830 with eight teachers from Tahiti. In 1836, the London Missionary Society sent six missionaries together with a number of teachers, who divided the country into districts of between 3,000 and 5,000 inhabitants and trained local 'teachers' as they could. When Turner began work in 1840, he had 15 teachers for his district and preached with them in 16 villages. In 1844, the missionaries opened a theological seminary (Malua). In 1859, 131 teachers had successfully completed the course; 70 were preaching in Samoa, the rest in missions further to the west (Tuvalu, Melanesia), and 70 were still in training. In 1859, there were 10 missionaries and 212 native teachers working in the field (see Turner 1861, Chap. 1–7). In passing I would point out the very rapid Samoanisation of the pastoral personnel: all these teachers were assigned a village and became its pastor (we should bear in mind that the New Testament appeared in Samoan translation in 1850, thanks to the unflagging efforts of Pratt, Turner, Murray, Nisbet, etc.); this explains that Samoans have long considered Christianity as part of their tradition. It also explains that the Christianity which was established in Samoa was the result of *interpretation* of the Bible by the Samoans who became teachers.

67 See Turner (1861: 19).

68 See Turner (1861: 32). In 1859, the 'members of the institution' (apparently trained in Malua and working in Samoa) numbered '70 teachers, 50 women, the wives of the teachers, 36 young non-Samoans, 98 children' (Turner 1861:33).

69 Turner (1861: 37). Was it the same ideology that led Turner to take on 'six male and six female' servants to help with household chores 'during nearly the whole time we spent in Samoa' (1861: 21)?

70 The distinctive division of humanity into two genders is comparable to the animal kingdom. In the Samoan culture, once outside the *faamatai*, 'living beings' (*mea ola*) are reduced to a world made only of 'males and females'; but this view begins precisely only where the *faamatai* leaves off: outside the circles of identity (Tcherkézoff 2003a: chapter 7, 475–478, 490–493).

71 This is a typical case: village exogamy is respected — which is still the general rule — and the couple's residence is virilocal, something which varies much more depending on the standing of the 'two families' *matai* names (furthermore, if the husband is already a *matai* or becomes one, the couple usually lives on the land that goes with the title; if this is not the case, the choice of residence is far more open).

72 See Turner (1861: 23, 67). The missionaries thus contributed largely to keeping the *matai*'s *pule* authority separate from the authority of the pastors — all this being consistent with the fact that a Samoan who became a pastor could not at the same time lay claim to a *matai* title and, if he held one, was obliged to give it up.

73 Turner (1861: 64–67, author's stress). These anecdotes also show how ambivalent the representation of the pastor figure was and still is: on the one hand, he is 'as a sacred sister' of the village and is called, on ceremonial occasions, *O le Faafeagaiga* — he is presented with gifts of food; on the other hand, as the missionaries would explain, following their logic of reciprocity, he does a job — and he must be given money. The second aspect is probably the origin of the other common term for pastor, which surprises at first: *o le faifeau*, from *fai*, 'to do' and *feau*, 'job, task' (*feau*, the thing to do, a task or chore, an occupation, business, in the sense of 'mind your own business', the errand one is running, or the message one is carrying: the Pastor 'brought the Good Message', of course, but in a way of 'doing a job'). The same ambivalence can be found in the relationship between *matai* and pastor. For some things, the pastor's decision is supposed to prevail in the event of conflict because he 'knows', through communication with God, what is supposed to be. For others, the *matai*'s decisions prevail, because the pastor, like the non-*matai* men in the village, is one of those who 'does' (the work), and not one of those who can sit in the 'sacred circle of the *matai*' of the village (for examples of conflicts of authorities between the Pastor and the *matai*, see Tcherkézoff 2003a: 220–227).

74 See Tcherkézoff (*op. cit.* above in note 38).

75 The phenomenon is a recent one and affects the generation of 40–50 year-olds, whereas the Samoan pastor has been, as everyone knows, a figure of the society since 1850. This goes to show just how great an impact intensification of monetary circulation and access to Western learning (English) must have had on this evolution. Today there can be a world of difference between a retired pastor who has spent his whole life in a little village on Savaii and speaks only a few words of English and a Church administrator who works at headquarters in Apia, speaks fluent English and drives a 4 x 4 imported at great expense.

76 One big cannery employs a large workforce in eastern Samoa; the salaries are incommensurate with those paid in the western part; it is heavily subsidised by the United States; obviously Western Samoans try to get work permits for Eastern Samoa, but these are granted sparingly.

77 For mats (or tapa) and the role of exchanges in Western Polynesia, see this vol., Chap. 9, on Tonga, by F. Douaire-Marsaudon. Samoa is essentially no different (Tcherkézoff 2002).

78 The traditional gift of cooked food wrapped in leaves may have led to admission of the first canned products into the circuit. These cans — and only these — are called 'white men's tins' (*apa papalagi*), whereas the other cans are simply 'tins of XX [the product name]' (on *papalagi*, see above, note 16).

79 For a recent overview of what is known about Austronesian languages, see Tryon ed. (1995).

80 See Wilson (1982).

81 For the kin terms, the reader will be wondering about the descendants: 'my son, my daughter, 'etc.': this is in effect the sole exception, but only if the subject of the stated ownership is female! (In the Samoan linguistic unconscious, the father is therefore not the origin of his offspring; we understand this when we realise that the father uses a terminology related to the succession of *matai* names, which is not the case with the mother.)

82 See Tcherkézoff (1992b, Introduction).

83 It should be kept in mind that the extended family includes everyone who can and wants to be connected with a founder's name. But only some of these people live on the founding land.

84 'These great circular roofs are so constructed that they can be lifted bodily off the posts, and removed anywhere, either by land or by a raft of canoes.' Yet these roofs can be huge (60 metres in circumference) and, Turner adds, in this case, they are dismantled into four parts, moved and then reassembled, because a Samoan house does not use any nails (everything is fitted together and lashed with cords made of braided strips of coconut bark). 'As Samoan houses often form presents, fines, dowries, as well as articles of barter, they are frequently removed from place to place' (Turner 1861: 164–165).

85 See Tcherkézoff (1992b, enlarged in 2003a: chapter 3).

86 See Tcherkézoff (1992b, Introduction).

87 There is a vast ongoing debate on this; the government even called in an American anthropologist, whose analysis tended to conclude that the sense of private property had become widespread. See Tcherkézoff (2003a: chapter 3) on this and for a critique of the analysis, which confuses two things: by tradition, children stay (if they so wish), where their father lived, but on condition, as we have said, that they routinely demonstrate their membership in the extended family; however this has nothing to do with the growing sense of private property (a new phenomenon, which appeared and is growing in the case of permanent houses with enclosed gardens).

88 The fact that he can be dismissed apparently dates far back, since the missionaries found this practice already established when they arrived (Turner 1861: 190).

89 See above, the paragraph corresponding to note 36.

90 We cannot go into further detail: the text of the Constitution is deliberately vague, but it uses the word 'election', and stipulates, in so many words this time, the majority rule in the case of parliamentary decisions. Furthermore, a number of ways and means were defined by law a short time later (Tcherkézoff 2003a: chapter 6).

91 See Turner (1861: 25).

92 Here too the text of the Constitution is incomplete. To be sure, it makes a distinction between election by the list of individual voters and election by the list of 'districts'; the second notion implies representation by land and not by individual voter, and therefore by the *matai*. But this is not stated in so many words. The question did not even come up at Independence. But it does today: Is it 'unconstitutional' to have introduced by law (after the 1990 referendum) universal suffrage for electors, as the present opposition to the government claims and wants to have recognised by a court of law? [This present tense refers to the early 1990s]. The

answer is 'Yes' if everything is made to rest on the question of the *aiga* land as the condition of political representativity. It is 'No' if one is looking for one sentence of the Constitution which would explicitly state that the only admissible electors are the *matai* (Tcherkézoff 2003a: 230–244).

93 From *fai*, 'to do'; the term was inherited from the earlier 'native' administration.

94 On the exchange of arguments about the referendum, see Tcherkézoff (1998). The question of gender distinction is clearly more complex. Furthermore, under the impact of the value assigned by the missionaries to the husband–wife pair (see above), the division of roles between persons and lines descended from a brother or a sister was weakened or blurred in a number of families. There too it is easy to glimpse a boundary line: the day when, in each family, no distinction is any longer made between a brother and a sister as candidates for the succession to the charge of *matai* will be the day there is a good chance that the role has become purely folkloric. Only as long as this role is governed by the logic of sacred/action, *tapuai/fai* will it continue to be part of the *faamatai* characterizing the long-term historical period in Samoa described in this chapter, which is still at work in this society today [until what I could see in my last extended stay, in 1994].

95 The statistics are not broken down by gender, so this remark is based on numerous discussions with Samoans in the vicinity of Apia and in northwestern Upolu, the most 'urbanized' zone, which now accounts for over one quarter of the country's population; its weight was absolutely decisive in the referendum, as the more remote zones had a high abstention rate (owing also to the fact that registering to vote was difficult and a completely new phenomenon for villagers, and the government had left little time to register and obtain a voting card).

96 It is striking to see how, in the recent years (early 1980s to early 1990s), a number of political parties have been created (with the practice of blocks of votes controlled by the party). This has greatly changed the functionning of Samoa's Parliament.

97 In ordinary language, the phonemes *t* and *k* sound alike, so *polokiki* is an entirely adequate transcription of the word *politic*; in Polynesian languages a consonant must be followed by a vowel.

98 See MacPherson (1997), Tcherkézoff (2003a: 250–251).

99 We are familiar with this logic for the chiefdom of pre-colonial Hawaii (Valeri 1985).

100 Traditionally, in choosing a successor to a 'great' name, war was the only alternative if rival families persisted in their disagreement. When it comes to those names whose origin goes back to the gods and is lost in the cosmogony, there is no higher authority (in this matter, Samoa was very different from Tonga; see Douaire-Marsaudon 1998a). In the second half of the nineteenth century, the Europeans in Apia, with their 'consuls' and their constant reference to the Kaiser or the King of England, had introduced the idea of a higher authority, which German colonisation merely actualised; it was able to do this because the first Governor (Solf) and the High Court judge (Schultz) were both local residents and familiar with the *faasamoa*.

101 This can be clearly seen in the division of powers between the Head of State and the Prime Minister. The Head of State, even though he is literally called as such (*Ao o le Malo*), is universally regarded as the supreme *matai* of the country (see above, Part One, on the appointment of Malietoa in 1962 and the plans for the future [it would still today be unthinkable that the Parliament would elect to this position a *matai* holding a middle ranking title]), while the Prime Minister may even hold an altogether middle-ranking *matai* name, even if he will try to have other higher titles be conferred on him as he goes on. This distinction appeared twenty or so years after independence, like the other phenomena discussed here and which followed: generalised voting, the notion of political career, etc. But, in the 1960s, at the start, it seemed obvious that the Prime Minister too should be chosen from among the country's 'great' *matai* (for a comparison between France and Samoa concerning the division of powers between Heads of State and Prime Ministers, see Tcherkézoff 1993b, part Two, and 1996).

102 We have used this notion of combination several times. There is not room here for a more thorough discussion, but the reader can refer to Jocelyn Linnekin's excellent article (1991a), which stresses a common error in historical anthropological work on cultural change: the desire to choose between an analysis that starts with the 'global' system and goes on to study the local consequences, and another system which starts with the local culture and observes how this culture interprets events. Yet it is only by combining the two that one can understand — this is the object of Linnekin's article — why contact produced totally different results in Hawaii and Samoa. What has been said here about religion, for example, may shed a complementary light on the subject. The Hawaiian 'taboos' were clearly visible to outsiders: these were in the form of cult objects or the many prohibitions organising the separation between men and women. Breaking these objects or

causing men and women to eat together, if only once, introduced an irreversibly new factor. But in Samoa, as we have said, the genealogy is the cult object. And even more generally it can be said that, in Samoa, the taboos are essentially in the words: a huge portion of the social organisation is conveyed by the obligatory distinction (on pain of 'shame' and punishment) between levels of speech (in the vocabulary and even in the phonetic system), as has been clearly shown by the ethno-linguistic studies of Duranti (1981, 1994) and Ochs (1988).

103 It should be noted once more, especially in regard to the pages describing the political situation, that this chapter was written in 1994–1995.

BIBLIOGRAPHY

Aiono, Dr. Fanaafi Le Tagaloa
1984   'The confessions of a bat', *Savali* (official Gazette), English edition (Apia, Samoa), July: 22–29.
1986   'Western Samoa: the sacred covenant', in *Land Rights of Pacific Women* (coll. Book, n.ed.). Suva, University of South Pacific (Institute of Pacific Studies): 103–110.
1992   'The Samoan culture and government', in Crocombe & *al.*: 117–138
1996   *O Motuga-Afa*. Apia, Le Lamepa Press.

Aiono-Le Tagalo, Fanaafi [Junior]
2003   *Tapuai: Samoan Worship*. Apia, Malua Printing Press.

Akerman, K.,
1979   'The Renascence of Aboriginal Law in the Kimberleys', in R.M. Berndt & C.H. Berndt (eds), *Aborigines of the West, their Past and their Present*. Perth, University of Western Australian Press.

Antheaume, Benoît & Joël Bonnemaison,
1988   *Atlas des Iles et Etats du Pacifique sud*. Montpellier / Paris, GIP RECLUS / Publisud ('les Atlas RECLUS').

Babadzan, Alain
1982   *Naissance d'une tradition. Changement culturel et syncrétisme religieux aux Iles Australes(Polynésie française)*. Paris, IRD [ORSTOM] Press ('Travaux et documents', 154).
1999   'L'invention des traditions et le nationalisme', *Journal de la Société des Océanistes* (special issue: A. Babadzan ed. 'Les politiques de la tradition. Identités culturelles et identités nationales dans le Pacifique'), 109: 13–35.

Bain K.
1993   *The New Friendly Islanders*. London, Holder & Stoughton.
Ballard, Christopher
1995   'The Death of a Great Land: Ritual, history and subsistence revolution in the Southern Highland of Papua New Guinea',
        Ph. D. Thesis, Canberra, Australian National University.

Bamford, S.C.
1997   'The containment of gender: embodied sociality among a southern Anga people'. Ph.D. Thesis, University of Virginia.

Barber, D.
1994   'A question of identity… as New Zealand develops into an Asian–Pacific country, Polynesians shoud be warned they will find Asians formidable fellow countrymen', *Pacific Islands Monthly,* 64 (11): 51.

Baré, Jean-François
1987   *Tahiti, les temps et les pouvoirs. Pour une anthropologie historique du Tahiti post-européen.* Paris, IRD [ORSTOM] Press.

Baré, Jean-François (ed.)
1992   'La terre et le Pacifique', *Etudes Rurales,* 127–8 (special issue).

Barr, J.
1983   'A survey of ecstatic phenomena and 'Holy Spirit Movements' in Melanesia', *Oceania,* 54 (2): 109–132.

Barrau, Jaques,
1961   *Subsistance Agriculture in Polynesia and Micronesia.* Honolulu, B.P. Bishop Museum ('Bulletin', 223).

Bataille-Benguigui, Marie-Claire
1976   '"Le salon de l'agriculture" aux îles de Tonga et sa relation avec le passé', *Journal de la Société des Océanistes,* 32 (50): 67–86.
1985   'La fonction socio-économique de la fabrication du tapa', in *Catalogue d'exposition sur le tapa en Océanie.* Musée d'Aix-en-Provence: 23–26.
1991   'Un des effets de l'insularité: les migrations aux Iles Tonga, Polynésie occidentale', in *Territoires et sociétés insulaires* (Symposium of Brest, 15–17 novembre 1989). Paris, Ministry
of Environnement: 231–238.

Bateson, Gregory
1971   *La cérémonie du Naven.* Paris, Ed. de Minuit (orig. ed.: *Naven: a Survey of the Problems Suggested by a Composite Picture of the Culture of a New Guinea Tribe Drawn from Three Points of View.* Cambridge, Cambridge University Press, 1936).

Beckett, J. (ed.),
1988   *Past and Present, the Construction of Aboriginality.* Canberra, Aboriginal Studies Press.

Beier, Ulli
1976   'Haus tambaran in Maprik: revival or tourist attraction ?', *Gigibori,* 3 (1): 20–29.

Bell, F. L.
1931   'The place of food in the social life of central Polynesia', *Oceania,* 2: 117–35.

Benguigui, Georges
1989   'The middle class in Tonga', *Journal of the Polynesian Society,* 98 (4): 451–463.

Bensa, Alban
1996   'Contexte, temporalité, échelle. De la micro-histoire vers une anthropologie critique', in J.
          Revel (ed.), *Jeux d'échelles: la micro-analyse à l'expérience.* Paris, Gallimard / Seuil / Ecole
          des Hautes Etudes en Sciences Sociales ('Hautes Etudes'): 37–70.

Berndt, R.M. (ed.),
1977   *Aborigines and Change — Australia in the 70's.* New Jersey, Humanities Press Inc.
          ('Canberra, AIAS, Social Anthropology Series', 11).

Biersack, Aletta (ed.)
1991   *Clio in Oceania. Toward a Historical Anthropology.* Washington, Smithsonian Institution
          Press.

Billings, D.K. & J.N. Peterson
1967   'Malangan and mamai in New Ireland', *Oceania,* 38 (1): 24–32.
Billings, Dorothy
1969   'The Johnson cult of New Hanover', *Oceania,* 40 (1):13–19.
1983   'The Play's the Thing: the Political Power of Dramatic Presentation', *Journal of the
          Polynesian Society,* 92 (4): 439–462.

Bischofs, P. J.,
1908   'Die Niol Niol, ein Eingeborenenstamm in Nordwest-Australien', *Anthropos,* 3: 32–40.

Blackwood, B.
1940   'Use of plants among the Kukukuku of Southeast-Central New Guinea', *Proceedings of the
          Sixth Pacific Science Congress 1939* (Berkeley, California), 4: 111–126.
1978   *The Kukukuku of the Upper Watut* (edited by C.R. Hallpike). Oxford, Oxprint
          ('Monograph series', 2).

Bodrogi, T.
1967   'Malangans in north New Ireland; L. BirÓ's unpublished notes', *Acta Ethnographica
          Academiae Hungaricae,* 16: 61–77.

Boluminski, F.
1904   'Bericht des Kaiserlichen Stationchefs Boluminski über den Bezirk Neumecklenburg',
          Deutsches Kolonialblatt, 15: 127–134.

Bonnemaison, Joël
1986   *L'arbre et la pirogue.* Paris, IRD [ORSTOM] Press (English translation by Josée Pénot-
          Demetry: *The Tree and the Canoe: History and Ethnogeography of Tanna.* Honolulu,
          University of Hawaii Press, 1994).

Bonnemère, Pascale
1996   *Le pandanus rouge. Corps, différence des sexes et parenté chez lez Ankave-Anga.* Paris, CNRS
          Press / Maison des Sciences de l'Homme ('Chemins de l'ethnologie').
1998   'Quand les hommes répliquent une gestation. Une analyse des représentations et des rites
          de la croissance et de la maturation chez les Ankave-Anga (Papouasie Nouvelle-Guinée)',
          in Godelier & Panoff (eds), vol. I: 81–113.

Bonnemère, Pascale, ed.
2004   *Women as Unseen Characters: Male Ritual in Papua New Guinea.* Philadelphia, University
          of Pennsylvania Press ('Social Anthropology in Oceania').

Borofsky, Robert
1987   *Making history. Pukapukan and Anthropological Constructions of Knowledge.* Cambridge,
          Cambridge University Press.

Borofsky, Robert (ed.)
1994   *Assessing Cultural Anthropology.* New York, McGraw-Hill.

Bott, Elizabeth
1981   'Power and rank in the Kingdom of Tonga', *Journal of the Polynesian Society*, (90): 7–81.

Bourke, R.M.
1980   'Visit to Menyamya and Swanson River areas' (unpublished report). Port Moresby,
          Department of Primary Industry.

Bowden, Ross
1983   *Yena, Art and Ceremony in a Sepik Society.* Oxford, Pitt River Museum.

Breton, Stéphane
1999   'Le spectacle des choses: considérations mélanésiennes sur la personne', *L'Homme*, 149:
          83–112.
2002   'The spectacle of things. A Melanesian perspective on the person and the self', in Jeudy-
          Ballini & Juillerat (eds): 123–156.

Bromberger, Christian
1982   'Pour une analyse anthropologique des noms de personnes', *Langages*, 66: 103–124.

Brouwer, E.C.
1983   'The shark callers of Kontu', *Bikmaus*, 4 (4): 56–68.

Brown, P
1969   'Marriage in Chimbu', in R. Glasse & M.J. Meggitt (eds), *Pigs, Pearshells, and Women.
          Marriage in the New Guinea Highlands.* Englewood Cliffs (N.J), Prentice-Hall: 77–95.
Brutti, Lorenzo
1993   'Du nom au pouvoir. Les anthroponymes informels comme indice de la bilinéarité à
          Ciago (Trentin italien)', DEA Thesis. Marseille, E.H.E.S.S.

Buck, Peter H. (Sir, Te Rangi Hiroa)
1930   *Samoan Material Culture.* Honolulu, B.P. Bishop Museum ('Bulletin', 75).

Burrows, Edwards G.
1939   'Breed and border in Polynesia', *American Anthropologist*, 41: 1–21.

Cain, Horst
1979   *Aitu. Eine Untersuchung zur autochtonen Religion der Samoaner.* Wiesbaden, Franz Steiner Vlg.

Campbell, Ian
1992   'The Emergence of Parliamentary Politics in Tonga', *Pacific Studies*, 15 (1): 77–97.

Carrier, James G. (ed.)
1992   *History and Tradition in Melanesian Anthropology.* Berkeley, University of California Press.

Chazine, Jean-michel,
1977   'Prospections archéologiques à Takapoto', *Journal de la Société des Océanistes*, 33 (56–57):
            191–215.
1985   'Les fosses de culture dans les Tuamotu. Travaux en cours et perspectives', *Journal de la
            Société des Océanistes*, 61 (80): 25–32.
1988   'Tradition et Développement aux Tuamotu', *Bulletin de la Société des Etudes Océaniennes*,
            243: 48–54.
1991   'Contraintes et ressources de l'environnement, l'exemple des Tuamotu', *Notes et Documents
            de Sciences Humaines*, 13. Papeete: IRD [ORSTOM] publications.
1992   'Les recherches en archéologie dans les îles du Pacifique sud-est', *Iles et Archipels*, 14:
            376–390 (special issue, CRET, Bordeaux, 'Le Pacifique, l'océan, ses rivages et ses îles: 30
            ans de recherche scientifique').
1993   'Les atolls des Tuamotu, contraintes et ressources de l'environnement', in Corinne Beck
            (ed.), *Pour une histoire de l'environnement.* Paris, CNRS Press: 259–268.
1996   'De surface et d'intérieur, notes sur un parcours polynésien',
            in M. Julien and M. Orliac (eds), *Mémoire de pierre, mémoire d'homme.* Paris, Sorbonne
            Press: 336–343.
1999   'Pêcheurs ou agriculteurs? Le compromis communautaire de Mitiaro aux Iles Cook', in G.
            Blanchet (ed.), *Les petites activités de pêche dans le Pacifique Sud.* Paris, IRD [ORSTOM]
            Press: 175–184.

Chevron, le Père,
1841   Letter, 21st October 1841 (Futuna), *Annales de la Propagation de la Foi*, 80–91.

Chinnery, E.W.P.
1929   'Studies of the native population of the east coast of New Ireland'. Canberra, Government
            Printer (H.I. Green) ('Territory of New Guinea Anthropological Report', 6).

Churchward, Clerk M.
1959   *Tongan Dictionary: Tongan-English and English-Tongan.* London, Oxford University Press.

Clay, B.,
1977   *Pinikindu: Maternal nurture, paternal substance.* Chicago, University of Chicago Press.

Coiffier, Christian
1990   'Sepik river architecture: changes in cultural traditions', in Lutkehaus & *al.*: 491–500
1991   '"Cannibal Tours", l'envers du décor. Mani bilong waitman', *Journal de la Société des
            Océanistes*, 92–93 (1–2): 181–188.

Collocott, Ernest E. V.
1923   'Marriage in Tonga', *Journal of the Polynesian Society,* 32: 221–228.

Coudart, Anick
1994   'Maisons néolithiques, maisons de Nouvelle-Guinée. L'ethnologie comparée du choix social
            et technique', in B. Latour & P. Lemonnier (eds), *De la préhistoire aux missiles balistiques.
            L'intelligence sociale des techniques.* Paris, La découverte: 228–252

Crocombe, Ron
1976   *The Pacific Way. An emerging identity.* Suva, Lotu Pasifika Productions.

Crocombe, Ron & Ueantabo Neemia, Asesela Ravuvu, Werner von Buch (eds)
1992   *Culture and democracy in the south Pacific.* Suva, University of the South Pacific Press.

Crumlin, R., (ed.),
1991   *Aboriginal Art and Spirituality.* Melbourne, Colin Dove.

Dark, Philip
1983   'Among the Kilenge, art is something which is well done', in M. Mead & Bernie Kernot
            (eds), *Art and Artists of Oceania.* Sydney, The Dunmore Press: 25–44.

Darwin, C.
1842   *On the Structure and Distribution of Coral Reefs.* London, Ward & Locke.

Davidson, J.W.
1966   'Problems of Pacific history', *Journal of Pacific History,* 1: 5–21.
1967   *Samoa mo Samoa.* Melbourne, Oxford University Press.

Dening, Gregory
1966   'Ethnohistory in Polynesia', *Journal of Pacific History,* 1: 23–42.
1980   *Islands and Beaches: discourse on a silent land, Marquesas 1774–1880.* Honolulu, University
            of Hawaii Press.

Derlon, Brigitte
1989   'Malanggan: objets, rites et société en Nouvelle-Irlande', Ph. D. Thesis. Nanterre,
            University Paris X-Nanterre.
1994   'Droits de reproduction des objets de culte, tenure foncière & filiation en Nouvelle-
            Irlande', *L'Homme,* 34 (2): 31–58.
1990   'L'objet malanggan dans les anciens rites funéraires de Nouvelle-Irlande', *RES,* 19–20:
            179–210.
1997a   *De mémoire et d'oubli. La fonction rituelle et sociale des objets malanggan de Nouvelle-
            Irlande.* Paris, CNRS Press / Maison des Sciences de l'Homme ('Chemins de
            l'ethnologie').
1997b   'La mort à bras-le-corps. Jeux de substitution et de régénération en Nouvelle-Irlande',
            Atelier, 18: 49–73.
1998   'Corps, cosmos et société en Nouvelle-Irlande', in Godelier & Panoff, vol. I: 163–186.

2002a   'Copy rights for objects of worship, land tenure and filiation in New Ireland', in Jeudy-Ballini & Juillerat (eds): 211–238.

2002b   'Vous, les Blancs, vous faîtes toujours la guerre. Changement social et conflit inter-villageois en Nouvelle-Irlande', in
C. Hamelin et E. Wittersheim (eds), *La tradition et l'état. Eglises, pouvoirs et politiques culturelles dans le Pacifique*. Paris, l'Harmattan (Cahiers du Pacifique Contemporain, 2): 25–57.

Douaire-Marsaudon, Françoise

1986   'Le travail des femmes dans le royaume polynésien de Tonga', in D. Champault & J. Jamin (eds), *Côté femme. Approches ethnologiques*. Paris, l'Harmattan ('Connaissance des Hommes'): 175–192.

1993   'Les premiers fruits. Parenté, identité sexuelle et pouvoirs en Polynésie (Tonga, Wallis et Futuna)', Ph. D. Paris, Ecole des Hautes Etudes en Sciences Sociales.

1996a   'Je te mange, moi non plus!' Meurtre et sacrifice cannibales en Polynésie (Tonga)', in Maurice Godelier et Jacques Hassoun (eds), *Meurtre du Père, sacrifice de la sexualité. Approches anthropologiques et psychanalytiques*. Paris, Ed. des Cahiers d'Arcane: 79–100.

1996b   'Neither black nor white. The father's sister in Tonga', *Journal of Polynesian Society*, 105 (2): 139–164.

1998a   *Les premiers fruits. Parenté, identité sexuelle et pouvoirs en Polynésie occidentale (Tonga, Wallis et Futuna)*. Paris, CNRS Press / Maison des Sciences de l'Homme ('Chemins de l'ethnologie').

1998b   'Le meurtre cannibale ou la production d'un homme-dieu: théorie des substances et contradictions hiérarchiques en Polynésie', in Godelier & Panoff (eds), vol. II: 137–167.

2001   'D'un sexe, l'autre. Le rituel du kava et la reproduction de l'identité masculine en Polynésie', *L'Homme*, 157: 7–34.

2002a   'Quand les dieux ne créent pas la femme: figures de femmes originaires en Océanie', in F. Lissaragues & J. C. Schmitt (ed.), *Eve et Pandora. La création de la première femme*. Paris, Gallimard ('Le temps des images'): 187–210.

2002b   'Le bain mystérieux de la Tu'i Tonga Fefine: germanité, inceste et mariage sacré en Polynésie occidentale, Tonga', Part I, *Anthropos*, 97 (1): 147–162.

2002c   'Le bain mystérieux de la Tu'i Tonga Fefine: germanité, inceste et mariage sacré en Polynésie occidentale, Tonga', Part II, *Anthropos*, 97 (2): 519–528.

Dumont, Louis

1966   *Homo hierarchicus. Le système des castes et ses implications*. Paris, Gallimard (English translation by Mark Sainsbury, Louis Dumont and Basia Gulati: *Homo hierarchicus. The Caste System and its Implications*. Chicago, The University of Chicago Press, 1980).

Duranti, Alessandro

1981   *The Samoan Fono: A Sociolinguistic Study*. Canberra, Australian National University (Department of Linguistics, 'Pacific Linguistic Monographs, Series B', 80).

1994   *From Grammar to Politics. Linguistic Anthropology in a Western Samoan Village*. Berkeley, University of California Press.

Durkheim, Emile

1968 [1912] *Les formes élémentaires de la vie religieuse*. Paris, Presses Universitaires de France ('Bibiothèque de philosophie contemporaine').

Emory, Kenneth, P.,
1975   *Material Culture of the Tuamotu Archipelago.* Honolulu, B.P. Bishop Museum ('Pacific
           Anthropological Records', 22)

Errington, Frederick
1974   'Indigenous ideas of order, time, and transition in a New Guinea cargo movement',
           American Ethnologist, 1 (2): 255–267.

Errington F.& D. Gewertz
1989   'Tourism and anthropology in a post-modern world', *Oceania*, 60 (1):37–54.

Feil, D.K
1981   'The bride in bridewealth: A case from the New Guinea Highlands', *Ethnology* 20 (1):
           63–75.
1987   *The Evolution of Highland Papua New Guinea Societies.* Cambridge, Cambridge University
           Press.

Fetchko, P.J.
1972   'Anga material culture', M.A. Thesis. Washington, George Washington University.

Field, Michael J.
1991[1984] *Mau. Samoa's struggle for freedom.* Auckland, Polynesia Press (revised ed.).

Fierens, G.
1872   Lettres, *Annales de la Propagation de la Foi*, 44.

Finsch, O.
1914   *Südseearbeiten. Gewerbe und Kunstfleiss, Tauchsmittel un 'Geld' der Eingeboren auf
           Grundlage der Rohstoffe und der geographischen Verbreitung.* Hamburg, Friederischen and
           Co.

Firth, Raymond
1940   'The analysis of *mana*: an empirical approach', *Journal of the Polynesian Society*, 49: 483–510.

Foley, W.A.
1992.   'Language and identity in Papua New Guinea', pp. 136–149 in R.D.Attenborough &
           M.P. Alpers (eds), *Human Biology in Papua New Guinea. The Small Cosmos.* Oxford,
           Oxford University Press: 136–149.

Forge, Anthony
1965   'Art and environment in the Sepik', *Proceedings of the Royal Anthropological Institute od
           Great Britain and Ireland*: 23–31.

Fournier, Marcel
1994   *Marcel Mauss.* Paris, Fayard.

Fredrikson, Charles
1991   'Certains l'aiment nature', *Sciences sociales et santé*, 9 (1):21–37.
1994   'La duplicité de la femme: sorcières jouisseuses et disqualification féminine', in minutes of
        the Symposium 'Ethnologie du Portugal: unité et diversité', Paris 12–13 mars 1992,
        Cultural Centre Calouste Gulbenkian: 225–257.

Freeman, Derek
1983   *Margaret Mead and Samoa. The making and unmaking of an anthropological myth.* Cambridge
        (Mass.), Harvard University Press.

Friedman, Jonathan
1981   'Notes on structure and history in Oceania', *Folk*, 23: 275–95.
1985   'Captain Cook, culture and the world system', *Journal of Pacific History*, 20: 191–201.
1993   'Will the Real Hawaiian, please, stand: anthropologist and natives in the global struggle
        for identity', in van der Grijp and van Meijl eds: 737–767.

Gailey, Christine W.
1980   'Putting down sisters and wifes: Tongan women and colonization', in Mona Etienne &
        Eleanor Leacock (eds), *Women and colonization. Anthropological Perspectives.* New York,
        Praeger-CBS / Bergin & Garvey: 294–322.
1987   *Kinship to kingship. Gender, hierarchy and state formation in the Tonga Islands.* Austin,
        University of Texas Press.

Garanger, José,
1987   'Le peuplement de l'Océanie insulaire', *L'Anthropologie* 91 (3): 79–92.

Gell, Alfred
1975   *Metamorphosis of the Cassowaries.* London, Athlone ('LSE Monographs', 51).

Gewertz, Deborah
1983   *Sepik River Societies.* Yale, Yale University Press.

Gifford, Edward
1924   *Tongan Myths and Tales.* Honolulu, Bernice P. Bishop Museum ('Bulletin', 8).
1929   *Tongan Society.* Honolulu, Bernice P. Bishop Museum ('Bulletin', 61).

Gilson, R.P.
1970   *Samoa 1830–1900: the politics of a multi-cultural community.* Melbourne, Oxford
        University Press.

Gizycki, Renate von
1982   'Tongan Handicrafts', *Pacific Islands Monthly*, February.

Glasse, R. M.
1987   'Huli names and naming', *Ethnology*, 26(3): 201–208.

Glowczewski, Barbara

1983   'Manifestations symboliques d'une transition économique: le 'juluru', culte intertribal du 'cargo' (Australie occidentale et centrale)', *L'Homme*, 23 (2): 7–35.

1989   *Les Rêveurs du désert, Aborigènes d'Australie*. Paris, Plon (reprinted by Actes-sud, 2000)

1991   *Du Rêve à La Loi chez les Aborigènes d'Australie*. Paris, PUF.

1996   'Histoire et ontologie en Australie aborigène', *L'Homme*, 137: 211–225.

1998a   'Le Corps entre deux vents: à propos du mythe 'Two-Men' dans le nord-ouest australien', in Godelier & Panoff (eds), vol. I: 203–227.

1998b   'The meaning of 'one' in Broome, Western Australia: from Yawuru tribe to the Rubibi corporation', *Aboriginal History*, 22: 203–222.

1999   'Dynamic cosmologies and Aboriginal heritage', *Anthropology Today*, 15 (1): 3–9.

2001   'Returning research through Multimedia and the Internet', in 'The Production and reception of contemporary media technology' symposium: AIATSIS conference 'The power of knowledge, the resonance of tradition' (18–20 September).

2002   'Culture cult. Ritual circulation of inalienable objects and appropriation of cultural knowledge (Northwest and Central Australia)', in Jeudy-Ballini & Juillerat (eds): 265–288.

2004   *Rêves en colère: avec les Aborigènes australiens*, Paris, Plon ('Terre humaine').

Godelier, Maurice

1969   'La monnaie de sel des Baruya de Nouvelle-Guinée', *L'Homme*, 9 (2): 5–37.

1973   'Le concept de tribu. Crise d'un concept ou crise des fondements empiriques de l'anthropologie ?', in M. Godelier, *Horizon et trajets marxistes en anthropologie*. Paris, Maspéro: 93–131.

1978   'La part idéelle du réel: essai sur l'idéologique', *L'Homme*, 18 (3–4): 155–188.

1982   *La production des grands hommes. Pouvoir et domination masculine chez les Baruya de Nouvelle-Guinée*. Paris, Fayard (English translation by Rupert Swyer: *The Making of Great Men. Male Domination and Power among the New Guinea Baruya*. Cambridge, Cambridge University Press, 1986).

1984   *L'idéel et le matériel, pensée, économie, sociétés*. Paris, Fayard (English translation by Martin Thom: *The Mental and the Material. Thought, Economy and Society*. London, Verso, 1986).

1985   'Ethnie-tribu-nation chez les Baruya de Nouvelle-Guinée', *Journal de la Société des Océanistes*, (61) 81: 159–168.

1990   'Société à Big men, sociétés à Grands homme: figures du pouvoir en Nouvelle-Guinée', *Journal de la Société des Océanistes*, 91 (2): 75–94.

1991   'L'Occident est-il le modèle universel de l'humanité? Les Baruya de Nouvelle-Guinée entre la transformation et la décomposition', *Revue internationale des Sciences Sociales*, 128: 411–423 (English translation: 'Is the West the model for humankind ? The Baruya of New Guinea between change and decay', *International Social Science Journal*, 128: 387–399).

1992   'Corps, parenté, pouvoir(s) chez les Baruya de Nouvelle-Guinée', *Journal de la Société des Océanistes*, 94: 3–24.

1994   'Monnaies et richesses dans divers types de société et leur rencontre à la périphérie du capitalisme', *Actuel Marx*, 15: 77–97.

1996   *L'énigme du don*. Paris, Fayard

1999   *The Enigma of the Gift* (English translation of *L'énigme du don*, by Nora Scott). Chicago, The University of Chicago Press.

2000   'Is anthrology still worth the while ? Some responses to voices from America', *Ethnos*, 65 (3): 301–316.

Godelier, Maurice (ed.)

1991   *Transitions et subordinations au capitalisme*. Paris, Ed de la Maison des Sciences de l'Homme.

Godelier, Maurice & Michel Panoff (eds)

1998   *La production du corps* (vol. I) and *Le corps humain supplicié, possédé, cannibalisé* (vol. II) [Acts of the Symposium on representations of the body, Maison des Sciences de l'Homme, nov. 1992]. Amsterdam, Archives Contemporaines.

Goldman, Irving

1955   'Status rivalry and cultural evolution in Polynesia', *American Anthropologist*, 57: 680–97.

Goodale, J.,

1987   'Gambling is Hard Work: Card Playing in Tiwi Society', *Oceania*, 58 (1): 6–21.

Grépin, Laure-Hina

1995   *Tikehau. Des paradoxes sociaux autour de l'adolescence masculine contemporaine dans un atoll de Polynésie Française*, DEA Thesis. Marseille, Ecole des Hautes Etudes en Sciences Sociales.

2001   « L'adolescence masculine aux Tuamotus de l'Est aujourd'hui. Le *Taure'are'a*: contradictions et transformations d'une catégorie sociale traditionnelle », Ph. D in Social Anthropology, EHESS. Marseille/Paris: Ecole des Hautes Etudes en Sciences Sociales.

Grijp, Paul van der

1993a   'After the Vanilla Harvest: Stains in the Tongan Land Tenure System', *Journal of the Polynesian Society*, 93: 233–53

1993b   'Women's Handicrafts and Men's Arts. The production of Material Culture in the Polynesian Kingdom of Tonga', *Journal de la Société des Océanistes*, 97: 160–169

1997   'Leaders in squash export: entrepreneurship and the introduction of a new cash crop in Tonga', *Pacific Studies*, 20: 29–62.

2004   *Identity and Development: Tongan Culture, Agriculture, and the Perenniality of the Gift* (with a foreword by Alan Howard). Leiden: KITLV Press) [Verhandelingen series].

Grijp, Paul van der & Toon van Meijl (eds)

1993   'Politics, Tradition and Change in the Pacific', *Bijdragen tot de Taal-, Land- en Volkenkunde*, 149 (4), special issue.

Groves, W. C.

1934–35   'Tabar to-day: a study of a Melanesian community in contact with alien non-primitive cultural influences', *Oceania*, 5: 346–360.

Gunson, Neil

1979   'The *hau* concept of leadership in Western Polynesia', *Journal of Pacific History*, 14: 28–49.

Haineline, J.,
1965   'Culture and biological adaptation', *American Anthropologist* 67: 1174–1197.

Hanson, Allan
1989   'The making of the Maori: culture invention and its logic', *American Anthropologist* 91:
           890–902.

Hanson, Allan & Louise Hanson
1990   'Introduction: Art, Identity and self-Counsciousness in Oceania', in Hanson and Hanson
           (eds), *Art and Identity in Oceania*, Bathrust, Crawford House Press: 1–14.

Harrison, S.
1985   'Names, Ghosts and Alliance in two Sepik River Societies', *Oceania*, 56 (2): 138–146.
1990   *Stealing peoples' names. History and politics in a Sepik river cosmology.* Cambridge,
           Cambridge University Press.

Hau'ofa, Epeli
1983   *Tales of the Tikongs.* Auckland, Longman Paul.
1993   'The social context of the Pro-democracy movement in Tonga', in *Convention on Tongan
           Constitution and Democracy.* Nuku'alofa (ms. multicopied): 90–92
1994   'Thy Kingdom Come: the democratization of aristocratic Tonga', *The Contemporary
           Pacific*, 6: 414–428.

Hau'ofa, Epeli & Vijay Naidu, Eric Waddell (eds)
1993   *A New Oceania. Rediscovering Our Sea of Islands.* Suva, University of South Pacific Press
           (School of Social and Economic Development).

Haudricourt, A.-G
1942   'Ce que peuvent nous apprendre les mots voyageurs', *Mélanges d'histoire sociale*: 25–30.

Haudricourt, A.-G. & M. Jean-Brunhes Delamarre
1955   *L'homme et la charrue à travers le monde.* Paris, Gallimard.

Hauser-Schaublin, Brigitta
1989   *Kulthäuser in Nordneuguinea.* Berlin, Akademie Vlg.

Hays, T.E.
1993   'The New Guinea Highlands'. Region, Culture Area, or Fuzzy Set', *Current Anthropology*,
           34 (2): 141–164.

Hays, T.E. (ed.)
1992   *Ethnographic presents. Pioneering anthropologists in the Papua New Guinea Highlands.*
           Berkeley, University of California Press.

Healey, P.M.
1981   *Angan languages are different.* Huntington Beach, Summer Institute of Linguistics
           ('Language sata', Asian-Pacific series,12).

Hecht, Julia
1977   'The culture of gender in Pukapuka. Male, female and the mayakitanga "sacred maid"',
         Journal of the Polynesian Society, 86: 183–206.

Helu, Futa
1992   'Democracy bug bites Tonga', in Crocombe & *al.* (eds):139–151.

Herdt, Gilbert.
1987   *The Sambia. Ritual and gender in New Guinea.* New York, Holt, Rinehart and Winston.

Hermann, Elfriede
1992   'The Yali movement in retrospect: rewriting history, redefining "cargo cult"', *Oceania*, 63
         (1):55–71.

Hertz, Robert
1970   *Sociologie religieuse et folklore* ('textes réunis par M.Mauss'). Paris, Presses Universitaires de
         France ('Bibliothèque de sociologie contemporaine') [first published: 1928].

Hill, R.C.
1991   'The 1990 Elections in Tonga', *The Contemporary Pacific*, 3 (2): 357–378.

Holmes, Lowell D.
1987   *Quest for the Real Samoa. The Mead / Freeman controversy and beyond.* South Hadley
         (Mass.), Bergin and Garvey.

Höltker, Georg von
1966   'Das Geisterhaus bei den Bosngun am unteren Ramu River, Neu Guinea', *Jahrbuch des
         Museums für Völkerkunde zu Leipzig*, 22: 17–39.

Hooper, Antony & Judith Huntsman (eds)
1985   *Transformations in Polynesian Culture.* Auckland, The Polynesian Society ('Memoir', 45).

Howard, Alan
1990   'Cultural paradigms, History and the Search for Identity in Oceania', in Linnekin &
         Poyer (eds): 259–279.

Howard, Alan & Robert Borofsky (eds)
1989   *Developments in Polynesian Ethnology.* Honolulu, University of Hawaii Press.

Hughes, I.
1978   'Good money and bad: inflation and devaluation in the colonial process', *Mankind*, 11:
         308–318.

Hunter, E.,
1993   *Aboriginal Health and History — Power and Prejudice in Remote Australia.* Cambridge,
         Cambridge University Press.

Huppertz, J
1977   'Zum Schädelkult in Porapora', *Verhandlungen der Naturforschenden Gesellschaft in Basel*,
            86 (1–2): 207–236.
HWS (anonymous)
1925   *Handbook of Western Samoa* ['compiled by the Administration of Western Samoa'].
            Wellington, Government Printer.

Islands Business (monthly magazine), Suva.

Iteanu, André
1990   'The concept of the person and the ritual system: an Orokaiva view', *Man*, 25 (1):35–53.

James, Kerry E.
1988a   'O, lead us not into 'commoditisation'... Christine Ward Gailey's changing gender values
            in the Tongan Islands', *Journal of the Polynesian Society*, 97 (1): 31–48.
1988b   *Making Mats and barkcloth in the Kingdom of Tonga*. Nuku'alofa, Australian Government's
            South Pacific Cultures Fund.
1993   'The Kingdom of Tonga', *Contemporary Pacific*, 3 (2): 163–166.

Jessep, O. D.
1977   'Land tenure in a New Ireland village', Ph.D. Thesis. Canberra, Australian National
            University.

Jeudy-Ballini, Monique
1988   'Entre le clair et l'obscur: les transformations de l'histoire', *L'Homme*, 106–107: 237–251.
1991   'Comme des chiens! Un point de vue sur l'évolution des rapports hommes/femmes en
            Nouvelle-Bretagne', *Journal des Anthropologues*, 45:13–18.
1998   'Appropriating the Other. A case study from New Britain', in Verena Keck & Jürg
            Wassmann (eds), *Common Worlds and Single Lives. Constituting Knowledge in Pacific
            Societies*. Oxford, Berg Publishers: 207–227.
1999   "Dédommager le désir'. Le prix de l'émotion en Nouvelle-Bretagne', *Terrain*, 32: 5–20
            (English translation: "Compensating desire': the price of emotion in New Britain (Papua
            New Guinea)', *Pacific Arts*, 19–20: 12–26.
2002a   'Le christianisme revisité ou: le meilleur de la tradition', in C. Hamelin et E. Wittersheim
            (eds), *La tradition et l'état. Eglises, pouvoirs et politiques culturelles dans le Pacifique*. Paris,
            L'Harmattan (Cahiers du Pacifique Contemporain, 2): 59–81.
2002b   'To help and to hold. Forms of cooperation among the Sulka, New Britain', in Jeudy-
            Ballini & Juillerat (eds): 185–209.
2004   *L'art des échanges. Penser le lien social chez les Sulka*. Lausanne, Payot ('Anthropologie-
            Terrains').
Forthcoming 'The lives of the mask. A few questions about the commercial valuation of the Sulka's
            ritual artifacts, New Britain', in Toon van Meijl & Jelle Miedema (eds), *Shifting Images of
            Identity in the Pacific*, Leiden, KILTV Press.

Jeudy-Ballini, Monique & Bernard Juillerat (eds)
2002   *People and Things: Social Mediations in Oceania*. Durham (N.C.), Carolina Academic
            Press.

Jolly, Margaret & Nicholas Thomas (eds)
1992   'The politics of tradition in the Pacific', *Oceania*, 62 (4), special issue.

Jordan, D.,
1988   'Uses of the Past, Problems for the Future', in Beckett (ed.).

Jorgensen, Dan
1991   'Big men, great men and women: alternative logics of gender difference', in Maurice
         Godelier and Marilyn Strathern (eds): 256–271.

Josephides, Lisette
1985   *The Production of Inequality. Gender Exchange among the Kewa.* London, Tavistock.

Jourdan, Christine & Jean-Marc Philibert
1994   '*Urbi et orbi:* constructions identitaires et cultures urbaines', *Journal de la Société des
         Océanistes*, 99 (2): 151–66.

Juillerat, Bernard
1979   'En route pour les plantations', *Journal de la Société des Océanistes* 64: 209–212.
1986   *Les enfants du sang. Société, reproduction et imaginaire en Nouvelle-Guinée.* Paris, Editions
         de la Maison des sciences de l'homme.
1991   *Œdipe chasseur. Une mythologie du sujet en Nouvelle-Guinée.* Paris, P.U.F.
1992   'L'univers dans un hameau. Cosmologie et histoire chez les Yafar', *Etudes rurales* 127–128
         (special issue'La terre et le Pacifique', J.-F. Baré, ed.): 159–176.
1993   *La révocation des tambaran.* Paris, Ed. du C.N.R.S.
1995   *L'avènement du père. Mythe, rite et représentation dans un culte mélanésien.* Paris, C.N.R.S.
         Editions et Editions de la Maison des sciences de l'homme ('Chemins de l'ethnologie').
1996   *Children of the blood. Society, reproduction and cosmology in New Guinea.* Oxford-
         Providence, Berg (translation of Juillerat 1986).
2001a   'Mère interdite, mère promise, ou la prophétie des origines', *Perspectives Psy*, 40: 40–45
         (special issue: 'Aspects de la notion de temps dans la prise en charge de la psychiatrie').
2001b   *Penser l'imaginaire. Essais d'anthropologie psychanalytique.* Lausanne, Payot.

Juillerat, B. (ed.)
1992   *Shooting the Sun. Ritual and Meaning in West Sepik.* Washington, Smithsonian Institution
         Press.

Kaberry, P.
1939   *Aboriginal woman, sacred and profane.* London, Routledge & Kegan Paul.

Kaeppler, Adrienne
1971   'Eighteen century Tonga: new Interpretations of Tongan society and material culture at
         the time of Captain Cook', *Man*, 6: 204–20.
1974   'Cook voyage provenance [*sic*] of the 'Artificial Curiosities' of Bullock's Museum', *Man*, 9:
         68–92.
1978   'Exchange patterns in goods and spouses: Fidji, Tonga and Samoa', *Mankind*, 11: 246–52.

Keefe, K.,
1988   'Aboriginality: resistance and persistence', *Australian Aboriginal Studies,* 1: 67–81

Keen, I. (ed.),
1988   *Being Black: Aboriginal Cultures in 'Settled' Australia.* Canberra, Aboriginal Studies Press.

Keesing, Felix M. & M.M. Keesing
1956   *Elite Communication in Samoa: a Study of Leadership.* Palo Alto, Stanford University Press.

Keesing, Roger M.
1989   'Creating the past: custom and identity in the contemporary Pacific', *The Contemporary Pacific,* 1: 16–35.
1990   'Reply to Trask', *Contemporary Pacific* 3: 168–171.

Keesing, Roger & Robert Tonkinson (eds)
1982   'Reinventing traditional culture: the politics of kastom in island Melanesia', *Mankind,*13 (4) (special issue),.

Keesing, Roger M & Margaret Jolly
1992   'Epilogue', in Carrier (ed.): 224–248.

Kele'a (monthly newsletter, created in 1986). Nuku'alofa.

Kempf, Wolfgang
1992   'The second coming of the Lord: early christianization, episodic time, and the cultural construction of continuity in Sibog', *Oceania,* 63 (1):72–86.

Kilani, Mondher
1983   *Les Cultes du Cargo mélanésiens. Mythe et rationalité en anthropologie.* Lausanne, Le Forum anthropologique / Editions d'en bas.

Kirch, Debra
1984   'Tourism as Conflict in Polynesia; Status Degradation among Tongan Handicraft Sellers', Ph.D. Thesis. Honolulu, University of Hawaii at Manoa.

Knauft, B.M.
1993   *South Coast New Guinea Cultures. History, Comparison, Dialectic.* Cambridge, Cambridge University Press.

Koepping, K.P.,
1988   'Nativistic Movements in Aboriginal Australia', in Swain & Rose (eds).

Köhnke, G.,
1974   *The shark callers.* Boroko (PNG), Yumi Press.

Kolig, E.
1973   'Progress and Preservation: the Aboriginal Perspective', *Aboriginal News*, 1 (4): 18–20.
1977   'From Tribesman to Citizen? Change and Continuity in Social Identities among South Kimberley Aborigines', in Berndt (ed.).
1988   'Mission not accomplished — Christianity in the Kimberleys', in Swain & Rose (eds).
1989   *Dreamtime Politics — Religion, World View and Utopian Thought in Australian Aboriginal Society.* Berlin, Dietrich Reimer Vlg.

Kooijman, Simon
1972   *Tapa in Polynesia.* Honolulu, Bernice P. Bishop Museum Press ('Bulletin', 234).

Kraëmer, Augustin
1902   *Die Samoa-Inseln* (2 vol.). Stuttgart, E.Naegele.

Küchler, Suzanne
1983   'The Malangan of Nombowai', *Oral History*, 11 (2): 65–98.
1987   'Malangan: art and memory in a Melanesian society', *Man* (N.S.), 22: 238–255.
1988   'Malangan: objects, sacrifice and the production of memory', *American Ethnologist*, 15 (4): 625–637.
1992   'Making skins: *Malangan* and the idiom of kinship in Northern New Ireland', in Jeremy Coote & Anthony Shelton (eds), *Anthropology, Art and Aesthetics*, Oxford, Clarendon Press: 94–112.

Kulick, Don
1992   *Language Shift and Cultural Reproduction. Socialization, Self, and Syncretism in a Papua New Guinea village.* Cambridge, Cambridge University Press.

Latouche, Jean-Paul
1984   *Mythistoire Tungaru. Cosmologies et généalogies aux îles Gilbert.* Paris, SELAF ('Langues et cultures du Pacifique', 5).

Lattas, Andrew
1992a   'Introduction. Hysteria, anthropological discourse and the concept of the unconscious: cargo cults and the scientisation of race and colonial power', *Oceania*, 63 (1):1–14.
1992b   'Skin, personhood and redemption: the doubled self in West New Britain cargo cults', *Oceania*, 63 (1): 27–54.

Latukefu, S.
1974   *Church and State in Tonga.* Canberra, Australian National University Press.
1975   *The Tongan Constitution.* Nuku'alofa, Tonga Traditions Committee.

Laufer, Carl, M.S.C.
1946/49 'Rigenmucha, das Höchste Wesen der Baining (Neubritannien)', *Anthropos*, 41/44: 497–560.
1955   'Aus Geschichte und Religion der Sulka', *Anthropos,* 50: 32–64.

Laycock, D.C.
1973   *Sepik languages: Cheklist and preliminary classification.* Canberra, A.N.U. (Pacific Linguistics Series, 25).

Lefébure, Cl.
1978   'Linguistique et technologie culturelle: l'exemple du métier à tisser vertical berbère',
           Techniques et culture, 3: 84–148.

Lemonnier P.
1981   'Le commerce inter-tribal des Anga de Nouvelle-Guinée', *Journal de la Société des
           océanistes*, 37 (70–71): 39–75.
1982   'Les jardins anga (Nouvelle-Guinée)', *Journal d'agriculture traditionnelle et de botanique
           appliquée*, 29 (3–4): 227–245.
1984   'L'écorce battue chez les Anga de Nouvelle-Guinée', *Techniques et culture*, 4: 127–175.
1986   'The study of material culture today: towards an anthropology of technical systems',
           Journal of anthropological archaeology, 5: 147–186.
1987   'Le sens des flèches: culture matérielle et identité ethnique chez les Anga de Nouvelle-
           Guinée', in Koechlin, B., F. Sigaut, J.M.C. Thomas & G. Toffin (eds), *De la voute céleste
           au terrain, du jardin au foyer. Mosaïques sociographiques*. Paris, EHESS: 573–595.
1990   *Guerres et festins. Paix, échanges et compétition dans les Highlands de Nouvelle-Guinée*. Paris,
           Editions de la Maison des sciences de l'homme.
1992   'Couper-coller: attaques corporelles et cannibalisme chez les Anga de Nouvelle-Guinée',
           Terrain, 18: 87–94.
1993a   'Introduction', in P. Lemonnier (ed.):1–35.
1993b   'Pigs as ordinary wealth. Technical logic, exchange and leadership in New Guinea', in
           Lemonnier (ed.): 126–156.
1995   'Fertile chimeras', *Pacific Studies*, 18 (4): 155–169.
1998a   'Maladie, cannibalisme et sorcellerie chez les Anga de Papouasie Nouvelle-Guinée', in
           Godelier & Panoff (eds), vol. II.: 7–28.
1998b   'Showing the invisible. Violence and politics among the Ankave-Anga', in Verena Keck
           (ed.), *Common Worlds and Single Lives. Constitution Knowledge in Pacific Societies*. Oxford,
           Berg: 287–307.
2000   'Se montrer partout'. Organisation sociale et 'semi-nomadisme' chez les horticulteurs-
           forestiers Ankave-Anga (Papouasie Nouvelle-Guinée), in Serge Bahuchet & *al.* (eds),
           L'homme et la forêt tropicale. Marseille, Société d'écologie humaine: 191–205.
2002   'Women and wealth in New Guinea', in Jeudy-Ballini & Juillerat (eds): 103–121.
n.d.   *Bribes d'ethnographie watchakes* (unpublished ms.).

Lemonnier, Pierre, ed
1993   *Technological Choices. Transformation in Material Cultures since the Neolithic*. London,
           Routledge.

Lévi-strauss, C.
1962   *La pensée sauvage*. Paris, Plon.

Lévi-Strauss, C. (ed.)
1977   *L'identité. Séminaire dirigé par Claude Lévi-Strauss*. Paris, Grasset ('Figures').

Lindstrom, Lamont
1993   *Cargo Cult. Strange Stories of Desire from Melanesia and Beyond*. Honolulu, University of
           Hawaii Press.

Linge, O.
1932   *The Erstwhile Savage. An Account of the Life of Ligeremaluaga.* Melbourne, Cheshire.
Linnekin, Jocelyn
1983   'Defining tradition: variations on the Hawaiian identity', *American Ethnologist* 10:
        241–252.
1991a   'Structural history and political economy: the contact encounter in Hawai'i and Samoa',
        History and Anthropology, 5: 205–32.
1991b   'Fine mats and money: contending exchange paradigms in colonial Samoa',
        Anthropological Quarterly, 64 (1): 1–14.

Linnekin, Jocelyn & Lin Poyer (eds)
1990   *Cultural Identity and Ethnicity in the Pacific.* Honolulu, University of Hawaii Press.

Lipset, David
1990   'Boars' tusk and Flying Fox: symbolism and the ritual of office in the Murik Lakes', in
        Lutkehaus & *al.*, 1990: 286–297.

Lipuma, Edward
1988   *The Gift of Kinship. Structure and Practice in Maring Social Organization.* Cambridge,
        Cambridge University Press.

Lloyd, R.
1973   'The Anga language family', in K. Franklin (ed.), *The Linguistic Situation in the Gulf
        District and Adjacent Areas, Papua New Guinea.* Canberra: Linguistic Circle of Canberra
        ('Pacific Linguistics Series', C 26): 33–111.

Lockwood, Victoria S. & Thomas G. Harding, Ben J. Wallace (eds)
1993   *Contemporary Pacific Societies. Studies in Development and Change.* Englewood Cliffs
        (N.J.), Prentice Hall ('Exploring Cultures').

Lomas, P.
1981   'The early contact period in northern New Ireland (Papua New Guinea). From wild
        frontier to plantation economy', *Ethnohistory*, 28: 1–21.

Lommel, A.,
1950   'Modern Culture Influences on the Aborigines', *Oceania*, XXI, 1: 14–24

Lory, Jean-Luc
1981–1982 'Quelques aspects du chamanisme baruya (Eastern Highlands Province)', *Cahiers
        O.R.S.T.O.M. (série sciences humaines)*, 18 (4): 543–559.
1982   'Les jardins anga', *Journal d'agriculture traditionnelle et de botanique appliquée*, 29 (3–4):
        247–274.

Lutkehaus, Nancy & *al.* (eds)
1990   *Sepik Heritage.* Bathurst, Crawford House Press.

Macdonald, Ch.
1977   *Une société simple. Parenté et résidence chez les Palawan (Philippines).* Paris, Institut
          d'Ethnologie.

Macpherson, Cluny,
1997   'The persistence of chiefly authority in Western Samoa', *in* G. White et L. Lindstrom
          (eds), *Chiefs today: traditional Pacific leadership and the postcolonial state.* Stanford:
          Stanford University Press (East-West Center Series on Contemporary Issues in Asia and
          the Pacific):19–48.

Maddock, K.,
1977   'Two law in one community', in R.M. Berndt (ed.).
1988   'Myth, history and a sense of oneself', in J. Beckett (ed.).

Maistre, Guilhem
1994   'Le village de Galue (Galowe), Nouvelle-Bretagne, Papouasie Nouvelle-Guinée. Traditions
          et mutations', report. Nouméa, IRD [ORSTOM].

Marcus, George
1977   'Contemporary Tonga. The background of social and cultural change', in N. Rutherford
          (ed.), *Friendly Islands. A History of Tonga.* Melbourne, Oxford University Press: 210–227.
1979   'Elopement, Kinship, and Elite Marriage in the Contemporary Kingdom of Tonga',
          Journal de la Société des Océanistes, 35 (63): 83–158.
1980   *The nobility and the chiefly tradition in the modern Kingdom of Tonga.* Wellington, The
          Polynesian Society ('Memoir', 42).

Martin, E.
1992   'The end of the body?', *American Ethnologist,* 19 (1): 121–140.

Martin, John
1817   *Histoire des Naturels des Iles Tonga ou des Amis, situées dans l'océan Pacifique, depuis leur
          découverte par le Capitaine Cook, rédigé par John Martin, sur les détails fournis par William
          Mariner* (translated from the English original edition). Paris, Gide.
1981   *An Account of the Natives of the Tonga Islands [...]; Compiled and Arranged from the
          Extensive Communications of Mr. William Mariner, Several Years Resident in Those Islands
          (facsimile* publication of the original edition, London, 1817, 2 vol.). Neiafu, Vava'u Press.

Maschio, Thomas
1995   'Mythic images and objects of myth in Rauto female puberty ritual', in N. Lutkehaus & P.
          Roscoe (eds), *Gender Rituals. Female Initiation in Melanesia.* London, Routledge:
          131–165.

Matangi Tonga (bi-monthly magazine, created in 1986). Nuku'alofa.

Mauss, Marcel
1904   'Esquisse d'une théorie générale de la magie' (with H.Hubert), *L'Année sociologique,* 7:
          1–146 (republished in M. Mauss, *Sociologie et Anthropologie.* Paris, Presses Universitaires
          de France, 1950: 3–141).

1906   'Introduction à l'analyse de quelques phénomènes religieux (1906)', in M. Mauss, *Œuvres,* vol. I *Les Fonctions sociales du sacré* (Victor Karady, ed.). Paris, Editions de Minuit, 1968: 3–39.

1925   'Essai sur le don. Forme et raison de l'échange dans les sociétés archaïques', *L'Année sociologique,* n.s. 1: 30–186 (republished in M. Mauss, *Sociologie et Anthropologie:* 143–279).

1938   'Une catégorie de l'esprit humain: la notion de personne et celle de 'moi'', *Journal of the Royal Anthropological Institute,* vol. 68 (republished in M. Mauss, *Sociologie et Anthropologie*).

1980   *Sociologie et anthropologie,* Paris: Presses Universitaires de France (1st publ. 1950).

1990   *The gift: the form and reason for exchange in archaic societies.* London, Routledge (translation of the 'Essai sur le don' of 1925, by W. D. Halls, foreword by Mary Douglas).

McDowell, Nancy
1988   'A note on cargo cults and cultural constructions of change', *Pacific Studies,* 11:121–134.

Mead, Margaret
1938   'The Mountain Arapesh: an importing culture', *The American Museum of Natural History Anthropological Paper,* 36: 138–349.

1930   *Social Organization of Manu'a,* Honolulu, Bernice P. Bishop Museum ('Bulletin', 76).

Meier, Joseph, M.S.C.
1945   'Reminiscences. A Memoir', Special issue of the 'Chronicle'. Aurora (Ill.), The Monastery Press

Meijl, Toon van & Paul van der Grijp
1994   *European Imagery and Colonial History.* Saarbrucken, Beitenbach. ('Nijmegen Studies in Development and Cultural Change', 19).

Meleisea, Malama
1980   *O tama uli: Melanesians in Samoa.* Suva, University of South Pacific (Institute of Pacific Studies).

1987   *The making of modern Samoa. Traditional authority and colonial administration in the modern history of Western Samoa.* Suva, University of the South Pacific (Institute of Pacific Studies).

Meleisea, Malama & Penelope Schoeffel-Meleisea (eds)
1987   *Lagaga. A short history of Western Samoa.* Suva & Apia, University of the South Pacific (Institute of Pacific Studies / Samoa Extension Centre).

Milner, George
1966   *Samoan Dictionary. Samoan-English, English-Samoan.* London, Oxford University Press.

Mimica Jadran
1981   'Omalyce. An ethnography of the Iqwaye view of the cosmos', Ph.D. Thesis. Canberra, Australian National University.

1991   'The incest passions: an outline of the logic of the Iqwaye social organization, Part 2',
            Oceania, 62 (2): 81–113.

Missionnaires Maristes
1890   *Dictionnaire Toga-Français-Anglais*. Paris, Chadenat.

Mitchell, W.E.
1994   Review of Strathern & Godelier 1991, *American Ethnologist*, 21(4): 1013–1014.

Modjeska, C.N.
1982   'Production and inequality: perspectives from Central New Guinea', in A. Strathern (ed.),
            Inequality in the New Guinea Highlands society. Cambridge, Cambridge University Press:
            50–108.

Moisseeff, Marika.
1989   'Représentations non figuratives et singularité individuelle, les *churinga* du désert central
            australien', in L. Perrois (ed.), *Anthropologie de l'art. Faits et significations (Arts de l'Afrique,
            de l'Amérique et du Pacifique)*. Paris, IRD [ORSTOM] Press
1994   'Les objets cultuels aborigènes ou comment représenter l'irreprésentable', *Genèses* 17:
            8–32.
1995   *Un long chemin semé d'objets cultuels, le cycle initiatique aranda*. Paris, Ed. de l'E.H.E.S.S.
            ('Les cahiers de l'Homme').

Monberg, Torben
1991   *Bellona Island. Beliefs and Rituals*. Honolulu, University of Hawaii Press ('Pacific Island
            Monograph Series', 9).

Monfat, A.
1890   *Les Samoa ou Archipel des Navigateurs, étude historique et religieuse*. Lyon, Emmanuel Vitte.
1893   *Les Tonga ou Archipel des Amis et le R. P. Joseph Chevron, étude historique et religieuse*. Lyon,
            Emmanuel Vitte.

Montiton, Albert
1874   'Les Paumotus', *Missions Catholiques*, 6: 339–504.

Mowaljarlai, D. & J. Malnic,
1993   *Yorro Yorro – Everything standing up alive – Spirit of the Kimberley*. Broome, Magabala
            Books.

O'Hanlon, Michael
1992   'Instable images and second skin: artefacts, exegesis and assessments in the New-Guinea
            Highlands', *Man*, 27 (3): 587–608.

Ochs, Elinor
1988   *Culture and Language Development: Language Acquisition and Language Socialization in a
            Samoan Village*. Cambridge, Cambridge University Press.

Otton, Ton & Nicholas Thomas, eds
1997   *Narratives of Nation in the South Pacific*. Amsterdam: Harwood Academic Publishers.

Panoff, Michel
1969   'Les caves du Vatican. Aspect d'un cargo cult mélanésien', *Les Temps modernes*, 276:
         2222–2244.
1979   'Travailleurs, recruteurs et planteurs dans l'archipel Bismarck de 1885 à 1914', *Journal de
         la Société des Océanistes*, 35: 159–173.
1985   'Une figure de l'abjection en Nouvelle-Bretagne: le *Rubbish man*', *L'Homme*, 94: 57–71.
1991   ' 'The Pacific way', un rêve évanoui ?', *Journal de la Société des Océanistes* (special issue:
         'une décennie de changements', M. Panoff, ed.), 92–3 (1–2): 3–6.

Parkinson, R.
1907   *Dreissig Jahre in der Südsee. Land und Leute, Sitte und Gebrauche in Bismarkarchipel und
         auf den deutschen Salomoninseln* (Stuttgart: Strecker und Schroder)
1926   'Thirty years in the south seas. The Bismarck archipelago land, natives and customs'
         (unpublished English translation of the 1907 German book, by N.C. Barry, Sydney,
         Hallstrom Pacific Library).

Pereira, Janet Aileen
1983   *A check-list of selected material on Samoa. Vol. 1: General Bibliography; vol. 2: Agriculture*.
         Apia, University of the South Pacific, Extension Center.
Petri, Helmut & Gisela Petri-Odermann,
1988 [1964]   'A Nativistic and Millenarian Movement in North West Autralia', (translated from
         German), in Swain & Rose (eds): 391–396.

Pirazzoli, Paolo A. & L. F. Montaggioni,
1986   'Late holocene sea-level changes in the north-west Tuamotu Islands, French Polynesia',
         Quaternary Research, 25: 350–368.

Read, K.
1952   'Nama cult of the Central Highlands, New Guinea', *Oceania*, 23: 1–25.

Reynolds, Henry
1972   *Aborigines and Settlers: the Australian Experience, 1788–1939*. Melbourne, Cassell
         Australia.

Robillard, Albert B. (ed.)
1992   *Social change in the Pacific islands*. London, Kegan Paul International.

Rogers, Garth
1975   'Kai and Kava in Niuatoputapu; Social Relations, Ideologies and Contexts in a Rural
         Tongan Community', Ph.D. thesis. Auckland, University of Auckland.

Rose, Deborah Bird,
1988   'Jesus and the Dingo', in Swain & Rose (eds): 361–375.

Rougerie, Francis & Bruno Wauthy,
1986   'Le concept d'endo-upwelling dans le fonctionnement des atolls-oasis', *Oceanologica Acta*, 9 (2): 133–148.

Ruff, Wallace & Ruth Ruff
1980   *Village studies. Part I.* Lae, University of Technology, Department of Architecture and Building.
1990   'The village studies project for the recording of traditional architecture', in Lutkehaus & *al.* 1990: 568–586.

Ryan, d'Arcy
1958   'Names and Naming in Mendi', *Oceania*, 29: 109–116.

Ryan, Dawn
1969   'Christianity, cargo cults, and politics among the Toaripi of Papua', *Oceania*, 40 (1):99–118.

Ryan, J.,
1993   *Images of Power – Aboriginal Art of the Kimberley.* Melbourne, National Gallery of Victoria (exhibition catalogue).

Sahlins, Marshall
1958   *Social Stratification in Polynesia.* Seattle, University of Washington Press ('American Ethnological Society Monograph').
1962   *Moala. Culture and Nature on a Fijian Island.* Ann Arbor, University of Michigan Press.
1981   *Historical Metaphors and Mythical Realities. Structure in the Early History of the Sandwich Islands Kingdom.* Ann Arbor, University of Michigan Press ('Association for the Study of Anthropology in Oceania Special Publication', 1).
1987   *Islands of History.* London, Tavistock (paperback; 1st published by The University of Chicago Press, 1985).
1992a   *Anahulu. The Anthropology of History in the Kingdom of Hawaii*, vol. I, *Historical Ethnography.* Chicago, The University of Chicago Press.
1992b   'The Economics of Develop-man in the Pacific', *Res*, 21: 13–25.
1995   *How 'Natives' Think: About Captain Cook, For Example.* Chicago University Press.

Schieffelin, E. L.
1976   *The Sorrow of the Lonely and the Burning of the Dancers.* New York, St. Martin's Press.

Schindlbeck, Markus
1990   'Tradition and Change in Kwanga Villages', in Lutkehaus & *al.* 1990: 232–240.

Schmid, Jürg
1990   'The response to tourism in Yensan', in Lutkehaus & *al.* 1990: 241–244.

Schnee, H
1904   *Bilder aus der Südsee; unter des kannibalischen Stammen des Bismarkarchipels* (Berlin, D. Reimer 1904).

Schoeffel, Penelope

1978 'Gender, status and power in Samoa', *Canberra Anthropology,* 1 (2): 69–81.

1979 'Daughters of Sina: a study of Gender, Status and Power in Samoa', Ph.D. Thesis. Canberra, Australian National University.

1995 'The Samoan concept of *feagaiga* and its transformation', in Judith Huntsman (ed.), *Tonga and Samoa. Images of Gender and Polity.* Chirstchurch, University of Canterbury Press (MacMillan Brown Center for Pacific Studies Publications): 85–105.

Schuster, Meinhard

1985 'The men's house, centre and nodal point of art on the middle Sepik', in Suzanne Greub (ed.), *Authority and Ornament: Art of the Sepik River, Papua New Guinea.* Basel, Tribal Art Centre: 19–26.

Schwab, Johann

1970 'Klan-Gliederung und Mythen im küstennahen Inland-Gebiet zwischen Sepik und Ramu (Nordost-Neuguinea)', *Anthropos,* 54 (5–6): 758–793.

Scragg, R.F.R.

1957 *Depopulation in New Ireland. A Study of Demography and Fertility.* Port-Moresby, Government Printer (Territory of Papua New Guinea health monograph).

Shore, Bradd

1981 'Sexuality and gender in Samoa: conceptions and missed conceptions' in Sh. Ortner & H. Whitehead (eds), *Sexual Meanings. The Cultural Construction of Gender and Sexuality.* Cambridge, Cambridge University Press: 192–215.

1982 *Sala'ilua: A Samoan Mystery.* New-York, Columbia University Press.

So'o, Asofou

1996 'O le fuata ma lona lou: indigenous institutions and democracy in Samoa', Ph. D. Thesis, Canberra, Australian National University.

Stair J.B.

1897 *Old Samoa: or flotsam and jetsam from the Pacific Ocean.* London, The Religous Tract Society.

Stanner, W.E.H.,

1979 *White Man Got No Dreaming, Essays 1938–73.* Canberra, Australian National University Press.

Strathern, Andrew J.

1970 'Wiru penthonyms', *Bidjragen tot de Taal-, land- en Volkenkunde,* 126 (1): 59–74

1971a 'Cargo and inflation in Mount Hagen', *Oceania,* 41 (4):255–265.

1971b *The Rope of Moka. Big-men and Ceremonial Exchange in Mount Hagen, New Guinea.* Cambridge, Cambridge University Press.

1974 'Anthropolgy and Problems of Social Change in Papua-New-Guinea', *Man in New-Guinea,* 6 (3): 15–25.

1977   'Melpa food-names as an expression of ideas on identity and substance', *Journal of the Polynesian Society*, 86 (4): 503–511.

1979/1980 'The red box money-cult in Mount Hagen 1968–1971' (two parts), *Oceania*, 50 (2):88–100 & 50 (3):161–175.

1982   'Witchcraft, greed, cannibalism, and death. Some related themes from the New Guinea Highlands', in M. Bloch & J. Parry (eds), *Death and the regeneration of life*. New York, Pergamon: 111–133.

1991   'Struggles for meaning', in A. Biersack (ed.) *Clio in Oceania. Towards a Historical Anthropology*. Washington, Smithsonian Institution Press: 205–230.

Strathern, Andrew & Marylin Strathern

1969   'Marriage in Melpa',in R. Glasse & M.J. Meggitt *Pigs, Pearshells and Women. Marriage in the New Guinea Highlands*. Englewood Cliffs (N.J.), Prentice-Hall: 138–158.

1971   *Self decoration in Mount Hagen*. Toronto & Buffalo, University of Toronto Press.

Strathern, Marylin & Maurice Godelier (eds)

1991   *Big Men and Great Men. Personifications of Power in Melanesia*. Cambridge/Paris, Cambridge University Press/Editions de la Maison des Sciences de l'Homme.

Strauss, H.

1990   *The Mi-Culture of the Mount Hagen People, Papua New Guinea* (ed. by G. Stürzenhofecker & A. J. Strathern). Pittsburg, University of Pittsburgh, Department of Anthropology ('Ethnology Monographs', 13) (1st publ.1962).

Swain, Tony

1988   'The Ghost of Space: reflections on Warlpiri christian iconography and ritual', in Swain & Rose (eds): 452–469.

Swain, Tony & Deborah Bird Rose (eds),

1988   *Aboriginal Australians and Christian Missions: Ethnographic and Historical Studies*. Bedford Park (S. Austr.), The Australian Association for the Study of religions (Special Studies in Religions, 6).

Tamahori, Maxine

1963   'Cultural change in Tongan bark cloth manufacture', M.A. Thesis. Auckland, University of Auckland

Taylor, Anne-Christine

1993   'Remembering to forget: identity, mourning and memory among the Jivaro', *Man*, 28(4): 653–678.

Taylor-Hubert, Mary

1990   'The Bishop' Progress: representation of missionary experience on the Sepik frontier', in Lutkehaus & *al.* 1990: 197–211.

Tcherkézoff, Serge

1983   *Le roi nyamwezi, la droite et la gauche. Révision comparative des classifications dualistes.* Cambridge/Paris, Cambridge University Press/Maison des Sciences de l'Homme [English translation by Martin Thom: *Dual Classifications Reconsidered.* Cambridge University Press, 1987].

1989   'Rituel et royauté sacrée: la double figure du père', in A.Muxel & J.P.Rennes (eds), *Le Père. Métaphore paternelle et fonctions du père.* Paris, Denoël ('l'espace analytique'): 273–302.

1991   Review of *Developments in Polynesian Ethnology* (R. Borofsky and A.Howard, eds), Honolulu, University of Hawaii Press, 1989, *L'Homme,* 119: 160–2.

1992a   'La question du 'genre' à Samoa. De l'illusion dualiste à la hiérarchie des niveaux', *Anthropologie et Sociétés,* 16 (2): 91–117.

1992b   'Les enfants-de-la-terre à Samoa. Tradition locale et développement imposé', *Etudes Rurales,* 127–8 (special issue: 'la terre et le Pacifique ', J.F.Baré, ed.): 15–40.

1993a   'The illusion of dualism in Samoa: 'brothers-and-sisters' are not 'men-and-women'', in Th. Del Valle (ed.), *Gendered Anthropology* (1st European Association of Social Anthropologists EASA Conference, August 1990, vol. 4). London, Routledge & Kegan Paul: 54–87.

1993b   'L'individualisme' chez Louis Dumont et l'anthropologie des idéologies globales: genèse du point de vue comparatif' (two parts), *Anthropologie et Sociétés,* 17 (3): 141–158 & 18 (1): 203–222.

1994a   'Hierarchical Reversal, ten years on (Africa, India, Polynesia)' (two parts), *Journal of Anthropological Society of Oxford JASO ,* 25 (2): 133–167 & 25 (3): 229–253.

1994b   'L'inclusion du contraire (L.Dumont), la hiérarchie enchevêtrée (J.P.Dupuy) et le rapport sacré/pouvoir. Relectures et révision des modèles à propos de l'Inde' (two parts), *Culture* 14 (2): 113–134 & 15 (1): 33–48.

1995a   'La totalité durkheimienne (E. Durkheim et R. Hertz): un modèle holiste du rapport 'sacré/profane'', *L'Ethnographie* (special issue: 'l'Ecole française de sociologie', M. Fournier & L. Racine, eds) 91 (1): 53–69.

1995b   'L'autocar à Samoa (Polynésie) ou la hiérarchie au quotidien', *Gradhiva* 18: 47–56.

1996   'Les oppositions dualistes 'droite/gauche', la politique française et l'anthropologie des classifications', *Gradhiva* 20: 67–81.

1998 'Is aristocracy good for democracy? A contemporary debate in Western Samoa', in Jürg Wassmann (ed.), *Pacific Answers to Western Hegemony: Cultural Practices of Identity Construction.* Oxford, Berg ('Explorations in Anthropology Series'): 417–434.

1999a   'Qu'est-ce qu'un acte sexuel, au Samoa Occidental ?', in Ph. Descola, J. Hamel et P. Lemonnier (eds), *La production du social. Autour de Maurice Godelier.* Paris, Fayard: 369–387.

1999b   'Who said that the 17th-18th centuries Papalagi ('Europeans') were 'sky-bursters'? Another Euro-centric projection onto Polynesia', *Journal of the Polynesian Society,* 108 (4): 417–425.

2000a   'The Samoan category *matai* ('chief'): a singularity in Polynesia? Historical and etymological comparative queries.', *Journal of the Polynesian Society,* 109 (2): 151–190.

2000b   'Are the Samoan chiefs *matai* 'out of time'? Tradition and democracy: contemporary ambiguities and historical transformations of the concept of chief', in Elise Huffer et Asofou So'o (eds), *Governance in Samoa.* Canberra / Suva, Australian National University (National Centre for Development Studies, 'Asia-Pacific' Series) / University of the South Pacific (Institute of Pacific Studies): 113–133.

2000c   'Multiculturalism and construction of a national identity. The historical case of Samoan /
          European relations', *The New Pacific Review*, 1 (1): 168–186.

2001a   *Le mythe occidental de la sexualité polynésienne: Margaret Mead, Derek Freeman et 'Samoa',*
          Paris, Presses Universitaires de France ('Ethnologies').

2001b   'Is anthropology about individual agency or culture? Or why 'Old Derek' is doubly
          wrong', *Journal of the Polynesian Society*, 110 (1): 59–78.

2002   'Subjects and objects in Samoa: ceremonial mats have a 'soul'', in Jeudy–Ballini & Juillerat
          (eds): 27–51.

2003a   *Faa-Samoa, une identité polynésienne (économie, politique, sexualité). L'anthropologie comme
          dialogue culturel.* Paris, L'Harmattan ('Connaissance des hommes').

2003b   'The unwarranted encounter between the etymology of *Papâlagi* and the apotheosis of
          Captain Cook', *Journal of the Polynesian Society*, 112 (1): 65–73.

2004   *'First Contacts' in Polynesia: the Samoan case (1722–1848). Western misunderstandings about
          sexuality and divinity.* Canberra/ Cristchurch, Journal of Pacific History Monographs /
          Macmillan Brown Centre for Pacific Studies.

n.d. 1   "Soeur ou épouse, il faut choisir !'. L'énigme de l'exogamie villageoise à Samoa', in
          F.Héritier et E. Copet-Rougier (eds), *Frère/soeur: la relation essentielle de parenté.* Paris, Ed.
          des Archives Contemporaines (coll. 'Ordres Sociaux')

Tonga Taimi (weekly magazine, created in 1989). Nuku'alofa.

Thiele, S.(ed.),
1991   'Reconsidering Aboriginality', *The Australian Journal of Anthropology* (special issue), 2 (2).
Thomas, Nicholas
1989   *Out of time. History and Evolution in Anthropological Discourse.* Cambrige, Cambridge
          University Press.

Threlfall, N.
1975   *One Hundred Years in the Islands. The Methodist/United Church in the New Island Region,
          1875–1975.* Rabaul (PNG), The United Church.

Tonga Coucil of Churches
1975   'Land and Migration'. Nuku'alofa (ms. multicopied).

Tonkin, Elizabeth, Maryon McDonald & Malcolm Chapman (eds)
1989   *History and Ethnicity.* London, Routledge ('ASA Monographs', 27).

Tonkinson, Myrna Ewart,
1990   'Is it in the blood? Australian Aboriginal identity', in Linnekin & Poyer (eds): 191–218.

Tonkinson, Robert & M. Howard,
1990   *Going it Alone: Prospects for Aboriginal Autonomy.* Canberra, Aboriginal Studies Press.

Trask, Haunani
1991   'Natives and anthropologists: the colonial struggle', *The Contemporary Pacific*, 2:
          159–167.

Trompf, Garry
1990   'Keeping the *lo* under a Melanesian Messiah: an analysis of the Pomio *Kivung*, East New Britain', in John Barker (ed.), *Christianity in Oceania. Ethnographic perspective.* Lanham, University Press of America ('ASAO Monograph', 12): 59–80.

Tryon, Darrell T. (ed.)
1995   *Comparative Austronesian Dictionary. An Introduction to Austronesian Studies* (5 vol.). Berlin, Mouton de Gruyter ('Trends in Linguistics', Doc. 10).

Turner, George
1861   *Nineteen Years in Polynesia.* London, John Snow [republished in 1986 with only the chapters concerning Samoa, under the same title, Apia, the Western Samoa Historical and Cultural Trust].
1884   *Samoa, a hundred years ago and long before.* London, Macmillan [republished in 1989, Suva, University of the South Pacific, Institute of Pacific Studies].

Turner, J. W.
1991   'Some reflections on the significance of names in Matailobau, Fiji', *Journal of the Polynesian Society,* 100 (1): 7–24.

Tuzin, Donald
1980   *The Voice of the Tambaran: Truth and Illusion in Ilahita Arapesh Religion.* Berkeley, University of California Press.

Valeri, Valerio
1982   'The transformation of a transformation. A structural essay on an aspect of Hawaiian history (1809–1819)', *Social Analysis,* 10 (republished as chapter 3 in Biersack, ed., 1991).
1985   *Kingship and Sacrifice. Ritual and society in ancient Hawaii.* Chicago, The University of Chicago Press.

Wagner, Roy
1969   'The Talk of Koriki: a Daribi contact cult', *Social Research* 46:140–165.
1972   *Habu. The Innovation of Meaning in Daribi Religion.* Chicago & London, The University of Chicago Press.
1986   *Asiwinarong: Ethos, image, and social power among the Usen Barok of New Ireland.* Princeton, Princeton University Press.
1987   'Figure-ground reversal among the Barok', in L. Lincoln (ed.) *Assemblage of spirits: Idea and image in New Ireland.* New York, G. Braziller, Inc., in association with the Minneapolis Institute of Arts: 56–62.

Walden, E. & H. Nevermann
1940   'Totenfeiern und Malagane von Nord-Neumecklenburg' (notes prises par Walden durant l'Expédition Navale Allemande de 1907–1909, et rédigées après sa mort par Nevermann), *Zeitschrift für Ethnologien,* 72: 11–38.

Wassmann, Jürg
1991   *The Song to the Flying Fox.* Port-Moresby, The National Research Institute (translated from the German,1982).

Watson, James B.
1990   'Other people do other things: Lamarckian identities in Kainantu Subdistrict, Papua New
            Guinea', in Linnekin & Poyer (eds): 17–42.

Weiner, Annette
1976   *Women of Value, Men of Renown. New Perspectives in Trobriand Exchange.* Austin &
            London, University of Texas Press.
1992   *Inalienable Possessions, The Paradox of Keeping-While-Giving.* Berkeley, University of
            California Press.

White, Geoffrey M.
1991   *Identity through History. Living Stories in a Solomon Islands Society.* Cambridge, Cambridge
            University Press.

Whitehouse, Harvey
1996   'Apparitions, orations and rings. Experience of spirits in Dadul', in Jeannette Marie
            Mageo & Alan Howard (eds), *Spirits in Culture, History and Mind.* New York & London,
            Routledge: 173–193.

Wilson, William H
1982   *Proto-Polynesian Possessive Marking.* Canberra, Australian National University ('Pacific
            Linguistic Series', B, 85).

Worms, E.A..& H. Petri
1972   'Les religions primitives d'Australie', in H. Nevermann, E.A. Worms, H. Petri, *Les religions
            du Pacifique et d'Australie.* Paris, Payot: 153–388.

Worsley, Peter
1977   *Elle sonnera, la trompette. Le culte du cargo en Mélanésie.* Paris, Payot (translated from the
            English original edition, *The Trumpet Shall Sound*, London, Granada Publ., 1957).

Zonabend, Françoise
1977   'Pourquoi nommer? Les noms de personnes dans un village français: Minot-en-
            Châtillonnais', in C. Lévi-Strauss (ed.): 257–279.
1980   'Le nom de personne', *L'Homme*, 20 (4): 7–23.

BIOGRAPHIES

Marie-Claire Bataille-Benguigui is honorary Associate Professor (Maître de conférences) at the Muséum National d'Histoire Naturelle. She has been researching ethnology in Oceania for numerous years for the Musée de l'Homme. Following several research projects in the Kingdom of Tonga she became interested in human relations with marine life, systems of representation linked to the marine environment and socio-economic changes in island micro-society. She has recently begun a more general study of human-animal relations.

Georges Benguigui is honorary Director of Research at CNRS. He has published work concerning managers and the middle classes, *La Fonction de l'encadrement* (with Griset and Montjardin), and the sociology of science. He has also written on prisons and prison guards, *Le Monde des surveillants de prison* (with A. Chauvenet and F. Orlic). Following several trips to Tonga after 1983, he became interested in the emergence of new social classes and other socio-political developments in Tonga.

Pascale Bonnemère holds a research position at the CNRS, is a founding member of CREDO, and teaches at the University of Provence and the EHESS. She is engaged in long-term fieldwork among the Ankave-Anga people of Papua New Guinea. Her main research interests are life-cycle exchanges and rituals, personhood and gender, on which she has published articles in journals and edited collections. She is the author of *Le Pandanus rouge. Corps, differences des sexes et parenté chez les Ankave-Anga* (CNRS-Editions, 1996) and is the editor of *Women as Unseen Characters: Male Ritual in Papua New Guinea* (University of Pennsylvania Press, 2004). She is also a member of the international cooperative program CREDO-RSPAS on the anthropology and history of 'Oceanic Encounters'.

Jean-Michel Chazine holds a research position at the CNRS and is a founding member of CREDO. He has conducted archaeological excavations and survey projects in French Polynesia (1975–80), the Cook Islands and the Republics of Tuvalu, Kiribati, Samoa and the Solomon Islands. He established and directed the Department of Archaeology in Tahiti from 1979 to 1982. Since 1992, his research interests have expanded to include Indonesian Borneo and Palawan in the Philippines. Regular expeditions have yielded a large amount of archaeological data, among them an unexpected rock art tradition in inland Borneo (http://www.kalimanthrope.com). In Palawan, around the Tabon Caves Complex, he has studied the location and dispersal of micro-settlement remains in small rock-shelters. After 2000, he returned to studying Tuamotuan archaeology. He discovered an unknown series of features and a regional pearl-shell technology while searching for the remains of the initial human settlement on the islands. He is the author of some 70 articles and was awarded the Cristal prize by CNRS in 2001.He is a member of the CREDO-RSPAS program on 'Oceanic Encounters'.

Brigitte Derlon is Associate Professor (Maître de conférences) at EHESS in Paris, deputy director of the Laboratory for Social Anthropology (CNRS/EHESS/Collège de France) and director of a CNRS research team on the anthropology of art. She has conducted ethnographic research among the Mandak mountaineers on New Ireland (Papua New Guinea). Her studies focus on ritual objects, shell money, exchange, land tenure, and the relationship to tradition and social change. Her book *De mémoire et d'oubli* (CNRS/Editions de la MSH, Paris, 1997) is dedicated to the analysis of the *malanggan* objects and rituals of New Ireland. She co-edited, with Michèle Coquet and Monique Jeudy-Ballini, *Les cultures à l'œuvre. Rencontres en art* (Biro éditeur/Editions de la MSH, Paris, 2005). Her current research, in collaboration with Monique Jeudy-Ballini, deals with the collective imagination of collectors of primitive art in France.

Françoise Douaire-Marsaudon is a Director of Research at CNRS, a founding member of CREDO and director of the Maison Asie-Pacifique (MAP). She has carried out numerous ethnographic studies in Tonga and Wallis and Futuna since 1983. She has studied the relationship between the (trans)formations of chiefly political systems and the construction of the person, particularly gender (*Les premiers fruits. Parenté, identité sexuelle et pouvoirs en Polynésie occidentale*, 1998). She is the co-director of several MAP programs centred on the Asia-Pacific region, these have been focused on the history of missions, the study of autochtony and migrations, and the methodology of historical anthropology. She is a participant, with P. Bonnemère and S. Tcherkézoff, in a comparative program on 'The gender dimension of culture and social life' with other groups from EHESS. She also directs a research project on youth sexist violence for the Department of Seine Saint-Denis, France. She is a member of the CREDO-RSPAS program on 'Oceanic Encounters'.

Barbara Glowczewski is a Director of Research at CNRS, a member of Laboratory of Social Anthropology (CNRS/EHESS/Collège de France) and is currently an Adjunct Professorial Research Fellow at James Cook University in Australia. She coordinates the 'Anthropology of networks: intercultural dialogs, global anger and local creations' seminar at EHESS in Paris. She is the author of six books and the award-winning multimedia works, *Dream Trackers: Yapa art and knowledge of the Australian desert* (Unesco, 2000) and *Cultural Diversity and Indigenous Peoples: oral, written expressions and new technologies* (Unesco, 2004). She has been documenting ritual dynamics with the Warlpiri in Central Australia; oral history and identity conflicts in the Kimberley; cognitive mapping in Arnhem Land with Aboriginal director and composer Wayne Barker (*Spirit of Anchor*, documentary CNRS Images/media); and investigating the criminalisation of Indigenous peoples in Queensland. She co-directs a research program on 'Indigenous strategies of communication: cultural festivals and new technologies' with Professor Marcia Langton and Dr. Rosita Henry.

Maurice Godelier is honorary Professor of Anthropology (Directeur d'études) at EHESS, a founding member of CREDO and a former director of science policy at CNRS (chairman of the department of social and human sciences from 1982–86). One of his main research interests is the analysis of economic forms of different societies, and the way that societies operate and evolve (see his works: *Rationalité et irrationalité en économie, Un domaine contesté, l'Anthropologie économique, Horizon, trajets marxistes en anthropologie*, and *L'Idéel et le* *matériel* (*The Mental and the Material*)). He was editor of the work *Transitions et subordinations au capitalisme.* He carried out extensive fieldwork among the Baruya people of Papua New Guinea from 1967–69, continuing until 1988 (*The Making of Great Men. Male Domination and Power among the New Guinea Baruya,* 1986; *Big Men and Great Men: Personifications of Power in Melanesia,* coedited with Marilyn Strathern, 1991). More recently he readdressed the theme of gift-exchange in his work, *The Enigma of the Gift,* 1996. The second major theme of his research is the relationship between body, kinship and power. He edited two volumes on this subject with Michel Panoff: *La Production du corps* and *Le Corps humain: possédé, sacrifié, cannibalisé,* 1998. These were followed by a work on incest and kinship, edited in collaboration with Thomas Trautmann and Tjon Sie Fat, *Transformations of Kinship* (Smithsonian Institute Press, 1998). He recently published a major synthesis on the topic, *Métamorphoses de la Parenté,* 2004.

Monique Jeudy-Ballini is a Director of Research at CNRS and a member of the Laboratory of Social Anthropology, (CNRS/EHESS/Collège de France). She conducted numerous ethnographic studies among the Sulka people of New Britain between 1980 and 1994. Her principal research themes concerned representations of sexual identity, the status of chief's daughters, the mythology of work, the process of Christianisation, the system of ceremonial exchange and of Sulka aesthetic ritual. She co-edited *People and Things. Social Mediations in Oceania* (Carolina Academic Press, Durham, 2002) with Bernard Juillerat and is the author of *L'art des échanges: Penser le lien social chez les Sulka* (Payot, Lausanne, 2004). Her recent research concerns the anthropology of art; she co-edited *Les cultures à l'œuvre. Rencontres en art* (Biro éditeur/Editions de la MSH, Paris, 2005) with Michèle Coquet and Brigitte Derlon. She is currently conducting an ethnographic study, in collaboration with Brigitte Derlon, of collectors of primitive art in France.

Bernard Juillerat is emeritus Director of Research at CNRS and a member of the Laboratory of Social Anthropology (CNRS/EHESS/Collège de France). After his studies in Modern Letters at the University of Lausanne (Switzerland) he taught high school in Kinshasa, Zaire. He later studied Anthropology in Paris. For his doctorate, which he obtained in 1969, he studied a non-Islamised society in North Cameroon. In 1970 he began his study of the Yafar, a group of forest dwellers in Papua New Guinea. He later conducted a critical study on the Banaro based on Richard Thurnwald's early 20th-century analysis. His recent theoretical efforts have been directed toward integrating the achievements of Freudian psychoanalysis with ethnographic interpretation. His principal publications are *Les Enfants du Sang* (1986); *Oedipe chasseur* (1991); *Shooting the Sun* (1992); *L'avènement du père* (1995); *Children of the Blood* (1996); and *Penser l'imaginaire* (2001).

Pierre Lemonnier is a Director of Research at CNRS, a founding member of CREDO, and teaches at the University of Provence. After repeated field research among various Anga peoples of Papua New Guinea from 1978 to 1982, he chose the Ankave valley for long-term anthropological fieldwork, a location to which he regularly returns. He has published several books on the anthropology of technology, including *Elements for an Anthropology of Technology* (1992) and *Technological Choice: Transformation in Material Cultures since the*

Neolithic (1993).   His works on Melanesia include *Guerres et festins: Paix, échanges et compétition dans les Highlands de Nouvelle-Guinée* (1990) and numerous articles. His book on witchcraft and mourning among the Ankave, *Le Sabbat des lucioles*, is to be published in 2006. His other fields of interest are the interpretation of Ankave male initiations and the comparative study of Anga cultures. He is a member of the CREDO-RSPAS program on 'Oceanic Encounters'.

Philippe Peltier is a Museum Conservator (Conservateur du patrimoine). He is in charge of the Oceania and Island Southeast Asia (Insulinde) Unit of the Musée du Quai Branly, Paris. His training is in ethnology and art history and he has participated in or curated numerous exhibits, including 'Primitivism in 20th Century Art' at the Museum of Modern Art in New York (1984); 'David Malangi' at the Musée des Arts d'Afrique et d'Océanie in Paris (1995); 'Altär' at the Kunst-Palast museum in Dusseldorf (2001); and 'Gaugin-Tahiti, l'atelier des Tropiques' in Paris and Washington (2004). He is currently preparing an exhibition on the art of New Ireland that will open in Paris in 2007. He has also spent more than two years among the Adjirab in the lower Sepik valley where his research focus was local history and warfare.

Serge Tcherkézoff is Professor of anthropology (Directeur d'études) at EHESS, a founding member and the Director of CREDO, Adjunct Professor of anthropology at Canterbury University, New Zealand and was recently ARC Linkage Fellow at The Australian National University. His works bring together the results of his field studies in Samoa during the 1980s and 1990s with an ethno-historical critique of European narratives about Polynesia. He has published two books concerning contemporary Samoan society in the domains of economy, politics and gender relations: *Le mythe de la sexualité polynésienne* (2001) and *FaaSamoa, une identité polynésienne*, 2003. His two other books on 'first encounters' between Polynesians and Europeans — *Tahiti 1768* and *First Contacts: the Samoan Case, 1722–1840* — were published in 2004. He has previously published on holistic French anthropological theory (*Dual Classification Reconsidered*, 1987) and is achieving a book on Mauss and the Polynesian gift. A historical study of the French 18th–19th century invention of the Polynesia/Melanesia racial distinction is currently in press (Société des Océanistes, 2006). He co-ordinates, with Professors Darrell Tryon and Margaret Jolly, the CREDO-RSPAS cooperative program on 'Oceanic Encounters'.

www.ingramcontent.com/pod-product-compliance
Lightning Source LLC
Chambersburg PA
CBHW061242270326
41928CB00041B/3364